J. W. Baldwin
Baltimore
1982

D1174315

CISTERCIAN STUDIES SERIES: NUMBER THIRTY-FIVE

THE CISTERCIANS IN DENMARK

CISTERCIAN STUDIES SERIES: NUMBER THIRTY-FIVE

THE CISTERCIANS IN DENMARK

Their Attitudes, Roles, and Functions
in Medieval Society

by

Brian Patrick McGuire

Cistercian Publications, Inc.

Kalamazoo, Michigan

1982

© Cistercian Publications Inc., 1982
Available in Britain and Europe from
A.R. Mowbray & Co. Ltd.
St Thomas House Becket Street
Oxford OX1 1SJ

Typeset by the Carmelites of Indianapolis

Library of Congress Cataloguing in Publication Data:

McGuire, Brian Patrick.
    The Cistercians in Denmark.

    (Cistercian studies series; 35)
    Bibliography: p. 343
    1. Cistercians—Denmark—History.   I. Title.   II. Series.
            BX3443.D4M37   271'.12'0489   81–6123
            ISBN 0–87907–835–9   AACR2

To
Lester M. Stewart

The Author

Brian Patrick McGuire was born in Hawaii in 1946 and graduated from the University of California-Berkeley in 1968. Two years later he completed a D. Phil degree at Oxford under R.W. Southern on the subject 'The History of St Anselm's Theology of the Redemption in the Twelfth and Thirteenth Centuries'. Since 1975 he has been a *lektor* in medieval literature and history at the Institute for Greek and Latin Medieval Philology at the University of Copenhagen, where he is also head of the medieval centre (Middelaldercentralen). He has published several articles in both English and Danish on various aspects of medieval life and thought, including a study of *Conflict and Continuity at Øm Abbey* (1976).

A Note on the Danish Alphabet

The Danish alphabet has 29 letters. The extra three (which are placed at the end of the alphabet) are Æ, Ø and Å.

Æ æ is a dipthong. It sounds like 'a' and 'e' rammed together, the same way it looks in print.

Ø ø is pronounced the same as 'oe'. The slash (/) can be looked upon as giving the same effect as the German (or Swedish) umlaut (··).

Å å is simply a double 'a' and until the Danish Spelling Reform of 1948 was written 'Aa'. Books in the bibliography from before this date us the old form (such as *Aarhus*, today *Århus*).

Contents

INTRODUCTION   1

I THE SOURCES   15

II ARRIVAL AND GROWTH 1144–1177   37

The 1140s: Darkness and Light   38
Eskil as a convert to Cistercian monasticism   44
Eskil in the 1150s and after: foundations, gifts, publicity   49
The Achievements of the 1160s and 1170s   60
    Absalon and Valdemar at Esrum   60
    Eskil's limited yet limitless influence   63
    Myths and realities: Sorø and Øm   74
    Danes in Wendland: Dargun, Colbaz, Eldena   79
    Coastal expansion: Esrum and Sorø   84

III THE CULMINATION OF THE CISTERCIAN ADVANCE 1178–1215   89

Absalon and the popes:
    protection and favouritism, 1178–1201   90
Abbot William of Æbelholt: anger and devotion   92
Cistercian monasteries for women   98
Troubles in Slesvig: Guldholm and Ryd   100
Looking back at Løgum   105
The Cistercian advance in retrospect   108

IV CONTINUITY AND GROWING TENSIONS 1215–1257   113

Major themes of the period   113
Travelling monks   115
Contact with the papacy   117
Dealings with the Order   120
Relations with the king   126
Cistercian limitations after 1220   132
Relations with bishops   136
Signs of change in the 1250s   142

V CATASTROPHE AND RECOVERY 1257–1307   145

Emotions in the chronicles   147
The Baltic fringe: Twilight of Danish influence   151
The decline of dependence on international structures   156
Troublesome royal women and generous female donors   166
Interminable cases and monastic compromises   172
Lasting changes and continuing themes   179

VI QUIET YEARS AND THEIR TRAUMAS 1307–1357   183

Change in the social base   183
Problems in the sources   187
Violence and the threat of violence   192
Episcopal relations as a compensatory factor   198
Problems with national and international institutions:
     The Monarchy   203
     The papacy   208
     The General Chapter   209
Finance and properties   213
The Cistercians in the context of a more varied society   215

VII COMPLEXITY, ISOLATION AND VITALITY
     1357–1414 AND BEYOND   221

The ambiguous royal attitude   222
Continuing—but limited—international links   228
Bishops: distance and accessibility   233
The growing role of towns   237
The continuing centrality of the lay aristocracy   239
Isolation of the abbeys from each other   245
Ramifications of the agricultural crisis   248
Looking forward: 1414 to the Reformation   251

Abbreviations   260
Citeaux and Clairvaux Filiations in Demnark   264
Danish Rulers   265
Danish Medieval Bishops   266
Danish Cistercian Abbots   271
Final Note   278
Notes   279
Bibliography   343
Maps:

    Danish Cistercian Monasteries   88
    Danish Bishoprics   112
    Danish Monastic Houses   220
    Administrative Districts   263

Photographs   355
Index   397

Foreword

THE CISTERCIANS undoubtedly set their stamp on Denmark's past. About a hundred years after the end of the Viking Age and two centuries after the Danes became Christians by decree of King Harald Blue-Tooth, Europe entered a new phase in her economical and socio-political development: a period in which cultural, political, and economic factors gradually combine to unite Europe in a new manner. It is at this particular turning-point in history—exciting in more than one respect—that the Cistercian monks appear on the Scandinavian scene. Always ready to try out new ideas, they act in contemporary society as a leaven of experiment and as protagonists of novel developments. Socio-politically they work to undermine the prevailing feudal system by attempting to become economically independent of royal and baronial power, thanks to their reliance on their own manual work. In consequence, they are seen to side with the Pope in the Investiture Struggle which, regarded under a positive aspect, tends to make the Church independent of secular power.

As monks of an ascetic tradition, the Cistercians succeed in combining a sense of the human factor with strictness of observance; thus, attaching themselves to whatever is genuine and down-to-earth, they manifest a peculiar devotion for the Humanity of Christ, the Word of God become flesh and blood among men. Through the work of their hands the desert is almost literally made to bloom. Through their industry, their monasteries become centres of new technical knowledge and proficiency, with a wide cultural influence on their contemporaries. In their communities the most practical sober-mindedness combines with a deep and genuine mystic approach to Christ—all in the utmost simplicity. Their tradition of hospitality and love of mankind, reflected in so many ways, is finally only an outward expression of their inner spiritual convictions.

But as so often happens, the train of events and the inevitable evolution both of their order and of society in general proved too powerful for their initial resolve. Their growing wealth and even their success as a monastic organization undermined the original ideal. Monasteries became feudal manors, embroiled in power struggles and intrigues. The development of the towns and the growth of the universities claimed other solutions than those the Benedictine tradition is capable of providing. Finally, when the Reformation was introduced—again by the stroke of the royal pen—the king simply dissolved all monasteries and thereby strengthened his own royal power.

A significant aspect of Denmark's history is reflected in the achievement of the Cistercian Order. This in itself is enough to make this book welcome and to make one wish that it may find a quantity of readers. May it be added that Brian McGuire is the opposite of a dry historian: he has a talent for perceiving the person behind the events and for portraying him with acuity and affection.

✠ Hans L. Martensen
Bishop of Copenhagen

Author's Preface

MY PURPOSE IN WRITING this book has been to present to a non-Scandinavian readership a fragment and *exemplum* of Cistercian medieval development. Because of the language barrier, Danish medieval history has been a subject mainly reserved to Scandinavian historians. It is time for Denmark to take its rightful place on the map of Cistercian history. I hope that other scholars will be able to use my results for a fuller understanding of the relationship between Scandinavia and the rest of medieval Europe.

The first draft of the book was completed in the summer of 1975, but its contents would never have seen the light of day if it had not been for the interest and support of E. Rozanne Elder, editor of Cistercian Publications. At the Cistercian Studies Conference in Kalamazoo in 1978, Dr Elder asked to see the by-now dusty manuscript. After delays due to the vagaries of the European and American postal systems, I was a year later given a green light to revise and update my findings. This has been a pleasure because of the secure knowledge which so few writers have, that the fruits of their labour will reach a public.

In the final draft, I have taken into account a large amount of important work on medieval Denmark that appeared between 1975 and 1980. I have profited greatly from the criticism of my Danish colleagues. They will probably find little new or unexpected in these pages, but my goal has not been to be original or to upset basic theses concerning Danish medieval history. I have chosen to limit polemics with colleagues to a bare minimum and instead to borrow from the best and most enduring of their results.

A book of history is just as much a result of innumerable contacts with living persons as an analysis of the sources involved. I should like to thank the following people for the dialogues, both written and oral, by which they have brought me through the last decade and to this final result. Sir Richard Southern and Beryl Smalley of Oxford have shown continuing interest and have provided many helpful comments. Jean Leclercq of Clervaux Abbey, Luxembourg, has caught many a slip and offered welcome new perspectives. Niels Skyum-Nielsen, my supervisor from 1972–74, when I held a postdoctoral fellowship at the Institute of History, Copenhagen University, has given me both his time and his patience. The same can be said for Troels Dahlerup of Århus University; Kai Hørby, chairman of the Institute of History in Copenhagen; and especially Jan Pinborg, chairman of my own Institute for Greek and Latin Medieval Philology. Olaf Olsen of the National Museum and Michael Gelting of the Royal Archives in Copenhagen, Tore Nyberg of Odense University, Ole Schiørring of Århus University, Niels Sterum of the Randers Museum for Cultural History. Graham Caie of the English Institute at Copenhagen University, Holger N. Garner of the Øm Abbey Museum, John Baldwin of the Johns Hopkins University, and Olga Bartholdy of Løgumkloster—all have shared their knowledge, criticisms and ideas with me. To my students, and especially to Birgitte Bentzon, I owe many a moment of enlightenment and renewed inspiration. Rozanne Elder has gone through the entire manuscript and has saved me from innumerable infelicities of style and expression. The many faults that remain are my own.

Much of the revision of this book has taken place at my home outside of Skamstrup, part of an area testamented to the Cistercians at Sorø by Archbishop Absalon before his death in 1201. As I have looked outside at the changing patterns of the Danish seasons, I have often felt an immediate bond with the past and present of this northern yet idyllic countryside. But I have also been aware of a link back to the world of my own youth. For whatever in its pages that provides a fuller understanding of the medieval world and its monastic population, I want to dedicate this book to my friend and first guide in medieval studies, Lester M. Stewart of Oakland, California.

Middelaldercentralen—The Medieval Centre
Copenhagen University
December 1981

Introduction
The Danish Cistercians

DENMARK, LIKE THE REST OF SCANDINAVIA, has long been on the fringes of European geography as well as consciousness. From Paris to Copenhagen by road today is a distance of 1200 kilometres (750 miles). By North American standards, this is only a moderate space, about the length of the state of California. But at each end of the two European points are different traditions, one bearing the deep influence by Roman domination and culture in the first centuries of our era, the other remaining outside Latin Europe and taking on Christianity only in the tenth century.

To many a foreigner, the mention of Denmark brings a vision of flat green fields and Viking ships. To this day the country shows many signs of pride in its Viking past. In official Danish histories, the Middle Ages do not begin until the Viking Age ends (about 1050). The adoption of the Lutheran faith in the sixteenth century meant the same rejection of the Middle Ages that took place elsewhere in Northern Europe. The period from about 1050 to 1536 remains for many educated Danes one of the least sympathetic and attractive in their history and many react with surprise when they are told that monasteries once dotted their countryside.

To anyone who takes the time to look, this countryside is full of surprises. Although the highest point in Denmark is only a few hundred feet above sea level, many districts have a rolling, almost hilly, landscape. There are flat areas in Southern Jutland, on the island of Lolland, and on the eastern end of Zealand, where the capital, Copenhagen, lies. But the popular image of

Denmark as a northerly Holland has more to do with social welfare than with physical geography.

Denmark is not as small as is sometimes thought. The individual geographical units are small, but distances can be significant by European standards. The peninsula of Jutland is 350 km from north to south and varies in width between 50 km at the narrowest to 170 km at its widest. The island of Zealand is about 140 km from north to south and on the average 100 km wide, while the island of Fyn, sandwiched in between Jutland and Zealand, is about 70 km by 60 km. Besides these three main areas there is a myriad of smaller islands, from Lolland and Falster south of Zealand to the archipelago south of Fyn. It is almost impossible to be further than 50 km from the sea anywhere in Denmark. A nation of seafaring people in the Middle Ages easily formed from so disparate a geographical collection a political entity.

Until the seventeenth century, the kingdom of Denmark also included what today is the southern end of Sweden, the districts of Skåne, Blekinge and Halland. They increased the area of the country by about one-third: Skåne itself, with its rich farming lands and great forest regions, is about 100 km from north to south and 120 km from west to east. From the eastern tip of Blekinge to the western shore of Jutland is a distance of 450 km, about 280 miles.

The present population of all these districts today nears eight million; in the twelfth century it was probably less than one million. As elsewhere in Europe, much of the landscape was covered with forests, though place names indicate land clearance from the tenth century onwards and the founding of new villages all over Denmark. If we mention briefly the sites of the various Cistercian houses, we can get an idea of Danish geography in some of its variations. Esrum, the mother house of the Clairvaux line (founded before 1152), is situated on the edge of a large lake in northeastern Zealand. It lies, in good Cistercian fashion, at the bottom of a valley, in excellent farming and pasturage lands. Like other Cistercian houses founded in the twelfth century, it is inland, for until the 1170s Danes still had to fear the inroads of Wendish pirates. Esrum's daughter house of Sorø (1161) was during the Middle Ages on an island in the middle of the west Zealand farming plains. The island was formed by three lakes and their connecting streams, sources of both protection and food for the monks. Another Esrum daughter, Vitskøl (*Vitae Schola*, 1158), is located on an arm of northwest Jutland's great bay, Limfjorden. Because of the narrow entrance to this fjord, the monks were given some protection from pirates. When one enters the verdant ruin of the abbey church, once one of the greatest in Denmark, the sea is forgotten and there is the same rich green landscape that characterizes Cistercian abbeys in France or England. Vitskøl's daughter house, Øm (*Cara Insula*, 1172), belongs to what might be called Denmark's Lake District in east-central Jutland, a favoured place for monasteries. Not far from urban centres like Århus and Horsens, Øm is probably the most beautifully situated of all the Cistercian houses, with lakes both north and south and pine woods on its edge.

In the Citeaux line, the mother house, of Herrisvad (1144), is in Skåne, not far from the archiepiscopal seat of Lund. It too is located in a lush valley and along a stream to provide power and drainage. Even though the site is now a military base, one can still pick out the typical Cistercian features of the area. Løgum Abbey (*Locus Dei*, c. 1171), belongs to the much more puritan landscape of Southern Jutland. Now on the edge of the town of Løgumkloster, the medieval abbey church was located near a winding stream and probably surrounded by great forests, some of which are still there. The sandy soil of the area made agricultural conditions less favourable than they were in eastern Denmark. Holme (*Insula Dei*, 1172), on the garden isle of Fyn, had better possibilities, with water, woods, and fertile agricultural lands around it. Even today it is one of the most idyllic Danish Cistercian sites. Tvis (*Tuta Vallis*, 1162), a few miles outside the town of Holstebro in western Jutland, manages also to give the standard verdant, valley-stream impression even if the region is generally flat and open. But the plain gives way to a rich river valley, and here along Storeå was exactly the terrain Cistercians liked.

South of the present Danish border (adopted in 1920), in what once was the duchy of Slesvig-Holsten, is Ryd (*Rus Regis*, c. 1210). Not far from Flensborg Fjord, Ryd's placement bears witness to the end of the era of coastal danger. In the fourteenth century a lone abbey was founded at Knardrup, a farm to the west of Copenhagen. Before 1200 three houses for women were started, in the episcopal seat of Roskilde, in Slangerup in northern Zealand, and in Bergen on the island of Rygen. Monasteries for women did not follow the male Cistercian practice of choosing sites distant from towns.

Even today, almost all of the Cistercian locations remain far from settlements and the marks of modern man. One of the most remarkable of all Scandinavian abbeys, Lyse, located in the Valley of Light (Lysedal) about 30 km from Bergen in Norway, sums up the special character of the Scandinavian Cistercian houses. To reach the site, one must drive through mountains and rough country. Finally comes the descent to a valley, in the summertime just as lush and almost as semi-tropical as the surroundings of any Burgundian abbey. Here are warmth and shelter from the cold sea winds; peace and light suggest the possibility of contemplation. The Cistercians knew what they sought when they came to Denmark and the other Scandinavian countries: protected sites, good agricultural lands, water, and drainage. But surely also they were looking for natural beauty to inspire them. The very names they gave their Danish homes indicate a sense of what they found: Isle of God, School of Life, Place of God, Protected Valley.

The Cistercians arrived about two centuries after the Danish royal house accepted Christianity. In the ninth century the missionary Ansgar had used the trading centre of Hedeby (near the modern Slesvig) as a base for journeys into Scandinavia, but he seems to have had no permanent influence. The exact moment of conversion for the members of the Jellinge family, the main royal dynasty of the tenth century, cannot be established, but it belongs to the third quarter of the tenth century. King Harald Bluetooth erected a monument to the memory of his parents and on one of the stones commemorated the Christianization of the Danes. Connected to this event is the legend of Poppo, a priest who is supposed to have gone through ordeal by fire in Harald's presence in order to convince him of the truth and power of the Christian religion. According to the German historian Widukind, Poppo 'by his unharmed hand . . . showed the truth of the Catholic faith to all'. There is an artistic tradition for this legend in Danish golden altars of the twelfth century, and during the Middle Ages Poppo may have been much better known in the North than Ansgar.

At such moments of crucial cultural change, fact cannot be separated from myth. But with the acceptance of Christianity by the royal house, a slow process started by which Christian beliefs, values, and attitudes began to penetrate the Danish population as a whole. Some historians would contend that Christianity was a veneer in the Middle Ages and did not really penetrate popular consciousness in Denmark until the Reformation. But here one can argue about the definition of Christianity, and it is at least clear that the cult of the saints, relics, devotion to Mary, the building of parish churches, and regular payments to church institutions, all became a part of Danish cultural and social life in the course of the Middle Ages.

Our knowledge of the eleventh century in Denmark, a difficult and confusing period, comes mainly from written sources from abroad. The adoption of Christianity by no means put an end to Danish expeditions of conquests, now perhaps better organized than in the previous century and part of royal policy. The union of Scandinavia and England under Canute lasted only a few years, but every royal son and great chieftain must have remembered this moment of triumph as an exploit worthy of imitation. Long after 1066, Danish kings plotted a return to England, and their failure to realise their plans was not always due to Norman cunning. With Svend Estridsen (1047–74), we meet for the first time a Danish king who can be known from a contemporary historian, Adam of Bremen. As the Danish historian Aksel E. Christensen has pointed out, Svend Estridsen is a Janus-like figure, looking back on the conquests of the Viking Age and trying to repeat them, while at the same time making contacts with the pope and furthering the organisation of the Christian church in Denmark. It was probably under Svend Estridsen that the medieval dioceses were formed, with a bishop at Børglum in Northern Jutland, another at Viborg in the centre of the peninsula, a third at Århus on the east side, a fourth at Ribe on the west, and a fifth at Slesvig (now in the Federal Republic of Germany). The islands of Fyn (Fünen), Lolland and Falster were under the bishop of Odense, while Zealand and later Rygen (Rügen, now in the German Democratic Republic) after the Danish conquest in 1170 were put under Roskilde. The eastern regions of Skåne, Halland and Blekinge came under Dalby, whose bishop soon moved to Lund. At the start of the twelfth century Lund became an archbishopric and the ecclesiastical seat of the North. It was thus able to block an attempt by the archbishopric of Hamburg-Bremen during the eleventh century to gain metropolitan status over Scandinavia. Danish royal intentions together with papal reform policy and opposition to the German monarchy combined to guarantee the Scandinavian church relative freedom from German hegemony.

The decades immediately before and after 1100 have been looked upon as a crucial turning point in Danish history, when the pagan culture of the Viking Age definitively gave way to the Christian culture of the south. In the course of the twelfth century almost two thousand romanesque stone churches were built in Denmark, many of them probably replacing wooden structures. Whoever built these churches—monarchy, nobility, or peasants—by them bore witness both to economic prosperity and to the penetration of Christianity into the everyday lives of the populace. One of the church leaders who ensured and coordinated this growth was Asser, archbishop of Lund, 1103/4–1137. Once looked upon as a rather crude figure with only a limited vision of the international church, Asser is, in the eyes of Aksel E. Christensen, the man who secured the independence of the Danish church. Under him the cathedral at Lund was built and the chapter organized. The first decades of the twelfth century brought the partial penetration of Gregorian reforms into Denmark. Although the celibacy of the clergy never quite became established, many cathedral chapters formed regular communities, while Benedictine monasteries were founded in several places. Dalby near Lund probably became an Augustinian community, while Lund itself acquired a Benedictine house. On Zealand Næstved was given a Benedictine monastery by a rich family, the Bodilsens; in Ringsted another Benedictine house was founded, as well as at Sorø. On Jutland, we can see the faint outline of Benedictine monasteries at Veng, Seem, and Slesvig. Odense cathedral had a Benedictine community from about 1100 made up of English monks from Evesham. They spread the cult of King Knud, who had been murdered in the cathedral in 1086 for political reasons but whose royal successors made sure he was elevated to martyrdom.

The first decades of the twelfth century in Denmark are characterized by a tragic attempt by the myriad grandsons of Svend Estridsen, both legitimate and illegitimate, to jockey their way to power. One after another was eliminated by death. Until the triumphant emergence of Valdemar I (The Great) in 1158, a state of on-again, off-again civil war existed. As in England under the anarchy of King Stephen, we find that civil war and social unrest do not seem to have hindered the foundation of Cistercian abbeys, for it was during this period that the first Cistercians came to Denmark (Herrisvad in 1144, Esrum before 1152). Their main support, as we shall see, was Archbishop Eskil of Lund (1137–77), who, because of disagreements with the king, spent much of his archbishopric abroad, where he met and formed a friendship with Bernard of Clairvaux.

The Valdemarian dynasty gave Denmark the political stability it had lacked almost since the death of Svend Estridsen. Valdemar I worked closely with the church in order to strengthen his power. His program was jeopardized by the papal schism between Innocent II and the German emperor's candidate, Anacletus. Valdemar was obliged to side with his feudal lord, Frederick Barbarossa, and Eskil, a supporter of Innocent, left the country. By 1170 the schism was over, however, and Eskil cooperated with the monarchy in establishing its legitimacy by participating in a great meeting at the Benedictine church of Ringsted. Here Valdemar's father, Duke Knud Lavard, who had been killed in 1131, was recognized as a saint. As elsewhere in Europe, a royal dynasty tried to guarantee its legitimacy by establishing a saintly ancestry. Eventually Valdemar extricated himself from his feudal bonds to the German emperor and by 1200 Denmark emerged as one of the strongest and richest kingdoms in Europe, with an independent church and monarchy and an active policy of conquest along the eastern and southern shores of the Baltic.

Valdemar's sons Knud (1182–1202) and Valdemar II (The Victorious, 1202–41) carried on his policies of foreign conquest and domestic consolidation. Valdemar II is remembered as a great legislator as well as a military strategist. In his day Danish military power reached all the way to Estonia. He cooperated with the learned archbishop of Lund, Anders Sunesen, a descendant of the rich Hvide family which had supported both Cistercian monasticism and the Valdemarian monarchy.

In 1223 Valdemar was captured by a German lord and held for ransom. This act is traditionally looked upon as the turning point in the good fortunes of the Danish monarchy. By the time of Valdemar II's death in 1241, the age of conquests was over and a new period of unrest had begun. From this point onwards in Danish history the political vicissitudes of Southern Jutland began to complicate royal succession. The region provided a centre for opposition to the monarchy. It became common for younger members of the royal family to become Dukes of Southern Jutland. In 1232, Valdemar II made his younger son Abel duke, and the latter was probably responsible for the assassination of King Erik Plowpenny eighteen years later. Yet Abel could only maintain his rule for two years. After his death his brother Kristoffer I ruled (from 1252–59). He too apparently came to a violent end. Rumour has it that he was poisoned, and there is even a story that the abbot of Ryd, Arnfast, put poison into the host that he administered to the king. Kristoffer's queen, Margrethe Sambiria, ruled Denmark while her son Erik Glipping was in his minority, with disastrous results for the Danish Cistercians. Erik Glipping held the throne until 1286, when he too was murdered in one of the most mysterious conspiracies in Danish history. All of this prompted papal envoys who had come to Denmark during these years to comment on the Danes' European reputation for murdering their kings.

The eldest son of Erik Glipping, Erik Menved, ruled from 1286–1319. Again a long minority gave prominence to the queen mother, Agnes of Brandenburg. As king, Erik Menved tried to reestablish royal power and set out on a program of conquests that ended unsuccessfully and almost bankrupted the country. Denmark, like other European countries, was suffering from economic decline due to crop failures and the first plague outbreaks, as well as other factors. Erik's brother, Kristoffer II, made two attempts at being king, from 1320–26 and 1330–32, and was followed by an interregnum during which the country was ruled by German lords who had managed to get mortgages on entire regions in return for loans to the failing monarchy. The 1330s are one of the darkest periods in Danish history, when it looked as if the country might become an appendage to Germany, a recurrent Danish nightmare still strong whenever economic decline or political chaos threaten.

In 1340 Kristoffer's son, Valdemar Atterdag (1340-75) began to consolidate his power. He eventually reunited the country and even set out on a new series of conquests. In the last decades of the fourteenth century, Denmark was ruled by a woman, Margrethe I (1387-1412), who managed briefly to unite the three Scandinavian kingdoms and provided relative stability to Scandinavia. Under this queen and her male predecessors was ruled and misruled the medieval Denmark which provided the setting for the Cistercians this book treats. From the half-legendary Gorm the Old in the tenth century to the larger-than-life Margrethe in the beginning of the fifteenth, a single dynasty in almost uninterrupted succession ruled Denmark. Not until the time of the Valdemars was an hereditary kingship established, and even then younger members of the family and illegitimate members often interposed themselves in the scramble for the throne. Only in France do we find another royal dynasty equally as successful in maintaining itself, and this continuous line must have given Denmark a strong sense of national unity. But there were murderous feuds, and no Danish king in the Middle Ages could feel secure, especially those who had younger brothers in Southern Jutland ready to take advantage of any weakness they might show.

Although there were various popular movements of protest against abuses in the Catholic church, the Reformation, like Christianity itself six centuries earlier, was imposed in the sixteenth century by royal choice. In 1536 King Christian III ordered the acceptance of the new faith, imprisoned the Catholic bishops and confiscated all church lands. The last decision immensely enriched the monarchy and gave it outright ownership of about half the land in the country, for the church by the end of the Middle Ages owned perhaps a third of the land. There was no organized Catholic resistance, and the transition was mild by comparison to what happened in other European countries. The Reformation in Denmark was a royal-urban event. The friars were thrown out of their priories in Malmø, Copenhagen, Flensborg and elsewhere, but the monasteries in the countryside were allowed to continue. They could not recruit any new members and as their numbers declined, the houses were closed and remaining monks were moved to a few centres. Sorø became the gathering place for the last Danish Cistercians. A number of abbots seem to have accepted the Protestant faith and so must have broken all juridical links with the Order, but in everyday life they still functioned as Cistercians. One of the last abbots of Øm interested himself in Protestant theology and built up a book collection of theological writings from both sides. Various inventories from Sorø show that the abbots lived well, with many servants, and that there continued to be a semi-monastic community into the 1570's. Meanwhile the abbey complex began to attract various outcasts from the new society: Catholic recalcitrants, mentally disturbed people, and old age pensioners. In this last twilight the abbey seems more than ever to have provided for the weak and helpless. In 1586 Sorø was turned into a school.

Other Danish Cistercian houses did not do as well under the new regime. Øm, for example, was converted in 1560 into Emborg, a royal hunting lodge. Although this new status lasted for only a year, the archaeologists under Olaf Olsen who in 1975-78 excavated the ruins assure us that before and after the hunting, a great deal of drinking was done. Seemingly endless quantities of broken glass were found. Much of Øm abbey ended up in the foundations of the castle at Skanderborg and even in town houses there, for stone could be transported there by water from the abbey site.

The sad story of the quarrying of the Danish abbeys resembles that of the English or North German Cistercian houses. For many of them, no trace remains of a once considerable foundation. Løgum Abbey provides the most complete Cistercian complex, but the east wing has been almost entirely rebuilt and the other wings are gone. At Sorø only the church remains intact, as at Løgum. In Esrum, we find the south wing of one quadrangle, from the fifteenth century. It has been much altered. The ruins of Tvis are all below ground level, while Herrisvad and Vitskøl both can be traced from the few bricks their excavations unearthed. Vitskøl's lay-brother wing, however, still remains, in remodeled form, while at Holme the monastic quadrangle exists, even though it has been converted into a family seat and has lost on the outside almost all signs of its medieval origins. The church there was savagely 'restored' in the nineteenth century. A good imagination is necessary to conceive the medieval size and contents of any Danish Cistercian house, but the fine churches at Løgum and Sorø bear witness to something of what once existed.

The Cistercians had no role to play in Denmark after the Reformation, and so it was natural that their buildings soon were handed over to other uses or left to decay. Hostility toward monasticism has been present in Danish culture ever since the end of the Middle Ages, and it has been difficult for Danish historians to accept the Cistercians as a positive part of the medieval landscape. One of the earliest indications of a challenge to the monastic way of life is the story of Brother Rus, a folk tale also known in German versions but which seems to have taken form in fifteenth century Denmark. The tale goes that the devil one day sought entrance at Esrum Abbey by dressing himself up as a young man. He gained the abbot's favor by becoming his personal cook and preparing for him all his best-loved dishes. The brothers too became dependent on the services of Brother Rus, who brought women into the abbey for their enjoyment. Finally his true identity was discovered, and in one version of the tale, the monks chased the intruder and corrupter all the way along Esrum Lake through Grib Forest to the village of Nødebo, where the devil disappeared into a well that still exists behind the parish church.

Danish ballads, some of which go back to the Middle Ages though their texts almost always are known only in later versions, have a favourite theme in the monk or nun who is forced to enter the monastery by his or her parents. The nun is inevitably rescued from her imprisonment by a handsome knight. One of the finest and best-known of medieval Danish ballads, 'Marsk Stig', tells the tale of the murder of King Erik Glipping in 1286 and transmits the tradition that the killers were dressed as Cistercians. This detail has inspired a modern Danish historical novel in which the Cistercians are made out to be involved directly in the murder.

The author of this work, Ebbe Kløvedal Reich, is the heir and torchbearer of a cultural tradition in Denmark which looks upon the medieval church and monasticism as a source of oppression for the Danish people. Another of Reich's books lionizes the nineteenth century priest, poet and politician, N.F.S. Grundtvig. One of Grundtvig's hymns, still included in the official hymnal (Den danske Salmebog, nr. 302, from 1817), thanks God for Martin Luther, who brought light to his people and opened mens' eyes from 'popes' lies and monks' dreams':

Herrens bog var lagt på hylden	*The Lord's book was left on the shelf,*
eventyr i kirken lød;	*In church one heard only fairy tales;*
for en krone, for en gylden	*For a crown or a guilder*
Himmerig til fals de bød;	*They offered heaven for sale;*
sandheds lys og korsets ord	*Truth's light and the cross's word*
var som sunket ned i jord,	*They were buried in the earth,*
at de skulle ej fordømme	*So that they need not condemn*
paveløgn og munkedrømme.	*Popes' lies and monks' dreams.*

This same attitude can be found in a school textbook from almost a century later, *Vor Historie*, from 1902. The author quotes an historian who praises the effects of the Reformation on the education of the layman:

> The religious concepts he had [prior to the Reformation] were gained from legends and from sermons by monks who never studied the Bible but instead were full of anecdotes and allegories, where God appeared as a hidden, mystical being, whom man could never approach directly, almost like an oriental despot.

A contemporary of Grundtvig's, Hans Christian Andersen, had a more sophisticated view of monasticisim. In one of his lesser-known stories, 'Psyche', a young Renaissance artist who had been rejected by the girl he loved found peace and consolation in a Roman cloister:

> Now for the first time he seemed to have understood himself, to have found the way to truth and peace. In the church were God's light and clarity, in the monastic cell the calm where the human tree could grow up through eternity.

But Andersen suggests Grundtvig's theme of monastic dreams in a later comment on the artist-monk's way of life. He is described as having given up his creative reality for a dream: 'Yes, this world was a dream, and the dream controls the hours and can return for hours, but cloister life lasts for years, long and many'. The artist's withdrawal from the pain of involvement in the world can be seen as the choice of an eternal dream. Andersen is more positive than Grundtvig, for the storyteller is a lover of the south, of romanticism, and thus is attracted by Catholic forms. But his reservations are typically Northern European.

Recent textbooks are usually much kinder to the Cistercians than their early twentieth-century predecessors. Danish popular culture, however, still looks upon monasticism as at best an exotic curiosity, at worst something suspicious. A popular children's song tells how a monk 'on the long summer days' goes into the fields, picks flowers, spreads out his cowl, and asks a 'lovely virgin to kneel on it'. The two end up dancing merrily. This innocent song sums up both the medieval critique and the post-Reformation tradition: the sexual charges against monks and the belief that many of them sneak away from their monasteries to live their merry lives. The shadow of Brother Rus lives on in popular consciousness.

This brief introduction to Danish geography, history, and cultural background can be ended with a quick review of the work already done on monastic and especially Cistercian history in this country. The first and so far only complete attempt to deal with the history of monasticism in medieval Denmark was made by a Protestant clergyman, J.B. Daugaard, in 1830. His book has long been out of date and has much that needs to be revised, but it can still be read with pleasure. It is an indication of a new interest in medieval religion and shows how Romanticism opened the way to medieval studies. Daugaard's review of the Danish monasteries is structured according to diocese, and he has little sense of the different orders. In 1838, A.C.A. Kjerulf wrote a little work on Esrum and published various charters connected with the abbey, the first serious work on a Danish Cistercian house I have been able to find. Esrum was excavated for the first time by J. Kornerup in 1879. The same year he published a description of his finds and of Esrum's links with its daughter houses. For the first time a Danish historian had tried to establish the evidence for links among the Cistercians in the North. But Kornerup felt obliged to apologize to his audience for even dealing with the subject: 'Medieval monasticism,' he wrote at the opening of his article, 'was apparently not based on any healthy idea or on a true understanding of the purpose of human life'.

German positivist source criticism cut a swath through the Øm monks' account of their abbey's history with the publication of an article by G. von Buchwald in 1878. An emotional and incomplete response the next year by A.D. Jørgensen was probably prompted by nationalistic pride. Here appeared a continuing theme in Danish historical writing: the determination to establish a Danish identity in the face of German assertions of superiority. And this meant defending the reputation of medieval monks!

One of the most sympathetic of nineteenth-century Danish church historians, Hans Olrik, made a trip to France to look at the archives and establish links between Clairvaux-Citeaux and the North. He published his findings in 1893 and apologized for their meagreness, but he had established a tradition, since followed by Danish historians and archaeologists, of establishing how Denmark imitated and altered European models in building, writing, and thinking.

At the turn of the century a young archaeologist at the National Museum, Ivar Hertzsprung, excavated Cistercian sites, such as that at Vitskøl, and wrote a description of Danish monastic history covering the period 1202–1319. It was published in 1904 after his early death in 1902. Hertzsprung was one of a long and imposing line of archaeologists at the National Museum, including C.M. Smidt, Poul Nørlund, and Tage E. Christiansen. In the twentieth century there has so far been no work on all the Danish Cistercian houses. Johannes Lindbæk planned a full history of monasticism but only completed volumes on the Danish houses of the Holy Spirit in 1906 and the Franciscans in 1914. A Catholic priest, Edvard Ortved, who died in 1930, published in 1927 in Danish a general history of the Cistercian Order and posthumously in 1933 a volume on the Swedish Cistercian houses. Ortved's scattered notes on Danish Cistercian houses are contained in the Royal Library in Copenhagen. He suffered from unfavourable working conditions and lacked the training of a historian. His chapters on Swedish abbeys are more the notes of an archivist than full treatments.

Probably the best exposition of a Danish Cistercian house is that done on Sorø by Poul Nørlund, published in 1923, while Hal Koch, a church historian, in 1936 wrote a seminal article on the early history of Danish monasticism. Koch based his analysis on legal concepts and thus was able to organize the limited material and see it in a European perspective. This canon law approach characterizes the work of more recent historians like Niels Skyum-Nielsen and Troels Dahlerup.

An architectural history of all Danish monastic houses was issued in the 1930s and completed in 1941 with a volume on the Cistercians by Vilhelm Lorenzen. Here he described in detail his diggings at Herrisvad in 1939, but most of the historical information is not trustworthy. Various individual treatments of abbeys have appeared since the Second World War; Tore Nyberg in 1972 looked at monastic wills and pointed out a need to look again at monastic history as a whole.

In a standard treatment of Danish medieval history, published in 1977, Aksel E. Christensen summarized the most recent work and pointed out how little we still know, for example, about the attitudes of royal founders of monasteries. We remain as far today from a new work on Danish monasticism as we have been for the last century. As we shall see, the sources are meagre and full of problems. A complete treatment may never be written. With the Cistercians, however, we are relatively well off in our materials, but some Danish historians would still claim that it is impossible to write good history about the Cistercians in Denmark. They would insist on attention to general ecclesiastical problems, such as patronage, incorporation of churches, and other phenomena that can be investigated as legal matters. The gravity of this challenge has scratched away like a devil on my shoulder as I have revised these chapters from the original form they took when first written in 1975. What follows is a book redone in 1979–1980.

The last five years have witnessed renewed interest in Danish monasticism, partly thanks to excavations at Øm from 1975–78, at Tvis in 1978, and also at Vitskøl. Further excavations need to be made at Sorø and Vitskøl, and new light will certainly be shed on Danish Cistercian history. In what follows I skip lightly over a thousand unclear matters and at times will be seen to fall and stumble badly in my own ignorance. But it is encouraging to hope that as I have profited from Daugaard, Olrik, Koch, Nørlund, and Skyum-Nielsen, others will gain something from this book.

I

The Sources

FOR FIVE OF THE TEN DANISH CISTERCIAN abbeys for men, we are fortunate enough to have collections of sources that originate from the Middle Ages. These are Esrum in Northern Zealand, Sorø in mid-Zealand, Løgum in Southern Jutland, Vitskøl in Northern Jutland, and Øm in mid-Jutland. These collections, or books as they normally are called, are of widely varying content and provenance. Instead of going through the sources for the Danish Cistercian houses abbey by abbey, we can form a better idea of the sources' shared and varying traits if we review them chronologically. In the first group are the works written between about 1150 and 1350, Danish as well as foreign sources that have bearing on Denmark. After about 1350 there is a lapse of almost a hundred years during which we have almost no information. In the third period, from about 1440 to the coming of the Reformation to Denmark in 1536, hectic activity left behind the bulk of the medieval Danish Cistercian sources that remain in our possession. But in the fourth period, the post-Reformation remainder of the sixteenth century, the abbeys still managed to provide a wealth of materials that other men came to catalogue and use. Naturally in this last period it was property documents that interested the new secular landowners, and so most of the sources dealing with matters of spirituality, liturgy, and hagiography were thrown out and forever lost to us. From the small collection of intellectual sources that remains, we still can get some impression of the minds of the Danish Cistercians. Because this book does not allow space for a close analysis of each of these intellectual sources, I shall try at the end of this chapter to characterize what we have.

THE HIGH MIDDLE AGES: c. 1150-c. 1350

The Øm Book

The Øm Book, also known as the Øm Abbey Chronicle, is our prize source for Danish Cistercian history and a constant point of reference. The original manuscript is in the Royal Library at Copenhagen (*E don. var.*135, 4°). A printed facsimile edition with an excellent introduction by C.A. Christensen reviews the different segments of this medieval Cistercian collection of chronicle, polemic, and hagiography.[1]

The Øm Book can be divided into five sections. The first, entitled *Exordium monasterii quod dicitur Cara Insula*, is a description of the abbey's foundation in 1172 and of the devotion shown by Bishop Sven of Århus to it (ff. 2r-23r, as published in *Scriptores Minores Historiae Danicae Medii Aevi*, SM, II, 158-92). Begun in 1207 and finished in 1217, the Øm Book provides our most complete account of how a Danish Cistercian abbey began. The copyist who in a clear and attractive hand wrote down this chronicle also initiated a list of abbots, which follows it immediately (ff. 23r-28v; SM II, 192-202) and contains short descriptions of Øm's first abbots. Afterwards other hands describe later abbots and take the list up to 1320. But the last abbots are little more than names (f. 28v); the full abbot list with brief biographies ends in the 1260s. On the abbots of the 1230s and 1240s, the list is extremely detailed and almost turns into political history. The author stops short, however, and refers to the monks' *cronica nostra et acta temporum* (SM II, 199). This is a lost work which indicates that Øm produced a treatment of history which probably dealt with secular as well as monastic events.

The page following the chaotic notations for the final half century of the abbot list begins a new quire in the manuscript (ff. 29r-43r; SM II, 206-63). This contains an account of the controversy between the monks at Øm and the bishops at Århus in the 1250s and 1260s. This, the best-known part of the Øm Book, may have had a separate existence before it was attached to the *Exordium* and the abbot list. The last page (f. 43r) is cut off, and although this has led to speculation that some of the text has been lost, recent studies have shown that the account as it stands is complete.[2] A short description of the monastery's property boundaries in Djursland from the 1300s follows (ff. 43v-44r; SM II, 263-4), another indication of the way the monks kept adding sections to the Øm Book. Finally, a new quire contains the biography of Bishop Gunner of Viborg, who was abbot at Øm from 1216-21 (ff. 45r-53r; SM II, 265-78). This unique Danish medieval biography begins by stating that Gunner has already been mentioned. Most historians have concluded that this refers to the short notice about him in the abbot list (f. 24r; SM II, 194). But the same section of the abbot list has several references to a more complete but now lost 'lives of the abbots', which was not intended to be made public.[3]

In an earlier work on Øm Abbey I dated this biography to the period soon after the culmination of a major controversy between the Øm monks and the bishops of Århus, in the late 1260s or in the 1270s. Apparently it was added to the Øm Book much later. The text is much less crammed onto the page than that of the controversy account; the biography is more carefully written, with fewer grammatical and spelling mistakes. The hurried quality of the monks' polemic against the bishop of Århus indicates they may have intended to use it as a legal brief in meetings with the Danish king or with the Cistercian General Chapter, or even with the bishop himself. In any case, the final assembling of these various sections into what today is known as the Øm Book came at some time after the end of the controversy (c. 1268).

The Sorø Donation Book

Even earlier than the first part of the Øm Book is the first segment of the Sorø Donation Book (Gl. kgl. S. 2485, 4°).[4] Assembled about 1440, its first segment is apparently a copy of a lost manuscript. This provided an account of the Benedictine abbey founded by the rich Skjalm family at Sorø in the mid-twelfth century, next a justification of the abbey's refoundation by Cistercians in 1161, and finally a description of the donations to the abbey by Absalon, bishop of Roskilde, and his relatives in the Skjalm family.[5] Poul Nørlund has given the only available analysis of this part of the Donation Book and concluded that at least the section about Absalon and other members of the Skjalms was composed sometime between 1205 and 1212.[6] He does not draw any conclusions about the very first section, on the scandalous Benedictines at Sorø, which probably goes back to the same period and perhaps even an earlier. It resembles the Øm Abbey Exordium in that both accounts attempt to justify newly-established Danish Cistercian abbeys and to secure the rights and holdings gained during their first period.

Sorø Annals and Chronicles

Sorø also provides us with two collections of annals, the first known as *Annales Sorani 1130–1300*, the Older Sorø Annals.[7] Its original was destroyed in a catastrophic Copenhagen fire of 1728 which wiped out almost completely the old University Library. But we do have copies and know that the Annals were included in a Sorø manuscript containing Adam of Bremen's *Gesta pontificum Hamburgensis ecclesiae* and William of Æbelholt's *Genealogia regum danorum.*[8] The existence of these two works at Sorø tells us something about the monks' historical interests, while the Annals shows that the monks themselves wrote history. Here we must add the reservation, however, that the *Annales Sorani 1130–1300* contain no internal proof that they were written at Sorø. Their title and attribution are the result of modern historical research, and although it is unlikely that they emerged from a non-cistercian intellectual milieu, they can in themselves tell us practically nothing about the attitudes of the Sorø community. Unlike the Øm Chronicle, these annals are brief and impersonal.

Even shorter, but not so problematic in terms of Cistercian origin, are the *Annales Sorani 1202–1347*, the Younger Sorø Annals, found in *Gl. kgl. S.* 450, 2°, a manuscript from the end of the 1100s containing the *Epitome Justini* and with a famous notation on f. 129r:

Liber sancte Marie de Sora. Per manum Absalonis Archiepiscopi.

The Annals were added on the last page of the manuscript by many different hands in the 1200s and 1300s. According to Ellen Jørgensen, the first hand covers 1202–31, the second 1231–88.[9] We do obtain a few valuable notations about Sorø abbots and monks, as well as a reference to two books once contained in the abbey's library and now lost to us.

Much more valuable than these two short annals is the Elder Zealand Chronicle, finished soon after 1307.[10] Again we no longer have the original and have to depend on post-Reformation copies. We are faced by the same problem: there is no internal proof of attribution to Sorø, but it would be pedantic to doubt that we are here dealing with a work composed in a Danish Cistercian milieu. The use of international Cistercian literature, emphasis on Danish Cistercian events, together with information about central Zealand families, all point to Sorø as the place of writing. The composers of the Elder Zealand Chronicle had at their disposal sources as diverse as the Clairvaux-Eberbach *Exordium Magnum Cisterciense*, the *Vita Prima* of Saint Bernard, Sulpicius Severus's *Life of St Martin of Tours*, and lives of Thomas of Canterbury, Dominic, and Francis of Assisi.[11] The Chronicle is more a compendium of extracts from such sources than an independent work of history, and the occasional entries concerning local and national history are for the most part annalistic. Assuming that Sorø is the place the Chronicle was written, we can conclude that its contents show a Danish Cistercian interest in saints popular all over thirteenth-century Europe.

The Ryd Annals

The Ryd Annals, which continue in Latin to 1288, have various Danish extensions into the early 1300s. The surviving manuscript is in the Hamburg Staatsbibliothek and is written in a single thirteenth-century hand.[12] At the time of the Reformation, other copies of the Annals were available, as one used by a Danish Franciscan friar, Peder Olsen. The Cistercian abbey of Ryd on Flensborg Fjord, today in the German Federal Republic, is considered the place of origin because of the many references to Southern Jutland and to Cistercian events. Again we are dependent on a learned attribution to a Cistercian abbey that is based on indirect evidence. It would be presumptuous to make conclusions about Cistercian attitudes solely on the basis of statements made in the Ryd Annals.

The Colbaz Annals

While the Ryd Annals deserve a more complete analysis, the Colbaz Annals have been thoroughly investigated by Anne K.G. Kristensen.[13] They are the only Danish medieval annals for which we have an original manuscript.[14] It is in two parts, the first from the 1100s and the second from the 1200s. The earlier section was written at the Danish archiepiscopal seat at Lund in Skåne in the twelfth century, and then before 1200 the codex was transferred to the Cistercian monastery at Colbaz, a daughter of Esrum founded in 1174 and located in what is now Poland. As we shall see, there are a number of problems with the datings given for Cistercian foundations in this manuscript.

The Vitskøl Narrative

Another narrative source that needs more analysis is the so-called *Narratiuncula* for Vitskøl Abbey.[15] Again we have only post-medieval copies, the earliest being a manuscript contained at the Arnamagnæan Institute in Copenhagen, AM 291, fol., from 1608. It is entitled *Sorensis Monasterii Antiquitates* and includes a copy of the Sorø Donation Book followed by the Vitskøl narrative. A note claims that the Vitskøl *Narratiuncula* was attached to the medieval manuscript and then the text is given in ff. 70r–72v.[16] In the fifteenth-century original of the Sorø Donation Book, there is no final section with the Vitskøl narrative. It is likely therefore that Vitskøl monks brought the narrative with them when they were transferred after the Reformation to Sorø where all remaining Danish Cistercians were brought after 1536. At Sorø the *Narratiuncula* may then have been transcribed. The account was originally composed sometime in the thirteenth century by a monk from Varnhem Abbey in Sweden. Varnhem's interest in Vitskøl lay in the fact that the Swedish abbey had been forced to disband in the 1150s and was later refounded at Vitskøl. Some of Vitskøl's monks, however eventually returned to Varnhem.

The Guldholm Foundation Narrative

Much easier to date is the narrative for the founding of the abbey of Guldholm outside Slesvig, which in the 1190s was moved to Ryd on Flensborg Fjord.[17] Again there is no medieval manuscript, only a copy contained in P.J. Resen's *Atlas Danicus*, which also has a copy of King Valdemar I's foundation document for Vitskøl and part of Duke Buris's charter for Tvis Abbey. The monk who wrote the brief narrative for Guldholm gave 1289 as the year of composition. It is probably no coincidence, as we shall see, that the Guldholm narrative was composed a year after the Latin version of the Ryd Annals came to an end.

Summary of the Danish Narratives

With this mongrel collection of chronicles and annals we have covered the narrative sources composed or likely to have been composed by the Danish Cistercians during the High Middle Ages. Only the Øm Book and the Colbaz Annals have come down to us in their original form. The other narratives have to be considered through late medieval or post-Reformation versions or copies. (Parentheses indicate a modern attribution of Cistercian provenance.)

1. Colbaz Annals:	end of 1100s and 1200s (for Cistercian parts)
2. Sorø foundation account:	soon after 1200, before 1212
3. Øm foundation account:	1207–1217 (*Exordium Carae Insulae*)
4. Øm abbot list:	1217–1320 (many pauses)
5. Vitskøl *Narratiuncula*:	sometime during the 1200s
6. (*Annales Sorani* 1130–1300:	sometime during the 1200s)
7. *Annales Sorani* 1202–1347:	c.1231, c. 1288, then intermittently
8. Øm controversy account:	1260s or soon after
9. The biography of Gunner:	1260s or soon after
10. (Ryd Annals:	1200s to 1288)
11. Ryd (Guldholm) Narrative:	1289
12 (Older Zealand Chronicle:	completed soon after 1307)

It can be noted at this point that the Cistercian accounts in Denmark emerged shortly after 1200, a time when the rights and privileges of the abbeys were under inspection, or in the 1260s or soon after, when they were directly being challenged by episcopal authority. The first wave of Danish chronicle writing thus corresponds to the international Cistercian surge of historical accounts from the end of the twelfth and the early thirteenth centuries, as summed up in the *Exordium Magnum Cisterciense*, but also seen in England in the narrative of the foundation of Fountains Abbey and even in Norway in the fragment we have from a foundation narrative for Lyse Abbey outside of Bergen, dated to c.1206.[18] Cistercian historical accounts can almost always be traced to a well-defined context in which the monastery involved fosters a narrative for the sake of establishing its claims. The classic point of departure for all such accounts is the *Exordium Parvum* which sets out the history and the documentation for the founding of Citeaux itself. We can assume that any Danish Cistercian writer who set about writing about the origins of his abbey was consciously or unconsciously influenced by the Citeaux narrative, where statements of purpose and descriptive passages alternate with copies of central documents from popes and bishops.

In the Danish narratives we discern a pattern which frequently was followed; in the annals, there is little Cistercian coordination of style or content. No single one of these narrative sources can in itself, aside from the parts of the Øm Book, shed clear light on the mentality of the Danish Cistercians. But a combined treatment of all the narrative sources, supplemented by the facts that can be extracted from charters about the abbeys, can still tell us much about monastic concerns, attitudes, goals, and frustrations. Even if we leave aside the annals whose Cistercians origin could be disputed, the narrative accounts have provided for me the raw material for a synthesis concerning the Danish Cistercians. Because of such sources, I have tried to consider the monks not only in terms of what they owned and what they were given, but also with regard to how they felt about their roles and position in church and society.

Clairvaux and Citeaux Sources

Because of the Cistercian Order's international structure, we have from Clairvaux and Citeaux a number of invaluable narratives that can illuminate the Danish Cistercians' earlier history. First of all, there is a letter written by Bernard's secretary, Geoffrey, to inform Archbishop Eskil of Lund, shortly after Eskil had returned to Denmark from Clairvaux in 1153, of Bernard's death. Next there is the *Vita Prima* (Bk IV, ch. 4) of Bernard, which mentions the devotion felt by Eskil towards Bernard and Eskil's desire to have Cistercian monks with him in Scandinavia.[19] The *Vita Prima* was completed shortly after Bernard's death and so provides an almost contemporary account of Bernard's links with Denmark and Sweden. Thirdly, we have the equally valuable *Liber Miraculorum* written by Herbert of Clairvaux soon after 1178, when Eskil had retired to the monastery after giving up the archbishopric of Lund.[20] The accounts of Eskil's conversations with Herbert provide a unique insight into the mind of Eskil and help us better understand his role in the early years of the Danish Cistercians. Some of the stories from the *Vita Prima* and the *Liber Miraculorum* are incorporated into the *Exordium Magnum Cisterciense* by Conrad, who after being a monk at Clairvaux became abbot at Eberbach.[21] This work can be dated to about 1200 and shows the further evolution of stories about Eskil, Bernard, and the Scandinavian Cistercians.

As a balance to these very personal literary sources, we are fortunate in having the decisions of the Cistercian General Chapter touching on Danish Abbeys.[22] There are only a few for the 1100s, but there is a wealth of them for the 1200s. Canivez's edition is by no means exhaustive, especially for chapter decisions in the later Middle Ages.[23] But for the period up to about 1300, Canivez was able, by collecting manuscripts in various Cistercian abbeys and collating them carefully, to present a more or less complete record of the decisions made at Citeaux.

These statutes can only rarely be coordinated with information given in Cistercian accounts emerging from the Danish abbeys. The cases that came to Citeaux from Denmark often concerned abbots who had failed to attend the Chapter or disputes between different factions within monasteries. Both situations, involving scandal and punishment, provided material that the monks themselves would hardly include in a chronicle of their abbey's history. For them history writing was a means of self-justification or even of self-preservation. The Citeaux decisions show a side of the Danish monasteries' existence that the monks themselves had no interest in revealing.

Non-Cistercian Documents

Documents originating from non-cistercian institutions can also sometimes illuminate Danish Cistercian history. Such sources were not included in the Danish Cistercians' own late medieval collections of documents. The monks' failure to transcribe them can have been due to a desire to include only documents that justified their claims to lands and privileges. Evidence for their defeats was usually omitted. Thus our knowledge concerning a controversy in the early 1200s between the Vitskøl monks and the Viborg canons comes from the latter, for the dispute did not end in a clear victory for the monks.[24] In the Vitskøl Book from 1499, there is no mention at all of the controversy. At times Cistercian abbots could be ordered by the General Chapter to destroy or give away all documents, once a case was finished and decided to their detriment, as happened at Esrum in the 1250s when it lost a dispute with Doberan over the parentage of Dargun Abbey.[25] Despite the monks' clear penchant for manipulating historical sources in their own favour and leaving out what they did not like, we occasionally get glimpses of the shadow side of their lives through documents from other sources.

Unfortunately the most brilliant narrator of the early Danish Middle Ages, Saxo, took no interest in the Cistercians as an Order and mentioned them only in connection with Eskil. Saxo's possible reasons for ignoring the explosion of Cistercian energy in Denmark during the second half of the twelfth century will receive attention in Chapter Three.

So long as we keep in mind the tendency of any institution to emphasize and preserve documents favourable to its own interests, we can use the records kept by the Danish Cistercians to supplement the literary sources and provide a fuller picture of Cistercian life in Denmark.

THE LATE MIDDLE AGES: c.1440–c.1520

For the second half of the 1300s and the first part of the 1400s, we have no narrative sources at all for the Danish Cistercians and can trace their history only through the documents that concern them. But after the mid-fifteenth century and especially during the thirty year period 1490–1520, there was an almost feverish attempt to collect and collate the documents of the previous centuries. While high medieval Danish Cistercian sources are dominated by chronicles, the late medieval sources are almost all collections of charters, dealing with the various abbeys' properties and privileges. These collections, as at Sorø, Esrum, and Vitskøl, stretch from the foundation right to the end of the fifteenth century and so furnish us with the bulk of our knowledge about how the Cistercians were legally situated in Danish society and the extent of the properties they had amassed over centuries.

It would be easy to assume that the years after 1490 brought so many collections because the monks were aware that their position in society was slipping. By such reasoning the monks would have anticipated the need to defend themselves, first of all by bringing together all vital documents in one place. But the causes of this activity are not so easily determined, precisely because we lack any narrative source from the same period in which a Cistercian would have revealed something about the monks' attitude towards society. Another factor that needs to be considered is the general tendency during this period among other groups of landowners (the crown, noble families, and bishops) to have property books drawn up. The late Middle Ages saw an economic upswing in Danish society that seems to have affected the Cistercians as well as other privileged groups. The compilations may actually reflect a new energetic optimism among the monks instead of any great fear of the future.

An immediate explanation for the collecting and copying of original documents done in these years is that dynamic abbots led Esrum, Sorø, and Vitskøl, men whose personalities and programs have left a mark on the period. But this impression may well result from the fact that these men were on the threshold of the Reformation and made up the last Cistercian generation. Many of the traces they left of themselves survived because they were preserved by post-Reformation Denmark. This was due not to reverence for the abbots but to the desire to determine exactly what the various abbeys owned prior to their secularization.

The Sorø Donation Book

The forerunner of the collections of the 1490s is the Sorø Donation Book (Gl. kgl. S. 2485, 4°), from about 1440 or shortly after. After an initial section on the founding and early donors of the abbey that probably goes back to the period before 1214, the Donation Book gives an account of the abbey's holdings at Broby in Alsted herred. As Poul Nørlund has pointed out, the monks had in 1440 recently acquired the last part of Broby from the Lunge family. This acquisition was the culmination of the monks' century-long attempt to get hold of this valuable property, located a few kilometres south of the monastery. Nørlund thought that the monks were very much afraid that the new holding 'would be challenged by the powerful and greedy Lunges', and so the monks 'armoured themselves for the possibility of a dispute'.[26]

There is no better explanation for the appearance of the Donation Book at this point in Sorø's history. But a few supplementary observations are perhaps in order. Once the monks began to compile their many records on Broby, they apparently decided it would be a good idea to collate all their holdings and to give short summaries of their acquisitions through the centuries. To this new register they added the early medieval chronicles. The result is a reference book to Sorø properties in very rough form, but in general organized so that the holdings near the abbey are described first, and the more distant later, with a section on new acquisitions in market towns toward the end. At the very end of the Donation Book is an extra section on Broby that in the main repeats earlier information but provides more evidence of the monks' concern for their holdings there. Once we have removed the initial chronicle section, there is thus a symmetry in the Donation Book, with Broby at the beginning and at the end of the property register.[27]

This structure has not previously been noticed, for Langebek's edition in the *Scriptores Rerum Danicarum* ends not with the Broby notations but with a summary of a case that has nothing to do with the contents of the Donation Book.[28] In the manuscript, the last page has been crossed out on the verso, the side which contains the extraneous account which Langebek nevertheless included. The monks probably used this leaf because it was only written on one side; they deliberately scratched out this side so they could finish their Property Book on the other side. The monks were expert at recycling writing materials. A careful inspection of the manuscript also reveals signs of its incompleteness. What we have may well be a rough draft of a register of the abbey's holdings meant for internal use and later amplification. But it was never converted into a finished work.

The monks were apparently right to be concerned over their Broby holdings, for various royal documents from later in the century bear witness to further disputes finally settled by a royal court.[29] But the complicated claims to Broby may have been only one factor that inspired the drawing up of the Donation Book. The abbacy of Niels Clementsen was nearing its end in the 1440s. Under him Sorø had expanded its properties, especially in market towns, and he may himself have wanted the achievements of his regime to be apparent to his successors.[30]

The Sorø Book

The next major source for the Danish Cistercians is the so-called Sorø Book, a collection of papal, royal, and episcopal privileges which was certified in Copenhagen by the archbishop of Lund in 1494. Here for once we can be almost certain that the collection resulted from outside pressure on a monastery, for in the years after 1489, the Bishop of Roskilde, Niels Skave, made life miserable for the monks because of a dispute concerning the occupation of a priest's farm. The question involved the legal rights of the bishop over the property, which the monks claimed as their own. The controversy manifested itself at many levels: moral, administrative, and political. In the end it was settled by the king. In an excellent account of the dispute, Johannes Lindbæk concluded that the Sorø Book may have been drawn up by the monks as early as 1490 to counter the bishop's attacks on their rights and privileges.[31] The situation is similar to that described in the Øm monks' thirteenth-century account of their bitter quarrel with Bishop Tyge of Århus. In both cases outside challenges inspired the monks to record their own history. But in the 1260s the result was a narrative full of documents, while in the 1490s the outcome was a collection of documents without any narrative aside from some marginal commentaries some of them written in Danish. The manuscript is deposited at the Arnamagnæan Institute (AM 290, fol.)[32]. Interestingly enough, the Sorø Book was sent prior to 1494 to the curia for papal confirmation, but this one never came. The best Abbot Jakob of Sorø could do was to get the Archbishop of Lund, Jens Brostrup's, confirmation, in 1494.

The Esrum Book

Three years later, the most valuable and complete collection of medieval privileges and property deeds for a Danish Cistercian monastery was made, the *Codex Esromensis* or Esrum Book (*E don. var.* 140, 4°). This bulky volume can be dated to 1497, for it ends with a Property Book listing all the abbey's holdings in that year and the rent paid on each of them to the monastery. There are two alternating hands, but one of them predominates. As in the Sorø Book, a couple of documents were added later than 1497, and in 1512 the papal legate, Itzardus, certified the collection at Helsingør. In his text he says that the Codex had 212 pages, as it does today. There are only a very few marks and corrections made by anyone other than the original writer. The editor of the Esrum Book, O. Nielsen, wrote in his preface that the monks almost certainly included all the documents for properties and privileges that the abbey still had at the end of the fifteenth century.[33]

It is impossible to attribute this collection to any outside event affecting Esrum. But Peder Andersen, who had been abbot since the 1480s, was apparently interested in creating the same orderly collection of privileges that already had been made at Sorø. He had been busy during the preceding decade with trading properties with influential aristocrats and getting hold of buildings in Copenhagen. As we shall see in the last chapter, the fifteenth century brought a flurry of interest among Danish Cistercian abbeys in acquiring and developing properties in market towns. Here the new wealth of society was being concentrated, and none of the original Cistercian statutes seem to have prevented abbots from acquiring such properties in order to rent them out and thus provide their houses with steady incomes. By 1497 Peder Andersen was probably near the end of his abbacy and wanted to put his house in order so that the monks would have an easy guide to the changes of the past years as well as to the situation of their property holdings and privileges in general.

The Vitskøl Book

In 1499 Abbot Henrik Kristiernsen Tornekrans of Vitskøl had the notary Bent Knudsen at Viborg transcribe the monastery's papal, royal, and episcopal privileges. When this was completed, two canons of Århus witnessed to the correctness of the copy, which became the Vitskøl Book. It is much closer to the Sorø than to the Esrum Book, for it does not contain documents concerning property transactions. Luckily the Sorø Donation Book makes up for this absence in the Sorø Book, but at Vitskøl there is no record of a similar property book. Thus we know much less about Vitskøl's holdings and can trace them only in the earliest period through lists included in papal and royal documents included in the Vitskøl Book.

After the Reformation, in 1574–75, the Vitskøl Book was copied by Albert Knoppert, a notary, and witnessed by Copenhagen University and the chapters of Århus, Viborg, and Ribe cathedrals. This copy and the original are lost to us, but seven later copies from the seventeenth and eighteenth centuries are extant, all of them dependent on the same source, the 1574–75 transcript.[34] The oldest was made about 1670 (Ny kgl. S. 1173, 4⁰) and is the basis for the only published version of the Vitskøl Book available, in the *Dänische Bibliothec*, Volume VI.[35]

The man responsible for the Vitskøl Book, Abbot Henrik of Vitskøl went on to become abbot of Esrum and finally, about 1510, of Sorø.[36] An aristocrat and politically active, he appreciated the need for collecting Cistercian sources. Abbot Henrik apparently felt as responsible for Løgum's records as for those of his own abbey's. In 1518 at Sorø he sponsored the writing of a Necrologium for Løgum Abbey and added at the end his desire to be listed among Løgum's benefactors and to be remembered in the monks' prayers.[37] By this time Sorø had become the undisputed leader of the Danish Cistercian abbeys in terms of wealth and influence. In 1524 Henrik had a *Catalogus Illustrium Sorae Sepultorum* compiled; even though it can at times be inaccurate or confusing, it provides a valuable supplement to the information we have in the Sorø Donation Book about lay families who showed generosity to the abbey.[38]

All the late medieval sources seem to have arisen out of local situations and disputes, or the threat of them, and point to dynamic abbots who wanted to clarify matters. In these sources there is more a sense of a local and isolated desire to protect the rights and holdings of individual abbeys than any indication that the abbots felt any general threat to the future of the Cistercians in Denmark.

POST-REFORMATION SOURCES: 1536–1606

The coming of the Reformation to Denmark meant a quick end to Franciscan and Dominican priories in the market towns, but the monasteries in the countryside, including the Cistercian houses, were frequently allowed to exist as Protestant religious communities for many decades after 1536.[39] The relatively peaceful transition from Catholicism to Protestantism in Denmark is iconographically expressed by the gravestones for the last abbots of Sorø. The last Catholic abbot, Henrik Tornekrans (d.1538), is shown as a Cistercian bearing the abbot's staff, while his successor, Niels Jespersen, (d. 1556), is represented in the Reformation garb common to Danish clergy with a small roll instead of a staff as the symbol of his authority. Sorø maintained its transitional status of a Protestant home for former Cistercian monks until 1586. A source from this period witnesses a continuing interest in the monastery's history.

The Sorø Abbot List

This is the *Series Abbatum Monasterii Sorensis*, completed soon after 1556.[40] It is a very undependable document,[41] and even though its compilier had better materials than we do for making a complete list of abbots, its information seldom agrees with the dates and names given for abbots in documentary sources for Sorø. An introductory paragraph indicates that the list was begun while Sorø was still Catholic; perhaps soon after the 1524 list of benefactors was completed.[42] But in mentioning the last, Protestant, abbots, the continuator could no longer have had the old motive of defending the Cistercian heritage.

The Løgum Book

At Løgum before the Reformation, no complete account of properties was made that has come down to us. At the end of 1575 and the beginning of 1576, negotiations took place in Kolding between the Danish crown and Duke Hans the Elder concerning spiritual jurisdiction over the churches in the southern part of Ribe diocese. Many of these churches had been administered by Løgum monks, so the original documents regarding acquisition by and rights of the monks were brought to Kolding and copied. In 1578 this original work was copied into what became the Løgum Book.[43] Thus we have for the Danish Cistercians a vital source which was not drawn up by the monks themselves to defend their rights and holdings. The source collection emerges from a post-Reformation dispute, so the contents do not in their arrangement reflect the interests of the Løgum monks. By this time any surviving Løgum monks had long since been transferred to Sorø, where after the Reformation the last Danish Cistercians were allowed to live out their days in peace, but not to recruit new members. The Løgum Book, like the Sorø Book and other collections, contains almost exclusively documents that established or guaranteed the rights and holdings of the former monastery. A gap in information about the monks' claims to Brede church indicates that they had been defeated and so did not keep any record of the decision that had gone against them.[44] But when the case was reopened in the 1300s and went in their favour, they were careful to begin once again to keep the documents involved.

The copyists of the Løgum documents were restricted to what the monks had decided to save in their archives. They followed the procedure of the Esrum Book: first they covered the monastery's properties in the immediate vicinity; later they branched out. The only significant difference between the pre-Reformation Esrum Book and the post-Reformation Løgum Book is that the former has papal and royal documents first, followed by property documents, while the opposite is the case for Løgum. The Esrum monks had been concerned first with establishing their general rights and privileges in church and society, while the post-Reformation copyists for Løgum were mainly interested in the monastery's properties. It is fortunate for us that they nevertheless decided to include the papal and royal privileges, perhaps as an afterthought in case one of these by now antiquated documents might have bearing on a property dispute.

The Øm Inventory and the Skanderborg Register

The post-Reformation sources, like the late medieval collections, are largely concerned with properties. This is the case also for the Øm Inventory from 1554,[45] and the Skanderborg Register of 1606.[46] But in the Øm records of holdings we are also given a careful list of the books in the monks' and abbot's libraries.[47] It is one of the most informative and exciting indications of the quality and depth of the intellectual life at a Danish Cistercian abbey. It also give us an opportunity to see how one of the last Øm abbots did his best to keep up with the newest developments in Protestant theology, a rare indication of how the former Cistercians adapted themselves to the new regime in Denmark.

All these sources, both narrative and documentary, have provided the basis for my attempt to look at the Danish Cistercians as a group of abbeys that had common interests and policies and a shared way of life throughout the Middle Ages. Fortunately many of the documentary sources have been included in chronological order in the *Diplomatarium Danicum*, so it has not always been necessary to wander among a number of the older printed collections. My method has required preliminary studies on Esrum, Sorø, and Øm, followed by an examination of all the sources for all Danish Cistercians abbeys from 1144 to 1414. This has necessitated much tedious wading through papal bulls and property documents that tell little about life at the abbeys themselves. Because of the limited narrative materials available, I have nevertheless welcomed this solid foundation of information. Without the guidance of the *Diplomatarium*, I would have been overwhelmed by problems regarding dating and provenance.

Upon completing my chronological tour through all documentary sources, I returned to the separate periods in Danish medieval history and combined documentary information with the available literary sources. Here I made the leap from being an archivist to being an historian; it remains to be seen whether the jump has brought Cistercian studies any distance.

The first period of the Cistercians in Denmark is relatively well covered by narrative and documentary sources that complement each other, both those from Denmark and those from Clairvaux-Citeaux. After about 1220, however, there is a gap that can be only partly filled in by information in the Øm abbot list. The Øm controversy in the 1260s provides the richest combination of documentation and emotional expression of an institution's situation that we have for any decade in Danish medieval history. From about 1270 to 1310, the narrative sources become much thinner, and we become ever more dependent on the documents. For a whole century after 1310, the documents are almost exclusively our guide. There is very little in the way of international material to direct us. This limitation encouraged me to use sources from the later 1400s to bridge the gap to the Reformation. But I have chosen not to write a final chapter on fifteenth-century developments, for this could easily turn into a book in itself.

THE INTELLECTUAL SOURCES

It is wrong to separate the 'intellectual life' of the monasteries from their economic and social involvement. If we use the term in its broadest sense, then every chronicle and collection of annals we have from the monasteries tells us something about the thoughts and attitudes that characterized the monks. The best introduction to the minds of the Danish Cistercians is the Øm Book itself, its grammar, style, sentence structure, and ideas—as well as its omissions. Yet not even here are we able to find the Danish Cistercians producing a full work of history. Their self-defence and polemics have an immediately practical goal, and thus no Danish Cistercian writer approaches the level of the twelfth-century clerk Saxo in writing history. As I have already indicated in my comments on the Older Zealand Chronicle, monastic authors saw their task in terms of guaranteeing the survival of historical traditions that supported their claims to a favoured place for their Order in society. Both in the Clairvaux tradition leading to the *Exordium Magnum* and in Danish materials, the Cistercians were mainly compilers and were not concerned about original approaches to writing history. In the brief life of Abbot Gunner at the end of the Øm book, we encounter a Danish Cistercian who was able to describe persons and events with originality and depth. The existence of such a biography makes it impossible to characterize the Danish Cistercians as intellectually impoverished. On the basis of what we do have, the monks seem to have been interested in history, biblical exegesis, theology, and law.

The Øm library list from 1554 supports the impression one gains from the few surviving medieval manuscripts from Danish houses that the monks had enough to give them the fundamentals of biblical and theological understanding. If they wanted to advance further, they had to go abroad to Cistercian houses of studies or to the universities themselves. In the 1200's Cistercians may have been among the Danish ecclesiastics who went to Paris for their higher education.[48] But in the later Middle Ages Cistercians, like monks at Esrum's daughter abbey at Colbaz, probably limited themselves to German universities.[49] By this time universities had become more local and regional in their recruitment and drew less on students from distant countries. And at the end of the fifteenth century the abbot of Sorø seems to have tried to establish his own house of studies in order to keep monks from leaving the country to follow a course of studies.[50]

The Danish Cistercians appear to have been intellectually isolated but by no means ignorant in grammatical and theological training. Such a perspective fits the social geography of Denmark itself. It was a country on the fringes of Christian Europe. Thanks to Eskil, the links between Clairvaux and the Danish houses under Esrum were highly personal. But by the end of the twelfth century, the Danish Cistercians no longer looked abroad for their main religious inspiration. They concentrated on consolidating their properties and privileges and on meeting the challenges they met in Danish society.[51] The Danish monks seen in the intellectual sources are solid citizens of the Christian commonwealth of Europe and of the Cistercian Order.

The Aurora of Peter of Riga (Løgum)

From thirteenth-century Løgum we have a copy of Peter of Riga's Aurora (*Gl. kgl. S. 54*, fol.). This is a versified version of the Bible written by a canon of St Denis in Rheims who died in 1209. Peter's paraphrase contains more than fifteen thousand verses with his own allegorical and moral commentary, and was written during the last quarter of the twelfth century at the request of his students and colleagues. At the end of the Løgum manuscript is the sentence: *hos Tuuo conversus depinxit metrice versus*, a valuable indication that a lay-brother at Løgum could copy a book as one of the tasks he performed for the monastery. There are a number of marginal notes, many of them simply headings, written in different hands and apparently there to make it easier for readers to find the sections they needed. Some of the explanatory notes indicate that the readers of the work were young novices or monks who could not have been expected to know the Bible and associated biblical legends well. On f. 74, for example, a note explains that Longinus was the soldier who opened Christ's side with a lance and later became a martyr. In such a versified Bible we can see a teaching instrument at a Danish Cistercian monastery. Through the *Aurora* the monks could easily learn biblical stories and perhaps memorize some of them. It may seem rather elementary, but such a method gave life to the Bible and made its text more accessible.

The Compendium of Theology (Vitskøl)

Just as the Cistercians would have been expected to know the Bible without ever having read through the entire Vulgate, so too they had to know something about theology without being called upon to follow the newest arguments of the scholastics. From Vitskøl Abbey we have a *Compendium theologice veritatis* (*Ny kgl. S.* 13, 8°), which was copied in the fourteenth century under an Abbot Peder and rebound with iron clips in the fifteenth century under an Abbot Henrik, whose name was engraved into the binding. The Compendium is a textbook for beginners and a reference book of problems, with short, easy sections on everything theological a monk might need to know. It starts with God and his attributes, turns in its second book to creation, the angels, man, and the immortality of the soul, and in the third book takes up sin and grace. The fourth book deals with the Incarnation and the Redemption, the fifth the virtues, the sixth the sacraments, while the seventh devotes a whole section to purgatory, an indication of late medieval concern for the remission of punishment for sin.[52]

This is in every way a school book, but for a monastic school and not a university. In order to assure that readers be made aware of the sources for the declarations in the text, names of authorities were placed in the margins. Patristic and moral theology does not go beyond twelfth century authorities. There is no trace of later scholastic writers. A final indication that the book was meant to be used by monks for their own moral betterment is a marginal note in the section on obedience referring to the *regula beati Benedicti* (f. 150v). The notator wanted to be sure readers were aware that the obedience spoken of in the Gospels was the same as that enjoined by Saint Benedict.

The Transitus Super Genesim (Herrisvad)

The fourteenth-century Vitskøl Compendium of theology and the thirteenth-century Løgum versified Bible are the two most valuable indications of the content of learning at Danish Cistercian houses. They deserve closer study and analysis, especially the Compendium. Another manuscript of Biblical content comes from the Cistercian abbey of Herrisvad in Skåne, *Transitus super Genesim* (*E. don. variorum* 138, 4°). There is a notation *Sancte Marie Herivadensis. Per manum Suenonis Symonis.* Thus we know another Danish Cistercian copyist, Sven Simonsen. This is from about 1200 and so, together with the first part of the Øm Book, is one of our earliest Cistercian manuscripts. The title given is:

> *Transitus super Genesim, Exodam, Leviticum, Numeros, Deuteronomium. Super duodecimos prophetas et super Isaiam. Augustinus de heresibus et sententie breves de sacramentis.*

The 132 pages, however, get only as far as Isaiah. The rest is missing. The *Transitus* is much more a proper Biblical commentary than Peter of Riga's versified Bible and shows an interest in understanding some of the most difficult books of the Old Testament. Another Herrisvad manuscript, only a fragment, is AM 392, fol., with a text from the 1200s ending with the words: *Expliciunt glose Gaufridi Babionis secundum Matheum. Liber sancte Marie de Herivado.* Finally some pages of the abbey's accounts now among the Royal Library's fragments contain parts of the *Miracula s. Thomae.*[53]

Esrum Materials

For Esrum we have only a manuscript at the Vatican Library, which Ellen Jørgensen in her study of Danish medieval libraries thought might have been taken to Rome while Esrum was still Cistercian as part of the efforts made by Italian humanists in collecting from monasteries codices that might be of value to them.[54] The contents of this manuscript are much more varied than the biblical, theological, or hagiographical fare we thus far have met. The manuscript, composed at the end of the twelfth or in the early thirteenth century, contains a treatise by Bede on sacred vessels used in the celebration of the mass, on the tabernacle and the priest's vestments, together with travel descriptions of Palestine and Rome, and finally part of Gregory of Tours' *Liber miraculorum.* One assumes it was the description of Rome which interested the humanists. The contents of this manuscript point to the breadth of the intellectual interests of the Esrum monks in about 1200: liturgy, travel, miracles, all could be included in a Cistercian abbey's book collection.

A lost Esrum work is the *Libri Esromensium nostrorum* mentioned in the Sorø Donation Book. These Esrum Books may have been a collection of notations about the monastery's lay benefactors, as we can see from the reference: 'That Jens [Sunesen] died at the Lord's sepulchre, and in him divine works shone forth, as is contained in a letter which the guardian of Jerusalem wrote about this to King Valdemar, the tenor of which has been annotated in the books of our Esrum men'.[55] The number of lost works for Danish monasteries vastly exceeds those which we have. For Øm we have already mentioned an independent lives of the abbots and the *cronica nostra et acta temporum* referred to in the Øm Book. The latter were supposed to give a full account of the tragic death of King Erik Plowpenny. [56]

Sorø Materials

Aside from the dozens of volumes mentioned in the Øm inventory of 1554, the greatest number of lost works whose titles we have were at Sorø. The

Liber qui dicitur Hervæus and the *Excerpta patrum* are mentioned in the Sorø Annals and will be considered later. There were also, according to Ellen Jør- gensen, a Valerius Maximus manuscript that burned in the University Library in 1728, the *Hexaemeron*, which was Anders Sunesen's renowned and practical school book of theology in verse, and the Adam of Bremen manuscript.[57]

But Sorø also had a wealth of manuscripts that we still have, including the Justin manuscript owned by Archbishop Absalon of Lund, used by the his- torian Saxo, and containing the *Annales Sorani* that were added between 1202 and 1347 (*Gl. kgl. S.* 45°, fol. membr.). Verner Dahlerup has written about the Justin manuscript and about Sorø's Jens Jyde.[58] He lived at the end of the thirteenth century and was responsible for AM 455, which con- tains legal documents of inestimable value to Danish medieval history: the preface to the Jutlandic Law, Valdemar's Sjællandic Law, the Church Law for Zealand (Sjælland), and a later version of Sjællandic Law. Jens Jyde also copied out parts of King Valdemar's Property Book, contained in the same manuscript.[59] Dahlerup realized that the copying of the Property Book and the kingdom's and church's laws at Sorø indicated a desire on the abbot's part to protect monastery properties by being able to refer quickly to Da- nish as well as ecclesiastical law. One could go even further and claim that Jens Jyde's work, done at about the time a Sorø abbot functioned as counsellor to King Erik Menved and when a Sorø monk held a doctorate in canon law, indicates that Sorø was a centre for legal studies, both secular and ecclesiastical.

Dahlerup also brought to light a Sorø manuscript containing a culinary and medical treatise, dealing in part with the healing properties of herbs (*Ny kgl. S.* 66, 8°). This was copied by the monk Knud Jul, who was at Sorø in 1310.[60] When Dahlerup wrote in the 1920s, excavations at Øm had not yet led to a thorough analysis of the skeletons found there. Work done in the 1930s showed the great surgical skill of the Cistercians who, like the Augustinians at Æbelholt, were able to treat wounds that normally would have been fatal.[61] Nevertheless Dahlerup could assert that Knud Jul's medical book showed that the monks 'medical knowledge was equal to the best that the Middle Ages knew'.

Law, medicine, theology, biblical studies, liturgical treatments, history writing, hagiography: all these pursuits were fostered at Danish Cistercian abbeys. We can see only a tiny fragment of what the monks knew and learned, but we can at least conclude that their interests were widespread. At the end of the Middle Ages in Sorø, the writing of history and the pas- sion for verse helped produce a secular history of the Danish kings written in Danish, the Rhyme Chronicle (*Rimkrøniken*). In writing such a chronicle, the Sorø monks were doing for Danish secular history what Peter of Riga had already provided for salvation history: they were offering a pleasant and simplified version of a long, otherwise difficult story that now could be read aloud, listened to, and learned.

The Øm library as it appeared in 1554 encourages us to look at the monks as intellectual plodders without great ambitions. But the middling quality of their learning left room for monks who went further and made original contributions, such as the writer of Bishop Gunner's biography and the authors of the Rhyme Chronicle. In order to understand the significance of these scattered works and chance allusions to lost books, it is necessary to remember that the Cistercians' lives were not centred on intellectual activities.[62] They spent their time primarily on prayer and the recitation of the divine office, activities whose content would have been the same in Denmark as anywhere else in the Order.

Because of their hidden lives lived around the liturgy, the monks are largely unknowable to us as human beings. Only in moments of passion and in terms of materialistic involvement do they let themselves be seen in our sources. However little the intellectual sources reveal about the monks' interests, they point out that we are dealing with a social group that was more than a collection of rich landowners. As Jean Leclercq has often pointed out, the monks used learning only in order to grow in the spiritual life. Thus the moralistic and allegorical content of their theological works, as at Vitskøl, should not be reason for disdain and comparison with the scholastics. The monks sought not learning in itself, but a path to God.

The monks' learning was thus immensely practical in character. Everything was to be used in moving towards divine union. There was no reason to get involved in tricky intellectual questions. Similarly when it came to medicine, the monks preferred remedies to theories. In writing history, they were interested not in speculating on the ages of the world but in getting down the basic facts about their foundations in order to avoid challenges to their rights and privileges. We can thus divide the monks' intellectual sources into two areas: monastic education and edification on the one hand, and monastic rights and privileges in society on the other. The first goal inspired the copying of works of theology, medicine, and hagiography, while the second led to modest works of history, the collection of property documents, and the copying of law books.

Basic education and spiritual advancement within the monastery; propaganda and self-defense without. These are the two mainsprings of the Danish Cistercians' intellectual activity. Surprisingly, the Cistercians in their limitations still have much to show us. Even if we had known them only through their painstakingly written manuscripts and had no traces of their churches and other buildings, they would still have something to say which is immediately understandable even in our culture. The Cistercians made the best use of the materials they had at their disposal. They almost never wasted space and they reused what they could. The Cistercians led the way in the twelfth century not only in cultural and religious renewal but also in the art of low consumption and recycling.

In the Danish abbeys of which we know something, the Cistercians seem only rarely to have been obsessed by a single idea or passion. The demands of the land and the neighbourhood and the stratified society of medieval Europe, together with the Cistercians' own chosen isolation, made it impossible for them to impose their own views and solutions on the rest of society. But with their material wealth and moral self-assurance, they could also be sensitive and responsive to what was going on around them. Time and again, they managed to adjust to new developments. The Danish Cistercians, like their brethren in other lands, lived on for centuries by finding ways to renew themselves in their relations with other groups in society. It is the story of this changing pattern of relationships that we best can trace from the sources we have at our disposal.

II

Arrival & Growth

1144–1177

TEN CISTERCIAN MONASTERIES were founded in Denmark between 1144 and 1215, an imposing number for such a relatively small area. Moreover, at a time in the history of the Cistercian Order when dependent houses for women were looked upon with disdain and distrust, three of these came into being.[1] It is tempting to look at this development in terms of a Cistercian revolution that transformed religious life in Denmark and gave it a depth and an international perspective it previously had lacked. Unlike the area to the south along the Baltic coast, Denmark had been Christian for a century when the Cistercians arrived. But in the meagre sources, we can see Christianity only as it manifested itself in the life of the upper classes. The building of hundreds of parish churches in stone in the twelfth century was once thought to reflect a surge of peasant Christianity, but the newest research indicates that here too we find mainly the imprint of the magnates.[2]

The Cistercians were not interested in bringing the Gospel to the masses. By founding their monasteries outside such traditional centres of politics and commerce as Ribe, Odense and Roskilde, the monks nevertheless contributed to the spread of Christianity in the Danish countryside. They quickly entangled themselves in the finances and functions of parish churches in the neighbourhood of their monasteries, even though Cistercian legislation strictly forbade such involvement. The first great period of Cistercian expansion in Denmark can be looked upon as a meeting of the old Christian south, now reinvigorated through Gregorian reform and mo-

37

nastic renewal, with the transitional culture of the north.³ Neither fully Christian nor still pagan, the northern magnates sought in the Cistercians a link to the spiritual riches of the south. The outcome of this meeting was fruitful in terms of architecture, education, farming methods, and religious inspiration.

It would be misleading, however, to accept Cistercian sources at face value and concede the medieval monks' deep conviction that their Order was the centre of earthly as well as heavenly society. In the twelfth century there were many other social groups and movements creating Danish culture and religion: the building of parish churches, the spread of other religious orders, the formation of cathedral chapters, and the activities of individual bishops. But the Cistercians were very much in the forefront. They could penetrate into the very dreams of a peasant in mid-Jutland. They could offer a burial place to the richest family on Zealand. They could involve themselves in the controversy over which pope the Danish king was to recognize during the schism of the 1160s. No account of Danish medieval history can leave out the roles played by the Cistercians; no account of medieval Cistercian history can ignore the functions of the monks in this distant northern clime.

THE 1140s: DARKNESS AND LIGHT

For the coming of the Cistercians to Denmark, we have nothing but a few stark words in two of the early annals, those from Colbaz, now in Poland, and from Ryd, now just south of the Danish border in the Federal Republic of Germany on Flensborg Fjord: *1144. Conventus venit in Herrisvad.*⁴ Herrisvad is in the province of Skåne, since the seventeenth century part of Sweden. It became the mother house of three other abbeys: Løgum in Southern Jutland, Tvis in Western Jutland, and Holme on the island of Fyn. Of these four houses, the only one from which we have sources of any significance is Løgum. We are thus at a loss to explain how and why the *conventus* or chapter of Cistercian monks came to Herrisvad. We know only that Herrisvad's mother house was Citeaux, the great mother of all Cistercians, and not Clairvaux, from which Archbishop Eskil of Lund drew a group of monks in the beginning of the 1150s. In most modern treatments of Danish Cistercians, the close relationship between Eskil and Bernard of Clairvaux has been strongly emphasized.⁵ This explains Eskil's activities and contributions after 1150, but what about the previous decade? Is it impossible for us to establish the moment at which the great northern archbishop became convinced that the Cistercians belonged in his part of the world? Or must we here, as in so many other aspects of Scandinavian history, merely utter a sigh and point to the lack of sources to provide any answer to the problem.

Since the beginning of the 1950s there has been a tendency to denigrate Eskil's role in monastic foundations.[6] It would be easy to strengthen the imposing evidence amassed for this view by minimizing Eskil's involvement in the founding of Herrisvad. But such a conclusion would ignore a tradition both in Danish and in Clarevallian sources for Eskil's central role in bringing the Cistercians to Herrisvad. The first part of the *Exordium Carae Insulae*, from 1207, specifies Eskil as Herrisvad's founder. This source comes from the culmination of the foundation period for Danish Cistercian houses and not from the beginning. It is full of controversial subjects, and its author assumes a defensive and, at times, polemical tone.[7] The Øm monastic author clearly wanted to establish the legitimacy of his abbey's foundation by pointing out Archbishop Eskil's role in confirming its early privileges. The words of praise given him thus had a very practical purpose. But this intent is not in itself grounds for rejecting the claims made:

> Archbishop Eskil worked always and everywhere for the building and strengthening of this house and was devoted to it. He had not previously given it a letter of privilege because it had not before been sought from him. He led forth two groups of monks, one from Citeaux, the other from Clairvaux, and founded two monasteries. From them many groups of monks have been scattered throughout Denmark. Afterwards he was made a monk at Clairvaux, and after some time ended his life there. He was buried honourably under marble before the great altar.[8]

We find here a number of statements concerning Eskil that are frequently made in medieval descriptions of him. He founded one monastery from Citeaux and another from Clairvaux. These monasteries gave rise to others. He became a monk at Clairvaux, died there, and was buried in a place of honour. This information agrees with what we find in early sources from Clairvaux, most specifically the *Exordium Magnum Cisterciense* from the turn of the century. Here Eskil is named as the man who 'obtained two houses of the Cistercian Order, one from the house of Citeaux itself, and the other from Clairvaux'.[9]

One of the sources from which the *Exordium Magnum* takes a great deal of its material, the *Vita Prima* of Saint Bernard, has a section written by Bernard's secretary, Geoffrey of Auxerre, in 1156.[10] Eskil is again named as the founder of the monasteries in his homeland, but Geoffrey does not specify the number for which he was responsible. Finally the *Liber Miraculorum* by Herbert of Clairvaux, composed between 1178 and 1181, while Eskil was living in retirement as a monk at Clairvaux, speaks of his 'several convents'.[11] But again we are left without any specific mention of Eskil as founder of Herrisvad.

Thus we cannot find a mid-twelfth-century source to back up the early thirteenth-century assertion that Eskil was responsible for Herrisvad. But it is still likely that as archbishop of Lund, Eskil did what he could to see to it that the Cistercians came to his diocese. Eskil spent much time and effort in securing the independence of his see from the archbishopric of Hamburg-Bremen, and so he had a great deal to gain by strengthening links with a French monastic order. One tradition must be dropped, however: the myth that Eskil gave Herrisvad his own patrimonial holdings and consecrated the new monastery on 1 July 1150.[12] Perhaps Eskil was there on that date, but our only confirmation exists in a sixteenth-century manuscript in Stockholm's Royal Library entitled *Antiquitates cenobii Herriswadensis in Schandia.*[13] Even though the list is very late, it is our one source for Herrisvad from the monastery itself that has not perished by fire, reform, or indifference. It contains inscriptions from the seats in the monks' choir and in the lay brothers' choir, together with information about daughter foundations, names of abbots, and inscriptions on the organ and on grave stones. Among these is mentioned an inscription in the monks' choir that the church was begun in 1158 and was made possible by the honoured lord, Eskil, archbishop of Lund, who was to be named with all reverence. We thus have late medieval documentation for Eskil's involvement with Herrisvad back to 1158.

If we do assume that Eskil was in one way or another active in 1144, as he apparently was in 1158, the question arises why he brought monks to Denmark from Citeaux and not from Clairvaux. The best possible explanation has been given by an authority on Løgum abbey, Jürgen Wissing. He points out that the year before the foundation of Herrisvad, in 1143, Cistercians had been sent from Clairvaux to found monasteries in Sweden: Nydala in Småland and Alvastra in Östergötland.[14] We can add the information that between 1140 and 1143, Clairvaux founded seventeen new daughter houses; in 1144 only one. Apparently the supply of novices at Clairvaux available for another emigration to the North had more or less dried up in 1144. Eskil had to look to Citeaux in order to find the required twelve monks and an abbot to make the long trip.

During the last decade of Saint Bernard's life, Clairvaux could not keep up with the popularity of the Cistercians. In 1152 the General Chapter forbade all further foundations.[15] The Cistercians were very much afraid of overexpansion. Within a few years, however, they again began to found new houses. But in the 1140s any Cistercian settlements in Denmark had to draw on a supply of monks that could not keep up with an extraordinary demand from all over Western Europe.

Our original questions still remain to be answered. Why Cistercian monasteries in the midst of the barbarian North, for so it must have seemed to the monks of Clairvaux? Can we concede the initiative to Eskil? Or was it the purpose and policy of Citeaux and Clairvaux to send monks to these lands? If we look at our Scandinavian sources, we get a perhaps unexpected but quite logical answer to these questions. The Cistercians came to the North because they were invited to come there, and not just by Eskil but also by royal figures. The *Narratiuncula* of the foundation of Vitskøl abbey, written sometime in the thirteenth century, provides the most detail.[16] It claims that King Sverker of Sweden and his queen Ulvilde Håkonsdatter (whose former husband was the Danish king, Niels) in Bernard's day founded two abbeys from Clairvaux on their patrimony, one at Alvastra and the other at Ludrö on Vånem. The site at Ludrö was unsuitable, and so the monks moved elsewhere, finally settling at Varnhem. Thus we have a thirteenth-century tradition which considered the foundations the result of royal initiative.

This story corresponds with an assertion in the *Exordium Magnum Cisterciense* that the 'pious woman who was the queen of Sweden' brought the brothers there.[17] Thus both the undated but fairly early Scandinavian narration and the Clairvaux source agree that the monks went north because they were called for. Elsewhere we are told how impressed the Swedish king was with the piety, devotion, and insight of the monk Gerard, who became the second abbot of Alvastra.[18] The author of the *Exordium Magnum*, Conrad of Eberbach, here reveals how the Cistercians functioned in close contact with the very top level of Scandinavian society.

By the early 1140s the Cistercians' reputation had spread as far as the Northern kingdoms. Why did they come when they were invited? Between the Rhineland Cistercian foundations of the 1130s and the Swedish-Danish territories lay a huge German area which the Cistercians did not begin to 'cultivate' until the last decades of the century. Why did the Order—at a time of relative harmony between the German emperor and the papacy—skip Northern Germany and instead settle Scandinavia at such an early date? The Cistercians were not a missionary order. They were founded in a traditionally Christian part of Europe in order to renew the monastic way of life. They withdrew to desolate and isolated places not in order to preach to a backwoods population but to have the peace and quiet that the Benedictines could not enjoy in their urban setting.[19] German historians from the late nineteenth and early twentieth centuries emphasized the missionary thrust of the Cistercians and concentrated on their expansion from the 1170s onwards into Slavic areas along the Baltic.[20] By then the original reform impulse had been replaced by a Cistercian willingness to carry out papal and episcopal policies in converting non-christians or in dealing with heretics, as in Southern France. But in the 1140s Bernard was still alive. By now he too was inflamed by the crusading ideal and seems to have contemplated using the Cistercians as missionaries.[21] But Cistercians at this time still centered their activities on the simple monastic life of withdrawal from the world, prayer, and manual labour.

The Cistercians did not come as missionaries to Scandinavia, nor can they be seen as instruments of any clear papal policy. Once again we must turn to our Clairvaux sources, whose pious language conveys a great deal of historical information. They emphasize Bernard's central role. Just as he is credited with the success of Cîteaux, so too he saw to it that the Cistercians found a place in Scandinavia. According to the *Exordium Magnum*, some of the monks were initially unwilling to leave France and go to Scandinavia to make new foundations. The settling of the North is looked upon in these French sources as a reluctant exodus made possible only by the determination and conviction of Bernard himself.

Here we can go directly to the language of the *Exordium Magnum*, composed on the basis of earlier narratives that frequently are contemporary with the events they describe. The author Conrad says that Bernard wanted to send the monks because they were to live among as many different nations as possible:

> That monastic order now began to be transferred across many bodies of water, that is, the obstinate and arrogant wills of many nations, which were like gloomy whirlpools of waves, in order to foster the practice of true religious devotion.[22]

At this point Conrad mentions the request of the Swedish queen, which Bernard used as a reason for sending out a group of monks. They are said to have hesitated at the thought of being sent to 'foreign and barbarian regions'. In some of his best prose, Conrad captures the sense of remoteness and strangeness that the thought of these places created in the minds of the monks. For them these nations were 'very remote and hidden in the last clime of northern winter'; the brothers were able to contemplate their trip only with 'a certain mental terror'. They shivered not only at the thought of the cold but also at the prospect of living among men who were 'primitive and uncultured'.[23]

Without the iron will and total conviction of Bernard, together with the brothers' absolute obedience to him, no one would ever have left Clairvaux. Bernard was even obliged to perform a miracle in order to show the brothers that it was God's will that they go. According to Conrad, he took a lavabo bowl (used for catching water when the priest washes his hands at mass) from the luggage packed for the trip. It was made out of hard metal, but as a sign that 'the spirit of the Lord' was sending the brothers, Bernard left a deep impression on it with his finger. At this the brothers were converted to their mission. The function of the anecdote is to impress us with the courage of the early Cistercians and to contribute to the hagiographical literature concerning Bernard. The fear of the brothers is vividly and convincingly described.

Yet even this miracle is supposed to have left the monk Gerard unhappy. He complained to Bernard that he had left his home in Germany to come and share in the community at Clairvaux. It was his fondest wish to be buried there, but now it looked as if his bones would come to rest far away from those of the other Clairvaux brothers and especially of Bernard. The abbot took pity on the young man and promised him that before his death he would be able to return to Clairvaux to be buried there. Gerard trusted Bernard and went with the others. He eventually became prior and cellarer at Alvastra and finally abbot. Conrad looks upon Gerard as one member of a courageous band of men who would do anything to follow Bernard—even though they might hesitate awhile.

These early settlements Conrad looks upon with the eyes of a Cistercian at the end of the twelfth century, a time when the Order had accepted a missionary role. Thus Conrad could praise the efforts of the early brothers who also seemed like missionaries. Because of the lack of priests in this region, says Conrad, the Lord sent his faithful servants with their monastic discipline and learning into that kingdom (of Sweden). The monks' work bore much fruit among people 'who had heard the name of monk but had never seen one'.[24] Through the influx of German, English, and French Cistercians from the heartland of the Order in Champagne-Burgundy, Scandinavian men and women must have gained a new impression of Christianity.

But it is the Cistercians who are speaking here, and so they are telling us more about their self-image than about the way Scandinavian society considered them. They became missionaries without intending to do so. But they did not proselytize in any open, direct manner. Their function was primarily to bear witness to the monastic life. Gerard, for example, is characterized as being so caught up in his 'spiritual pursuits' that he came to hand over all his 'temporal and external functions' to his cellarer, Abraham. What is important in Conrad's mind is the example of spotless monastic life the Cistercians provided for ignorant men. Genuine spirituality can win the favour of secular society. According to Conrad, the Swedish king came to respect the Cistercians and especially Gerard so much that he felt himself in their power. Whenever the king visited Gerard, he was struck by fear. It was, as he said, as if 'all the secrets of my heart would lay exposed' to him.

Again, such lines reflect an idealization of a past situation by a Cistercian writer. There is no corroboration from any Scandinavian source. But the very clarity of the Clairvaux writer's intent in including such anecdotes makes it easier for us to understand what the Cistercians sought in spreading their Order to a far corner of Europe. They sought to convert the world by living outside of it. Simply by being good themselves, they could exercise a profound influence on society—starting at the very top. There is a Cistercian sense of superiority implicit here, an emphasis on the centrality of the mother abbeys for all Cistercians. In a sense, the monks feel almost too valuable for these barbarous lands. Gerard in old age was able by another miracle to travel all the way back to Clairvaux to die. When the king heard of this, he remarked that the soil of Sweden was not sufficiently holy to contain the bones of such a saint.

The Clairvaux Cistercians who put these words into the king's mouth looked upon the North as an uncivilized area which they had a duty to penetrate. But Clairvaux remained their home. If they could not live there, then at least they would die and be buried there. If we return to our original question, why the Cistercians came, we can conclude that the Clairvaux sources are sufficiently informative to let us know that the monks were invited, that Bernard wanted them to go, and that its members went north with great fear and a desire to return. There are a number of indications that the northern monks frequently did visit Clairvaux later in the century.[25] Abbots were obliged to meet in the General Chapter at Citeaux once a year in mid-September. A few twelfth and early thirteenth-century statutes from the Chapter indicate the presence of Danish or Swedish abbots, but we can by no means establish how often they came.[26] In 1217 a rule was established that monasteries at a great distance from Citeaux, for example those in Sweden, would only have to send representatives once every five years.[27] But Denmark is never mentioned in such provisions.

Nevertheless, there was good reason for Danish and Swedish Cistercians to maintain contacts with their mother houses. The fledgling abbeys needed both moral and political support. Eskil's travels often brought him to Clairvaux, as in 1156, when he may have been there together with two Swedish abbots, our friend Gerard and Henrik, who then was abbot of Varnhem and in 1158 became abbot of of the newly-founded Vitskøl.[28] Henrik may have been attending the General Chapter at Citeaux and at the same time have paid a call at Clairvaux, where he talked with Geoffrey, Bernard's friend and secretary. Thus were transmitted memorable miracle stories about Eskil and his kin.

ESKIL AS A CONVERT TO CISTERCIAN MONASTICISM

So far I have drawn on the good source materials for the 1150s and 1160s or even later and thus neglected the 1140s. In the uncertain beginnings we cannot get away from Eskil. We can consider him in three contexts, even though only the last tells us immediately about Eskil and the Cistercians. First we will examine the foundation charter for a Benedictine abbey at Næstved on Zealand from 1135. Then we will try to determine the way a Benedictine historian in Normandy in the same year looked at the Cistercian Order. These preliminary steps will enable us to have greater understanding for some of the earliest documentary sources we have for Eskil, especially his great charter for Esrum Abbey, dated to 1158.

The Benedictine foundation at Næstved

In looking at the language of Eskil's charter for Næstved, we will first of all examine his attitude towards monastic foundations in general and then try to reach some tentative observations about how these attitudes could determine Eskil's reception of the Cistercians.[29] In the first place, Eskil did not found the Benedictine monastery in Næstved in the sense that he gave a huge chunk of land to it and thereby provided an economic foundation for the community. It was the Bodilsen family, consisting of Peder and his brothers Henning and Jørgen, who gave the land. Eskil merely confirmed their property transfers and gave the monastery the churches in Næstved, Tjæreby, and Hårslev. Moreover he, in his capacity at the time as bishop of Roskilde, transferred to the monks the episcopal third of the tithe on various properties.[30] Here we find the establishment of a pattern that would repeat itself in later charters drawn up in Eskil's name: he gives churches and fractions of tithes to monastic houses, but very rarely does he provide them with his own lands. The grandiose claims for Eskil's gift-giving, found especially in Herbert of Clairvaux's *Liber Miraculorum*, can almost never be backed up by the actual monastic charters we are lucky enough to have.[31] Eskil can be seen as a benevolent organizer, who coordinated the good intentions of a landowning family with the practical needs of a new monastery. In giving the monks churches, he diminished the revenues of the bishopric of Roskilde, but there is no indication that he provided the new foundation with anything that had belonged to him personally.

The next question, why he acted in this role, is much more difficult to answer. Should we look at his episcopal function as that of a notarial service, merely recording a transaction and providing it with his official stamp? Such a conclusion would ignore the fact that Eskil committed episcopal revenues and so was institutionally involved in the new foundation. So long as we remember that the language of individual charters ultimately must be seen in terms of the official language of groups of charters, we can consider the reasons given here for the foundation.[32] The foundation charter mentions first of all the 'divine charity' that inspired the Bodilsen family and their desire to increase the honour of God by founding such a religious house:

> On the foundation which has been constructed, like a city, in which they participated, they have placed a structure of jewels, polished and precious stones.[33]

The language here emphasizes the Bodilsen family's desire for eternal salvation. They entrusted to Eskil the task of initiating in their Næstved church the monastic life according to the Rule of Saint Benedict. The monks are looked upon as men fighting for God. This military metaphor was enormously popular in medieval life and is echoed in the Rule itself.

These lines and the actions they describe cannot in themselves reveal anything individual or personal about Eskil's attitude to the monastic life. The phraseology does indicate, however, that Eskil as bishop was dealing with categories that easily could be adjusted to Cistercian concepts. In phrases dealing with tears and love (*in hac igitur convalle lacrimarum ascensiones in corde suo disponentes . . .*), the charter emphasizes intention as a mainspring of human action. This is a theme that corresponds to Cistercian concerns.[34] There are only hints of the literary forms and mental attitudes that the Cistercians developed in their early literature, but there is enough for us to speak of a potential receptivity to Cistercian thought and life.

We do not know how and when Eskil changed from supporting new Benedictine foundations to aiding the introduction of the Cistercians into Denmark. In 1138 he became archbishop of Lund, and this may have been the central turning point. From then on his actions for the furtherance of ecclesiastical interests in his archdiocese had international import. There is no evidence that Eskil himself went to France in the beginning of the 1140s to bring the Cistercians from Cîteaux to Herrisvad. Our only indication of his activities in this period comes from two charters for Lund church which were drawn up under his name on 1 September 1145.[35] The first charter made known that he had founded new offices at the cathedral and had improved those already in existence, the second that he had consecrated the church to Saints Mary and Laurentius.

At some point between 1135 and 1143, Eskil became interested in the Cistercians, so much so that he decided to see to it that they started a monastery in Skåne. As bishop, he had to give his permission for the foundation of any monastic house in the area under his jurisdiction. In keeping with Cistercian practice, the new house was set far away from the ecclesiastical centre, Lund. It would not be troubled by the business of the cathedral's properties and the rivalry of other religious foundations in the town. Like the new cathedral at Lund and Skåne's Premonstratensian houses, Herrisvad must be looked upon as Eskil's creation. They all appear at almost the same time and indicate a desire on his part to be a dynamic leader in consolidating the church in Scandinavia. Eskil sought out the Cistercians apparently because they could bring the best elements of international church reform to Denmark and thereby contribute to a church province independent of German interests and interference. Eskil had been educated at Hildesheim, an episcopal seat since Carolingian times. His learning, as we shall see, was probably traditional and out of touch with the French cathedral schools of the early twelfth century. And yet, when it came to inviting monks to Denmark, he chose the new French orders. With them and with his expanded cathedral chapter he apparently planned to strengthen the future of his diocese, his country, and of the church itself in Scandinavia. In the 1160s, when Uppsala in Sweden became an archbishopric, Eskil saw to it that its first bishop was one of his own Herrisvad Cistercians, Stephen. Likewise at Ribe in the early 1170s he seems to have furthered the election of another Herrisvad veteran, Ralph, as bishop. In the business of European diplomacy during the schism Eskil also used the Cistercians. They were his loyal monks and though we cannot speak of a Cistercian faction in Denmark in the conflicts between Eskil and the Danish monarchy we can at least see the traces of an effort to secure the international interests of Eskil's position through a close alliance with the international Cistercian Order.

A foreign interpreter

Once again we have jumped the gun and abandoned the 1140s for a more certain period. The gap in our knowledge about the precise motivation and time of Eskil's conversion to the Cistercians makes it natural to turn to one of the early twelfth century's most informative and imposing narratives, Orderic Vitalis's *Ecclesiastical History*.[36] Normally it would be questionable to fill out the gaps in Denmark's limited source materials by taking a foreign account from the same period and then assuming that similar attitudes apply to Denmark. But such a procedure can be justified in view of the man and mentality we already have found in the Næstved and Lund charters. Eskil's thoughts and reactions were probably never as precise and well-articulated as those of Orderic, but the historian can at least show us how Eskil might well have regarded the new monks.

As a Benedictine in an old-style house with its own pride and traditions, Orderic was not likely to be wildly enthusiastic about the Cistercians. But the grudging recognition he gives them and their work tells us much more about their success than a Cistercian source ever could do. Orderic looked upon the Cistercians as one part of a general expansion of monastic foundations:

> Monasteries are being founded everywhere in mountains, valleys and plains; observing new rites and wearing different habits, the swarm of cowled monks spreads all over the world.[37]

In this sentence we can detect Orderic's hesitation. The monks are almost being compared to an anonymous crowd expanding by some blind force. He does not approve of novelties, such as wearing white habits rather than the black of the Benedictines. Black stands for humility, while white draws attention and shows the desire to be different for its own sake, something that Orderic could not accept. His judgment on the Cistercians is clear and forthright. Many of these new monks live exemplary lives, but some of them are fakes:

> In my opinion voluntary poverty, contempt for the world, and true religion inspire many of them, but many hypocrites and plausible counterfeiters are mixed with them, as tares with wheat.[38]

This is a theme to which Orderic returns at the end of his account in order to underline it. During the intervening sketch of the origins of the house of Citeaux, Orderic is also careful to show that the new monks were far from perfect.

Orderic reports that the new order started when the abbot of Molesme, Robert, discovered through a careful examination of the Rule of Saint Benedict that there was a great gap between the monks' daily lives and the Rule's provisions. He wanted his monks to give up their comfortable existences supported by the labour of others and to return to working for a living. The answer to Robert's challenges which Orderic puts into the mouths of the Molesme monks represents his own attitude. Hardships should not be suffered for their own sake. Benedict's Rule was a guide that allowed adjustment to varying conditions.[39] It was up to each abbot to make dispensations for special circumstances. Moreover, the idea that the monks should engage in manual labour distracts from the true monastic vocation, which is prayer and the liturgy. Peasants should take care of manual labour so that the monks can have more time for their spiritual labour.[40] These functions should not be mixed up. Orderic clearly reveals his sympathies by making the monks in opposition to Robert much more eloquent than the reformer himself. He even goes so far as to say that the breakaway community wanted to 'observe the Rule of Saint Benedict according to the letter as the Jews observed the law of Moses'.[41] But he does give them credit for their monastery 'of great austerity and piety' and points out how Robert did everything possible to maintain good relations between Molesme and Citeaux.

Orderic concludes by telling us that thirty-seven years had gone by since the foundation of Citeaux, thus dating the writing of this passage at 1135.[42] This is confirmed by his statement that sixty-five abbeys had been founded in the intervening period. It is purely a coincidence that this Benedictine account was composed in the same year as the foundation of one of Denmark's richest Benedictine abbeys. But through Orderic's reluctant but honest acceptance of the Cistercians as a reformed monastic order, we can see how the Order might have appealed to the innovative and ambitious Eskil:

> . . . by the great good they do, [they] shine out in the world like lanterns burning in a dark place. They maintain silence at all times and wear no dyed garments. They toil with their own hands and produce their own food and clothing. From 13 September until Easter they fast every day except Sunday. They bar their gates and keep their private quarters completely enclosed. They will not admit a monk from another religious house to their cells, nor allow one to come with them into the church for Mass or any other offices.
> . . . They have built monasteries with their own hands in lonely, wooded places and have thoughtfully provided them with holy names, such as Maison-Dieu, Clairvaux, Bonmont, and L'Aumøne and others of like kind, so that the sweet sound of the name alone invites all who hear to hasten and discover for themselves how great the blessedness must be which is described by so rare a name.[43]

If the established monk-aristocrat, with his sense of tradition and hierarchy, could admit the virtues of these revolutionaries, then so much the more would Eskil, a member of a new church aristocracy in a developing European fringe country. Eskil almost certainly never read Orderic, who was practically unknown outside his own monastery, but the Cistercian reputation for austerity and effectiveness reached him and convinced him that the new order fitted into his program for strengthening his position at Lund and his contacts with the international church.

ESKIL IN THE 1150s AND AFTERWARDS: FOUNDATIONS, GIFTS, PUBLICITY

Sometime between the end of the 1130s and the beginning of the 1140s, Orderic's sweet Cistercian sound penetrated Eskil's mind and helped bring about the 1144 foundation at Herrisvad. A few years later, Eskil started a monastery at Esrum in Northern Zealand. As at Herrisvad, we have problems in determining how Esrum started, but once again we cannot separate the beginnings of this monastery from the personality and activities of Eskil.

Until recently it was generally accepted that Esrum was founded in 1153 on the site of a Benedictine house,[44] but the most recent research has rejected this tradition.[45] Esrum's earliest papal bull, from 29 December 1151, is of a standard type issued for Cistercian houses.[46] There is no clause in this charter that reserves the rights of the bishop, and so the bull must have been issued for an exempt house. The only monasteries of this type in Scandinavia were Cistercian. The dating, 1151, conflicts with the Ryd and Colbaz Annals, which give 1153 as the date that *conventus venit in Esrom*. As we pointed out before, these Annals came from later in the twelfth century. The notation in the Colbaz Annals was not added until the manuscript was moved from Lund to Colbaz in the 1170s,[47] and even if it was added before the end of the twelfth century, it could not have been written down before twenty years had separated the writer from Esrum's beginnings.

The 1153 date cannot be rejected out of hand, however, for we know that Eskil in this year visited Clairvaux and for the last time saw his friend Bernard. After the great abbot's death on the twentieth of August, his secretary Geoffrey wrote Eskil a memorable letter to inform him of the event. On the basis of this letter and of Eskil's own statements, Danish historians earlier assumed that Eskil in 1153 brought monks and lay brothers from Clairvaux to start a new Cistercian abbey at Esrum. In Eskil's 1158 privilege for Esrum, he does say that he had brought monks back with him from Clairvaux to Esrum. But he does *not* say that it was this group that had originally founded Esrum. They apparently provided reinforcements for an already extant monastery.[48]

Another problem is that, as archbishop of Lund, Eskil had no legal basis for founding a monastery in the diocese of Roskilde.[49] But the Ryd Annals, despite their late date of composition, may suggest a solution on the basis of a tradition otherwise lost to us. Under 1150, they have the strange sentence, '*Conventus mittitur* [in Warnhem] *kal. Maii qui profectus est postea in Esrom*'.[50] Under 1153, in the Colbaz Annals and several others, is the usual *Conventus venit in Esrom*. Thus the monks were apparently first sent elsewhere but came to Esrum, where they were met by Eskil's party from Clairvaux. In the meantime their new abbot, William, had been to Rome to obtain the papal privilege for the new abbey from the Cistercian pope Eugenius III. A royal privilege for Esrum, issued sometime between 1151 and 1157, indicates that Eskil, as archbishop of Lund, at some time before 1146 under King Erik Lam acquired the immediate area for himself and subsequently handed it over to monastic use. Even if Eskil was not the episcopal *fundator* of Esrum, he provided it with its first properties.

The dating of the founding of Esrum to 1150 or 1151 at the latest has to take into account the fact that the first abbot of the other monastery is said in the Lund Book of the Dead to have been Folmer.[51] This is feasible if there was a preliminary party in 1150/51 at Esrum with an abbot who died soon after the monks' arrival in Northern Zealand. This dating also makes sense in terms of the General Chapter's prohibition in 1152 against the establishment of new houses. Although this provision was ignored after a few years and the Order again began to spread, it was at least for a few years maintained with some rigidity.[52] The 1153 dating in the various annals may be due to a confusion of the influx of Eskil's Cistercian party from France with the actual beginnings of Esrum a few years earlier.

Now that we have some idea of how Esrum began, the sources for the rest of the 1150s dealing with Eskil open to us. The essential source is the 1153 letter from Geoffrey to Eskil. It shows genuine sorrow at the death of Bernard and indicates that Eskil was one of the people to whom Geoffrey felt it natural to turn to express and make public these feelings: 'Bernard your friend sleeps; but all of him does not sleep; his heart is waiting and watching'.[53] Geoffrey praises Eskil for his desire to listen to Bernard's wisdom and for coming from the end of the earth to be with him. Nothing could hold Eskil back. Neither distances, nor dangers at sea, nor the fear of barbarian peoples were enough to give him pause. Now Geoffrey sends Eskil a description of Bernard's last days. He asks him and all who read the letter not to be displeased by his style. They should forgive him because of the great emotion he experiences in writing it.[54]

In this magnificent yet difficult letter one penetrates deep into Cistercian spirituality. Geoffrey conveys in both formalized and emotional terms the strength of the monks' belief in personal salvation. The death of Bernard unites the entire Cistercian community, monks as well as patrons, and intensifies their solidarity. The impulse that makes Geoffrey write to Eskil is the same one that motivated Gerard the Clarevallian novice to insist on staying at his monastery: the need for Bernard, the great abbot. Why should all of this be conveyed to Eskil in particular if not for the existence of something more than a diplomatic relationship between abbot and archbishop? Eskil is expected to understand what the loss of Bernard means to Geoffrey and his fellow Clairvaux monks. In this moment of sadness, Eskil is to be sought out, for Bernard had put his trust in him. Geoffrey's letter initiates the rich tradition of Eskil's importance to the Cistercian Order, a tradition carefully developed by Clairvaux writers.

Eskil returned to Clairvaux in 1156. In the *Vita Prima Bernardi*, Geoffrey wrote of a conversation he had had with Eskil. The archbishop had told him that the bread given him by Bernard and blessed by the saint before Eskil's last departure from Clairvaux was still fresh after three years.[55] This story was so attractive to the Cistercians that they reused it in the *Exordium Magnum*.[56] Geoffrey mentions Eskil in his narrative elsewhere and helps us see his role as a defender of Cistercian interests. He starts his section on

Eskil with a generalized portrait of him as an important churchman devoted to Bernard. But this is not enough for Geoffrey. He goes into detail, saying he had heard Eskil claiming that 'he had spent on that journey more than 600 marks of silver'.[57] Geoffrey tells the story to impress, but if we look at it in terms of the 1158 charter for Esrum, where Eskil makes his own donations sound much more important than everyone else's,[58] we begin to see how willingly Eskil publicized what he was doing for the Cistercian cause. If we only had charters as sources for Eskil's life, any statements about his personality would be unwarranted, for charters often used language common to monastic documents in general. But the presence of narrative sources from Clairvaux opens to us a dimension of Eskil that has not been sufficiently understood.

Geoffrey makes it clear that Eskil greatly impressed the brothers at Clairvaux. They noticed his devotion not only to Bernard but also to the rest of the community:

> Here [at Clairvaux] it is difficult to describe how much he wept and how he acted not only towards him [Bernard], whom he esteemed above all others, but also towards even the least of the brothers.[59]

Geoffrey probably wrote these lines on the basis of personal experience and was referring to himself when he mentioned 'the least of the brothers'. We have a strikingly similar description of a bishop's devotion to the Cistercians in the first part of the Øm Abbey Chronicle's description of the respect shown by Bishop Sven of Århus towards the monks.[60] In both cases the authors may be exaggerating their enthusiasm in order to impress contemporary ecclesiastics and encourage them to treat the Cistercians as well as their predecessors had done. But the Clairvaux source is still very close to Eskil, for Geoffrey wrote immediately after his visit, providing a fresh, clear portrait of a man who had convinced the Clairvaux community that he was invaluable to them.

Geoffrey included in his account of Eskil another story which normally receives much less attention than the more charming tale about the loaves of bread. He says the events happened in the monastery founded by Eskil in Denmark, and so the story has traditionally been attached to Esrum.[61] It is interesting to note that Geoffrey here speaks of only one monastery as the result of Eskil's efforts. A few dozen lines earlier, Geoffrey had written something similar: 'He was not satisfied to see him [Bernard] in his sons when he had founded a new convent'. Geoffrey emphasized here Eskil's desire to see Bernard in the flesh as the reason for his first visit to Clairvaux. Geoffrey says little about Eskil's outward achievements (the number of monasteries he founded) but concentrates on his spiritual bond with the Order and especially with Bernard. Thus it is impossible to tell from the *Vita* how active Eskil had been in establishing the Cistercian Order in Denmark. Only in the later Clairvaux tradition, from the end of the 1170s, when Eskil himself had settled at Clairvaux, did writers begin to emphasize his material accomplishments.[62] It seems likely that this change in emphasis was due at least in part to Eskil's own talent for publicizing his activities.

Returning to Geoffrey's story, we find that it is centred on a young relation of Eskil's who lived a wayward life but then became ill.[63] Eskil visited him and decided to take him to the monks. The young man assented but after his arrival at the monastery grew even more ill. A demon, knowing he soon would die and resenting the brothers' success in securing the young man's salvation at the last moment, took his revenge by invading one of the monks. The poor man cried out with terrible sounds and could hardly be held down by the other monks. He spoke a language which no one ever before had heard. The brothers were quite desperate and placed on the brother's heart relics of Saint Bernard which Eskil had given them. Then the brother began to scream again, but now in German: 'Take it away, take it away, get Bernard away . . . Oh, how heavy you have become, Bernard, how intolerably hard you are on me'.[64] Afterwards there was silence, and the brother opened his eyes and immediately recovered his former health. Geoffrey concluded the anecdote with the information that Eskil himself had told it to him. Again we see Eskil obtaining not just glory for the Cistercians but also an aura of saintly power for himself. He had been proud to tell Geoffrey of the bernardine relics he owned and the way they had proven themslves.

Why had the brother cried out in German? Did the Danish monks think of this as the language of demons? Or does this chance mention indicate the presence of many German monks in the first decade of the Danish Cistercians? From the Sorø abbot list, we know that many of the early abbots there were foreigners, and at least one was German.[65] Similarly for Herrisvad we have a few names of abbots. One of them, Robert, was probably French.[66] Finally we have a letter from Hildegard of Bingen to an Esrum monk, who apparently had come from Germany and was still in contact with a friend there about whom he seemed concerned.[67] These are only scattered fragments of information, but there is no doubt that the first Cistercian houses in Denmark were international communities, composed of brothers who had come to the Order from many different countries. Many first came to Clairvaux or Citeaux as novices and then were sent north, as Gerard of Alvastra, who was probably born in Utrecht, came to Clairvaux, and then went to Sweden.[68]

A final aspect of this story worth noting is that the young man was a relative of Eskil's. It is understandable that Eskil encouraged male relatives to leave the world and join a monastery he had founded. The Trund or Trugot family to which Eskil belonged came originally from Jutland but had settled in Skåne during the twelfth century and become a considerable political factor able to challenge even the new royal dynasty under Valdemar I. Eskil could use his Cistercian foundation to take care of family members who could not be placed at Lund or for whom there was no available inheritance. But for the Clairvaux Cistercians, Eskil's family and its link with their monastery are only a background detail. Their interest is how a man's salvation can bring down the wrath of the devil on a Cistercian house.

We notice here a general tendency in Cistercian writings after the death of Bernard: concentration on the miraculous in order to confirm the power of Bernard as a saint. Such incidents as the one at Esrum provide a guarantee for the holiness of the Order. For anyone today interested in psychological motivation behind conversion to the Cistercian Order during the period, such stories have only limited value. But the very emphasis on the miraculous helps explain how the Cistercians could attract a person like Eskil, who was fascinated by outward achievements and heroic gestures.

Leaving behind the Clairvaux sources and turning to Eskil's 1158 charter for Esrum, we find evidence of many of the personality traits we have already noted: Eskil's desire to make his accomplishments known, his pride in his relationship with Bernard, his self-image as a great patron. But for once we also find real evidence that Eskil had indeed done something to give the Danish Cistercians the security they needed. He had given them land. When Eskil returned to Denmark after his trip to Clairvaux, Valdemar was now established on the throne, having defeated his rivals in 1157. The years from 1158 to 1161 mark a period of what looks like relative harmony between Eskil and Valdemar, ending in 1161 because Eskil could not accept the German king's and Valdemar's candidate for the papacy, Octavian.[69] It is precisely in these years that Esrum obtained some of its most important charters from Valdemar, and we can detect behind them Eskil's efforts on behalf of the abbey. He opens his great charter to Esrum by emphasizing how much he has worked for the spread of Christianity all over Denmark. This is a common theme in royal and episcopal charters for the period and tells us nothing exceptional about Eskil. But in the next sentence he becomes more concrete and describes how he has brought monks of various religious orders to Denmark:

> ... so that the brothers of the Cistercian Order not be wanting among us, we—despite great difficulties and expense—went to the father of the monastery of Clairvaux, the blessed dom Bernard, and from his sons brought with us into our land the seed from which a harvest of souls of the faithful can be prepared.[70]

The agricultural image based on the parable of the sower and his seed illustrates Eskil's adoption of biblical metaphors dealing with cultivation of the land that are so common in Cistercian language. Eskil's image is relatively simple compared with some of the involved Cistercian metaphors. Once again we note his talent for publicizing his own efforts. But he does not use the word *fundare* or any of its synonyms for his work at Esrum. He simply says he brought brothers from Clairvaux to Denmark.

In order to provide for the brothers' 'practical needs and peace', Eskil gave them the place called Esrum, which he had obtained from King Erik. Eskil apparently also gave the Esrum monks the charter King Sven Grathe had issued him confirming this transaction, for a copy of it appears in the Esrum Book.[71] So that the 'poor of Christ' would have what they needed and even have an abundance, Eskil provided them with fields, forests, lakes, fishing places, and meadows, adding a village called Villingerød, a location which still exists today in the fertile farming area a few kilometers north of Esrum. Two themes are contained in this charter which will be enormously popular in the remainder of the twelfth century: the Cistercians as the poor of Christ, and their benefactors' desire to give them more than what they needed to stay alive. These are more than literary clichés, for the intentions were realised in practice. By 1200, the Cistercians at Sorø, Esrum, and Vitskøl really did have an abundance. The poverty theme drops out of the charters after that time, perhaps because it would have seemed absurd to call the well-heeled Cistercians the poor of Christ.[72] Even literary conventions sometimes give way to changing material realities.

Eskil claims in the same 1158 charter that the number of monks at Esrum increased in the course of time. He came to feel that their 'few possessions' no longer sufficed for them. 'So that they not be in need of anything',[73] he gave them the village of Asserbo, which he had obtained partly by cash purchase and partly by trading other land. Eskil's remark concerning an increase in numbers at Esrum may refer to his 1153 contribution to the original group there from 1150 or 1151. But Eskil does not make this distinction clear. His blurring of the circumstances of Esrum's foundation may even reflect a conscious desire on his part to be remembered as the man who single-handedly started a Cistercian house at Esrum.

The place names mentioned in this charter indicate that the area already was settled. When we read that the Cistercians came to desolate and isolated places, it does not necessarily mean that no one had been living there before them. The Øm monks had to buy up land from unwilling peasants. One of the rustics could be convinced to sell only after being threatened by Mary in a dream.[74] And in the Esrum charter Eskil mentions a peasant (*bundo*) who lived in Tjæreby and sold his patrimony there to the monks for ten marks silver. This is the earliest Danish reference we have to the buying up of land by Cistercian monks, a practice that was looked upon with disdain in the *Exordium Parvum* and finally forbidden by the General Chapter in 1182. But Esrum's monks were interested in obtaining an economic base and so bent the rules to their needs. This seems to have been common practice in many Cistercian houses after about 1150.[75]

The fact that Esrum was founded in a relatively well-settled and farmed area meant that the monks had to acquire their holdings individually. Wendish abbeys south of the Baltic founded in the 1170s or later were apparently from the start given huge tracts of land, mini-baronies.[76] Esrum never had anything like that at any time in its existence. In the course of the century the monks did reorganize their holdings and apparently were responsible for the abandonment of many peasant settlements. This development is hinted at in charters from the 1170s and 1180s, in which many of the early place names in the Esrum area have disappeared.[77] This provides a valuable indication that the monks built larger units of production by consolidating the smaller holdings they had come to own. They either hired the former peasant owners to work for them or encouraged them to settle elsewhere. A good example of this practice is the village of Tanga, which was probably in the immediate vicinity of Esrum. Tanga is named, together with Villingerød, in a papal charter issued on 29 December 1151 to Abbot William of Esrum. By 1178 it no longer exists. Absalon's charter from that year mentions 'the place in which was the village which once was called Tanga'.[78]

We can begin to see here how a Danish Cistercian abbey would build up a block of holdings in the vicinity of the monastery and also willingly acquire land at a greater distance, as at Tjæreby west of Hillerød and Asserbo on the north coast. These distant holdings would become the nuclei of granges. Eskil personally gave the monks a number of holdings: Villingerød; the nearby village of Aveholm; a farm in Såne near the eastern shore of Esrum lake; as well as Asserbo. But the abbey also profited from dealings with King Valdemar (another farm in Såne) and Count Niels, Eskil's kinsman and probably the young man mentioned in the Clairvaux story about Esrum's demon. Bishop Absalon of Roskilde exchanged the land the brothers bought in Tjæreby for other property. Finally kings Valdemar and Knud Magnussen had given the brothers properties in six villages. Aside from this last entry, which cannot be specified, we get a very complete picture of the early holdings of Esrum and of the way Eskil cooperated with the Esrum monks in seeing to it that they could obtain favourable arrangements with landowners in the area.

In this charter Eskil devotes much space to his own property contributions to the monks. But he reveals little about any efforts he might have made to secure land for them from his relatives or the king. Near the end of the document, Eskil adds that he hopes his example will be imitated by the faithful 'so that they both can rejoice—he who sows and they who reap from what has been sown'.[79] Eskil intended the document to be an incentive to all potential benefactors of Esrum. The personality evidenced here, the brashness and almost aggressively self-centred piety, is the same as we found at Clairvaux.

Eskil's involvement with the Cistercians during the 1150s can also be seen in the 1158 foundation of Vitskøl Abbey on Limfjorden in 1158. If ever we have a truly royal foundation, a Cistercian house that owes its existence to a Danish king's desire to initiate a community of monks, it is Vitskøl. But Eskil is still there. The royal charter is taken from the 1499 collection of charters known as the Vitskøl Book. It has been dated to sometime between 23 October 1157 and 18 April 1158.[80] The first date is that of the defeat of Valdemar's rival for the monarchy, Sven Grathe. The second marks the death of Bishop Asser of Roskilde, a witness to the privilege. The historical background can be summarized thus: Valdemar and Knud were allies in fighting Sven, but on 9 August 1157 at a banquet in Roskilde celebrating an agreement by which Valdemar obtained Jutland, Knud Fyn and Zealand, and Sven Skåne, Sven's men killed Knud. Valdemar was wounded but managed to flee to Viborg. In a final battle between the two, Sven was killed. The foundation document for Vitskøl was drawn up in a dramatic recollection of the preceding events and indicates that the new monarchy had already allied itself with the Cistercian movement.

This very political document recounts Sven's perfidy. Divine mercy had been with Valdemar, for he had managed to escape from Roskilde. God was on his side, as history's victors so often would have posterity believe. The betrayers were stopped after allying themselves with criminal types and after having upset the hard-won peace of the kingdom. At a synod in Roskilde after Eskil had returned from abroad in April of 1158, Valdemar promised to found a Cistercian house on his own patrimony. The thirteenth century account of Vitskøl's foundation states that Valdemar, prior to the decisive battle, had made a vow that he would found a Cistercian house if he were victorious over his enemies.[81] But this is the way the monks preferred to record history. The Øm monks also remembered their foundation as the result of a promise made by a powerful man in need of God's help, in this case an Århus bishop in danger of shipwreck.[82] Whatever the proper chronology may be, the myth was created, and in royal privileges to Vitskøl the monastery's status as a royal foundation is usually mentioned. The monarchy and the monastery were intimately involved with each other, and neither the king nor the monks wanted it any other way.

Even if Valdemar's privilege emphasizes strongly his own role in Vitskøl's foundation, he adds that he made his donation 'with the venerable archbishop, legate of the apostolic see, Eskil, being present and confirming it',[83] together with six bishops and many abbots. Eskil's legal role is recognized.

The king could not found a Cistercian house without having backing from the Church. Eskil had no special prerogative to approve the foundation, for he was not bishop of the diocese involved. But as archbishop, legate, and patron of the Cistercians, his involvement was central.

The thirteenth-century narration concerning Vitskøl's foundation adds more about Eskil's role. The probable author of this account is a monk from the Swedish abbey of Varnhem.[84] As such, he would have had less reason than a Danish monk from Vitskøl itself to manipulate the facts at hand. After the death of Sigrid, the foundress of Varnhem, life became impossible for the Varnhem monks because of the treatment they received from Queen Christina, the wife of King Erik.[85] Finally the monks were forced to abandon their monastery. Abbot Henrik headed south with some of his monks, intending to appeal to Clairvaux, their French mother house, for help. On the way they stopped at Roskilde, where a church synod was being held, the same one mentioned in King Valdemar's charter. Here both King and Archbishop were 'presiding'.[86] When Eskil was informed of Henrik's predicament, he reminded Valdemar of his promise before the 1157 victory to found a Cistercian abbey. Eskil argued that Henrik was just the man to become abbot of such a new house. The King sent the monks to Jutland to look at his properties there and to decide which of them would be most fit for a monastery. After making his inspection, Henrik sought out Eskil for his opinion and also consulted many others. He finally decided on the farm at Vitskøl on the eastern shore of Limfjorden north of Viborg. Messengers were sent to Varnhem for the remaining brothers. Later on, when Gerard had become Alvastra's second abbot and secured Varnhem's refoundation, some brothers returned there, while others remained at Vitskøl.

The narration concerning Vitskøl's foundation, despite its uncertain dating, is extremely helpful in filling out our knowledge about what was involved in starting a Cistercian house in Scandinavia. The Varnhem writer describes how twenty-two monks and a larger number of lay brothers came with their chalices, books, silver, vestments, and cattle to Vitskøl. Here we have clear evidence that lay brothers were present in the Cistercian settlement of Scandinavia. Only at Lyse Abbey near Bergen in Norway does the small size of the church, together with the absence of a west wing in the cloister (where lay brothers would have lived) point to the absence of lay brothers from a Scandinavian abbey. Another valuable piece of information in the foundation narrative is the description of the articles that the brothers brought with them. These are in accordance with the Cistercian statute from 1134, which specifies that the brothers were to have both liturgical necessities and 'temporal necessities so that they can both live and immediately observe the rule there'.[87] But the mention of cattle indicates that the brothers were by no means impoverished. Finally our author specifies Eskil's concern that the new abbey at Vitskøl come under Esrum as its mother house and not, as might be expected, Alvastra, which was Varnhem's mother abbey.

The archbishop accepted the importance of the Cistercian system with mother and daughter houses. That he negotiated Vitskøl's obedience to Esrum shows his awareness of the complications that could arise from a Danish abbey with a Swedish mother. As can be seen with Lyse Abbey, whose mother was Fountains in Yorkshire, great distances and political differences could ruin international mother-daughter links.[88]

Eskil is looked upon in the Vitskøl narration as a key figure who smoothed the way for Abbot Henrik. First he saw to it that Valdemar kept his promises, then he arranged for a suitable property, and finally he took care of whatever objections Alvastra might have had to losing a daughter house to Esrum. This impression of Eskil as being close to the needs of the Cistercians is confirmed by Esrum's charters until the 1170s. Eskil frequently defended the abbey in disputes over its rights and privileges. But Eskil rarely again acted as a property donor. In comparison with King Valdemar or Bishop Absalon, he gave very little to the monasteries. But it should be added that Eskil hardly needed to give very much himself when he was able to recruit others to provide for the Cistercians. Whether in terms of acquisitions of property, the solution of land disputes, or the avoidance of disagreements among the monasteries themselves, Eskil was very active in Esrum's success.

The first such indication comes from Eskil's witness to a donation by his relative, Count Niels, to Esrum in the village of Veksebo. After Niels' death, two men from whom he had bought the land, Sven and his son Rane, had tried to get the sale revoked. As usual Eskil is extremely informative about his own involvement. Visiting the area in order to consecrate an altar and say mass, he was met by the two challengers to the monks' claims. They conceded the case: 'The land which they had previously claimed in calumny, they deeded to me, with many witnesses present, so that it by an eternal right would be under that church [of Esrum]'.[89] Eskil does not indicate how Sven and Rane had been convinced to return the property to the monks, but he implies that he was responsible for their change of heart. As in the confusion about his exact role in the foundation of Esrum, Eskil does not actually claim all the credit. But he manages to leave that impression.

Another instance in which Eskil defended Esrum's holdings has been dated to the years 1167–74.[90] This time Villingerød was being challenged. The claimant was a canon of Lund cathedral, Florentius, who was nephew of the Dean of the Lund chapter, Johannes, from whom Eskil had bought Villingerød. The Esrum Book contains no copy of a deed recording this early transaction. But there is a charter of King Sven Grathe to the effect that

Eskil had bought Villingerød from the heir of Bishop Herman of Slesvig.[91] This was apparently Johannes, and so even if a document for the transaction itself is missing, it seems odd that Florentius would challenge a title the monks held by royal confirmation.

Eskil's reassertion of the monks' holding makes short work of Florentius's claim. This 'young man' had begun to calumniate the monks' right by saying the land had not been legally alienated from him. Eskil then summoned Florentius and made him promise that he would in future leave Esrum's property alone. Once again we have a charter in which Eskil leaves the impression that he took quick and decisive action. But when we return to the precise language of the document, there is nothing concrete to back up the impression. As clearly as Eskil indicates he cleaned up the case for the monks, so vague is he about how he convinced Florentius to abandon his claim!

These documents exhaust our knowledge about Eskil's involvement with Esrum. We can see from Bishop Absalon's charter for the monastery that its possessions grew considerably from 1158–78.[92] But none of the new holdings can be identified as Eskil's gifts. It seems that Eskil's main commitment to Esrum after 1158 consisted in defending the monks' title to lands that he had given them earlier. Although some charters may have been lost, it is clear from those we do have from this period that the two persons who contributed most to expanding Esrum's possessions were the bishop of Roskilde, Absalon, and King Valdemar. Eskil gave the monks vital psychological backing and some material beginnings, but Absalon and Valdemar saw the experiment through and made the new foundation viable and prosperous.

THE ACHIEVEMENTS OF THE 1160s AND 1170s

Absalon and Valdemar at Esrum

The first hint of Bishop Absalon's role comes in a charter dated between 1158 and 1160 in which King Valdemar deeded the forest of Villingehoved to Esrum.[93] The king says that Absalon, by now bishop of Roskilde, and his relative Sune Ebbesen had established the boundary of the property by riding around it. The arenga of this charter, which may have been composed by Absalon himself, idealizes the relationship between king and monks. They are devoted to the service of God and, like other subjects, are protected by the royal peace and generosity. Thus they are not to lack anything, especially since 'in their prayers our salvation is protected and the stability of the kingdom is guaranteed'.[94] The function of the monks, their worth in the kingdom, and the royal duty to help them, all these themes are carefully interwoven. In the next sentences we find more familiar ideas. The monks fight for Christ the King, and the Danish king seeks to provide for his and his parents' souls. But the first sentence remains as a clear statement of an idealized royal relationship to the monks.

In confirming the monks' right to Villingerød, which might have been challenged because the abbey had only the charter of Valdemar's infamous predecessor Sven, the monarchy adopted the language of the earlier document and its image of shipwreck in this world but added a mention of the royal desire to honour God and Saints Mary and Benedict. As in other early charters dealing with the Cistercians, the name of Mary appears frequently, acknowledging her role in the Order.[95]

Another indication of the monarchy's treatment of the monks can be found in a charter from the same period, 1158–60, in which the king gave the village of Stenholt to Esrum after an initial misunderstanding.[96] The acquisitive monks had bought the village from the peasants there for six marks. According to the charter, they had not known then that the property belonged to the king. He was willing to forgive this oversight and to hand over all his rights in the village in return for four marks silver. He gave nothing for free but at least helped avoid what could have ended in a nasty dispute. Once again in the arenga the monks are said to provide for the king's own salvation and the stability of the kingdom.

These charters bring us to the vexing problem of the relationship between royal power and monastic foundations. Why did kings encourage monasteries? Are the monks mere instruments of royal policy? The most famous instance in which the monks let themselves be used to carry out a royal policy appears in the first of Valdemar's privileges to Esrum.[97] Here the monks handed over one mark in gold as their contribution to the gilding of King Valdemar's father's shrine at Ringsted Benedictine Abbey. Knud Lavard had been murdered by his cousin Magnus in 1131. Now at the end of the 1150s his son Valdemar had won the civil war that had ensued for decades. By advancing Knud as a saint, King Valdemar sought to strengthen his throne. The Esrum brothers' payment thus acknowledged the holiness of Knud Lavard and thereby fitted into Valdemar's political program. Just as in the foundation charter for Vitskøl, Valdemar in the aftermath of his battlefield victory established the legitimacy and dignity of his position by linking his house with sainthood.

Another possible instance of Cistercians being used to further political ambitions is the foundation in 1163 of Tvis Abbey near Holstebro in Jutland. Its founder, Duke Buris Henriksen, was a relative of Valdemar and a potential claimant to the throne. Tvis may express Duke Buris's desire to build up his power and prestige in the area.[98] The foundation of Guldholm in the 1190s by Valdemar, bishop of Slesvig, the illegitimate son of the defeated King Sven, has also invited speculation about his intentions of using the 'Cistercian party' to fight the royal power clique.[99] Finally, and most importantly, the activities of Eskil in founding Cistercian abbeys outside his own diocese of Lund have inspired speculation about his intention to use such abbeys, exempt from the power of local bishops, to consolidate his power over the Danish Church.[100] As archbishop, Eskil had authority over other Danish prelates, but by obtaining Cistercian support, he would be better able to resist those bishops who sided with the Danish king in the great controversy of the 1160s over the legitimate pope. These interpretations of royal or episcopal relationships to the Cistercians are too one-dimensional. They easily reduce the new foundations to pawns in an elaborate political chess game.

In my view the monks were liable to political manipulation, but the most they could do was to lend an aura of spiritual authority to established political facts, such as Valdemar's new monarchy after 1157. When we see the monks together with secular or religious magnates whose position is unclear, men like Bishop Valdemar or Buris Henriksen, we are merely making intelligent guesses if we claim that monastic foundations were part of their political policies. The monks were necessary for such magnates primarily because they could assuage their consciences. In a society whose upper class lived and died violently, it was important to have men dedicated to peace and prayer. The monks came to Denmark because they were invited and cared for by the top level of society. It is nearly impossible to see how magnates and monks interacted, for the arengae of monastic charters cannot be used directly to read the intentions of founders. But indirectly these statements, together with gifts and legal settlements, all indicate enthusiasm and interest for this still young Order.

Absalon's involvement with the Cistercians can be seen from a charter for Esrum by which he gave the village and forest of Tømmerup. He had bought them from King Valdemar in return for other property.[101] In a medley of scriptural allusions, the charter's arenga expresses the donor's desire to use rightly the talent given to him so that he may have nothing to fear on Judgment Day. The language indicates that what men own is merely what they are given by God to administer; to Him they are sooner or later accountable. The charter describes the transaction itself, which Absalon says 'seemed to me in no way to wander from the path of righteousness'.

Absalon defended his transaction in careful detail. The property had once belonged to the bishopric of Roskilde, and Absalon anticipated a possible charge that he had been reducing his own diocesan holdings in favour of the monks. He pointed out that Roskilde had received Esrum holdings in Gentofte and Ordrup in exchange. Such a transaction should be permitted, especially when what was taken away from Saint Lucius at Roskilde had been given to the mother of God. How can any gift to her diminish the position of Lucius? This formulation aptly defends the transfer by emphasizing Mary's primary position among the saints. Here Cistercian devotion to the Virgin is used to support a potentially controversial land transfer. Roskilde, as Lucius's home, cannot be offended by an act acknowledging Mary's position:

> For what does the vicar of St. Lucius take away, subtract, or diminish
> in his bishopric of Roskilde when he cares sincerely for and honours
> more fully the mother of the Lord with suppliant offerings and a
> devout gift?[102]

The charter as a whole indicates Absalon's desire to guarantee for the monks a rather complex transaction which could easily be challenged. Absalon emerges from the charters issued in his name as a central figure in the preservation and extension of Cistercian rights and properties in Denmark during the last decades of the twelfth century. The monks found in him a bishop and politician who cooperated with them even if cooperation meant manipulating the holdings of the Roskilde bishopric. A similar pattern of cooperation can be seen at Sorø. Here a Cistercian commentary to the Sorø Book points out that even if lands were taken from Roskilde, the bishopric did not lose any wealth, for Absalon made up the difference from his own pocket.[103]

The monks realized that Absalon took risks in their favour and faced potential criticism from Roskilde canons. Similarly Absalon supported the Cistercians' claims when local opposition forced the monks to petition the king to confirm their holdings. There are two Esrum charters from 25 February 1174 by which the monks' claims to Såne are recognized. One is in King Valdemar's name, the other in Absalon's.[104] A man named Peder Scalle had laid claim to Såne, even though Esrum's title to it had been recognized at the end of the 1150s. But now the matter was once again settled in favour of the monks, and Peder Scalle had to back down. The role of defender of the monks, in which Eskil had once gloried, had been transferred to Absalon. This is natural in view of his position as bishop of Roskilde, but it is hardly something we would expect if we looked at the Danish Cistercian houses only through the eyes of Clairvaux writers. For them Absalon did not exist, but that may well be due to Eskil's domination of their consciousness.

Eskil's limited yet limitless influence

What happened to Eskil in these years? Had he lost interest in Esrum? Why do the charters tell us so little about him? We do have a few indications of his position. As archbishop of Lund, his main field of activity was his own diocese. Here he may have been close to Herrisvad, whose records we lack. We do know that Eskil was involved in the building of the abbey church, begun in 1158[105] Excavations made on the site in 1939 revealed many signs of what must have been an imposing Cistercian church in the romanesque style, with all the strictness and simplicity that Bernard could have desired.[106] Usually we cannot detect any signs of Cistercian austerity in the early Danish abbeys. Esrum, as we have seen, began buying property almost from the start. Sorø got episcopal shares of parish tithes from an early date, even though the *Exordium Parvum* and early Cistercian legislation forbade this practice.[107] But Herrisvad, despite the gaps in our knowledge of its history, at least in terms of architecture, apparently remained faithful in its first decades to the ideals of austerity and simplicity. Could Eskil have been involved in this assertion of idealism?

One consideration may help clarify Eskil's absence from the Danish sources. The archbishop simply did not spend enough time in Denmark to carry through any consistent policies to the advantage of Esrum or the other houses west of Öresund. As we have seen in the sources of Vitskøl's foundation, Eskil was back in Denmark in 1158 after having spent some time abroad (a good part of it involuntarily, as the prisoner of an ally of the Emperor Frederick I). By 1161, Eskil left Denmark again. His last recorded act before his exile was to witness a donation by King Valdemar in March.[108] Then he disappeared to France, where he remained until 1167 and supported Alexander III—during a period (1161–67) when most of the Danish bishops sided with the antipope, Victor IV. This would have meant a total moratorium on new Danish Cistercian foundations had they depended on Eskil. But monks from Esrum were sent to Sorø in the spring of 1161, probably solely on the inspiration and encouragement of Absalon and other members of his family.[109] In 1163, Tvis was founded, and among those signing its charter were Robert, abbot of Herrisvad, Frederick of Esrum, and Henrik of Vitskøl. One can hardly look at this foundation as a defiant act carried out in spite of Eskil. The business of spreading the Cistercian Order in Denmark continued as if there were no schism at all.[110]

Yet we cannot totally disregard the role which Eskil played for the Cistercians even in these years. Most of our information comes from the Øm Abbey Chronicle, which is extremely sensitive to events of this period. Its attention results from the fact that the bishop of Århus, who founded and endowed the monastery, supported Valdemar and thus the antipope, Victor. The Øm writer shows that his community feared challenges to its rights and holdings because of the schismatic position of the bishop of Århus, who was also named Eskil:

It should not be left to silence, something we should have written about in the beginning, how Abbot Henrik wrote to the lord pope concerning the place which Bishop Eskil [of Århus] offered to him, and what the pope replied. For Bishop Eskil was stained by the schism of Octavian, as also certain other bishops and the king himself, and therefore the abbot delayed receiving the place from his hands without consulting the pope.[111]

As I have pointed out in *Conflict and Continuity at Øm Abbey*, the Øm writer waited until he was well into his account about the abbey's beginnings before bringing up this unpleasant and dangerous issue. But once he did, he provided a wealth of detail and copies of papal privileges which clearly show Archbishop Eskil's continuing involvement not just in the affairs of the Danish church but also in a proposed new Cistercian foundation. Abbot Henrik of Vitskøl made a trip south to the papal court-in-exile at Sens in order to legitimize the gift of the schismatic Århus bishop. Archbishop Eskil was with the pope, Alexander III, at Sens in the beginning of 1165. The meeting resulted in papal confirmation of the transfer by the new community to the locality of Sminge (from there it later moved to Veng, then to Kalvø, and finally in the spring of 1172 to Øm). The papal letter says that the pope had conferred with Eskil 'our brother' on the matter and that the decision to allow the monks to leave Vitskøl for Sminge met with the archbishop's approval.[112]

As it turned out, the brothers did not settle in Sminge but instead took over a Benedictine house at Veng. Once again papal permission was sought for the move. The first abbot of the new community, Brienne, went south to the papal court in 1165 or 1166.[113] The Øm Chronicle includes a copy of a charter issued by Alexander III to King Valdemar. The first part has no surprises. There is the usual story of the decline of the Benedictines and the Cistercian desire for reform. Similar descriptions can be found in Cistercian accounts for Sorø, Guldholm, and other houses. The pope confirms the new foundation at Veng and asks King Valdemar to protect it. The bishop-elect of Århus, Sven, is also named. The letter then introduces a matter hardly germane to the Cistercian foundation. The pope asks Valdemar to request Eskil, archbishop of Lund, who is a religious and discreete man and 'as we believe, very acceptable to God and men, most faithful to you and your kingdom', to come home.[114] He is to be given due honour and the chance of defending and protecting his rights and lands.

Here we catch Eskil *in medias res*. Probably at his instigation, an innocent communication between pope and king became a highly political document. The transmission of such a request to a schismatic king reveals the way Cistercian emissaries at the papal court could be used as mediators. The king could have had nothing against the Cistercians at this point and had no reason to refuse the papal request. But merely by receiving it, he recognized the position of Alexander III as rightful pope. Thus a seemingly trivial, matter-of-fact document takes on a significant political dimension. It is not apparent whether Brienne brought the letter back to Valdemar personally, but the Øm monks kept a copy in their archives. This copy was considered valuable enough to be included in the Øm Chronicle when it was begun in 1207 or soon thereafter.

In this affair the Cistercians were used by the pope and the archbishop to carry out their designs. In one sense they are merely messengers, but in another they provide a warning to the king that he can disregard neither this international society living in his realm nor his rightful archbishop.

The events of these years have been looked upon as a grand battle between, on one side, Eskil, Alexander, and the Cistercians, and, on the other, Valdemar, and his schismatic bishops, with the first party winning out in the end.[115] This interpretation ignores the lack of evidence of any opposition between Cistercian houses in Denmark and King Valdemar. Eskil's role in furthering Cistercian interests in Denmark, as we have seen, becomes unclear after 1158. The new foundation which settled at Øm in 1172 did seek Eskil's support. Similarly, a newly-elected bishop like Sven of Århus needed to be consecrated by his archbishop, Eskil. But even if Eskil is a central figure, the Danish Cistercians did not place all their hopes in him. They used him, first at Sens, and then in 1165–66 at Clairvaux, to obtain help in legal matters. But there is nothing to indicate that the Danish monks allied themselves exclusively with Eskil.

When the monks at Veng were forced to move a second time and refounded their community at Kalvø on Skanderborg Lake in 1167, Abbot Brienne went south a second time to obtain papal approval.[116] Stopping at Clairvaux, he found Eskil and obtained from him a letter approving the transfer. The text of the letter reveals the reciprocal use Eskil and the Cistercians made of each other. Eskil consented to the transfer of the monastery not only because the monks wished it but also because King Valdemar, Bishop Absalon of Roskilde, and Bishop Sven of Århus had requested it: 'To them we can deny nothing'.

Eskil was on the verge of being able to return to Denmark, and so this remark was a careful piece of flattery. During Eskil's exile in the 1160s, it was not so much the Cistercians who made use of Eskil as he who used the Cistercians. Through them he maintained contacts with the royal party, emphasized his links with Pope Alexander, and hinted at his good will towards King Valdemar and Bishop Absalon.

During these decisive years, Eskil also laid plans to found Carthusian abbeys in Denmark. He established contact with the brothers of La Chartreuse, who sent to him a brother Roger to discuss the sending of a group to the North. In a letter sent to Eskil between 1160 and 1162, Peter, abbot of La Celle, described the difficulties of getting such an abbey started.[117] In another letter from 1162–63, Peter, abbot of the Benedictine house St

Remi at Rheims, wrote to Basilius and other priors in that Carthusian Order and used on behalf of Denmark the biblical image that the harvest was great but the workers few.[118] The priors were urged to complete the work they had begun there and to send some of their brothers North. These two letters reveal traces of Eskil's efforts. But just as at Esrum, the man who completed the task was not Eskil but Absalon. According to the Sorø Donation Book, Absalon exchanged Esrum's holdings in Asserbo for lands in the forest of Ørved, a vanished locality that is supposed to have been near Esrum.[119] He then called the Carthusians to Asserbo, where they remained only a short time before returning to France. According to the Sorø writer, the Carthusians found the place unfit for habitation. Whatever happened, the practical task of obtaining land titles for the new settlement was carried out by Absalon. This fact contributes to an impression of Absalon as a man both practical and useful to the monks in completing Eskil's initiatives.

From 1167 until the middle of 1174, Eskil was back in Denmark. During this period two more Cistercian abbeys were founded: Løgum in Southern Jutland (1170 or 1171) and Holme, now Brahetrolleborg, in southern Fyn north of Fåborg (1172). About Holme we know next to nothing. Even the date is uncertain, for it comes from the unreliable Colbaz Annals. The first certain indication of the abbey's existence comes from 1175, when Abbot Thomas of Holme signed a confirmation of the privileges of St Knud's Abbey in Odense.[120] Both Løgum and Holme were daughters of Herrisvad, and it would not be surprising if their foundations were due at least in part to Eskil's efforts. Eskil was involved during this period in the foundation of the Premonstratensian abbey Væ in Skåne. Even if his support consisted entirely of privileges and not of property gifts, he was still an essential participant in the new religious foundation.[121] In Løgum's case we know that its early privileges were issued by Eskil. These were lost in a fire before the end of the century.[122] In Holme's case, Bishop Simon of Odense legally had to be involved. But here we may have a link with Eskil. Bishop Simon had given Eskil's foundation at Væ the church of St Mary and so can be looked upon as Eskil's ally in starting the new house. Eskil may have reciprocated by helping Bishop Simon found a Cistercian house on Fyn.[123]

By now we have almost exhausted what we can know or surmise about Eskil and the Cistercians by using Danish sources. The further we get from the 1150s, the less clear his role at home in Denmark becomes. From about the middle of 1174 until mid-1176, Eskil for a fourth time travelled outside Denmark and so could only have aided the Cistercians indirectly.[124] When he returned, only a few months remained before he resigned his archbishopric and left the country for good to become a monk of Clairvaux. In such circumstances he had little opportunity to carry out any business for the

Cistercians, such as helping them with disputes, arranging exchanges and purchases of property, or confirming transactions.

Our last glimpse of Eskil from a Danish source comes from Saxo and is not a favourable one.[125] Eskil's castle was being beseiged by the king; this may have been Søborg in Northern Zealand, not far from Esrum.[126] The archbishop refused to let the men defending it concede defeat. Valdemar wanted to conclude the action as quickly as possible and took Eskil's grandson hostage. He had grown up in Esrum monastery and had been educated by the monks. The king threatened to have the boy executed unless Eskil gave in to his demands, but Eskil remained adamant. Saxo describes with his usual flair for style and setting how the Esrum monks came crying to King Valdemar and begged him not to take the poor boy's life.[127] This glimpse of the monks, though marked by Saxo's antipathy for Eskil, tells us something about Eskil and the Cistercians. Eskil had used them to look after his grandchild; now when the boy was in trouble, it was the monks who pleaded for him.

To complete our picture of Eskil and the Cistercians, we are fortunate in having Herbert of Clairvaux's *Liber Miraculorum*, written soon after Eskil went south in 1178. In many ways this is a rather crude account, for Herbert was concerned exclusively with the supernatural and so only indirectly reveals anything about Eskil as a person. Herbert's central story deals with Eskil's youth when he was at school in Hildesheim.[128] Ill with fever, he had a dream in which he was burning up but obtained some relief when he came into the presence of a very dour, strict woman, whom Herbert would have us believe was Mary. He offered her everything he could for his release, practically bribing her with visions of gold from his parents. The boy was terrified of being relegated to the fire. The Virgin answered that from five types of grain he was to render five measures to her. This command was interpreted as an order to found religious houses in her honour. When the boy awoke, he could say nothing except, 'Blessed be God. I am free. I shall burn no more.' When he finally recounted his vision, a listener predicted that one day he would found five monasteries and become a great man in the Church. Here Herbert adds a detail that tells as much about Eskil's work as anything we can find elsewhere: 'He did not want to be content with the founding of those five houses but made an effort to build many others, both with his own gifts as well as with those of other believers'.[129] So he brought groups of brothers from many different orders to his country: Cistercians, Carthusians, and Premonstratensians, and provided handsomely for them from his own funds, settling them in the best locations. These foundations increased and multiplied like the shoots on a great vine and sent forth buds among the Saxon, Slavic, Swedish, and Norwegian nations and many others, bringing a new grace of religion to barbarian tribes. And today 'they are increasing more than ever'.[130] These hyperbolic claims in Herbert's account are worth investigating. They vary from anything recorded earlier by Geoffrey of Auxerre. Significantly enough, the later *Exordium Magnum* modified Herbert's assertions and said only that Eskil had seen to the founding of a number of religious houses, among them two Cistercian abbeys. Either the author of the *Exordium*, Conrad of Eberbach, lacked sufficient interest in Eskil to give him as much attention as Herbert had, or else he felt his predecessor had used too many exaggerated expressions. The latter may be the case, for Conrad was willing to devote a great deal of space to recounting Eskil's childhood vision. He lifted his narrative almost word for word from Herbert and could easily have taken the few sentences about Eskil's foundations just as literally. But in modifying Herbert's claims, Conrad indicated he knew that Eskil could not be credited, even indirectly, for Norwegian houses, founded by English abbeys, or Saxon houses, which had nothing to do with Danish expansion.[131]

Herbert's overheated account nevertheless provides a symbolic truth. For the Clairvaux Cistercians, Eskil was the great apostle of the barbaric, dangerous, and unknown North. They felt indebted to him for the spread of their Order northward. At a time when many statutes adopted by the General Chapter indicate fear that the Order was losing its early purity, a man like Eskil could give assurance and a sense of security.

Occasionally Eskil almost overplayed his role in telling exciting stories to Herbert. The *Liber Miraculorum* has one tale from Eskil about a rich and powerful knight who married a woman already the wife of another knight. Eskil admonished and finally excommunicated him. On Holy Saturday night the devil suffocated the couple as well as their two children. In the morning they were found dead in their beds. When this story became known in Denmark, many terrified sinners repented. Herbert tells the story in great detail, while Conrad only summarizes it.[132] Conrad left out totally an account in Herbert concerning Bishop Elias of Ribe.[133] Once as Eskil visited Elias and celebrated mass, he found to his consternation that the Eucharistic host shattered into five segments. He finished celebrating mass as quickly as possible and was very much afraid. A few days later he received news about the papal schism between Alexander and Octavian. Elias sided with Octavian. For Herbert (and his mentor Eskil), the disintegration of the host was a sign of Elias's coming apostasy. Herbert provides a gory description of Elias's death, apparently something which Eskil enjoyed telling. On his deathbed Elias was to have refused to confess or to receive communion. When one of his sons begged him to do so, Elias exploded, 'You evil son of a whore. Your intention is not hidden from me. I know that you desire my death so that you can get hold of my riches.' When his friends returned, they could not find Elias in bed. Looking up they found his corpse hung over the highest beam in the room. They concluded that devils must have thrown him up there. The lesson is clear: those who allow themselves to be separated from the body of Christ deserve such a death.

The disturbing aspect of such tales told by Eskil to Herbert—and there are many others—is their emphasis on divine punishment and the justification of Eskil's acts as churchman and prelate. A Danish noble married a woman to whom he was closely related; Eskil excommunicated them. After a time the woman, who is called incestuous, was found dead in her bed next to her husband, strangled by the devil. Such lurid tales were material for daily consumption in the rough and tumble of medieval life. Their entrance into a Cistercian milieu merely underlines the double quality of Cistercian life: for those inside the fold there are warmth and receptivity; for those outside there are contempt and suspicion. You are either with me or against me. Eskil was with the Cistercians, and Herbert accepted what he must have thought was the Archbishop's brave fight to compel the barbarian Danes to live according to the rules of the Church on marriage. But the deletion of the most violent stories or their summarization in Conrad's *Exordium Magnum* indicates that such stories could be too vindictive or self-righteous for the polishers of Clairvaux literature. Thus we can see a distinction between Eskil's crude vengefulness, typical of a more primitive type of warrior Christianity, and Conrad's high Cistercian emphasis on monastic righteousness.

The question remains whether we are directly in touch with Eskil through Herbert's narrative. How can we draw a line between narrator and informant? Did Herbert write down verbatim what the retired archbishop told him? It is likely that the narrative is essentially Eskil's, but some of the details may be Herbert's. The latter was accountable to the entire Cistercian community for what he wrote and so could not have merely fantasized. Herbert could make Eskil into a hero whose actions reflected the triumphal spread of the Cistercian Order. At the same time Eskil, as often before in his life, was keenly aware of his own role and wanted to make posterity aware of it.

Even if many of the stories Eskil brought to Clairvaux reflect violence and hatred, the retired archbishop could also impress the brothers by his quietness. Herbert tells how Eskil, praying one day in Clairvaux's oratory, had a vision of his dead brother.[134] The scene recreated here enables Herbert to comment that Eskil normally spent the whole day 'almost until the hour of dining' in constant prayer. The description of the vision itself shows a different aspect of Eskil than the stories about devils, but even there Eskil's emphasis is in punishment for sins. The brother said nothing but bowed his head in grief. Eskil was also silent. He was terrified, for he could only see the man's head, neck, and the top of his shoulders. The rest of his body was on fire, and Eskil could only see the flames.

After the vision had left him, Eskil felt great sorrow for the man and his sufferings. On the next day, coming into the monks' chapter, he begged their prayers and masses for his dead brother. At this point Herbert adds, 'These and almost all other things, which we above related, we heard from the venerable and holy father himself'.[135] Because Herbert insisted that the stories came directly from Eskil, we can use them in an attempt to understand the archbishop and his relationship with the Cistercians.

In this case the spiritual bond between the monks and the former archbishop is eloquently expressed. Eskil was deeply affected by the vision and used the chapter, when brothers were supposed to confess their sins and to discuss the business of the day, to convince the brothers that he was a visionary. We see here the essential role of oral communication in creating moral edification in the Cistercian community. Eskil's way of communicating his vision to the brothers shows the receptivity of the Cistercian milieu to tales of the marvellous and miraculous.

Especially in the twelfth and early thirteenth centuries, monks were encouraged to write down experiences that could both heighten the reverence and respect due the Order and their monastery and inspire future members to holy lives. This combination of hagiography and self-justification began at Clairvaux with the lives of Bernard, was expanded by Herbert and Conrad, reached its height in the many works of Caesarius of Heisterbach, and appeared in Denmark in works like the Øm Abbey Chronicle, the short *Vita* of Bishop Gunner of Viborg, or the 1289 account of the founding of Guldholm. These narratives, except for the lives of Bernard, often concentrate on a figure external to the monastery, frequently a bishop who was a special benefactor and is supposed to have loved the Cistercians without reservation.

In concentrating on such a personality, the Cistercians reminded themselves, as well as any secular clergy who might read their accounts, that they were a unique order in the Church. They had been well treated by great churchmen and deserved continued special consideration and generosity. There is nothing exclusively medieval about this need to believe in oneself and defend oneself through the praise and devotion of others. But the Cistercians developed this practice into a literary genre, most clearly expressed in the *Exordium Magnum*. Here some of the Cistercians' main benefactors are mentioned, their help remembered, their example praised.

It is noteworthy that this particular episode of Eskil's vision and his narration of it in chapter are also included in the *Exordium Magnum*.[136] The author follows the Herbert text rather closely and thus shows us he accepts almost completely an edifying episode about a patron's vision, while elsewhere he has deleted the patron's stories of violence and revenge. This selection of Eskil's stories in Conrad is not, as one might assume, merely a question of which ones have direct application to Cistercian interests. In at least one case, Conrad apparently included a story told by Eskil simply because it was a good story. It had nothing to do with the Cistercians. It is the account of Eskil's uncles, the one a violent and sinful man, the other a saintly bishop.[137] The bishop, named Sven, encouraged the other, called Eskil, to go on crusade to atone for his sins. This Eskil refused to go unless his brother came with him. So they both went and visited the places where Jesus had walked. Finally they came to a dilapidated church called Pater Noster. Here was supposed to be the spot where Jesus had given mankind the Lord's Prayer. Eskil the elder was so overwhelmed that he asked God to grant him a special favour. Afraid that after his repentance on the pilgrimage, he might revert to his bad habits once he returned home, he asked to die on the spot so he could go directly to heaven. His prayer was answered. His brother made the same request, and immediately died too. The other pilgrims were so impressed that they repaired the church in memory of the event.

Again we see Archbishop Eskil as a magnificent storyteller, who knew how to make anecdotes memorable and at the same time to assure his own fame. After this account, the *Exordium Magnum* adds a few lines summarizing Eskil's career and praising him especially for leaving his archepiscopal office to come to Clairvaux. He gave up his riches to become one of the poor of Christ. He was buried in the presbytery in front of the Lady altar. The last sentence puts Eskil's contribution into the context of all the holy men who followed Bernard's example and preferred the Way of Christ:

> And so such persons so high in position and revered in office were drawn by the virtues of our blessed father Bernard and by the purity of the holy Cistercian Order. They preferred the taunts given Christ to all the pomps of the Egyptians. They would rather suffer under the discipline of the Order for a time than for all eternity be tormented because of false favours and honours given them.[138]

Herbert and Conrad record a number of other episodes mentioning Danish monks, especially concerning Abbot Henrik of Vitskøl. He seems to have been a frequent visitor at Clairvaux in the 1170s.[139] Likewise an unnamed Esrum lay brother managed to come there before his death.[140] But most of the space given to Danish Cistercians concerns Eskil. His gift as a storyteller enables us to use his anecdotes to gain an impression of his personality. Despite his efforts to bring about the triumph of the Cistercian Order in Denmark, Eskil belongs to the first half of the twelfth century and not to the second. His world is dominated by a wrathful Old Testament God who lets the devil string up sinners or suffocate them. Eskil's childhood vision of Mary as a mean woman has little to do with the loving mother and intercessor appearing in twelfth-century collections of miracles of the Virgin, to say nothing of Cistercian literature about Mary. Eskil's Mary had to be bribed into dismissing the boy on promise of future payment; Bernard's Mary was the mother of grace and mercy, always available to the sinner and setting very few conditions.

The qualities of Eskil's mind can be found elsewhere in the twelfth century: repressed sexuality and thinly-veiled sadistic impulses can lie just beneath the surface of edificatory literature. But in accentuating the anger of God, the arbitrariness of Mary, or the praiseworthy value of a death wish, Eskil shows that he is psychologically at home in the archaic and tougher world of the early Middle Ages. His mind was shaped by membership in an old, aristocratic, landowning family and by the pre-gregorian atmosphere of Hildesheim. Eskil functioned in a world formed before the endless wanderings and pessimism of epic literature had given way to the arrival and hope of romance. As a product of a land where Christianity was still only a thin veneer, as a man educated not in a French cathedral school but in a Carolingian episcopal seat, Eskil apparently adopted the most punitive aspects of Christianity. Later on, his friendship with Bernard may have softened some of the harsh lines in his thinking, as we can see in his letter from captivity in 1157, where he emphasizes the fact of Christ's redemption.[141] But in the late 1170s Eskil was still a self-righteous defender of his actions and roles in Danish politics, a seeker after divine justification. Conrad of Eberbach found this side of him unattractive, while Herbert was hypnotized by him.

If we apply this view of Eskil, tentative as it must be, to his relationship with the Cistercians in Denmark, we can see why he contributed so little and yet did so much for their beginnings. He provided powerful incentives to other men, inspired and excited them, was a strict taskmaster and a careful planner. Such a personality was ideal for starting a foreign monastic order in a distant European country. Eskil's courage and belief in the Cistercian mission stem from an unquestioning and unsubtle grasp of what was right in a given situation. But in practical terms, Eskil dispersed his energies. His off-on relations with the monarchy, his concentration on other orders such as the Carthusians and the Premonstratensians, and the abrasiveness of his personality—all these factors made it impossible for him to complete many of his projects. In the end, he felt more at home and spent more time with the monks of Clairvaux than he did in the northern expanse of Denmark with King Valdemar and his court.

The myth of Eskil was much more valuable for the Cistercians, both at Clairvaux and in Denmark, than were the actual contributions he can be seen to have made to Danish houses. There is very little that can be said for property contributions after 1158. And even regarding privileges for the houses, Eskil was content with affirming what he had already given rather than broadening the monastic base. Eskil is the only person in twelfth-century Denmark besides the Augustinian Abbot William of Æbelholt who reveals himself to us as a person. These indications of his character and attitudes have been interpreted and used in quite different ways. In my view Eskil was a great mythmaker at a time when such myths of power and creativity were just as essential to Danish and French Cistercians as concrete gifts of land.

Myths and realities: Sorø and Øm

Leaving Eskil and returning to the Danish Cistercian sources themselves, we can summarize events and tendencies in the 1160s and 1170s. We find new foundations every few years, a widespread myth of Benedictine decline, the frequent necessity for the monks to leave one place and try another one before finding a suitable location for their monastery, their dependence on benevolent founders, rapid and sometimes almost too hasty land acquisitions not only near but even at great distances from the monastery itself.

The history of Sorø Abbey in central Zealand illustrates some of these developments and concepts. Sorø started out in the 1150s as a Benedictine house but quickly went into decline. It was dependent in both its Benedictine phase and its Cistercian refoundation on one family of benefactors and probably would not have survived without their support. And even though the site of the monastery was not moved, there were times when this must have seemed likely because of troubles with unfriendly neighbours.[142] The most fascinating aspect of the pre-1215 chronicle that tells us virtually all we know about early Sorø is the agreement of its interpretation of events with what we find in the almost contemporary Øm Abbey Chronicle.[143] The Benedictine houses that the Cistercians in both cases replaced were, according to the Cistercians, hopelessly decadent. The Cistercians had their work cut out for them from the very beginning. At Veng the repentant Benedictine abbot was convinced to withdraw to Vitskøl and become a simple monk, to the great rejoicing of the Cistercians.[144] At Sorø there seems to have been nothing left when the Cistercians arrived on the scene in 1161. The place, which had been founded by the sons of Skjalm Hvide (Asser Rig, Ebbe Skjalmsen, and Toke Skjalmsen), had been left 'desolate' by the last Benedictine abbot, Robert.[145] He had come from Sweden and, after being made prior at Sorø, had lived more for the sake of his stomach than of his soul.

Once again, the myth easily visible on the surface of the narration is far more important than any historical fact which might be submerged beneath. The Cistercians justified their arrival on the basis of the decline of their predecessors. The monks saw themselves as champions of reform. On a local level they implemented the international mission of the Cistercians: a return to authentic monasticism. In this sense almost all the Danish foundation accounts—whether for Øm, Sorø or Guldholm—build on the literary and moral structure already present in the *Exordium Parvum*. We are told of a reform party which replaced or separated from the original, decadent community.[146] Just as with the austere church at Herrisvad, we get a rare chance in these chronicles to see how early Cistercian ideals were at work in the minds of Danish monks. It is impossible to show that the very first generation of Danish Cistercians viewed themselves as reformers of a monastic tradition in decline. But the thirteenth century monks who wrote about this first generation certainly looked upon their predecessors in such a light.

In this sense the Sorø Donation Book, with its initial chronicle, is more than a register of lands given by the Skjalm family. The writer indicates that his predecessors had had great ambitions, which he seeks to justify. At Øm the chronicler seems to be apologizing when he minimizes the community's takeover of the Kalvø Benedictine house by claiming that there were only two monks left there.[147] Whatever the historical truth may be, the Øm writer envisioned the possible charge that the Cistercians had been intruders.

Similarly the chronicler of Ryd, writing about the foundation of Guldholm Abbey in the early 1190s, added some entertaining stories about an event that justified the Cistercian beginnings.[148] The Slesvig Benedictines found their abbot dead drunk in a tavern and brought him back to the abbey in procession, as if they were celebrating the rites for the dead. This symbolized that the abbot was dead in his soul. Likewise the community was dead to all the genuine impulses of monasticism. It was time for the Cistercians to replace it, but the takeover had to be defended even as late as 1289, when the account was written. The author insists that the old Order was in decline and that the house had become so disorderly that the monks not only lived in quiet sin but also scandalized the neighbourhood.

Such accounts emphasize an unshakable and polemical belief by the Cistercians in themselves. Could it not be the very strength of this conviction that accounts for the Cistercian successes in twelfth and early thirteenth century Denmark? And cannot this understanding of the Cistercian advance in one country shed light on the amazing expansion of the Order in the twelfth century? Behind the self-confidence of the chronicles there may have been a great deal of insecurity about the present situation of the Order. But in emphasizing the purity of their mission the monks could convince others to support them. This seems to have been the case whether the monks dealt with the Skjalm family at Sorø, King Valdemar, or Bishop Sven of Århus.

The pervasiveness of Cistercian self-assertion in early thirteenth-century sources should provide sufficient warning against reducing foundations like that of Tvis in 1163 to purely political moves by an ambitious prince. Tvis is just as much a product of Herrisvad's growth in the preceding years as and perhaps even an indication of its Abbot Robert's desire to spread houses of his Citeaux line all over Denmark instead of limiting them to Skåne. Holme on Fyn and Løgum in Southern Jutland give a fine balance to the Citeaux line. The only part of the country with no house affiliated to Herrisvad is Zealand, where Esrum and its daughter Sorø had their own preserve.

Best accounted for in this period is the history of the abbey that started at Øm in the spring of 1172. Here we can see the central role a mother abbey played in the foundation of a daughter house. Henrik, abbot of Vitskøl (the same who visited Clairvaux and is mentioned in the works of Herbert and Conrad), and Brienne, the first abbot of Øm, saw to it that the monks got a decent place to live. Only the tireless travels of these two to the papal court made the final settlement at Øm possible. All along there was resistance. The Øm chronicler naturally tried to make his story as heroic as possible, but the documents he includes back up the basic truth of the account. Again we find the influence of the *Exordium Parvum* and other early Citeaux writings on later Cistercian chronicles. The narrator builds up his account around documents which he copies in full. Without such Cistercian use of charters, our knowledge of Denmark—and Western Europe—in the twelfth century would be much poorer.

The difficulties in establishing Øm can be seen in a dispute with a relative of King Valdemar, Margrethe, sister of a Count Erik. The Cistercians had settled at the former Benedicine house of Veng. But Margrethe, who owned a third of the property, did everything possible to get the brothers to leave. She wanted instead to found a community of nuns there and so offered King Valdemar 'a great deal of land in Fyn' if he would give her the whole of Veng.[149] She is also supposed to have bribed the queen with jewellery and other gifts which the Øm chronicler described in detail. The monks fought fire with fire by sending two of their lay supporters, probably influential landowners, to the royal court to ask for the king's help, but in order to convince these two men to look after their interests, the monks had to pay them with valuable properties.

Despite genuine pious generosity, the give and take of life in the thirteenth century did not preclude financial transactions between the monks and their representatives. From the very start the Danish Cistercians engaged willingly in whatever methods were necessary to get what they wanted. This is not to accuse the monks of being unscrupulous but to show that they tried to survive in a society where their claims were by no means automatically accepted. In this case, however, the monks' rival was not simply a greedy landowner, unwilling to part with his properties. Margrethe opposed the monks because of a desire to further her own ambitions by founding a convent.

In the fourteenth century, opponents to the monks' property claims sought to obtain the land for their own use. Margrethe belongs to an earlier period when the problem seems not to have been lack of religious enthusiasm among lay persons but competition between religious orders for their favour. This episode in the history of Øm and the bitter remark of the author that even at the time of writing (1207), the monks' claims had not been met, warns us against looking at the twelfth century as an easy time when the monks always were welcome.[150] The Vitskøl narration about the fierce but totally unexplained resistance of another woman to the monks at Varnhem parallels this account of Margrethe's treatment of the Øm community. The monks naturally wanted their readers to think they had a difficult time so they could gain sympathy and support.[151] But the disputes that they document tell us in themselves, regardless of their commentary, that if monastic gains in twelfth-century Denmark were huge, they were often hard-won.

Another important aspect of the relationship between the monks and lay society that emerges from the account of the Veng dispute is the ambivalent royal attitude. Here we see the worth of narrative, which reveals attitudes hidden from us in charters. If we had to describe Valdemar's treatment of the monks solely from charters, he would seem always to have backed the monks. But they only copied and included in their collections the charters in their favour, as we can see from the Esrum Book. In the Øm Chronicle, the writer had to show the king in another light, for the property claims from the 1160s were still outstanding in 1207 when he wrote. The Øm author describes how the monastery's two advocates managed to convince the king to give the monks back their share of Veng in return for a 'gift' of three marks in gold and a number of villages that on Valdemar's death would go to his son Knud. Actually, our writer admits, two of these villages went to the king's concubine.[152]

Even this transaction was insufficient to convince King Valdemar to defend the brothers' rights against Margrethe. The writer claims that because Valdemar was related to her, he was unwilling to force her out of Veng: 'He did not want to offend her while he lived, and so justice was neglected'.[153] The monks' frustration is revealed here more openly than in any other Danish Cistercian source. Despite papal letters to the king, the monks could not get the land. Finally Margrethe obligingly died and the monks almost regained Veng. But the king, after further delaying the matter, had the discourtesy to die suddenly. And so the brothers, 'as they always complained, today are complaining. They will not stop complaining until justice is done to them for the things unjustly taken away from them.'[154]

This, one of the most remarkable and revealing sentences in the Øm Chronicle, summarizes the Cistercians' attitude to a world treating them badly. They will persist for generations in order to get the rights they believe theirs. But lay families that gave them trouble likewise continued to do so from one generation to the next. We see this dilemma best at Sorø with the descendants of Esbern Snare. Just when one of them is on his deathbed and has handed over to the monks Esbern Snare's original legacy, as had been intended for the monks, another family member comes on the scene and resists the monks until he too is on his deathbed and having thoughts about eternity.[155] At Øm the dispute, which may have transferred to Margrethe's descendants, seems to have continued for more than forty years. At both Sorø and Øm the monks never forgot anything done against their interests and nurtured their claims until the day came when they once again could assert them.

This Cistercian fear of being mistreated takes on central importance in the dispute that arose during the 1260s between Tyge, bishop of Århus, and the Øm monks, the best-known episode in Danish Cistercian history.[156] But the attitude was already latent in the 1160s, when one might think the monks still the darlings of the upper class. If we consider only their privileged and guaranteed position in society, this image is correct. But the monks still had a major disadvantage in their need to acquire vast agricultural holdings. From the first, they had to compete with the children of their benefactors and with people, like Margrethe, who were interested in other religious orders. Only rarely could the monks as a religious family even begin to compete with the tightly-knit lay families of the aristocracy. Only with strong bishops like Absalon could they break through the monopoly of family interests and get what they considered their rightful holdings.

When the king was obliged by family bonds to look after his relatives, the monks had even less chance of obtaining what they sought. King Valdemar apparently adopted a tactic of delay in the monks' case against Margrethe. All the legal weapons the monks could summon from the pope or elsewhere could not overcome the basic fact that Valdemar was related to this determined woman.

No matter how hard the Danish Cistercians pushed their claims in society, and regardless of how well they succeeded in establishing a solid place in it, they were still pained by the reminder that they were an import. Like exotic flowers the monks were attractive but inevitably less important to the magnates than their own offspring. In the twelfth century the Cistercians were favoured by male society. In the thirteenth century, at the very time when male family members abandoned their parents' concern for the monks, great women of the realm came to fill the role of benefactor and enabled the monks to continue to gain new holdings.

In the face of Margrethe's resistance, the Veng monks were forced to Kalvø, a marshy and insignificant island at the south end of Skanderborg Lake. Here they were unable to stay for more than a few years because of difficulties of communication and transport, and perhaps also because of the lack of running water to provide power.[157] So in the spring of 1172, they came to the place called Øm, which they latinized to *Cara Insula*, beloved isle. Here at last, after buying land from local peasants, some of whom were reluctant to sell, the monks could settle down to daily life. The foundation narrative for Øm not only shows how difficult such beginnings could be; it also indicates how much work the monks had to do themselves, both in acquiring privileges and guaranteeing property rights and in measuring the altitudes of nearby lakes to see if a canal could be dug to provide running water, as well as in negotiating reasonable terms with difficult peasants.

Again we are warned against thinking of the early Cistercians as solely the offspring of the upper class and its ambitions. At Sorø, Herrisvad, Esrum, and Vitskøl, royal and episcopal help were substantial and made for an easy start. But at Øm it was another story. Bishop and king had to be cajoled into helping the monks. The first abbot, Brienne, had to shuttle back and forth to the papal court three or four times to confirm the movements of the monks from one inadequate or unsuccessful site to another. These difficulties may well be the mainspring for the composition of a detailed account. After what the monks had been through, they wanted the world to know their gains. If necessary, they would fight again. The troubled origins of Øm and the modest endowment of land it got from its patrons hint at the likelihood that early Danish Cistercian houses, with the exception of the 'big four' already named, were unassuming residences for the monks.[158] The Danish expression *herrekloster* that has crept into the language, despite decades of resistance,[159] is a misleading description for a place like Øm in the thirteenth century, with its small church and unimposing buildings, seen in the excavated ruins.[160] In the late Middle Ages, however, Øm did take on a much more prominent place among Danish Cistercian houses, and so the term *herrekloster*, as we shall see, has some relevance.

Danes in Wendland: Dargun, Colbaz, and Eldena

In 1172, the same year as the monks arrived at Øm, a new foundation was made from Esrum at Dargun, located in eastern Mecklenburg in a district called Circipanien, on the boundaries of the province of Pomerania. Our only reference to this emigration is in the Colbaz Annals.[161] We can have some confidence in this particular dating, for Colbaz itself was founded from Dargun a few years later and this notation was added before the end of the century.

The historian Albert Wiese, whose little book on Dargun is still the best treatment of the abbey's history, looks upon the foundation as a direct result of King Valdemar's wars against the Wends, which started after his capture in 1168 or 1169 of the independent island of Rygen in the Baltic.[162] In a campaign in the summer of 1171 in Circipanien, Valdemar captured a fortress where the keeper of the castle was named Otimar.[163] Saxo says Otimar was pardoned by Valdemar, and Wiese identifies this man with Chotimar, one of three noble brothers who first gave lands for a monastery at Dargun. Wiese assumes Chotimar's life was spared because he promised to give land for the foundation of a Danish Cistercian abbey. Niels Skyum-Nielsen is more careful and accepts the warning of Hans Olrik, who in 1908 wrote that any connection between the Danish advance into the area and the founding of a Cistercian daughter house of Esrum is only a possibility.[164]

Even if Wiese's interpretation of Chotimar's pardon because of his promise cannot be substantiated, the monastery at Dargun did begin at the time of Valdemar's victory in the region. It also belongs to the time when the abbot of Esrum was Walbert, the only twelfth century Esrum figure whose activities can be seen in a number of charters instead of only one or two. Abbot from 1170 until the 1190s, Walbert seems to have been very active in the spread of the Cistercians to Wendland.[165] His name appears at the head of the list of signatories to Bishop Berno of Schwerin's confirmation from 30 November 1173 of Dargun's foundation.[166] Documents from Dargun later in the 1170s have the notation: *Walbertus abbas de Esrom, sed tunc tantum monachus.*[167] It looks at first sight as if he had abandoned his post after 1173, but he was abbot again in the 1180s.[168] The practice of giving up the abbacy and later being recalled to it is known from an Øm abbot list. Here Walbert's temporary abandonment of his post might be linked with his involvement in the foundation of Dargun.[169] His activities at such a distance from Esrum may have required his resignation. But once he returned to Denmark, Walbert took office again.

Walbert was signator to the most important documents concerning Dargun's foundation. He seems to have been cooperating with Bishop Berno, who a few years before had been instrumental in convincing a Wendish prince to found the abbey of Doberan, a daughter of Morimund.[170] It is indicative of the Danish presence that it was Esrum that founded a daughter house here, instead of Doberan's mother abbey, Amelunxborn, in the diocese of Hildesheim. In Berno's 1173 charter for Dargun, Kazimir I, duke of Pomerania, is said to have offered at Dargun's altar ten marks income from a market booth he had, plus a salt supply, together with half the fish caught in the upper reaches of the Peene River.[171] The other half of the catch Kazimir had previously donated to the brothers. The charter also mentions gifts the three brothers had already made, including forests, fields, lakes, and a mill. All this was done at Dargun's altar, which Berno himself had consecrated and which he claimed was the first Christian altar in all of Circipanien.[172] Berno himself, from 'the small income' of his episcopacy, gave seven marks yearly to the monks. This extremely valuable charter points out how different were the Cistercian beginnings in Wendland from those in Denmark. In the former they were said to be among the first representatives of the Christian religion who settled in the district. They contributed by their very presence to the Christianization that accompanied the Danish conquests so carefully described by Saxo. And yet the great Danish historian never mentions the Cistercian involvement in this process, a problem to which we will return in the next chapter.

The second great charter for the early history of Dargun was issued after 1176 by Kazimir I of Pomerania. He confirmed all earlier gifts to the monastery and encouraged the Dargun brothers to have colonizers come to settle the area around the monastery.[173] In his invitation we can see how North German monasteries often started out with a huge, unsettled land area, while Danish houses normally received only individual villages and limited tracts of land. Kazimir's charter concedes permission to the monks to call Germans, Danes, Slavs, or people of any other nation to them so that these men can practise their respective trades. Moreover the monks can arrange for a division of their lands into parishes and call parish priests to them. Finally they can have booths or trading places or do as they wish, 'in the manner of our people or of the German and Danish peoples'.[174] This extraordinary passage gives us the impression of a huge and thinly populated Circipanien in which the monks were used as spearheads both of colonization and of Christianization. Kazimir was extremely generous, probably because he gave very little. The monks were simply allowed to take whatever measures needed to get the tillers of the soil, craftsmen, tradesmen and of course priests necessary to take care of the new population's spiritual needs.

We can thus look upon the 1170s at Dargun as a period when the Danes were invited as one people among many to cultivate Wendland and fill some of the empty spaces. We do not know what effect the invitation had. But Berno and Duke Kazimir cooperated in giving the Danish monks and whatever colonizers they could attract to them the greatest possible freedom. Moreover Berno supplemented the monks' income with the tithes he had from villages which once had been under the old fortification of Dargun.[175]

This privilege speaks of problems the monks had been having and threats to their peace. No Danish abbot signed the document. For the rest of the century our knowledge about Dargun is very limited. The Colbaz Annals claim that the Dargun monks emigrated to Eldena on the coast in 1188, but Wiese has shown that this cannot be correct.[176] Sometime in the 1190s the prince of Rygen, Jarimar, bore witness to a gift by his master of the mint, Martin,[177] who handed over to Dargun a salt supply that the prince had given him. The abbot of Dargun is called Ivan, a name that could be Danish or German. Thus monks were still at Dargun after 1188.

Wiese has looked at the chronology of conflicts in the area in order to determine when the monks started their trek to the coast. He pointed out that the period between 1175 and 1178 witnessed a bloody conflict between Saxons, Brandenburgers, and Danes on one side and the troops of Bogislav I and Kazimir, Pomeranian princes, on the other. Another conflict extended from 1184 to 1185, and this time the Danes were victorious. There was no reason for Danish monks to abandon their house. The next period of hostilities, 1198–99, led to a Danish defeat and, Wiese concludes, 'bitterness between the nations forced the Danes to leave Dargun'.[178] This is logical but cannot be proven. In any case the Colbaz Annals once again show a lack of dependability, even for an event at the mother house and at the very end of the century, when the Annals themselves were being written!

The earliest documentary mention of Dargun's refoundation comes in a 1216 letter by the bishop of Kamien.[179] It mentions the wars that the earlier occupants had experienced. Thus Wiese's explanation for the monastery's abandonment draws on a near-contemporary source. The bishop wrote that after the monastery had been vacant for some time, it was taken over by a colony from Doberan. According to our fickle Colbaz Annals, this happened in 1209. The transfer can be dated, Colbaz Annals notwithstanding, to the first years of the thirteenth century.

That the Eldena monks did not return to Dargun can be explained by the altered political situation. Danes were probably no longer welcome in Circipanien. Moreover, the duke of the island of Rygen, Jarimar I, who also controlled the area on the coast around Eldena, was very much attracted by the Cistercians. He helped found a monastery of Cistercian nuns from Roskilde in the island's main settlement, Bergen, in 1193. Apparently he had no desire to let the Eldena Cistercian monks depart again.[180] In any case they stayed put.

The emigration from Dargun to Eldena at the end of the 1100s is a turning point in Danish Cistercian history. It marks the defeat of Esrum's policy under Abbot Walbert of vigorous expansion into Wendish lands. From then on abbots at Esrum concentrated on areas closer to home. Even if we occasionally meet an Esrum abbot at Eldena, mother and daughter house seem to have existed largely independent of each other.[181] In the 1250s Esrum made one great effort to get back its title over Dargun. But this attempt ended in ignominious defeat. So long as Danish political hegemony in Mecklenburg and Pomerania was on the wane, the Danish Cistercians had to give way to their German brethren from rich and powerful abbeys like Doberan.

The story of Danish expansion into the southwest Baltic in the 1170s would not be complete, however, without mention of the founding of Colbaz (Kolbacz), attributed to 1174. There is no documentary evidence concerning its foundation near Stettin (Szczecin). But as the exhaustive and exhausting historian Hoogeweg puts it, we can assume but not prove that the first monks here came from Esrum.[182] It is just as likely that the first monks were sent from Dargun. In any case, the Esrum abbot appeared in a later document as Colbaz's visitor.[183] Even if we cannot claim that Esrum founded Colbaz directly, there was a legal bond between the two houses.

Once again we find a keeper of a castle being considered responsible for a Cistercian foundation. In 1173 King Valdemar sailed with his fleet to the area and began the siege of Stettin.[184] The *castellanus* handed over the city to him and at the same time is to have promised to found a Cistercian abbey. But the diocesan bishop, Conrad of Stettin, was also involved. The Colbaz Annals say he died in 1186 and gave properties to the new house, together with the tithe from a number of villages in the monastery's vicinity.[185] Without such notations in the Annals, we would know almost nothing about Colbaz abbey's early history. The first abbot was named Everard and died in 1195.[186] In 1210 the building of the monastery (apparently in stone) was begun under Abbot Rudolph, who died in 1217. Even with these bits of information, there are problems. According to another Colbaz source, the first abbot was called Reinhold and he held his post for only a year before resigning.[187]

The Colbaz Annals are most useful in terms of what they do *not* say about Esrum's role in the new abbey's early life. We cannot conclude from their silence that Esrum was totally inactive. But we are unable to establish any role at all for the mother abbey. Even if Esrum did involve itself at first, the nearly total silence about Esrum in much more adequate later sources for Colbaz, together with the monastery's own phenomenal success in acquiring property and becoming a cultural centre in the area, would indicate that the daughter abbey had only a tenuous link with Esrum.[188]

Esrum's involvement in the abbeys south of the Baltic was thus ephemeral. It was supported by King Valdemar and Abbot Walbert in the 1170s, but not pursued once the Danish advance was halted. Because early historians who dealt with the Cistercian houses in this part of Europe were German, they looked upon the monasteries mainly as spreaders of German culture.[189] Consequently the period of Danish influence in the later part of the twelfth century has been lightly brushed over. Certainly, the Danish impact was limited. The military campaigns of the 1160s and 1170s brought the Cistercians south from Denmark in the wake of the invaders. But the decades of conflict that followed prevented any continuous involvement and finally forced the Dargun monks to find a new home, closer to Denmark and more securely under Danish rule.

Coastal expansion: Esrum and Sorø

The monks' move from landlocked Dargun to coastal Eldena is more than a sign of receding Danish influence in Pomerania. From 1140–1172 new Cistercian houses in Scandinavia and Northern Germany were founded inland, protected from the marauding Wendish pirates. The only exception is Norway.[190] This period ended thanks to the vigorous campaigns of Absalon and Valdemar in the 1160s to subjugate the Wends, first in the conquest of Rygen and the capture of its town Arkona, and afterwards in operations on the mainland. Dargun in 1172 is the last inland monastery. Its immediate successor, Colbaz, is near water routes. Herrisvad, Esrum, Sorø, Øm and Løgum were all landlocked and so relatively secure from pirates. Vitskøl provides a special case, but the narrow mouth of Limfjorden could have made the area uninviting to pirates who needed to escape quickly to the open sea.

After thirty years of Danish expansion in the Baltic and along its southern shores, however, it was the *inland* monastery of Dargun that at the end of the century was exposed to depredation. At this point the Dargun monks had to seek protection at a coastal site. Similarly Sorø in 1194 founded a daughter house in Halland (today on the west coast of Sweden). The new abbey was probably placed on the coast to simplify communications with Zealand. The conquests of Valdemar and Absalon opened up new areas for expansion to the Danish Cistercians.

It is no accident that the first mention we have of Esrum gaining coastal possessions outside of Zealand is from 1176. In that year King Valdemar gave the monks a property in Halland with the right to fell trees there.[191] At about the same time or soon afterwards, Bishop Sven of Århus gave the Øm monks extensive holdings in the southern part of the peninsula of Djursland but admitted in one version of his testament that these lands were not worth much because of the incursions of 'pagans'.[192]

A growing house like Esrum could welcome such an addition to its holdings. Valdemar's gifts show the monarchy's continuing involvement in Esrum at a time when Archbishop Eskil had dropped completely out of the picture. In a surprising arenga, the charter mentions how we can read of the humanity of princes in olden times who 'after a short time in administering a temporal realm' were united forever with the princes of a more happy homeland.[193] This is one of the more original formulations in any royal charter for the Danish Cistercians and gives us a vivid picture of an aristocratic view of heaven as a place where worthy magnates assembled after a life of service on earth. At the beginning of the century monks like Anselm at Bec had been almost convinced that only through monastic life was salvation possible.[194] Now the Danish king—or his clerical composer—argued for an extension of salvation to all those who governed well. The charter's emphasis on the Danish monarchy's link with the generosity of past princes perhaps reveals some of the spiritual opportunism behind the continuing endowment of monasteries. Esrum was well established by 1176, and Valdemar had no obligation to continue the policy of generosity that had marked the opening of his reign. His death was only a few years distant, however, and it may well be that the ageing Valdemar had begun to think seriously about the 'purchase of paradise', as the idea so aptly had been called.[195]

This Esrum charter heralds the beginning of a new period of expansion that came to mean much more for Esrum and Sorø than new foundations in Wendland. It is difficult to explain why the two Zealand houses wanted properties in Halland along the coast of what today is Sweden. The charters mention lumber, fishing, and an 'iron works' which probably means a water wheel which propelled a bellows for a foundry.[196] Except perhaps for iron, one would think that the monks could get what they needed in Zealand. Moreover, many of their acquisitions were bitterly contested by the local population, which looked upon their new neighbours as intruders. Only the regular intervention of Absalon and the king himself secured the monks' possessions. And yet they held on to what they had obtained until the end of the Middle Ages.

This expansion culminated in Sorø's 1194 foundation of a daughter abbey at Ås, north of Varberg. We know almost nothing about this house, but if we look at it in terms of Sorø's own holdings in the area, it may be that Ås was meant as an outpost to protect Sorø's interests in Halland. Too distant to be administered by lay brothers as a grange, the Sorø possessions were ideally suited for the foundation of a daughter abbey. We do not know how close contact Sorø maintained and how much her abbot guided the affairs of the daughter house. Statutes from the Cistercian General Chapter mention Ås only rarely.[197] It would not be fair to look upon the new foundation as merely a glorified priory for Sorø, but the placement of a daughter house here instead of on Zealand indicates that Sorø wanted to consolidate its Halland property interests.

In this period of acquisition in Halland, we often find traces of Absalon's activity. He may be the unnamed archbishop of Lund who, according to a charter issued by King Valdemar and dated to 1177, had given the monks a forest area in Glumsten, in Halland's Faurås herred.[198] The local inhabitants were ordered to allow Esrum to make use of the resources in this locality. Until then they had done their best to keep the monks away, but now they were to let them fell trees, remove those that the wind had knocked down, make salt, and feed their pigs on the forest's acorns. Finally the monks were to be allowed to transport to Zealand, by land or by sea, the products they collected in Halland. The detailed listing of the exact rights for the brothers and the carefully reasoned defence of them indicate the likelihood of cooperation between Sorø and Esrum, with Absalon as a possible link between them.

The next charter, from 1182, also deals with the monks' rights to a forest property.[199] Again, local inhabitants had resisted the monks' rights, this time that of felling trees. The document, drawn up in Absalon's name, emphasizes in its arenga the difference between the saintly monks with their 'small possessions' and the 'evil men' (the local inhabitants) who harass them.[200] The poverty theme we noticed in earlier charters has disappeared, but there is still emphasis on the brothers as helpless men who do not have much land, giving the archbishop all the more reason to look after what the monks did have.

About fifteen kilometers north of Morup, near the Halland coast, lies Tvååker, just outside Esrum's sphere of interest. According to the Sorø Donation Book, Absalon as archbishop gave this village to the monks. The Sorø compiler says Absalon was 'concerned about the house's needs, especially its lack of wood, which was necessary for them for finishing their buildings'.[201] There may be something to this statement, for we know that Sorø's great church was finished soon after 1200.[202] In this period it had only a wooden roof; after a devastating fire in 1257 the church was rebuilt with stone vaulting. Consequently the monks would have needed huge timbers to reach across the ceiling, and these they may have had to travel to Halland to find.

As in the 1177 charter for Esrum concerning Glumsten Forest, the value of the location for collecting salt is emphasized here. But a new resource is also mentioned; 'They could . . . extract iron from the earth'. Once again we get a glimpse of the Cistercians' wide-ranging economic activities, the way their creative ambition took on material forms. According to the Sorø writer, Absalon bought part of the forest from the inhabitants of the district. A very careful description of the boundaries is given. This attention to detail points to the possibility that the writer was concerned about potential challenges to Sorø's holdings there. Normally, for Zealand possessions, he does not note boundaries. Similarly in the Øm Book, a fourteenth-century addition describes the abbey's property boundaries in Djursland, its most distant and trouble-plagued holdings.[203]

We soon find the exact reason why our Sorø monk (writing soon after 1200 and probably before 1215) devoted so much space to Tvååker and emphasized Absalon's role in obtaining the land for the monks from the inhabitants. After his death 'the villagers engaged in litigation with the brothers over those forest boundaries',[204] but Absalon's successor, Archbishop Anders Sunesen, settled the matter. The forest was to remain 'whole and undivided'. All the area stretching from the sea to the road leading to Morup (a valuable indication that there was communication by land between Esrum and Sorø holdings in Halland) belonged to Sorø. In the eastern forest (apparently on the other side of the road), the monks' share stretched from the mill 'where iron is made' through the road 'which leads to the southern ironworks'.

These provisions deserve special mention because they show how precise and detailed the monks could be when defending their holdings, qualities that we see repeatedly throughout the Danish Middle Ages. In the outcome of this litigation, it is also apparent that Absalon's work left a solid foundation for Sorø which even the local population's strong resistance could not overcome. Anders Sunesen had merely to reassert what Absalon already had made clear. The case was often the same on Zealand. Because Absalon cooperated with the monks in looking after details during this period of painstaking consolidation, the monks had a favourable legal foundation when they had to assert their rights after Absalon's death in 1201.

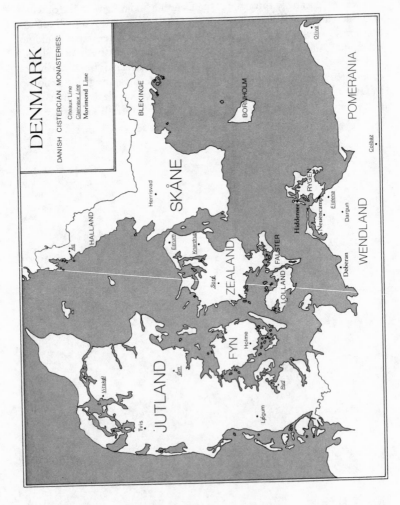

Danish Cistercian Monasteries

III

The Culmination of the Cistercian Advance

1178–1215

D URING THE LAST DECADES of the twelfth century two personalities dominate our attention: Archbishop Absalon of Lund and William, the Augustinian abbot of Æbelholt abbey in Northern Zealand. As with Eskil, we are forced to look at the Cistercians from the outside, but this is even more the case now. Absalon never identified himself with the Cistercians as Eskil had done. To him the monks seem to have been welcome and necessary in the Danish church, but he showed none of Eskil's enthusiasm for the Order as an international brotherhood. Nevertheless, Absalon's involvement with the Danish Cistercians is evident from the charter material, and however limited this type of historical source is in revealing the attitudes of individuals, the charters when taken as a whole point to continuing good relations between the archbishopric of Lund and the Danish Cistercian movement. Without Absalon, the Danish Cistercians would never have been able to guarantee the gains made under Eskil. If we had had a fuller Cistercian narrative for this period, we would probably have found Absalon described as a great patron of the Order. The Sorø account at least considered Absalon's contribution invaluable. This is understandable in view of his family connections with this monastery, but he seems to have been just as active at Esrum and possibly at other Danish Cistercian houses.

ABSALON AND THE POPES:
PROTECTION AND FAVOURITISM, 1178–1201

In 1178, soon after Absalon became archbishop of Lund, he issued a charter to Esrum that summarizes its growth during the two decades after Eskil's charter.[1] The basic properties in the vicinity of Esrum remain the same as in 1158: Villingerød, Såne, and Havreholm. Asserbo, which had been given to the Carthusians and finally ended in Sorø's hands, has disappeared. A number of place names have dropped out. This may well be the result of consolidation of farm lands and initiation of the grange system. Real gains can be seen to the east of Esrum Lake and at its south end, places like Stenholt and Toelt. Finally the Morup holdings in Halland and a location called Saxolfstorp, which may have been in Skåne, had been added since 1158.

Along with this steady growth of properties, Esrum—and assumedly many other Danish houses whose cartularies are lost to us—began to obtain a number of papal privileges. These show us that the Danish Cistercians sought and gained the same rights and exemptions from the jurisdiction of their local bishops that their sister monasteries abroad obtained in the last decades of the twelfth century. The existence of such privileges in the Esrum and Sorø sources indicates that the frequent trips to the papal court made by Øm's first abbot, mentioned in its Chronicle, were probably fairly common to many Danish Cistercian abbots.[2] After the long trek south to the mid-September General Chapter, it would have been possible to continue to Rome, perhaps wintering there and returning to Denmark in the spring.

A comparison of the earliest papal privileges for Esrum with the 'great privilege' given Cistercian houses during the reign of Innocent III reveals a change of emphasis from concern for the monks' stability to clarification of the exact relationship betwen the diocesan bishop and the Cistercian house.[3] In the course of the century the Cistercians became an exempt order. The local bishop had no right to intervene in the abbot's election, or to order Cistercian abbots to local synods or courts.[4] In many cases these exemptions seem to have been mere formalities, unimportant in an era of good relations between the monks and their bishop. Later, in a more competitive age, they would play a central role for both sides. In the Cistercian century, however, the monks of Øm did whatever they could to make the bishop of Århus welcome on visits to them, even providing a special house for him. The Løgum monks arranged for the bishop of Ribe to obtain a property near the abbey where he could build a house for himself.[5] In the 1260s the Øm monks tried to define more precisely the exact extent of the Århus bishop's rights over them, and precipitated a catastrophe. But in the twelfth century in Denmark, cooperation between bishops and Cistercians was more prevalent than conflict. We can look upon the issuing of papal privileges to Danish houses as formal acts intended as insurance against a rainy day but rarely invoked in practice.

One concrete problem does seem to have cropped up in the last two decades of the century: the question of the Cistercian monks' payments of tithes to churches in whose parishes they owned land. In a letter to Absalon, the abbot of Citeaux informed the archbishop that a papal immunity given one Cistercian house was valid for all houses of the Order;[6] sometimes the pope wrote specially to a single house or to a group of them, but this did not narrow the general applicability of the pope's command. The abbot asked Absalon to allow 'in no way that our brothers who are with you are troubled' by any measures that would be 'against the so evident command of the supreme pontiff'.[7] The abbot then quotes a bull of Pope Lucius III stating Cistercian immunity from the payment of tithes. The general history of the Cistercian Order during these years reveals a chronic dispute concerning payment of tithes by Cistercian houses on lands they owned.[8] Parish priests and bishops usually wanted the monks to render tithes at least for newly-acquired lands that until the time of Cistercian purchase or donation had been subject to tithes to the local church. These were called predial tithes to distinguish them from novel tithes, those levied on newly cultivated land that had never before been a source of income to the local parish.

Two charters contained in the Øm Chronicle provide evidence that here and possibly elsewhere in Denmark the Cistericians were under pressure to pay predial tithes.[9] The first papal statement came from Alexander III and can be dated only to some point between 1166 and 1181.[10] The community had asked the pope whether the monks were obliged to pay tithes. The answer is the customary one: they are fully exempt for all lands which they cultivate with their own hands or at their own expense and also from payment on the offspring of their animals. The problem emerged again in the 1180s when Urban III (1185-87) wrote to Absalon, who again appears as a questioner on the matter.[11] The pope accused the monks' opponents of deliberately confusing the issue. They had claimed that the monks were exempt only from payment of tithes on newly cultivated land. This assertion contradicted what the pope and his predecessors frequently had stated. Cistercians were exempt from tithes on all lands they work at their own expense. The strong language of this bull cannot be necessarily applied to the Danish situation in particular, for it was issued to bishops and archbishops all over Europe.[12] But it does show that Absalon conferred with the pope as well as the abbot of Citeaux in order to clarify the matter. Absalon apparently did his best for the Danish Cistercians by consulting the highest authority possible.

Absalon's death at Sorø Abbey in 1201 tells the rest of the story about his relations with the Cistercians in the twelfth century. His burial there confirmed the Skjalm family's attachment to the abbey, an important fact until at least the 1280s. The Sorø records show the personal devotion of Absalon to the Cistercians, while many charters for Sorø, Esrum, Øm and Løgum issued by the Archbishop bear witness to his continuing involvement with the Order. The Sorø monks naturally wanted to emphasize Absalon's role as their great founder and supporter, but the number of possessions and rights Absalon guaranteed for the Cistercians should be sufficient for us to see him as the driving force behind their fruitful years at the end of the twelfth century.[13]

Saxo saw Absalon as a military hero whose Christianity had little to do with anything the Cistercians would have applauded. We have seen him as an efficient, practical, and generous bishop. There are many Absalons, but it is clear that he was a competent spiritual and political leader, able to reconcile the spiritual family ideal of the Cistercians with his own sense of physical family bonds. In his missionary and military form of Christianity, Absalon can seem crude and even repellent. But another side of him is seen in the religious houses he founded in Denmark. His international position can best be seen in the letters of Abbot William of Æbelholt. This fiery French abbot made it clear that had it not been for Absalon, he would never have left his beloved Parisian abbey to come to this dark and hostile land. When William had trouble in his initial settlement at Eskilsø in Roskilde Fjord (where he arrived in about 1175), he turned to Absalon for help. Absalon helped him with the ensuing move to Æbelholt.[14] Just as with the Cistercian monks of Zealand, Absalon saw to it that Augustinian canons at Æbelholt got the lands and rights they needed. We see him indirectly, through the witness of others, but his family loyalties and his international involvements both led him to strengthen the position of the Danish Cistercians.

ABBOT WILLIAM OF ÆBELHOLT: ANGER AND DEVOTION

Our most talkative source for the Danish Cistercians during these last years of the twelfth century is the letter collection of this same Abbot William of Æbelholt. The most recent work on the letters indicates that they were originally intended to make up 'a collection of examples for dictation', the art of letter writing, as well as to provide the materials for an impression of William's life.[15] Unfortunately we lack any medieval copy of the letters and therefore we cannot see how they were used. But the preface to the collection says the letters were intended not for the learned but to aid those who were beginners in *dictamen*, 'so that if there is anything in them which might develop their awareness and intelligence, they might together with us thank God and memorize them'.[16]

One possible objection to the authenticity of the letters is the statement in the preface that the names of magnates have been included in them so that 'greater authority be associated with them by these names'.[17] This sentence might be interpreted as indicating that William invented appropriate names in order to give the letters more appeal. But a closer look at Latin text indicates that William tried to reconcile his desire to give examples of *dictamen* with the purpose of having the letters accepted as worthwhile specimens of the art. By emphasizing to his readers the importance of the recipients of the letters, William probably thought the letters' contents would gain more weight. Normally a set of letters in a medieval course of *dictamen* would leave out personal names. William may have known he was going against this practice and felt obliged to explain himself. He composed his letters at a time when, in the words of Jean Leclercq, 'the art of letter writing was to be codified with greater and greater precision in the *artes dictandi* whose technicality was soon to become as complex as that of the *artes praedicandi*'.[18] In William's attempt to live up to the demands of codification, while at the same time using the collection to assert his own importance in church and society, something of his personality emerges. He sought acceptance as an authority and recognition for his work.

The letters are genuine products of William's mind, but we cannot know which of them ever were sent. The editors of the *Diplomatarium Danicum* consider many of the letters to have been William's own drafts in the solution of disputes. In some cases we find William taking on the *persona* of other persons and writing a letter in the name of Bishops Absalon or Peder of Roskilde.[19] William's proposals as outlined in such drafts were not always accepted, and so we should be on guard against accepting William's letters as representations of historical facts. The letters can best be used as sources for exploring the attitudes shown and poses taken by Abbot William in dealing with institutions and people in his adopted land. It is here we can learn something about the problems and conflicts, as well as the respect, that the Danish Cistercians could engender.[20]

There are a number of letters drawn up by William and addressed to the abbot of Esrum. In one of them William's declarations of devotion to Abbot Walbert clarify his conception of friendship, a theme that appears in several other letters.[21] After many flattering lines, William asked the abbot for any news he might have on the activities of the royal chancellor, Anders Sunesen. Here is the point of the letter: William was concerned about negotiations concerning the marriage of the Danish princess Ingeborg to King Philip Augustus of France. He was interested in the latest news on the matter. Besides revealing William's curiosity, this letter is an invaluable indication of the way Cistercian abbots, in this case Walbert of Esrum, in making trips south to the General Chapter, could have picked up pieces of political information highly prized back in Denmark. The Cistercians can be seen here as part of Denmark's communications network with the rest of Europe.

In another letter to the Abbot of Esrum (named as W., which may also be Walbert), the heading specifically mentions his return from Citeaux.[22] William speaks again of friendship but this time hints at black clouds on the horizon. Someone has tried to stir up trouble between the two abbeys, but they will not succeed because of the 'fraternal love between us'. William assures the Esrum abbot that he is grateful for all his favours (*beneficia*) which indicate his love. If anything not in this spirit of harmony had ever manifested itself in William's words and works, or in the abbots of Esrum, it should be forgotten, so that they can serve God 'in innocence and simplicity'. The text deserves the original Latin. My translation cannot capture the ingratiating, double quality of William's words:

> *Si quid igitur operibus nostris vel verbis vel etiam vestris contradictionis emerserit, quod tamen non arbitramur, illud totum antiquet oblivio, deleat et abstergat, ne quid morum nostrorum gratiam devenustet, quos semper oportet in innocentia et simplicitate cordis divinis obsequiis mancipari. . . .*
> (If then any contradiction should emerge from our works or words or also from yours, which, however, we do not think will happen, let forgetfulness age, destroy and remove it wholly, so that it does not take away the beauty and grace of our ways with each other, which always must be maintained in innocence and simplicity of heart in obedience to God.)

In itself this letter is too general to indicate anything about the relationship between Esrum and Æbelholt, except that at some point there could have been friction. But in the next letter William became much more specific.[23] He had apparently been accused of making false charges against the Esrum monks. He admitted that he had been led astray by false rumours and by the envious and now confessed his fault. But having done so, William turned the tables and pointed to false rumours also at Esrum. Of course the abbot there was not to be held responsible for them, but it was being said at Esrum that Abbot William and his monks 'like lions in ambushes tried to attract men wishing to leave your house and by greediness for their possessions would join them to our community'.[24] The particular instance was that of a boy named Philip who, according to local gossip, was taken into Æbelholt only because Abbot William wanted to use the money given him by his father to buy clothing for himself and his monks![25]

Also it was being said (apparently by the offended Esrum monks) that William habitually called them man-eaters.[26]

William appealed for peace between the Esrum Cistercians and his own Æbelholt Augustinian canons. After quarrels are settled, the sweetness of friendship will increase. His letter is both aggressive and reconciliatory. He admits his own faults but accuses the Esrum monks of spreading stories about him and his canons. Here we see how abbeys of different orders in late twelfth-century Denmark could collide with each other over the matter of recruitment. There was probably only a limited pool of aristocratic sons available to the Zealand abbeys. Sorø would have taken the offspring of the greatest family, the Skjalms. That left Esrum and Æbelholt to compete for the available recruits in northeastern Zealand. We have no other references to gossip and slander in Danish houses as a result of such competition, but William's letter at least makes it clear that the entrance of a young man to a religious house could be accompanied by a substantial gift from his father. This practice was probably not mandatory, but clearly the material situation of a monastery could be vastly improved by such a semi-voluntary gift. Æbelholt had rich properties, but during these years it was likely to have been tapping them to the limit in order to pay for the building of its church.[27]

Like most medieval sources, this one tells only one side of the story, and Esrum's records say nothing to provide balance for Abbot William's assertions. But we can use the letter to establish that in Denmark as elsewhere in Europe (as can be seen in Bernard of Clairvaux's letters), good relations between abbeys of different orders easily could be soured by rivalry in recruitment. The tone and content of this letter also indicate that William valued good relations with Esrum and at least went so far as to draft a letter to resolve a dispute between the two houses.

Abbot William's desire to maintain friendly contacts with Esrum can be seen again in a letter he wrote to the abbot sometime in the 1190s. It deals with negotiations in France to reconcile King Philip with his by now estranged wife, Ingeborg.[28] William does not tell the Esrum monks anything they could not have found out by listening to court gossip about the proceedings. The letter is a gesture of courtesy, but at the same time another indication of William's personality. He wants to remind the Esrum monks that he is engaged in an important task. It is his duty to see that the integrity of the sacraments is preserved. He attaches great significance to the case and hopes its outcome will contribute to the glory of the Danes. It might be appropriate, he thought, to send the monks a copy of the papal letters that had been sent to the French king on the matter and which William had obtained. But he is certain that the Esrum monks can easily obtain a copy from those he is sending to Æbelholt! William's letter to Esrum points to a conviction on his part that it was worthwhile to impress these monks. As in other letters, he seems to have been keenly aware of Esrum's prestige and position in the kingdom and wanted its abbot and monks to think highly of him. There may have been other motives, and the letter may well never have been sent in the form we have it. But the contents still reveal an Augustinian abbot and diplomat who sought recognition from the Cistercian community at Esrum.

Just how important was Esrum at this time in Denmark? H. N. Garner calls it 'in a certain manner the Cistercian Order's spiritual centre' in the country because of the number of houses Esrum or its daughters founded.[29] As we have seen, Esrum's role in many of these foundations was quite limited, and abbeys like Colbaz add hardly anything to Esrum's sphere of influence. Abbot William is in fact our only narrative source indicating Esrum's central position, and he may have exaggerated because of his geographical proximity or his own inflated ego. But in one of his drafts that apparently was not effectuated, William gives a rare insight into the membership of the Cistercian abbey. The document purports to have been drawn up by Abbot Walbert of Esrum and concerns a dispute over income in the parish of Tjæreby, just south of Æbelholt. William provides the names of the Esrum monks at the close of the letter. They include Torben, prior; Helge, subprior; Peder, cellarer; and three other brothers.[30] The fact that Esrum had both prior and subprior indicates that it had grown to such an extent that it needed to divide up functions into two offices instead of one. We are in the presence of a significant abbey, even if we can only dimly perceive the outline of its size and influence. Similarly C. M. Smidt of the National Museum in Copenhagen concluded after excavations at Esrum and other ruins in Northern Zealand that the abbey in the later twelfth century was the area's centre of architectural influence.[31]

The other letters of Abbot William are more practical but again show us an emotional and even a material dependence on Esrum. There is a request to keep for a few days a Brother Stephen of Esrum, who had been sent down to Æbelholt to help with the placement of a water conduit.[32] As usual William tries to embellish what could have been a simple request with figurative language and ends with pure flattery: 'Who could be more suitable for this [project] than Brother Stephen?' The Æbelholt monks were probably building their cloister at the time, and their dependence on Cistercian skills confirms our picture of the monks as highly qualified in many practical areas of life. They were able to build and to pray. Clairvaux and Citeaux had not just sent pious men to Scandinavia; they had given the North the technical knowledge of Western Europe.

In a letter to Jens, subprior at Esrum, William expressed his friendship and said that the bearer of the letter would tell him about the business at hand.[33]

William did not want to tire the subprior with a long explanation. He may also have felt that it would be easier to communicate effectively by using oral Danish instead of written Latin. But he also used a letter in the manner we can see as well in Saint Anselm's communications to his monastic friends. Written contact was intended primarily to convey emotional messages. Practical problems could be conveyed orally by the letter carrier. What is worth remembering for the future (and for the readers of the collection) is the declaration of friendship and love.[34] This practice is clearest in a fragment of a letter from William which has the heading 'to the abbot of Esrum'.[35] Here only the opening lines, with the usual protestations of affection, have been kept. The function of the collection as providing examples for letter writing is evident here. The first lines are all that is necessary. But William was apparently so enamoured by his own stylistic felicities and by the self-assumed importance of his activities that he frequently kept the entire text of letters in the collection.

Abbot William's contacts with the Cistercians were not limited to Danish houses. In the difficult affair concerning Queen Ingeborg, he seems to have obtained some much-needed help from the abbots of Cîteaux and Clairvaux. We have one of these 'ghost-written' letters, ostensibly composed by the royal chancellor Anders Sunesen and sent to Absalon. In it William describes how, after he and Anders had left Rome for Paris with papal letters, they were held captives by the Duke of Burgundy for six weeks and deprived of the bulls.[36] But through the efforts of the Cistercian abbots, they were released and were able to appear before the king. The debt and affection owed to the Cistercians are as considerable as William's rhetorical artifice:

Quantus autem fuerit circa nos praedictorum abbatum affectus, multiplex rerum approbatione dignus designat effectus.

There followed a meeting at which the archbishop of Sens, the bishop of Arras, the abbots of Cîteaux and Clairvaux, and Peter the Chanter met with Anders and William. Apparently no progress was made, and William complains about expense and delay. But it is clear from this letter that he looked to the Cistercians for immediate practical help and legal guidance in the matter. We also know that Cistercians later on were close to Ingeborg, so close that one abbot was criticized by the General Chapter for allowing Ingeborg and her ladies to stay overnight at his abbey, something absolutely forbidden by Cistercian statutes.[37]

William's letters are a unique witness to the presence and influence of twelfth-century French monastic culture in Northern Europe. It is impossible to characterize William's effect on Denmark without using his own words. But the legend he created about himself, his quick canonization, and

the fame Æbelholt obtained as a place of pilgrimage all indicate that he succeeded in his life work of establishing the success of his community of Augustinian canons.[38] For all their brashness and egotism, William's letters to
Esrum illuminate aspects of the complex relationship between neighboring
abbeys of different orders during a period of monastic growth.

Unlike the great letter writer of the preceding century, Saint Anselm,
William did not express the literary convention that contact between
friends is unimportant to love.[39] He insists on contact, both written and
oral.[40] And yet there is an archaic and fulsome quality about the letters that
cannot be ignored. With their overgrown rhetoric, delight in word play,
and cultivation of the obscure, William's letters, like Eskil's theology, belong to the earlier part of the century. But William lacks the vitality of these
earlier letter writers. One contemporary figure he does resemble is Peter of
Blois, who like William often felt out of place in society and never quite settled down in his functions.[41] Whenever things became difficult for William
in Denmark, he threatened to return to France. But this was bluff. William
remained a blustering, prickly outsider who even in the 1190s did his best
to impress the people who counted for him. In evaluating his letters as a
source for Cistercian history, we must always keep in mind his complicated
personality. He combines the best and worst aspects of twelfth-century
learning: its curiosity, enthusiasm, and ambition, together with its narrow-
ness, self-centeredness, and naïvety.

CISTERCIAN MONASTERIES FOR WOMEN

Abbot William's collection includes letters written to Cistercian nuns at the
monasteries of Roskilde and Slangerup. As Nanna Damsholt has pointed
out, these letters fall into a category that was semi-obligatory for any full
twelfth century collection, letters of counsel to women.[42] Roskilde's Cistercian monastery for women was founded some time before 1177, while
Slangerup cannot be dated with certainty before about 1200.[43] Roskilde
was under the care and administration of the Sorø abbot, while Slangerup
was under Esrum. The fact that the two greatest Danish Cistercian houses
west of Øresund had their own women's houses may reflect Absalon's initiative. As bishop of Roskilde he made a substantial donation to the new Cistercian house there.[44] It is a sign of the Danish Cistercians' flexibility that at
a time in the history of the Order when monasteries for women were
founded only with great reluctance and not nearly in proportion to the demand, Sorø and Esrum went ahead and took the reponsibility for such houses. Roskilde can be looked upon as a probable residence for unmarriageable

women in the Skjalm family.[45] One of the main sources of its income came from pilgrims visiting the grave of Saint Margrethe, a member of the Skjalm family. Her body was brought to the church of St Mary in 1177. Thanks to Absalon, the Sorø monks were given a share in this income. Here is a rare instance of contact among the nuns, the monks, and Absalon.[46]

Just as the Roskilde nuns seem to have been connected with the Skjalm family, Slangerup may have had links with the royal family.[47] This would supplement what we already know about Esrum's close links with Valdemar. Its privileges from him and his son Knud VI show a continuing involvement with the monks. The triangle made up of Skjalm family – Sorø – Roskilde may well correspond to a similar triangle of Valdemar family – Esrum – Slangerup.

Amid these meagre facts and assumptions, the letters of Abbot William provide welcome light. We have one letter to the Roskilde nuns and three to the Slangerup community. In the Roskilde letter William was concerned about a certain Niels, who was son of the nuns' prior.[48] By *prior* William referred to a layman who took care of the house's business, a title that the Cistercian General Chapter later changed to *procurator* in order to avoid confusion with the monastic office.[49] This young man, Niels, had become a canon at Æbelholt, an interesting choice in view of Roskilde's affiliation with Sorø, but perhaps an indication of William's powers of recruitment. As in the case with Esrum, there was trouble, this time because Niels would not accept a punishment William had decreed for him and had instead returned to Roskilde to stay with the nuns. Now William asked them to send Niels back to Æbelholt, where he belonged. The outcome of the matter is unknown to us, but once again we get a glimpse of cooperation among religious houses on Zealand over recruits and runaways.

Of the letters to the Slangerup nuns, one is merely a formal answer to an unspecified query from them.[50] William writes to the prioress 'A' and to the nuns 'K' and 'J' that he has tried to answer their request as quickly as possible. He says that friendship does not grow old if it is based on sincere affection and is kept up by frequent contacts. The second letter is one of admonition.[51] William had heard from Thomas, apparently an Æbelholt brother who had visited Slangerup, that the nuns were devoted to him. He expresses his love for them and warns in the rest of the letter against *cupiditas*. Here we find one of William's favorite themes: the interior person as the essential part of the human being. 'Because you are daughters of the king [of heaven] and his spouses, let your glory be from within and not from exterior things'.[52] It is difficult to see if William is writing a general moral exhortation or if he is warning against some mispractice in the monastery.

The third letter is more specific, but so full of biblical allusions that it has been looked upon as a collection of literary clichés whose main purpose is to warn the Slangerup nuns against the evils of drinking.[53] Because William writes here to two royal daughters at Slangerup monastery, it is this letter which indicates the royal link. William was worried that these women were more concerned about their comforts and social position than in the discipline of the monastic life. He emphasizes as before the inward person and asks the nuns to be happy in sharing not with the rich but with the poor, 'because God's word is in the simple and the poor'. Only in a single sentence does he mention the evil of drinking at the nuns' table and adds the memorable remark: 'That vice is the custom of the country'.[54] William acts here as spiritual adviser for two women from the very top of society. His dissatisfaction with their pride may indicate that they were put there because of royal expediency and not genuine devotion. Here as elsewhere William involved himself in the lives of others. In so doing he followed a well-established tradition according to which abbots gave advice and criticism to nuns. The unusual aspect of this example is that the nuns belonged to a Cistercian house, while William as an Augustinian abbot really had no business there. But the proximity of the convent to Æbelholt together with William's interest in everything around him are probably sufficient explanations for these letters.

We are thus in the ironic position of knowing something about the dealings between an Augustinian abbot and a Cistercian house for women, while the relation of the Esrum abbot with these same nuns is practically unknown to us. The fact that William could take on such a role with the Slangerup nuns could indicate tolerance on the part of Esrum to an involvement that could have been interpreted as interference in its affairs. But this is of course only one possibility. The frustrating aspect in dealing with Esrum, to which so many roads lead us, is that the monks can be seen almost exclusively only through the eyes of others. Even the one letter drawn up in the name of Abbot Walbert and the chapter at Esrum to solve a dispute over lands near Æbelholt turns out, as we have seen, to be a draft composed by William of Æbelholt.[55] So often when we think we are catching sight of the Esrum monks in William's letters, we are actually seeing only an extension of his personality trying to get this community (or the Slangerup nuns, the king, or the bishop of Roskilde) to do what he wants. His very involvement with the Cistercians, however, reveals how much he valued them and sought their respect and acceptance.

TROUBLES IN SLESVIG: GULDHOLM AND RYD

William's dealings with the Cistercians can also be seen in his letters concerning a dispute between the Cistercians at Guldholm, outside Slesvig, and the Benedictines of St Michael's monastery at Slesvig. Here we are fortunate also in having a Cistercian account, written by a monk of Ryd Abbey, the successor of Guldholm. This chronicle, however, is as late as 1289.[56] The first problem we meet is the usual one of dating. When was Guldholm founded? The date given in the Ryd Chronicle for the abbey's foundation by Bishop Valdemar of Slesvig, 1192, disregards the fact that Valdemar, a member of the royal line defeated in 1157 by Valdemar I, was at that time rebelling against the Danish king. It is unthinkable that he would at this point have been able to summon a group of monks from Esrum. Therefore Bishop Valdemar's contribution to Guldholm's foundation has to be dated to 1191.[57] On 23 May of that year, Bishop Valdemar dedicated the cemetery and buildings of the new monastery. It was intended to replace the Benedictine house of St Michael's, which had been plagued by a great scandal. The new monastery was to take in the discredited monks of St Michael's and make Cistercians of them. The Ryd writer's late story about the bad behaviour of the Benedictines is backed up by a near-contemporary source, a royal privilege from 1196 referring to Benedictine abuses at Slesvig.[58] Bishop Valdemar's reform of the monastery of St Michael and its transfer to Guldholm on Langesø outside of Slesvig can be looked upon as an episcopal initiative similar to what had happened already at Sorø and at Veng-Øm. There is no evidence that Valdemar refounded the house as a part of his political resistance to the Danish king.

In 1192 (traditionally on 12 June), a group of monks came from Esrum to settle at Guldholm.[60] Thus Bishop Valdemar in 1191 had prepared the conversion of the Benedictine community into a Cistercian one, while in 1192 the Cistercians themselves arrived. Since the bishop was imprisoned on 8 July, it is unlikely that he was among those who welcomed the mother abbey's contingent in the summer of 1192.[61] We can accept the Ryd Chronicle's portrait of him as the reformer of St Michael's and the founder of Guldholm. But after Valdemar's first initiative in 1191, the Cistercians themselves completed the work he had begun.

The monks at Ryd never forgot Bishop Valdemar and his interrupted work. The 1289 writer lamented the contrast between the bishop's great plans for the new house and the all too brief a time he had to carry them out. As so often before, we find a strong and ambitious bishop behind a Cistercian foundation in his diocese, but we also see that once the bishop had begun the process, the monks themselves could finish it.

But not without difficulty. By the 1190s it seems to have been considerably more difficult to reform and reorganize a former Benedictine community than it had been thirty years earlier. The Benedictines who came to Guldholm from Slesvig to be converted—willingly or unwillingly—to Cistercians, soon returned to St Michael's.[62] A 1289 Cistercian account of their attacks on the remaining Cistercians at Guldholm is probably coloured by time and prejudice, but here the letters of William give us much-needed detail. The Benedictines from St Michael's at Slesvig sought the support of the duke of Southern Jutland, who was the brother of King Knud and of the Valdemar who would in 1202 succeed Knud on the throne. Here entered Abbot William, who supported the Cistercians. We have two different versions of a letter he wrote in which he adjudicated the patronage of Guldholm to Duke Valdemar and thus thwarted the desires of the Slesvig Benedictines, who had linked the continuing existence of their monastery to the duke's patronage.[63]

Abbot William's drafts are in his own name and in that of Omer, Bishop of Odense. Both had apparently been appointed papal judge-delegates in the case. At the same time as he confirmed the duke's patronage, Abbot William also recognized the right of the Cistercians to hold property in Slesvig. This apparently was the real bone of contention. Now that the Benedictine monks had returned to Slesvig from Guldholm, it was not clear if the former properties of their Benedictine monastery which had been turned over to the Cistercians also reverted to them. William sided exclusively with the Cistercians and showed once again a desire to maintain good relations with them.

William also included in his collection a draft of a letter to Pope Celestine announcing the judge-delegates' decisions.[64] Far more informative are two letters apparently written (but not necessarily sent) before William had been appointed judge-delegate.[65] The first is general and only mentions the scandal and the need for a speedy solution. William is at his rhetorical best in describing the Benedictines' revolt against the Cistercians:

> Black monks rise up against grey, one monk against another, and, as it is said, have clubs and swords prepared for battle so that now the days of tribulation are believed to draw near.[66]

William dramatizes but does not make his purpose clear here. In the second draft he is more precise.[67] The Benedictines had appealed to the pope and were doing everything possible to justify their return to Slesvig. But at the same time they had been insulting the Cistercians cruelly and robbing them of their goods. William added fuel to the fire by referring to the base lives of these Benedictines, another indication that the 1289 account resulted from contemporary tradition and was not a later invention. William's passion for the cause of justice reaches a new climax here. He warns the pope against believing anything the Benedictines might claim:

> Behold these men come into your presence, as if they would obtain justice and judgment and yet they are armed with the javelin of im-

piety, by which they attack the fortress of holiness. But they will not conquer it, for wisdom always conquers evil.[68]

Let those sons of confusion be themselves confounded so that they will not find a place of refuge with you, William begs the pope. They rejoice in letting their tongues speak lies.

Why such strong language and passionate involvement? Once again the personality of William must be considered. He was a man of causes. Here he seems to jockey with the papal court in order to get an appointment as a judge-delegate in the matter. Apparently he succeeded, perhaps not through this strong letter, but by means of his own persistence and the influence of Archbishop Absalon, the king, and possibly the Esrum monks. Even if we have no direct evidence of how Esrum behaved in this dispute, the papal concession of authority to William and the subsequent decision, totally favourable to Guldholm point to an agreement, whether explicit or not, between William and Esrum to provide for Esrum's newest daughter. William's actions are completely consistent with the pattern we already have seen in his letters to Esrum. Passionate, explosive, and self-righteous, William the Augustinian abbot sought good relations with his neighbour Cistercian abbey.

William's efforts on behalf of Guldholm only led to a temporary victory. In 1209 the monks emigrated thirty kilometres north to Ryd on Flensborg Fjord.[69] They settled at a spot known in Latin as *Rus Regis*, a name indicating that the area belonged to the king and that it was a forest clearing. There is no reason to look upon this move as anything but a geographical necessity. The site of Langesø outside Slesvig consisted of a narrow peninsula with bad drainage.[70] The move north may perhaps also indicate a desire to live in an area more politically stable than Slesvig. Just as their confrères in the trek from Dargun to Eldena in 1199, the Guldholm Cistercians sought out a place where they might be more adequately protected by Danish royal power. Two of the Danish versions of the Ryd Annals add the curious note that before the monks themselves came north, they sent a lay-brother to collect the monks' share of parish tithes.[71] We can see here the importance of lay-brothers, so infrequently mentioned in Danish Cistercian history and yet essential at least during the first century because of their labour on the granges and assumedly also because of their abilities as builders and engineers. These lay-brothers were probably responsible for constructing a magnificent system of drainage and mills so efficient that its pipes were incorporated into the plumbing of Glucksborg Castle, built on top of the abbey after the Reformation.[72] As at Sorø with its great engineering feat in the canal Møllediget or at Øm with its three canals, the monks at Ryd demonstrated how skillfully the Danish Cistercians could make use of the watercourses at their disposal.[73]

The move to Ryd signals the end of Cistercian expansion in Denmark. There is no recorded attempt at a new foundation until the 1320s. By the start of the thirteenth century, Cistercian Denmark had taken the shape it would maintain until the Reformation. In the course of sixty-five years, ten abbeys of men (plus Dargun, Colbaz, and Eldena outside Denmark) and two monasteries of women (plus Bergen on Rygen in 1193) had been founded. Except for the 1180s there is no decade from the 1140s until 1200 which did not bring new foundations.

Looking back over the course of the century we can see how gradually it all had happened:

Herrisvad (no special Latin name)	—1144
Esrum (no special Latin name)	—1150 or 1151
Vitskøl (*Vitae Schola*)	—1158
Sorø (*Sora*)	—1161
Tvis (*Tuta Vallis*)	—1163
Sminge-Veng-Kalvø-Øm (*Cara Insula*)	—1165–72
Seem-Løgum (*Locus Dei*)	—1170 or 1171
Dargun (no special Latin name)	—1172
Colbaz (*Mera Vallis*)	—1174
Holme (*Insula Dei*)	—1174
Guldholm (*Insula Aurea*)	—1192
Ås (*Asilum*)	—1194
Dargun to Eldena (*Hilda*)	—1199
Guldholm to Ryd (*Rus Regis*)	—1209

Notice how the Cistercians, if at all possible, latinized the local place names of the sites where they founded their monasteries. Sometimes these latinizations could be made without much difficulty. Vitskøl can easily be turned into *Vitae Schola*. But Holme, which just means island, has to be endowed with a religious connotation, thus *Insula Dei*. It is interesting that the two earliest Danish Cistercian houses had names that never were latinized. In general the names given show great affection for the abbey sites: *Cara Insula* or *Tuta Vallis*.

Only the beginning of the 1170s is crowded with new foundations, a possible reflection of King Valdemar's consolidation of power which culminated in festivities at Ringsted Abbey in 1170 and with the start of Danish conquests in Rygen and Wendland. After that period there is a pause of almost twenty years, and the final foundations are on the fringes of medieval Denmark. So the great age of new monasteries lasts from 1158–1174. It seems as if it took Herrisvad and Esrum a few years to con-

solidate their own possessions and establish themselves before they could initiate daughter houses. The instability and wars that plagued Denmark until
1157 could also have hindered new foundations immediately after 1151.
Here we must be on guard, however, for the greatest period of Cistercian
foundations in England coincides with the years of the Anarchy in the late
1130s and the 1140s.

LOOKING BACK AT LØGUM

A summary of this age of Cistercian expansion in Denmark can be found in
the great charter for Løgum issued by Bishop Omer of Ribe and dated between 1191 and 1197.[74] Because of a fire in the 1180s or early 1190s, all the
abbey's early documents perished, so Omer was obliged for the sake of the
monks to tell the story of the monastery's first years and at the same time
define his own relationship with it as diocesan bishop. The narrative elements
in the charter provide a mini-chronicle that probably reflects the early history
of Løgum as the monks wanted the bishop to see it. It is impossible to state
that the monks 'dictated' the charter, but from the cooperation of monks and
bishop resulted an authorized account of Løgum's beginings intended to
assure good relations between the abbey and future bishops of Ribe.

First Omer confirmed the gifts to the monks made by Ralph, his
predecessor. He mentioned the participation of Archbishop Eskil in this donation. He explained that the Cistercians had first come to a place called
Seem, not far from Ribe, where there was a Benedictine double abbey. But
the white monks moved to Løgum under Bishop Ralph, who died in 1171,
and this act was approved by his successor, Stephen, who had previously
been abbot of Herrisvad.[75] In these lines, Bishop Omer traced the first years
at Løgum until the time when he assumed the bishopric.

The historical account gives way to a warm declaration of affection for
the monks. Omer builds carefully on biblical phrases, but the language is not
just a string of clichés. The emotional style and medley of quotations recall
the writings of St Bernard himself. But we are not far from Abbot William
either: 'We bound the monks of Løgum to our heart', Omer writes, 'and
though because of limited resources we could give less than we desired,
nevertheless, in order to benefit them, we have cared for them, wishing to
gain God's recompense through their prayers.' Using a reference mainly
based on Luke 16:3, Omer sums up his link with the monks that can lead
him to heaven: '. . . since after our period of labour we no longer could dig
and would be ashamed to beg, we might be received into the eternal taber-
nacles'.[76] It is noteworthy that Omer's conclusion contains no directly biblical language but states baldly his preference for the Cistercians: 'Because of
this hope we venerate all religious men in the intimate devotion of the

heart, but since they are more familiar and more our own, we especially embrace [the Løgum monks] with all our affection'.[77] This choice of the Cistercians among monastic orders and the desire to achieve heaven through the monks' prayers are familiar literary themes in Danish foundation charters. But here they are combined in a new fullness.

Omer continues the charter by confirming the privileges of collecting tithes given by his predecessors to Løgum.[78] He himself gave them the church of Nørre Løgum as well as Ginnegård, which cannot be identified but may have been within that parish. He then described the tribulations the Løgum monks had suffered. Many brothers had died. Cattle had been ravaged by disease. Sheep had drowned. Two granges had burned down. Finally a fire had devastated the cloister. Surviving charters and other valuable records had been collected in the monastery's bakery, a separate building, but some days later this too burned down. Fire was one of the great dangers for the Cistercians—as for all medieval people. The Ryd Annals mentions two fires at Esrum during this period.[79] But at Løgum we are told how much damage was done.

In the following lines, Omer consoled the monks and spoke of the purpose behind such sufferings:

> Blessed be God, who consoles their weakness in these tribulations (Cf. 2 Cor 1: 3–4), so that they do not give up, but revert to him all the more fervently, he who forgives so much and takes such pity, and who afterwards brings to gentleness those who have suffered the confusion of punishment and wrath (Cf. Is 55: 7).[80]

We might become lost in this language of divine punishment and recompense if it were not for the regular reversion to the practical matter at hand. At the end of the charter, Omer claimed he had composed this 'long narration' of the Løgum community's trials and tribulations so that their rights and possessions would not be challenged in the future, despite their loss of documents. He thus gave the Cistercian house exactly what it needed, especially in its first decades: a legal basis, an historical tradition, and a clear link with its founder bishops. For a monastic order that was supposed to be exempt from episcopal jurisdiction, the Cistercians revealed frequently how much they depended on their local bishops to guarantee their position in society. But as Louis Lekai has pointed out, the Cistercians in the twelfth century underwent a 'process of gradual and eventually total exemption' and local and regional differences were probably more significant than any blanket exemption for the Order as given by the papacy.[81]

Omer's charter is addressed to a Løgum abbot named Vagn. Here we are unmistakably in the presence of a native Danish abbot. By the 1190s the original French, English, or German abbots seem to have been replaced by

Danish successors.[82] Together with this apparent transformation of the monasteries to Danish-member institutions, we find in charters after about 1200 a more business-like tone. This resulted from the standardization of legal formulae in documents. At the same time appear the first signs of strong resistance to the monks' claims. We have already noticed the Øm dispute over tithe payment. A similar problem seems to have developed at Løgum. Between 1202 and 1204, Bishop Omer ratified an agreement between Løgum and the parishioners of Nørre-Løgum which entitled the monks to two-thirds of the tithe income from the church, despite the earlier resistance of the parishioners.[83]

In the face of such problems the monks looked especially to the local bishop and to the king for guidance and protection. During the years from 1202 to 1214, Løgum obtained from Valdemar II a charter confirming all the abbey's possessions and rights and adding a provision unique among royal charters. [84] The king imposed a *madban* on runaway monks: no one was to feed them. The king's officials were to seize such monks and deprive them of anything they had with them. This charter, because of its uneven formulations, has been declared a product of the monks' own composition.[85] If so, it reflects needs they felt and shows they were plagued by members of the community who broke their vow of stability. We have no idea why they ran away, but the fact that such a provision is found in a Cistercian charter from the early thirteenth century and not in any of the early Esrum charters issued in the king's name suggests that this problem of discipline may not have existed earlier.

Even more revealing, the charter has the king declare that his father Valdemar and brother Knud 'had chosen to love and honour the Cistercian Order above all [other] orders under heaven'.[86] Such an assertion cannot be found in any of Valdemar I's or Knud VI's extant charters. We can only conclude that the Løgum Cistercians felt uncertain that the new king had for the Order the same concern his predecessors had manifested. By emphasizing the devotion earlier kings had shown, they could bind the new Valdemar to a similar policy. There is an uneasiness here, a sense of an urgent need to manipulate the past by formulating a version of it favourable to the Cistercians.[87] In this way the monks could guarantee the gains of previous decades and prevent future challenges. This charter's declaration of devotion to the Cistercians summarizes the direction of chronicles in Denmark after 1200. They attempted to create an acceptable past that glorified the monks and focused on their value to kings and bishops. The Danish lay and ecclesiastical authorities were on the whole generous to the Cistercians, but their involvement cannot be characterized with the exclusiveness with which the Løgum monks try here to stamp it.

THE CISTERCIAN ADVANCE IN RETROSPECT

Looking upon the first decades of the Cistercians in Denmark as a whole, we might feel tempted to compare events with the ideals expressed in the *Exordium Parvum*. The Cistercians did not live up to strictures against the collection of tithes or the ownership of churches or mills. We find examples of such acquisitions almost from the very arrival of the Order in Denmark. But the Order's general history shows a similar development elsewhere. After Bernard's death in 1153, the impulses to austerity of life and independence from unearned incomes became weaker.[88] This was the case even with Clairvaux, the mother house of the majority of Danish abbeys. Here a conscious policy of buying up lands for granges can be traced through the second half of the century.[89]

Such developments, which Bernard would have opposed, came as a result of the tremendous growth of the Order, especially of the Clairvaux line. It was impossible for such a large international organization to maintain the simplicity of the first communities of monks. This pattern repeats itself in the Franciscan Order in the thirteenth century. But there a group of friars tried to resist the tendency and to maintain the original ideals. The resulting tragic split is symptomatic of the collapse of the medieval church's reform movement by the end of the thirteenth century. The Cistercians apparently did not experience this tension between progressive and conservative parties. The only evidence we have of occasional pangs of conscience concerning aberrations from early principles is provided by the decisions of the General Chapter, especially in the 1180s and 1190s.[90] These statutes can be looked upon as an attempt by zealous abbots to return to early practices. But in Cistercian abbeys all over Europe, local customs and entrenched traditions could not be eliminated. After about 1215 the Cistercian reform impulse died out. The General Chapter began to concede a number of practices, such as the buying of property, that it had vainly tried to limit before 1200.

The Danish situation is typical of the general European pattern in the second half of the twelfth century. Since the Danish abbeys were founded relatively late they were not deeply influenced by the initial reform impulse. This original concept of the Cistercians was articulated by Stephen Harding, third abbot of Citeaux and author of the *Carta Caritatis*. Eskil's conversion to the Cistercians as an order worthy of transplantation to Denmark seems to have owed more to Cistercian success and to the magnetic personality of Bernard than to any interest in asceticism. Eskil was fascinated with the monks not as austere men but as makers of a strong community. It was this sense of community that drew him to Clairvaux. After 1158, the dominant figure of Cistercian expansion in Denmark was Absalon of Lund. As a practical, political man whose first concern was unity and centralized rule, Absalon could hardly have been attracted by concepts of poor monks, independent of all worldly powers. Absalon was a born aristocrat who made the monks into spiritual and material aristocrats.

If we leave the question of monastic reform and look at the Danish Cistercians in terms of colonization, the opening up of new areas to cultivation and to Christianity, we run into new problems. German historians once justified the monks' special privileges, such as that of collecting tithes given to Wendish abbeys, on the basis of their unique situation and unusual difficulties in getting started. But, as we have seen, the Danish Cistercians can hardly be looked upon as colonizers of great tracts of virgin land. They should rather be considered as new settlers in old areas, such as Halland, Northern Zealand, or in the Gudenå lake area in Central Jutland, in areas where peasant cultivation long had existed

Another way to understand how the early Danish Cistercians functioned in their new surroundings would be through attention to the needs expressed by members of the Danish ruling class: bishops, great landowners, and the royal family. These groups wanted to share in the spread of the monks across the face of Denmark in order to have an outlet and means of expression for their religious feelings. Such a class-oriented interpretation of the Cistercians' role in Danish society still leaves room for the idealistic appeal that made their success possible. The Cistercians were worth paying for because they provided a safety valve for divine wrath, a means of contact between the ruling class and the divine, a balm for consciences, and a high degree of prestige for protectors. Purely political motives, such as the strengthening of anti-royalist factions, find no support in the sources.

In the twelfth century almost everyone who mattered in society wanted the Cistercians in their midst, except the Benedictines. If the magnates could not live like saints, then they could share in the prayers and good works of the monks whose material existence they made possible. The charters and records of land disputes indicate that the monks provided frequent reminders to the upper class of their existence and needs. We can see a lively exchange of members, money, land, and feelings between monks and magnates. At least in this initial period, the Cistercians provided Denmark with an international link—diplomatically invaluable during the schism of the 1160s—and with a focus for the aspirations and hopes of the ruling class. Later the Cistercians would settle into the landscape and look after themselves without gaining the same attention and involvement from the ruling class. But in the twelfth century they were explosively active and apparently able to obtain what they wanted and needed to make a permanent settlement in Denmark.

What the peasants thought of the monks is anyone's guess. The peasant

Api at Øm first resisted and then gave in to them because he had dreamed he saw Mary threatening him.[91] At Sorø some peasants apparently became lay brothers.[92] At Esrum a peasant sold the monks land.[93]. In the course of the thirteenth century the Cistercians became more and more dependent on hired labour as the number of lay brothers dwindled.[94] But it is impossible to evaluate attitudes between peasants and monks as we can with the ruling class. Whatever peasants felt about the expanding monasteries and their accumulative land policies, the monks, thanks to the rich Danish landowning class, were able by the first years of the thirteenth century to settle down and gain in privileges and possessions the security they wanted and needed.

In the midst of the generally positive reception given the monks by bishops, kings, and magnate families, we have one prime source for twelfth century Denmark that hardly mentions the Cistercians at all: the historian Saxo. If he was Absalon's clerk, as is generally assumed, then Saxo was a member of the secular clergy and would have had no special reason to sympathize with the Cistercians.[95] But Saxo's attitude is difficult to understand in view of his master Absalon's overwhelming devotion to the monks and all the measures he took for their welfare. Saxo seems otherwise to have approved almost everything Absalon did. Saxo was more interested in warriors than monks, while Absalon was concerned with both. There seems to have been a gap of understanding between patron and author. Saxo only speaks of the Cistercians when he writes about Eskil, and then he makes the monks from Esrum almost ridiculous. He may have identified them with Eskil, while Absalon apparently had a much more sophisticated view of the Cistercians and their usefulness to Danish society. Could Saxo even have been jealous of the way Absalon took their monasteries under his care and gave them great tracts of land? Instead of conceding Absalon's generosity to the monks in the *Gesta Danorum* and perhaps criticizing him for it, thus flawing the portrait of Absalon as the perfect leader and churchman, Saxo merely left out the Cistercians. His silence about these monks in the face of their tremendous expansion during the very years about which he writes needs to be noted and discussed.[96] Concentration on the Cistercians would perhaps have distracted from Saxo's idealization of Absalon as hero and fighter. Either Saxo did not like seeing Absalon in such roles as efficient businessman or monastic patron, or else he minimized the importance of this side of Absalon's life work.

Whatever the reason, Saxo's silence indicates that in the twelfth century the Cistercians in Denmark did not inspire everyone in the upper classes. They had a firm hold on the top level of society, but at the very next level, among the people who served the magnates, there could have been others who shared Saxo's suspicion and contempt for these seemingly naive and useless monks. In an age of military prowess, conquest, and blood, the Cistercians seemed out of place. Saxo reveals an archaic quality in his work here, for in France and England the new, more courtly aristocracy of the High Middle Ages felt an immediate solidarity with Cistercian values. Saxo is thus not just a remarkable historian who acquired a fine knowledge of Latin and points to a high intellectual standard in Denmark at the end of the twelfth century. He was one of Absalon's retainers and immediately dependent on him. He had reason for resenting others whom Absalon favoured.

Saxo's pregnant silence about the monks, his lack of interest in their activities, his concern for military prowess instead of monastic life—all these qualities warn us against thinking that Danish Cistercians always found enthusiam and immediate acceptance. The right people were eventually won over to the idea of providing for the Cistercians, but the going could still be tough. After 1215 the situation became much more difficult, for even the elite then would sometimes feel that the Cistercians were in the way of their ambitions. The open, receptive society of the twelfth century gave way to a harsher, more demanding hierarchy of the thirteenth. The Cistercians had to fight for the rights and privileges they had come to assume were theirs. The source that they left us in the next period emphasize legalism and property disputes. Such records, and the dogged determination behind them, distort the historical reality that within the monasteries, the vast majority of the monks devoted themselves to interior lives of self-denial and prayer.

In the summer of 1978 a new aspect of twelfth century Cistercian achievement came to light in preliminary excavations of the ruins of Tvis abbey in West-Jutland.[97] The foundations of an impressive church and cloister quadrangle came to view. In the following year the west end of the church was found a few inches beneath the surface. The church was apparently built of brick and was forty-nine metres in length, a considerable size for a Cistercian house about which we know almost nothing from written sources and which once was assumed to be a poor or at best modest foundation. Most surprisingly of all, architectural evidence so far points to the construction of the church in one uninterrupted period and its completion by about 1200, before the impressive Cistercian church at Løgum, which still stands today, was even begun. Thus at Tvis, as at Sorø and probably also at Esrum and Vitskøl, substantial Cistercian churches were well under way before the end of the fifth decade of the Cistercian presence in Denmark. Only the combined effort of all the moneyed and propertied elements in Danish society could have made such buildings possible in such disparate parts of the country. These churches in themselves bear witness to the early success of the Cistercians in Denmark.

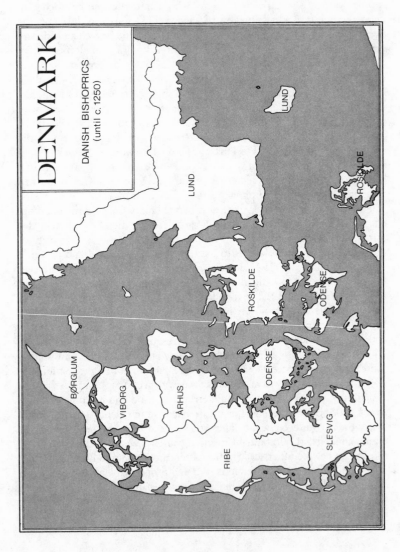

Danish Bishoprics

IV
Continuity and Growing Tensions
1215–1257

MAJOR THEMES OF THE PERIOD

BY LOOKING AT THE DANISH Cistercian abbeys in terms of their relationships to each other and to power groups in Danish and international society, we can watch the abbeys lose their status as communities favoured by lay society. They became traditional institutions more or less taken for granted as part of the monastic landscape. By the interval 1215–1257, the Cistercians now had to fight to maintain the gains of the preceding decades. At the beginning of this period, the Fourth Lateran Council clarified the question of paying tithes and thus removed a major source of controversy for the Danish Cistercians. Løgum Abbey planned to cultivate larger areas of land and so sought and received permission by royal charter to reorganize peasant settlements at the abbey's will and convenience. The monks could thereby make larger and more productive farms.[1] Both Sorø and Esrum were engaged in complicated negotiations with rich landowners who went on crusade and needed to borrow money to finance their expeditions.[2] Often such local magnates either never came back or were unable to repay the amount borrowed, which meant that land handed over to the monasteries as security then remained with the monks. In Ryd the Cistercians settled down in a new location. Even though they had some difficulties with their former holdings in Slesvig, they were able to enjoy a number of years of peace and stability.[3]

Outwardly all looks settled and prosperous until we turn to the Sorø Donation Book or to the chronicles composed during these years. The Sorø monks were beginning long and frustrating negotiations to get properties in Stenmagle from the sons of the great donor of the Skjalm family, Esbern Snare. This matter was not settled until the end of the century.⁴ At Øm, Sorø, and perhaps Varnhem in Sweden, chronicles were being written to legitimize the first half century of the abbeys' existences and to justify the monks' claims against possible challenges. The Øm chronicler, in looking back on the first abbots of the house, emphasized their concern with spiritual matters, while for those of his own time he concentrated on practical concerns. He praised abbots like Thorkil (1199–1216), under whom the account was written, for being able to cope with material demands.⁵

Despite some danger signals, the monks remained confident that they could achieve whatever they wanted and needed. They were still the favoured childen of bishops, kings, and large landowning families, and many of the privileges we have from this time still give great flexibility to the monks and indicate episcopal confidence in their usefulness to the life of the church.⁶

By 1257, much of this had changed. Esrum had lost, and been humiliated in, a long litigation with Doberan Abbey in Mecklenburg over its paternity of Dargun Abbey.⁷ Sorø had its first difficulties with the bishops of Roskilde over the monks' right to install priests in parish churches.⁸ Løgum was being plagued by continuing dissatisfaction among the parishioners of Nørre-Løgum about the monks' collection of tithes from the church.⁹ Øm had just consecrated its abbey church but for the first time was dealing with a bishop of Århus who was unsympathetic to the Cistercians.¹⁰ The coming of the friars to Denmark in the 1220s and 1230s ended the status of the Cistercians as the aristocracy's fashionable order. The Franciscans and Dominicans became the favoured sons of the church. As elsewhere in Europe, the Cistercians in Denmark could not compete with the friars' immediate appeal to the population of growing market towns.

What had gone wrong? Apparently the monks kept on expecting the special treatment they had obtained in the twelfth century from kings, bishops, rich landowners, and the international organization of the Cistercian Order. But in the meantime the world had changed. After the 1220s the Danish monarchy became less expansive and more unstable. Bishops became more concerned with consolidating their cathedral chapters and diocesan rights. They began to look upon the monks as competitors rather than protégés.¹¹ Landowners began to regret their ancestors' great donations to the monks and tried to devise ways to regain some of these 'losses'. The Cistercian Order itself no longer gave special attention to Danish and other Scandinavian houses. Its new area of expansion was Eastern Germany and Poland. Here it was the offspring of Morimund and not, as in the twelfth century, Clairvaux and its daughters, that were active and aggressive.

At the same time as the Cistercians shifted their attention from the North to the East, the influx of English, German, and French monks and abbots to Denmark dried up. The monasteries became more Danish and less international. It was no longer expedient for kings and bishops to call on Cisterican abbots to look after matters of diplomacy for them.[12] The Danish Cistercians nevertheless did their best to maintain their earlier positions. They did their best to maintain the *status quo*. This attitude prepared the way for the confrontations of the 1260s at Øm Abbey. The monks continued into the thirteenth century as if nothing had changed and as if they could still count on broad support from privileged groups in society. Thus they became easy prey for aggressive and acquisitive members of these groups.

This view might make the monks appear as innocent victims of powerful men when they were in fact one of several factions trying to exercise and keep power. The monks did try during this and later periods to acquire as much land as possible and to create huge estates in the vicinity of their monasteries. But the exploitation of opportunities for increasing their holdings forms only one aspect of the monks' existence, an aspect disproportionately represented in our surviving sources, because of the interest notaries and royal officials in sixteenth-century Denmark had in preserving sources which established the dissolved monasteries' exact holdings. Monastic sources containing only historical, liturgical, or biographical material often perished.

TRAVELLING MONKS

The monks apparently did their best to secure what they had already gained. One source that illuminates the human difficulties behind such efforts during this period comes not from a Cistercian house but from Prémontré, the mother abbey of the Danish 'Norbertine' house at Børglum in northern Jutland.[13] The abbot of Prémontré, Gervais, headed an order close in structure to the Cistercians and a product of the same reform impulse at the start of the twelfth century. He wrote a letter concerning a Børglum canon, Eskil, who had been sent to the Lateran Council in 1215 to obtain papal privileges for his house, and had subsequently disappeared. His story reveals something of the problems that could arise when thirteenth-century Danish institutions sent members south to obtain guarantees for their rights, privileges, and holdings.

Abbot Gervais wrote that when he met the monk Eskil at the Council, the poor creature was so impoverished that 'he seemed not to have come from the hands of men, as it were, but from those of devils'.[14] This lively comparison initiates a detailed account of how Gervais, as father abbot, had taken Eskil under his wing, had seen to it that he was given decent clothing to replace his rags, and had paid his expenses for food and lodging. Eskil was given an amount of money to pay the notary at the papal chancellery who had been charged with renewing the abbey's privileges. Gervais describes how he had chatted up another notary who was favourably disposed to him so that the matter could be more easily expedited. He also complains about inflated prices for food and lodgings because of the Council, an indication of a connection between church meetings and the cost of living in thirteenth-century Rome.[15]

Gervais's letter is full of welcome details about travel and money. After he left Rome, he sent Eskil money from Viterbo. Later that year, he met him in Hesbaye. Eskil claimed that he had been attacked by robbers and was now 'as thin as a skeleton'. Once again Gervais looked after him. He remarks that the papal letter giving the monks permission to transfer the site of their monastery was incorrect because it did not mention Børglum as an episcopal seat. One more problem for the hapless Premonstratensian canon Eskil!

About the first of September 1216, Eskil arrived at Prémontré and stayed there until the General Chapter. Once again he received new clothes. Gervais also fortified Eskil with a general Premonstratensian privilege which protected the Børglum canons from being forced to take over the administration of women's houses, and with another general privilege for the whole order. Both were properly endorsed with the seal of the General Chapter. Eskil then went on his journey again, apparently to return to Rome, for Innocent III had meanwhile died and the papal privilege for Børglum had to be renewed by the new pope, Honorius III. Gervais advised Eskil to secure a new privilege, but he adds in his declaration that he had no idea what happened to the wandering Dane after he left Prémontré and characterizes Eskil as a stubborn man who did not like to receive advice.[16]

This detailed letter shows how difficult it could be for Danish abbeys to maintain contact with Rome and with the international structure of their Order. Eskil's penniless arrival in Rome may have been due to his own carelessness, but it could also have been the result of insufficient funds given him to make the trip. Abbot Gervais makes it look as if Eskil would never have obtained the desired papal privilege without his help and connections with the papal notary. Despite all Gervais' efforts, Eskil disappears from our view into the darkness of history. But the letter makes clear the risk any Danish community took in sending one or more of its members south to a General Chapter or to the papal court. The trip was expensive and dangerous, and even with the help of the Order itself, success was not guaranteed.

The experience of Eskil shows what it meant for Danish religious to obtain papal privileges and travel about in Europe. Danish Cistercians could come back with empty hands and pockets. Or they could fail to return at all. In September 1215, the Cistercian General Chapter ordered the abbots of Øm and Tvis to come to its next meeting or be punished. They had sent their excuses 'because of the dangers of wars'. We do not know which wars they referred to, but Øm's abbot did not come the following year, and so the abbot of Holme on Fyn was ordered to announce the General Chapter's punishment to him.[17] No excuse is given this time, but this is only one of a number of instances during this period when the General Chapter issued decrees against Danish abbots who failed to attend.[18] It is easy to understand why they stayed away. Even if they came only once every five years, as the Swedish abbots did, the journey was long and difficult.

CONTACT WITH THE PAPACY

Cistercian monasteries in one way or another nevertheless maintained lively contacts with the papal court as well as with the Cistercian General Chapter. This might seem superfluous after Innocent III had given Esrum, Sorø, and Løgum (perhaps together with other Danish houses) the valuable general privilege that covered all possible varieties of exemption or immunity from episcopal power.[19] But changing relationships between bishops and monasteries, as well as the growing importance and development of canon law, meant that Cistercian houses were well-advised to take nothing for granted and to seek out papal authorization that old privileges took on the appropriate new legal forms. There could also be individual points on which Cistercian abbots felt they needed papal clarification. Thus Abbot Gunner of Øm, even if he did not personally go to Rome in the beginning of 1217, saw to it that Pope Honorius confirmed his abbey's rightful possession of a much disputed church at Veng.[20] In the same document, the monastery's move in 1171 from Veng to Øm was confirmed. The bishop of Århus and the archbishop of Lund, Anders Sunesen, are said to have provided counsel in this matter. The 'urgent necessity' of the brothers is spoken of, an indication that the monks were still having problems with their possession of Veng. This evidence of a continuing dispute is confirmed by the nearly-contemporary first part of the Øm Chronicle.[21]

From the dating of these papal privileges, 30 and 31 January, it is clear that they were issued at the same time as a whole string of papal bulls dealing with requests from Sorø, from the chapter of Århus, and from Anders Sunesen.[22] Århus' interests are in this case intermingled with those of Sorø. Two bishops of Århus, Peder and Skjalm Vognsen, members of the Skjalm family and benefactors of Sorø, left behind property both to the Århus chapter for founding new prebends and to the Sorø monks for their own use.[23]

If we look at this group of privileges as a whole, we can conclude that in January 1217, a delegation of Danish churchmen were at the Lateran to do business with the new pope's chancellery. We do not know if any Cistercian monks were present in this delegation. It seems unlikely that the newly-elected abbot of Øm would have missed the General Chapter in September yet have managed to be in Rome the following January. In any case, Cistercian interests were represented in a way that must have been satisfactory to both the Sorø and Øm monks. Here we have an outstanding example of cooperation between officials of the diocesan church in Denmark, representing the Århus canons and the archbishop of Lund himself, and the Cistercian monks. It seems apparent that there was sufficient unity and harmony in Denmark at this point for monks and canons to pool their resources and either send a neutral messenger or form a common delegation to the pope.

They may have cooperated again in 1244, when Esrum, Sorø and Århus all obtained privileges at the papal court in February, March, and the beginning of April. This time the issuing of the various privileges is not so chronologically close together. Sorø obtained its privileges at the end of February and the beginning of March, while Esrum's are dated the last week in March, and Århus 29 March and 9 April.[24] This time there were no overlapping matters, as in the case of the Vognsen legacies. Even if it is not easy here to see a common interest between the secular canons and the Cistercian monks, they did appear at almost the same time in Rome and may well have traveled together or hired a common representative. In this instance, as in the preceding one, other Danish Cistercian abbeys may also have been represented at the papal court. Since our collection of these abbeys' papal privileges are less complete than those of Sorø and Esrum, however, we have no trace of their participation.

The provisions of the papal privileges given in these years continue Innocent III's practice of treating the monks as members of an exempt order.[25] All abbeys received more or less the same privileges. But the Danish houses sometimes obtained papal bulls which provide specific information about their property holdings. Typical of this group is a privilege issued by Gregory IX in 1228; in it he confirmed for Sorø a number of possessions acquired since the 1198 privilege of Innocent III.[26] Most of these new acquisitions can be dated before 1215, but a few belong to the period 1215–1228. On the same day as Sorø obtained its privilege from Gregory, Esrum received a very detailed bull that listed all its granges and a number of village holdings.[27] Esrum had just been given a papal privilege in 1223, so even in the course of five years, the abbey had managed to add to its properties.[28]

In 1223, too, it looks as if Esrum and Sorø sought papal privileges in a common delegation to the chancellery, for their privileges were issued only a few days apart from each other.[29]

Just as Danish Cistercians cooperated in gaining routine confirmations of their land acquisitions, they also went to the papal chancellery in unison to settle problems with the diocesan church. Pope Gregory IX showed special interest in the Cistercians in a 1234 series of bulls for Sorø, Esrum, and Løgum.[30] His helpfulness may, of course, have been due to a need for allies in his battles against the Emperor Frederick II.[31] These bulls follow a formula often employed for Cistercian houses, but they still point to individual Danish problems. In one document, Gregory ordered three officials of Ribe, the bishop, the prior of St Nicholas Abbey, and the choir dean, to see to it that those who had acted unjustly against the Cistercians provide them with reparations. Such a bull points to concrete wrongs done to the monks.

The other bulls are more general: Gregory freed the brothers from summons to courts at a distance of more than two days' travel; he ordered diocesan officials to protect Sorø and to excommunicate those who harmed the monks; he forbade anyone to challenge the authenticity of the seals on letters carried by the brothers on the abbey's business. The first and third of these privileges were issued to Sorø alone, while the second was also give to Løgum and to Esrum. It could be that Sorø was being harassed by representatives of the bishops of Roskilde and that Løgum and Esrum merely obtained the same privilege as a precautionary measure. Although we can, in a general way, point to increasing unrest in Denmark up to the death of King Valdemar II in 1241, there is no further evidence of conflict between diocesan authorities and Cistercian abbeys at this time.

On a European level, the period was a crucial one for the Cistercians. During it their privileges and exemptions were under constant attack. In one of Gregory's many bulls defending Cistercian privileges, he says that the abbot of Citeaux and his fellow abbots had complained to him about lack of respect for their properties and privileges.[32] From this period date many of the general privileges given to Cistercian houses and collected in the Sorø Book, such as a renewal of the prohibition against intervention by the bishop in election of abbots or his requirement of compensation for giving the new abbot his blessing.[33]

From 1228 to the end of the 1240s, we know more about Sorø and Esrum's dealings with the papal chancellery than about these abbeys' land transactions. Acquisitions may have come to a standstill, or the monks may have been busy trying to hold onto what they already had.[34] In the 1240s Sorø, Esrum, and Løgum, as we have mentioned, acquired a group of privileges from Innocent IV. These for the most part simply reaffirmed such traditional rights as freedom from being summoned to secular or ecclesiastical courts or freedom from the threat of excommunication by a diocesan prelate. Once again we cannot focus on specific problems. We need also to consider that after 1220 the Cistercian Order had two permanent representatives at the papal court to take care of its affairs.[35] Thus renewals of privileges could have been effected without the presence of any Danish monks. We therefore do not know whether or not the Esrum monks were at the papal court in 1249, but they obtained copies for themselves of a number of bulls issued between 19 and 24 September by Innocent IV reaffirming various privileges of the Order.[36] Such copies were probably available to the Danish abbots when they attended the General Chapter at Citeaux.

Innocent expressly forbade the issuing of excommunications and interdicts against those who worked for the Cistercians and against their benefactors. He confirmed all the Order's liberties, but especially the monks' freedom from being summoned to diocesan courts. The Cistercians could also have members ordained to the priesthood without examination by the local bishop. No bishop or other church officials were allowed to make visitation of the abbeys. Only the officials of the Order itself, especially appointed to the task, could do so. Finally Innocent conceded the tithes on newly cultivated land to the Cistercians if they already had the right to collect the tithe in the parish where the land was located.

We can see here a number of the matters that were turned into burning issues in the 1260s and nearly destroyed Øm Abbey: the complex relationship between bishop and exempt monastery involving jurisdiction, visitation, and economic independence. The Danish Cistercians may have been a few years behind their brethren in central Europe in confronting these problems.[37] But the Danish houses clearly looked to the papacy for support during this period, as they did in the 1260s during the Øm controversy. In the 1240s, problems were not yet large or immediate enough to provide a real test of the papal chancellery's effectiveness in guaranteeing Cistercian privileges. In the 1260s problems became so overwhelming that the Danish monks and their complaints got lost in the shuffle.

DEALINGS WITH THE ORDER AS AN INTERNATIONAL ORGAN

It is impossible to tell how often Danish abbots attended the General Chapter at Citeaux, but there were apparently years when one abbot or another was expected by mutual agreement to appear on behalf of the Danish houses.[38] As we might expect, the two mother abbeys, Esrum and Herrisvad, most frequently appear in Chapter records from 1220–1260. Esrum is mentioned thirteen times, Herrisvad twelve. The only other Danish abbey which even comes close to this number is Ås in Halland, probably because its geographically central position made it a logical house for dealing with Norwegian problems.[39] Løgum and Holme are not named at all, Ryd and Vitskøl only once, and Tvis and Øm three times each. Even Sorø, which probably by now had become the wealthiest of the Danish Cistercian houses, rated only two mentions.

The number of times a name appears cannot be used to determine a monastery's importance. Often an abbey is named only because it has neglected its duties and is to be punished. But it is noticeable that the three Wendish offspring of Esrum—Eldena, Dargun, and Colbaz—are much more frequently named in the General Chapter's decisions. This is partly due to the task given these houses to provide for the establishment of new monasteries in what today is Poland.[40] This activity shows how North German and Polish abbeys were still being founded and were spreading in the first half of the thirteenth century. Danish Cistercian houses, by contrast, had already finished their era of foundation and expansion by 1200.

These decisions by the General Chapter shed some light on Esrum's situation. We can see the Esrum abbot functioning in his capacity as father immediate in a 1232 decision of the General Chapter. He was charged, together with visitors from Clairvaux, with investigating a scandal at Eldena.[41] This source is doubly valuable, for it is one of the few indications we have of a continuing relationship between Esrum and Eldena. Apparently the monks at the daughter house had attacked their abbot with physical force and had thrown him out of the monastery and elected a replacement. Investigators from Esrum and Clairvaux were charged with punishing the guilty and finding out if the abbot's deposition had been carried out justly. Afterwards they were to report back to the General Chapter. This is a typical decision: it suggests a great deal about a conflict but gives little precise information.

In only one other instance do we find a Danish abbot intervening to clear up a problem in a daughter abbey. Herrisvad received authority over Colbaz in 1237. For the 'correction and reformation' of Colbaz, about which rumours had reached Citeaux, the abbot-visitor was to go 'personally' to the abbey and see what was to be done.[42] Esrum—Colbaz's mother house—is not mentioned.

The Esrum abbot during this period acted so highhandedly on two occasions that the General Chapter disciplined him. In 1229 the abbot was given six days of light penance, two of them on bread and water.[43] Moreover, he was not to occupy his abbot's stall in choir for forty days. He had arranged the resignation of an abbot at a daughter house and appointed a successor without consulting anyone else. But his offence was mitigated by the deposed abbot's bad reputation. As usual, we lack specific facts. But it is clear from the Chapter's text that an abbot-immediate was not supposed to take such a drastic step without consulting his fellow abbots. The fact that the Esrum abbot tried to do so indicates that he exercised real power over daughter abbeys.

The second occasion when the Esrum abbot overstepped his prerogatives is mentioned in a 1241 decision.[44] The abbot of Clairvaux was to deal with an abbot of Esrum who had appointed a monk of Clairvaux as abbot of an unnamed abbey without obtaining permission from Clairvaux. Once again we see the abbot acting unilaterally, this time ignoring the clear rule that no monk can be elevated to an abbacy without the consent of his own abbot.

In 1241 the abbot of Esrum was ordered to discipline monks and lay-brothers of Tvis, Øm, and Herrisvad who had created a scandal by drinking in a pub.[45] But the 1242 General Chapter complained that the abbot had not reported how he had punished the offenders.[46] The Herrisvad abbot was brought into the matter to announce the General Chapter's punishment for the Esrum abbot. The year before, the abbot of Herrisvad had been given another task involving Esrum. Together with the abbot of Neuencamp, he was to settle a dispute between Esrum and Doberan.[47] This conflict may well have been over the question of Dargun's rightful mother abbey, a dispute that would drag into the late 1250s. Neuencamp was apparently chosen because it belonged to the same line as Doberan, that of Morimund, while Herrisvad would be expected to see the problem from the point of view of the Esrum filiation.

Esrum's position as proto-abbey in the Clairvaux line brought it into the centre of events in one of the greatest Scandinavian Cistercian scandals of the period. In 1254 the Chapter ordered the abbot of Esrum to inform Sorø's and Ås's abbots that they had been deposed.[48] These two had come to Herrisvad as visitors, a function that normally would have been carried out by Herrisvad's own mother abbey, Citeaux.[49] The fact that Sorø and Ås, daughters of Esrum, were called upon to visit Herrisvad, shows flexibility in thirteenth-century Cistercian administration. As it turned out, the Sorø abbot misused his rights by deposing the Herrisvad abbot without giving him any chance to defend himself. The General Chapter ordered its deposition of the Sorø and Ås abbots to be made known in all the houses of the Order, so that such a crime would not be repeated.[50]

Esrum acted not only as messenger of the General Chapter but also as the mother abbey of Sorø and Ås in seeing to it that the General Chapter's decisions were carried out. In 1243, the abbot of Esrum together with the abbot of Varnhem was ordered to investigate a scandal in Norway at Hovedø monastery on Oslo Fjord.[51] Here we are given precise details about what had gone wrong. The monks and lay brothers at Hovedø had marooned the prior, sacristan, and sub-chanter on islands to die of starvation. They had publicly stripped their own abbot and their visitors of their clothes and other possessions and had gravely harmed two of their own monks. The conspirators were excommunicated and were to be disciplined by the abbots of Esrum and Varnhem. The abbot of Ås was to make this task known to these two abbots. This final clause indicates that the abbots of Esrum and Varnhem were not present at Citeaux, while the Ås abbot was. Esrum's prestige and position among Scandinavian houses are clearly indicated here.

The violence at Hovedø was as extreme and primitive as some of the uprisings David Knowles points to in Welsh and other isolated British abbeys.[52] The geographical and cultural situation seems to have been similar. In these locations the Cistercians did not have the same possibilities for frequent contacts with sister abbeys that they did in areas like Jutland or Yorkshire. The problems of the Norwegian abbeys can be seen all through the decade of the 1210s, when the General Chapter tried to arrange a satisfactory system of visitation for them.[53] They were too far away and unimportant for Fountains to continue to oversee them. They appear to have been equally unwanted by the Swedish abbeys.[54] So they were left to fend for themselves. When visitors finally did come to Hovedø, their efforts to reform irregularities wrought by isolation ended in violence.

Looking at Esrum and its daughters in the records of the Norwegian dispute, we can appreciate their relatively tranquil existence during this period. Until mid-century, Esrum and Herrisvad apparently cooperated in furthering the interests of the Cistercian Order in Denmark. In 1243, for example, the General Chapter ordered both abbots to inspect a proposed new site in Halland for Ås.[55] But in 1250 Esrum was passed by when Herrisvad was ordered to resolve a quarrel between Dargun and Eldena.[56] The two houses may have had claims to properties that had been owned by the Eldena monks before they had emigrated from Dargun. Herrisvad was to be helped by the abbots of Sorø and Doberan. Esrum, the mother of Eldena, was not given the same chance as Dargun's refounder, Doberan, to influence the outcome, but was represented only indirectly through a daughter house, Sorø.

Esrum's troubles had just begun. In 1252 the dispute between it and Doberan over the paternity of Dargun was referred to the abbots of Herrisvad, Neuencamp, and Renfeld, the last two being Morimund foundations likely to back Doberan.[57] By 1254 the General Chapter had become impatient about the lack of progress in the matter and charged the same abbots to resolve the dispute by its next meeting.[58] This must have happened, for in 1255 Esrum fought the 'evil decision' of these abbots at the General Chapter, which not very obligingly handed over the matter to the Abbot of Morimund himself.[59] Esrum's abbot refused to admit defeat. His efforts to reverse an unfavourable decision apparently went beyond what the General

Chapter could allow, for in 1256 it summarily deposed him. A year later the Chapter allowed for the possibility that the former abbot might in future be reelected, if he reformed himself.[60].

This dispute went back at least as far as 1241 and may have been simmering ever since the resettlement of Dargun in 1209. In 1258 the General Chapter handed over Dargun's paternity to Doberan and imposed perpetual silence in the matter on the abbot of Esrum.[61] Thus ended a frustrated final attempt by Esrum to assert its power and influence over an abbey for whose first foundation it was responsible. Esrum's efforts seem remarkable in view of the fact that the Dargun refounded in 1209 was clearly the product of Doberan's initiative.

In this particular case, we can supplement the records of the General Chapter with documents from the Doberan archives. The abbey kept the full text of the 1258 decision subsequently endorsed by the General Chapter.[62] The abbots of Clairvaux and Morimund had summoned the abbots of Doberan and Esrum at the time of the General Chapter and had listened to the opposing arguments. They had adjudicated full right of paternity to the Doberan abbot and ordered Esrum to refrain from future complaints. Thus the General Chapter's decision emerged from the findings of an *ad hoc* Cistercian tribunal made up of the abbots whose daughter houses were involved in the dispute. The Chapter merely certified its decision.

The Clairvaux abbot, who would have been expected to side with his daughter-house, Esrum, apparently bowed to the legal arguments and conceded the case to Doberan. But he also secured some compensation for Esrum to save face. In 1258 or 1259 Abbot John of Clairvaux ordered Abbot Ture of Esrum to hand over to Doberan all the documents he had concerning Dargun after he had received thirty marks silver from Doberan. The language leaves no room for doubt: 'We wish and command that you' hand over everything you have pertaining to the right of paternity which 'you were claiming' over Dargun.[63] The matter was closed, but Esrum was compensated for its loss. The offer was accepted, for on 7 June 1259, at Esrum itself, Abbot Ture gave over to Abbot Conrad of Doberan all his documents concerning Dargun and acknowledged that he had received the money.[64] At the same time he gave up all his rights over Dargun.

All the information we have about this dispute and its solution comes either from the Doberan archives or the decisions of the General Chapter. The most upsetting event at Esrum in the 1250s only becomes known to us from non-Esrum sources. The Cistercians, like other interest groups, often reveal most about their concerns when they preserve little or nothing for prying posterity.

Abbot Ture who had to accept this defeat in 1259 had advanced to his position at Esrum after first being abbot of Vitskøl. He had thus attained the highest post possible for a monk in the Esrum family of monasteries in Denmark. Four years later, he stepped down to become abbot at Øm during the height of its bitter controversy with the bishop of Århus.[65] Ture's defence of what he considered the abbey's rights long after the cause was lost parallels his earlier action in the Dargun affair. Ture probably had replaced the Esrum abbot deposed in 1256; there he did his best to clean up the mess others had made. At Øm he did the same. In both instances he was fighting for a lost cause.

In the course of this review of the General Chapter's decisions regarding Danish abbeys, we have occasionally seen the abbot of Clairvaux summoned to deal with the Danish abbeys in one capacity or another. Cistercian regulations obliged him to visit the Danish abbeys of his filiation, and we do have some evidence that he fulfilled his duty during this period. In 1217 the General Chapter ordered the abbot of Clairvaux to settle a dispute which arose after a monk of Clairvaux came to Denmark. He had pretended to be the regular visitor and reputedly had slandered the abbot of Herrisvad.[66] This is one of a very few indications of tension between the Herrisvad and Esrum lines. As far as the Chapter was concerned, it was an unfortunate act committed without the knowledge or consent of the Clairvaux abbot.

A royal charter issued by Valdemar II on 27 January 1230 granted Clairvaux monks full exemption from all tolls in purchasing and transporting skins and wax in Denmark, in whatever quantities they needed for their monastery.[67] The document says that the brothers had ships to move the goods. We get a glimpse of a rich trading activity between Denmark and France fostered by Cistercian contacts.[68] The privilege also points to frequent visitations by Clairvaux representatives to Danish daughter houses.

The tradition of burying Danish churchmen at Clairvaux established by Archbishop Eskil, continued into the 1240s. Niels Stigsen, bishop of Roskilde, died there in 1249.[69] The Clairvaux source claims he was a relative of Archbishop Esklil, but Hans Olrik, whose article on contacts between Clairvaux and Denmark is still the most complete review of the relationship, says a family connection cannot be established. The exile of Niels at Clairvaux was interpreted by the monks as an act necessary 'for the liberty of the church', while a number of Danish sources give no reason for his exile.[70] The Clairvaux source is probably referring to a dispute between episcopal and royal power in Denmark that eventually led to catastrophe for the Archbishop of Lund, Jakob Erlandsen, and for the Cistercians. The fact that Niels Stigsen sought Clairvaux as a place of retirement after he had lost his bishopric indicates that there still were strong links between the Danish episcopacy and Clairvaux.

Looking back over the decisions of the General Chapter affecting Danish abbeys, we must remember that this body concentrated mainly on abuses and complaints. Its records give only a limited idea of the normal and natural contacts being maintained at the time between Danish and French abbeys. Valdemar II's privilege to Clairvaux monks travelling in Denmark indicates much more clearly that Cistercian exchanges between North and South could benefit both parties. The Danish abbeys could profit from an international structure that gave them guidelines for common liturgy and discipline. These kept them from stagnating as religious institutions or being ripped apart by internal quarrels. At the same time Clairvaux and Citeaux were able to keep their positions in the Order, despite the rapid expansion of the filiation of Morimund. Up until about 1260, the Cistercian Order's centralized structure seems to have functioned as it was meant to do.[71] The many decisions involving Scandinavian houses in this period are only part of a whole encompassing all parts of Cistercian Europe. The government of the Cistercian Order enabled Danish houses in the first half of the thirteenth century to maintain discipline, to check up on each other, and to keep in contact with the Order as a living organism.

RELATIONS WITH THE KING

Just as important as the international links is the bond Danish Cistercians maintained with the monarchy. It is during this period that the concept of immunity from royal as well as episcopal interference in the affairs of Cistercian monasteries was clarified and categorized.[72] Thus many of the royal charters issued to Danish houses should be seen as the result of a conscious effort on the part of the Cistercian leadership to guarantee rights and privileges in the more precise legal language of an era stricter and more formalistic than the twelfth century had been.

Sometime between 1202 and 1214, Valdemar II provided Esrum with immunity from royal duties and services for all those who worked its lands in Halland.[73] But full exemption from such burdens for all Esrum's properties and labourers did not come until 1237.[74] In 1211 Løgum obtained immunity from all royal rights and duties: but the charter mentions only the inhabitants of Nørre Løgum parish.[75] Just as with Esrum's exemption for Halland properties, the Løgum deed leaves open the question of the status of the monastery's other lands and labourers. In the first extant copy of a royal privilege for Sorø, the monks were freed from all royal duties on the lands they had obtained from Esbern Nielsen, as well as on their other holdings. But the document specifically states that the 'brothers . . . because of the favour of this liberty have deeded to us whatever they had in Snertinge and a hundred marks of pure silver . . .'.[76] Such a clause shows us that the monks had to pay for what they got: royal good will could be expensive, especially at a time when the monarchy needed hard cash.

In order to establish their independence from lay society, the monks had to see to it that their workers did not pay the military tax, *leding*, or offer any of the other services that peasants normally gave the king or his officials. At least as early as the time of King Sven Grathe, in the 1150s, the monks' workers in Esrum were exempted from such payments and services.[77] The same was true in Sorø from the reign of Knud VI (1182–1202) and probably as far back as that of Valdemar I (1157–1182). But just as new popes called for new privileges, so too new kings in Denmark reminded the monks of the cost of royal protection and immunity from services.

In this area of exemption, the monks had to pay attention not only to the monarchy but also to the local nobility. In 1237 Ryd obtained from Duke Abel of Southern Jutland exemption from all exactions on its labourers. The monastery had to pay a tidy sum. The Ryd Annals set the price paid by Abbot Peder at fifty-three marks. But the monastic writer claims that future dukes thereby would have no right to require further payments before guaranteeing the privilege.[78] The Ryd annalist wrote in the 1250s and after, when Ryd was in a dangerous and exposed position in an unstable kingdom. His assertion may well have been nothing more than wishful thinking.

The normal practice of Danish abbeys was to acquire new charters of liberties on the accession of new kings. It is likely that some payment, even if only a token, was made when the document was drawn up. Although we cannot generalize from the single instance we have for Sorø in King Valdemar II's time, we can at least look upon the relaxation of Valdemar's restraints in the 1230s and his granting of more generalized charters as a concession that he had not been eager to make earlier in his reign. In May 1236, two months after his privilege to Esrum, he granted the Vitskøl monks the same privileges that they had enjoyed before 'the time of the General Council'.[79] The monks were guaranteed that their labourers would not have to pay taxes or provide services.[80]

After Valdemar's death in 1241, the type of royal privileges granted to Danish abbeys remained basically the same. The monks were guaranteed exemption for themselves and all their workers from royal exactions. But the arengae or introductory formulae of the charters change drastically. Under the two Valdemars and Knud, interference in the monks' affairs by lay or ecclesiastical powers was mentioned as only a theoretical possibility.[81] Under Erik Plowpenny (1241–50), Abel (1250–52), and Kristoffer (1252–59), abrogation of the monks' rights and immunities is mentioned as a fact. Just as the Ryd Annals claim that at Valdemar's death in 1241 the crown fell from the Danes' head and disorder took over,[82] so too royal privileges reflect the period's fear and uncertainty. At the same time, however, the rapid succession of kings probably had these charters drawn up as instruments of propaganda to emphasize their own vital roles in defending the monks against enemies. When Abel was still duke of Southern Jutland but jockeying to become king, he issued from Copenhagen a privilege of protection for Esrum.[83] At this point in his career he needed Esrum much more than it needed him. Three months later, King Erik Plowpenny, whose royal power was in danger, gave the monks a similar privilege. He was probably trying to reassert his authority.[84]

Soon after Abel became king, he issued another privilege to Esrum which reasserted the old exemptions. The document links his patronage of the monastery to that of his father Valdemar and uncle Knud.[85] Erik Plowpenny, now murdered and out of the way, is naturally not even mentioned. Similarly, when Kristoffer replaced his brother Abel, he mentioned his predecessor Erik and left out Abel. Kristoffer deliberately ignored the claims of Abel's son to continue the line.[86] By the 1250s the charters of protection and exemption given to Danish Cistercian houses had become political documents expressing royal policies and ambitions in the same way as Valdemar I's 1158 foundation charter for Vitskøl had done. The monar-chy's attempt to use the monasteries to legitimize itself is most evident in Vitskøl charters. On 30 August 1250 King Abel issued a charter to this monastery.[87] The Vitskøl monks had complained to him that royal officials as well as other unnamed persons had been attacking them and the liberties given Vitskøl 'by our forefathers'.[88] In the very first sentence, Abel established himself as a legitimate member of the royal line, ignoring the death of Erik Plowpenny. The language emphasizes the king's desire in no way to abrogate the established liberties of the monks. Three times in the first three sentences, Abel's writers managed to mention his royal forefathers.

Abel thus appears as a king protecting the abbey founded by his ancestors and continuing their care for the monks. But his protection may have cost a fair price. A few days after issuing the Vitskøl document, at Viborg on 3 September, he renewed the exemption of the canons' labourers from all royal payments.[89] He mentioned that the canons' provost had given an island worth thirty marks to his father in return for the privileges. Abel does not say whether he collected money himself, but the possibility is there.

Thanks to the section of the Øm Chronicle devoted to the abbots of the 1240s and 1250s, we know that Abel's reference to complaints against attackers is more than royal propaganda.[90] The chronicle shows how the abbey was caught in the crossfire between the supporters of Abel and those of Erik Plowpenny. Here Abel is excoriated as a shameless exploiter of monks, not Abel but Babel, who had brought confusion to the land. Moreover 'that wretched fratricide was not afraid to extort three hundred marks money from Abbot Olav and the brothers' in giving the monks the privileges and liberties 'of our peasants and labourers which his predecessors and ancestors, his father and brothers, the pious kings of Denmark, gave us previously freely and as a favour'.[91]

The mention in the Vitskøl privilege of the monks' complaints against royal officials who were unfairly taxing its lands and labourers may well point to a real attempt by the men behind Abel to milk the Cistercian abbeys. Abel's actions towards Øm indicate that there was more propaganda than sincerity in his declaration of devotion to the Cistercians.

The Ryd Annals again reinforce our impression of this period in their entry for 1247. In this year there were fires at Sorø and Colbaz; Odense was burned by the Germans, and King Erik burned Svendborg:

> What more? Once they had wretchedly destroyed the kingdom, then they were not afraid by their fraternal bloodletting not much later to impose perpetual infamy on themselves and the kingdom.[92]

The Ryd annalist expresses the same bitterness with the royal dynasty as did his Øm brother. The Cistercians had reached a turning point in their relationship with the monarchy because of its volatile state. The crown no longer could guarantee the monks its old benevolence or, at worst, neutrality. The monasteries had become pawns in the Danish political game.

The Cistercians were not alone in this situation. Abel and Kristoffer were quick in handing out similar guarantees to houses of the Benedictine, Augustinian, and Johannite observance.[93] The formulations for exemption from all military taxes and other payments to the king become standardized in such documents. But sometimes royal intentions and policies become apparent behind the stock phrases.

In Kristoffer's second privilege to Vitskøl, such desires eventually show up clearly.[94] In the arenga he uses the familiar theme that the monks' prayers contribute to the prosperity of the realm but he employs it to justify his desire not just to renew the monks' privileges but also 'to increase them in all ways'. Kristoffer's charter borrows from some of Abel's language about royal officials who harass the monks and demand undue payments from their labourers, but the language is much more specific than Abel's had been in now stating that all judicial fines levied on the brothers' labourers are to go to the monastery and not to such royal officials. Such fines were usually in one of two classes: either for three marks or for forty marks.[95] In both cases the brothers are to have full power to collect them. This provision covers not only the monks' peasant labourers; it also protects donors who give the *halv hovedlod*, the maximum allowable part of their inheritance, to the abbey (in medieval Danish law a daughter was allowed the *halv hovedlod*; a son twice that). Finally, in order to make quite clear his good intentions to the brothers and to show he is increasing their privileges, Kristoffer handed over to them the right of collecting the salvage from shipwrecks that washed up on a section of Jutland's east coast where the monks had land. Salvage rights normally belonged to the king. By handing them over unconditionally to the monks, Kristoffer gave Vitskøl a special sign of royal favour. This may have been due to the dynastic link going back to 1157. In general, Cistercians houses did not get much special attention from the monarchy in this period, and Vitskøl is the exception proving the rule.

If we compare the Vitskøl royal charter with two that were granted the year before to Esrum,[96] Vitskøl's uniqueness is made clear. Esrum received the usual exemptions and nothing more. King Abel's text about royal favour for the Cistercians as a monastic order drops out completely. For Løgum, the full text of Abel's charter was simply repeated.[97] It would be wrong to use generalized charters of this kind to characterize the royal attitude towards the Cistercians. What was issued in the king's name may well have been left vague and general precisely because the monks wanted it that way. In the 1250s there was no consistent staff in an established royal chancellery.[98] Kristoffer seems mainly to have used whatever writers were available in the different places to which he travelled. Texts of Cistercian privileges could vary according to the sympathies of their individual composers (who could be bishops) and so do not allow us to postulate clear patterns of royal policies towards individual abbeys, except for Vitskøl.

Besides granting general privileges to Cistercian houses, Danish kings were among their leading donors of properties. But it is much easier in the pre-1215 period to see them in this role. Valdemar II showed none of the same generosity towards the Cistercians his predecessors had done. In 1239 he sold two properties to Esrum.[99] We know of no gifts he made to either Esrum or Sorø. He may have contributed to Vitskøl's wealth, whose property greatly increased up to 1252.[100]

Perhaps the best way to evaluate Valdemar II's role in the life of the Danish Cistercians is through an analysis of his contribution to the settlement of a dispute between the chapter of Viborg cathedral and the Cistercians of Vitskøl. Thanks to the Viborg chapter, we have the full text of a large number of charters dealing with the affair. At first the royal role is not at all apparent, and it is not even clear against whom the Viborg canons were fighting. In May 1216, Pope Innocent III ordered Bishop Ebbe of Århus, the abbot of Øm, and the provost of Vestervig to intervene against the citizens of Viborg, who had moved boundary markers and made invalid judgments concerning the Viborg canons' properties.[101] Thus far the Vitskøl monks are not involved at all, but on 3 June a bull was issued in which Innocent ordered the bishop of Børglum, the provost in Vestervig, and the prior in Grinderslev to judge a land dispute between the Viborg Chapter and the Vitskøl monks.[102] The abbot of Øm has dropped out of the picture, perhaps because, as a daughter of Vitskøl, Øm would be expected to side with its mother house.

The matter had been brought to the papal chancellery by the canons of Viborg, who claimed that the Vitskøl monks had deprived them of their land. The Cistercians were here looked upon as aggressors and troublemakers. Until now most of our sources have reflected a Cistercian point of view, so this set of documents is particularly useful for revealing the other side of the story. After four days the delegation representing Viborg's interests was able to obtain a bull in which the pope ordered the abbot of Vitskøl, the provost of Vestervig, and the archdeacon in Århus to protect the provost and canons of Viborg from attacks by clerics and laymen in the dioceses of Viborg, Ribe, and Børglum.[103] This bull reasserts that the canons were having problems with the townsmen of Viborg. Oddly enough, the Vitskøl abbot was being called upon to help the very community which was accusing his house of unfair practices.

For three years our sources are silent about the outcome of these two, perhaps related, disputes. Then in 1219 came a judgment by King Valdemar II in which the content of the controversy between the monks and the canons was fully revealed and theoretically settled.[104] The monks claimed that they had received a fourth part of the island of Læsø from the canons and had held it unchallenged for years. The canons on the other hand contended that the monks had got only a part of the forest on the island and none of its new fields and clearings. The matter was referred to the king apparently because the papal judges had been unable to reach a decision. Valdemar's decision gave half the meadows that the monks had in their possession to the use and ownership of the canons, while the rest of the meadows and the entire forest area were to remain under the monks. The king tried to impose a compromise by which the monks gave up some of their holdings, while the canons abandoned some of their claims.

If we had this document alone, Valdemar would appear to be an arbitrator in what looks like a reasonable decision. But in another charter from 1219 we learn of the role of Abbot Gunner of Øm.[105] He had been appointed executor of the king's judgment and so worked out the practical details. Together with Jens, the provost of Viborg, and Peder, the prior of Vitskøl, he had gone to the island of Læsø and made a tour of inspection. They had established boundaries by removing bark from trees. In the island's main village, Byrum, Gunner decided that whatever the monks already had taken for building a church or had plowed, they were to keep, while the rest of Byrum was to be used by monks and canons in common. The remainder of the island was so carved up that the western half was left to the canons' meadows, while the monks kept their forest. To the south a meadow area went to the canons. Each party was to have transit through the land of the other and to pasture their cattle in common and to have unrestricted hunting rights for their workers.

Gunner's descriptions of the new division of Læsø are so clear and detailed that one could easily draw a rough sketch of the island's divisions from the charter's contents. In this case a number of institutions cooperated to bring legal settlements without conflict. Cistercian Vitskøl came to terms with the Viborg chapter through the intervention of a Cistercian abbot and the Danish king. The cooperation between Gunner and Valdemar expresses something of what must also have taken place in the drawing up of the Jutlandic Law (*Jyske Lov*) in the 1220s. There too Gunner was active.[106]

The fact that the abbot of Øm was called upon to enact the king's decision in the Læsø case points to Gunner's special position as a man who was trusted and respected not only by other Cistercians but by the very canons who, because of his monastic affiliation, had reason to suspect him of partisan motives. Gunner's election in 1222 to the see of Viborg perhaps occurred partly as a tribute to his successful arbitration. The Læsø problem flared up only once again. In 1274 Vitskøl and Viborg settled a disagreement over a chapel on the island.[107] The outcome in 1274 indicates that the 1219 agreement as a whole was sufficiently solid to last. Only one aspect of it required later clarification. Gunner and Valdemar had succeeded in reaching what so seldom is achieved by arbitrators in property disputes: a lasting and satisfactory settlement.

Nevertheless the Vitskøl monks were not completely happy with what they had gained and given up. In 1221 Abbot Jens and the monks of Vitskøl confirmed the decision on Læsø and mentioned all the terms contained in Abbot Gunner's charter.[108] But when it came to a mention of the meadows stretching from the monks' forests to the east, they were said to have been given 'to the canons' use' by the monks, whereas in Gunner's decision these lands are described as having been 'granted to be possessed by the canons in eternal right'.[109] The monks left themselves a loophole. Another indication of their displeasure is the fact that our only charters mentioning the agreement come from the Viborg canons. It is likely that if the monks had triumphed in the Læsø dispute and obtained all they had wanted, they would have kept a copy of the decision and included it in the Vitskøl Book.

CISTERCIAN LIMITATIONS AFTER 1220

The Læsø settlement provides our last group of documents that shows in detail the monarchy acting in the capacity of protector and judge. After the 1220s the monarchy's relationship with the Cistercian houses of Denmark is less visible, unless it is in terms of royal propaganda. At the same time the Cistercians no longer held a central place in Danish monastic and religious life. As elsewhere in Europe, the Dominicans and Franciscans had arrived. By 1240 at least ten Franciscan houses and three Dominican priories had been founded in Denmark.[110] No new Cistercian houses were begun in thirteenth-century Denmark.

The friars' attention to the spiritual well being of lay people had an immense attraction.[111] The Cistercians could no longer expect the same number of gifts and favours from the privileged and propertied section of lay society that they once had obtained. They responded by doing a great deal to improve and expand their relations with the aristocracy of the countryside and to strengthen their hold over parish churches in the neighbourhood of the abbeys. The only source we have for Danish Cistercian attitudes to the coming of the friars is neutral. The Ryd Annals (AD, p. 109) say quite simply that 'The Franciscans came on bare feet to Denmark and founded a house at Ribe'. The Cistercians did not need to look at the friars as direct competitors because their areas of activity—countryside vs. towns—were different. The danger existed, however, that the Cistercians and their ways would seem uninteresting by comparison with the friars' energy and boldness.[112]

The Cistercians depended on the habits and riches of the countryside to sustain their position, while thirteenth-century Denmark, like the rest of Western Europe, was becoming more urbanized. Friars, universities, and cathedral chapters all did well in this period. Scholasticism was a system of thought ideally suited for crowded and competitive urban centres of learning to which monastic schools now had to take a back seat. But there are also special Danish factors which account for the slowing of Cistercian growth. The decline of Danish military prowess and the weakening of royal power after the 1220s was a blow to the Cistercians. From that time onwards, they no longer could reckon on a strong, supportive monarchy. They became the pawns of kings' attempts to consolidate their power. It is no accident that it was during this period that Esrum failed miserably to reassert its hold over Dargun. Once Danish military power had been removed from Northeastern Germany, the Danish Cistercians could maintain no influence. Similarly Colbaz during this period dealt with neighbour foundations apparently without any intervention by Esrum.[113] Only Sorø can be seen to be involved abroad—with a German Cistercian house—and this is a spiritual bond of no great significance.[114] The attempt by Valdemar to obtain as much money as possible from Cistercian houses by renewing their privileges may very well reflect his own acute need for funds in order to carry on his military program. But the great age of Danish expansion to the south was over, and with it ended the Danish Cistercians' most creative period not only in Mecklenburg and Pomerania but in Denmark itself.

On a local and regional level, however, Danish Cistercian houses seem to have done quite well for themselves during these decades, especially when we take into account the general instability and land ravaging in the 1240s. Vitskøl doubled its properties between the beginning and mid-years of the century. Øm began its church and consecrated it in 1257.[115] Løgum started to build its abbey church in the 1220s and continued it all through these hard years.[116] It gained land to the south and east of the market town of Tønder, around Store Jyndevad, a large complex of fishing and milling properties on a number of streams.[117] Esrum's main building period may have been over by this time, but as at Sorø its monks were busy getting papal and episcopal confirmations of their privileges and exemptions.

During the 1240s Esrum won a great victory in a property dispute. The monks were able to complete their circle of holdings around Esrum Lake by convincing a Nødebo property owner, Saxo Torbernsen, to give up his part in the village to the monks.[118] Nødebo is already mentioned as Esrum property in a 1228 papal charter, so this disagreement may well have lasted for up to twenty years.[119] Saxo had claimed the village as his wife's inheritance but finally admitted that he was only entitled to a small part of it. In the end he chose to maintain good relations with Esrum. His parents and wife's parents were buried there, he pointed out in the charter; apparently he wanted the same for himself and his wife.[120] This is one of our first mentions of lay burials at Esrum, while Sorø, ever since Absalon had moved the Skjalm family graves to the church, had allowed them (regardless of early Cistercian legislation).

Both Sorø and Esrum during this period experienced continuing generosity and devotion from leading local and regional families. When in 1248 Jon Jonsen Lille of Hørsholm (today a prosperous suburb north of Copenhagen) exchanged his property in Lille Værløse with Esrum's holdings in Ordrup and Copenhagen, he was initiating a long series of transactions with the monks. By the time of his death in 1307, Esrum had gained a strategic and valuable new set of properties between the abbey and Copenhagen.[121] Jon Jonsen has been identified as one of the greatest landowners of Northern Zealand and a grandson of Ebbe Sunesen of Knardrup, an important benefactor of Sorø.[122] While some branches of the Skjalm family concentrated their patronage on Sorø, then, others favoured Esrum.

In 1247, on the thirteenth of May at three in the afternoon, a fire broke out at Sorø which badly damaged both the church and the monastic buildings. The compiler of the abbot list left an inventory of the buildings that were destroyed.[123] Among the ruined structures were the monks' and lay brothers' dormitories, the 'greater and lesser guest houses', a bakery, a brewery, the *domus vestiarii*, a house for the subcellarer, a chapel for the bishop, a house for the sacristan, a room for the cellarer, storehouses for tools and garden materials, a weaver's house, stables for horses, a gatehouse, a barn, 'a pumphouse run by artificially contructed wheels', a mill with four paddle wheels, and a mill using horsepower. One of the few objects saved from the outlying buildings was a bell, spared when the fire 'by a miracle' changed its course.

This fascinating list of buildings and rooms gives us an idea of the size and complexity of a great monastery like Sorø. There may have been two quadrangles, the one bordering on the church with the brothers' living quarters, and the other lying to the west and attached to the monastic quad-rangle, where household functions would have been taken care of. It may be, however, that there was only a single quadrangle, and a number of the buildings mentioned were not contiguous with the cloister complex but were independent structures in the immediate vicinity (as surely were the mills described). The existence of two guest houses together with a bishop's chapel points to frequent demands on the brothers' hospitality by the bishop of Roskilde and his entourage, as well as by other dignitaries. The description of the mills shows that the Cistercians had lost none of their twelfth-century interest in using the most advanced engineering techniques of the day.

This great fire could have meant the end of Sorø's greatness, but recovery seems to have been swift. In 1250 Ingeborg of Kalundborg, wife of a Peder Strangesen, a niece of Archbishop Absalon, the daughter of Esbern Snare of the Skjalm family, gave the monks for the remission of her sins her holdings in Bringstrup and Ørslev Østre together with a nearby mill.[124] The income was to provide for the purchase of wax candles which were to 'burn con-tinuously day and night in front of the great altar'. Stone vaulting was also to be constructed in the church. Ingeborg's pious gift facilitated the church's rebuilding. One can almost look upon the 1247 catastrophe as a *felix calami-tas* that incited the monks and their patrons to improve the church.

The account of the 1247 fire and all the buildings that were destroyed reveals not only the extent of Sorø's economic activities but also shows how the monks were able still to obtain valuable gifts from descendants of the Skjalm family. The old spontaneous generosity was nevertheless gone. Inge-borg's gift to the monks was nothing more than her share in the patrimony of Esbern Snare that had all along been owed to Sorø. Ingeborg had waited decades before finally handing it over. This delay may have been due to her husband Peder Strangesen, one of the key figures in a protracted dispute with the monks over Stenmagle properties.

Although local aristocrats continued to support Danish Cistercian houses, their efforts must still be looked upon as sporadic. The problem was that the old rich families like the Skjalms had branched off into lesser clans which did not have the same unlimited land ownership. A gift of land to a monastery meant a reduction in income for the coming generation. What the father gave, the son often held back in order to keep his lands together. Only an unusual son or a loyal wife would see to it that the monks got what had been testamented them. No Cistercian abbey could count on such relationships for anything more than chance additions to its land holdings during this period. Sorø provides a model of the careful, rational care of its property holdings that characterizes Cistercian houses in general. By the time of Innocent IV's 1248 bull, the number of granges under Sorø had grown in twenty years only from nine to ten. But the granges named here show a consolidation of holdings near the monastery and the alienation of properties that were at great distance.[125]

RELATIONS WITH BISHOPS:
NECESSARY COOPERATION AND COMPLICATIONS

Sorø's consolidation of its holdings would have been impossible without the support of the Roskilde bishop and his officials. The bishop was the greatest landowner on the island of Zealand, and Sorø properties were often located in parishes where the archdeacon of Roskilde had special rights.[126] The Sorø Donation Book praises Bishop Peder Sunesen of Roskilde for his determination in seeing that the will of his predecessor Absalon was carried out and that the Sorø monks got the properties rightfully coming to them.[127] In a solemn ceremony at the high altar of Sorø in 1214, the year of his death, Peder Sunesen handed over to the monks all that they were entitled to have.[128] His successors were not as easy to deal with. In 1257, Pope Alexander IV forbade Bishop Peder of Roskilde to fill vacant positions in churches in Sorø's gift.[129]

In the first half of the thirteenth century the Cistercian Order's governing body, the General Chapter, did its best to keep its abbeys free of involvement in parish churches. A 1214 decision is quite uncompromising: 'No one is to receive parish churches'.[130] As Louis Lekai has pointed out, reception of parish churches did not necessarily mean that Cistercian priests acted as pastors.[131] Vicars could be hired and their salary paid out of the *mensa* segment of tithe payments. But such incorporations inevitably meant involvement in the diocesan church. The Order did its best in the 1230s to deal with the tide of incorporations. General Chapter decisions emphasized that no monks should do parish work.[132] But these statements indicate that the Order had accepted an increasing number of parochial incorporations. The General Chapter was fighting a rearguard action to keep abbots from using their own personnel to look after these churchs. Such a procedure was less expensive than the hiring of a secular priest but meant sending a monk for shorter or longer periods out into the world, a practice hardly in accord with early Cistercian ideals and legislation.

Here the Danish Cistercians seem to have followed the international trend. The 1257 papal bull for Sorø indicates that it had parish churches and was already involved in controversy with the bishop of Roskilde in choosing priests for them. Such contact with parish affairs meant that Danish Cistercian abbeys put themselves, at least in this function, under the direct jurisdiction of the ordinary. Exempt from episcopal power in 'home' affairs, the monks were now vulnerable in their ever more pronounced and legalized involvement in lay society.

Open conflicts between bishops and Cistercian houses are nevertheless still rare in this period. The necessary cooperation of the Roskilde bishop can be seen in one legal settlement. In 1254 Sorø and heirs of the provost of Roskilde, Tyge Bjørundsen, decided that the monks were to get two-thirds of a disputed property in Suserup, and the heirs the other third.[133] Also sometime between 1237 and 1241, Pope Gregory IX confirmed the Bishop of Roskilde Niels Stigsen's excommunication of the Lady Margrethe because she had not handed over her son Esbern Snerling's testamentary gift to Sorø.[134] This bishop ended his life at Clairvaux, continuing a twelfth-century loyalty between Cistercian houses and Danish bishops.

But all was not well. Some sources for the activities of bishops and cathedral chapters during the first part of the century indicate that episcopal institutions were heading for clashes with the Cistercian monasteries. Twelfth-century bishops like Sven of Århus and Absalon of Roskilde had handed over to monks rights and properties that had belonged to the bishopric itself. This could be done as long as the bishop was strong, the Cistercian cause attractive, and the chapter weak. But after about 1215, bishops in Ribe and Århus built up their chapters into strong and wealthy institutions. In 1215 Anders Sunesen confirmed Bishop Tue of Ribe's gift of the income of Tønder and Ballum churches to feed and clothe three new canons at Ribe cathedral.[135] Sometime between 1215 and 1224 Bishop Ebbe of Århus set up two new prebends at his cathedral and arranged for their incomes.[136] During the same interval, Bishop Ebbe made a gift both to his canons and to the building of the cathedral. He claimed that under his two predecessors, the construction of the cathedral had been neglected.[137] This unusual criticism by a bishop might help explain what happened between Århus and the abbey of Øm. The bishop and canons may have come to feel that because of generosity to the Øm monks, earlier bishops had not spent enough time and money on the church at Århus.

A growing consciousness among canons of their privileges appears in the so-called Ribe Bishops' Chronicle (*Bispekrønike*), dated to the end of the 1220s.[138] The writer was almost certainly a Ribe canon. He praised Bishop

Tue for his work in reforming the cathedral chapter and evaluated his predecessors mainly on the basis of their work for that cause.[139] Among the
few allusions to Løgum is mention of Bishop Ralph's 1166 visit to Eskil in
France that led to the monastery's foundation. The chronicle also names
Løgum in the cases when the abbey was chosen as a burial site for a Ribe
bishop.[140] So far as the chronicle's author was concerned, the monks hardly
existed. Besides mentioning Tue's efforts for the cathedral chapter, the Ribe
author concerned himself with Tue's attempt to separate priests from their
wives and his mission to Reval in Estonia, where he was captured during
one of Valdemar's campaigns. An attractive personality for the Ribe writer,
Tue was the first bishop of Ribe who is known to have been buried at his
see and not at Løgum.

On the whole, however, the period from 1220 to the end of the 1240s
brought continuing good relations between diocesan bishops and Cistercian
abbeys. Sources other than the Ribe Chronicle show that Bishop Tue probably did as much for Løgum as had some of his predecessors. He was willing
to continue the earlier Ribe tradition of generosity to the Løgum monks,
even if he was caught up in establishing his own diocesan authority. In a
document dated to sometime between 1214 and 1227, Tue took the monks
under his protection and confirmed their possessions.[141] In 1227, Tue handed Daler church over to Løgum.[142] This church, located west of Tønder,
did not have the same strategic importance to the monks as the one at
Nørre-Løgum, but an additional church could mean added income because
of parish tithes. Tue speaks of the monks' 'lack' or 'need'.[143] Although this
may be merely a rhetorical device, it could also indicate that the building of
the abbey church at Løgum, now underway, was causing the monks financial difficulties. They were to provide a vicar for the church and to pay his
expenses, and so the incorporation did not necessarily give Løgum any
financial advantage. Anything left over from the vicar's fee was handed over
'by perpetual right to the convenience of the said brothers'.[144] However little this may have been, it was still offered as a gesture of friendship. Normally in the transfer of a church to a monastic institution, the conditions attached by the bishop emphasize more specifically the rights of the diocesan
organization.[145]

Tue was also responsible for a very important document drawn up by the
Ribe chapter confirming all that the bishops of Ribe had given the abbey.[146]
This written recognition of the Løgum holdings guaranteed the monks
against future quarrels with the chapter. The canons' charter specifically
mentions a number of the monks' holdings that they had obtained from
Ribe bishops. Besides Daler church, the monks also received Lydersholm
southeast of Tønder. The canons say that Løgum gave the bishop something 'equivalent' in return, so there is no question of an episcopal gift. Nev-

ertheless, we can see cooperation among chapter, bishop, and monastery here. The charter ends with a declaration that may have been formulated by the monks themselves, but its affectionate tone is consistent with a respect the canons had for the interests of the Løgum monks:

> Therefore since we love in Christ all religious with intimate and heartfelt devotion, nevertheless we especially embrace these who have been examined by us, with all our affection, because they are more our own beloved ones. And so we confirm all these immunities and collations, and all possessions whatever they are.[147]

Whether or not the canons themselves are the authors of this statement, they allowed it to be drawn up in their name. They gave Løgum a special status not because it was Cistercian but because it was a *local* foundation to which they felt strong bonds. Løgum and other Cistercian abbeys did well in acquiring properties and privileges because the monks managed to maintain the good will of their diocesan bishops and cathedral chapters. It was apparently a matter of pride and prestige for a diocese like Ribe to have a healthy and flourishing Cistercian house within its borders. Monasteries in Denmark became in the course of the thirteenth century local foundations, deeply involved in the life of the countryside and of the aristocracy, and less concerned with their status as part of an international order. This was a natural development once the monks were accepted as part of Danish society, but it made them less attractive to churchmen who looked to religious institutions for spiritual inspiration. Here as elsewhere the friars took over, and the Cistercians had to count more on their legal prowess and on local patriotic appeal than on their international reputation.

Danish Cistercians could usually count either on the friendly neutrality or the active cooperation of their diocesan bishops. Tue's successors, Gunner and Esger of Ribe, were both buried in Løgum abbey church. Esger received this honour despite the fact that he was identified with the royal party and so acquiesced in measures taken against Øm Abbey in the 1260s.[148] Bishop Peder Elavsen gave the monks of Øm beautiful volumes with gold lettering (despite early Cistercian regulations) and chose to be buried there.[149] At Vitskøl the monks could count on the Cistercian bishop Gunner, once the abbot of Øm. His Cistercian biographer emphasized his respectful ways in telling of a visit he as bishop paid to a house of the Order.[150] So long as Gunner was bishop of Viborg, Vitskøl had no reason to fear episcopal encroachments. His successor at Viborg, Niels, who was also royal chancellor, confirmed all of Gunner's privileges to the Cistercian house.[151] Niel's brief charter merely says that the monks could continue to enjoy the same rights and immunities over their labourers and incomes as they had under Gunner, but he thereby endorsed the policies and favourable treatment of his popular predecessor.

Although the record of episcopal-monastic relations is scanty for the Zealand abbeys and for Vitskøl and even for Øm, we have a wealth of privileges from Løgum that deserve mention. In 1237 Bishop Gunner of Ribe confirmed a property transfer.[152] A certain Keld, first in the presence of Bishop Tue and then before Gunner, had handed over to Løgum all that he owned in fishing places south of the town of Tønder, and in Lydersholm mark, a few kilometres to the east. In return he had received from the monks lands in Lydersholm with a number of fishing places. Keld was entitled to fish in all of Lydersholm mark, except in the pond next to the monks' mill. He promised that after his death all his rights would revert to the monks, who thereby gained entrance to the rich fishing and milling area south and east of Tønder. The Løgum monks' boldness in striking out to the south in a completely new area parallels the Esrum monks' first attempt in the 1240s to build up a new belt of holdings between themselves and Copenhagen.[153]

Bishop Gunner of Ribe issued the charter between Løgum and Keld while staying at Løgum. Apparently the bishop spent as much time as possible there, for in a document from 1238, also drawn up at Løgum, he received a gift of property near the abbey site from the monks.[154] The location is described as being next to the chapel of Omer, Gunner's predecessor as bishop of Ribe.[155] At Øm there is also mention of a so-called bishop's house and documentary proof that the bishop of Århus visited the abbey once each year for a few days.[156] Despite Cistercian legal immunities and full exemption from episcopal jurisidiction, we find in Denmark a close relationship between diocesan bishops and Cistercians which until about 1250 manifested itself in frequent episcopal stays at Cistercian houses. Eventually permanent quarters for the bishop close to the abbey were established as the most convenient arrangement. The 'bishop's chapel' mentioned in the 1247 Sorø fire indicates that the bishops had all they might need in the Cistercian house in their dioceses.[157]

In the charter for his new property, Bishop Gunner received as much land as he might need for the buildings, but he was to put them up at his own expense. He would be allowed to use them as he liked for as long as he lived, but after his death the title to them would revert to the monks. Future Ribe bishops were thus not to have an automatic *pied à terre* at Løgum without first negotiating the matter with the monks. As at Øm, the monks welcomed the bishop but did not concede that the ordinary had a right to stay with them or occupy a permanent residence in or near the abbey.

Løgum also had dealings with the bishop of Slesvig, for even though it was in the diocese of Ribe, some of its properties were located in the diocese of Slesvig. In 1238, the same year as Bishop Gunner was allowed to make his property purchase, the bishop of Slesvig took Løgum's side in a dispute over land.[158] In a letter to the archbishop of Lund, the bishop of Slesvig recounted his efforts to mediate between Løgum and a certain Ubbe Tordsen. He had called the 'best men of the whole province' together to judge the matter: almost two hundred of them. Only two spoke against the monks, and one of them was Ubbe's own brother. Summoned to state his case, Ubbe had refused to come. The bishop of Slesvig delineated the boundaries of the Løgum property, a fishing and marsh area with mills about twenty kilometres southeast of Løgum, to the east of the area where the monks had recently made significant gains.

Like the bishop of Ribe, his colleague at Slesvig also sought the monks' hospitality. In a 1248 renewal of Løgum's reception of the tithe from Bylderup parish, Bishop Eskil of Slesvig stated that he and his men 'very often' came to the abbey 'for the sake of its hospitality'. Claiming that he did not want the brothers 'to be excessively burdened by expenses',[159] he confirmed a donation given long before by his predecessor, Bishop Valdemar of Slesvig.[160] One little phrase in this confirmation weakens the monks' position and strengthens Bishop Eskil's use of the privilege in establishing his right to expect hospitality. Bishop Eskil hinted that the original donation may not have been legitimate in the first place: 'We approve [of it] if it was made legally'. Eskil may be indicating that Bishop Valdemar's ill-fated revolt against the king invalidated his donation.[161]

Bishop Eskil used a possible objection to the legitimacy of the Løgum holding in order to appear as a benefactor rescuing the monks from embarrassment and any challenge to their property rights. At the same time he asserted a right to be fed and housed. Long before a bishop of Århus in the 1260s insisted on his right to stay at Øm with his servants and men at the monks' expense, the issue was being discussed at other Danish Cistercian abbeys. The close involvement and interdependence of bishops and Cistercian abbeys shows how far we have come from theoretical statements in standardized papal bulls concerning Cistercian exemption from episcopal power. The monks' involvement with bishops seems an inevitable fact after the death of Valdemar II in 1241. Distant from Clairvaux and Citeaux, the Danish houses had to live with a weakened monarchy and lay landowners who often regretted the generosity of their ancestors. The Cistercian abbeys as institutions became more dependent than ever on good relations with diocesan bishops. With this practical motivation and the Benedictine Rule's clear insistence on reception of all guests, the Danish Cistercian houses had little choice but to bid their bishops welcome. In the process they conveyed the impression that bishops had a right to visit them yearly and to expect good treatment.

The expenses and demands of hospitality are clearly expressed in a 1251 agreement between Bishop Esger of Ribe and Løgum.[162] He gave the monks a farm east of Tønder, close to the area where they had been making gains during the preceding decades. Like Eskil at Slesviĝ, Esger stated that he and his men often came to Løgum.[163] The brothers were to be compensated by being allowed to keep two-thirds of the dairy production on the farm for their own use, while they were to reserve a third for the needs of their guests. The wheat and other products from this property were to be at the abbot's disposal. To ensure against future trouble, Esger added the seal of his chapter to the deed. This arrangement is a case of *donations-gæsteri*, hospitality given in exchange for donations to the monks.[164]

SIGNS OF CHANGE IN THE 1250s

The Danish Cistercian abbeys succeeded in a number of ways in gaining material wealth and prosperity by the 1250s. Vitskøl vastly increased its property holdings. Sorø constructed a great complex of buildings and workshops that were probably replaced after the 1247 fire. Løgum's mill and fishing system in the streams around Tønder meant a solid source of income, while the farm from Bishop Esger guaranteed milk production for the monastery. Løgum continued to gain properties in the 1250s and in about 1256 was sufficiently well off to take in a community of monks from a disbanded Frisian abbey.[165] This was the abbey of Marienhafen, which in 1250 had been attacked by various lay magnates. Forced to flee, some of its monks came to Denmark and settled down at Løgum. The fact that the monastery could take in the extra numbers indicates that it had a surplus of wealth, something every Cistercian abbey in Denmark was constantly trying to achieve by land acquisitions. Løgum's arrival at this goal can also be seen in a 1257 privilege by King Kristoffer giving the monks freedom from tolls for their ships in all of the kingdom's harbours, especially that of Åbenrå.[166] This indicates that the monks were carrying on commercial activities by ship from Jutland's eastern coast.

Whether as merchants or as patrons of parish churches, the Cistercians exposed themselves to the ways of the world. So long as they could count on sympathy and cooperation from the powerful men of church and state, they had nothing to worry about. But once society was polarized and one upper class faction fought another, the monks were in trouble. In taking sides they jeopardized their relationship with at least one of the social groups on which they depended: bishops, local landowners, the royal circle, or the peasants. In the 1260s when ideological and personal divisions rocked the kingdom, the monks could not remain neutral.

In the next chapter we will consider where the various Cistercian abbeys stood in a dispute between King Erik Glipping (1257–86) and the Archbishop of Lund Jakob Erlandsen. This conflict ended for good the days of

royal and episcopal protection and favour for the Danish Cistercians. Without the continuing support of the bishops, the good era would have come to
an end by 1230, but here the Cistercians were fortunate. The activity and
personality of Bishop Gunner of Viborg may also have played a role. As a
courteous, diplomatic man, he could see to it until his death in 1251 that his
religious order and all its claims and rights were given fair and even preferen-
tial treatment by the other bishops of the kingdom.[167]

A sign of the approaching end of good relations is the Roskilde Cistercian
nuns' acquisition in 1257 of a cluster of privileges and confirmations from
Pope Alexander IV. He confirmed Absalon's gift of property.[168] The bull
explains that the nuns had asked the pope to establish Absalon's gift of two
mills and land because Roskilde was a new foundation and needed a solid
economic base.[169] Another charter confirmed Absalon's gift of the incomes
from various villages on Zealand together with a third of all gifts brought to
the grave of the local Saint Margrethe.[170] Most revealing of all, Alexander
forbade laywomen to lodge in the monastery for more than a brief
period.[171] The nuns feared the burden and expense of semi-permanent
women who wanted a comfortable home without taking vows of religion.
In the words of the charter, the monastery suffered 'a serious loss, and the
leisure of holy contemplation is greatly disturbed there'.[172] For a moment
the otherwise unknown history of the Roskilde Cistercian nuns comes alive.
The nuns must have had great difficulties in trying to attract gifts of land
from noble ladies who could easily end up as permanent pensioners indifferent to the discipline of religious life.

By the 1250s Sorø and Esrum, like Roskilde, seem to be more caught up
in defending already-gained privileges and properties than in trying to get
new ones. Løgum, however, was still extending its holdings. But even
Løgum was no match for the Augustinian house at Æbelholt in Northern
Zealand, not far from Esrum. At the end of the 1240s it came out of what
looks like a thirty year pause in new acquisitions and began profiting from
devotion to the cult of its founder, now Saint William.[173]

If we look outside Denmark to Esrum's daughter Eldena, the contrast between the mostly settled Danish abbeys and the still expanding Pomeranian
neighbour is apparent. In the 1240s Eldena had obtained a number of valuable charters from the princes of the island of Rygen and Pomerania. In
1252 it acquired its first property on Rygen.[174] During the same period, Eldena became involved with the neighboring town of Greifswald, over
whose market the abbot Andreas obtained full rights in 1241. When Eldena's possessions were confirmed in 1248, the possibility that Danes as well
as Slavs and Germans might settle on them was mentioned. Colonists were
to observe the law of the community where they settled.[175]

Danish Cistercians played little or no role in the growth of Eldena. From the time in 1232, when the Esrum abbot was called in by the General Chapter to settle a dispute there, until 1273, when the Eldena abbot was removed from office and then became prior at Esrum, the mother and daughter abbeys seem to have had little to do with each other.[176] The Esrum abbot may well have performed his visitation regularly, but Eldena's growth and prosperity during these years had nothing to do with its connections with Denmark.

By the mid-thirteenth century, the Danish Cistercians had not stopped growing in terms of adding new buildings and lands to their abbeys. But in terms of relations with the leading groups in Danish society, the monks had become less important. Bishops had begun to concentrate on their cathedral chapters. Towns in general took up more episcopal attention than before, and so did the friars. The shaky monarchy still tried to prop itself up by making declarations of loyalty to the monks in order to emphasize links with ancestors. Lay landowners still looked to the monks for burial and prayers, but for most of their lives they treated the monks as nuisances and irritations rather than as allies.

The Cistercians had by no means outlived their usefulness to upper-class Danish society. But they had begun to demand more from this segment of society than it felt it got from them. Thus began conflicts between stubborn monks, who could not see how things had changed in the preceding decades, and angry opponents, who could not understand how the monks could be making such unreasonable claims. It is not here a matter of the secularizaton of society or the failure of Cistercians to live up to their spiritual mission. The sources normally only allow us to see the monks in their economic function, so we can say almost nothing about their religious life. But it is clear that the appeal the monks had because of their spiritual function became weaker for the upper class. At the same time the monks refused to see or concede that they had become any different than their brethren had been a century earlier.

V
Catastrophe and Recovery
1257–1307

I N THE SECOND HALF OF THE THIRTEENTH CENTURY the Cistercians continued to play an active and significant role in Danish society. The consecration of the abbey church at Øm in 1257 and the settlement of a complex and vital property dispute at Sorø in 1307 are two events among many that bear witness to the monks' ability to build, grow, attract gifts, and, despite challenges, to keep them. In this respect nothing had changed since the halcyon days of the twelfth century.

Behind this facade of continuity, however, much was changing. Bishops began making demands on Cistercian houses within their dioceses that the monks felt they could not meet. For a century the abbeys had been able to count on the benevolence or at least the neutrality of local bishops, but at Ryd, Sorø, Øm, and even Vitskøl, differences that had long remained beneath the surface now emerged. In the cases of Ryd and Øm, the results were disastrous.[1] Vitskøl and Sorø did not experience the same bitterness, while Løgum seems still to have been favoured by helpful bishops. The confrontation was basically due to the fact that old rights and privileges were being taken up again, investigated, questioned, and reformulated. In such a process many Cistercian abbeys felt their prerogatives and immunities from episcopal interference were being undermined.

A related problem was the relationship between the Cistercians and the monarchy. Here too the monks had long been able to rely on either benevolence or neutrality. Now, however, they had to take sides in a violent quarrel between the king and the archbishop of Lund, Jakob Erlandsen. Initially all the Danish Cistercian houses backed the archbishop and therefore faced a hostile monarchy. Many of the abbeys quickly became reconciled to the expediencies of the political situation. Only Øm and Ryd remained loyal to the archbishop to the bitter end. Trying to remain on good terms with both factions, the monks attempted a difficult balancing act.

No longer able to count on either bishops or kings, the monks could also expect little support from the Cistercian General Chapter. The yearly meeting took on much less importance for the Order as a whole after a dispute between Clairvaux and Citeaux broke out in the early 1260s. The number of decisions involving Danish abbeys during these years diminishes drastically in comparison with the preceding period. Danish abbots went to Citeaux less often, probably because the General Chapter's decisions made little difference in solving the problems they faced at home. For a brief moment in the 1260s the Danish abbots worked together, meeting, discussing the controversy between Øm abbey and Bishop Tyge of Århus, trying to settle a revolt at Tvis abbey, looking for a common policy in the dispute between king and archbishop over the church's rights and privileges in society. These efforts did little good in providing a settlement between Øm and its attacker, the bishop of Århus. From this spurt of energy and cooperation resulted withdrawal into localism, with each abbey fending for itself. After the 1260s it looks as if Cistercian abbeys in Denmark abandoned their sense of belonging to an international order and concentrated on looking after themselves.

In the economic life of the abbeys, we also find that old structures and relationships were giving way to less ambitious forms and practices. The number of lay brothers in Danish houses, as elsewhere in Western Europe, declined significantly during this period.[2] Vitskøl and Øm curtailed their building programs before the naves of their churches reached half their projected length. Economic instability followed a decline in gifts and a lack of vocations. There was no longer any need to add extra space for a large choir of lay brothers. The monks had to hire more peasant labour to cultivate the old granges, while scattered holdings were no longer consolidated into new. By the end of the century, grange farming had become outdated, and the monks began to lease individual small holdings to peasants and require a yearly payment. The Cistercians, who had begun by cultivating the land with their own hands, alienated themselves from the soil in every sense except the administrative.

During these difficult transitional years, it appears at times as if the entire Cistercian Order in Denmark was on the verge of collapse. The Cistercian abbots themselves in one of their appeals to the cardinal legate, Guido, during the Øm controversy expressed precisely this fear.[3] The Øm monks end their chronicle with a pitiful statement on the condition of the monastery in which they leave the impression that the abbey will not last out the year and soon all the monks will be dispersed.[4] The realization that society—the king, the bishops, and parishioners in neighbouring local churches—was willing to sacrifice the interests of the monks came as a shock to the Cistercians.

But the monks' pessimism was not completely justified. Despite loss of profitable gifts from male members of aristocratic families, the monasteries remained attractive to widows and continued to gain new holdings. In a few cases Cistercian houses took on the task of administering the testaments of such women. At the same time the monks were able to solve some property disputes without alienating their opponents. By showing a willingness to compromise, they gained most of what they considered rightfully their own. Thus there is a gap during these years between what the monks could feel about their position in society and what they actually accomplished. Sometimes we find Cistercians consciously or unconsciously manipulating the truth. Like members of many established institutions, they came to look upon their survival and prosperity as ends in themselves.

EMOTIONS IN THE CHRONICLES:
BITTERNESS AND NOSTALGIA

Perhaps the best short introduction to what the Danish Cistercians felt during this period is the Ryd Annals, probably composed some time during the last half of the thirteenth century.[5] They compass Danish history from mythical antiquity to 1288. The problem of its composition and relationship to various other annals is a thorny one that calls for the same detailed and exhaustive study already done for the earlier period by the Danish historian Anne Kristensen.[6] Fortunately the Ryd Annals are much more informative than some of the other contemporary annals. Even if we cannot establish their exact dependence on predecessors, the thirteenth century entries clearly reflect the attitudes of a monk or monks at Ryd Abbey who experienced events after the death of Valdemar II (1241) as one long series of catastrophes for the kingdom of Denmark and for their own exposed borderland monastery. The Ryd Annals are closely related to the Ryd Chronicle.[7] The Annals end in 1288, while the author of the Chronicle dates his composition to 1289. While the Annals deal with contemporary history and show how events had conspired against the abbey, the Chronicle records the abbey's foundation and claims that the monks had been deprived of the security and prosperity they should have had.[8] Both accounts reflect a monastic institutions's yearning for peace and stability, for strong bishops and strong kings who would take monasteries under their wings and provide for them. The problem was that almost a century had gone by since such kings and bishops had existed in Denmark or had been so partial to the Cistercians.

The closer the Ryd Annals get to mid-century events, the more pessimistic the tone. The death of Valdemar II in 1241 brought war and dissension.[9] In 1247 King Erik Plowpenny burned down the castle of Svendborg, and fierce quarrels between him and his brother Abel devastated the countryside. In 1259 a third brother, Kristoffer, died and was succeeded as king by Erik Glipping, far worse for the monks than his father or uncles had been:

> Erik his son reigned. He brought many evils on the churches by plundering and did no justice for those who had been injured and harmed. Also the monasteries, which his forefathers had built through their own efforts and those of their followers, he impoverished wretchedly by his horses and dogs.[10]

When Erik assumed the throne, he was only a boy of 10, so it is likely that our writer at Ryd remembered him from the vantage point of the 1270s or early 1280s, when Erik followed his mother, Margrethe Sprænghest, in treating the Cistercians harshly and demanded their loyalty in the monarchy's conflict with the archbishop of Lund.

The Ryd author makes no mention of a charge made against the abbot of his house, Arnfast, that he had poisoned King Kristoffer.[11] He says merely that Kristoffer died. The Sorø Annals, which cover the years 1130 to 1300 and are known as the Older Sorø Annals, claim that Kristoffer died by poison.[12] This difference can perhaps open up an aspect of Danish Cistercian history not sufficiently appreciated: the analysis each individual house makes of the situation and its independence of its sister abbeys. Sorø may have sided with the monarchy, while Ryd and Øm defended themselves at the cost of royal sympathy and even risked outright enmity by their harsh criticism.

A further indication of different approaches to history at Sorø and Ryd is the way the Sorø Annals in reporting the same events as the Ryd Annals, abstains from making similarly critical remarks.[13] For Ryd the decades after 1240 were a bitter experience, while for Sorø the period receives no particular characterization in the Annals. The entire controversy between the monarchy and the church is left out. Jakob Erlandsen is first mentioned in 1274 at his death.[14] The Sorø Annals end in 1300 and so were composed either in the preceding decades or else soon after that date. Their lack of polemics may point to a Cistercian desire at the end of the century to cooperate with the monarchy and forget past disputes.

Leaving the sparse annals and turning to more generous chronicles, we find more material for comparison. Despite differences of approach, the narratives originating from Sorø and Ryd reveal the same Cistercian attitudes. At both houses the monks looked back on an earlier, easier period in their history. Both chronicles yearn for a strong, friendly monarchy. In the Ryd Chronicle of 1289, the writer describes the abbey's foundation history in order to wax nostalgic about a golden age that would have come about if only Bishop Valdemar of Slesvig had been allowed to remain at his post. The bishop's memorable words, 'You are called Golden Isle (Guldholm), and if I live, I shall gild you', sound the keynote for Ryd's history. Our writer mourns that such a beautiful sentiment had not been realized:

> But alas! His hope deceived him, and he was not allowed to carry out his so pious proposal. For, not long afterwards, he was taken captive and expelled from the kingdom.[15]

By themselves these lines explain why the account was written. All coming generations were to be shown that Ryd had been deprived of the realization of its true greatness because its greatest patron had been imprisoned.[16] The Cistercian writer rams his message through because it is so vital for his interpretation of Ryd's tragic history:

> Therefore, Guldholm and your sons, weep and lament for the quick and untimely fall of your most pious father because while he lived, an abundance of all good things flowed forth for you, but once he was taken away, you remained impoverished and hidden away, insignificant among your sisters and despicable.[17]

Our writer's lament involves an explicit comparison between Ryd and its sister houses. His claim that Ryd was worse off than other Cistercian abbeys cannot be substantiated, but that he should have made it is surprising in view of the state Øm seems to have been in at the end of the century, after years of dispute and impoverishment.

But the assertion can be understood better if it is looked at in terms of the entries in the Ryd Annals for the decade. In 1283 Bishop Jakob of Slesvig deprived the monks of the tithes of parish churches that they collected despite the original Cistercian prohibition against such incomes. Ever since the monks moved to Ryd in 1209, they had been getting parish tithes deeded them by the bishop of Slesvig.[18] Bishop Jakob is also alleged to have had some of the monks thrashed.[19] His attack seems to have led to a dispersion of the community in 1284.[20] In one of the Danish versions of the Ryd Annals, the writer adds that the monks were scattered to their 'great sorrow and unhappiness'.[21] When in 1287, Bishop Jakob of Slesvig died, the Annals commented that he was 'more a tyrant than a bishop'.[22]

Normally the Danish Cistercian narrative sources are extremely cautious and do not make bald accusations. Only charges by the Øm monks against Bishop Tyge of Århus contain a similar harshness of language. One of the Danish versions of the Ryd Annals merely says that the bishop of Slesvig was dead and makes no personal comment about him;[23] this may point to a later revision at a time when the monks desired peace with the bishop's successor.[24]

If we look at the Ryd Annals and the Ryd Chronicle as a unity expressing prevailing Cistercian attitudes in this abbey, one consistent theme stands out: the desire for a strong, stable monarchy.[25] The Annals begin by listing Danish kings from mythological times.[26] Here they draw on earlier annals but they emphasize consistently that only a wise monarch can rule the country properly and provide the necessary conditions for monastic survival. The anger of the Annals and the nostalgia of the Chronicle reflect a frustration with internecine strife in the royal family, with greedy kings, rapacious bishops and their indifference towards monastic needs.

At Sorø, we find less transparent attitudes. The part of the Elder Zealand Chronicle covering the period to 1251 was probably composed at this monastery during the second half of the thirteenth century.[27] The author was satisfied to take excerpts from other chronicles or hagiographies he found interesting or relevant, and to summarize, shorten, or take them over wholesale. The partisan prejudice of the Ryd Annals gives way to a seemingly impenetrable neutrality.

If we analyze the Elder Zealand Chronicle in terms of the author's choice of borrowings, however, a clear pattern of preference reveals something about monastic attitudes. In a way much more subtle than the glosses of the Ryd Chronicle author, the Sorø compiler looks back on an earlier period in which the Cistercians were the driving force of monastic renewal in Europe and were accorded a privileged position in society. He borrows from the account in Bernard's *Vita Prima* of how he spread the Order and points out Eskil's praiseworthy desire to save it. Saxo's passage on Eskil's withdrawal from his post as archbishop is used—but only a favourable section of it. This is followed by accounts of Eskil's childhood dream of punishment and reward, his foundations in Denmark, and his last days at Clairvaux.[28] Our Sorø monk also mentions the martyrdom of Thomas Becket and some of his miracles, thereby implying the link between the great archbishop and the Cistercian Order.[29]

The Sorø writer concentrated on the efforts of the Clairvaux Cistercians under Bernard to open the North to the new monasticism. He borrows the story from the *Exordium Magnum* about the monk Bernard promised would be able to return from Sweden to die at Clairvaux.[30] As in the bulk of Danish Cistercian literature, to which the Øm and Ryd sources provide significant exceptions, the writer reveals himself only indirectly. But his purpose is clear. Whatever benefits the Cistercian Order he emphasizes.

By its careful selection of narrative sources, the Elder Zealand Chronicle becomes just as much Cistercian propaganda as the Ryd Chronicle. An earlier, better age is posited, in direct or indirect contrast to the present situation in which Cistercians are either ignored or openly attacked. This yearning for a better past is also apparent in the Life of Bishop Gunner, which belongs to the 1260s or 1270s.[31] The author of the Life was not angry, like his Ryd colleague, or impersonal, like the Sorø compiler. He extols Gunner's virtues and his attraction on people from all levels of society. But by his biographer Gunner was transformed into a mythical personality radiating kindness, gentleness, well-being and, most of all, security. So long as Gunner was bishop at Viborg, the place of the Cistercians in Danish society was clear. The author mentions nothing about the troubled decades that followed Gunner's death, but the very attractiveness of the portrait hints at the pain of loss felt by the monks.

The second half of the thirteenth century brought a new wave of Cistercian historical writing in Denmark that exceeded in quantity if not always in quality the productivity of the first period of Cistercian history writing shortly after 1200. The Ryd Annals and Chronicle, the Øm Chronicle and the Life of Gunner, the Elder Zealand Chronicle, and the Sorø Annals for the years 1130–1300 all belong to the years after 1250. Their content points to a Cistercian desire for a strong and generous monarchy, fear of the incursions of local bishops, and a fierce defence of rights and privileges. Most of all, these works reflect a growing nostalgia for better days when the Cistercians in Denmark were well treated and did not have to assert their claims in the legal and political mazes of an increasingly complex society.

THE BALTIC FRINGE: TWILIGHT OF DANISH INFLUENCE

Danish Cistercian frustrations at home are reflected in an almost total disengagement from the chain of abbeys by then established along the southern shores of the Baltic. By the 1250s Esrum had lost forever any claim to paternity over Dargun abbey. Even with its two daughters in the region, Eldena and Colbaz, Esrum's involvement seems to have been extremely limited. In 1283 at Colbaz Abbot Mogens of Esrum ordered the abbot there to send a confessor to Cistercian nuns at the nearby town of Stettin.[32] The abbot of Esrum affixed his seal to the document, as did Herman, abbot of Colbaz, and Johannes, abbot of Eldena. The abbot of Eldena must therefore have accompanied the Esrum abbot on his visitation. It is likely that earlier the same year Abbot Mogens had visited Eldena and taken Johannes with him on the long trip east to Colbaz.

Despite a lack of other documents indicating cooperation among the three abbeys, the abbot of Esrum probably made fairly regular visitations of

Eldena and Colbaz. In 1275 the Cistercian General Chapter ordered the abbot of Clairvaux to travel personally to Eldena to find out why the abbot had been deposed.[33] This monk was now prior as Esrum, and indication that its abbot had in some way been involved with Eldena's events. A decade later, Eldena again had trouble, and now the role of Esrum is clearer. Some documents belonging to the abbey of Ourscamp in France had been taken by the monks of Eldena. Its 'father abbot', which must mean the abbot of Esrum, was ordered to enquire into the matter. [34] Like most of the General Chapter's records, this notation is disappointingly short but it indicates that the recognized system of mother-daughter abbeys still functioned in the Baltic despite the eclipse of Danish political influence in the area.

Most decisions of the Cistercian General Chapter regarding Colbaz indicate little about contact between daughter and mother house. In 1277 the abbots of Colbaz and Doberan were ordered to look into a quarrel between the abbots of New Doberan (or Pelplin) and Oliva, both near Gdansk. In the same year Colbaz and Chorin (Brandenburg) were ordered to inspect a location in Poland proposed for a new monastery. This seems to have been the abbey of Himmelstädt, for in 1278 the abbots of Colbaz and Chorin were given full powers to make a foundation there.[35]

Another indication of Colbaz's development outside the sphere of Danish Cistercian influence, aside from occasional visitations during this period, comes in the Colbaz Annals.[36] They say nothing at all about Denmark, but concentrate either on local events in Pomerania or what today is Poland or on matters of concern for the entire Cistercian Order. The Clairvaux-Citeaux dispute is referred to in an entry for 1264 saying that in this year the abbots of the 'Clairvaux and Morimund line' were not present at the General Chapter. Similarly it mentions a dispute in 1275 between the Franciscans and Cistercians which led to a decision by the General Chapter that the monks were to have no association (familiaritatem) with the friars until fitting satisfaction was provided by the Franciscans.[37]

In 1247 Colbaz burned down. The Colbaz Annals mention this fire only, while the Ryd Annals state that in this year both Colbaz and Sorø were destroyed by fire.[38] This slight addition points to an essential difference in cultural orientation between the Southern Jutlandic Danish abbey and the Polish house. The Ryd chronicler wanted to give a cross section of important Cistercian events in the whole area associated with Denmark, while the Colbaz writer was more regional in his outlook.

Colbaz may have had good reason for concentrating on its own problems. In 1269 local magnates attack monks and lay brothers of the house on what apparently was one of its granges. The monastic personnel were 'violently ejected' and at the time of writing, the usurpers were 'still holding' the property 'without any right'. Similiarly Oliva, Colbaz's daughter further east, was having trouble. In 1226 and 1236 it was also ravaged by fire, the second time 'totally' and by 'pagans'. In 1271 unnamed laymen did a great deal of damage to the monastery and laid waste the whole district. The same fate came to Colbaz itself in 1273 when the neighbouring area was 'seriously ravaged' and the monks' church damaged.[39]

Colbaz and Oliva thus experienced in the 1260s and 1270s the same exposure to secular magnates' quarrels and destruction that Øm and Ryd had lived with ever since the 1240s.[40] As seen through its Annals, Colbaz was a relatively isolated Cistercian house trying to make its way in a violent society. This parallel to the situation of Danish Cistercian houses could have fostered new links between Esrum and Colbaz, but there is no evidence at all for such contacts. It would be wrong to argue from silence, but Colbaz appears from its Annals to have had no concern for Danish events and did not look to Denmark's Cistercians for aid.

During this period, too, Eldena seems to have functioned more or less independently of its mother house, Esrum. At the end of the century it bought property on the Danish island of Rygen in the Baltic and began a conscious program of expansion there.[41] The monks readily accepted the social conditions of the island and bought rights as feudal lords.[42] Similarly the Cistercian nuns at Bergen on Rygen, who had made their foundation from Roskilde, did what they could to buy up villages as feudal fiefs.[43] We do not know if Sorø was concerned for the nuns at Bergen, as it was for those of Roskilde, but in at least one instance we find Eldena involved with Bergen.[44]

The foundation of a Cistercian house at Hiddensee just off Rygen points to continuing growth for the Order in the South Baltic despite the general stagnation of new foundations in Denmark and elsewhere in Europe. Along the Baltic shore, there was a steady increase in the number of Cistercian houses.[45] These foundations come from daughters and granddaughters of Morimund, whose line dominated the area, because of Doberan. After its victory over Esrum, Doberan seems to have grown into the leading Cistercian house of the region.[46] Hiddensee was actually founded by Neuencamp south of Stralsund, which had itself been founded in 1231 by Doberan.[47]

The case of Hiddensee shows how complicated it could be to assure the existence and continuity of such late foundations. On 13 April 1296, a charter drawn up by which Prince Wizlaus II of Rygen gave the new abbey the island of Hiddensee and the village of Zarrentin.[48] In June Bishop Jens of Roskilde, as bishop of Rygen, gave his permission for the foundation.[49] In a property sale a year later by Ingefred, widow of Anders Erlandsen, and her son, the monks had to untangle a number of rights and claims before they could hold the island in peace. Ingefred claimed that Wizlaus's simple transfer of half the island and full legal jurisdiction over it was improper, for he ignored her property and rights.[50] The Neuencamp monks bought out Ingefred's claim on the island for a hundred marks of pure silver and two hundred marks in Wendish money. A number of conditions were added: inhabitants of the village of Schaprode would continue to have the right to collect wood; Ingefred's pigs could still forage on the island, and a number of fishing places were reserved for her men.

It looks like an amicable settlement, even if the monks had to pay for it. But continuing rights on Hiddensee for Ingefred's descendants made future quarrels likely. Another party now came forward with claims against the monks: Wulfard, parish priest in the village of Schaprode on Rygen. Because the monks had been given the care of souls on Hiddensee, formerly in his care, Wulfard may have regretted the loss of income now that he had fewer parishioners. On 23 March 1299, a settlement was arranged.[51] Wulfard claimed he had done everything possible to prevent the building of an abbey on Hiddensee and had been helped in his efforts by two canons of Roskilde cathedral. But Wulfard was eventually convinced that the new Cistercian house would be doing a spiritual service to the community by providing the sacraments at all times, while he 'because of the difficulty of crossing the arm of the sea' often was hindered from rowing over to Hiddensee.[52] Wulfard's unselfish motives in giving up his resistance may well have been genuine, but his sudden recollection of the importance of having priests on the spot makes it seem likely that the monks had made it worth his while to consider pastoral needs.

We should add here that the founding of a new parish by separating an area from an old parish almost always created problems in the medieval church. There were vested interests which had to be placated, especially when there was a question of monks taking over functions from secular priests. The role of the Roskilde canons is not made clear, but they were trying to defend the assumed rights of a priest in their diocese against monastic incursion. Such resistance was common in the diocesan church but seems to have increased in the course of the thirteenth century because of stagnation of incomes and a greater awareness of canon law procedures.[53]

After the settlement with Wulfard, Hiddensee continued its efforts to obtain secure legal and economic foundations. In 1302 Duke Valdemar II of Jutland sold the abbey additional property on Rygen for 1000 Wendish marks.[54] Thanks to the abbot of Neuencamp the new community had met the challenges of secular landowners and parish priests and could now begin a program of expansion. Among the witnesses to this sale were Arnold, abbot of Neuencamp, and John, abbot of Dargun. The Neuencamp abbot's presence is natural on such an important occasion for the new daughter-house while the Dargun abbot's participation indicates Hiddensee's link to the Morimund-Doberan family of Northern Germany. It would be easy to forget that Hiddensee-Rygen were in the diocese of Roskilde and part of the kingdom of Denmark, for almost all the spiritual links were to the south. But the bishop of Roskilde is not completely invisible. In September of 1302, the bishop-elect, Oluf, transferred the jurisdiction of the island of Hiddensee from the parish church of Schaprode to Hiddensee Abbey's chapel at Gallen. This transfer was confirmed in 1306.[55]

From the initial agreement with Wulfard in 1299 to the final confirmation by the Roskilde bishop, in 1306, the Hiddensee monks had done all they could to normalize their relationship with the diocesan church. The Cistercian abbeys' willingness to take over parish functions was probably partly due to the alteration of the Cistercian economic base: now that the abbeys were more dependent on lay tenants than on lay brothers, they began to interest themselves in the pastoral needs of these workers.

At the same time Hiddensee was dealing with the bishops of Roskilde, Doberan became involved with the Danish king, Erik Menved (1286–1319), because of his feudal sovereignty over Rostock.[56] Once again a Danish authority and a Morimund-branch monastery dealt independently of any apparent contact with the Cistercians of Denmark. One might think that Erik Menved's increasing involvement in Northern Germany at this time would have led to a renewed Danish Cistercian interest in reclaiming lost houses like Dargun or even in starting new daughter abbeys. But the Danish houses were either too weak or too caught up in their own affairs to be tempted by the opportunity. In the twelfth century Danish Cistercian expansion followed faithfully the Danish political and military advance southward. The whole area along the Baltic shore and inland was open to new religious foundations. But now the situation was quite different. The Morimund line had established its hegemony over the southern shore and islands. There was hardly any room for Danish Cistercian expansion. In the 1330s when the first new Danish Cistercian house in one hundred thirty years was founded, it was on the island of Zealand itself, about half-way between Esrum and Sorø, on the site of one of the old estates belonging to a branch of the Skjalm family. The new foundation of Knardrup would have to face even more claims and privileges than Hiddensee. The age of expansion for Danish Cistercians was decisively over, both inside and outside of Denmark. Neither the ephemeral foreign policies of Erik Menved nor Sorø abbey's surplus of lands could make any real difference in giving the monks opportunities for new foundations.

THE DECLINE OF DEPENDENCE ON
INTERNATIONAL STRUCTURES

The few papal bulls issued to Danish houses and a halving of the number of decisions from the Cistercian General Chapter concerning Denmark indicate that the Danish monks were much less involved on the international scene than they had been in the preceding period. During the Øm controversy in the 1260s, however, when the monks sought support abroad, there was lively contact between Danish Cistercian houses and the south. After it contacts became much less frequent. The frustration the Danish Cistercians felt over the impotence of international institutions in influencing the outcome of the Øm controversy probably led them to depend less on these bodies.[57] In positing such a cause-effect relationship we are making a conclusion that cannot be directly substantiated from our sources. As so often, the Danish Cistercians are tremendously loud when fighting for something dear to them, but after they give up the battle, their silence and inactivity could mean almost anything. But certainly disillusionment played a role here.

The monks' mistake during the 1260s was their failure to realize the basic connection between their troubles at Øm and the greater issue of the dispute between king and archbishop. The monks turned for help to Archbishop Jakob Erlandsen and thereby transferred a local dispute to the national stage. In siding with the archbishop, they became enemies of the monarchy. The other abbeys, except for Ryd in Southern Jutland, were much more cautious. All the Danish Cistercian abbots became embroiled in the Øm controversy and soon experienced the futility of their solidarity when it came to dealings with the king, with his mother Margrethe, with the papacy, or even with the Cistercian General Chapter.

The first appeal of the Danish abbots to the pope came on 6 May 1263, when they informed Urban IV that Øm had been attacked by Bishop Tyge of Århus and asked for papal protection.[58] The Øm controversy had grown out of a disagreement between the monks and Bishop Tyge concerning his right to collect from the abbey yearly procurations, the benefits of hospitality, as his predecessors had done. The monks insisted that such procurations were given voluntarily, while the bishop considered them his right.[59] The abbots of Herrisvad, Esrum, Tvis, Vitskøl, and Holme all signed the appeal to the pope. On the same day they were joined by the abbots of Sorø, Løgum, and Ryd in appealing to the abbot of Citeaux and the General Chapter.[60] Also on 6 May, all these abbots asked Jakob Erlandsen as archbishop to punish Bishop Tyge for his behaviour.[61] At the start of the controversy, the Danish Cistercians seem to have had faith in international organizations' power to further their interests. Queen Margrethe likewise tried in the years around 1263 to influence the General Chapter.[62]

But Bishop Tyge was far too quick for the Danish abbots. His master stroke was to forbid the Øm monks from carrying out priestly functions in the parish churches incorporated under the abbey.[63] This decision in itself reveals Øm's dilemma: as a Cistercian abbey fiercely aware of its exempt status from episcopal jurisdiction, Øm like so many other Cistercian houses had submitted itself to episcopal authority because of its involvement in the parish system. The monks now had to choose between defying the authority of their bishop or recognizing his rights over them. The Øm monks defied him, and this act may have alienated some of the other abbots. While in May the Danish abbots had reacted in a solid front, in October only the abbots of Esrum, Løgum, and Ryd complained to Pope Urban against Tyge.[64] But during that spring and summer, Øm still could count on the other abbots. On 10 May the abbots of Vitskøl, Holme, and Tvis assembled in Århus cathedral, transmitted Abbot Bo of Øm's second appeal and witnessed that Tyge had denied Bo the letter of appeal for which he had asked.[65] Niels, bishop of Viborg and royal chancellor, was present. Both he and Bishop Esger of Ribe managed to stay on the king's side during the dispute with Jakob Erlandsen and yet did everything possible to resolve the dispute between Øm and Tyge.

In January 1264, the new abbot of Øm, Ture, sent two monks, Lars, and Bo, to represent the abbey at the curia, and their visit seems to have done some temporary good.[66] In May, Pope Urban ordered the Benedictine abbots of Ringsted and Næstved to punish Bishop Tyge if he did not stop his attacks on Øm.[67] A whole string of papal bulls was issued on 22 May, yet their effect was so minor that it has been suggested that they were only drafts which the Øm monks brought home despite their lack of authority.[68] By now the other Danish abbots seem to have begun to distance themselves from Øm's cause. In June 1264, Esbern of Esrum, witnessed a charter at Greifswald.[69] He was probably making a visitation at Eldena. The fact that he went south instead of going to Jutland to help Øm as he had done in the spring of 1263 points to a desire on his part to conduct business as usual instead of expending all his efforts on the Jutlandic abbey.

Clairvaux now entered the fray. In September its abbot sent a letter to Queen Margrethe encouraging her to protect Øm against Tyge. The abbot of Clairvaux championed the Øm monks without using the bitter, hysterical language that they themselves had come to employ.[70] This letter may have done some good, for in November at a meeting in Århus cathedral the bishops of Ribe and Viborg tried to gain acceptance for a compromise by which Abbot Ture of Øm was to give Bishop Tyge of Århus the same amount of yearly procurations as Øm had given his predecessor Peder Elavsen.[71] This solution would have saved face for all parties concerned and shows that a sincere effort was being made on the part of the episcopacy to reach a solution. But it was not accepted.

From the autumn of 1263 onwards, abbots from other Danish Cistercian houses seem to have done their best to avoid involvement in the Øm controversy. On 21 May 1263, Bishop Niels of Viborg gave Vitskøl exemption from paying the tithe even if its property was worked by secular labour.[72] This was a landmark recognition of a change in the status of Vitskøl's agricultural land. The monks had probably been long dependent on tenants instead of laybrothers, but the bishop now accepted the monastery's economic immunity despite the change. It can hardly be a coincidence that this privilege was issued by Bishop Niels, who supported the king, only a fortnight after the complaints made by the Danish abbots against Bishop Tyge. Similarly, the absence of Vitskøl in the October appeal to the pope suggests a desire to play a less vocal role and thus reach a compromise with the help of its own Bishop Niels.

The height of the Øm controversy, 1263–64, is marked by a number of incidents that emphasize a close relationship between bishops loyal to the king and Cistercian houses in their dioceses. In December 1263, Bishop Esger witnessed the deeding of a shop in Ribe to the Løgum monks, the first instance we have of Cistercians' gaining town property in Denmark.[73] A few months later, March 1264, Bishop Esger forbade parishioners in Daler, where Løgum already had had probelms, to appoint their priest or make any decisions without the consent of the abbot of Løgum.[74] The contrast with contemporary events at Øm is striking. At Løgum bishop and monks cooperated to maintain the monks' rights in a parish. At Øm, Bishop Tyge did his best to isolate the monks by severing them from pastoral duties. Both Løgum and Vitskøl, which were among the Cistercian houses geographically closest to Øm, had reason to maintain good relations with their bishops and not get too involved in Øm's dispute. Similarly Esrum in the summer of 1265 was given a motive for keeping to benevolent neutrality. In June it gained its first new possessions for a number of years, and its charter to them was confirmed by King Erik Glipping.[75] In July the abbey was given general exemption from payments to the king and a guarantee of royal protection.[76] The king and his advisors may have been trying to isolate Øm from its mother house at Esrum by making the latter indebted to them.

While the papal legate and Cistercian cardinal, Guido, was on his way to Denmark to solve the disputes between king and archbishop and between Øm and Århus, the Danish Cistercians' main concern was to protect themselves from any extra expenses he might impose on them. So in March 1266 they met at Sorø and witnessed a 1257 bull from Pope Alexander IV by which the Cistercian Order was exempted from collections and all other papal exactions.[77] After Guido arrived, he was convinced to issue a charter for Løgum in August stating that the monks there were not obliged to pay anything for his stay as legate.[78] In 1221 a previous papal legate to Denmark, Cardinal Gregory of Crescenti, had stayed at Løgum. The collective memory of the monks, or tales about other papal legates, may have encouraged the Cistercians to apply for such guarantees.[79] So we have the irony of Danish Cistercian abbots arming themselves against their own Cistercian confrère coming as papal legate!

At a time when one would expect the other Danish abbots to be backing up the abbot of Øm, they were seeking to protect their own interests. Sometime before 21 May 1266, they did issue a complaint to Guido about Bishop Tyge's attacks on the abbey and asked him to punish the bishop,[80] yet their interest in Øm seems to have stemmed from a fear that the dispute threatened their own abbeys. The Cistercian abbots asked Guido to punish Tyge because 'it is to be feared . . . that by his example other bishops in the kingdom of Denmark' might be encouraged to turn against their Cistercian houses. 'Already', they claim, this possibility 'is evident for us by their threatening words'.[81] Diocesan bishops were apparently warning the Cistercians that unless they reconciled Tyge's claims with the demands of Øm, they could expect rough treatment. The Cistercian abbots had a common fear to unite them in welcoming Guido to Denmark, but as earlier in the dispute, their solidarity did not last for long. In the ensuing months, only the Ryd and Øm abbots remained with Guido, as they were in September at Slesvig when Guido ordered the king to put Jakob Erlandsen back into office.[82] A month earlier, the abbot of Løgum had obtained from Guido an important confirmation of its holdings in Brede.[83] It would have been appropriate for him to back up the legate in the affair of Øm. But the abbot of Løgum was conspicuously absent. From this time onwards Danish abbots put up only token resistance to the bishop of Århus and gave little visible support to Øm.[84]

It is easy to understand why the abbots reacted this way. When Cardinal Guido came in the spring, they had been taken in by Øm's euphoria that now all wrongs would be righted. The other abbots had apparently made no objection to the Øm monks' insistence on total vindication. Øm had collected all its old grievances against Bishop Tyge and sought to crush the bishop completely and avenge what he had done to them.[85]

The alliance with Guido did not pay off. In November 1266, the Løgum monks had to chase after him to Lübeck to get the legate to issue a charter ordering the Brede parishoners to cease hindering Løgum from exercising its rights over their church.[86] Apparently Guido had issued a charter to the inhabitants of Brede which supported them and contradicted an earlier charter to Løgum.

The Brede mixup is symptomatic of Guido's failure to bring clear, consistent solutions to Danish disputes. After doing no good at all for Øm, he left Slesvig in October and headed south, hotly pursued by the Øm abbot, who in Lübeck complained to him about Bishop Tyge's continuing attacks.[87] On 30 November in Magdeburg, Guido appointed a protector for Øm, the bishop of Slesvig, the man most likely to raise suspicions at the Danish court. Such a move could easily convince the monarchy that the Øm monks were playing mid-Jutland into the hands of the enemies of the crown in Sles-vig.[88] Bishop Bonde vainly summoned Tyge to his court at Slesvig in 1267, and his procedures had little effect on the situation.[89]

In the beginning of February 1267, the Danish Cistercian abbots begged King Erik Glipping to order Tyge to stop his attacks, threatening that, if he did not, he would have to accept that the abbots might pursue the matter before the rightful spiritual judge.[90] The letter is a strange combination of desperate plea, threat, and apology for the actions about to be taken. The abbots claimed that if they did not react immediately, then the monks would have to be sent away and Øm would cease to exist as an abbey.

The decisive act that ended Danish Cistercian support for Øm came on 22 February 1267, when Duke Erik Abelsen declared his protection for the ab-bey. The cousin of King Erik Glipping and the son of King Abel (1250–52), Erik threatened the throne of Erik Glipping. After this time there were no more joint appeals to the king. The trial of Tyge at Slesvig continued under Bishop Bonde, but the procedure had become irrelevant. On 3 August 1267 Tyge was excommunicated. In September Cardinal Guido at Lübeck con-firmed the judgment.[91] King Erik Glipping had already been excommunica-ted in 1266, and Denmark placed under interdict.[92] Aside from Peder Olsen, a Franciscan historian who wrote in the sixteenth century, there is no evidence that the Danish Cistercians observed this interdict, which specifically included them, and stopped celebrating the liturgy.[93] In April 1268, Erik Glipping renewed Esrum's privileges.[94] Since he had just done so in 1265, Erik's move must be looked upon as a political one, occasioned either by his own ambitions or by the request of the monks themselves that the monarchy and the Danish Cistercians reach a quiet understanding. Skyum-Nielsen has already pointed out how unlikely it is that Cistercian houses keeping the interdict would have gone to the king for a renewal of privileges.[95]

In June 1268, the king confirmed Esrum's labourers' exemption from mil-itary services and other payments to him. A week later he did the same for those working for the Roskilde Cistercian nuns.[96] Since this monastery was administered by Sorø, the privilege indicates an understanding between the king and Sorø. Sometime in 1268, Erik confirmed a boundary for a Sorø property.[97] An indirect hint of the Cistercians' non-observance of the inter-dict is a bull from Clement IV, who in asking the Danish people to stop per-secuting those who kept the interdict mentioned only Franciscans.[98]

There were nevertheless apparently some Cistercians in Denmark who were upset about their Order's cooperation with the monarchy. In 1268 the General Chapter ordered an inquiry into a 'conspiracy' at Tvis Abbey.[99] Monks and lay brothers had revolted against their abbot and harmed him bodily. The matter was handed over to the abbots of Herrisvad and Ryd, the first because of its status as mother abbey. Prior to the chapter's decision, all nine Danish Cistercian abbots wrote it about the matter and asked that the abbot of Tvis be restored to his former position.[100] This revolt may well have been connected to the Øm dispute and the question of whether or not to obey the interdict.[101] It was the prior of Tvis and not its abbot who had been involved in summoning Bishop Tyge to the court at Slesvig. This could indicate that the abbot of Tvis had disagreed with the prior and had refused to accept the authority of a court set up in order to try the bishop of Århus for his treatment of Øm.[102] In any case, Tvis was split. For a last time in their history, all the Danish abbots can be seen coming together in order to rectify a scandalous situation.

The Tvis revolt could indicate that the desire of the abbot for reconciliation with the monarchy had not been accepted by some of the monks and lay brothers. Such unrest among the monks is underlined by a 1269 decision from the General Chapter in which the abbot of Holme on Fyn is said to have physically ejected the father visitor, the abbot of Herrisvad.[103] This incident may have no connection at all with the Øm controversy itself, but it is another sign of the failure of the Danish Cistercians in these years to form a united front and to respond with a common voice to the threat facing them.

All during this controversy we find the monarchy reaping the benefits of the lack of agreement among the Cistercian houses by issuing charters that the individual houses needed. In January 1269, King Erik increased Løgum's privileges. In February, he guaranteed Vitskøl's.[104] Løgum was still plagued by its Brede controversy, but Bishop Esger backed the monks in an appeal to the pope.[105] In 1269 King Erik took Løgum under his protection.[106] In August he exempted the labourers of Sorø from being drafted into work on fortifications.[107] The charter was issued just north of the abbey at Pedersborg, a symbolic and significant spot, for it was from the fortress here that the monks in the early years of the century had been subjected to attacks and insecurity. Finally in June 1270, King Erik extended his benevolence to Øm itself and forbade anyone from hindering the work of the monks' caretaker of their farm at Purup.[108] Thus the very king whose men had so harassed the monks a few years earlier acted now as their loyal protector. The monastery at Øm had come full circle into the fold of royal favour.

The Danish abbots risked a great deal in ignoring the interdict and turning to the monarchy for protection. Jakob Erlandsen of Lund and Bishop Peder of Odense, a Cistercian himself, attended the Cistercian General Chapter in 1269 to gain support for their cause against the Danish monarchy.[109] The fact that the Danish abbots were indifferent to what happened at Cîteaux shows how convinced they had become of the greater importance for them of maintaining good relations with the king than depending on the international structure of the Order.

In a 1270 decision the General Chapter ordered the Danish abbots to obey the papal legate, Cardinal Guido's, findings.[110] The only edict issued by Guido that the abbots had reason to disobey at this point was the interdict itself, for Guido's other decisions involving the Danish Cistercians had almost all been in their favour. The Chapter ordered the abbot of Esrum to make this decision known to his brethren, so he was probably present at the Chapter. The abbot somehow managed to return to Denmark and temporize until the interdict was lifted in 1274. But Esrum especially had every reason to continue its policy of maintaining good relations with the monarchy.

On 29 October 1271, Esrum received from the king a mill and adjoining properties at Sode, immediately north of the monastery on a stream linking Esrum Lake with the sea.[111] In exchange Abbot Esbern had to hand over Esrum's properties in Lille Værløse, relatively far to the south, a minor sacrifice in view of what the monks gained. The transaction gave Esrum economic independence in its home region. The monks likely had a mill of their own further upstream near the monastery itself, but the king's previous ownership of a mill a very few kilometres away meant that the grinding of grain could have taken place either at the monks' or at the king's mill. Now the Esrum monks had no more competition.

The detail and precision of the terms in this charter indicate the importance of the mill as a source of income.[112] With it is mentioned its toft, the dam backing up the stream, and all of the surrounding inundated area, together with whatever marshy areas lay between the mill and the monastery. All of this, claims the charter, once belonged to the king. For more than a century the monks had had to accept the fact of alien ownership and rights on their doorstep. They were also given all the roads leading to the mill, together with a special road that went from the monastery across royal land to the public road beneath a hill called Sodebjerg. The roads are different today, but Sodebjerg hill to the northwest of Esrum gives us an excellent idea of locations.

The document states a desire to prevent both Sode Mill and a mill further downstream at Hulerød from changing ownership. The monks agreed not to retain too much water at Sode and to assure that Hulerød Mill would be able to get what it needed. At the same time royal officials were to allow the peasants who had done their milling at Sode to continue there instead of being sent downstream to Hulerød. No new mills were to be constructed between Sode and Hulerød, and water levels were to remain as they were.

The witnesses to the charter, issued not far from Esrum at the royal fortification of Søborg, point to the solemnity of the occasion: Jens, bishop of Børglum, who had been a pupil of Bishop Gunner of Viborg and now was close to the king; Otto Count of Ravensberg; Junker Erik, brother to the Swedish king; Absalon Andersen and Oluf Haraldsen, descendants of the Skjalm family and involved in many transactions with both Sorø and Esrum during these years; Junker Erik, son of Duke Knud; Jens, provost on Falster and the royal notary; Erik, the king's chaplain and a canon of Lund; and Poul Hvid, the royal bailiff at Søborg.

Such a document points to a continuing alliance between Cistercian houses and King Erik Glipping. Regardless of the efforts made by Archbishop Jakob Erlandsen and Bishop Peder of Odense at Cîteaux in 1269 to get support, most Danish Cistercian abbeys by this time had decided it was best to go quietly over to the royal party, or at least to withdraw from the fray. Only Ryd and Øm showed solidarity with Jakob Erlandsen. Because of its immediate dependence on the dukes of Southern Jutland, Ryd had good reason to resist the royal party. Even Øm, despite its spectacular confrontations with Bishop Tyge, eventually found it expedient to seek reconciliation with Tyge's royal backers. In 1270 the monks gave way to the need for royal protection.

In the autumn of 1272, at the time of the Cistercian General Chapter, Bishop Peder of Odense, again at Cîteaux, witnessed a bull of Pope Gregory IX from 1234 in which he gave the Order his protection against magnates who misused their right of patronage to burden the abbeys with unjust levies and demands on their hospitality.[113] Bishop Peder was doing a favour for the Cistercians in backing their claims and in verifying the authenticity of their documents, but there is an air of unreality about his actions. He was operating in a vacuum, for no matter what he did at Cîteaux, he could expect no help back in Denmark from the Cistercians in regaining his diocese.

A final indication of the revised political situation which drove the monks into the king's camp and away from the General Chapter, can be seen in an appeal by the abbots to King Erik Glipping.[114] It came sometime during 1272 and concerned Løgum's rights to Brede church. This right of patronage to the church had been given to Løgum in 1252 by King Abel, and confirmed by Bishop Esger of Ribe in 1272.[115] Various efforts had already been made by Cardinal Guido as the papal legate in the late 1260s to reconcile the conflicting claims of the parishioners and the Løgum monks.[116] Guido's help was just as inadequate for Løgum as it had been for Øm. The monks had had to appeal to the pope. In October 1272 their efforts paid off. From Pope Gregory X they received confirmation of their rights to Brede. He assigned the provost in Slesvig to protect the monks against robbers and plunderers.[117] A month earlier, the General Chapter had given the Løgum abbot a special dispensation. This indicates that he had gone first to Cîteaux and then to the papal court at Orvieto.

Instead of supplementing the papal action by asking help from the General Chapter, the Danish abbeys turned to King Erik and asked him to prevent his men from attacking Løgum's access to the right of patronage over Brede. The document asserts that the Løgum monks had performed 'devout services' and provided 'voluntary tasks' to the kings predecessors in time of peace and war.[118] The monks promised that if the king heard their request, they would offer prayers for him throughout the whole Order. There is no hint here of the traumas of the preceding decade, no indication that Erik or his mother had treated the Danish Cistercians far from well. As in the Øm controversy, the Danish abbots as a group were diplomatically forgetting an unpleasant side of life. In disputes like that at Brede, where royal officials, privileges and involvement are clear, and where local peasants made trouble for the monks, the Cistercians realized that only royal good will and actions could safeguard them.[119] Rather than making wild claims with tactless bitterness as had the Øm monks, the Løgum abbot and his monks mobilized brother abbots to secure a royal response.

This rapprochement with the monarchy seems to have been led by the abbot of Esrum. Esrum was the first Cistercian house during the Øm conflict to gain a royal privilege, and the Sode Mill exchange provides supplementary evidence of the abbey's closeness to the monarchy. In June 1273, still a year before the interdict was lifted, King Erik, once again at his Søborg fortress, conveniently close to Esrum, for the third time in less than a decade exempted the abbey from all payments to him, and he handed over to the monks the right to collect judicial fines.[120] The proximity of this privilege to those of 1265 and 1269 provides more evidence that both sides wanted a new understanding. The steady flow of royal privileges for Esrum, Løgum, Vitskøl, Sorø, and even Øm during these years indicates that the Cistercians were seeking a settlement with the king after their accusations a decade earlier against his trusted ally, Bishop Tyge of Århus.

After the abbots' common appeal to the king in 1272, we find no more instances in which Danish Cistercians join in common cause. The documents we have from the period point to the abbeys' concentration on local concerns and individual survival. The decisions of the General Chapter in the 1270s show little about the situation of the Danish abbeys. In 1272 it granted a petition by Løgum that it be allowed to observe the anniversary of its founders in the abbey.[121] In 1227 Ås and Ryd's abbots were given permission to be absent from the Chapter for a single time.[122] In 1281, however, Vitskøl's abbot arrived with a dramatic request: he asked if his house could be dispersed.[123] Later in the decade Ryd was dispersed, but it lodged no similar request with the General Chapter. This and similar omissions have been ascribed to the likelihood that the Danish Cistercians simply chose the occasions when they appealed to the General Chapter and when they ignored its authority and took care of matters themselves.[124] This latter tendency becomes more marked than ever during these decades.

Vitskøl's problems seem to have originated with the appearance of a Franciscan bishop, Peder of Viborg. Chosen by Jakob Erlandsen in the 1260s, he was able to assume office only in 1281. He encountered some resistance from the cathedral chapter, which had favoured another candidate, whom Peder put in chains. This action led to a papal inquiry.[125] The Vitskøl dispersal may have resulted from subsequent unrest in the diocese. It is clear from a later document that the monks quarrelled with Bishop Peder, but the exact issue is not clear. In 1286 a settlement was reached and ratified by Archbishop Jens Dros of Lund, who refers to the bishop's insistence on a 'right which he had against those monks'.[126]

Problems continued. In 1287 Vitskøl burned down. In 1291 fire consumed Herrisvad.[127] The abbeys of the region were ordered in 1291 to contribute to the rebuilding of Herrisvad, though the General Chapter took into consideration the possibility of resistance to its provisions for help.[128] In 1293 the appeal for contributions had to be renewed, and this time Vitskøl was also included among the abbeys to be aided.[129] The 'intolerable poverty' of both houses was mentioned, and this observation seems justified by architectural evidence that the west end of Vitskøl's church never reached its projected length. The building programme apparently stopped soon after 1290. The materials used for the west end of the church, added after the fire, are shoddy and cheap, a pitiful contrast to the solid and carefully hewn stone of the pillars in the proud ambulatory built earlier in the century.[130] Also the floor tiles are plain and mostly unglazed. The purpose of the building operation seems to have been merely to finish the church in a subdued and hasty way. Funds had run out. There were fewer lay brothers. Little help seems to have come from sister abbeys.

The very General Chapter that had tried to inspire, encourage, and finally enforce cooperation among Danish abbeys was ignored or resisted in the 1290s. In 1291 it ordered an inquiry into the 'insolence' of the abbeys in Denmark, Friesland, and Sweden towards their rightful visitors from Clairvaux and Citeaux.[131] In 1292 the General Chapter insisted that Clairvaux and Citeaux's authority over the abbeys in these regions remain in force despite resistance so that these abbots in their visitations could employ full powers of punishment and correction.[132]

Efforts to help Danish abbeys seem to have been vain. In 1294 the appeal for aid to the burned abbeys from 1293 was renewed because the abbeys still lacked funds.[133] During the rest of the 1290s the General Chapter's decisions for Denmark are routine. In 1292 the abbot of Løgum requested that his attendance that year could be counted for the year on which he was supposed to come, one more indication that Danish abbots had an arrangement about attending the Chapter only once every few years.[134] Five years later Ås was granted permission to celebrate the anniversary of its founder.[135] In 1297 the abbot of Herrisvad was excused from attendance at the General Chapter for five years.[136] The abbeys seem to have been having trouble in getting back to normal.

During the 1280s and 1290s, the General Chapter continued to involve itself in the affairs of the Danish Cistercians, but it no longer functioned as a rallying point for Danish Cistercian solidarity as it had done in the 1260s. Even the system of visitation by Clairvaux and Citeaux came under attack. As we near the end of the century, centrifugal forces pulling the Scandinavian abbeys away from the centre of the Cistercian Order increase. A similar development is apparent elsewhere in Europe, as at the abbey of Balerne in Franche-Comté.[137] In 1281 this abbey, like Vitskøl and Ryd, was dispersed. It had been unable to meet the financial demands being made on it. After this time there are no decisions in the General Chapter involving Balerne until 1389. The abbey seems to have maintained a shadow existence during the intervening years and may have continued as a Cistercian house. Available records suggest that it survived only because of a close alliance with a powerful magnate. In order to survive it had to accept the new political facts and give up any hope of getting help from Citeaux.[138] The quarrel of the 1260s between Citeaux and Clairvaux had weakened the international structure of the Order.[139] Each abbey had to find its own most practical course of action. At Balerne as at Esrum and other Danish abbeys, the most common response was to look for help from secular powers and to expect little from the General Chapter.

The language of the appeals to Danish abbeys to help their sisters reveals the General Chapter's impotence. Charity towards those nearby is emphasized first, but in the end force is mentioned as a means of making charity work: 'Let them contribute from the goods given them by God for the sake of charity. But if they are negligent or remiss, they are to be forced to do so by inquisitors or visitors sent there by the authority of the General Chapter, if it be necessary.'[140] The General Chapter anticipates the role that it would play in Scandinavia and elsewhere after the fourteenth century's wars and schism: it would appoint one abbot after another to collect levies due the Order. Esrum and Sorø would be made into tax collectors for the entire northern region.[141]

TROUBLESOME ROYAL WOMEN
AND GENEROUS FEMALE DONORS

The Øm controversy of the 1260s might well have gone in the monks' favour had it not been for the interference and involvement of Erik Glipping's mother Margrethe.[142] She had already given the monks a taste of her arbitrary demands in 1260 when she and her soldiers took up quarters in the monastery.[143] From the death of King Kristoffer in 1259 until Erik reached his majority, she virtually ruled Denmark and made life miserable for the Cistercians. Margrethe's contempt for Øm stands out against her devotion to the Cistercian Order as an international organization. But this contrast underlines the local and national problems the Danish abbeys faced and their inability to turn to the international structure of the Order to cope with their everyday problems.

During these decades from 1270 onwards into the first years of the fourteenth century, the Danish Cistercians had to come to terms both with royal women as well as with female benefactors. In both cases the problems were exceedingly complex, for the women, with all their special desires and attitudes, could only function in relation to a male-dominated society. Thus even if the monks over a period of decades could cultivate cordial relationships with women, they might find at the end that all their efforts had been made in vain because male heirs had run off with property testamented by a widow to the monastery.

The monks' most visible problems were with royal figures who used them for their own political purposes. Such is the case with Agnes and Jutta, daughters of King Erik Plowpenny. In 1263 Agnes founded a Dominican convent in Roskilde and then a number of years later, after both she and her sister Jutta had been prioresses there, they abandoned their vocations to run off with men.[144] The scandal and its implications created a wealth of documents and attestations. It was a source of embarrassment and even danger to the monarchy, where descendants of former Danish kings might all too readily assert their claims. Also the properties with which the royal sisters had endowed the new convent were extremely valuable and important for the monarchy itself. The queen mother, Margrethe, and her advisors had vainly tried to divide the inheritance of King Erik Plowpenny in a manner acceptable to all parties involved. In the 1280s the case reached the royal court itself and was handed over to a special commission.[145] Agnes and Jutta did their best to get the lands back in order to keep them for themselves or else to hand them over to others. Agnes especially showed great political cunning in transferring some choice Zealand holdings to none other than the monks of Sorø.[145] She thereby gained an ally in her attempt to separate herself from her convent.

Cistercian abbeys, like other institutions collecting documents important for their social or economic wellbeing, could occasionally omit what was not in their favour. In the case of Agnes we find in the Sorø Donation Book an instance in which the monks' manipulation of facts for their own purposes can be seen in all clarity.[146] The Cistercians fought hard to maintain their security and the intactness of their membership. The greatest threat to them was the possibility that their members would find the Cistercian way of life too hard and decide to try another. But in the Agnes dispute we find the Sorø monks giving moral support to a woman who had left her convent. The Sorø writer tried to rationalize her action by blaming a strict and unfair discipline in the religious community that Agnes could not accept.[147] This sympathy camouflages the fact that so long as Agnes held to her decision to leave the convent, the Sorø monks would be able to keep their new property. The Sorø compiler was either naive or consciously biased in expecting his public to accept his excuses for Agnes as the expression of a disinterested concern for her vocation. Sorø had everything to lose if Agnes were forced by the secular and ecclesiastical establishment to return to her convent.

In the end the Sorø monks managed to keep the land they had obtained from Agnes, despite the fact that King Erik Menved took the monastery under his protection and demanded the return of all its holdings no matter what had happened to them.[148] The nuns fought Sorø for as long as they could, but by 1300 they apparently gave up and came to terms with the monks.[149] In other property disputes during the latter part of the thirteenth century the monks might go on for many decades without getting what they wanted. But this time they were able to overpower the resistance of a convent of nuns. In both this and the Øm controversy we can see the same Cistercian stubbornness and manipulation of the truth for the sake of property and rights.[150] The Sorø monks had an opponent they could overcome, while the Øm monks lashed out against the one man whose support or at least neutrality they could not do without.

The alliance between Sorø and Agnes shows how the monks could profit immensely from taking up the cause of women in need. In the period between 1272 and 1292 a good number of land transfers involving Danish Cistercian monasteries were carried out with women. Even if we are seldom given any idea of the personal relationships behind such transactions, it is very likely that the monks had made themselves known to such women years before they had drawn up their wills and had managed to convince them of the value and efficaciousness of their lives. The popularity of the Cistercians is surprising when we note that on Zealand two mendicant convents for women had been founded in Roskilde and were eminently successful in attracting female donations. In giving to the Roskilde Dominican or Franciscan convents, women were often assuring themselves of a place to retire in peace and to be taken care of in their old age.

One of the most informative of all Danish wills, that of Gro, the widow of Esbern Vagnsen, from 1268, follows this pattern.[151] She handed over the administration of all her bequests to the nuns of the Roskilde convent of St Clare and herself became one of its members. Among Cistercians abbeys, only Øm was remembered, for it belonged to the part of mid-Jutland to which Gro had family bonds. Otherwise, her generosity was lavished on the

Dominican houses all over Denmark. The very best legacy was for the Ros- kilde convent itself. The only exception to this pattern of generosity is a comparatively large gift of eight marks to the Johannite priory in Antvor- skov, while three marks were handed over to each of the Zealand Franciscan and Dominican houses.

Such a testament, from which the Cistercians are almost absent, can hard- ly come as a surprise in view of the impact the friars had on Denmark after 1220. The Cistercians were from 1220–1270 caught up in securing and consolidating their earlier gains. But after about 1280 donors again began to name the Cistercians in their wills. A new period of enrichment began for many of the Cistercian houses, largely through the generosity of female donors. This is the case with a testament drawn up in 1287 by Lady Juliane, daughter of Tule Bosen and a descendent of the Skjalm family.[152] She ex- pressed the wish to be buried with her parents at Sorø and with them to await the last day. The family bonds of life were to be continued in death. The lands Juliane gave were of great value, for they were south of Sorø near the stream called Susâ in an extremely fertile area. In return she also asked that the monastery send a pilgrim to the Holy Land in Jerusalem, another to St Peter's tomb in Rome, and a third to St Nicholas' in Bari. A grave monu- ment once at Sorø showed a handsome young man dressed for travel as a pilgrim. This man may well have been a representation of the traveller sent by the abbot on one of Juliane's pilgrimages.[153] Juliane's request for both burial and three pilgrimages shows that her bond with Sorø was more than a matter of family custom. It was a commitment involving specific demands on her and on the monastery.

Juliane lived at least another fifteen years. When she renewed her agree- ment with Sorø in 1287, she gave her property only in return for other Sorø holdings.[154] The monks consented to the arrangement and mentioned Juliane's 'great friendship' with them, even if they had to give up lands which they claimed were worth ninety marks in silver. The Sorø monks had to accept hard bargains to get what they wanted in this period, and even apparently generous women who were devoted to Cistercian houses could set strict terms.

Sometimes, however, there were no strings attached. In 1274 Lady Cecilie, daughter of Peder Ebbesen and a relative of one of Northern Zea- land's biggest landowners, Jon Lille, gave Esrum property in Kollerød, along the belt of land Esrum had been accumulating during the previous decades. In her charter Cecilie named Esrum specifically as 'the place which I love more affectionately than others'.[155] During this period and even more so in the fourteenth century, lay donations focus only secondarily on the Cister- cians as an order. They concentrate their attention on individual houses. Cecilie expressed her attachment to Esrum not because of its Cistercian af- filiation but because it had played an important role in her life.

Cecilie was only one member of an extended family that felt a bond with Esrum. All through this period Jon Lille and his relatives were endowing the monastery with gifts and asking for prayers in return.[156] Cecilie's donation was made in the presence of King Erik and Queen Margrethe, one more indication of royal cooperation with Esrum after the Øm controversy was over.

In 1275 Esrum received a gift from another Cecilie, this time the sister of Jon Lille. The transaction was confirmed by her son Anders Pedersen Vædder.[157] A third Cecilie is mentioned in Sorø in 1279, when Bishop Stig of Roskilde ordered Oluf Tagesen to hand over to the abbey a farm which he had taken into possession even though his sister, the Lady Cecilie, had willed it to the abbey.[158] Here we have a classic case of a male relative's resistance to a woman's gift to a Cistercian abbey. Once again we have run into descendants of a branch of the Skjalm family which was so important for Sorø from its very beginning. Now in the 1270s its female members were continuing the family tradition of generosity towards both Zealand Cistercian male houses.

Other women, named as 'noble' in the Sorø Donation Book, also made sure they would be remembered. The widow of Jakob Havre, Juliane, in 1281 gave the monks property in Tølløse and asked them to remember her with 'pittances' on the feast of St Juliane.[159] The brothers were to pray for Juliane's soul daily, apparently by including her name in their necrology of patrons and benefactors. Whether by asking for pilgrimages or providing pittances, female benefactors to Sorø show ingenuity in finding ways to make themselves remembered by the monastic community.

Such women were not always widows. In 1291 a certain Margrethe with the permission of her husband, Knud Rød, gave Esrum her farm in Boserup in Esbønderup parish, a few kilometres from Esrum itself.[160] The property had great strategic value in filling out one of the many areas in this district where the Esrum monks had not yet been able to get a monopoly on land. The land was just outside the village of Esbønderup. Just as at Sode, the monastery had been slow in gaining hegemony over the district immediately to the west of Esrum. As with Sorø, which took two centuries to increase its 25 per cent share of Alsted to 82 per cent, Esrum's expansion in its own neighbourhood was painstakingly slow.[161] Once again we see how much the Cistercians of Zealand needed the generosity of women in order to keep adding to their lands. The number of charters involved do not allow statistical comparison, but women are in evidence now in a way they were not a century earlier.

The success of Zealand Cistercian houses in collecting female bequests during this period is underlined by the 1292 testament of Gyde, daughter of Skjalm Bang and widow of Esbern Karlsen. We have both the full text of this will and a mention of it in the Sorø Donation Book. The monks were fully aware of the will's importance for them.[162] Seeking burial at Sorø, Gyde gave it twenty marks money plus what she owned at St Martin's parish in Roskilde. This is the first time we find Sorø acquiring property in the town of Roskilde, an event that could have hardly been looked upon with favour by the Roskilde canons. Already involved in the town because of the Cistercian house for nuns there, the monks now had a base from which to foster their own commercial ambitions in the growing community.

Gyde's testament contains details that give it a personal quality frequently present in female donations to Cistercian houses. She ordered that the velvet pall on her coffin afterwards be used to make a chasuble for the monks. In this direct way her bequest to the monastery would be attached to every monk who wore the vestment while he said mass.

The testament is long and complicated. It names almost all monastic and religious foundations on Zealand, including leper houses and hospitals of the Holy Spirit, neither of which belonged at this time to any international religious order.[163] Gyde seemed to recognize the importance of the charity dispensed by these new houses, as well as the activities of the friars. But her heart was with Sorø, perhaps because her home was the village of Broby, just south of the abbey. Here she drew up the testament and richly endowed the parish church. She asked that three wax votive candles always be kept burning there for her, on the Lady Altar, on the altar of St Nicholas, and on that of St Margaret.

Gyde's loyalty to her local origins and to the great neighbouring monastery underlines the tendency for lay donations to concentrate on individual local houses and to ignore links according to religious order. To the distant Cistercian abbey at Esrum, Gyde gave only two marks, while to the nearby Ringsted Bernedictine monastery, she gave ten, half of what she left to Sorø. If the testament can be used as a guide, Gyde was not interested in religious affiliations but was expressing personal bonds with the people and houses she remembered. To the prioress of the Cistercian nuns at Roskilde, she left a gold ring with a crucifix on it, and to her granddaughter Kristine at the same house, she gave a chest, two marks in money, and a cooking pan. Cistercian nuns were no more than monks entitled to personal property, but such fine points apparently made no difference to Gyde.

Gyde distributed her legacy as she wished and showed her preferences. She could do so because she had no sons to press their demands. The male relatives she mentions are all sons of her daughters. She took care of them handsomely, but still had plenty left over for the Cistercians at Sorø and Roskilde, and for many other houses. Gyde patronized the Cistercians not as a religious order but as extensions of her biological family. The spiritual communities at Sorø and Roskilde were for Gyde individual houses to which she felt a personal and a family loyalty.

Women's generosity was often spoiled by male relatives waiting until the givers were dead. One of Gyde's beneficiaries and her executor was her nephew Ingvar Hjort, a knight who in later years caused Sorø considerable legal and financial problems by opposing the new foundation at Knardrup. Sorø records make it look as though he considered the monks as rivals in his landholding plans. Even though he finally settled with Sorø, Ingvar Hjort long did everything possible to make life difficult for the monks.[164] The generosity of his grandmother seemed not to influence him in the same direction. As available land became more scarce, liberal gifts to Danish houses by rich widows became more and more frequently contested by kinsmen.

If we turn to Løgum, we find no similar tendency among Southern Jutland women to hand over handsome legacies to Cistercian houses. The land Løgum does gain in these years comes from bishops or male landowners.[165] Only at Ryd do we find a woman handing over land to the monks. In 1306 Abbot Niels and his monks recorded a widow's gift to the brothers' table of various properties on the condition that they never be alienated.[166] Female donors, especially widows, played a significant role in the growth and social relevance of Esrum and Sorø in the years from 1272–92, but the materials we have for other Danish Cistercian houses do not reflect this same development.

INTERMINABLE CASES AND MONASTIC COMPROMISES

If we turn from the role of laywomen to that of laymen in their involvement with Danish Cistercian abbeys, we meet a number of complex disputes. Sorø was plagued by a controversy over properties at Stenmagle. This area, about fifteen kilometres north of Sorø, was a good farming country. The dispute lasted for almost the whole of the century. Litigation was transferred from father to son and from one abbot to another.[167] The royal role was decisive in assuring that the monks got what they believed to be theirs. The property was conveniently confiscated by the crown in 1290 because its lay claimant was declared an outlaw on the basis of his alleged involvement in King Erik Glipping's murder in 1286. Only at this point was it possible for the monks of Sorø to go to a court of justice and secure the lands which they so many times had seen slipping through their fingers—or which had been wrenched away from them.[168]

Another classic dispute at Sorø concerned Søtorp, another good farming property a few kilometres to the northwest of the abbey. The monks acquired the land in a 1253 exchange, but on the death of the former owner thirty years later, trouble began which lasted until 1307.[169] The situation was complicated when Katherine, a sister of a knight, Bo Bred, donated another parcel in Søtorp to the monks. She made this gift in union with her son Henning, subsequently a monk of Sorø, a unique instance in which we can see a likely connection between a parent's land gift and a son's entrance to a Danish Cistercian abbey. We are aware of many instances in which women entering religious houses in Denmark made contributions.[170] It is much more difficult to determine what men had to do in order to gain entrance.

Another heir of Bo Bred, Jens Kok, refused to accept this donation and appealed to both ecclesiastical and secular courts to get it nullifed. The Sorø Donation Book does not make clear whether or not Jens challenged the entire Søtorp holding or only Katherine's bequest. But the former seems to be the case. Jens occupied the holding and soon arranged for a hearing on the rightful title to the property. Refusing even to listen to the Sorø version of the story, Bishop Ingvar of Roskilde declared the exchange by Anders Ägesen legally invalid and awarded the entire property to Jens.[171]

The monks at Sorø were confronted by a hostile bishop of Roskilde. Ingvar was the first bishop there who had no relation to the Skjalm family's descendants and who had been a dean of the cathedral chapter prior to his election. There may be a link between his complete familial independence from Sorø, his service to the chapter, and his lack of sympathy for the monks.[172] Sorø appealed to the archbishop of Lund, Jens Dros, who appointed two judges, both canons of Roskilde cathedral, Master Rane and Jens Rude.[173] They followed their bishop's decision, and so the abbot of Sorø appealed through the archbishop of Lund to the pope.[174] Abbot Niels's list of grievances reflects the same bitterness and frustration that we find in the Ryd Annals from the same decade. He claimed that the monks had been mishandled and given a so-called 'definitive sentence' that was 'no sentence at all'. In the same appeal Niels described his appearance in 1288 before the canons of Roskilde. When Master Rane had asked if he and Jens wanted to reach an amicable compromise, Niels had replied that the lands had first to be returned to the abbey. The judges would hear no more of this but simply read out Bishop Ingvar's decision from 1285.

The matter became even more serious after the bishop's death in 1289. Jens Kok, whom the Sorø compiler accuses of being afraid 'that he had lost his support because of his lord's death', handed Søtorp over to a certain Asser Jensen.[175] The monks were convinced that this knight had absolutely no respect for them. He not only held onto Søtorp; he seized the fields and meadows of nearby villages, including Krøjerup, and extended his plundering even into Kindertofte parish. In a forest there he cut down trees to his heart's content. He also refused to allow the monks to fish in Maglesø, which bordered the Søtorp properties.[176] In general it seems he considered the area to the northwest of Sorø his own domain. The nightmare of a hostile knight providing a threat only a few kilometres north of the abbey came true for the monks, just as it had at the start of the century at Pedersborg.

Asser pulled up the monks' boundary markers, ignored ecclesiastical judgments, and followed his own will. Sorø had met an enemy that could not be intimidated in any way:

> Neither the discipline nor the judgment of the church did any good, for he was recalcitrant in all matters, and an excessive hardness remained fast in his heart, so that there was no hope of getting anywhere in this matter.[177]

The monks were superb at dramatizing their own dilemmas and naturally saw God's intervention when new mediators appeared. They were the new bishop of Roskilde, Olav, and two knights: Ingvar Hjort, a future enemy, but still at this time sympathetic to the monks, and Herlug Jacobsen. In their 1307 decision, they gave a quarter of Søtorp to Sorø, as willed by Katherine.[178] Asser Jensen was to give the remainder of Søtorp to Sorø as well, but the monks were to compensate him with Tersløse in Merløse herred. The usurper was to be put at a good distance from the monks, but he was not punished. As so often, Danish Cistercians preferred to reach an amicable settlement with an enemy instead of pushing their claims to the hilt. Had they done the same at Øm in the 1260s the outcome might have been less tragic.

Near the very beginning of the Søtorp dispute, in 1285, the abbot of Sorø transferred the bones of the founders of Benedictine Sorø from their twelfth-century church to the newly rebuilt Cistercian abbey church.[179] Absalon's relatives at last joined him in Cistercian surroundings. At about the same time, a frieze of shields was placed around the church. It showed the coats of arms of families that had traditionally supported the monastery and whose members were buried there.[180] At this very time donations from these families were drying up, and the abbey needed very much to inspire and encourage the new lines if they were to maintain the accustomed generosity. These actions in the 1280s should also be seen as manifestations of the general Danish tendency toward localism, emphasizing contacts and bonds with the nobility and clergy of the district instead of the house's membership in the Cistercian Order.

As late as 1180, the Cistercian General Chapter had decreed that only royal patrons and founders of abbeys were to be buried in the Cistercian church.[181] The Sorø monks had long since ignored this decision, and now they merely made their long-standing policy visible. Sorø's move should thus not be looked upon by themselves but in the context of the history of the Danish Cistercians as a whole. Just as individual abbeys in Denmark resisted visitors from Clairvaux and had to be forced to contribute to their sister abbeys, so too they did their best to be on good terms with the local landowning aristocracy. Only as local and regional institutions, riveted to the soil, with loose national and international bonds, could the Danish Cistercians survive.

The departure of the Cistercians from their founders' ideals in order to maintain their position in society may have brought conflicts inside monasteries. For these we have no sources. In the relationship between the abbeys and the representatives of the secular church, however, there is at least one superb indication that a diocesan official was aware that the Order had not developed in the way it had been meant to do. This occurs during a dispute over the patronage of Brede church which kept cropping up during these years. In 1276, the provost of Slesvig, after being appointed to inquire into claims and counterclaims for Brede church, arranged a hearing between Løgum and Mogens, the archdeacon of Århus, concerning the right of patronage.[182] The protocol drawn up for Bishop Tyge of Ribe is one of the most articulate legal documents of the century involving the Cistercians and points out that the Øm controversy had taught the diocesan officials of Århus to argue well.

Mogens claimed first of all that the monks could not have received the patronage of Brede from King Abel because he had never had the church under his patronage. He had neither built it nor given it land or money. Moreover, even if he had been the true patron, he had never actually presented the monks with Brede but only had given them the right of patronage. The subtle point is that the monks may have gained the patronage of Brede, but the same party could not both receive such a right and bestow it on itself: the monks could not keep the right of patronage for themselves but had to hand the church over to a secular priest. Finally, if it is assumed that the king was the true patron, the king kept for himself the right to appoint others than the monks to the patronage of the church, and this is exactly what King Erik had done!

These arguments are linked to a passage from the Decretals of Gregory IX forbidding Cistercian monks from possessing churches of their own.[183] This decretal itself cites a famous letter from Pope Alexander III to the Cistercians warning them against the decline of discipline brought about by their acquisitiveness. Alexander had reminded the Cistercians of their earliest statutes, which did not allow them to have parish churches. The Cistercians of Løgum had replied to this argument that such a prohibition did not exist at all. What they were saying here was apparently that they no longer were bound by such a law; they admitted indirectly that they long since had left behind the early twelfth-century idealism with its non-involvement in the affairs of the secular church. The Løgum monks simply pointed out the status quo as it long since had been: that Cistercian houses took on, in limited numbers, nearby parish churches. It is fascinating here how the Århus churchman used the decretals to get back to twelfth-century criticism against the Cistercians for becoming too worldly and concerned with ownership.

Even though the monks replied carefully to all the assertions Mogens made and brought out the charter given by Bishop Esger of Ribe guaranteeing their rights in Brede, the decision of Bishop Tyge apparently did not go in their favour. The parties were to meet again, but we have no further documents involving the Brede controversy until 1324, except for a 1277 verification of the validity of Bishop Esger of Ribe's documents on the matter by the Bishop of Slesvig. This verification indicates that the bishop of Ribe, Tyge, had contradicted his predecessor's decisions, causing the Løgum monks to turn to the bishop of Slesvig for his support, and thus to ask him to play the role of rival that recalls some of his predecessors' actions. The actual Ribe decision was not included in any of the monk's document collections because its result probably was not what the monks wanted to record and remember.

The monks of Løgum, like their brethren at Sorø, could no longer count on episcopal backing. Bishop Esger was the last bishop of Ribe to be buried at Løgum. With his successors the monks had to accept a more business-like relationship. Fortunately for the monks, Bishop Tyge of Ribe does not seem to have had the same animosity for Cistercians that his namesake at Århus had felt toward Øm. He arranged an agreement between the abbey and the parishioners at Daler, who had long been giving Løgum problems. Thereafter parishioners would be allowed to pay their tithes to the monks with threshed grain instead of sheaves.[184] In a dispute over land in Draved Forest, a wooded area part of which still exists today south of Løgum, Tyge again backed the monks.[185]

In 1283 Løgum was attacked by a magnate named Jon Iverson and his men. The monastery appealed to Archbishop Jens Dros, who ordered a Ribe canon to pass judgment in the matter.[186] A few months later, in a case perhaps connected with Jon Iversen's, the abbot of Løgum demanded that a certain Jens Urne return property wrongly taken from the monks and give full compensation.[187] Løgum received the backing of the Ribe bishop in a decision issued on 11 October. The protocol of the hearing shows how subtle and complex such a matter could be.[188] Jen Urne's lawyer had tried to delay the decision by various procedural manoeuvres. He had claimed the court had no power because in the summons to Jens the judge's name had not been given!

For a moment we can perceive the thirteenth century's increasing legalism.[189] In Denmark as elsewhere in Western Europe, it had become essential for any self-respecting Cistercian abbot to be learned in at least the rudiments of both canon and civil law if he was to protect his abbey. Jens Urne's lawyer claimed that because the monks had gone to the king for justice, they could not also take their case to an ecclesiastical court. The abbot could answer that he and his monks had suffered violence from Jens, and so they could litigate before the judge of their choice. The abbot could quote canon law to back up this assertion, but the lawyer blocked further progress by appealing to the papal court. Judges were appointed, but the case was delayed for a year until the monks themselves in September 1285 appealed to the pope and described the legal complications they had experienced while Jens Urne kept the land he had taken from them.[190] For the first time a legal representative (*sindicus*) for the monastery is mentioned, an office we also find at Esrum at about this time.[191]

The case dragged on until June 1290. In the meantime Jens Urne became involved in another dispute with the monastery, solved through the intervention of the Duke of Southern Jutland.[192] The Duke's role in Løgum's history became increasingly significant after a declaration of his protection for the abbey in 1284, apparently the start of a campaign to gain influence.[193] The 1290 settlement with Jens Urne satisfied few of the monks' initial claims. They were forced to give Jens the choice between buying the land from them for 500 marks or letting them keep the property at a cost of 100 marks. He chose the land. The monks gained a tidy sum of money, but in view of the legal expenses of these years, it was a Pyrrhic victory.

The Løgum disputes and their outcome are particularly valuable indications of Cistercian relationships with secular magnates. Rarely do we get so much detail or see so closely the legal exchanges of the courtroom. Just as the monks during this period entered into the business of administering parish churches, so too they accepted the legal complications of defending their rights and privileges. Diocesan bishops incorporated parish churches and duties under Cistercian abbeys during these decades. After years of controversy and definition of jurisdiction and rights in mid-century, the Cistercians and the episcopal church were settling down to a *modus vivendi* which emphasized cooperation in taking care of parish needs. Sorø got the right of patronage over Lynge church in 1297 from Bishop Jens Krag.[194] In 1305 Bishop Oluf of Roskilde confirmed the Sorø monks' right to exercise pastoral care in his diocese. In was the same at Vitskøl. The monks received the right of patronage over Nørresundby church north of Ålborg from Bishop Niels of Børglum in 1293.[195]

The monks belonged to solid institutions that could afford to compromise in the long run. Moreover, they could often count on the backing of bishops and secular magnates. Therefore Cistercians seldom came out as total losers in their land disputes. Even when they did lose, they could concentrate their efforts in rounding out the possessions they already held and in exchanging distant properties for nearby ones.

The monks could no longer count on great benefactors as in past days. The last major donor for the Cistercians in Denmark is Jon Jonsen Lille, who in his 1306 testament bequeathed the monks a great number of holdings and a request that a special altar be placed for his family in the abbey church at Esrum.[196] Otherwise we can see at Esrum how some of the most important local donations, which filled out gaps in the abbey's nearby holdings, came not from great aristocrats but from relatively obscure parish priests. Niels Attesen, priest in Blistrup, stated in his testament that he had been devoted to the monks for more than thirty years and wanted to share the family's tradition of attachment to the monks.[197] His brother, a parish priest in Tibirke, did the same.[198]

Parish priests had every reason to be suspicious of the incursions of the monks into their parochial incomes and the souls in their care, and yet here are warm declarations of affection. Perhaps the attachment can be explained by Esrum's relatively quiescent policy of land acquisition during this same period. The monks welcomed new holdings, but five years often went by without any new acquisitions being named in the Esrum Book. Some may have been omitted, but in comparison to the twelfth century, expansion was almost at a standstill, aside from the marked generosity of Jon Jonsen Lille's relatives.

The Cistercians manifest during these years an ability to reconcile themselves with their enemies. Løgum came to terms with Jens Urne, Sorø with Peder Olufsen of Tystrup. In a fit of anger Peder had destroyed Sorø's mill at Kongskilde, perhaps because he resented the monastic incomes from this source so near his home. But a few years later he deeded property in Bringstrup to Sorø in reparation and gained a reference in the Sorø Donation Book as an 'outstanding man' who had had a change of heart.[199] The monks constantly tried to convince knights, priests, and magnates in their regions that their work was invaluable and worth all the land it took from them.

One means by which the Cistercians could attract landowners to give them some of their holdings lay in confraternities. According to this arrangement a layman or woman received in return for a gift to the monastery a secondary membership in the Order and thus obtained full participaton in the abbey's spiritual benefits. In German abbeys like Himmerod this practice can be seen from the middle of the thirteenth century. At Sorø the first instance of confraternity comes in 1298 when Esbern Hammer handed over Døjringe properties in exchange for lands belonging to the abbey.[200] By no means a generous gift, this transaction was attractive enough for the monks to bestow confraternity on Esbern. Most of those who were received into confraternity asked for and obtained the right to withdraw to the abbeys in their declining years and be taken care of by the monks. This happened at Esrum, where Niels Attesen, priest in Blistrup, guaranteed himself such old age care at the monastery.[201]

Through such arrangements the Cistercians continued to attract secular attention and land gifts. The most important factor on their side was the essential conservatism of rural society. The friars might come and go, but the Cistercians were always there in the countryside, a manifestation of the dream of permanence and stability so central to the lives of medieval women and men. When Jakob Herbjørnsen, a landowner in Northern Zealand, drew up his testament in 1299, he was careful to spread cash gifts around to the Franciscans and Dominicans on the island. But like Gyde of Broby before him, Jakob's first loyalty was to his local church and monastery. In Jakob's case, they were Græsted and its neighbouring monastery, Esrum. Here he chose to be buried, and so he left the monks twenty marks by mortgaging a large piece of land for them in Græsted parish. Not once in this will does the name Cistercian appear. Esrum is simply Esrum, the local centre of spiritual security. 'Considering that in human affairs nothing is secure except that which helps the salvation of the soul', Jakob can find rest at Esrum after he has made his peace with God.[202] Jakob's words are traditional and formulaic. But the choice of such a formula and the gift behind it point to a continuing attraction the Cistercians exercised on propertied members of society.

LASTING CHANGES AND CONTINUING THEMES

In this busy period of disputes and controversies, Cistercian houses managed to emerge relatively unscathed. Despite the bitterness and nostalgia of some of the Cistercian chronicles, our documents bear witness to a stabilization of the Cistercian role in society after 1270. The period brought new risks and uncertainties, but legal disputes with local bishops were clarified, and contested properties were defended. On the whole the monks showed flexibility in getting away from the humiliation brought on by the Øm controversy and Jakob Erlandsen's vendetta with the monarchy. After the death of King Erik Glipping in 1286, the Cistercians at Sorø exposed the Order to possible royal displeasure, for at least one of the Zealand nobles who was close to Sorø was implicated in the king's murder.[203]

Sorø managed to allay any suspicion that might have arisen, and new charters confirming monastic rights and privileges were drawn up in the same manner as earlier.[204] Likewise the death of Bishop Ingvar of Roskilde brought successors who recognized the role of Sorø in incorporating churches and taking on parish functions in guaranteeing the abbey a foothold in the expanding trading town of Copenhagen.[205] During the same period Løgum obtained a number of new properties and even shops in Ribe, another indication of Cistercian success in adapting to the times.[206] The late Middle Ages in Denmark is characterized by the growth of towns; the Cistercians saw the value of urban properties and did not hesitate to buy them.

Symbolic of the harmony reached between bishops and Cistercian abbeys at the end of the thirteenth century is a settlement between Løgum and the bishop of Ribe on the question of procurations (payments of hospitality). In the charter, drawn up in the bishop's name, he admitted that the monks had been burdened by the demands made on them to provide hospitality for himself and his men on their visits to Løgum. The custom had brought such a mob of people that the monks hardly knew how to cope with the demands being made on them. In return for some properties the bishops now released them from all future obligations to provide procurations.[207] Two years later the agreement was renewed at Løgum, and the abbot said he had consented to it with the permission of his superior, Abbot Peder of Herrisvad.[208] The main obligation for the monks, stated here, was to serve God; all that distracted from this duty was to be kept out of their lives. The monks were willing to give up land in order to gain privacy and isolation. At Løgum and assumedly elsewhere, the monks were eventually able to get what they needed by paying for it.

Why were bishops at the end of the thirteenth century amenable to such settlements, while their predecessors had held out and demanded their rights? No doubt different personalities were involved now, but the roles of monastery and bishop towards each other had also been more clearly defined in Denmark. The archepiscopal-royal dispute brought a crush of legalism that at first created new disputes and problems but eventually provided the language and procedures for settlements. The Cistercians and the bishops learned in the process to distinguish what was essential to them from what was peripheral in importance.

At the same time as abbeys and bishops were coming to terms with each other, recruitment to the Danish Cistercians changed drastically. A 1263 decision for Vitskøl indicates that the brothers no longer were able to recruit a sufficient number of lay brothers to cultivate their lands.[209] In 1306 Esrum obtained a ratification of a 1302 papal bull which stated that the monks did not have to pay tithes on their lands even if they leased them out.[210] From this time onwards, the monks could split up the old granges and allow single peasant families to live on them without having to be concerned about the legal consequences. These bulls may be only formal recognitions of a situation that long had existed. But the acceptance of their validity by the bishop of Roskilde shows that both he and the abbot of Esrum wanted to legitimize the changes being made in the Cistercian system of tilling the land.

An indirect indication of crisis in recruitment to the lay brotherhood comes from the period after 1250, when the Sorø Donation Book mentions the reception of some small landowners into the monastery as lay brothers.[211] At the same time they handed over their property to Sorø. This transaction and the resulting recruitment are mentioned so specifically probably because the compiler wanted to emphasize the event. He would not have done so if there had been plenty of lay brothers. Although these recruits certainly did not belong to the aristocracy, we do find cases in Denmark in which lay brothers came from noble families.[212]

The most convincing evidence for the noble origins of a significant portion of the men recruited as lay brothers in the twelfth and thirteenth centuries occurs in the Older Donation Book for Lund cathedral, begun in the middle of the twelfth century and continued to about 1500.[213] Here we find a very large number of monks and lay brothers from Esrum and Herrisvad mentioned in the notices giving the days of death. This is not in itself surprising, for Lund was the cathedral church of Eskil, Absalon, and Anders Sunesen, all of whom had close links to the Cistercians. Of sixteen names from Esrum, six are lay brothers. For Herrisvad's twenty-one notices, nine are lay brothers. Adding up the figures, we find fifteen lay brothers, fourteen monks, three abbots, two novices, and three who cannot be classified. Almost as many lay brothers as monks and abbots gave Lund cathedral gifts significant enough to get them a place in the Donation Book.

Considering that a memorable gift was the sole criterion, aside from sanctity, for being included in such a list, one can only conclude that a surprising number of lay brothers at both Esrum and Herrisvad were well-off.[214] Moreover, such Cistercian donors could not have shown their generosity towards Lund without also taking care of their own abbeys. First of all, in gaining entrance they would have given something; secondly, in their testaments they would have given most of any properties they might have inherited during their lifetimes to their own abbeys. Thus these Esrum and Sorø donors to Lund must have had considerable holdings. Consequently, a significant number of lay brothers from Danish Cistercian abbeys would have come from wealthy landowning families. To use the expression 'noble' would be to stretch the meaning of the word, for Denmark's nobility in the 1200s was not a feudal one and did not have the same fixed social or legal position as its German counterpart.[215] But there were landowning families whose members called themselves knights, and it is with this class we are dealing.

Using this evidence, we can draw a preliminary conclusion about the decline of lay brother recruitment after 1250. In the last half of the thirteenth century, the old established branches of the Skjalm family died out, moved away, or lost their interest in Sorø. Only a few lateral lines kept up the old patronage. This was also the case at Esrum after the death of Jon Jonsen Lille. Even before this time, as we have already pointed out, the abbey was growing very slowly. It seems likely that with fewer recruits to the lay brotherhood from noble families, the monks had to try to attract independent peasants to fill out the thinning ranks of those who cultivated the land as lay brothers. A landmark study of the ownership of property in Alsted herred, where Sorø was located, showed that such independent peasants were hard to come by.[216] The monks, on the one hand, or the descendants of the Skjalm family, on the other, had already absorbed most of the land in this district. The result for Sorø, and perhaps also for Esrum, may well have been that the monks no longer had a base for recruitment. The new noble families that became their supporters did not continue the old tradition of sending their sons to become lay brothers or monks. As the supply of lay brothers dwindled, the monks came to depend first on hired peasant labour and finally had to allow peasants to rent land from them and pay a yearly amount.

The evidence is fragmentary here, but a general tendency is clear. As the monks lost contacts with old aristocratic families, they also lost their supply of lay brothers and had to devise new ways to cultivate the land as well as new contacts with families whose social position was rising. The 1280s may have been a turning point, witnessing land disputes with the Roskilde bishop at Sorø, fire and dispersion at Vitskøl, total collapse at Ryd, a number of disputes at Løgum, and a fire at Herrisvad.

During the next decades, the Danish Cistercian abbeys reformed and reformulated their relationships with bishops, king, and the new aristocratic families. Once the bottom had been reached, the abbeys fell back on their properties, privileges, and spiritual traditions. They seem to have given each other little help. Except for an occasional glimpse of cooperation between the abbots of Løgum and Herrisvad, we lack a sense of the regional solidarity that the monks had tried to express in the 1260s. This may be an impression due to gaps in the sources. But when Danish Cistercian houses appear in the records, they are alone. Making their own way in a world ever more complex and demanding, the monasteries functioned as if local bonds and associations were the only earthly salvation available for them.

VI

Quiet Years and their Traumas 1307–1357

CHANGE IN THE SOCIAL BASE

THE FOURTEENTH CENTURY is for the Danish Cistercians an almost uncharted period, which no historian so far has treated in detail. This may be due to the near-disappearance of narrative sources. The sources that are available are quite rich and varied, even in comparison with those of the preceding half century, but these materials are spread about in short notices, property deeds, and chance references. Looked upon as a whole, they give detail and clarity to our picture of the monks' relationships with other groups in Danish society. The monks can be seen anticipating and adjusting to changes within society's economic and political structures. At the same time their way of life and claim to a spiritual dimension continue to make them attractive to lay donors.

In 1307 Jon Jonsen Lille's daughter, Cecilie, at Hørsholm in Northern Zealand drew up a will that in many ways resembled her father's of the preceding year in favour of Esrum.[1] Like her father, Cecilie wanted to be buried at Esrum, to which she gave sixty marks, so that the monks would observe the anniversary of her death every year and enjoy pittances in her memory. She also gave them a farm in Smørum, northwest of Copenhagen, a smaller gift than that of her father, but still substantial. To the abbot of Esrum, Jens Hvid, Cecilie made a personal bequest of ten marks, and to Brother Heuze Krabbe she gave four. Cecilie's devotion to Esrum was not a vague gesture to a local monastery; her choice of individual monks for some of her bequests points to a personal relationship with them.

Cecilie's will is the last instance we find of a woman who had connections with religious houses and clerks all over Denmark and provided for all of them. In Copenhagen alone, she left fourteen different endowments, some as small as a mark each, but including groups as diverse as the canons at the church of Our Lady, Franciscan friars, the sick at the house of the Holy Spirit and lepers at their hospital. Because of her wealth, Cecilie could be generous to a great number of religious foundations, from the oldest and most established houses, like Benedictine Ringsted and Næstved, to the newer communities that cared for the sick and which had not yet been organized into religious orders. In Roskilde she remembered with gifts from one to eight marks the cathedral, its poor scholars, the Franciscan priory, its convent, the Cistercian female house, one of its nuns, the Dominicans, their convent, one of their sisters, Franciscan nuns, the house of the Holy Spirit, the leper hospital, and individual parish churches. Besides giving to Dominican and Franciscan priories in the rest of Zealand, Cecilie also left money to parish churches.

Cecilie's generosity was not limited to the island of Zealand. In North Jutland, where she had properties of her own, she named parish churches and Dominican and Franciscan houses. In Slesvig and Sønderborg she also made bequests. And finally, in Skåne she included parish churches and Franciscan brothers.

Such a broad swath of endowments, with its starting point at Esrum, shows Cecilie's faithfulness to her family's traditional piety and devotion to the North Zealand house. At the same time she must have felt the importance of the contributions being made to religious life in Denmark both by the friars and by the brothers of the Holy Spirit, and by parish churches. A single Cistercian house did not receive all the gifts, but its central role in family piety was maintained.

Without such detailed wills we might have thought that the Dominicans and even more so the Franciscans, who were especially active in Denmark by this time dominated pious bequests. The friars led an active life and were closely involved with the laity, something which the Cistercians could never allow themselves. Cecilie's will, like that of her father, points to the traditionalism of upper class religious devotion in Denmark. New orders and houses were taken into the orbit of secular generosity, but family ties with older monastic houses were maintained. In such a hierarchical society, with continuing bonds to magnate families with their great land holdings, the Cistercians at Esrum and Sorø had nothing to worry about.

After the death of Cecilie, it is unclear what happened to the cluster of estates with their headquarters at Hørsholm and to the family which had been so generous to Esrum. In the 1340s we find property owners at Hørsholm whose link to Cecilie's family cannot be determined.[2] One development is clear. At Hørsholm as elsewhere on Zealand, the day of the great landowning families was over.[3] A new class of landowners was more numerous, but its members were not as fabulously well endowed as their predecessors. This new group did not have the capital in land and money necessary to make bequests to religious houses on the same magnanimous scale. A good example of the new tendency occurs in 1308, when the Lady Kristine, widow of Jakob Blåfod, made her testament.[4] The Lady Kristine belonged to a family that had central importance in the affairs of Denmark during the reign of King Erik Menved (1286–1319). Her son-in-law, Niels Rane, was a member of a prominent family on Stevns, and his brother, Rane Jonsen, had been an important figure at court, but was outlawed and exiled for the murder of King Erik Glipping in 1286. Jakob Blåfod had been among the exiles. Although Niels Rane rose to the high status of King Erik Menved's advisor and in 1313 sat in judgment over rebellious peasants in Jutland, by 1316, he himself had been implicated in this revolt and was executed.[5]

The Lady Kristine's main endowments were to the Franciscan nuns of St Clare in Roskilde. She gave them two farms on Stevns plus sixty marks and in return asked for burial in their church. The reason for her devotion to the nuns is clear. Her daughter Margrethe was a sister there. The gifts may well fulfill an earlier obligation incurred by the girl's entrance. In any case, Kristine showed concern for the well-being of the nuns, especially for their clothes. She gave them various fabrics so that they could make new garments.[6]

The Cistercians had reason to be alarmed by such a testament. With only two monasteries for women on Zealand and none in the rest of Denmark, they could attract only a few of the daughters of rich families. Kristine did remember one Cistercian house for women; the Cistercian nuns in Roskilde received ten marks, and two of their members, Gertrud Jonsdatter and her sister Kristine, received four marks each. Lady Kristine's largesse to this house apparently was due to her relationship with the two nuns. No Cistercian monastery for men was on her list. As so often, personal bonds rather than devotion to the Cistercians as a religious order seems to have occasioned the bequest.

The Franciscan and Dominican friars in Roskilde are named in Kristine's testament, as are the Dominican nuns, the Holy Spirit Hospital, and the lepers' house here. Kristine also included some priories the friars had in central and north Jutland, and six marks to the 'hospital in Antvorskov'. Thus her will is not a narrow document concentrating all bequests on a single house. Kristine does not show the same broad spectrum of contacts with people and religious foundations that Cecilie maintained. The lavish generosity of Cecilie's testament has been replaced by a narrower concentration on the Poor Clare convent and other houses in Roskilde. Because neither had direct male heirs, both women could give away a substantial part of their inheritance and manifest personal tastes and preferences. But Kristine's will points to a change in attitude towards the Cistercians in the early four-teenth century. Even though Cistercian houses were still noticed, the old primary loyalty to individual Cistercian monasteries was gone. Our material is limited, and it is dangerous to draw sweeping conclusions. But Cecilie's testament is the last in the old style for the Cistercians, while Kristine's points to a new and less favoured status for the monks.

Even when a noblewoman did leave her major bequest to a Cistercian house, it was often small by comparison to thirteenth-century gifts. When Ingerd Pedersdatter, wife of Ølrik Skaft, in 1341 asked for burial at Esrum, she left the monks only a single farm in Udesundby and no money at all.[7] Her gifts to other Zealand religious house were individually small. She re-membered all the hospitals on Zealand, her parish church at Bjergby, Søborg church near Esrum, the Slangerup Cistercian nuns and all Roskilde's monasteries, plus Augustinian Æbelholt and the church of Our Lady in Co-penhagen. She also left clothes to her sister, a nun in the Poor Clare convent in Roskilde. The Esrum monks kept a record of Ingerd's testament, but neither they nor other Zealand houses were made much richer by her good intentions.

With the disappearance of the old families and their generosity, the Cis-tercians had to revise and broaden their relations with various social groups. From the 1140s to the 1220s the monks had been able to count on the loyalty both of strong bishops and of rich magnate families. During the rest of the thirteenth century, even though both groups failed to provide consis-tent support, the Cistercians usually could obtain backing from individual bishops and members of great families. Moreover, they could always go to the pope or to the Cistercian General Chapter for help. But, as we have seen, by the end of the thirteenth century, international structures no longer played a vital role. With the disappearance of the great landowning families and their replacement by new and less wealthy ones with no tradition of loyalty to the old orders, the Cistercians had to depend more than ever on their local bishops. Yet diocesan bishops had no reason to feel the same devotion to the monks that their predecessors had done, for the Cistercians no longer represented the vanguard of spiritual life in Europe. The monks responded to their devalued status in the upper echelons of church and society by seeking support and sympathy from a much broader segment of lay and religious society. In the twelfth and thirteenth centuries, the Cister-cians did not really need to deal with more than the elite of society—kings, bishops, and great families. Contacts with peasants could be limited because lay brothers either did or at least supervised agricultural work. In the fourteenth century, because of changes in society's structure, the monks had to give the same attention to the country gentry (called *armigeri* in the sources) as to magnate families. Even peasants took on a new importance when the monasteries no long had lay brothers and had to recruit agricultural labourers or to lease out lands to lay tenants. Interdependence and localism are the two great themes of the first half of the fourteenth century. As the monks needed village labourers and knights, these very different social groups looked to the monks for both spiritual and material benefits.

PROBLEMS IN THE SOURCES

Before considering the documentary sources that underline these changes, we should review the few narrative sources composed during this period. At Øm the abbey chronicle continued its list of abbots until 1320.[8] The earlier practice of giving a brief characteristic of each abbot was discontinued, and sometimes we have nothing but a name, with no indication of how long the particular abbot held office.

The reason for this brevity may well be lack of space; the abbots are listed on a page wedged in between the earlier abbot list and the account of the dispute with Bishop Tyge on the following leaf.[9] But there is another possible explanation. There may well have been other chronicles at Øm which told the lives of the abbots in much greater detail and which now are lost.[10] A more tangible indication of the situation of Øm abbey after its defeat in the 1260s can be seen in the text of the original manuscript describing the events. The account of the dispute with Bishop Tyge was left unaltered and incomplete for the rest of the Middle Ages. There are no corrections or marginal notes. In the early thirteenth century account of the abbey's foundation, the handwriting and language all point to a carefully finished product. In the description of the conflict with Århus, we are reading a draft, not a complete polished narrative.[11]

This failure to round off the account could indicate a loss of interest in the writing of history at Øm. It may well be that the Øm monks did not continue writing because history no longer could be a practical tool by which to defend their claims and privileges.[12]

The disappearance of chronicles at Øm is paralleled by a similar development at Sorø. The Older Sorø Annals end in 1300,[13] while another set, the Younger Sorø Annals, carries on until 1347.[14] The latter have come down to us because they were added to the last page of a magnificent twelfth-century Justin manuscript once owned by the Danish historian Saxo.[15] Like the last part of the abbot list in the Øm Book, the Younger Sorø Annals are mere notations with no attempt to give a detailed summary of events. Nevertheless they provide some fascinating bits of information that point to Sorø as an intellectual centre.

In an entry for 1247, for example, the fire that destroyed the monastery is mentioned, and the remark is added that an account of it can be found 'in the book Excerpts of the Fathers'.[16] The title alone would seem to indicate a *florilegium* or collection of passages from the Christian fathers of the type that was popular in monasteries.[17] It seems odd that an account of the fire at Sorø would be included in such a collection, but if we consider the physical placement of the Later Sorø Annals themselves at the end of the Justin manuscript and the general tendency of monastic manuscripts to contain miscellaneous collections of materials, this entry may be pointing to the existence of an historical account contained in what otherwise was a theological collection. Besides mention of the fire in the Sorø Annals, there is an extremely detailed account of the fire's destruction from the sixteenth century that could be based on the entry in the 'Excerpts of the Fathers'.[18]

Another indication of Sorø's intellectual life is an entry for 1340: 'In this year there was a great war in Spain between pagans and Christians, as you can find at the end of the book which is called *Herveus*'.[19] This book title probably refers to Hervé, monk of the Benedictine monastery at Bourg-Dieu in Berry in the first half of the twelfth century.[20] Hervé's commentaries on Isaiah and the Epistles of St Paul have survived, and manuscript evidence suggests they were popular in Cistercian circles. These and other now lost commentaries by Hervé existed at Heiligenkreuz in Austria and at Clairvaux itself. His works were so highly valued at the end of the Middle Ages that the authorship of some of them was attributed to Anselm of Canterbury. As with the 'Excerpts of the Fathers', we hear of a theological manuscript containing a separate element, in this case the chronicle of a foreign war. It is impossible to determine if this account of the Spanish war points to the Sorø monks' writing of a larger chronicle of international events. If this were true, we could speak of historical studies at Sorø. But in the absence of the manuscript, it is impossible to draw such a conclusion, for the monks may well have copied such a chronicle from elsewhere.

In terms of Sorø's political and intellectual importance during this period, however, the Younger Sorø Annals' short notices give invaluable information. Under 1313 is mentioned the death of Jakob, 'Master in Decretals and monk at Sorø'.[21] Surviving manuscripts from Sorø in this period indicate a pronounced interest in legal studies at the monastery.[22] In the political sphere, Abbot Henning of Sorø, who is said to have died in 1308, is called 'counsellor of King Erik of the Danes'.[23] Henning's name appears frequently in documents of this period.[24] The title given him here places him in the very centre of political events at the opening of the century and points to Sorø's importance.

In one instance these brief annals are bolder in taking a political stand than were the Older Sorø Annals. For 1331 the Younger Sorø Annals mention the interregnum in Denmark: 'In those days and times there was no king in Denmark, but the men of Holstein ruled for many years and did great evil'.[25] Like the Older Sorø Annals, however, the Younger claim that King Kristoffer died in 1258 of poisoning. They may merely be continuing the tradition that seems to have been accepted at Sorø in the thirteenth century concerning the matter.

The Younger Sorø Annals also note that in 1300 the bishop of Roskilde, Jens Krag, was buried at Sorø. It is one more tribute to the continuing influence and vitality of the Danish Cistercians at the opening of the fourteenth century that they could attract so important a bishop to choose burial at Sorø instead of at his own cathedral.[26] This is the last such instance of episcopal burial known to us. Thereafter bishops were generally interred at their cathedral churches.

Another account which has been attributed to Sorø, the Younger Zealand Chronicle, tells us little or nothing about the abbey.[27] This chronicle is so political in its concerns and secular in its outlook that some Danish historians have even concluded that it was written by a layman.[28] In 1973 Leif Szomlaiski, in a study of the chronicle, argued that the work was composed at Sorø.[29] A review of his reasons and a study of the Chronicle's content make it necessary for me to disagree with him.

Szomlaiski's strongest argument is that a manuscript (F 42), destroyed in the fire at the Copenhagen University Library in 1728, probably contained both the Older and the Younger Zealand Chronicles.[30] The Older Chronicle belongs to Sorø, for there is a clear interest in Cistercian history and a concentration on mid-Zealand personalities and events. But the fact that the two works were together in a manuscript that also contained other narrative sources having nothing to do with Sorø does not seem to me to establish a Sorø provenance. Szomlaiski also argues that the Rhyme Chronicle, written in Danish in the fifteenth century at Sorø, names the Younger Zealand Chronicle.[31] But again such a relationship does not necessarily point to Sorø composition. The monks who wrote the Rhyme Chronicle could easily have seen or borrowed a copy of the Younger Zealand Chronicle from another religious house.

Other arguments for Sorø provenance included the fact that the Younger Zealand Chronicle starts up where the Older one leaves off, in 1307. Actually, the Younger Chronicle begins with annalistic materials from the 1200s, and even if it does become more independent and detailed after 1307, it can hardly be looked upon as a continuation of the Older Zealand Chronicle in content and approach. The Older Chronicle is compilatory and unoriginal, merely taking chunks of foreign narrative material and condensing them.

The Younger Chronicle totally lacks such excerpts and also shows no interest at all in Cistercian history. If the Older Chronicle is indicative of a tradition of history writing at Sorø, the Younger Zealand Chronicle would represent a radical transformation. Szomlaiski concludes his arguments based on 'external criteria' with reference to 'the milieu at Sorø', where the writing of history was strongly encouraged.[32] The Elder Zealand Chronicle and the two Sorø Annals do indicate historical work at Sorø, but only one of them goes significantly beyond 1300, and the sketchy Younger Sorø Annals alone hardly point to an active historical milieu there. The abbey after 1300 seems to have been a centre much more for legal than for historical studies. The manuscripts we have point to a continuing interest in law and perhaps also medicine or at least herbology.[33] For more than a century Danish historians have fought the literary myth fostered by B. S. Ingemann in his *Valdemar den Store og hans Mænd* (Valdemar the Great and his Men) that the historian Saxo was a monk at Sorø. The ghost of this myth still contributes to the tendency to see the Sorø monks as great historians. They may well have been, but what remains from Sorø in the fourteenth century indicates that the intellectually-inclined monks were more interested in law than in history.

One aspect of the Younger Zealand Chronicle which convinces Szomlaiski that it was written at Sorø is its careful mention of the burial there of King Kristoffer and his sons.[34] This is a powerful argument until we notice that the same chronicle describes how King Valdemar Atterdag's son was buried at Roskilde in 1363.[35] It would have been an admission of defeat for a Sorø monk to end his chronicle with such a piece of information, for it would be showing that while the weak and ineffectual Kristoffer chose Sorø, the strong and awesome Valdemar chose Roskilde for his son's last resting place.

The rest of Szomlaiski's attempt to provide external evidence for accepting Sorø is marred by the same tendency to emphasize facts that could just as well point to other religious communities on Zealand. Of a careful list of families important to Sorø and mentioned in the Younger Zealand Chronicle, Szomlaiski has to admit that the same people were involved with other religious foundations in business transactions and benefactions.[36]

For me the acid test of the Younger Zealand Chronicle's provenance lies in the outlook and concern of its author or authors. Any Cistercian orientation is totally missing. The historian Ellen Jørgensen, aware of this absence, said the Chronicle shows knowledge of central Zealand and the Næstved area but no special interest in either Sorø or Næstved.[37] Szomlaiski's attempt to decide the thorny question of provenance is not convincing. The writer(s) of this central chronicle in Danish fourteenth-century history is more likely to be found among the canons of Roskilde cathedral.[38] The death and accessions of Roskilde bishops are carefully noted in the Younger Zealand Chronicle, together with information concerning Roskilde episcopal and capitular activities. For example, in 1353 the baptism of King Valdemar's daughter Margrethe by the bishop of Roskilde is given prominence.[39] The accession of Jakob Poulsen as bishop of Roskilde is included for 1344,[40] and we are told he had once been dean of the chapter. King Valdemar's interference in the election of a bishop of Børglum in Northern Jutland is mentioned without any criticism of the king. The writer excuses him apparently because he had chosen a Roskilde canon and 'was providing for him in all his needs, and kept him with himself for along time honourably at his court'.[41] When Valdemar is criticized, it is in connection with his annexation of the lands of Roskilde church in 1357.[42]

Events at Roskilde are given a prominence they otherwise do not deserve in comparison with the Chronicle's concentration on conflicts of monarchy and the fate of Denmark as a whole. Our writer (or writers) usually deals with the whole of Zealand and uses its trials and tribulations as a point of departure for a description of events elsewhere in the kingdom. But his regional concern is combined with a local loyalty to the bishop and chapter at Roskilde. Thus it is likely that the Chronicle was written by a canon or canons or Roskilde during the years when Bishop Henrik Gertsen held office, 1350–68.[43] After 1357 Henrik had his duties diminished by papal permission because of the weakness of old age, and it may have been during this time, between 1357 and 1368, that one of his associates in the cathedral chapter worked on the Chronicle.

The theory that the Chronicle was written at Roskilde can help explain the surprising combination of secular and religious elements in it. A cathedral canon's way of life, with daily secular affairs in an important town and the administration of huge estates, would mean frequent contacts with lay society. Our author(s) clearly accepts a divine scheme and sees God punishing evil, but the theological point of view is a secondary, not a primary, theme. The Chronicle gives a sustained and consistent account of secular history from the viewpoint of a religious institution directly involved in political events. This sense of closeness to what is happening in the lay world points to a canon and not to a monk as the chronicler. In the fourteenth century canons and monks led quite different lives: a Roskilde canon had a different relationship to lay society and politics than a Sorø monk. If we look at the Younger Zealand Chronicle as a whole, we find a secularizing world quite distant from the one presented by the Sorø monk who wrote the Older Zealand Chronicle and concentrated on pious acts and saintly persons.

VIOLENCE AND THE THREAT OF VIOLENCE

Even if life for the monks continued in its old pattern of prayer and administration, they were more exposed than ever to an increasing tendency to the
use of force in the society around them. It is impossible to determine if the
amount of violence actually increased in Danish society in the first half of
the fourteenth century, but the sources indicate that institutions like Cistercian monasteries now had to deal with it as a regular and recurrent problem.
At Øm during the political unrest of the 1240s and the disputes with Bishop
Tyge of Århus in the 1250s and 1260s, attacks by armed men had been a
problem, but Øm's situation among Danish Cistercian houses was almost
unique. In the early fourteenth century, however, almost every Danish abbey of which we have records had its daily routine upset in one way or
another by violence or the threat of it.

Our sources do not usually allow us to see the monks' reaction to this
state of affairs, as does the Øm Chronicle. The Cistercians no longer could
count on strong bishops or monarchs to protect their house from raiders
and outlaws. By 1307 it was becoming clear that King Erik Menved's grandiose plan to reestablish Danish hegemony in Northern Germany was failing. From this time until midcentury, political and social upheavals characterized Danish life. The worst period came in the 1320s and 1330s, when
Denmark was ruled either by a weak king or by none at all. But both before
and after these decades, the Danish Cistercians were implicated both directly and indirectly in episodes that manifested lay society's powerlessness to
maintain the rule of law.

Sometime before 29 August 1308, the Norwegian King Haakon complained of the Danish King Erik Menved's treachery towards the banished
Danes accused of the murder of King Erik Glipping. These men had long
since fled to the Norwegian court. [44] At one point a representative of King
Erik, Tule Ebbesen, came to Ås Cistercian abbey in Halland, today on the
Swedish west coast but then part of Denmark. They sent for Niels Jakobsen, bailiff for Count Jakob of Halland, who was one of the magnates exiled
from Denmark. Tule asked Niels to come to confer with him and promised
not to harm him, in keeping with an agreement made between the two
kings. Niels Jakobsen arrived with some companions at a stream called Viskan, where the abbey had a farm, Iderås (the name suggests it was near Ås
itself). From there Niels sent a message to Tule asking him if he should
come to Ås or whether Tule would come to him at Iderås. He was told to
come to Ås.

According to the Norwegian King's account, Niels Jakobsen arrived without weapons and with only a few companions, including a peasant, so that
they were thirteen in all. While Niels sat and talked with Tule Ebbesen,

Tule sent his companions away. But in the midst of the conversation, these men returned armed, took Niels's men prisoner, and cut off the heads of two archers and the peasant. The capture of the bailiff and the murders all took place at Ås itself. If Tule was staying as a guest of the monks, they may well have been eyewitnesses to this bloody betrayal.

Even allowing for the propaganda quality of the account, we are provided with a powerful commentary on the situation of the Danish Cistercian monks. In a violent society still split into factions more than twenty years after the death of Erik Glipping, the Cistercians were but helpless spectators. We know almost nothing about events at Ås during these years, but this single account provides a flash of light over the Danish Cistercian landscape. We see the parlay, the massacre, the dead bodies, and the abbey in the background. How the monks reacted we do not know. They could hardly feel secure in a society where powerful laymen took such violent revenge on each other.

In 1313 the monks of Ås again experienced the use of force, this time in the service of legitimate power. Ås was involved in a dispute with the nuns of Gudhem Cistercian monastery, located in central Sweden about 180 km northeast of Ås, over fishing rights in the nearby stream Viskan.[45] The nuns accused the monks of taking over illegally the part of the stream where they had exclusive rights. In an earlier confrontation about the same matter, the women had received help from the Swedish king Erik, who had had the monks' fish trap totally destroyed. The monks had rebuilt it, and the nuns now turned to King Birger, who wrecked it a second time. This is a very rare instance of a Scandinavian Cistercian house for women asserting its rights against a male monastery by appealing to secular power. The fact that Ås and Gudhem were isolated houses, far from normal centres of law and administration, may have made the nuns feel that such dramatic measures were necessary. The elimination of the Ås fish trap is a far cry from murders in the monastery, but both point to the monks' subjection to laymen's use of force to carry out their purposes.

In 1309 Pope Clement V ordered the dean of the cathedral of Slesvig to defend and protect members of the Cistercian Order, who were subject to persecution.[46] The language of the bull is formulaic and can tell us nothing about the Danish situation in particular. We do not even know which abbey or abbeys had complained. The bull is contained in the *Codex Esromensis*, but we know of no contemporary problems at Esrum. The fact that the Dean of Slesvig was ordered to intervene may point to Esrum's appeal to the papal court at Avignon on behalf of its daughter house Ryd. Whatever its cause, the papal bull points to the monks' fear of violence and their desire to protect themselves. Another such bull was issued in 1320 under John XXII for Løgum abbey.[47] The prior of Odense and the provost and chanter in Århus were to see that Løgum was shielded from all attacks on its rights and possessions. Again it is impossible to establish details, but the matter may have been concerned with inheritances by individual monks of properties from their families, for six weeks later Pope John allowed the monks to inherit all property which would have come into their possession had they not entered the monastery. [48] Sorø obtained the same privilege in 1334. [49] It may be that the Cistercians were having trouble at this time in gaining new lands through new members because of resistance by other family members.

All these signs of trouble are borne out decisively and concretized by the Knardrup affair, a turning point in Danish Cistercian history. According to the Younger Zealand Chronicle, Knardrup was founded by King Kristoffer in 1326, but in the same year, after Kristoffer died, the monks were thrown out by two knights, Ingvar Hjort and Knud Porse. [50] If we had only this one sentence, it alone would suggest a massive change in the attitude of secular society to the Cistercians. Despite all the troubles experienced in founding Cistercian abbeys in the 1100s, there had been no instance in which laymen ejected monks bodily.

The Sorø monks, who apparently had sponsored the foundation with Kristoffer, appealed to Avignon. In 1329 Pope John XXII's decision was made. [51] The abbot of the Benedictine house at Cismar and the treasurer in Holstein and precentor of the cathedral church at Lübeck were to see to it that Knardrup was returned to the status of an abbey. The man who had hired the knights against the monks was Barnum Eriksen, son of Duke Erik of Halland, who was himself the son of Valdemar II's illegitimate son Knud. [52] Knardrup had once been a royal possession and in the chaos that followed Kristoffer's exile in 1326, Barnum asserted an old claim. The dispute was thus not an ordinary one over property rights. It involved royal property, the families around the throne, and their relative strengths and political prowess.

After the death of Barnum, Ingvar Hjort, who had married into his family, took possession of Knardrup. The pope's description mentions the cooperation of 'some other laymen of the same diocese' who had occupied the village of Søsum, which also belonged to the estate. [53] For an instant we see what looks like land-hungry villagers of the 1300s jumping at a chance to take over new holdings and ally themselves with an acquisitive nobility.

The papal bull explains why the case was handed over to churchmen outside Denmark: 'Because of the unstable condition of the said kingdom, [the monks] are unable to obtain the full complement of justice in that kingdom from those who have seized [the property]. [54] The papal commentary probably reflects the description of the situation sent to the pope by the archbishop of Lund and the monks themselves. It was apparently a fair analysis of the breakdown of legal processes in Denmark. The monks were unable to return to Knardrup until 1343,[55] when Valdemar Atterdag came to the throne and began to reestablish domestic peace. The pope in 1329 had given the judges the right to use 'the secular arm' should the guilty parties refuse to obey their decision, but in view of Denmark's political confusion, it is not likely that the papal judges were able to take advantage of this clause.

Gertrud, the wife of the original claimant, Barnum Eriksen, cooperated with Ingvar Hjort in holding onto Knardrup after her husband's death. She was the daughter of Peder Tygesen of Vedby, a grandson of Jon Lille, the man who had given so much for the Zealand Cistercians.[56] The changed attitude of his descendant shows how insecure life had become for the monks.

Yet another indication of the hostile world the Cistercians had to face in the fourteenth century comes in a case involving the attempt by a rich widow named Valborg to start a Cistercian monastery for women at Opager in mid-Lolland.[57] Valborg's husband had been a member only of the rural gentry,[58] but the great number of properties she left to her proposed foundation indicates that such persons could be more than minor landowners. Valborg started her initiative during the reign of King Erik Menved who, according to a 1329 bull of John XXII, ratified the foundation and gave it the necessary privileges and exemptions. But before the monastery could be founded or the prioress and nuns enter it, two knights, Morten Due and Peder Vendelbo, made legal demands on Valborg because of debts they claimed her late husband had owed them. The papal bull on the matter indicates that the nobles had managed to obtain a favourable decision from a secular court but does not give details. In any case the knights occupied the estate, which consisted of forty-one different holdings. Valborg herself went to Avignon to pursue the matter, and there she died sometime during the 1320s. The papal decision indicates that her determination made an impression. The abbot of Holme on Fyn and the prior and provost of Odense were ordered to see to it that her property be given to the abbot of Sorø so that he, in accordance with her wishes, could found a Cistercian house for women at Opager. The abbot of Sorø was to act as 'father abbot' for the nuns and to look after their needs.

All the proceedings at Avignon were extremely complicated, especially for a woman who spoke only her own 'vulgar idiom', as the papal bull puts it. The knight Peder Vendelbo came to Avignon and had himself represented by counsel, a parish priest from the archdiocese of Lund, while Valborg apparently had with her no legal advisors from Denmark. The bull points out the efforts made to expedite the matter. Despite an intervening holiday, the pope asked the appointed judge to continue the case and reach a decision. This was achieved on a technical point. Valborg and Peder Vendelbo's priest each chose lawyers at Avignon. When Peder's lawyer, Ferrand, failed to appear in court, Valborg's lawyer, Recuperus, accused the absent lawyer of contempt of court and asked that the matter be terminated. The judge, a papal auditor, decided that Ferrand had indeed shown contempt, and ruled that Valborg should regain possession of the lands. Ferrand was to see to it that the knight made reparation for her lost income and for her expenses incurred in the case.

The decision of the papal auditor points out the weakness of the process, however. The judge reinstated Valborg in her properties 'so far as he was able'.[59] The rest was up to her. Her death at Avignon, probably shortly afterwards, guaranteed the impotence of the decision. Despite the stern papal command to the abbot of Holme and the Odense officials, nothing seems to have come out of it. We know only that in 1397 the property at Opager was owned by a member of the country gentry (an *armigerus*). Valborg's ambitious project vanished into thin air, and she remains one of the unsung women of Danish history, a woman whose determination to realize her project took her all the way to the papal court. Valborg won her case, but in the end nothing mattered except the realities of power in Denmark. The kingdom was in confusion, and no papal bull could alter the hold that a single knight could maintain on a property. With a strong king to back the papal decision, the outcome might have been different.

This case points to some of the problems and limitations of monastic life in fourteenth-century Denmark. Monks could still count on occasional clusters of gifts, even to found new houses. But at Opager, as at Knardrup, it was impossible to realize the good intentions of founders. Society was split into so many factions and conflicting groups that the monks became victims to their ambitions and gained little from the international institutions in which they participated. Despite the complex and subtle papal machinery at Avignon, and despite Valborg's insistence in using this machinery, the decisive factor remained the desires of the male members of aristocratic lay society. Valborg's husband was accused, rightly or wrongly, of not paying his debts and so his widow lost her land, regardless of papal courts or Cistercian reactions. Real power remained with the landed nobility. It had become localized and fragmented but help from anyone outside this limited sphere was impossible.

The dominance of the lay nobility is emphasized by another bull from Pope John XXII.[60] In 1328 he ordered the archbishop of Lund to obtain compensation for the losses suffered by a Swedish Dominican, who on his way to Avignon had been attacked in the diocese of Ribe by a knight and his companion. No one was safe in Denmark in the late 1320s, yet the business of the church had somehow to be continued. In 1336 Bishop Jens Nyborg of Roskilde threatened excommunication and interdict against those who acted violently against clerks and church property:

It is horrid to admit that they indiscriminately injure, mutilate, kill, kidnap, hold captive, maim, and torture priests and others, diminishing their privileges and taking away their liberties. And as far as is in their power—alas—they do grave harm to the church by repecting nothing and having no fear for the divine judgment of its ministers.[61]

This, one of the harshest declarations of the Danish medieval period, gives depth to the general impression of the 1320s and 1330s as a period of near-anarchy.

The sufferings of the church were probably small in comparison to those of the hapless peasants. It is no wonder that it was during this half century that many independent peasants finally gave up their status and sought to be accepted as tenants by strong landowners.[62] The bottom rank of society accommodated itself to the new situation by altering its legal status. A similar development seems to have taken place among monks: they too sought the protection of a strong man. In 1343 King Valdemar Atterdag placed Esrum under the guardianship of Niel Eriksen of Hørsholm.[63] For the first time a Danish abbey was given a formalized and legalized bond with a secular noble. The royal charter says nothing about the monks' own request or desire in the matter, only that Niels was to be their defender from all injuries and molestation.[64]

In the same year Sorø revealed its fear of attack by buying the church and property of Pedersborg from the dean of Roskilde. In the charter Henrik, abbot of Sorø, stated he had asked the bishop and chapter of Roskilde to exchange this holding of theirs for Sorø lands in Lyng and Mulstrup because of 'grave problems caused to us and our monastery, and dangers and vexations threatening us, especially if the said church be made into a fortification by those who are enemies of the peace'.[65] Abbot Henrik expected trouble and wanted to protect the monastery from a repetition of the situation experienced before 1205, when a powerful landowner held Pedersborg and used it to harass the monks. The monastery's collective memory of the old days seems to have been especially keen on this point. Pedersborg had since become a peaceful parish church, but the monks could still see the possibility of a new fortress on the hill overlooking their home. There was fighting on Zealand in the 1340s in King Valdemar's attempt to gain full power over the island,[66] and the Sorø monks were girding themselves for all eventualities. So far as we know, they never had to carry out their emergency plan, for the medieval church remains atop the hill today.

Sorø was fortunate to be able to turn to Roskilde for help. In 1349 the bishop of Roskilde forbade anyone on pain of excommunication to cut down trees in Sorø's forests without the abbot's permission.[67] Once again the bishop supported the Cistercian monastery in its attempt to secure its holdings and rights. The vast forest areas around Sorø today bear witness to the even greater holdings of the medieval period. The monks' wealth was partly based on such lands, and it was essential to secure them.

Violence and the threat of violence thus play a central role in the affairs of the Danish Cistercian houses in the first half of the fourteenth century. The Cistercian monasteries can rightfully be looked upon as barometers of the pressures in Danish society as a whole. Even if no catastrophe befell any abbey, except for the fledgling Knardrup, the documents indicate more clearly than at any other time in Danish Cistercian history how almost all the abbeys were threatened by the social, political, and economic upheavals that the country as a whole was experiencing.

EPISCOPAL RELATIONS AS A COMPENSATORY FACTOR

Despite their troubles, the Danish Cistercians continued during these years to count on cooperation from local bishops, who seem on the whole to have looked upon the monks with at least benevolent neutrality. Exempt from episcopal jurisdiction, the monasteries were a potential threat to the power of any energetic bishop. This realization seems to have been one of the mainsprings for Bishop Tyge of Århus's attacks on Øm in the 1260s. But in the early 1300s, bishops and monasteries cooperated with each other through the parish system. In several instances bishops conceded the right of patronage over churches to monasteries, especially to the Cistercians.[68] The monks accepted what had inevitably to have been an ambivalent situation: formally, they were exempt from episcopal power; but because of their parish involvement, they were very much subject to the bishop. The legal distinction between the Cistercians as an exempt order and other non-exempt religious orders in Denmark thereby lost practical significance. It is not the first time we hear of the Danish Cistercians having parishes. During the Øm dispute, 'their' church at Dover is mentioned. But the process of parochial acquisition seems to be more widespread now than it had been earlier. Nevertheless, no Cistercian abbey ever came to hold more than a few parishes at a time.

In one case we are told exactly why a bishop conceded a parish church to a Cistercian abbey: the church was simply too poor to support a priest. Spandet, about twenty kilometers north of Løgum, was handed over to the monks by Bishop Jens of Ribe in 1323. The bishop defended his action: 'It should not be judged reprehensible by anyone if because of changing times, human statutes are altered'![69] Such a concession to change would have been unthinkable in the twelfth-century formulae of charters. Its appearance indicates that the fourteenth-century crisis had so much affected consciousness that the sense of uncertainty had altered the way legal statements justified themselves.[70] Spandet's lands had once been adequate to provide for a curate, but they no longer were so, and therefore the bishop gave the monks of Løgum the responsibility for providing a priest to administer the sacraments. The Cistercian monastery was thus given more than the simple right of patronage over the church. In this case it was to supervise the day-to-day functioning of the parish.[71]

Aside from getting new churches, the Cistercians strengthened their rights over those they already held. The bishops of Viborg twice in these years recognized the monks of Vitskøl's holdings of four churches which the monastery had received from former bishops.[72] At Løgum and Sorø, bishops assured the monks of their exclusive legal jurisdiction over their labourers in matters involving the violation of the sabbath.[73] Bishop Jens of Ribe helped the Løgum monks to get hold of Brede church, lost to them for more than half a century, by recognizing both Duke Erik of Jutland's patronage over it and his transfer of the right to the monks.[74]

In return for such services the Cistercians could facilitate the situation for bishops who wanted to change the *status quo* at their cathedral chapters. In 1329 Abbot Stig and the monks of Sorø gave their consent to the annexation of Stillinge church to the newly introduced chanter's stall at Roskilde.[75] In 1315 this office had been added to the other positions in the chapter and the church at Stillinge placed under it.[76] But the Sorø monks seem to have had some claim on its patronage, and the matter remained unsettled for more than a decade. In the document of recognition, the monks of Sorø did not directly state that they had been patrons of the church but clearly indicated that their consent was imperative to any change of status.

In 1331 Duchess Ingeborg of Halland granted the abbot of Esrum her claim to patronage over Esbønderup church.[77] According to the charter, the rector of the church, Michael, had recently died, and now Ingeborg was handing over the right of provision, or appointment of the new priest, to the monks, although the charter also shows that the monks already claimed the right of patronage over the church.[78] The bishop of Roskilde, Jens, recognized the transfer and indicated that he, like other Danish bishops during this time, welcomed and encouraged the role of Cistercian houses in taking over parish churches. Jens emphasized the central role of the sacraments and the liturgy in the church's life and stated that these functions are cared for 'most carefully' by 'religious men'.[79] In this extraordinary declaration a bishop points to monks as among the best parochial administrators.

Jens also indicated that the monks' takeover of the church could help relieve their poverty, a startling assertion when one thinks of Esrum's landed wealth at this time. But he seems to have accepted a Cistercian claim that Esrum needed parish incomes, especially those of nearby parishes like Esbønderup, in order to maintain its wellbeing (and perhaps to secure a regular cash income). The Cistercians were not alone in using the theme of poverty. The Augustinians at Æbelholt and the Premonstratensians on Skåne were also given parish churches during this period on the basis of their claims of poverty.[80] It seems correct to characterize the Cistercian acquisition of patronage rights over parishes as a result of a general movement within Danish religious life to acquire parish incomes.[81] This tendency is hardly surprising. The unexpected element is the way bishops seemed to welcome the transfers of patronage to such institutions.

One possible explanation for the bishops' changed attitudes, besides the poverty of the parish churches themselves, is the appearance during these years of absentee or pluralistic holders of prebends in cathedral chapters. A number of wills issued at Lund, for example, come from canons who were also connected with other Danish cathedral chapters.[82] This practice had been frowned upon by the church ever since the Gregorian reform, but it seems first to have become widespread in Denmark about this time. An assertion in 1312 that clerks needed two benefices because they could not live from the income of one alone suggests a decline in parish incomes resulting from the agricultural crisis.[83] Moreover we begin to hear of clerks who had the income of Danish parishes but were studying abroad, chiefly at Paris.[84]

With so many absentee clerks and smaller incomes from individual parishes, Danish bishops may well have looked upon monastic willingness to take over nearby parish churches and their functions as a necessary solution. Both absentee clerks and monastic patrons upset the ideal ordering of parish life, but at least the Cistercians were accessible and accountable for their acts. Moreover the bishop would be dealing with a stable institution and not a changeable individual. It is impossible to establish a clear connection between clerks who were absent and monks who were willing to take over parishes, but the simultaneity of the two phenomena indicates a link.

One more indication that bishops did what they could to maintain good relations with the Cistercians during these years can be found in the matter of procurations, payments made in lieu of hospitality offered by a monastery to a bishop. The Ribe bishops regularly renewed the agreement of their predecessor Kristian from 1298 and thus apparently spared the monks any more trouble or expense on the question.[85] At Vitskøl procurations became a problem after Bishop Peder was elected at Viborg. The outcome of deliberations is carefully described in a document he issued to the monks in 1322, a source which reveals a great deal about the way Cistercians and their local bishops coexisted.

Peder states that after his election 'some of our clerks and lay persons of our diocese' had encouraged him to seek the payment of these procurations from the monks. But no matter how often or how adamantly he insisted on them, the brothers of Vitskøl were 'constantly and always denying them, saying that we had no right or jurisdiction over them nor ever had any'.[86] Such a statement recalls the Øm controversy during which the monks claimed they had no obligation to feed and lodge the bishop of Århus in return for benefits his predecessors had given them. For a while neither side would budge. The dispute that arose cause 'not only our church but also the said brothers' many expenses and burdens.

Bishop Peder went to the magnates of the realm, both ecclesiastical and secular, to settle the matter once and for all. Again the procedure resembles the preliminaries to the Øm controversy. To a meeting at Viborg came the Cistercian abbots of Tvis and Øm, both named Niels, together with various diocesan officials, the Franciscan guardian from Ålborg, the prior of Vitskøl, and the bailiff of the Danish king's seneschal. The presence of the abbots of Øm and Tvis shows continuing Cistercian cooperation in a period when it otherwise seems to have disappeared.

Bishop Peder states in the document drawn up afterwards that the outcome satisfied all parties. With an elegance and a decisiveness never shown at Øm, the bishop discussed the question of procurations with his cathedral chapter and concluded it was not worth pursuing it any further because he found that the right of procurations 'as it were had arisen in the past from an indeterminate author, when we decided that they [such procurations] were uncertain or insufficiently established'.[87] So, with the chapter's consent, Peder renounced all claims to procurations and declared invalid all earlier documents on the question. The monks would be totally immune in the future from any payment to the bishops. The language is clear and decisive, and when at the end with the list of witnesses and their seals it is said that the persons named were present 'at this friendly agreement', the expression seems to have been justified.

This settlement, on 12 May 1322, seeems to have been part of a general legal clarification between the Vitskøl monks and the Viborg bishops. On 14 May all the rights and privileges that Peder's predecessors had given the monks were confirmed.[88] First the gift of four churches they had received from earlier bishops was mentioned, together with a statement that it was completely up to the abbot to see that his monks took care of parish duties. Secondly, in all cases when the monks' labourers violated the sabbath, the abbot alone was to mete out punishment. This provision is known to us from both Sorø and Løgum, but the next one is new. The abbot is allowed to force his lay employees to pay their debts by threatening excommunication. If any of his labourers, or anyone else, demanded payment from one of his workers, then the abbot could use the same threat to make him pay. But if the abbot proved to be an inadequate judge in such a case, then appeal to the bishop would be permitted. The abbot's authority over his workers was not absolute. But if the abbot decreed a just punishment over one of his workers, and this person subsequently left his service, then the bishop was not to give him absolution until he had carried out the penance the abbot had imposed on him. In general the abbey's labourers could never be summoned by diocean officials into the bishop's court unless the bishop himself had expressely ordered it.

Unfortunately we have no documents with similarly specific provisions from other Danish Cistercian houses, but the good relations maintained between Løgum and Ribe or Sorø and Roskilde indicate that the Vitskøl-Viborg settlement was probably not unique. It expresses in specific terms the general direction of episcopal-Cistercian relations in the fourteenth century. The process of defining legal rights and obligations that began in the thirteenth century was carried still further. At the same time bishops admitted both implicitly and explicitly that good relations with the Cistercian monasteries in their dioceses were of importance to them.

Exactly why the Vitskøl monks wanted their jurisdiction over their labourers so precisely specified at this time is not clear. But the careful enumeration of the abbot's almost unlimited rights over his labourers points to the primary role such agricultural tenants had come to play in Cistercian monasteries. The Vitskøl-Viborg agreement can be looked upon as a final indication that lay brothers had ceased to play an important role in Danish Cistercian houses. It was more vital now than ever before for the monks to have a ready supply of agricultural workers and to have full jurisdiction over them. The Viborg bishop was in effect conceding to the Vitskøl abbot the rights of a manorial lord over his labourers, rights the Cistercian abbots had probably long since exercised. But the desire to specify the relationship of the abbey with its labourers may point to the beginning of the agricultural crisis of the fourteenth century, when labour became more scarce and landowners, both lay and religious, had trouble in holding onto their workers.

The third document from this major rapprochement between bishop and abbey came on 16 June 1322 and merely states that Bishop Peder had given up all letters and records which could ever support the demand of the Viborg church for procurations from Vitskøl. Fulfilling an agreement reached in the previous month, the abbot and the bishop had met in the church of Nørre-Tranders and destroyed all documents having to do with the dispute and declared that if any were found in the future, they would have no validity.[89] Like the first two documents, this declaration was kept at Vitskøl and helps explain why we have no record at all of any procuration dispute before 1322. As in the Dargun affair of the 1250s, the Cistercians tended to destroy historical records when a dispute was over in order to guarantee safety from future manifestations of the same problem. In such instances we can already see the medieval monks' attitude towards history, an attitude that the Viborg bishop clearly understood and accepted: all records that contradict the official and advantageous point of view were to be committed to the fire for they were potentially dangerous.

In view of this tendency to get rid of outdated materials, it is difficult to accept completely this settlement between the bishop and the monks for what it claims to be: a reasonable and amicable discussion of issues that led to a clear and disinterested outcome. The bishop of Viborg may well have been paid for his logic, as the bishop of Ribe had been in 1298.[90]

Nevertheless, such documents give the marked impression that the bishops and the Cistercians got on so well during these years because they were good businessmen and lawyers who could see a mutual advantage in harmony, compromise, and restraint. The emotionalism of Bishop Tyge and the monks of Øm had been replaced by precise reasonability. The polished surface of such documents may well hide disputes and tensions that would have been clear to us if we had better narrative sources. But the transactions whose record we have in episcopal and monastic collections point to a high degree of cooperation between bishops and monasteries in meeting the challenges and threats of the age.

PROBLEMS WITH NATIONAL AND INTERNATIONAL INSTITUTIONS: THE MONARCHY

The Cistercians needed the bishops more than ever during the first half of the fourteenth century, not only because of unrest and social chaos but also because the monarchy had become a real burden on monasteries. During the years after 1307, Erik Menved flooded Danish monasteries with privileges.[91] The Cistercians were not the only order to get renewals of their royal privileges and immunities every few years. We have similar records from Æbelholt, Næstved, and the Roskilde convents.[92] On the surface it looks as if Erik Menved was being generous to these houses, but in reality the frequent issuing of privileges was very likely a means of increasing royal income.[93] There is no direct proof, but it is a well know fact that Erik Menved, to finance his compaigns in the south, made use of every chance he had to raise revenue through various forms of taxation.[94]

In 1300 King Erik Menved indicated the tentative quality of a privilege renewal to Esrum by adding the unique clause that Esrum could maintain the customary privileges 'until we should deliberate with our counsellors what is to be done with these and other monastic liberties of this type'.[95] This phrase can be looked upon as a potential threat to the monasteries, even if Erik's probable intention was only to leave open the possibility that the monks would have to obtain further confirmations, as happened in 1308 and again in 1310.[96]

At the same time as the king used the abbeys as a source of income, the monks may have welcomed the opportunity to get hold of unprecedented privileges, as happened in 1301 when Erik gave the Esrum monks the right to buy freely in the town of Hälsingborg.[97] The monks still needed the king to back up important changes in their monastery's existence and probably took the initiative in approaching him, as happened in 1307 when Erik Menved took under his protection Esrum's newly acquired properties in Uggeløse.[98] Later in the century the monks had trouble with claimants to this valuable property, which they had received from Jon Jonsen Lille.[99] In asking the king for recognition of their property rights, the monks indicated a continuing desire to seek the protection of the monarchy, weak as it was.

With the accession of Kristoffer in 1320, it would appear that the Cistercians gained a champion for their cause. In 1315, he had issued a supremely generous charter to Sorø by which he handed over valuable properties in what today is the town of Frederikssund in return for burial in the abbey.[100] He promised the monks two days of pittances twice a year and described exactly what they were to consume, from split cod and imported beer to fine spices and mead. No matter where Kristoffer died, the monks were to fetch his body, at their own expense, and bring it to the abbey for a stately funeral. He was to be buried in the choir of the church, next to his brother, Duke Valdemar, who had been interred there in 1304.[101] Before the high altar of Sorø, wax candles of the most expensive kind were to burn night and day in his memory and for the repose of his soul. As a magnanimous indication of this grandiose figure, the candles were always to be replaced as soon as they had burned to half their original length. The 1315 testament and property gift may signal Kristoffer's attempt to emphasize his own claims to the throne and his disapproval of his brother, Erik Menved. The fact that Erik chose to be buried, like the Valdemars, in Ringsted's Benedictine abbey church, while Kristoffer chose Sorø for himself and his wife, indicates his intention of establishing his own position in Denmark.[102]

Immediately after Kristoffer became king, Sorø also seems to have benefited from his attentions. In March of 1320, the papal court dispensed a Sorø monk from the impediment of his illegitimate birth, which would have prevented him from entering the monastery.[103] This was done 'on the request of Duke Kristoffer'.

Probably in the same year, Kristoffer helped settle a dispute between Vitskøl and the canons of Viborg concerning possessions in Limfjorden, the great bay on the northwest coast of Jutland.[104] In July 1320, again on his request, Danish monks who attended the king were dispensed from the prohibition against eating meat. The dispensation came at the very time when the

Cistercian General Chapter was trying to tighten up this provision in the monastic rule, and Kristoffer's action may well have been intended primarily for the benefit of the local Cistercians.[105] In 1320 while he was a guest at Sorø, he confirmed the privileges of one of the Roskilde monasteries.[106]

Generosity and benevolence were only part of the story. In 1340 the monks of Vitskøl documented a sale of property on the island of Læsø to the chapter of Viborg and explained why it had been necessary for them to do so.[107] They had been obliged at the time to pay Kristoffer a 'not immodest' sum of money for their privileges and liberties. The language shows they had no choice. The monks claimed that they were 'forced by mere necessity, not having any other alternative except to alienate our goods for the sum of money required'.[108] Thus what appeared in 1320 as the benevolent intervention of Kristoffer to facilitate the sale of Læsø to the canons turns out to have been an act of compulsion by the king towards a Cistercian monastery.

The Sorø monks kept their promises to Kristoffer and, after his death in poverty and defeat, they brought his body to their monastery. Kristoffer's cash-on-the-barrel treatment of Vitskøl in 1320 points out decisively that royal attachment to one monastery of an order by no means guaranteed devotion or favouritism to the order as a whole.

In an age of confusion and bankruptcy it was of course impossible for a king like Kristoffer to act as his predecessors had done in the twelfth century in assuring incomes to the Cistercians. Whatever pious considerations Kristoffer may havce felt, he needed the money he extorted from Vitskøl, just as he needed the prestige that Sorø as a burial church could give him. The problem for the Cistercians was that they had become more useful to the monarchy by their money than by their prayers.

With the expulsion of Kristoffer in 1326 and the takeover of the country by Count Gerhard of Rendsborg, Valdemar Eriksen, the young Duke of Southern Jutland, became Valdemar III of Denmark. The privileges issued to Danish monasteries during his reign reflect Gerhard's vain attempt to consolidate his power in the eastern part of the country. Valdemar's generous charters suggest that the weaker the Danish king knew himself to be, the more liberal were the privileges he gave. Such is the case with Valdemar III's charter of 1328 to Sorø in which he exempted the abbey and its subjects from all payments to the king.[109] This was nothing new, but the jurisdiction handed over to the abbot of Sorø over his labourers covered every crime from theft to homicide. This may have been an explicit extension of powers the abbot was already exercising in secular cases.

The monks may well have welcomed this clarification, and it is probably no coincidence that such a charter came in the same decade in which Vitskol received almost unlimited spiritual jurisdiction over its labourers from the bishop of Viborg. The Cistercians were concerned with defining the legal restraints they could exercise over their workers. Count Gerhard and his puppet Valdemar fulfilled the monks' wildest dreams. A later generation at Sorø, however, aware that such a charter was not worth anything once a strong monarchy ascended the Danish throne, failed to include it in the Sorø collection of privileges drawn up in 1490. In November 1327 Valdemar III had already given the monks an unusual privilege: the right to buy and sell leather, food, and other necessities at markets everywhere in the kingdom.[110] But this privilege again was not included in the monks' 1490 collection.

Another privilege Valdemar III granted to Sorø but not renewed by his successors was exemption for the abbey's monks, lay brothers, and servants from paying tolls on crossing the Baltic.[111] Other Danish abbeys received royal privileges in 1327–28, but most of them are mentioned only in registers, so we lack full texts.[112] Nevertheless, it is likely that Gerhard, like Erik Menved, was liberal in his charters to Danish monasteries because he needed their support and, even more, the payments these institutions probably made in obtaining such documents.

With the accession of Valdemar Atterdag in 1340, Denmark finally got a strong king. As might be expected, he broke the tradition of his predecessors in handing out privileges to monastic foundations. In a July 1340 royal confirmation of privileges to Vitskøl, he ignored dynastic links with predecessors who had founded the monastery and merely mentioned Kristoffer and other 'illustrious kings of the kingdom of Denmark'. A general statement follows on the worth of monasteries for the kingdom.[113] The language has the polish and sophistication that hint at the new king's ambition to become a Christian prince who would gain recognition all over Europe for his achievements. The phrases may well have been borrowed from foreign charters, while the formulae are a departure from those of the 1200s.[114]

Like the Danish royal privileges of the mid-thirteenth century, this business document does not allow any speculation about the king's personal relationship with the monastery. Valdemar seems to have accepted as valid the traditions of his ancestors in giving the Cistercians specific privileges and full jurisdiction over their labourers. He also seems to have been aware of the difficulties experienced by Zealand monasteries during these years because of the unsettled political situation. In 1341 he forbade forced hospitality and attacks on clerks and monks and their property on Zealand.[115] Although this decree was probably meant mainly for the canons of Roskilde, it automatically gave protection to all houses on Zealand.

As we have seen, Valdemar placed Esrum under the guardianship of one of his men. Royal protection turned into something that may have been a little too intimate for the monks' liking.[116] We have no record of a general royal privilege for Sorø from this time, only a confirmation of the monks' holding of the Udensundby property obtained from Kristoffer.[117] Although it is likely that such a general privilege was given, Valdemar did not show the same interest in endowing Sorø and assuring his burial there that Kristoffer had done.

Valdemar Atterdag was a pragmatic king who governed his realm and expanded his power without sentiment. When a monastery could do him a favour, he did something in return. But when he had no particular need of a monastery, he tended to ignore it. Thus the Slangerup Cistercian house for women received a substantial and strategically-placed land gift from Valdemar in return for taking in a royal daughter, Agnes, the daughter of King Birger of Sweden.[118] Valdemar said he had settled the matter with the nuns and with his queen, Helvig. She is the first Danish queen we know of to have been buried at Esrum,[119] but her husband did not share her devotion.

Another instance of Valdemar's generosity to a religious house that had done him a service occurred at Næstved. There the Benedictines gave him a piece of land where he could build a stone residence for staying overnight on trips south. In return, Valdemar exempted the monks from the duty of providing hospitality for the king and his entourage whenever they came to the town.[120] All through this period there are complaints from the monasteries about nobles who imposed themselves, with their horses and hounds, on the monks and demanded lodging and feeding. The notation in the Næstved Book that Valdemar freed the monastery from 'hospitality and the burden of his servants, horses and dogs' is more than a formality. It indicates an important royal privilege that any Danish monastery would have envied.

The silence of the sources on the relationship between Valdemar Atterdag and the Danish Cistercians prevents any conclusions about his attitude towards the white monks.[121] Esrum received from Valdemar an important confirmation of its holdings in the disputed Uggeløse.[122] Three times during Valdemar's reign, in 1348, 1358 and 1359, the Swedish King Magnus took Esrum under his protection and gave it privileges for its holdings east of Øresund. These acts hint that the Swedish king was eager to exert a certain influence on Esrum.[123] He may have seen a unique opportunity at a time when he temporarily held Danish lands in Skåne and Halland, and the Cistercians thus needed his recognition of their rights and holdings. Whatever the triangular relationship among Swedish and Danish kings and monks may have been, the fact remains that neither Esrum nor Sorø gained any lands from Valdemar Atterdag. He was a tough businessman, and he was not about to give away anything without getting something worthwhile in return.

During this same period the Danish monastery at Ås in Halland seems to come into the orbit of the Swedish monarchy. In 1346 it was included in a testament of the Swedish royal family that otherwise benefited only Swedish foundations.[124] Before this time in at least two instances Swedish magnates had grouped Ås together with their own country's religious houses in their list of benefactions.[125] A clearer indication of the Swedish king's involvement with Ås is a request by King Magnus to Pope Clement VI in 1347 asking for confirmation of the privileges he had given the abbey.[126] The bestowal of such privileges is natural at a time when Magnus was still lord of Halland, but in the same request he speaks of 'great devotion' to Ås because some of his children were buried there. Thus a Danish Cistercian abbey whose fate is otherwise almost unknown to us turns out to have gained a bond with a Swedish king during the same years when the Danish king apparently had little to do with the Cistercians.

This situation emphasizes the way each Cistercian monastery had had to come to terms with the secular prince in its own region. Løgum had many dealings during these years with the Duke of Southern Jutland. He was responsible for helping the monks regain Brede church.[127] In the thirteenth century, the Danish king had intervened in the case for the monks, while now Duke Valdemar was the key figure.

During these uncertain years, the Cistercians had had to adapt themselves to alternating periods of strong and weak monarchy, and even to no monarch at all. They could not expect royal generosity and at time must have feared economic exploitation by the king. But in general Cistercian monasticism and Danish monarchy had few contacts with each other. Only Kristoffer tied his fortunes to those of the monks, but they could do little for him until his life was over.

THE PAPACY

At first glance one might think the Avignon popes were just what the Danish Cistercians needed.[128] They were excellent lawyers and administrators, had able staffs, and the number of documents they left that dealt with Denmark indicate they were well-informed about Danish problems. Despite their bureaucratic machinery, however, the popes could do little or nothing to alter a relatively minor land dispute in Denmark. The monks could appeal to their hearts' content and get all the papal privileges or decisions they wanted, but in Denmark as elsewhere in Europe excommunication or interdict had become outmoded threats.

A decree in 1320 that the prior of Odense and the provost and chanter of Århus were to protect Løgum abbey may have some connection with the monks' attempt to assert their claims over Brede.[129] In 1327 Pope John XXII confirmed their holdings there.[130] But after 1334, when Sorø monks were given the right to accept inheritances, until 1357, we have no record of any papal privileges issued for Danish Cistercian abbeys.[131] In the case of Esrum, whose record collection is more complete than that of any other Cistercian house, this gap suggests that the monks may have stopped applying for such priviliges. We have no papal confirmation of Esrum's rights from 1309 until 1382, an apparent gap of more than seventy years.[132]

One reason for this hesitation to use the papal court may have been that Danish churchmen were increasingly being ordered by the court to carry out various legal tasks. As part of the extensions of canon law into all aspects of church life, it became a common practice under John XXII and his successors to delegate matters brought to the attention of the papal court to local ecclesiastics. Often these on-the-spot officials merely had to see that a papal appointee was properly installed as a cathedral canon in Denmark.[133] Sometimes they had to help an institution in trouble, as in 1320 when Abbot Peder of Esrum was ordered to see that the Johannite monks in Norway were given restitution for harm done them by King Haakon.[134] Often the appointees could delegate their powers to others, or only one or two of the appointees actually went ahead with the task given them. But clearly in many situations Danish Cistercian abbots were involved in difficult controversies that demanded time and expense. Unfortunately we have only the papal appointments and no record of outcomes or monastic reaction, but the decline of Danish Cistercian applications to Avignon may well be due to a desire to steer clear of close involvement with the papal machinery of justice. At the same time monks would have been more reluctant than ever to make the long journey south and traverse areas of social and political unrest on the way, as well as burden their own less prosperous houses with the expenses involved.

THE GENERAL CHAPTER, NORTH GERMAN ABBEYS, AND CONTACTS AT HOME

Just as the monks stopped using the papacy to get help in solving their problems, they also stayed away from the Cistercian General Chapter. In 1321 the Chapter ordered the abbots of Friesland and Denmark to send two of their number from each of the provinces every year or to be punished severely.[135] This suggests that the Danish abbots had stopped coming regularly to Citeaux. There are no further decisions on the matter, but the records of the General Chapter from the decades after 1320 indicate that the Order as a whole was going through a structural crisis. With the beginning of the Hundred Years' War in 1337, the General Chapter became all the more difficult to reach.[136]

Nevertheless, it was during these years after the bull *Fulgens sicut stella*, issued in 1335 by the Cistercian pope Benedict XII to reform his order, that we find evidence for a consistent attempt to regulate the financial system of the order. The Citeaux accounts for 1337–47, brought to light by the British historian Peter King, manifest the usual Cistercian determination to regulate practices and to ensure the order's international structure.[137] They are especially revealing in their silences concerning various Danish abbeys. As King has pointed out 'Herrevad, Ås, Vitskøl, Øm, Holm and Knardrup do not occur in the payments at all'.[138] There are payments from Sorø in 1339, 1343, and 1347; from Esrum in 1337, 1341, and 1343; Tvis in 1339, 1343 and 1347; Ryd in 1339, and Løgum in 1347. The overlapping would indicate that Danish abbeys may have joined forces to send a monk off to the General Chapter to pay for his own house and others, as for Sorø and Tvis in 1343, or Tvis and Løgum in 1347. In 1339 Andrew, a monk of Esrum, brought payments to Citeaux for Sorø, Tvis, and Ryd.[139] Andrew's money was looked upon with some contempt: the 'fifteen florins of lesser weight' he brought for Sorø was valued at eleven *livres tournois* and five shillings; Ryd's sixteen florins 'of good weight' was worth twelve *livres*, while Tvis's five florins 'of light weight' were reduced to three *livres* and fifteen shillings.[140]

The Danish houses had to contend not just with the dangers of war and the inconveniences of long distance travel but also with the bad reputation of their money. In the face of these obstacles, King's comment on the order as a whole seems especially apt for Denmark: 'That the taxation system did not work perfectly is not, perhaps, as surprising as the fact that, in the turbulent fourteenth century, many houses were still prepared to take their obligations to the order seriously'.[141]

Perhaps so many Danish houses are missing from the Citeaux rolls because they did not necessarily have to send representatives to the General Chapter in order to pay their assessments. During this period the General Chapter was beginning to appoint abbots as collectors of 'contributions' from the individual monasteries. Løgum and Tvis refused to pay, and their abbots were severly disciplined in 1352.[142] The Esrum abbot, who was appointed comissioner of the General Chapter, had first denounced the two abbots and forbidden them to exercise their priestly duties. Despite this grave sentence, the abbots had continued to celebrate mass and thus had completely ignored the General Chapter with its insistence on regular payments. It called for an enquiry into the charges by the abbot of Esrum and declared that, if they were correct, then the abbots of Tvis and Løgum were to be deposed. The Herrisvad abbot, as father immediate of the two houses was to carry out this investigation.

In 1254, the deposed abbot of Sorø was accused of disrupting the peace of another Danish monastery and going beyond his rights as visitor. By the mid-fourteenth century the problem had become not a dispute between two Danish monasteries but the refusal of Danish abbots to carry out the decrees of the General Chapter. The period witnesses a culmination of the crisis of power for international organizations that we already noticed at the end of the thirteenth century. Monastic institutions concentrated on local, and de-emphasized international, bonds.

In one instance, however, a daughter of Esrum did turn to the General Chapter for help with an internal problem. But this daughter was not a Danish house but the North German Eldena. The 1347 General Chapter recorded the petition of abbots Heinrich of Stolpe, Heinrich of Neuen-camp, and Jakob of Esrum, that the abbot of Eldena be allowed to sell some property that was causing the monastery excessive expenses.[143] Fortunately we have the full text of a charter describing the matter in detail. Written at Esrum on 5 August 1347, it seems to have been drawn up for the sake of an Eldena messenger, perhaps the abbot himself, on his way to the General Chapter. Abbot Jakob stated that he recently had performed his duty of annual visitation at Eldena,[144] a valuable indication to us that the mother-daughter relationship among Cistercian houses in the North was more than an empty formality in the fourteenth century. Abbot Jakob says that he found the abbey of Eldena in desperate straits because of immense debts mounting up because of high interest owed on money the monastery had had to borrow. The cause of the abbey's indebtedness is not given but debt was not unusual in a period of bad harvests, social unrest, and declining income from agricultural properties.[145] Jakob called together the abbot of Eldena, Martin, and all the monks to discuss the problems. For the first time in Danish Cistercian history outside of the Øm dispute we see the function-ing of an abbey's own chapter at a time of visitation. The visitor consulted with all the monks, not just with the abbot.[146]

It emerged from the chapter that Eldena held some properties at a great distance from the monastery, at Strippau, and these lands had for a long time been more a burden than a benefit. In the last several years they had provided no income at all but had caused many difficulties to members of the community who had had to travel to them to administer them. The un-settled quality of the period is suggested in these lines. Travel over long dis-tances had become a dangerous undertaking, and the Eldena monks felt jus-tified in their desire to concentrate their efforts on nearby holdings. It was proposed that the monastery sell the goods, and all the monks gave their consent, 'beginning with the older ones and in descending order to the younger ones'. This together with the assertion that 'no one opposed' the measure, is almost a formula but it also gives a glimpse of the Cistercian decision-making process, with formal consent required from the entire chapter for a matter of great importance to a house.

The abbot of Esrum agreed that the properties could rightly be sold to help the monks out of their financial dilemma. An elegant conclusion, full of rich metaphors and repeated phrases, sums up the various arguments of the letter and gives the monks full power to make the sale.[147] Better than any other document from this period, it illustrates the continuing functioning of Cistercian structures: the individual abbey's chapter, the practice of visitation by the mother abbey, and the involvement of the General Chapter.

Another indication of Esrum's international contacts during this period is a copy in the Esrum Codex of a letter obtained by the abbots at Citeaux and giving papal permission for the monks to sing the office during interdicts.[148] The abbots of Dargun, Colbaz, and Eldena all witnessed that they had seen the original document's attestation by the abbots of Clairvaux, Citeaux, and Morimund. Thus Esrum's acquisition of a copy indicates the abbey had been in contact with one of these North German abbeys, Eldena or perhaps Colbaz.

Despite growing localism, national and international structures were still there to be used occasionally.[149] Even if we do not find the Danish abbots functioning in unison as they had in the 1260s, cooperation between individual abbeys warns us against looking at each monastery as a totally isolated entity. Sorø maintained its relationships with the Roskilde Cistercian nuns,[150] while Esrum and the Slangerup nuns engaged in a property exchange which seems to have been to the monks' advantage.[151] Sometimes, however, Cistercian nuns clearly benefited from their dependence. When Swedish Cistercian nuns were having troubles with their land holdings on Zealand, they received help from the abbot of Varnhem in central Sweden.[152]

During the period when the monks of Knardrup were unable to return to their monastery, they may well have been lodged at Sorø. In a document from 1339, Peder, abbot of Knardrup, and one of his monks, Brother Jens of Sweden, appear as witnesses at Sorø.[153] Esrum became increasingly involved at about the same time with commercial activities. When a citizen of Hälsingborg, Peder Pedersen, deeded two market stalls to Esrum in 1338, he did so in the presence of Abbot Anders of Herrisvad.[154] Because of his geographical proximity, the abbot of Herrisvad took care of a business matter for his colleague at Esrum.

Of all the Cistercian abbeys for which we have substantial sources, only Løgum does not manifest contact with other houses. This may be an accident of the sources, but it may also reflect Løgum's isolated situation in Southern Jutland and the fact that the monks there normally could count on help from the bishop of Ribe and his chapter and so did not have to turn to their sister abbeys.[155] The instances that we do have of cooperation among the abbeys are so undramatic that it would be easy to minimize their importance. But the presence of such bonds shows that the monks still in some situations looked upon each other as fellow members of an international order with natural links among its components.

FINANCE AND PROPERTIES: ADJUSTMENTS AND EXPANSION

After 1300 Danish Cistercian abbeys began to lend money to landowners and in return to receive land mortgaged to the monks as collateral. In 1309 at Sorø a mortgage was arranged with the express provision that so long as the monks held the debtor's land, they could not collect the full amount of the property's yearly income for themselves.[156] While the debt remained outstanding and the monks profited from the land's income, they promised to pay their debtor, the Roskilde citizen Niels Torstensen, three marks yearly.

The mortgaged property is likely to have given a yearly profit of more than three marks, so they were making money from the transaction. Later mortgages usually specified that the monks would be allowed to keep the full annual income of the property involved. To avoid the charge of usury the borrower would state that he was freely giving the income 'as alms' to the monks.[157] Sometimes the monks' reception of this income would be subtracted from the principal of the loan, and so if the monks held the land for long enough, the borrower would soon be free of debt. But normally the Cistercians got hold of properties in which the annual income was given to them as their right and not deducted from the principal.[158] This meant that after the agreed number of years had elapsed, the monks could ask for repayment of the full amount of the loan.

Sometimes the borrower convinced the monks to renew the loan and even managed to borrow more money on the same property. At Alsted near Sorø Jens Nielsen Hviding in 1329 renewed a mortgage made by his grandmother, the Lady Ingeborg. Jens was given the monks' own land in Døjringe to keep freely for three years.[159] The dry notations of the Donation Book do not reveal Sorø's motivation for being so generous in this case. The probable motive was a desire to stay on good terms with an influential local family whose gifts could still enrich the monastery.

In 1333 Jens Nielsen Hviding had to give up the Døjringe but soon regretted his act and made trouble for the monks.[160] He finally convinced the monks that it was worth his while to give up Døjringe only if they bestowed on him some of their most valuable spiritual benefits. He was to be named among the main benefactors of the house, and the monks were to promise to meet the expenses of his funeral. The agreement shows that it was important for Jens to be buried among his ancestors at Sorø, but it also indicates that a landowner with strategic holdings could sometimes almost blackmail the monks into marketing their own spiritual benefits and giving up material advantages for a while to get what they wanted in the long run. Normally when a mortgage ran out and the principal had not been repaid, the monks appropriated the land. But knights like Jens Nielsen could make this process extremely difficult and tedious. The Alsted property had originally been mortgaged by Hamund Hamundsen in 1316, but Ingeborg, his widow, had managed in 1326 to extend the mortgage and to borrow a hundred marks more of silver on it. Now, three years later, Jens Nielsen gained further concessions on it. Finally in 1343 the monks' patience paid off. They gained a liberal mortgage on a nearby rich property at Fjenneslev from Jens Nielsen Hviding's widow, Kristine.[161]

In such transactions Sorø and other Danish Cistercian houses appear almost as banking institutions. Even kings borrowed money, as Erik Menved did in 1319 from Sorø.[162] In 1340 Ingefred, daughter of the knight Peder Jonsen, mortgaged her properties in Lindholm and Mødrup in Uggeløse parish to Esrum for a hundred marks of silver.[163] The charter is especially valuable for her statement that now, as previously when she had been in financial trouble, she looked to the monks for help and was grateful to them for giving it so willingly. She mentions her 'frequent need, not once but often', and how the monks replied to her 'both promptly and kindly' so that with her 'difficulties resolved', she could now again feel free.[164] The monks were hardly doing her a favour, for if she could not repay the principal, they would certainly appropriate her land. But her statement shows how the Cistercians functioned in lay aristocratic society. They were there, willing to lend a hand, for a good mortgage. In the midst of economic crisis the Cistercians were privileged to have ready cash to lend out in return for mortgages on lands.

Normally when the monks themelves purchased property, they paid cash or exchanged others of their holdings for it.[165] They were interested in consolidating their holdings and seem to have had a certain success. Esrum gained lands in Northern Zealand, while Sorø added properties to the south of its main holdings in Alsted herred. Løgum seems to have been extremely active in the area to the east and north of the abbey, while even Øm managed to add to its lands in Dover and Illerup parishes. At times we discover the monks selling their property, apparently for cash, but this usually happened with distant holdings of little value to the abbey's agriculture. Similarly the monks at times could be forced to purchase new property in installments because they lacked sufficient liquidity.[166]

In 1318 for the first time a Sorø purchase included an indemnity clause, another sign of the more sophisticated financial dealings in which the monks were engaging.[167] The seller agreed to compensate the monks if for some reason they were deprived of taking possession of the property. Symptomatic of this monastic high finance is the development of the office of procurator to look after the legal affairs of Cistercian monasteries. When Niels Jakobsen, probably in 1330, renounced all rights to the properties in Skåne testamented to Esrum by his brother Jens Jakobsen, his oath was recorded by 'Brother Michael, procurator of the reverend lords in Esrum'.[168] Apparently a Cistercian monk with legal training, Michael's job was to represent the interest of the abbey in contacts with noblemen who did business with the monks. The office of procurator apparently grew out of that of cellarer, and it is impossible to tell here if Michael was cellarer too. The phrase, 'the reverend lords of Esrum', innocuous as it looks shows how far we have come from twelfth-century charters when the Danish Cistercians were described in terms of their poverty. Now they are described as monastic lords, aristocratic gentlemen who are careful to assure their rights and holdings.

The charters we have for property sales in the years after 1300 betray a steep inflationary tendency in prices, and here also the monks had to adapt. They soon gave up computing prices in marks of money (based on the coinage system with its reduced silver content) and went over to evaluations in pure silver.[169] This secured their economic transactions from the risk of inflationary loss. In this way as in others, the monks coped with a tough noble class that had few sentimental bonds with them. In return for the liquid capital these landowners needed during a time of war and invasion, the monks got more land, something of which they never could get enough.

THE CISTERCIANS IN THE CONTEXT OF A MORE VARIED SOCIETY

The Cistercians did well during these troubled years not merely because they were financially able and legally astute. They learned how to deal with all elements within Danish society, from the poorest of their own tenants to the richest of religious institutions like the chapter at Roskilde or the Benedictine abbey at Næstved. The variety and relative fullness of our sources for this period enable us to see the interdependence of groups in Danish society.

At the lowest level, the sources after 1307 for the first time mention individual peasant holdings that owed rent (*landgilde*) to the Cistercian houses.[170] The breakup of the old grange system after the decline of lay brother recruitment seems to have been followed by the abandonment of large estates with peasant labour for the sake of individual plots held by rent-paying tenants. This was the dominant agricultural system for the Danish Cistercian monasteries from about 1300 and until the Reformation.[171]

The decline of grange farming and the increased use of the rent system may be connected with a general European agrarian crisis, with declining population, abandoned farms, and the consequent need for big landowners to give peasants an incentive to stay on the land. The careful enumeration of individual tenants in Danish monastic land transactions after about 1320 indicates that their landlords were aware that, in selling a piece of property, they needed to let the new owner know who his tenants were so that he could hold onto them. Just as the specific mention of independent peasants who became lay brothers at Sorø in about 1250 points to a shortage of *conversi*, so too the new tendency to record the names of tenants indicates that they were in short supply.

If the new relations with peasant tenants formed the backbone of the late medieval system of cultivation, the monasteries' relations with the village gentry (*armigeri*) and with the parish priests continued important. Without the cooperation of these groups the monks would have lacked an essential link with the power structure of the rural landscape. When the Århus canon Jens Jakobsen handed over his Vejby property to Esrum, he said he did so under the seal of his 'beloved friend Michael, pastor of the church at Søborg'.[172] Jens may well have come from the area and this may explain his devotion to the monks. But he could also have been encouraged by his friend Michael to give the land. If so, the Esrum monks had succeeded in convincing yet another local priest of their worth, just as they had done at the turn of the century. Also present at this property transfer were Jakob Karlsen, Jens Pedersen of Hillerødsholm, Henrik Isulvsen, Niels Pedersen of Slangerup, and Jakob Jensen of Havelse, who are collectively named *armigeri*. They and men like them guaranteed Esrum's position in the lay community. Their legal participation strengthened such a charter, and they were the men Esrum would call upon first if it felt itself in physical danger.

The same pattern of dependence on local priests and gentry is apparent at Løgum, to which in 1347 Hågen, parish priest at Skærbæk, handed over land in the town of Varde.[173] In Southern Jutland it is difficult to distinguish the gentry from the knights, whose social position was higher. It has been asserted that the nobility in this part of the country were weaker and less rich than elsewhere.[174] An investigation of the Løgum Book's property charters supports this observation. Løgum did business with knights only very occasionally. Most of its transactions were carried out with local landowners who were probably either independent peasants or *armigeri* at best. Only a few rich families benefited the monks of Løgum in the same way as nobles on Zealand did Sorø and Esrum. The relative paucity of noble families who gave support and business to the monks may have also been the case at other Jutlandic Cistercian houses, but our records for an abbey like Vitskøl are very scanty. The Skanderborg Register for Øm, however, does suggest that the monks here were almost exclusively involved with small owners who would have come at best from the lower nobility.

A vivid description of how local landowners handed over holdings to the monks is given in a 1343 charter by Duke Valdemar III of Jutland for Løgum. His appointed judge, Vagn Nielsen, set up a court at the very gate of Løgum Abbey, and here Tyge Esbernsen gave up property in four villages to the monks. The locations are given together with the names of the peasants living on each property. Also the inhabitants of the *berred* (county) are said to have witnessed the transaction. In 1345 the gifts were renewed, with the specific provision that daily masses were to be said for Tyge at the altar of Mary Magdalen.[175] The deed is noticeable for the specific details of its provisions. The donor required a given number of masses at a named altar in the abbey church and not just general spiritual benefits.

During this period knights continued to hand over properties to Løgum, sometimes for spiritual benefits alone, sometimes also for payment in land or money. In 1334 a knight, Jakob Roost, gave rich holdings to Løgum and said the thought of death had inspired him. He asked for burial at Løgum and claimed that he had been devoted to the monastery since childhood: '...*affectum cum consorte mea, pro ipsius profectu, a primeva aetate habeo specialem*'.[176] In such an unusual declaration we can visualize the fascination the building of the still incomplete abbey church might have exercised on a member of the local aristocracy. At the monastery whose construction had provided a background of both childhood and adulthood, the knight could look forward to burial.

Likewise wives of knights often gave rich donations to the monks, even if the gifts were not always as extravagant as they had been earlier.[177] A new group in society that during these decades began to have dealings with the monks consisted of citizens of towns. Tønder, Slesvig, Søborg, Roskilde, Slagelse—all began to figure in the economic life of Cistercian monasteries.[178] This development can be seen most clearly at Ribe, where the monks of Løgum were able to gain several properties.[179]

Finally, in their relations with other religious houses, the Cistercians seem to have done well. They managed to attract canons of Roskilde and Lund to Sorø as monks—apparently without causing complications in the abbey's dealings with their cathedrals.[180] The period witnessed a great number of property exchanges between Cistercian and Benedictine houses. Løgum and Ribe cathedral continued their longstanding cooperation with each other. But there are signs of the changed times. The testaments of Lund canons, who in the thirteenth century had usually left token gifts to Skåne Cistercians, became purely local bequests. The same is usually the case at Ribe.

For a donor looking around for the most needy recipient of his wealth, the Cistercians hardly stood out. He was more apt to think of the Holy

Ghost houses and leper hospitals which had an immediate social function. Education was becoming more concentrated at cathedral schools, and here too were worthy objects of pious gifts.[181] When an archdeacon of Ribe drew up his will, probably in 1344, he left half of what he had to the Holy Ghost house and the other half to the poor scholars of Pughus.[182] Such local concern was only natural, but it isolated the Cistercians from the cultural changes taking place around them. The monks' main duties now—when seen in terms of society as a whole—were to collect rents and to say masses for the innumerable dead. The Cistercian houses were in danger of becoming archaic rural institutions, self-perpetuating but inward-looking in a way Bernard and his monks never had been.

An indication of the Cistercians' conservative outlook is provided by the case of a Franciscan friar who left his convent and tried to becomer a Cistercian.[183] The pope gave him permission to transfer, but after repeatedly being turned away from Cistercian houses, the poor fellow had to settle for becoming a Benedictine at Odense. The Cistercians claimed they were unable to take him because of their poverty and the devastation of their monasteries by the wars Denmark had suffered (apparently in the period both before and after King Valdemar's takeover in 1340). The Cistercian appeal also mentions the destruction wrought by the plague, one of the few references in contemporary Danish sources to the event. Certainly the Cistercians were not as rich as they had been in 1300. But their failure to accommodate a potential new member who had sought papal permission to join them points to a certain stiffening in their organization. In all fairness, however, it should be added that two former Franciscans did manage to join Løgum and Ryd in 1334, despite resistance put up by the friars' superiors.[184]

The relative popularity of the monks on all levels of society, as seen in the documents of this period, could not have been achieved if the treatment of Bartholomaeus Jensen, the rejected Franciscan, had been typical. Cistercians prospered because they managed to be useful to all segments of Danish society on both spiritual and material planes. Looking back over this rich and confusing period, one realizes how few individual personalities have emerged. We have no abbots like Gunner or Bo of Øm to reveal the inner Cistercian mind. No remarkable bishops like Sven of Århus in the twelfth century or his successor Tyge in the thirteenth cast their shadows over the monks of the fourteenth century. Only the people who managed to convey their stories to Avignon have survived for us as personalities involved with the monks: Valborg, the disappointed foundress of Opager, or Bartholomaeus, the rejected friar. We have dealt with groups and classes in society instead of with individuals, and it may seem we have lost track of the Cistercians as persons.

The usual explanation for this lack of penetration to the individual's situation is a lack of necessary sources. But a more fruitful point of view is that our very lack of such sources tells us about the character of the age we have been dealing with and thus reveals something essential about fourteenth-century monks. In Denmark, as elsewhere in Cistercian Europe, the sources for the twelfth and thirteenth centuries are abundant in narratives because the content of life during these centuries invited representation in this historical form. In the twelfth century, the Cistercians looked upon themselves and were looked upon as heroes, and so it was only natural to emphasize individual monasteries and their members, their trials and tribulations in getting started in Denmark, and the individual bishops who helped them. In the thirteenth century, the Cistercians had to fight to establish their rights and privileges in society, and so it was natural for the monks at Øm, Sorø, and Ryd to write accounts of themselves to establish those rights. But in the fourteenth century, the Cistercians had a guaranteed place in society, even if its life was full of violence. In such a social context the monks no longer needed chronicles and their polemics, only records to keep track of the business of everyday life. Twelfth-century sources tell about heroes; fourteenth-century materials reflect shrewd businessmen. This difference is not due just to the arbitrary disappearance of monastic sources in Denmark after the Middle Ages. It is a reflection of the development of the Cistercian Order in Europe as a whole. The advantage for us is that such mundane documents reveal the everyday concerns of the monasteries instead of emphasizing the great polemical issues as thirteenth century narratives had done.

Beneath all this practicality and common sense, the monks still sang the liturgy and spent a good part of their lives in prayer. All this is beyond our grasp in the sources we have. Despite all economic explanations and class analyses for the Danish Cistercians, they should be looked upon also as men steeped in an almost inexhaustible spiritual tradition.

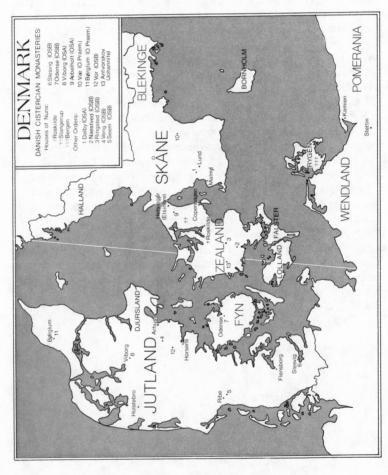

DENMARK

DANISH CISTERCIAN MONASTERIES:

Houses of Nuns:
†Roskilde
††Slangerup
†††Bergen

Other Orders:
1 Dalby (OSA)
2 Naestved (OSB)
3 Ringsted (OSB)
4 Veng (OSB)
5 Seem (OSB)

6 Slesvig (OSB)
7 Odense (OSB)
8 Viborg (OSA)
9 Aebelholt (OSA)
10 Væ (O.Praem.)
11 Børglum (O. Praem.)
12 Vor (OSB)
13 Antvorskov (Johannite)

Danish Monastic Houses

VII

Complexity, Isolation and Vitality

1357–1414 and beyond

THE LAST HALF OF THE FOURTEENTH CENTURY and the beginning of the fifteenth take us a long way from the Cistercians we first met on their way to Denmark from Citeaux and Clairvaux in the 1140s and 1150s. The twelfth-century Cistercians in their energy and piety depended institutionally and emotionally on close links between Citeaux-Clairvaux and Denmark. In the early thirteenth century, the Danish successors of these French monks consolidated their gains, while in the second half of that century they faced challenges to their position in church and society. They emerged neither unscathed nor triumphant, but Cistercian monasteries continued to play a significant role in Danish society. After about 1300 the abbeys began to function less as members of an international order and more as individual units. They could depend on the generosity of the local aristocracy and especially its female members. This continued to be the case in the second half of the fourteenth century. A significant reduction in the number of documentary sources we have may point to a slowdown of business and property gains as a result of the shock of the agricultural crisis and the Black Death. But the paucity of sources may also be an accident of history.

In the last half of the fourteenth century, we lack for the first time, even the briefest chronicle or annals to provide something of the Cistercian view of historical events. Consequently we can only look at the monks as others saw them. Because of this limitation, I shall include material in this chapter from later in the fifteenth century when it helps illuminate the development

221

of Cistercian monasticism during the remainder of the medieval period. This more thematic approach has the advantage of showing how some aspects of Danish Cistercian history continued to have importance until the Reformation. The king's role, for example, remained just as important for the monks at the end of the fourteenth and in the fifteenth centuries as it had been earlier. The aristocracy also continued to patronize Cistercian monasteries, to use them as burial places, and to request the monks' prayers. Among both royalty and nobility, however, changes were taking place in their relationship with the Cistercians. The king asked more from the monks than he apparently had done in the thirteenth century, while the aristocracy required better land deals and made exhaustive lists of specific spiritual services the monks were to provide for them.

The Cistercians could cope with such demands, but only in the context of their individual abbeys. The old Cistercian brotherhood in an international order leaves few traces. A number of monasteries showed vitality and initiative, keeping up to date with the requirements of society as a whole. We can see the culmination of this Cistercian openness to secular society in the fifteenth century when the monks began to use the Danish language instead of Latin in charters and made a political commentary on Danish history in the Rhyme Chronicle at Sorø. A vivid, if unconscious, expression of the monks' rapprochement with the secular world is an altarpiece made for Esrum in 1396 and still in existence. Its iconography, as we shall see points to both continuity and change in Danish Cistercian values. In what follows I shall try to use such diverse memorials of the Danish Cistercians in order to complete our picture of the monks in medieval Denmark.

THE AMBIGUOUS ROYAL ATTITUDE

In examining the relationship of the Cistercians with King Valdemar Atterdag until 1375 and then with his daughter Queen Margrethe until her death in 1412, we are limited mainly to Sorø and Esrum. Our sources for Vitskøl during this period reveal nothing concerning royal privileges, while Løgum seems to come more than ever into the orbit of the dukes of Southern Jutland and Holstein.[1] In only one instance do we find a charter from Løgum including King Valdemar.[2] This is natural in view of the fact that neither Valdemar nor Margrethe succeeded in limiting the very strong German political and social dominance of Southern Jutland during this period.[3] The monks of Løgum seem to have accepted the political situation and to have done their best to cooperate with the dukes.

The Zealand houses found it absolutely essential to forge a positive relationship with the newly-established monarchy. As we saw in the last chapter, Valdemar did very little to encourage the Cistercians. He was caught up in building strongholds at strategic points all over the island. When religious foundations occupied the site he had chosen, Valdemar sought papal permission to get their houses moved, as was the case at Kalundborg.[4] In direct competition with established monasteries, Valdemar founded chapels in his new fortifications and obtained papal permission to make places of pilgrimage of these new centres of royal power. Pilgrims could obtain indulgences from visiting them.[5]

The Cistercians were irrelevant to Valdemar's schemes. He concentrated either on fortifications in the countryside, as at Gurre in Northern Zealand, or in the growing market towns of the island. At Næstved on Southern Zealand he made agreements with the important abbeys and gave them benefits in return.[6] But Cistercian monasteries tucked away in the countryside had no strategic value to him. In the area around Esrum he did acquire estates from landowners who were in trouble. Previous Danish kings would then have made them available to the monks, either as gifts or to purchase. But Valdemar seems to have tried to regain as much property as possible in Northern Zealand for the crown and never once made the slightest gift or exchange with Esrum.[7] Valdemar wanted to make the fortification of Gurre into an impregnable stronghold, and in order to do so he confiscated some of the properties of the Augustinian community at Æbelholt. After the king's death, the keeper of the castle, Olav Bjørnsen, probably on the order of Queen Margrethe, compensated the canons for their losses.[8] They as well as the Zealand Cistercians may have felt some relief when the restless Valdemar was lowered into his grave at his castle of Vordingborg.

After the winter of silence or hostility following the anarchy of the 1330's, the wars of the 1340's and Valdemar's reign, the assumption of power by Margrethe in 1375 marks a new flowering in the relationship between the monarchy and the Cistercians. Margrethe had her father's body moved to Sorø, where he was buried in the monks' choir, a significant event in the monastery's history.[9] Royal burial at Sorø, which so far had been the case only for the unfortunate Kristoffer II, now looked as if it might become a regular practice. With the body of the king who had brought stability back to Denmark, Sorø took Ringsted's place as the preferred burial church for the royal family.

In death Valdemar conceded the place of the Danish Cistercians. The executor of his testament handed over fifty marks in silver to Abbot Swederus of Esrum in 1378 so that the monks would say a daily mass for Valdemar at the 'altar of the holy confessors' in the southern part of the abbey church. The monks were to enjoy pittances once a year in Valdemar's memory and to have 'three good courses aside from the usual meal' and be refreshed by 'one barrel of German beer' (considered to be of better quality than Danish!).[10] A similar arrangment was made with Troels, the abbot of Næstved, also in 1378, while at Ås abbey in Halland, Abbot Peder received from Queen Margrethe a gilded table with relics enclosed in it so that he would say a daily mass in the abbey church for the souls of Valdemar and his queen, Helvig.[11] All the monks who were priests were to participate in an annual commemoration of the couple. Moreover, they were to summon as many secular priests as they could from surrounding parishes.

In this last endowment the role of Margrethe is clear, while the earlier arrangements may have been made by Valdemar himself on his deathbed. But it was more likely Margrethe who arranged the masses and pittances at Esrum and Næstved. It is ironic that a king who had done so little good in his life for the Danish Cistercians should have been remembered so methodically at Sorø, Esrum, and Ås. But Margrethe's reign brought new royal attention to the white monks.

From our knowledge of Margrethe it is impossible to explain why she was drawn especially to the Cistercians, but the fact that she was a woman is significant in this connection. Cistercian monks were often able to form spiritual bonds with women, relationships manifested materially in wills.[12] From the moment Margrethe assumed power, she forged such links. It could be that her devotion to the monks stemmed from her childhood upbringing at the fortress of Akershus, at the bottom of Oslo Fjord.[13] The most prominent sight from the parapet of this imposing structure is an island where the Cistercian house of Hovedø (or Hovedøya) had existed since the twelfth century. The substantial ruins still there today point to a great medieval complex. Geographically at least, Margrethe was close to the Cistercians during her formative years.

To the Cistercian nuns of Zealand, Queen Margrethe played an important role. In 1387 the prioress of the monastery of Our Lady at Roskilde leased out a property in return for an annual sum in payment. She obtained the consent of her father immediate, the abbot of Sorø, and also that of Queen Margrethe.[14] The Cistercian nuns of Slangerup in 1391 reached with Henneke Olufsen of the powerful Grubbe family an important settlement which gave them compensation in return for the nuns' withdrawal of certain charges they had made against him.[15] The abbot of Esrum, Troels, sealed the agreement, showing that he still functioned as father immediate for Roskilde. Margrethe was present at the transaction.

For many decades the Cistercians had had to function without the monarchy's help or with a weak king whose benevolence toward the abbeys meant very little. With Margrethe the monks were blessed with a strong ruler who was there when they needed her. But the good old days of twelfth-century monarchs had not returned. Danish society was different now, and Margrethe did not give landed bequests on the scale that her illustrious predecessors had done. She made only a single gift to Sorø.[16] Esrum she could hardly have pleased when in 1377 she obtained papal permission to transfer the body of her mother Queen Helvig from its resting place there to Sorø. The excuse she gave was that Esrum was threatened by collapse, an assertion worth examining later.[17] The monks apparently had enough of a surplus to put up resistance to Margrethe's decree, for her body was never removed from Esrum.

Eventually Margrethe bestowed her favour on the monks of Esrum too by giving them in 1400 valuable properties in Ods herred.[18] She had originally obtained them from influential aristocrats, Jens Falk and Niels Sivardsen, but she handed them over to Esrum for the sake of the souls of her father and mother, for their parents, and for herself and her son. The conditions attached are just as detailed as those in the 1315 testament of Kristoffer for Sorø, but the document deals less with the monks' pittances and more with the services they were to perform. A daily mass was to be said at the altar in the monks' choir, where Queen Helvig was buried. Also a candle was to be kept burning there daily, and after high mass, the hymn *Salve Regina* was to be sung. As in Kristoffer's will, the brothers were to enjoy pittances, but immediately after eating, they were to be sure to sing a hymn to Mary's praise, *O florens Rosa*, in the choir in front of the statue of Our Lady.

Such details show how Danish Cistercians continued to give special devotion to Mary in the late Middle Ages. From Løgum we have an altarfront dated to about 1325 that has scenes from Mary's life.[19] This adds to the impression that the Cistercians in Denmark as elsewhere in Europe cultivated forms of art as well as liturgy that gave homage to Mary. The Esrum bequest indicates that one of the bonds between Esrum and Margrethe may have been a common devotion to Mary. The Queen of the North joined with the Danish Cistercian mother house in celebrating the Queen of heaven. In remembering her own mother, Margrethe showed devotion to God's mother. At such a moment we can see how the royal relationship with the Danish Cistercians now contained dimensions not evident in the twelfth century. Margrethe had to build up her own property holdings and get land from the nobility, and so she could not let the monks increase their holdings at her expense.[20] Moreover, they were already rich in lands. Her bequests of property were more of a symbolic nature, emphasizing spiritual links between herself, her parents, the monks, and Mary.

The concern Margrethe showed for both Esrum and Sorø provided all the Danish Cistercians could have hoped to receive from a fourteenth-century ruler. When Margrethe died, her body was taken to Sorø for burial in the church. For the moment the link between the monarchy and Cistercian house seemed secure. But sometime in the first six months of 1413, either the bishop or the cathedral chapter of Roskilde managed to move

Margrethe's body from Sorø to Roskilde. This single transfer ended the tradition of royal burials at Sorø and began a period when Sorø as well as other Cistercian houses could no longer hope for royal protection and involvement on the terms the monks preferred.

The significance of the transfer of Margrethe's body has long been recognized.[21] In a thoughtful article, Tage E. Christiansen of the National Museum in Copenhagen has discussed the reason for the move.[22] According to him, the monks had no desire to give up the body, a feeling reflected in the Sorø Rhyme Chronicle's lines in which Margrethe says that if she had had a real friend, she would have been left at Sorø.[23] Just before the Reformation, the Sorø Necrology claimed that the body had been 'violently' transferred, but the word is vague and the source is late.[24] We have no contemporary source for any physical confrontation between monks and canons or their men. According to Christiansen, it is much more likely that the monks were pressured into giving up the body by Margrethe's successor, King Erik of Pomerania, who wanted Margrethe in the centre of the choir at Roskilde to start a line of kings and queens descended from her as the first ruler of a unified Scandinavia. A great celebration, with the king participating, at Roskilde cathedral indicates that Margrethe's transfer was intended to mark the initiation of a new age in Scandinavia. At the same time, the bishop of Roskilde, Peder Jensen Lodehat, who had been Margarethe's chancellor and was still very powerful, was probably also behind this move. The transfer was bound to establish the preeminence of his church in the kingdom.

This interpretation of events, even though Christiansen concedes he lacks verification in contemporary sources, provides the best understanding of what happened in 1413. A massive exchange of properties between Sorø and Roskilde that followed a year later was probably also behind this move. The Roskilde bishop apparently intended to heal the monks' wounded pride by handing over to them a string of properties of great value to them.[25] A number of parish churches, together with scattered properties in the vicinity of the monastery in Alsted herred, enabled Sorø to consolidate many holdings. For centuries the church of Roskilde had held these lands. In letting them go, the bishop handed over to Sorø almost total control of this part of the island. He also obtained Sorø's holdings west of Køge and east of Kalundborg for his own church, but this was an insignificant loss for the monastery when compared to the nearby gains. It is difficult to say who received more land in the exchange, but Sorø obtained holdings that enabled it to concentrate its agricultural base in a more compact area and to eliminate the problem of sending men at a great distance to collect rents for the monastery.

The removal of Margrethe's body from Soro in 1413 and the transfer of lands with the church of Roskilde in 1414 provides a central turning point in Danish Cistercian history. Until this time at least one Cistercian house had managed to hold a central place in the political and religious aspirations of the monarchy. After 1414 Sorø became just one more monastery, receiving its share of privileges from the king or his clerks in the usual businesslike manner. The old fire of devotion and ancestral bonds were gone. The bodies of Kristoffer and Valdemar Atterdag remained in the abbey church, but these kings remained ambiguous figures in Danish history and myth, while Margrethe at Roskilde was given an elegant Gothic tomb that became a centre for pilgrimages and miracles. Sorø's loss was Roskilde's gain. In 1413 monasticism lost out to the diocesan structure in Denmark, the first sign of its diminished status in the church and society.

Looking ahead to the rest of the fifteenth century, we can see that the Danish Cistercians' relations with the monarchy made the monks vulnerable to any royal attempt to administer the monasteries. An important dispute between Sorø and the bishop of Roskilde, Niels Skave, was settled in 1493 by a royal decision[26] which supported the monks and ended the violent attacks on them and on their peasants that probably had been arranged by the bishop of Roskilde. But when the dust cleared and the legal matters were settled, something fundamental had changed. Sorø submitted itself to the juridical power of the king in a matter that was fundamentally an ecclesiastical affair and belonged to the pope's jurisdiction. Papal intervention had even less relevance in the last years of the fifteenth century than at Knardrup in the 1320s or in the Øm controversy of the 1260s.[27] The Cistercians who had once fought so stubbornly for independence both from diocesan and royal power ended up casting themselves into the arms of the monarchy in order to save themselves from a violent bishop. Such a reaction was understandable, but little more than forty years later the king would take the next step and appropriate the monasteries.

In 1443 a royal ordinance gave King Kristoffer of Bavaria and Archbishop Hans Laxman of Lund common responsibility for reforming Danish monasteries. Intended mainly for impoverished Premonstratensian houses and monasteries for women, the order can still be seen as an important indication of the monarchy's interventionist policy in monastic affairs.[28] As late as the time of Margrethe, the relationship between the Cistercians and the monarchy had fostered mutual advantages. The ruler gained spiritual benefits and prestige from connection with the order, while the monks obtained protection from attackers and legal support. In the 1490s, however, the monks sacrificed their ecclesiastical immunities in order to get legal help from the king. The reciprocity of the old relationship was replaced by one-sided dependence on royal good will. In a sense the monks had returned to the precarious situation of the twelfth century, when the success or failure of monasticism in Denmark depended starkly on the reception the kings gave the monks. But then the Cistercians had been able to offer something the kings clearly wanted and needed: a recognition of their legitimacy. In an increasingly secular society, the monks' charters and acts no longer legitimized a dynasty; they could only give a sense of personal religious bonds to kings. This had meant a great deal to Margrethe, but after her time the monks needed the monarch much more than he them.

CONTINUING—BUT LIMITED—INTERNATIONAL LINKS

Just as in the first half of the fourteenth century, the stream of business involving the Danish Cistercians with the papacy moved almost exclusively one-way. Communications were sent from Avignon or Rome to Denmark, and we have little idea of what requests were sent in the other direction.[29] There is one instance of an Esrum monk, Konrad of Bokelem, going to Avignon to ask for help. He had abandoned his monastery and wandered about, eventually regretting his decision, and now he used the legal processes of the papal court to ensure that he could be accepted back at Esrum without being too severely punished.[30] We do not know if the abbot of Esrum obeyed Pope Urban V's command, but all the church officials appointed to reinstate the monk at Esrum came from Roskilde cathedral. This is only one of the many indications during these years of contacts between Roskilde and the Cistercians of Zealand.[31]

In at least one situation we find the Cistercians showing open resistance to the papacy and its assertion of authority. In 1383 the bishop of Slesvig, Jens, who had been appointed *nuntius* by Urban VI, reported that Sorø, Esrum, Knardrup, and the nuns of St Mary of Roskilde and of Slangerup, together with those of St. Clare and St Agnes at Roskilde, had refused to pay a procuration.[32] This obstinacy may be a result of the great schism that plagued the church after 1378 and continued until after the Council of Constance in 1414.

During these years the Cistercians generally followed the papal allegiance of their country. Thus the English and German Cistercians, and apparently also the Danish, were loyal to the pope at Rome, Urban VI, while the French Cistercians and their Scottish brethren naturally supported the Avignon pope.[33] General Chapters kept meeting, but now there was one for the Avignon bloc at Cîteaux or Dijon and one for the Roman bloc at Rome itself, at Vienna, or at Heilsbronn. At the Roman General Chapters held by Urban VI in 1382 and by Boniface IX in 1390, the abbot of Esrum was ordered to function as collector of a *caritativum subsidium* in Scandinavia, Russia, and Slavonia. The 1383 report by the bishop of Slesvig may well indicate the Esrum abbot's negative response. In any case, a General Chapter held at Vienna in 1393 ordered the abbot not of Esrum but of Dargun to collect contributions for the order in the North and in Baltic countries.[34] In 1398 came a decree by the General Chapter at Heilsbronn concerning the feast of the Visitation. The abbot of Alvastra in Sweden loyally tried to implement it in a letter to a daughter abbey and to nuns under his care,[35] but we hear nothing about the Danes here. There is no direct evidence that the abbot of Esrum or of any other Danish Cistercian houses attended these General Chapters. But it is likely that some at least attended one or more of these meetings, for it is apparent that demands were being made all the time on Danish and other Scandinavian houses for financial contributions.

Before the outbreak of the schism, during it, and afterwards, the Cistercian General Chapter was mainly concerned with ensuring that contributions were collected promptly and efficiently. A number of declarations and accusations in records for the 1360s indicate that this was an ideal seldom realized.[36] In 1403 Boniface IX made Esrum's and Sorø's abbots vicars general for the whole North.[37] Thereby they became responsible for collections of the so-called contributions.

When we look at what the Danish abbeys actually paid, we can hardly call them overburdened in comparison to other houses. Thanks to the careful editing of Peter King and Arne Odd Johnsen we can look at the taxbook of the Cistercian Order, the *Secundum Registrum monasteriorum ordinis Cisterciensis*, drawn up in 1354-55 and extant in a manuscript about a hundred years younger.[38] There are many textual problems with names which King and Johnsen have done their best to puzzle out, but so far no one has been able to explain why Esrum, one of the richest Scandinavian houses, was assessed at a *contributio moderata* (the lowest amount that was levied) of only three *livres tournois*, while Hovedøya near Oslo owed eighteen.[39] The average payment to be made by Danish abbeys was about 7.7 *livres tournois*, below that of the average Norwegian, Swedish, or Pomeranian abbey.

Here are the figures for all the Danish houses (excluding Knardrup, which may not have existed when the list was drawn up). The figures are in *livres tournois*, shillings, and pence. I do not include the *contributio duplex*, which is double that of the *contributio moderata*, nor the *contributio excessiva*, which is double that of the second-lowest amount levied, the *contributio mediocris*:

	contributio moderata		contributio mediocris
Tuta Vallis (Tvis)	6 l.t.	15 sh.	9 l.t.
Insula Dei (Holme)	4	10 sh.	6
Locus Dei (Løgum)	4	10	6
Herrisvad	4	10	6
Esrum	3		4
Ryd	12		16

	contributio moderata		contributio mediocris
Vitskøl	4	10	6
Sorø	18	15	25
Ås	6	15	9
Øm	11	5	15

(for Øm elsewhere in the list there is another set of figures: 15 and 20)

As the editors point out, it is by no means certain that such figures reflect the relative wealth of the abbeys. There was probably a good deal of political manoeuvering involved in setting the figures, and the fact that so many houses are assessed at the same amount (as with 4 1.t. and 10 shillings for several of the Citeaux daughters in Denmark) points to a perfunctory evaluation of such houses' wealth. There is no doubt, however, that these Danish houses were far from the richest in the order, but by no means the poorest. Many Northern French and Belgian abbeys provided a *contributio moderata* of 45 1.t. or more, while the average contribution was a little more than 12.[40] One can conclude that the distance of the Danish houses from Citeaux made it difficult to collect from them, so the relatively light evaluations may have been made in order to assure that these houses did not feel overburdened and would be more willing to contribute to the distant motherhouse. For Esrum's low evaluation there are two possibilities. In the first place, Queen Margrethe's claim that it was in bad straits may have had some truth to it. But it is more likely that credit was given to Esrum for its responsibilities and expenses as motherhouse to several distant daughter abbeys that had to be visited. We see that Herrisvad, the other main Danish motherhouse, also had a low assessment, while in Hildesheim diocese Amelungborn, which was supposed to be rich, likewise had a modest 4 1.t., 10 shillings to pay, and at the same time had several daughters to visit (Marienthal, Riddagshausen, Doberan).[41] This explanation must remain tentative until more work has been done on Cistercian finances and some of the list's inconsistencies have been clarified. For the moment one can only agree with one of the editors that the Cistercian Order in the fourteenth century continued to show its ability to maintain its international structure.[42] But it must be added that the Tax Book says nothing about how often these payments were levied or whether the Danish Cistercian houses actually paid what they owed.

A single instance during this period points to the relative isolation of the Danish Cistercians from the rest of the Order. In 1358 the pope claimed he had reserved for himself the right to choose the abbot of Colbaz on the death of the incumbent abbot. But the monks, lacking knowledge of this arrangement, had gone ahead and elected the monk Nicolaus as their abbot.

Innocent VI asserted his right on paper but to avoid trouble at the abbey, he appointed the same man the monks had already chosen.[43]

Apparently Nicolaus had himself gone to Avignon to straighten out the matter after he had discovered the inconsistency. On his election he had seen to it that he received the necessary episcopal blessing, but the approval of the Esrum abbot had been given through the abbot of Buckow, Johan, who had had this power delegated to him by Herman of Esrum. After the matter had been submitted at Avignon and resolved, the pope sent a letter to the abbot of Esrum as the father immediate of Colbaz.[44] The pope asked the abbot to accept what had happened. In all this confusion, the abbot of Esrum appears to have remained passive. No one challenged his position, but he had handed over his prerogative to approve the new abbot to the abbot of another house. The election and confirmation of the abbot at Colbaz was decided there and at Avignon, while Esrum remained almost totally outside the picture. One wonders if this passivity may have been due to the abbey's situation in some kind of crisis.[45]

For the period between 1410 and 1451 we have many much clearer indications of connections between Citeaux and the North. In 1410 reform and the collection of contributions to the General Chapter in Norway and Denmark were handed over to the abbot of Sorø, while Alvastra received the same task for the Swedish abbeys. This function was to last three years. In 1412 the Sorø abbot was ordered to visit, reform, and make collections together with another abbot of his own choice in all three Scandinavian countries and to do so for the ensuing seven years. At the same time a number of Danish monasteries were absolved from arrears in their payments of contributions to the General Chapter.[46] Citeaux was apparently trying to resume relationships with the Scandinavian houses by cleaning the slate and using Sorø as its main contact instead of dealing with the monasteries individually.[47] The General Chapter had given up some of its power, a situation that must have meant a burden for the abbot of Sorø and for the abbot of Esrum who succeeded him in 1419 for a term of six years, during which he was to collect 6000 florins in Norway, Sweden, and Denmark.

In 1423 the abbot of Doberan was ordered to make collections in the three Scandinavian kingdoms, as well as in the province of Bremen and the diocese of Cammin, but by 1425 the task in Scandinavia had once more been turned over to the abbot of Sorø, this time for six years.[48] There is no indication whether or not this charge was removed in 1431, but in 1434 and again in 1443, the abbot of Clairvaux was ordered to visit the Danish and Swedish abbeys in his filiation.[49] For the first time in more than a century, we see continuing the bond between Clairvaux and the Scandinavian houses, but we have no idea if the motherhouse obeyed the General Chapter. In any case, these frequent provisions about collections and visitations indicate that the international structure of the Cistercian Order was once again functioning in Scandinavia after what might have been a pause at the end of the fourteenth century. It is an indication of the flexibility and endurance of medieval institutions and especially of the Cistercian Order's government that the General Chapter could still place such demands on Danish abbeys.

The burden was apparently too great at times, however, for in 1451 the abbots of Esrum and Sorø were summoned before the General Chapter and accused of 'many enormities' that are not specified but probably involved failure to collect these contributions or to deliver them to the General Chapter.[50] No matter what the outcome of the summons, the task of reforming monasteries and collecting money from them was immediately handed over to the abbots of Øm and Reinfeld. The transfer of these duties to Øm implies that this abbey now had a significant position among the Danish Cistercians (as also might be indicated by its relatively high assessment). But the naming of the Holstein abbey of Reinfeld, with which the Danish Cistercians had no historical bonds, could have been taken as an insult to the abbeys of Denmark. The language used against Esrum and Sorø is exceedingly strong and shows a sense of outrage because the two abbeys had made decisions with no regard for Cîteaux.

In the same 1451 General Chapter at which Esrum and Sorø were excoriated we hear that the abbot of Vitskøl, though excommunicated from the order for an unspecified crime, had continued to celebrate mass. He had defied not only the Order but the whole church.[51] The abbot of Øm was ordered to investigate the matter. If he found the charge to be true, he was to suspend the abbot of Vitskøl from office and, if necessary, summon him to the General Chapter. Once again the abbot of Øm was given a task involving a large responsibility.

The General Chapter tried to keep up its Scandinavian collections by appointing the abbot of Ås to the task in 1462.[52] By 1472 the abbot of Sorø had been reconciled to the General Chapter and was cited for his 'many outstanding works' (whose nature is as unspecified as his previous 'enormities') and given the power of visiting and reforming all the abbeys of Scandinavia.[53] At the end of the Middle Ages, the Sorø abbot seems to have become the main contact betweeen the General Chapter and Scandinavia, at least when he behaved according to its wishes. The Chapter in 1473 ordered Sorø's abbot to intervene at Herrisvad when a man who claimed to be its abbot had been guilty for many years of 'the gravest excesses and enormous abuses'.[54] Either the Sorø abbot was to go to Herrisvad himself and settle the matter, or he was to summon the offender to Cîteaux before the first of April 1474.

Even if the abbot of Sorø obtained in the fifteenth century a *de facto* preeminence among Danish Cistercians because of his monastery's wealth and Citeaux's need for him, the General Chapter still recognized Esrum's *de iure* preeminence. In 1478 it noted that the new abbot of Sorø had been confirmed by the abbot of Esrum, who was still Sorø's father immediate.[55] In 1487 the abbot of Esrum's appointment of a prior at Colbaz was quashed, and provision was made for situations in which the abbot of Esrum neglected to visit Colbaz once a year and failed to send a substitute because of the great distance and the dangers of travel. Nevertheless, the General Chapter carefully pointed out that Esrum's abbot was the father immediate of Colbaz and had the right of visitation. It was only in years when the abbot of Esrum did not come that the monks of Colbaz could call upon another abbot.[56]

Such adjustments to problems of discipline and organization point to the same decision-making structure in the General Chapter and the same practice of visitation by father abbots in the 1480s as in the 1170s when Colbaz had been founded. The revival of contacts between Citeaux and Denmark, at least after 1451, meant not just unpleasant financial burdens for the monasteries but also the continuation of the General Chapter's function as a forum for the resolution of problems in Danish monasteries. However timeworn the structure may have been and however less international Europe and the church were in the 1480s than they had been in the 1170s, the Cistercian Order had managed to reassert its old structure in Scandinavia and to adapt it to the needs of the time. This flexibility in self-renewal is one of the most extraordinary facts about the Danish Cistercians and their international contacts.

BISHOPS: DISTANCE AND ACCESSIBILITY

Local bishops continued to carry out the business that the monks brought to them, but their willingness to defend the monasteries against threats usually extended only to routine matters. The continuation of the old cooperation on a superficial level can still be seen in 1360, when Bishop Henrik of Roskilde handed over the income of Alsted church to the monks of Sorø. He claimed he shared the 'principal right of patronage' to the church with the monks.[57] In recognizing the monks' claim and giving up his own, the bishop enabled them to hold an important church and its incomes in an area close to Sorø where the abbey already owned most of the land.

At Vitskøl, the two documents that we have to illustrate the monastery's relationship with the bishop of Viborg both point to a cautious truce between them. Both times the bishop drew up a document at the request of the monks in order to affirm that his recent stay at the abbey was an expression of the monks' hospitality towards him and not a payment of procurations owed him.[58] In this echo of the Øm controversy and later settlements at both Vitskøl and Løgum, the bishop of Viborg was asked to put into writing something that in a less legalistic age would have required no formal record. But the monks had to be sure that they could lodge a guest only as an expression of hospitality without creating any regular obligations. Otherwise the bishop or one of his successors might try to make use of this precedent.

At Løgum, from 1367 to 1399 no bishop of Ribe confirmed the monks' privileges and possessions, an unusually long gap in comparison with the frequency of earlier confirmations.[59]Earlier they had often gone to him to obtain confirmations of agreements and wills, or else to back them up in their property dealings in the town of Ribe. In this period, the monks only had one property there which caused problems.[60]

The abbey of Øm had contact with its diocesan at Århus but only for a routine matter. In 1376 Bishop Oluf of Århus drew up a charter witnessing the deeding by Niels Gødsen and his wife of all their rights on Hårby Mark.[61] In this area northeast of the abbey, the monks gained considerable properties after about 1373.[62] They apparently went to the bishop of Århus to strengthen the validity of the transaction.This is the first time in more than a century that a bishop of Århus can be seen involved with an Øm property. Even though our knowledge of the abbey is incomplete because we have only a register of transactions and lack the full texts of its charters, this instance does indicate that the monks of Øm could now turn to the bishop of Århus for legal support.

Such backing, however, can hardly be regarded as indicative of warm relations between bishop and abbey. A much more convincing example comes from Sorø in 1375, when the archbishop of Lund handed over to the abbot, Michael Skåning, the right to choose the priest in the church of Tvååker, near Sorø's estates in Halland. The monks' 'principal right of patronage' was recognized, and because of the voluntary resignation of the priest, a Lund canon, the monks were promised the right to choose his successor.[63] As with the church of Alsted in 1360, the brothers of Sorø increased their influence over a parish church and were guaranteed a share of its income.

More significant than these infrequent signs of continuing good relations is a steady stream of bequests from diocesan officials or canons in Roskilde and Lund. Such men could not have handed over land to the Cistercians without at least the passive consent of their chapters and bishops. In 1363, for example, a canon of Roskilde and provost of Østersyssel, Peder, handed over to Sorø an attractive property in Roskilde with a number of buildings on it and thereupon joined the monks' fraternity.[64] Likewise in 1400, Jakob Knudsen, provost in Roskilde, gave Esrum three farms in Hågendrup and one in Tollerup in Northern Zealand.[65] The document was drawn up at

Roskilde, and the seals affixed were those of the episcopal officers of the church of Roskilde. It may well be that what appears to us as a gift was actually the payment to the abbey of a debt owed by Jakob Knudsen. Whatever the background Roskilde and Esrum had reached an understanding to the benefit of the monks.

A typical example of a settlement involving bishop, his officers, and a Cistercian monastery is a 1358 decision by Jakob Falster, canon in Roskilde, whom Bishop Henrik of Roskilde had appointed judge delegate.[66] Esrum and the heirs of Torben Pedersen of Vejby had disputed his gift of land in that village to the abbey. Jakob claimed he was able to convince the peasants making the claims to accept what belonged to the monks. The formulation used here is very unusual. The peasants are described as having taken into consideration the 'courtliness' (*curialitatem*) which they said the monastery had showed them.[67] This word, unusual for such a charter, points to the monks' high social status. In the eyes of the canon of Roskilde, the Cistercians had not just been decent or kind; they had been courtly and thus identified themselves with upper-class propriety in the face of a lower-class challenge (the local peasantry and disappointed claimants to the property).

Such a settlement, routine as it may have been in the relationship between monastery and cathedral church, points to a continuing pattern of cooperation. Naturally the cases in which matters did not go as the monks would have wanted are not included in their records, but there is enough material to show that the Cistercians could use the standard machinery of canon law in their diocese and sometimes obtain what they sought. A similar instance is the resolution of a long dispute over Uggeløse in 1362, when a knight, Hartvig Krummedige of Kærstrup, and his sons dropped their claims to the village, which supposedly had safely gone to the Esrum monks after a judgment by King Valdemar in 1353.[68] The settlement was drawn up at Odense, for the Krummedige family resided on Fyn, and it was sealed by Niels, bishop of Odense, who had been the judge, together with the prior of St Knud's monastery and the bishop's officials. Thus the church hierarchy on Fyn, led by the bishop, gave their support to the monks of Esrum, even though they had nothing to gain in favouring the Zealand abbey's claim. The monks were not really being favoured, however: they were merely successful in using canon law and a diocesan bishop to assert their rights.

The Cistercians did not gain a great deal from bishops during this period, but at least they could count on their benevolent neutrality. Despite the lack of open enthusiasm and support, Sorø, Esrum, and apparently also Øm, Løgum, and Vitskøl all could still enjoy a basic legal security. Everyday business says almost nothing about attitudes, but the old alliance between episcopal church and monastic institutions, going back to the twelfth century, still seems to have continued.

Looking ahead to the end of the fifteenth century, we see what could happen when a diocesan bishop turned against the Cistercians. A confrontation between Niels Skave of Roskilde and the abbot of Sorø,[69] after the fomer had dismissed a priest from property in Undløse because he had refused to pay rent to the abbey, ended in a display of violence that exceeded anything that had happened at Øm.[70] There in the 1260s the bishop of Århus had been satisfied with harassing the labourers of the abbey by summoning them to his courts, first at one place and then at another. But now the bishop physically harmed the abbey's peasants. Violence which had been a threat in the thirteenth century, became a reality at the end of the fifteenth.

In the resulting verbal attack on the Sorø monks, Niels Skave made charges of a type that had never, even in the heat of the Øm dispute, been launched against a Danish Cistercian house. The abbot was said to be totally immoral, associating with women and violating chaste wives when he was visiting his parish churches.[71] He was charged with raping a nun at Roskilde. Moreover, the monks of Sorø in general were supposed to have taken girlfriends, who hung around the abbey and had a good time! The bishop needed such assertions to justify his direct intervention at Sorø. Such involvement was otherwise forbidden by the Cistercians' exempt status. The unprecedented content of the charges and the violent character of Niels Skave makes it impossible to take them seriously. But the very fact that a bishop, no matter how fallaciously, could have unleashed such accusations, shows that the situation of the Cistercians in Danish society had changed. They were being slandered in a way that monks in general were attacked in Reformation polemics, when it became good church politics in Denmark as well as elsewhere for bishops and nobles to accuse monks of sexual immorality.[72]

The Cistercian General Chapter encouraged the monks of Sorø to resist the charges of the Roskilde bishop. For a moment in its declaration, it looks as if the old machinery of Cistercian exemption and privilege could still function.[73] But it was the king and not the General Chapter or the pope (to whom the matter was also taken) who concluded the dispute. Just as the path to royal takeover was prepared by such an outcome, so too the falling out between bishop and abbey after an alliance of centuries heralds the coming of the Reformation. In 1413, as we have seen, an act of violence was also perpetrated against Sorø, the removal of Queen Margrethe's body. But already the next year the monks were compensated for their loss. Their position in church and society was respected and recognized in this settlement. In 1489 another bishop of Roskilde permitted another act of violence against the monastery, but this time there was no amicable settlement quickly reached between Sorø and Roskilde. The old bonds were severed, and a once mutually beneficial alliance was thrown away.

THE GROWING ROLE OF TOWNS.

The Danish landscape became less rural after 1300. Despite the population decline caused by plagues and wars, towns had become extremely important factors in Danish society by 1400.[74] The Cistercians were aware of this development and did their best to come to terms with town councils and to gain properties in these trade centres. This process accelerated in the last decades of the fourteenth century and even more so in the first years of the fifteenth. This was not always the case, however. Properties in the town of Ribe were not added to during these years. Løgum failed to acquire any holdings in the town of Tønder, although the monks had a number of dealings involving the town council there, as when in 1360 the councillors approved the gift of a woman who already owed money to the monks.[75] Her husband may have been a citizen of Tønder. Likewise at Åbenrå in 1360, another woman, this time clearly the wife of a former citizen, gave property to Løgum. In the same year the councillors of Flensborg declared that a certain Svend Lille on his deathbed had testamented property to the abbey.[76] In such instances, Løgum's lack of contact with Ribe was compensated for by profitable dealings with the market towns of Southern Jutland.

The Cistercians had been founded as a rural order, but in the fourteenth century they willingly followed urban development. Like Løgum, Esrum established contacts in neighbouring market towns. In 1389 part of a Tisvilde property was deeded to the monks. The witnessess include not only a priest of Tikøb, a nearby village, but also a priest from the thriving town of Helsingør on the coast.[77] Esrum, however, was slow in establishing holdings in such towns; not until the 1420s did it gain land in Søborg and Roskilde.[78] Hälsingborg and Helsingør lands were added to the abbey in the 1450s. In 1452 the mayor of Helsingør deeded a building site bordering on the Sound. This may indicate the monks' interest in constructing warehouses and a pier for their trade.[79] Esrum's Copenhagen properties first appear in the 1480s. Abbot Peder Andersen acquired lots bordering on Gammel Torv and Vestergade in the centre of the old town.[80]

Perhaps because of a better financial situation, Sorø had already made significant gains in towns by the end of the fourteenth century. In 1403 the monks redeemed a mortgage in the town of Næstved. It had been held by a priest, Bennekin Albrectsen, who in that year became a monk at Sorø.[81] By drawing townspeople and priests into their confraternity or fraternity, which gave them a share in the spiritual benefits of the monastery, the monks of Sorø were able to exercise an influence on towns out of all proportion to the geographical limitation as a rural foundation. One wonders what the Næstved Benedictines thought about Sorø involvement in their town, especially at a time when the Benedictines were increasing their holdings in

Næstved enormously. But as at Roskilde, Sorø was able to gain entrance probably because the monks felt it was essential to maintain bases for trade in neighbouring towns. A good example of the brothers' conscious program of acquisition and consolidation of town properties can be seen in Slagelse, where in 1384 a widow whose husband had been a citizen gave the monks half a property that included a stone house and courtyard. Two years later, the industrious monks gained the other half of the holding from the deceased man's brother, who was a priest.[82]

Sometimes Sorø was cheated in its attempt to obtain town properties. This happened twice at Malmø, where the brothers obtained valuable holdings only to discover later to their chagrin that there were complicating financial factors which the former owners had chosen not to reveal to them.[83] Poul Nørlund has already told the gloomy story of how the brothers had to buy off their competitors in order to get the land title.[84] Another instance in which Sorø had problems in obtaining town properties can be seen at Køge, another market town where the monks had substantial interests. In 1412 they purchased property there for ten marks of silver, but they had to allow the former owners to keep and use the holding for their lifetimes without making any payment at all to the monks.[85] Not until twelve years later did the monks actually get hold of the property. This is the reverse of the situation in the early fourteenth century when the monks would gain the mortgage on a property in return for lending a sum of money and at the same time be allowed to collect the income from the holding so long as the principal was not repaid. Now in the early fifteenth century, even though the monks bought a property lock, stock, and barrel, the former owner could have free lifetime tenure on it. These conditions show how expensive it could be for an institution to gain town properties. But it should be added that in 1408 the brothers of Sorø gained another property apparently as a free gift.[86] The monks' transactions in these years show varying combinations of generosity and recalcitrance on the part of the people with whom they dealt.

The main attraction exercised by the Sorø monks on their town contacts was apparently still the spiritual benefits the monastery could offer. But unlike monks of earlier times, the brothers usually had to offer both spiritual and material advantages to potential sellers. Thus in Holbæk in 1410, Magnus Pedersen and his wife expressed a desire to participate in the spiritual benefits of Sorø and asked to join the monastery's fraternity,[87] a term which is used interchangeably with the earlier 'confraternity'. But the property they handed over to the monks they were able to keep and enjoy until their deaths.

Even Øm, one of the most rural of Danish Cistercian houses, began during these years to deal with towns. The monks negotiated with the town council of Grenå, on the coast north of their Djursland holdings, in order to acquire lands just to the north of the town.[88] Except for Vitskøl, no Cistercian house for which we have records for this period seem to have been unaffected by the attempt either to gain town properties or at least to come to terms with town authorities

THE CONTINUING CENTRALITY OF THE LAY ARISTOCRACY

Despite the increasing role of towns in the lives of the Danish Cistercian abbeys, the basis of their support in society continued to be the lay aristocracy. Both knights and gentry went on contributing land to the monks. Without them the steady, if slow, increase in holdings at Sorø and Løgum would have come to a total stop. Esrum did not do so well during these years, perhaps because the knight landowners of Northern Zealand were being squeezed out by royal expansion there.[89] One change in the pattern of Cistercian advances is clear at several abbeys: the monks seldom acquired lands close to their houses without great difficulty and expense, while most of the gifts with no strings attached were areas at a great distance from the monasteries. In an age when tenants paid a fixed yearly rent, such distant holdings were not as troublesome as they would have been earlier, when the Cistercians had their own granges and would have had problems in maintaining communications. But the monks, like the secular nobles themselves, still preferred well-rounded boundaries for their holdings instead of scattered bits of land over the whole island of Zealand.[90]

Just as it became harder for the monks to obtain town properties without paying out large sums, so too choice rural lands were available to them only at a high price. Even when the monks had to pay a tidy sum, they often also had to take on spiritual obligations to their sellers. In the thirteenth century it had been common for lay aristocrats to hand over properties with a vague phrase about the good of their souls. Now both female and male donors usually provided a precise list of spiritual benefits the monks were to provide. They had to say frequent masses for the deceased, sometimes once a day, often at a particular altar.

As we move into the fifteenth century we find bequests which concentrate not on monasteries as institutions but on their particular altars. The altar of the Eleven Thousand Virgins at Esrum became extremely popular, perhaps because of the donors' feeling that with so many saints associated with one altar, he was sure to get some heavenly attention.[91] In Britain the practice of endowing chantry chapels meant that aristocratic families took over whole spaces in large churches for the construction of a closed-off area to which one priest was to be attached and whose main duty in life was to be the saying of masses for the family's deceased. Although the arrangements made by Danish aristocratic families for altars in Cistercian abbeys were not so elaborate or exclusive, the monks had to give a great deal to their benefactors and to remember them in specific, detailed ways.[92]

It is difficult for us to know how the monks reacted to this stream of requirements from their benefactors, but it must have been tedious to keep up with all of them. The monasteries had been accumulating patrons since the twelfth century, and the Sorø and Løgum necrologies from the sixteenth century indicate that all donors, from the very earliest, were still being commemorated.[93] The late medieval insistence on individual mention at separate masses at named altars meant that Cistercian abbey churches had become prayer factories. The description by R.W. Southern of this period as an age of inflation certainly applies to the Danish Cistercian houses, where the quantity of remembrances became an obsession with aristocratic patrons.[94]

Sometimes, however, the monasteries were only asked to say a yearly requiem mass, as happened at Sorø in 1362 when Peder Troelsen in Tyvelse deeded property.[95] So far as we can tell from the entry in the Sorø Donation Book, this was a gift in an area where the monks were eager to make gains. The monks were thus occasionally able to attract new lands in return for limited spiritual benefits.

Sorø learned in these years to deal with two new prominent families of western Zealand, the Lunges and the Grubbes.[96] From the first family the monks in 1384 gained property in the village of Broby on Suså south of the abbey.[97] Folmer Jakobsen, the son of Jakob Lunge, handed over the property there, a large farm (curiam villicalem), in return for the favour 'that the brothers keep him in solemn and perpetual memory and that they do for him what they continually do for other benefactors of the house'.[98] In 1402 and 1417, Folmer's brother Anders exchanged his share in the Broby properties with the monks for other land on the condition that he be allowed to keep the entire village of Broby at a nominal rent of two marks a year. As the Sorø compiler points out, Anders was more than compensated for his generosity and for his brother's kindness, for he was able to collect the income from the whole of Broby for thirteen years. Nevertheless, the Sorø compiler praises the 'great wisdom' of the abbot responsible for the transaction, Niels Clementsen, because by allowing the man to keep property for his lifetime and handing over to him some of the abbey's 'own and ancient goods' the monks finally gained the land.[99] Broby is only a short distance from Sorø itself, and the monks had been after it since the thirteenth century. In 1440 the Sorø compiler admitted that it was difficult to make gains without great expenditure. The monks had to make temporary sacrifices in order to attain their goals, but they could do so if their abbots were clever and they were willing to accept short-term losses for the sake of long-term gains. One thinks of the economist John Maynard Keynes's much-quoted remark, 'In the long run, we're all dead'. But in the long run, a medieval abbey could maintain life for centuries.

The Cistercians frequently show an ability to distinguish the essential from the secondary in their economic and judicial efforts. In 1362 Esrum was awarded Uggeløse, after Hartvig Krummedige had dropped his demands. The monks were to have their legal expenses paid by the knight, but they waived the right. If any future challenge was made, then Hartvig would have to pay in full.[100] Clearly the monks wanted peace and quiet and by this reconciliatory but firm gesture, they tried to soften the blow that a potentially dangerous and hostile knight may have felt in losing the case. Esrum preferred to have good neighbours and lose some money to pressing its legal rights and risking renewed hostilities.

Women in such transactions often required fewer material benefits from the monks than did men. But the requests women did make were often much more detailed in terms of pious services the monks were to perform for them. Such donors could use gifts to the Cistercians to obtain a home where they would be cared for in their old age. Many of them probably ended up in monasteries for women, as at Roskilde, but in this period some aristocratic women began to choose Sorø itself as a last home. In 1396 Gertrude, widow of Erik Barnumsen and daughter of the knight Peder Grubbe (who, ironically, was the son of a plunderer of Knardrup), made known that she had given Abbot Niels of Sorø and the chapter her holdings in Svinninge. In return the monks made her a 'spiritual sister' at Sorø. This meant that she would share in all their good works, while at the same time they would care for her. In return, all her personal possessions, including money, jewels, and clothes, were to go to Sorø on her death, along with whatever else 'can be found in their monastery after my death'.[101] This last line makes it clear that Gertrude would be living at Sorø. As Nørlund has pointed out, such an arrangement for both men and women of Sorø as an old-age pensioners' home for the rich seems to have been rather common at the end of the Middle Ages.[102]

In other documents from the same years, we can see how the abbot of Sorø helped out Gertrude in her financial settlements, as if he had become guardian of her estate. In October 1396 Abbot Niels Clementsen placed his seal on an arrangement by which Gertrude gave to her granddaughter and the girl's future husband, Bent Bille, sixty marks in silver, to cover the expenses, clothes, and other requirements of their marriage.[103] Similarly in 1398 Gertrude handed over to Bent all her property in Skippinge Herred, and once again Niels Clementsen affixed his seal. When, in the same year, Gertrude's son, Barnum Eriksen, gave Bent Bille some land, the Sorø abbot again affixed his seal.[104] The participation of the abbot of Sorø in the affairs of this great aristocratic family points to the residence of Gertrude at Sorø and the abbot's desire to avoid family disagreements that might have jeopardized the settlement for the monks.

Another instance of the involvement of a Danish monastery in the affairs of an aristocrat can be seen clearly in four versions of a will made by Jens Jakobsen in 1359. All are included in the Esrum Codex.[105] In the first draft Jens, who was a canon of Århus, mortgaged his property in Saltrup, immediately west of Esbønderup and very close to the monastery, to Esrum for twelve marks silver. In the second draft, he mortgaged this property to the monks for the same amount of money, but on the condition that the mortgage not be redeemed for ten years. This was more favourable to Jens, for it meant he would have a whole decade before having to repay the principal. From the sum he borrowed the monks were to subtract a mark each year because of the income they collected from the land. This was a very disadvantageous arrangement for Esrum in comparison to earlier agreements, when land rents rarely if ever were deducted from mortgage sums. After ten years, Jens would owe the monks only two marks instead of twelve. In the third draft, Jens sold three farms in Saltrup, Pårup, and Bannebjerg to Esrum and in return gained twenty marks. For once we are able to see the monks at work on a potential donor, giving him various choices, but in the end getting what they wanted all along: a gift. In the apparently final draft, Jens handed over the three farms to Esrum as a gift, on the advice of his 'beloved friend' Asser, of the church at Helsinge.

In the 1350s this Asser had other contracts with Esrum.[106] All through the century Esrum made sure that local parish priests were involved in the drawing up of testaments and the giving of lands to the monastery. This practice continued into the fifteenth century. In 1415 Esrum gained property in Vejby from Asser Olavsen, curate of the church at Blistrup. His charter has an almost twelfth-century spiritual quality about it and indicates that the monks' spiritual benefits still could attract local priests.[107]

Tedious negotiations leading to an acceptable outcome, such as the one finally worked out at Saltrup, may well be hidden away in simple notices at Sorø. Usually the monks were ready and willing to give something in return, as they did in 1400 when a member of the village gentry and his wife were made members of the monks' confraternity in return for lands in Stevns herred, or the year before when Niels Jensen Grubbe and his wife Helena joined the same confraternity and were to be buried at Sorø in return for two farms.[108]

Even if the records for Esrum before about 1450 indicate a period of stagnation, Sorø, Løgum, and Øm all show constant gains in property holdings. Sorø's success parallels Margrethe's reign. From 1380 to 1413 the monks, after a very quiet period, made substantial additions. From the death of Margrethe until 1440, their main advances were limited to market towns.

The good years under Margrethe, despite her limited direct generosity, may have been due to an upper class 'rediscovery' of Sorø because of the renewed royal attention. Royal patronage could have stimulated aristocratic benevolence.[109] At Øm the net gains, already carefully computed by Poul Rasmussen,[110] are steady at seven or eight a decade from 1350 to 1380, then drop to half that from 1380 to 1400, only to shoot up to the old level between 1400 and 1409 and to climax at nineteen from 1410 to 1419. After that comes a steady descent that ends only during the last decades of the fifteenth century. Because of the summary nature of the Øm records, it cannot be determined if the lay aristocracy of central Jutland was responsible for most of these gains. Considering the large number of independent peasants still in this area, I find it likely that a mixture of village gentry, priests, and peasants did business with the monks.[111]

At Løgum the monks continued to deal with all levels of society in order to increase or strengthen holdings. But at the same time the influx of nobility from Holstein in Germany meant a fundamental change in the social composition of Southern Jutland. Most of the new nobles settled in the eastern third of the area.[112] But one great family, the Limbæks, took up residence at the fortress of Trøjborg not far from Løgum. The monks seem to have established good relations with them from the time they came to Southern Jutland. In 1376 Henning Nielsen Limbæk, a key figure in the politics of Southern Jutland,[113] took the monastery under his protection and emphasized that his ancestors had looked after the monks. He would maintain the tradition, he claimed, especially because the monks had showed such kindness in the past toward his family.[114] The monks probably supplied the Latin phraseology, but Henning Limbæk certainly consented to it. There are dark phrases about the chaotic state of the countryside and emphasis on a long respectable lineage, with the conclusion of benefaction.

In 1379 Johannes Limbæk of Trøjborg gave the abbey all his property in Kumled and Alslev, both near Løgum, the former situated between Løgum and Brede and so an important link between them.[115] He admitted that he and his relative Niels, together with their men, had mistreated the monastery and its labourers by not respecting their rights. But now they were asking for burial in the abbey church in return for a hundred and fifty Lübeck marks, to be paid to the monks through donated properties. Among those who sealed the document were various family members, the pastor of the church at Ballum, and a number of other local people. This agreement ended a conflict otherwise unknown to us and provides one more indication that the Limbæk family had adopted Løgum as its family monastery.

The Cistercians at Løgum as elsewhere had adapted to the changed composition of the aristocracy and won over a new ruling group to their side. Even if Johannes for a while had plagued the monks and their labourers, he and his relatives finally saw the advantage of being on good terms with them and using the monks to gain eternity.[116] The continuity of such settlements from the twelfth into the sixteenth centuries shows that the alliance between landed monasteries and landed aristocrats was based not only on social factors but also on deeply-felt spiritual needs.

The Rantzows were another Holstein family that came into Løgum's orbit during these years. In 1389 Henrik Rantzow witnessed that he held property from Løgum in Højer, apparently as a mortgage. He held also Sulsted, which was not to be redeemed for ten years. The document drawn up in Henrik's name indicates that there had been a dispute in which Henrik had claimed that the monks and their men had acted wrongly. Now he assured them of his forgiveness, asked for their friendship, and hoped that 'they will regularly intercede to God for me'.[117] As so often happens in monastic records, we see only a hint of underlying disagreement and controversy. But the monks once again had come to terms with a local aristocrat, this time a member of the village gentry. It is impossible for us to say from the monks' selective records whether such settlements were exceptional or whether the monks normally had good relations with their lay neighbours. But the monks doubtlessly profit from such agreements by gaining new families to be buried in their churches and favourable testaments.

In 1380 Niels Vind, with whom the monks had settled a dispute five years earlier, handed over properties about ten kilometres north of the abbey in Seem parish near Ribe.[118] Lage, priest of Sønder Hygum, about fifteen kilometres east of Ribe, drew up the document and made it known that Niels Vind was one of his parishioners who had desired in his last hours to provide for his soul. Such a gratuitous deathbed gift is a rather rare phenomenon in this period. As the examples above indicate, families were demanding more and more of the monks. Single liturgical acts did not have the same value they had had earlier. In 1400 the monks gained a number of scattered properties on the condition that twenty priests would celebrate an annual requiem mass. The donor wanted to be buried at Løgum together with his parents. His generosity was explained by the belief that 'mortal man takes nothing from the world except the works by which he either is justified or damned'.[119] In this faithful expression of late medieval piety are implied both the central argument for having monasteries and the threat that would make them irrelevant once Protestantism came to Denmark and eliminated the popular dependence on good works. The donor, by having such a large number of celebrants for the requiem mass, was contributing to the inflation that was devaluing the currency of spiritual benefits offered by the monasteries.

Inflation or no, Løgum became during the last decades of the fourteenth century the great burial church for the new aristocratic families of Southern

Jutland. At the same time Sorø became a favourite of new families in western Zealand, not only for burials but also for membership in the monastic confraternity. Although the evidence is only indirect—the testaments that speak of devotion to the monks—we can assume that behind such declarations there were monks active in making such families aware of the benefits they could offer them and convincing them to hand over some of their land. Sometimes the monks had to purchase land outright, but even here there can be an element of piety. In a typical Løgum transaction, the monastery in 1412 bought land on Alslev Mark near Brede from Anders Troelsen, who came from Dyreborg in Brede parish.[120] Although he was selling them the land, Anders also asked the brothers to pray for his soul, and the following persons sealed the document: Anders of Falster, priest in Visby and episcopal officer for Bishop Esger in Ribe; Niels, bailiff in the fortress of Trøjborg; Jakob Nielsen, *armigerus* in Gærup near Visby. These people are local dignitaries from the neighbourhood where Anders Troelsen lived. They participated in an ordinary legal act, in which one always can claim that the words 'that they [the monks] constantly intercede with God for my soul and the souls of all members of my family' are a mere formula. But here as with most documents there is the matter of *consent*: this is not a mechanical act but a choice made by a property owner that gave him a spiritual as well as a material link with the monastery.

The monks of Løgum accepted the importance of contacts with people like Anders Troelsen, who was a member of the village gentry, and cultivated them carefully. It is tempting to try to distinguish between such local aristocrats and the great aristocrats like the Limbæks and their respective influences on the monasteries. Both were essential to the monks.

ISOLATION OF THE ABBEYS FROM EACH OTHER

In looking at most of the sources for the late fourteenth and early fifteenth centuries, one can easily forget that we are dealing not with individual, separate abbeys but with a group of monasteries belonging to the same order. In earlier periods we find occasional indications that the abbot of Esrum was at Vitskøl or that Løgum and Herrisvad had dealings with each other. One can assume that such contacts were renewed whenever the abbot of a mother house visited a daughter house or vice-versa.

During this later period there is a single indication of contact. In February of 1400, Niels, abbot of Sorø, and Esbern, abbot of Knardrup, together with Peder, bishop of Roskilde, drew up a charter describing the arrangements involved with Queen Margrethe's gift a few days earlier of property in Ods herred to the monks of Esrum.[121] The transaction was so important that it brought the three Zealand abbeys together for a moment and gave them a chance to manifest their membership in a common order.

The lack of contact that otherwise characterizes our sources for these years by no means shows that Cistercian abbots had stopped visiting daughter houses. This activity probably did continue, but records, if there were any, have long since disappeared. Until the end of the thirteenth century, however, other indications of contact survived, as during the controversy at Øm. Now in the business of everyday life, in property disputes and transactions, and in dealings with local aristocrats and peasants, the various Cistercian houses seem to have been more than ever on their own.

The local isolation can best be seen in the abundant Sorø records. Because the same names often appear in the Næstved Book as in the Sorø Donation Book, we know that Sorø had to compete with the Benedictines for the same group of donors from the Grubbe family. In 1391 Bent Byg of Gunderslevholm mortgaged to Sorø a number of farms in Sigerslev in order to procure the hundred marks necessary to ensure burial for himself and his wife and a weekly mass for them.[122] In the same period Bent was defending Næstved's right to a property he had given that monastery in 1350.[123] There are no clear indications of rivalry between the neighbouring Benedictine and Cistercian abbeys, but in the 1390's Næstved did as well as Sorø in gains made, if not better.[124] Even though it is difficult to compare their acquisitions, it is clear that Sorø's monks had to face the possibility that the Grubbe family and others might totally abandon them for the Benedictines.

The nearby Johannite house of Antvorskov, moreover, became at the end of the fourteenth century the banker and creditor of the Zealand aristocracy in a much more effective way than Sorø had done. It mortgaged out its own property or acquired mortgaged property from landowners.[125] The vitality of the Antvorskov monks, as evidenced in the short notices, we have, does not mean that Sorø was directly threatened. Like Næstved and Sorø, Antvorskov usually limited its dealings to the vicinity of the abbey and kept out of its neighbours' way. Nevertheless, when Barnum Eriksen and his wife entered Antvorskov in 1399 in return for the monks' promise to care for them so long as they lived, the monks of Sorø indirectly suffered a major defeat. Barnum and his wife had also been involved with Sorø but now bestowed twelve farms upon the Johannites. For a man who owned more than 150 farms, this was no great sacrifice, but even for a rich house like Antvorskov, it was a very substantial gain.[126]

Forced by the competitiveness of the age to cultivate contacts with nearby aristocrats, houses like Sorø had every reason to concentrate on local connections. They had little to gain from traditional Cistercian travelling and visiting of each other's houses, and even though they probably continued to do so to some extent, the success or failure of their abbeys now depended more than ever on the bonds they could forge with influential lay-men and women living within a radius of fifteen to twenty kilometres of their houses. The Cistercians also had good reason to deal with neighbour-ing monasteries of other orders, their potential rivals for lands and bequests. Sometimes local exchanges could be worked out, as when Herrisvad gave up a property near Lund to a Benedictine house of nuns, Bosjö in mid-Skåne, and in return gained a farm closer to the monastery.[127] Only deal-ings with Cistercian nuns continue to show contacts between abbots of Sorø and Esrum and other houses of their own order.[128] According to canon law, the nuns needed male protectors and so had good reason to em-phasize their dependence on father abbots in their charters.

During this period after the death of Queen Margrethe, the abbot of Sorø took on the leadership of the Danish Cistercians.[129] We have already seen that he was usually preferred to the abbot of Esrum for making collections. From now until the Reformation, the earlier advancement from the abbacy of Sorø to that of Esrum was reversed, as happened in the case of Henrik Tornekrans. He started as abbot of Vitskøl, was moved to Esrum, and in about 1510 became abbot at Sorø.[130] Sorø was still the daughter of Esrum, but in prestige and wealth Sorø preceded it.

As we already have seen from the taxation Citeaux levied on the Danish houses, their relative wealth is difficult to compare. But there is no doubt that Sorø was better off than Esrum. In 1497 Esrum had about 280 farms, while Sorø had about 625 in 1536, so by this scale Esrum was half as rich as Sorø. Løgum had in 1530 about 193 farms and so was approximately as third as rich as Sorø,[131] while in the payments to Citeaux (if we use this as a scale), it was a quarter as well off. Of the other Cistercian houses we know much less about their landed wealth at the end of the Middle Ages. The fact that Ryd and Øm were so much ahead of the other houses in payments to Citeaux indicates that they may have been very well endowed in the four-teenth century. Again, however, one must take the precaution of adding that some payments, as for Herrisvad, may have been commuted because of the duties of visitation.

With the threat of collections from Citeaux, sometimes administered by sister houses, with all their riches tied up in land leases, and with ever-present dependence on the local aristocracy, the Danish Cistercians had lit-tle to gain and perhaps much to lose from cultivating close relations with each other. The sources leave the impression that each abbey was more or less on its own. Løgum had a special political and social situation in Southern Jutland to deal with, while Sorø had its own personal relationship with Queen Margrethe. Esrum was apparently cut off and perhaps even in trouble during this period. A 1377 papal bull allowing Margrethe to move her mother's body from Esrum speaks of grave problems there.[132] This has been considered to be merely a formula added by Margrethe and her son to justify the move.[133] But the fact that Esrum gained absolutely no property for thirty years, from 1359 to 1389, while Sorø, Næstved, Antvorskov, and other Zealand abbeys were doing quite well, suggests otherwise. At Øm the last decades of the fourteenth century brought a slowdown in gains, but there were major advances after 1400. Each abbey was caught up in its own development and in its own characteristic set of local and regional circumstances.

RAMIFICATIONS OF THE AGRICULTURAL CRISIS

Although there are no substantial indications in the surviving materials that the agricultural crisis, which set in during the 1330s in Denmark, greatly harmed the Danish Cistercians, there are a few clues that they too felt its effect. Bequests for Øm during the years when the Black Death reached Denmark in midcentury were increased, followed by a number of years when the abbey got nothing at all.[134] We begin to hear of abandoned properties.[135] Most important of all, the monks began to lease out their own properties to lay landowners in return for an annual rent, apparently because they could not find labourers to cultivate them.[136]

For a few years one can see the difference the labour shortage due to the Black Death made for the peasants' situation. In Esrum's dispute over Vejby, the monastery's procurator, Peder of Græsted, had to deal with two peasants (bondones) who had a legal claim on the land through their wives. The issue was not finally settled until it had been all the way to the landsting for Zealand in 1358.[137]

In general the monks were careful to consult with the laity in the parishes where they were involved in land transactions, as Sorø did when it exchanged property with Reerslev church in 1362.[138] The bishop of Roskilde, who confirmed the act, mentioned the consent 'both of the guardians (tutorum) and of all the parishioners of the church'. Perhaps this was a matter of form. But the fact that parishioners are mentioned here, while in the thirteenth century no such phrase appears in similar documents, points to the new importance of this group.

In all this material we lack the kind of dramatic indications of economic crisis apparent in the records of the churches of Odense and Lund. At Odense, the Benedictine monks claimed that because of disease and wars the incomes of benefices had so declined that a single benefice no longer could support a canon.[139] The canons of Lund complained to the pope about violence done to their church. Its benefices were impoverished; many of the monasteries and convents and over two hundred parish churches were 'wholly derelict'. The point was to show that wars inflicted by the king of Sweden on the diocese and 'many evil times and burdens' made it impossible for one benefice to support a clerk.[140]

In the 1360s and 1370s, life seems harsh, even for the church's privileged canons and monks. It had become difficult to maintain old privileges and incomes in a society that had become so much poorer than it had been at the opening of the century. Cistercian houses probably followed the lead of Løgum and began to mortgage out their own land. In such a response lay the salvation of large institutions in an economic crisis.[141] So long as there were new members of Valdemar Atterdag's nobility willing to take on such mortgages and hold onto the land in hopes of better times, the monks would have enough income in cash and goods to see them through the bad times. By the 1380s the monks began to redeem such mortgages and to become creditors once again, so that by 1400 to a large extent they had won back their old position as bankers and ready sources of cash for the landed aristocracy.[142]

What began as a period of liberation from old burdens for the peasants and a chance for social mobility apparently ended in a reassertion of the old ways. During the dispute between Bishop Niels Skave and Sorø in the 1490s, the abbot defined for the benefit of the bishop the relationship between the monastery and the peasants who rented land from it. He made it absolutely clear that the peasants were not free to move about at will and were in fact considered to be part of the property. He reasserted over the monastery's labourers rights that had been in effect since the thirteenth century, such as that of collecting fines from them, but he also showed that his jurisdiction over these people was so broad that the abbey could and often did sell them.[143] Sorø's abbot in this document (which naturally converted reality into Latin phrases and is part of a polemic) looked at his tenants as property of the monastery. The situation may have been different at Cistercian abbeys on Jutland, where villeinage never became widespread during the Middle Ages.[144] The entire question of peasants' conditions in the fifteenth century is still being debated,[145] but at least on Sorø's properties the fourteenth-century crisis does not seem to have bettered the situation of its agricultural labourers.

In 1497 Abbot Peder Andersen of Esrum had a survey made of all the abbey's holdings. The result, the Esrum Property Book, was added at the end of the Esrum Codex. It lists the rents owed by the occupants of the monks' properties.[146] This is the only pre-Reformation survey of a Danish monastery's holdings and presents some fascinating insights into the way the monks had built up their estates. Out of a total of eighty-three place names given in the list, I have been able to determine from the earlier charters contained in the Codex the dates of acquisition of fifty-six of the properties. The properties were acquired as follows:

18	names	pre–1215	32%
12	names	1216–1301	21%
6	names	1302–1400	11%
20	names	1401–1497	36%

At least some of the remaining twenty-seven names should be attached to the very first period, when we know least about Cistercian gains because we have only a few charters of acquisition. But one cannot assign to this period a number disproportionate with later periods, for it is precisely in the twelfth century and the first part of the thirteenth that we are best informed about property names because papal confirmations included lists of a monastery's holdings.

The high figures for the fifteenth century represent additions mostly in distant Ods herred, lands obtained through exchanges and in giving up lands in the Asserbo area and near Esrum Lake that had belonged to the abbey since earliest times. A much larger proportion of Esrum's actual landed wealth than seems evident from the figures came to it during the first period. The same seems to have been the case for Øm, where 'up to half of the farms that belonged to the abbey in 1554 came into its possession in the course of the first twenty-five years after its foundation'.[147]

For Esrum I would estimate that between 1151 and 1215, a little more than sixty years, the abbey acquired between forty and fifty percent of the total land area it held in 1497. It is also possible to conclude from these figures that the fourteenth century did bring a property crisis in comparison with the thirteenth, for the rate of acquisition was halved. The fifteenth century saw a revival of property transactions, at the cost of alienating some of the abbey's oldest possessions. In the last years of the fifteenth century, the Cistercian General Chapter ordered an investigation into Esrum's spiritual and material status, perhaps an indication of concern that Abbot Peder Andersen was being reckless in his transactions.[148]

It would take a much more careful survey than there is room for here to compare the rents paid by Esrum's peasants with other rents on peasant holdings in the fifteenth century.[149] But it is clear that even at this late date, Esrum had not yet succeeded in filling out all its farms with tenants, so it was in the monks' best interest to treat its workers well.[150] More than a century after the height of the agricultural crisis, land was still lying fallow. Most of the tenants' payments to the abbey were in kind, the bulk in grain, with a lamb, a goose, and five chickens being handed over by the average farm. Some of the peasants had to give labour services a few days a year, and often a whole village in common had to give a measure of butter as summer tax and, for winter tax a 'fat ox'. Some of the payments had been commuted to money instead of products, but grain remained the main source of income for the monks (except in coastal holdings like Hornbæk, where they obtained fish). The Property Book distinguishes clearly *landboer*, who rented their farms from the monks, from *gårdsæder*, the villeins who had nothing more than a house and a small patch of land.[151] Villages that are very close to Esrum often had what appear to be higher burdens that villages at a distance, especially the obligation to help the monks at harvest time. This is the case, for example for Saltrup in Esbønderup parish.[152]

The Esrum Property Book presents the hard facts of the relationship between peasant tenants and monk landlords but says nothing about how well it worked. On paper, the monks had managed to develop a system in which they were guaranteed goods and services and some cash. They can be seen here as great landlords, far removed from personal involvement with the land. We are far from the work ethic of the earliest Cistercians. In the twelfth and early thirteenth centuries, Danish Cistercian monks had been one degree removed from the land, for their lay brothers had done the agricultural work. But by now the monks were twice removed from the soil, for those who tilled it for them were merely their tenants and had no place within the monastery.

LOOKING FORWARD: 1414 TO THE REFORMATION

The popular idea of monastic decline in the fifteenth century leading almost inevitably to the Protestant rejection of monasticism does not agree with the impression to be gained from the materials left by the Danish Cistercians. Excavations made at Øm abbey between 1975 and 1978 have revealed that whole segments of the monastic complex were first built in stone in the course of the fifteenth century.[153] The south wing of the monastic quadrangle has been dated to this period, while the west wing was built about 1500, just at the time when the monks were again making substantial property gains. At Vitskøl and Holme, the west wings also belong to the end of the Middle Ages, and it has been suggested that excavations at other abbeys, such as Løgum, might reveal further instances of such late building projects.[154] The evidence already gathered during the 1970s points to a revival of wealth in both land and buildings in the Danish Cistercians' last century. This development corresponds to events elsewhere, as in Florence, where the Cistercians also showed a surprising vitality in adapting to new social conditions and making their presence felt.[155] Further work on the Cistercians in the fifteenth century is likely to reveal more clearly this renewed display of classical twelfth-century Cistercian energy and activity. For now, however, I shall limit myself to the written sources that we have, especially for Sorø and Esrum, during this period.

In the second half of the fifteenth century, both Sorø and Esrum made substantial advances. Peder Andersen of Esrum was a very active abbot who did everything possible to link his monastery with rich Copenhagen families, to reconcile it with the family of Johan Oxe, which was building up its estates around Asserbo, and to maintain good relations with the monarchy. Likewise the abbot of Sorø, Henrik Tornekrans, showed an ability to further the interests of his house.[156] Henrik contributed to the collection of records at Sorø, already begun in 1490 with the Sorø Book, which resulted from the abbey's legal dispute over its rights with Bishop Niels Skave of Roskilde.[157] He saw to it that Sorø's records were put in order and even supervised the drawing up of a necrology for Løgum Abbey. The fact that Løgum had Sorø take care of such a task has been used by one historian as a comment on the sorry state of Løgum's intellectual life.[158] But we know so little about Løgum at this time that such a conclusion is unjustified. It can at least be contended, however, that Sorø's action points to its continuing prominence and even to its possible leadership in organizing the charters and other documents of the Danish Cistercians in the years after 1510.

That Sorø became an important cultural centre in the fifteenth century can be seen in the creation of the *Rimkrønike* there, the Rhyme Chronicle, the first substantial piece of Danish poetry and in 1495 the first book printed in Danish. Research on the provenance of the Rhyme Chronicle asserts that it came to light at Sorø but probably had several different authors who added to it and changed it.[159] Sorø can thus be seen as something of a literary workshop for the composition of a popular work of history. The monks behind the Rhyme Chronicle used the abbreviation or *Compendium* of Saxo, various annals, and a book on the relationship of Alexander the Great and Aristotle. But instead of simply editing and borrowing, as in the composition of the Elder Zealand Chronicle two centuries earlier, the monks composed an independent work of literature and history.

Just as the Ryd Chronicle turns out on investigation to be an expression of the Cistercian desire and need for a strong and benevolent king, so the Rhyme Chronicle expresses this yearning. It starts with mythical kings and continues into the fifteenth century, each ruler being given a speaking text and describing his exploits and failures. Thus Erik Glipping is made to castigate himself for taking away from the churches and monasteries what rightfully belonged to them, an echo of the Øm controversy and an indication that the Cistercian collective memory was very long.[160] Queen Margrethe, on the other hand, does well and is depicted as a great unifier of the Scandinavian kingdoms, while the monks' regret about losing her body to Roskilde emerges in the lines at the end of her statement.[161]

The Rhyme Chronicle is by no means self-centred propaganda for narrow monastic interests, but Cistercian attitudes contained in it deserve closer investigation than they previously have been given. King Sven Estridsen, one of the earliest non-mythical Danish kings, is remembered especially for his good treatment of monasteries.[162] At no time does exclusively monastic history outweigh national history. The central concern is the exploits of the kings themselves. The foundings of Herrisvad, Esrum, and Sorø are all mentioned, but Archbishop Eskil is named only in connection with his withdrawal to Clairvaux and not because of his patronage of Danish Cistercian houses.[163]

At one point, the Chronicle attributes the success of a Danish king to the fact that during his reign the Cistercian Order was founded.[164] It has been said that the passage could not have been intended to attribute Danish military victories to God's pleasure with the new order,[165] but the text is unmistakable, and such an interpretation of history to emphasize the coming of the Cistercians is logical and understandable in a Cistercian context.

The authors of the Rhyme Chronicle make few such attempts to link Cistercian and national history. Only in their hatred of Erik Glipping and their justification of his murder because he mistreated monasteries do the monks make a clear example out of a Danish king who had harmed their interests. In their concentration on the royal line and emphasis on the elements of character and personal achievement that made good rulers, the Sorø monks reveal the perennial Cistercian yearning for the wise and sympathetic monarch. Kristoffer II is something of an embarassment to them. He favoured Sorø but was a weak king. Instead of trying to apologize for his failure, the authors simply have Kristoffer say that a man is responsible for his own fate. From Kristoffer to Valdemar Atterdag and Margrethe's son Oluf, all royal burials at Sorø are named.[166] The Sorø Cistercians can thus point to a central bond betweeen their monastery and the royal family. But they have to admit that they had lost the most important royal body of all, that of Queen Margrethe.

The Sorø Rhyme Chronicle is neither great history nor great literature, even if its rhyme and cadence are often pleasing and its content entertaining. It is unfortunate that the Chronicle has been so neglected, for it provides a unique late medieval glimpse into the minds of the Sorø monks. It shows how their concerns were essentially the same as those of their predecessors at Øm in the thirteenth century: the desire to ally themselves with the monarchy, to obtain the favour of a good ruler, and to comment on their relations with the society around them.

Because the Rhyme Chronicle is written in Danish, it distances itself from all earlier history writing in Cistercian monasteries. Its involvement in battles and royal problems also creates a vastly different impression of the monks than emerges from their writings as late as the first half of the fourteenth century. In the various Sorø Annals and the Older Zealand Chronicle, the Cistercians looked at the world from the viewpoint of their cloister. In representing the personalities of Danish rulers in the Rhyme Chronicle, the monks had to immerse themselves in the mentality of the secular world. Something was still left of the old Cistercian protective mentality, however, for there is an insistence that these kings are to a great extent to be judged on how they handled the monasteries.

The intellectual environment which produced the Sorø Rhyme Chronicle remains something of a mystery. A decision from the 1473 Cistercian General Chapter hints that there were plans for establishing a centre of studies at Sorø. In this year the Chapter praised the abbot of Sorø and placed under him all Scandinavian abbeys. The Chapter underlined a need to have a place of learning located in 'the excellent kingdom of Denmark and for bordering provinces'. Monks who wanted to begin courses of studies were to be brought together so that they could be instructed in the order's discipline in both morals and learning. The needs of such scholars were to be cared for 'according to the requirements of their fatherland', so that they not be obliged to 'wander about' (evagari) in search of a suitable place of learning. Nor were they to remain 'ignominiously ignorant and unlearned'.[167] Although much is vague in the General Chapter's decision and does not clarify the relationship of this new centre of studies with North German universities, it still points to ambitious plans to make Sorø an intellectual headquarters. Cistercian monks who wanted to complete their educations would not have to go to the College of St Bernard in Paris or to the order's house of studies at Greifswald.[168]

We do not know the outcome of these efforts, but the Rhyme Chronicle may have been part of this attempt to make Sorø a centre for Cistercian learning. The very form of the Rhyme Chronicle, in easily memorized verse, would have been appropriate to the young scholars spoken of in this decision. By learning such a poem, they could become practised in verse and at the same time be trained in the Danish Cistercian interpretation of national history.[169]

Another indication of the monks' interest in involving themselves in secular society is the new practice of translating Latin charters into Danish 'for the sake of lay people' who could not read Latin but whose acceptance of the content of the charters was essential to the monks.[170] The Cistercians had always needed the consent of the laymen involved in the charters they drew up, but now it was not enough just to tell these 'illiterates' (those who did not know Latin) what it was about. The monks had to give their business partners a chance to read it for themselves in their own language. One historian has characterized the end of the Middle Ages as a period when the monks became less inward-looking and began to attend to the needs of the 'common people'.[171] This is an idealization of the situation, but there is no doubt that the monks spent much effort and expense in looking after guests from both high and low society and in treating the sick, as can be seen at Øm.[172]

One important monument to Danish Cistercian concerns at the end of the Middle Ages is an altar piece from Esrum, made in 1496. It replaced an earlier altar with a painting of the Virgin Mary.[173] The central section of the 1496 altar is today exhibited in the National Museum in Copenhagen. Like the Rhyme Chronicle it is a provincial piece of work, with some fine and some rather amateurish parts. There are many other altars like it in Denmark and elsewhere in Europe, especially in Northern Germany, from this period, and so it could be asserted that this altar in itself shows nothing in particular about the Danish Cistercians. Golgotha scenes crowded with figures cut out of wood were the rage of the day, and Esrum's abbot Peder Andersen was simply following fashion when he ordered the altar.

When I first viewed the Esrum altar in 1973 and tried to relate it to the Danish Cistercians, I thought that the crowded figures and the lack of space suggested something of Johan Huizinga's hysterical waning of the Middle Ages. Since then I have come to look at the Esrum altar in another way. What follows is meant as a personal interpretation and not as a definitive historical explanation. That the monks of Esrum still identified themselves with the Cistercian Order can be seen in a panel in which Bernard of Clairvaux is shown receiving Christ from the cross in one of his visions. In the background is a hill with a monastery and a wall, apparently surrounding a graveyard. Here we have the early myth of the Danish Cistercians still alive at the very end of the medieval period: their link with Bernard the saint and mystic, Clairvaux in the hills of Burgundy and its graveyard, to which so many of the emigrants to the North wanted to return.

But the panel showing Bernard is only one of four flanking the central Crucifixion scene. The main occupants of the others are all female, from Ursula and some of her eleven thousand virgins to Juliane, who has lost the devil she was supposed to have whipped before throwing into a latrine. The last panel shows Saint Felicitas together with an unknown female saint. Felicitas has seven minature sons, all of whom, according to legend, she watched die as martyrs before having her head chopped off. Just as Bernard meant much to Esrum, so too did these female saints. The altar of the Eleven Thousand Virgins became the most popular in the church to donors during the fifteenth century. In the side panels' themes, the monks may be indicating that through their devotion to female saints of great renown, they could draw female donors.

In the Golgotha scene, there are almost as many women as there are soldiers. Of course some of these figures are historical, and among them are the mother of Christ and the other Marys. But the scene is drawn into the present by the placement in the center of a woman in the habit of a Cistercian nun. The monks of Esrum remembered their Slangerup sisters. Pious women who came to the church to see the altar would be able to identify with the Mary figures. Their husbands could see themselves in the rough soldiers, some of whom at least are placed to the right of Christ, the saved position.

Abbot Peder Andersen may not have deliberately meant the altar to please potential donors. But the contents of the altar piece reflect the attitudes, tastes, and concerns of the monks. They are very much caught up in a spirituality that emphasizes the universal nature of Christ's death on the cross, an act which embraces and involves not just monks but all men and women, good and evil. The distinctively late-medieval quality of the scene is its crowding: we see here a cross-section of humanity and realize the monks envisioned the Crucifixion in terms not just of their community but of Christ's involvement with the whole human race.

A close look, however, reveals that one very central group in Danish society is not represented here, the peasants. The Cistercians have been taken care of by Bernard and the nun; rich women have been signified by the well-dressed Marys, and knights and landowners by the soldiers. But there is neither physical nor psychological room on the altar piece for anyone in the humble dress of a peasant. We have here a superb unconscious exposition of Danish Cistercian mentality a few decades before the Reformation. The monks' world of religious devotion is wide open to the secular world. It is in fact inviting the outside world to come in and share the benefits of the monastery. But it is the landed and the privileged who are being invited. The backbone of the abbey's and of society's wealth have no place here. This may seem obvious, but obvious facts about a society can be the most important ones, and at the same time the easiest to ignore.

In leaving out the peasants, the Cistercians of Esrum showed they took the structure of society for granted. The peasants were ubiquitous and thereby invisible. There is no hint of cultural decadence in the Esrum altar, but it points to the opening of a world that had not yet existed for the Cistercians of fourteenth-century Løgum who obtained their altar front with scenes from the life of the Virgin Mary.[174] At Løgum religious art was intended to inspire inner meditation on the religious truths concerning Mary, while in Esrum's crucifixion, the monks invited lay persons and religious to participate in their celebration of Christ's sacrifice.

The acceptability of such a spirituality is underlined by the fact that in the seventeenth century the Esrum altarpiece was moved to a parish church and allowed to remain there with only one minor but fundamental change. The pious figure of the abbot Peder Andersen in the foreground was changed into a Protestant clergyman with a rounded collar! Nothing else had to be altered, not even the nun, a stunning witness to the relative mildness of the Danish Reformation in comparison to the violence of the English and the German. The survival of the Esrum altar to our day in a Protestant country, and especially its display in a Lutheran village church in the seventeenth century show that the transition from late medieval Cistercian spirituality to the new Lutheranism was a gentle one. The Esrum altar piece did not offend and could easily be integrated into the new ecclesiastical milieu.

With his altar and his property book, Abbot Peder Andersen showed the traditional Cistercian ability to pursue both practical and spiritual goals and to cultivate good relations with the aristocracy of Northern Zealand in the 1490s. Similarly the Rhyme Chronicle, the Sorø Book, and the Cistercian General Chapter's decision on education at Sorø all point to this monastery's deep involvement in lay society.

The Cistercians had come a long way from their alien origins and uncertain beginnings in the twelfth century. They had become part of the very fibre of Danish society. This was in itself no mean achievement and is perhaps an illustration of Toynbee's theory of challenge and response. The monks gave the Danish countryside their interpretation of the Christian religion and way of life. Over the centuries they met one challenge after another and managed despite bad periods in the 1260s and in the fourteenth century to emerge in good condition on the eve of the Reformation. They convinced kings to respect, grant, and renew their privileges. They saw to it that their diocesan bishops were aware of their usefulness and did not neglect them. They accepted new waves of religious life from the thirteenth centuries onwards, first the friars and then the orders devoted to acts of charity. The monks saw to it that the landed aristocracy remained spiritually and sometimes also financially dependent on them. In nearby parishes they often gained incomes and rights. Close to their abbeys and sometimes also far away, the Cistercians saw to it that the peasants tilled their lands and paid a good sum every year to them.

Our sources show the monks to have been patient, careful administrators and reveal little of the passions that must have motivated at least some of them to choose the monastic way of life. Only at Øm in the 1250s and 1260s do we touch on the anger and determination of the Danish Cistercians to win in a conflict with another power in society, no matter what the price. But elsewhere the monks were just as determined to maintain their way of life. They survived because they were able to adapt themselves and profit from new social conditions such as the growth of towns and the transition of agricultural economy. In the twelfth century it was by no means certain that the Cistercians would find a permanent home in Denmark. Like the Carthusians at Asserbo, they might well have turned around and gone home to France after a few bleak years. But they stayed and prospered.

How important were the Cistercians in Danish medieval history? The records indicate that they played a major role in royal and ecclesiastical diplomacy in the twelfth century. Their buildings from that time represented some of the most advanced architecture in the country, as at Sorø, and apparently also at Esrum and perhaps Tvis. The monks in these and other ways were at the centre of Danish politics and culture. In the thirteenth century, in a more varied and complex society, they were less prominent, as elsewhere in Europe, and had to cope with competition from cathedral chapters and the new orders. The fourteenth century brought the great crisis for the Cistercians as for all other groups in Danish society, while in the fifteenth century they regained some of their agricultural wealth and began to build again.

The monks' wealth depended, of course, on the work done for them by the peasants, and it is impossible to determine from the records we have whether the peasants were better off for being associated with a monastic institution than they would have been under secular lords. It can at least be claimed that the monks' labourers could count on the stability of the estates on which they lived. For peasants living on Esrum's estates around the Lake, it must have been some confort to compare their situation with that of peasants around Hørsholm, whose lords seem to have changed frequently. But there is no way around the Marxist interpretation of medieval feudal life: the peasants did submit themselves to an exploiting upper class, in this case the Cistercian houses.

After the twelfth century the Cistercians left the centre stage of Danish medieval history, but their late medieval revival shows their continuing potential ability to acquire lands, cultivate them, and deal with all groups in society. The monks after 1300 depended less on their international organization and more on their links with the countryside or with their diocesan bishops. If there had been no Reformation in Denmark, it is possible to imagine the Cistercians continuing into the eighteenth century, for they seem to have been a healthy order in the 1530s when the Reformation came. It was the mendicants, not the Cistercians, who were thrown out of their houses. In the less politicized countryside the Cistercians were granted permission to continue as religious institutions but not to take on new members. Eventually the surviving Danish Cistercians were brought together in Sorø, where the last of them died before the century's end. The death certificate for the order in Denmark was sealed, but instead of a summary execution there was a quiet old age.

Today there is a small community of Cistercians on Bornholm, a Danish island in the Baltic. It has no direct connection to its medieval predecessors in this country. The work of this community will probably take no greater place in annals of twentieth-century Denmark than that of the Cistercians in the fourteenth century occupies in history books of medieval Denmark. But who knows what effect the silent fourteenth-century monks had on their surroundings or what influence these modern Cistercians may have on the society around them? Quiet and easily ignored in the landscape, the Cistercians represented in the Middle Ages and still today represent a form of human community that can speak to our tortured age.

ABBREVIATIONS
(unless otherwise noted, place of publication
is Copenhagen)

AD — Ellen Jørgensen, *Annales Danici Medii Aevi*. Selskabet for Udgivelse af Kilder til dansk Historie. (1920).

Analecta — *Analecta Sacri Ordinis Cisterciensis* (Rome, 1945–64). Since 1964: *Analecta Cisterciensia*.

BD — Alfred Krarup, *Bullarium Danicum*. Pavelige Aktstykker vedrørende Danmark, 1198–1316. (1931–32).

Canivez — J. M. Canivez, *Statua Capitulorum Generalium Ordinis Cisterciensis*. Bibliothèque de la Revue d'Histoire Ecclésiastique 9–14B. (Louvain, 1933–41).

Cod. Esrom. — O. Nielsen, *Codex Esromensis*. Esrom Klosters Brevbog. Selskabet for Udgivelse af Kilder til dansk Historie (1880 –81. Photographic Reprint, 1973).

Conflict and Continuity — Brian Patrick McGuire, *Conflict and Continuity at Øm Abbey* (Museum Tusculanum 8: 1976).

DAM — G. Thorkelin, *Diplomatarium Arna-Magnæanum* I (1786).

DD — *Diplomatarium Danicum*, published since 1938 by Det danske Sprog- og Litteraturselskab. References in Roman numeral are to series (I Række, etc.), in Arabic numeral to volume (2 Bind, etc.)

DRB — *Danmarks Riges Breve*. Det danske Sprog- og Litteraturselskab. Rækker I–III (1938 ff.). Translation to Danish, often with notes of the documents in DD.

Hoogeweg — H. Hoogeweg, *Die Stifter und Klöster der Provinz Pommern* I (Stettin, 1924).

HT — *Historisk Tidsskrift*. Den danske historiske Forening (1840–   ). Noted according to series (*Række*) and volume (Bind).

Kirkekampen Niels Skyum-Nielsen, *Kirkekampen i Danmark 1241–1290:* Jakob Erlandsen, samtid og eftertid (1963).

KLNMA *Kulturhistorisk Loksikon for Nordisk Middelalder* I–XVII (1956–72).

KS *Kirkehistoriske Samlinger.* Selskabet for Danmarks Kirkehistorie (1849–   ).

Lekai *The Cistercians: Ideals and Reality* (Kent, Ohio: Kent State University Press, 1977).

Meck. Ur. *Meklenburgisches Urkundenbuch.* Verein for Mecklenburgische Geschichte und Alterthumskunde (I: 786–1250, published Schwerin, 1863. II: 1251–80, pub. 1864).

MGH, SS *Monumenta Germaniae historica. Scriptores rerum Germanicarum.* ed. G. H. Pertz (Hannover, 1839–96).

PL J. P. Migne. *Patrologiae Latinae Cursus Completus.* (Paris, 1844–1905).

Pom. UB Rod. Prümers and Rob. Klempin, *Pommersches Urkundenbuch* I–VI (Stettin, 1868–1907. Volume I reprinted in 1970).

Rep. Kristian Erslev, *Repertorium Diplomaticum Regni Danici Mediaevalis.* Danmarks Breve fra Middelalderen II (1896–98).

SM II *Scriptores Minores Historiae Danicae Medii Aevi,* M. Cl. Gertz (1922, reprinted 1970).

Sorøbogen *Sorø: Klostret, Skolen, Akademiet gennem Tiderne* I (1923) with articles by Poul Nørlund, "Klostret og dets Gods" (pp. 53–131) and Verner Dahlerup, "Tre Litterære Munke i Sorø Kloster" (pp. 132–145). *Sorøbogen* as cited here is not to be confused with the medieval manuscript known as the Sorø Book.

SRD Jakob Langebek and P. F. Suhm, *Scriptores Rerum Danicarum Medii Aevi* I–IX (1772–1878).

Winter   Franz Winter, *Die Cistercienser des nordöstlichen Deutsch-lands* I–III (Gotha, 1868–1871).

ZGSHLG *Zeitschrift der Gesellschaft für Schleswig-Holstein-Lauenburgische Geschichte* (Kiel u. Neumünster, 1870–   ).

ÆA   T. A. Becker, *De ældste danske Archiveregistraturer* I (1854) and IV (1885).

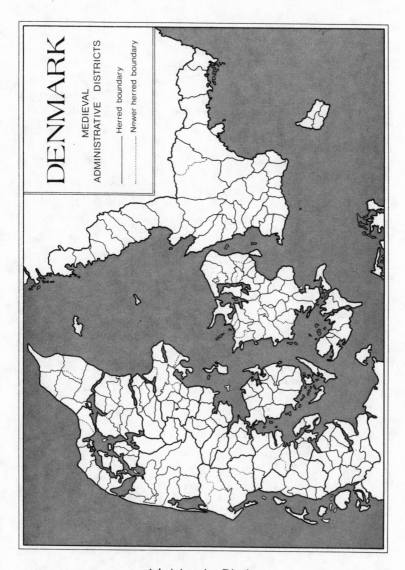

Administrative Districts

THE CITEAUX AND CLAIRVAUX FILIATIONS IN DENMARK

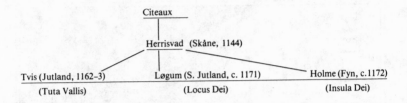

Citeaux

Herrisvad (Skåne, 1144)

Tvis (Jutland, 1162–3)   Løgum (S. Jutland, c. 1171)   Holme (Fyn, c.1172)
(Tuta Vallis)   (Locus Dei)   (Insula Dei)

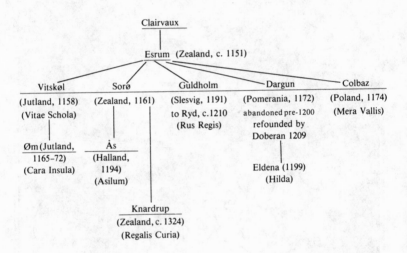

Clairvaux

Esrum (Zealand, c. 1151)

Vitskøl	Sorø	Guldholm	Dargun	Colbaz
(Jutland, 1158)	(Zealand, 1161)	(Slesvig, 1191)	(Pomerania, 1172)	(Poland, 1174)
(Vitae Schola)		to Ryd, c.1210	abandoned pre-1200	(Mera Vallis)
		(Rus Regis)	refounded by	
Øm (Jutland,	Ås		Doberan 1209	
1165–72)	(Halland,			
(Cara Insula)	1194)		Eldena (1199)	
	(Asilum)		(Hilda)	

Knardrup
(Zealand, c. 1324)
(Regalis Curia)

DANISH RULERS 1080–1412

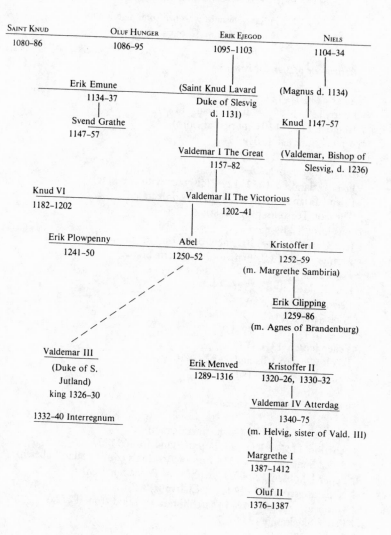

DANISH MEDIEVAL BISHOPS (c.1140–1400)

according to Andreas Nissen, *Danske Bisperækker* (Copenhagen, 1935)

† indicates bishops who had some significance
in Danish Cistercian history

Archdiocese of Lund (Skåne)

† Asser c. 1103–1137
† Eskil 1137–1177 (d. at Clairvaux 1181)
† Absalon 1177–1201 (buried at Sorø)
† Anders Sunesen 1201–23
† Peder Saksesen 1223–28
† Uffe Trugotsen 1228–52
† Jakob Erlandsen 1252–1274 (disputes with the king)
  Erland Erlandsen 1274–76 (never consecrated)
  Thrugot Torstensen 1276–80
† Jens Dros 1280–89
† Jens Grand 1289–1302 (new disputes with monarchy)
† Isarnus 1302–1310 (native of Southern France)
† Esger Juul 1310–25
  Karl Eriksen Røde 1326–34
† Peder Jensen Galen 1334–55
  Niels Jensen 1361–79
  Mogens Nielsen 1379–90
  Peder Jensen 1390–91
  Jakob Gertsen Ulfstand 1392–1410
  Peder Kruse 1410–1416

Diocese of Roskilde (Zealand)

† Asser c. 1145–1158 (Augustinian canon)
† Absalon 1158–91 (archbishop of Lund from 1177)
† Peder Sunesen 1192–1214 (son of Absalon's cousin, Sune Ebbesen)
† Peder Jakobsen 1214–25 (nephew of Peder Sunesen)
† Niels Stigsen 1225–49 (d. at Clairvaux)
† Jakob Erlandsen 1249–54 (archbishop of Lund from 1252)
† Peder Skjalmsen 1254–77
  Stigot 1277–80
† Ingvar Hjort 1280–90 (dispute with Sorø)
† Jens Krag 1290–1300 (buried at Sorø)
  Olav 1300–1320

Jens Hind 1320–30
Jens Nyborg 1330–44
Jakob Poulsen 1344–50
Henrik Gertsen 1350–68
Niels Jepsen 1368–95
† Peder Jensen Lodehat 1395–1416

Diocese of Odense (Fyn)

† Rikulf 1139–1162
† Livo 1162–1164 (schismatic)
† Simon 1163–86
† Jens Jensen 1186–1213
  Lojus 1213–28
  Ivar 1239–45
  Niels 1245–47
  Jakob 1247–52
† Regner 1252–66 (disputed at election)
† Peder 1252–76 (French Cistercian)
  Jens 1282–86
  Gisico 1286–c.1304
  Peder Pagh 1305–1339
  Niels Jonsen 1339–62
  Erik Jensen Krabbe 1362–75
  Valdemar Podebusk 1376–92
  Teze Podebusk 1392–1400
  Jens Ovesen Jernskæg 1400–1420

Diocese of Slesvig

† Occo 1141 (exiled but 1161 recalled and 1164 removed by King
  Valdemar)
† Esbern 1141–1161
† Frederik 1167–79 (buried at Sorø)
† Valdemar (illeg. son of King Knud Magnussen) 1184–1191 (buried at
  Citeaux, 1236)
† Niels 1192–1234
  Tyge 1234–38
  Jens 1238–44
† Eskil 1244–55
† Niels 1255–65
† Bondo 1265–82

† Jakob 1282–87
Berthold 1287–1307
Jens Bockholt 1308–31
Hellembert 1331–43
Henrik Warendorp 1343–c.1351
Niels Brun 1351–c.1368
Henrik 1368–70
† Jens Skondelev c.1370–1421

Diocese of Ribe (Jutland)

† Nothold 1134–c.1139 (reformer)
† Asker 1139–42
† Elias 1142–62 (schismatic)
† Radulf 1162–1171 (English)
† Stefan 1171–77 (formerly abbot of Herrisvad)
† Omer 1178–1204 (buried at Løgum)
† Olav 1204–14 (buried at Løgum)
† Tuvo 1214–30
† Gunner 1230–49
† Esger 1249–73 (buried at Løgum)
Tyge 1273–88
† Kristian 1288–1313
Jens Hee 1313–1327
Jakob Splitaf 1327–45
Peder Thuresen 1345–64
Magnus (Mogens Jensen) 1365–69
Jens Mikkelsen 1369–88
Eskil 1389–1409

Diocese of Århus (Jutland)

† Eskil c.1157–1166 (schismatic. Not to be confused with Archbishop Eskil of Lund)
† Svend 1166–1191 (buried at Øm)
† Peder Vognsen 1191–1204 (member of the Skjalm family, buried at Sorø)
† Skjalm Vognsen 1204–1215 (brother of Peder, buried at Sorø)
† Ebbe 1215–24
† Peder Elavsen ?–1246 (buried at Øm)
† Peder Ugotsen 1249–1260 (hostile to Øm)
† Tyge 1260–72 (arch-enemy of Øm)

† Peder 1273–74
  Tyge 1276–88
  Jens Askersen 1288–c.1305
  Esger Juul 1306–1310 (then archbishop in Lund)
  Esger Bonde 1312–c.1325
  Svend 1326–c.1352
  Poul 1354–1369
  Olav 1371–86
† Peder Jensen Lodehat 1386–95 (then bishop in Roskilde)

Diocese of Viborg (Jutland)

† Svend 1133–53
† Niels 1154–1189
† Asker 1191–1208
† Asgot 1208–20
† Thorsten 1220–22
† Gunner 1222–51 (former abbot of Øm)
† Niels 1251–67 (royal chancellor)
† Peder 1267–85 (disputed election)
  Laurentius 1286–97
  Tyge 1297
  Peder 1298–1322
  Tyge 1323–c.1330
  Simon after 1330–after 1342
  Peder c.1345–after 1360
  Jakob Moltke 1367–96
† Lave Glob 1396–1429

Diocese of Børglum (Jutland)

† Sylvester 1134–c.1146
† Tyge c.1146–c.1178
† Omer 1179–c.1183
† Thrugot c.1187–c.1200
  Omer c.1200–?
  Jens 1238–47
  Rudolf 1247–52
† Elav Glob 1252–1260 (murdered)
† Jens 1264–c.1280 (trained by Gunner of Viborg)
  Svend c.1281/3
† Niels 1283–97 (buried at Løgum)

Joseph 1298–c.1302
Niels 1304–1328
Tyge 1328–c.1341
Anders c.1345–54
Magnus (Mogens Jensen) 1354–65 (then bishop of Ribe)
Jens Mikkelsen 1365–69 (then bishop of Ribe)
Svend Moltke 1370–96
Peder 1396–c.1425

DANISH CISTERCIAN ABBOTS
(TO THE EARLY FIFTEENTH CENTURY)

The only contemporary medieval abbot list we have is from Øm. The Sorø list is very late and full of inconsistencies and problems. This means that C.A.J. France 'A List of Danish Cistercian Abbots', *Analecta Sacri Ordinis Cisterciensis* 20 (1964) is not trustworthy, for it is based on the Sorø list. The dates given in what follows are usually references to abbots in charter material. Since such documents usually tell us nothing about the abbots, except their presence, only the more interesting situations will be noted. In general it can be said that of all the Danish Cistercian abbots, only Gunner of Øm emerges to us as a person, and he only because he later became bishop of Viborg and was the subject of a brief biographical sketch. What follows makes no attempt to be an exhaustive review of Danish Cistercian abbots. It is a listing of the information to be gleaned from accessible charter and narrative material for the Danish Cistercians.

HERRISVAD (*Skåne*)

Robert 1158 (present at confirmation for Esrum properties)
      1163 (at foundation of Tvis)
Stefan (left to become bishop of Ribe in 1171)
Ake 1183
Thomas c.1206
Peder 1299 (charter defining Løgum's duty of hospitality to the bishop of Ribe) 1303 (confirms gift to Løgum)
Anders 1338
Jakob 1346

ESRUM (*Zealand*)
for more information on these abbots, see
Mediaeval Scandinavia 6 [1973] 127–32

Folmer 1151?
William 1151
Gerard c.1160
Frederick 1163 (present at the foundation of Tvis)
Walbert 1170, 1173, 1193 (active in Esrum foundations on the South Baltic)
William 1195?

Thorkil 1203 (present at the funeral of Abbot William of Æbelholt)
Eskil 1211
Jens I 1220s (formerly abbot of Sorø)
Jens II 1230s (Jens Kaare, abbot at Sorø a number of times)
Jens III 1248
Niels Skjalmsen (probably from mid-1250s after being abbot at Sorø briefly)
Ture 1258/59 (formerly abbot of Vitskøl, later of Øm)
Esbern 1263 (Øm dispute), 1264 (visiting Eldena), 1271 (Sode Mill exchange
   of land)
Mogens 1283 (orders abbot of Colbaz to send confessor to nuns of Stettin),
   1286
Niels 1290
Martin late 1290s (previously abbot at Sorø)
Jens Litle 1300
Peder 1319, 1320, 1331
Jens 1338, 1339, 1343
Jakob 1347
Sweder 1378
Sven 1425, 1437

SORØ

Notations taken from the untrustworthy Sorø Abbot List (*Scriptores Rerum Danicarum* IV, 534) are given in parentheses, while the dates given outside parentheses are from charter material.

Egbert (German, 1161–63)
Simon (English, 1163–86) 1164/78, c.1180, 1181, 1183
Godfred (English, 1186–1211) 1202/14
Atte (Zealand, and all his followers noted as Danish, 1211/18) 1223/28
Jens (three years, then abbot of Esrum)
Godfred (two years)
Peder of Vitskøl (ten years; then returned to Vitskøl as a simple monk)
   1227
Saxo (three years; cellarer at Esrum, subsequently returned there)
Jens Kaare (three years, nine months; then abbot of Esrum)
Joseph (abbot in 1247 at the great fire)
Jens Kaare (for a second time, 1247–49)
Ingemar (four months in 1249)
Jens Kaare (for a third time)
Isaac of Jutland
Niels Skjalmsen (then abbot of Esrum)

Niels (four years, four months; then went to Ås)

Isaac (for second time)

Niels (for a year)

Jakob and Jonas (they were brothers and ruled by turns for twenty-one years) Jakob is named in 1263 during the Øm controversy

Avo (less than a year)

Niels (five and a half years) 1288 appeal against judgment against the abbey by archbishop

Martin (had been subprior at Esrum, eight years as abbot of Sorø, then elected to Esrum) 1291 end of controversy over Stenmagle properties

Henning 1298, 1304, 1307, 1309, 1310

Niels Rytze (doctor of decretals) 1310

Gottschalk (for a year)

Henrik Berle (short time)

Master Niels 1322

Jakob of Copenhagen (four and a half years)

Herbert (no information)

Stig (six years) 1329, 1334, in 1337 named as former abbot of Sorø

Peder (six months)

Jakob Krag (four years) 1337

Henrik of Copenhagen 1343

Peder (a few months)

Jens Swede (six months)

Paul (a year)

Henrik of Copenhagen (a second time)

Jakob Weslev (1346, for six months)

Peder (1347, for sixteen years)

Henrik of Copenhagen (for a third time), 1364

Niels Klinkhammer (for sixteen years, but this impossible by evidence for his successor's dates)

Michael of Skåne 1375, 1378, 1383, 1385 (for twenty-six years)

Jens 1387 (not in the abbot list)

Niels of Halland (seven years, former abbot of Ås, died 1392) 1387, 1391, 1392

Niels Clementsen (fifty-two years, 1392–1444 when he died) a great number of references in documents back up these dates

ÅS (*Halland*)

Peder 1377

Niels of Halland pre-1392 (then abbot at Sorø)

COLBAZ (*Poland*)

main source is the Colbaz Annals

Everard (called the first abbot, died 1195)
Radulf (died 1217)
Herman 1283
Burchard (fifteenth abbot, died 1323)

KNARDRUP (*Zealand*)

Peder 1339 (at Sorø, probably in exile)
Esbern 1400

DARGUN (*Pomerania*)

in the Danish period before the refounding by Doberan in 1209

Herman 1176
Ivan pre-1200

ØM (*Jutland*)

until 1320. The main source is the abbot list contained in the Øm Book
and printed in *Scriptores Minores* II, 192-206

Brienne (English) 1165-73
Amilius (German) 1173-80
William (Norman: succeeded Henry at Vitskøl afterwards) 1180-92
Brendan (Danish: afterwards became abbot at Vitskøl) 1193-97
Niels (resigned his office and went to Vitskøl as a simple monk) 1197-99
Thorkil (raised by monks from boyhood) 1199-1216
Gunner (became bishop of Viborg) 1216-21
Jens ('in interioribus satis ydoneus, in exterioribus minus eruditus')
    1222-28
Niels II (raised by monks from boyhood, good at both externals and
    internals) 1228-32
Magnus (from Viborg, first a monk at Vitskøl; he asked God for release
    from the post and died soon after) 1232-34
Michael (raised by the monks; clever and capable) 1235-46
Jens II (at a time of civil disorders) 1246-49

Olav (disorders continue) 1249–56

Asgot (former cellarer at Vitskøl, he consecrated the new church at Øm in 1257. In 1260 became abbot of Vitskøl) 1256–60

Jens III Dover (Dover was one of the abbey's churches) 1260–62

Bo (beginning of controversy with bishop of Århus) 1262–63

Ture (a former abbot at Vitskøl and Esrum; the climax of dispute) 1263–68

From this point onward, there are no regular notations of the length of each abbacy, so no chronology can be made.

Jens III Dover (for a second time)

Conrad of Ribe

Jens IV of Horsens

Conrad of Ribe (a second term of seven months)

Jens III Dover (for a third time)

Jens IV of Horsens (for a second time)

Olav II (for six months)

Peder Pave (monk of Vitskøl and former prior)

Jens IV of Horsens (for a third time, for one and a half years)

Tyge Fisk (three and a half years)

Jakob Cordal (cellarer in Esrum, abbot at Øm for four and a half years, then abbot at Vitskøl)

Torben (two years)

Jon Røøth (eleven years)

Torger of Horsens (one year; then abbot at Vitskøl)

Jon Røøth (for a second time, then he became abbot at Vitskøl and Torger was translated to Esrum)

Jon Ubbe (one year)

Peder Gylbo (cellarer of Vitskøl. After two years at Øm, became abbot of Vitskøl)

Tyge Lang (one year)

Master Niels

Olav III

Kjeld (former abbot at Vitskøl)

In 1320, with the election of Niels Finsen (former cellarer at Esrum), the Øm abbot list stops.

Hans, 1376—otherwise there is no documentary information about abbots at Øm.

VITSKØL (Jutland)

information prior to 1320 is based mainly on the list for Øm

Henry 1157/58-1193 (transfer from Varnhem)
William (from Øm) 1193-97
Brendan (from Øm) 1197-after 1216 (still abbot of Vitskøl when the
     Øm Exordium was completed in 1216)
Ture (abbot of Vitskøl, then Esrum, then Øm in 1263)
Sven (gave up the office in 1260)
Asgot (from Øm in 1260) 1263 appeal to pope for Øm
Jens (mentioned in Gunner of Viborg's biography as abbot of Vitskøl,
     but no date is given. At least prior to 1280)
Jakob Cordal (from Øm) 1293 acquisition of church at Nørresundby
Torger of Horsens (from Øm)
Jon Røøth (from Øm)
Peder Gylbo (from Øm)
c. 1315 Kjeld (afterwards became abbot at Øm)
Bo 1320, 1322, 1340
Peder Andersen 1392
Niels 1397

RYD (Slesvig)

Peder 1237 (bought the liberty of the abbey from Abel, duke of Southern
     Jutland)
Arnfast prior to 1260. In that year Arnfast was chosen bishop of Århus by
     archbishop Jakob Erlandsen but he was never able to gain the position.
     Supported by the Øm monks, Arnfast was accused in royal circles of
     having poisoned King Kristoffer in 1259.
Mads 1263 (in appeal for Øm abbey against the bishop of Århus)
Michael (died in 1273 according to the Ryd Annals)
Jens (died in 1275 according to the Ryd Annals)
Niels 1303, 1306, 1316
Jakob 1321

LØGUM (Southern Jutland)

For more information, see the abbot list given by M. Mackeprang, Sønderjydske Årbøger 1945, pp. 39-40, which I have followed, with a few changes,
and supplemented with the dates in which abbots are mentioned in the
charters.

Vagn c.1200 (most probably Danish)

Poul before 1214
Tyge c.1213
Niels 1224
Jens 1263 (Øm controversy), 1267, 1272, 1278, 1279
Jon 1283
Thorkil 1293 (a gift of property in Ribe from the bishop)
Gunner 1296, 1303
Henrik 1313, 1324
Thomas 1340, 1343, 1347, 1349
Poul 1352
Oluf 1365, 1369
Thomas 1375, 1376, 1383, 1389
Sven 1397, 1405
Troels 1420

TVIS (*Jutland*)

Niels 1263 (Øm appeal)
Sven (mentioned in Gunner's biography, so before 1280)

HOLME (*Fyn*)

Thomas c. 1175, 1183
M (?) 1263 (Øm appeal)

FINAL NOTE

As this book goes to press, I would like to mention only a few of the recent Danish studies that have relevance for Cistercian history. Esben Albrectsen has completed his work on Southern Jutland's history in the fourteenth century with a beautiful book, *Herredømmet over Sønderjylland 1375 -1404* (Den danske historiske Forening: København, 1981), with frequent references to Løgumkloster. The sixtieth birthday of Professor Niels Skym-Nielsen occasioned a Festschrift, *Middelalder, metode og medier* (Museum Tusculanum: Copenhagen, 1981) in which Tage E. Christiansen rightly points out the correct origin of the *Life* of Bishop Gunner at Vitskøl and Svend E. Green-Pedersen deals with twelfth-century Cistercian foundations in Denmark and their political background.

The journal *Løgumkloster Studier* (Refugiets kulturforening: Løgumkloster) has reached its third volume and now provides a forum both for Cistercian studies and work on Southern Jutland's history. The editors of *Danmarks Kirker* continue to shed light on the construction and use of churches in medieval Denmark, and here the work of Ebbe Nyborg provides many fascinating insights. The results of the excavation at Øm Abbey from 1975-78 remain to be published in full: it is to be hoped that Ole Schiørring will make more information available.

Other work of interest includes Niels Lund and Kai Hørby, *Dansk Socialhistorie*, Vol. 2 (1980), where Kai Hørby has a helpful list of medieval Danish monasteries. Thelma Jexlev at Rigsarkivet continues in a number of nearly-completed studies on women's history in medieval Denmark to draw on her deep knowledge of monastic sources. Nanna Damsholt of Copenhagen is finishing a book on medieval Danish literature in terms of women's history, and she will provide a reevaluation of Cistercian literature from this viewpoint. Grethe Jacobsen's work on women's history and Danish social history illuminates new sides of the difficult late Middle Ages in Denmark: see her 'Sexual Irregularities in Medieval Scandinavia' in a forthcoming selection of essays on the church and morality edited by James Brundage and Verne Bullough (Prometheus Press, 1982).

My own students, Birgitte Thye and Jesper Ballhorn, are at work on subjects as diverse as Cistercian *exemplum* literature and Cistercian art in Denmark. A subject which once was considered an arcane corner of Danish and European medieval history is beginning to receive the attention it deserves: the Cistercians in Denmark in the context of medieval society.

March, 1982   B.P.McG.

Notes

CHAPTER I

1. *Øm bogen. Corpus codicum Danicorum medii aevi* II (Cpn., 1960). There is also a discussion of the Øm Book's various sections in Sv. Green-Pedersen, 'Øm klosters grundlæggelse og dets forhold til bisp Sven af *Århus', Århus Stifts Årbøger* 57 (1964), pp. 174-81. The page numbers given in my text refer to Gertz, *Scriptores Minores Historiae Danici Medii Aevi* (SM), Volume II, which contain most of the Danish Cistercian chronicles.

2. C.A. Christensen (note 1), p. XIV. The myth that the Øm Book has a lost final section continues to manifest itself in Danish cultural life, most recently in a historical novel by Ebbe Reich Kløvedal, *Festen for Cecile* (1979), where it is asserted that the Øm writer on the last half page of the chronicle for the latter part of the thirteenth century told the story of King Erik Glipping's murder and revealed the killers' identities. The abbot of Øm could not tolerate such an admission of the facts and so had the page cut out.

3. *Øm-bogen* f. 28v; SM II, 204-205. For a more complete treatment of the Life of Bishop Gunner, see *Conflict and Continuity at Øm Abbey* (Museum Tusculanum, Opuscula graecolatina 8: Cpn., 1976), pp. 110-13. For a treatment of the biography, see my article, 'Monastic and Episcopal Biography in the Thirteenth Century: The Danish Cistercian Account of Bishop Gunner of Viborg' (forthcoming). I am indebted to Ebbe Nyborg of *Danmarks Kirker* for providing proof that this biography was actually written at Øm's sister abbey, Vitskøl, and at some time in the late Middle Ages must have been copied for the sake of the monks at Øm. This place of origin gives me an entirely new perspective to the biography.

4. Printed in *Scriptores Rerum Danicarum* (SRD) IV, 463 ff. Unless otherwise noted, all the manuscripts named in this chapter are found in the Royal Library (Det kongelige bibliotek) in Copenhagen. For a guide to the manuscripts, see Ellen Jørgensen, *Catalogus Codicum Latinorum Medii Aevi Bibliothecae Regiae Hafniensis* (Cpn., 1926). This does not include manuscripts from the Copenhagen University Library now transferred to the Royal Library and listed in Alfr. Krarup, *Katalog over Universitetsbibliotekets Haandskrifter* 1-2 (Cpn., 1929-35).

5. SRD IV, 463-75. The Skjalm family, from their founder, are also known as *Hviderne* (the Whites).

6. 'De ældste Vidnesbyrd af Skyldtaxationen', HT 9 Række, 6 Bind (1929), 54–95.

7. Ellen Jørgensen, *Annales Danici Medii Aevi* (Cpn., 1920), abbreviated as AD, pp. 73–128.

8. AD, p. 17.

9. AD, pp. 24, 142–43.

10. SM II, 2–72.

11. SM II, 6–7.

12. AD, pp. 14–17, 62–70, 73–125. The Hamburg MS was catalogued as nr. 18b *in scrinio.*

13. AD, pp. 5–7, 39–43. *Danmarks Ældste Annalistik.* Studier over lundensisk Annalskrivning i 12. og 13. Arhundrede. Skrifter udgivet af Det historiske institut ved Købehavns Universitet III (Cpn., 1969).

14. Originally Berlin cod. theol. 149, 2°, and now in Marburg University Library.

15. SM II, 134–42.

16. SM II, 135–36.

17. SM II, 142–44, 146–47.

18. Arne Odd Johnsen, *De norske cistercienserklostre 1146-1264* (Det Norske Videnskaps-Akademi: II. Hist. Filos. Klasse Avhandlinger Ny Serie, No. 15: Oslo, 1977), pp. 72–3.

19. Geoffrey's letter is printed in *Diplomatarium Danicum* (DD) I, 2, 114 (dated to 1153). The most accessible text of the *Vita Prima* is still J. P. Migne, *Patrologia Latina* (PL) 185, col. 334–37. Much of it has been translated into Danish by C.P.O. Christiansen, a teacher who did much to encourage interest in the Cistercians in Denmark: *Bernard af Clairvaux. Hans Liv Fortalt af Samtidige og et Udvalg af hans Værker og Breve* (Selskabet for Historiske Kildeskrifters Oversættelse: Cpn., 1926). For the *Vita Prima* in general, see Adriaan Bredero, 'St. Bernard and the Historians', *St Bernard of Clairvaux: Studies Commemorating the Eighth Anniversary of his Canonization,* ed. M. Basil Pennington (Cistercian Studies Series 28: Kalamazoo, Michigan, 1977), 27–62. Also Bredero's 'Etudes sur la Vita Prima de Saint Bernard', *Analecta Sacri Ordinis Cisterciensis* 17 (1961) and 17 (1962), especially the section on the books of Geoffrey (1962), pp. 3–23.

20. Lauritz Weibull, 'En samtida berättelse från Clairvaux om ärkebiskop Eskil af Lund', *Scandia* IV (1931), pp. 270–90. The parts of the *Liber Miraculorum* published in PL 185, col. 1273–1382, do not include the section on Eskil.

21. Critical edition ed. Bruno Griesser (Series Scriptorum S. Ordinis Cisterciensis II: Rome, 1961). For a treatment of the organization, content, and ideology of this central Cistercian source, see my 'Structure and Consciousness in the *Exordium Magnum Cisterciense:* The Clairvaux Cistercians after Bernard', *Cahiers de l'Institut du Moyen-Age Grec et Latin* 30 (Cpn., 1979), pp. 33–90.

22. J. M. Canivez, *Statuta Capitulorum Generalium Ordinis Cisterciensis* (Bibliothèque de la Revue d'Histoire Ecclésiastique: Louvain). Fasc. 9, (1933), covers the years 1116–1220. Fasc. 10 (1934) 1221–61. Fasc. 11 (1935), 1262–1400.

23. See the criticism made by Bruno Griesser and his additions to the statutes in *Cistercienser-Chronik* December 1955, pp. 65–83 and July, 1957, pp. 1–20. Peter King, 'Cistercian Financial Organization 1335-1392', *Journal of Ecclesiastical History* 24 (1973) treats a Citeaux taxation register beginning in 1337 that has bearing on Danish abbeys.

24. DD I, 5, 197–98, from 1221.

25. Canivez 1258, nr. 52.

26. 'De ældste Vidnesbyrd' (note 6), p. 57: 'Man har aabenbart næret en intens Frygt for, at Adkomsten dertil skulde blive bestridt af de mægtige og gridske Lunger, og man har væbnet sig til eventuel Proces'.

27. SRD IV, 484, 530.

28. SRD IV, 531.

29. *Lokalarkiver til 1559. Gejstlige Arkiver* I: *Ærkestiftet og Roskilde Stift*, ved Thelma Jexlev (Rigsarkivet, Cpn., 1973): Sorø, nr. 14 and 15 from 1469 and 1470.

30. According to the Sorø Abbot List, he is supposed to have been abbot for 52 years and to have died in 1444 (SRD IV, 537). But this list is undependable, and it is safer to trust the scattered mentions of him in the years up to 1440 in the Donation Book itself.

31. 'Biskop Niels Skave og Sorø Kloster', HT 8 Række, 1 Bind (1907), 254–83.

32. The contents of the Sorø Book have never been published in full, for many of the papal bulls are general ones issued to all Cistercian abbeys. See the list of the contents of the MS provided in SRD IV, 558–69. The documents that have special application to Sorø have been published in DD.

33. *Codex Esromensis. Esrom Klosters Brevbog* (Selskabet for Udgivelse af Kilder til Dansk Historie, 1880–81/ 1973), p. IV. See also the helpful remarks in Thelma Jexlev, *Fra dansk senmiddelalder: Nogle kildestudier* (Odense University Studies in History and Social Sciences, Vol. 29: Odense, 1976), pp. 41–45.

34. A full explanation is given in DD II, 1, 12.

35. *Dänische Bibliothec oder Sammlung von Alten und Neuen Gelehrten Sachen aus Dännemarck* VI (Cpn., 1745), 129–84.

36. SRD IV, 538–39.

37. SRD IV, 575–87: Abbas Hinricus prefatus petit humiliter propter Deum, se inscribi ad librum istum, cum obitus ejus, utinam in Domino felix, primo patribus Loci Dei intimatus fuerit.

38. SRD IV, 539–45.

39. See Poul Nørlund, 'Klostret og dets Gods', *Sorøbogen* I, pp. 116–31: 'Klostret efter Reformationen'.

40. SRD IV, 534–39.

41. DD I, 5, 51.

42. See my 'Patrons, privileges, property: Sorø Abbey's first half century', KS (1974), pp. 35–36. The first sentence of the Series (SRD IV, 534) says that if future abbots of Sorø continue to show the piety displayed by past abbots, the monastery will flourish, an indication that the Reformation had not yet affected the abbey: *Quorum officiosis conatibus pientissimus Deus semper incrementum dedit, posthac nimirum dabit, si successores solidam fidem et sinceram pietatem coluerint.*

43. Printed in SRD VIII, 1–258. The background is given in DD II, 1,58.

282 The Cistercians in Denmark

44. See Chapter V, section 6, 'Interminable cases and monastic compromises'.

45. P. H. Suhm, *Nye Samlinger til den Danske Historie* 3 (1794), 302-26.

46. T. A. Becker, De Ældste Danske Archivregistraturer (ÆA) I (1854), pp. 161-276. For a close analysis of the Øm registers, see P. Rasmussen, *Herreklostrenes Jordegods i det 16. århundrede og dets Historie. Østjydsk hjemstavn* (Skanderborg, 1957), pp. 22f, 36f.

47. See my analysis in *Conflict and Continuity* (note 3), pp. 128-35.

48. SM II, pp. 268-69.

49. H. Hoogeweg, *Die Stifter und Klöster der Provinz Pommern* I (1924), pp. 243-44.

50. See Ch. VII, note 172.

51. For the Danish Cistercians and preaching, see Anne Riising, *Danmarks middelalderlige prædiken* (Cpn., 1969), pp. 22-23.

52. I have not been able to establish the authorship of the Compendium. The manuscript gives no hint at all, but considering the popularity of such works, it is unlikely the Vitskøl monks themselves would have had to compose such a treatment.

53. Ellen Jørgensen, 'Studier over danske middelalderlige Bogsamlinger', HT 8 Række, 4 Bind (1912-13), p. 45.

54. *Ibid.*, pp. 44-45. The codex is described in M. Vattasso and P. F. de Cavalieri, *Codices Vaticani Latini* (Roma, 1902) I, nr. 636.

55. DD I, 4, 91 (SRD IV, 478): *Iste Iohannes obiit apud sepulcrum domini. et claruerunt in eo divina opera sicut continetur in epistola quam gardianus Iherosolimitanus super hoc scripsit Waldemaro regi. cuius tenor annotatus est in libris Esromensium nostrorum.* See also my 'Property and Politics at Esrum Abbey', *Mediaeval Scandinavia* (1973), p. 146, n. 99, for mention of a letter from Hildegard of Bingen to the monk Frederick of Esrum.

56. SM II, 199.

57. 'Studier' (note 53), p. 45.

58. 'Tre Litterære Munke i Sorø Kloster', *Sorøbogen* I, pp. 132-45.

59. For a modification of Dahlerup's views, however, see Svend Aakjær, *Kong Valdemars Jordebog* (Cpn., 1945), pp. +53-+54.

60. Dahlerup (note 58), pp. 137-38.

61. Kr. Isager and Ejnar Sjövall, *Skeletfundene ved Øm Kloster* (Cpn., 1936). Also *Krankenfürsorge des dänischen Zisterzienserkloster Øm* (Cpn.-Leipzig, 1941).

62. I should especially like to thank Olga Bartholdy, former librarian at Løgumkloster Højskole, for making this point to me after I had claimed that the Danish Cistercians were intellectually backward. A quiet life can also be a rich and deep life.

Chapter II

1. R. W. Southern, *Western Society and the Church in the Middle Ages* (Penguin, 1970), pp. 315-16. For typical examples of the Cistercian attitude towards women, see the decisions of the yearly General Chapters of the Order contained in J. Canivez, *Statuta Capitulorum Generalium*

Ordinis Cisterciensis (Bibliothèque de la Revue d'Histoire Ecclésiastique: Louvain, 1933–41, Vol. IX–XIVB. A good example is in the 1154 chapter decision nr. 24. Abbreviation: Canivez 1154, nr. 24.

2. For general treatments, see Erik Arup, *Danmarks Historie* I (Copenhagen, 1926; photographic reprint, 1961), pp. 141–45. Lucien Musset, *Les Peuples Scandinaves au Moyen-Age* (Paris, 1951), pp. 154–55. Also Niels Skyum-Nielsen, *Kvinde og Slave* (Cpn., 1971). For the question of parish churches, see the section written by Aksel E. Christensen in Inge Skovgaard-Petersen, Aksel E. Christensen, Helge Paludan, *Danmarks historie* I (tiden indtil 1340) (Cpn., 1977), esp. pp. 309–12. Ebbe Nyborg, an editor for the series *Danmarks kirker* lectured at the Løgum Abbey summer course in July of 1979 on the question 'who built the parish churches' and replied that evidence points to the magnates.

3. The earliest statement of Cistercian practice can be found in the *Exordium Parvum*, now in a much-needed critical edition by Jean de la Croix Bouton and Jean Baptiste Van Damme, *Les Plus Anciens Textes de Citeaux* (*Citeaux: Commentarii Cistercienses*, Studia et Documenta, II: Achel, 1974), p. 77: *Et quia nec in regula, nec in vita sancti Benedicti eumdem doctorem legebant possedisse ecclesias vel altaria, seu oblationes aut sepulturas vel decimas aliorum hominum, seu furnos vel molendina, aut villas vel rusticos, nec etiam feminas monasterium ejus intrasse, nec mortuos ibidem excepta sorore sua sepelisse, ideo haec omnia abdicaverunt . . . .* For the twelfth century as the great watershed in Danish history, see Poul Nørlund *Gyldne Altre* (Cpn., 1926).

4. AD, p. 43. Abbreviated as AD. For the provenance of these chronicles, see Anne K. G. Kristensen's *Danmarks Ældste Annalistik* (Skrifter udgivet af Det historiske Institut ved Københavns Universitet III, 1969).

5. Hal Koch, *Kongemagt og Kirke* (Politikens Danmarks Historie, 3: Cpn., 1963), p. 249. Niels Skyum-Nielsen, (note 2), pp. 120–21, but see the reservation, p. 122. See also my 'Clairvaux og Nordens cisterciensere i 1100-tallet' (with an English summary), *Løgumkloster Studier* 1 (1978), 11–29, esp. pp. 17–18.

6. The breakthrough came with Niels Skyum-Nielsen's article, 'De ældste privilegier for klostret i Væ. Et nyfund', *Scandia* XXI (Lund, Sweden: 1951), pp. 1–27. Skyum-Nielsen showed that Eskil's contribution in terms of property to the new Premonstratensian abbey previously had been overstated. The same conclusion was reached concerning the mother abbey of Væ, Tommerup or Tomarp, in Curt Wallin, 'Ärkebiskop Eskil som klosterstiftare', *Scandia* XXVII (1961), pp. 217–34. Skyum-Nielsen's work emphasizes the legal importance of the local bishop in founding a monastery but warns against concluding that bishops were always active contributors to new houses.

7. The Øm Chronicle, as well as the narrative sources for Danish Cistercian houses, were printed in 1922 in Volume II of *Scriptores Minores Historiae Danicae Medii Aevi* (SM) (photographic reprint, Cpn., 1970), edited M. Cl. Gertz. Eskil is mentioned on p. 169. See also my *Conflict and Continuity at Øm Abbey: A Cistercian Experience in Medieval Denmark* (Museum Tusculanum, Opuscula Graeco-latina 8: 1976), esp. pp. 27–34.

8. SM II, pp. 169–70: *Iste archiepiscopus Eskillus semper et ubique edificationi et confirmationi huius domus intendit et devotus fuit, licet ante privilegium suum non dederit, quia prius non petebatur. Ipse eduxit duos conventus, unum de Cistercio, alterum de Claravalle, et fundavit duo monasteria, Herivadum in Scania et Esrom in Selandia, de quibus plura examina monachorum diffusa sunt per Daciam; et postea in Claravalle est monachus factus, et in ea aliquantum temporis vite sue spacium consummans ante magnum altare honorifice sub marmore iacet tumulatus.*

9. Migne *Patrologia Latina* (PL) 185: col. 1086–87. I shall refer to the *Exordium Magnum* in the critical edition published in Series Scriptorum S. Ordinis Cisterciensis II (Rome, 1961), ed. Bruno Griesser, here p. 212: *Cisterciensii Ordinis duos conventus obtinuit, unum scilicet de ipsa*

domo Cistercii et alterum de Claravalle. The sections of the EM dealing with Eskil have been printed in SM II, 428–42, entitled by Gertz 'De Eskillo et Patruis Eius'. The dating of the EM is sometime between 1178 and 1206 (Griesser, p. 34), with the 1180s as the most likely time for the composition of the first four books. The author, Conrad, who later became abbot of Eberbach, was at this time monk at Clairvaux. See my 'Structure and Consciousness in the *Exordium Magnum Cisterciense:* The Clairvaux Cistercians after Bernard', *Cahiers de l'Institut du Moyen Age Grec et Latin* 30 (Copenhagen, 1979), pp. 33–90.

10. PL 185: 335.

11. Lauritz Weibull, 'En samtida berättelse från Clairvaux om ärkebiskop Eskil av Lund', *Scandia* IX (1931), pp. 270–90, esp. p. 279: '... *conventus plurimos fratrum cisterciensium, car-tusiensium ac premonstratensium evocans ...* '. Weibull brought this source to light but did not analyze its information about Eskil.

12. See Edvard Ortved's unpublished typescript on Herrisvad at the Royal Library in Copenhagen: Ny kgl. Samling 2043, II. Note that Hamsfort's seventeenth century *Chronologica Rerum Danicarum Secunda* does not say that from 1151 Herrisvad was enlarged by buildings and fields, but we do not know what source he is using: *Scriptores Rerum Danicarum* (SRD), ed. Langebek and Suhm (Cpn., 1772), I, 275. For the conflict between Lund and Hamburg, see *Danmarks Historie* I (note 2), 281–4, 295–6. Also Aksel E. Christensen, 'Archbishop Asser, the Emperor and the Pope', *Scandinavian Journal of History* I (1976), 25–42.

13. Stockholm Kung. Bibl. MS. K 7 is from the sixteenth century. The same entry that deals with Eskil says that the monks' choir was finished in 1513. Thus the inscriptions cannot be older than the beginning of the 1500s.

14. Jürgen A. Wissing, *Das Kloster Lögum in Ruckblick: Erinnerungen, Betrachtungen und Vermutungen.* Heimatkundlichen Arbeitsgemeinschaft für Nordschleswig. Heft 26 (Apenrade, 1972), p. 30. Again we depend on the Ryd and Colbaz Annals for the foundation dates: AD, p. 43.

15. Canivez 1152, nr. 1.

16. SM II, pp. 138–39.

17. PL 185: 444: 'petente religiosa femina regina Sueciae conventum fratrum ad illas partes direxit'.

18. Griesser (note 9), p. 262. See also Fr. Hall, 'Beiträge zur Geschichte der Cistercienser Klöster in Schweden', *Cistercienser Chronik* 15 (1903), pp. 193–5. Gerard is identified as abbot of Alvastra in the narration on the founding of Vitskøl Abbey in Jutland, SM II, 140.

19. The Cistercian tradition of withdrawal to isolated spots goes back to the very beginnings of the Order, as can be seen in the *Exordium Parvum:* '... *suscepturos terras ab habitacione hominum remotas',* (note 3) p. 78. Only later on in the century, as in the *Exordium Magnum* (EM), is the missionary ideal partially accepted as desirable and praiseworthy. For this development, see the chapter, 'Crusades and Missions' in Louis J. Lekai, *The Cistercians: Ideals and Reality* (Kent State University, 1977), 52–64.

20. A classic example is Franz Winter's, *Die Cistercienser des nordöstlichen Duetschlands* (Gotha, 1868), I: 89–152, 'Die Festsetzung im Wendenlands von 1169–1198', esp. pp. 121–31.

21. Bernard's letter concerning a crusade in Wendland, dated 1147, is in *Mecklenburgisches Urkundenbuch* (Meck. Ur.) (Schwerin, 1863), nr. 43, p. 35. See Jean Leclercq, 'Saint Bernard's Attitude towards War', *Studies in Medieval Cistercian History,* ed. John R. Sommerfeldt (Kalamazoo, Michigan: 1976), 1–39.

22. EM IV, 28: Griesser, p. 258: ... *coepit iam religio ipsa transplantari super aquas multas,*

id est, diversarum nationum cervicosas ac tumidas voluntates tamquam caeruleos undarum vertices ad verae pietatis cultum inclinare.

23. *Ibid.*, p. 259: ... *licet remotissimas et in ultimo climate aquilonaris brumae abstrusas nationes non sine quodam horrore spiritus adire possent* ....

24. *Ibid.*, p. 260: *Quia vero propter paucitatem clericorum vix aliquis de terra illa convertebatur, Dominus fideli famulo suo de partibus Germaniae et Angliae litteratas et discretas personas mittebat, per quos disciplina monasticae religionis in regno illo fundata crescebat et fructificabat compententer in populis, qui monachi quidem nomen audierant, sed monachum antea non viderant.*
Note the mention of German and English monks who probably, like Gerard, had first gone to Clairvaux and from there had been sent to the North.

25. A typical example is the monk Henrik, who was at Clairvaux in 1156, according to the *Vita Prima* of Bernard, PL 185: 334–40. Henrik seems to have been once again at Clairvaux in the 1170s, when he gave Herbert a memorable miracle story. See Weibull (note 11), p. 288.

26. The most sensational reference to a Danish abbey in the statutes is from 1191, nr. 41, concerning a plot against the abbot of Herrisvad by the Løgum abbot and the chanter at Herrisvad. See also 1203, nr. 27 and 50. In 1215, nr. 19 the abbots of Øm and Tvis were ordered to come to the next General Chapter. They had stayed away that year because of 'dangers of wars'. This entry indicates that Danish Cistercian abbots were expected to come to Citeaux at least once every few years.

27. Canivez 1217, nr. 11. See Ed. Ortved, *Cistercieordenen og dens Klostre i Norden* II (Cpn., 1933), p. 19.

28. PL 185: 334, 340.

29. Næstved is one of the few Danish abbeys whose history has been written in full detail: H. J. Helms, *Næstved Sct. Petri Kloster* (Næstved, 1940). Unfortunately Helms does not bring many of his rich details into a European context and is satisfied with a more antiquarian approach.

30. DD I, 2, 64 (19 November 1135). Eskil was bishop of Roskilde until 1138, when he became archbishop of Lund.

31. Weibull (note 11), p. 279: ... *propriis sumptibus munifice procurans in optimis terre sue locis tanquam vites fructiferas pastinavit.*

32. Nanna Damsholt has treated the language of charters in her 'Kingship in the Arengas of Danish Royal Diplomas, 1140–1223', *Mediaeval Scandinavia* 3 (1970), 66–108. Although she has found a striking borrowing from a French royal charter for a Danish one, Ms. Damsholt has at the same time used these opening passages from the early period in order to describe how conceptions of royal power and authority were expressed. See also Thomas Riis, *Les institutions politiques centrales du Danemark* 1100–1332 (Odense University Studies in History and Social Sciences, Vol. 46: Odense, 1977), 'L' idéologie royale dans des arengae des diplômes royaux', pp. 66–85.

33. *Diplomatarium Danicum* (DD) I, 2, 64: *Et fundamento eius qui edificatur ut civitas cuius participatio eius in idipsum. gemmas. lapides politos, preciosos. superedificaverunt.*
Note that the images and language are biblical and are direct quotes but have been dexterously manipulated so that they fit into the desired context. Psalm 121:3: ... *quae edificatur ut civitas, cujus participatio ejus in idipsum.* 1 Cor 3:12: *si quis ... superedificat super fundamentum hoc ... lapides pretiosos.*

34. Again the phrases are biblical, but their combination gives new meaning. Psalm 83:7: *in valle lacrymarum.* Ps 83:4: *ascensiones in corde suo disposuit.*

35. DD I, 2, 88 and 89. Michael Gelting of Rigsarkivet has kindly pointed out to me that in August 1139 there was held a provincial synod at Lund, probably to initiate reforms at Lund as legislated by the Second Lateran Council. Cardinal Theodewin participated in this council (see DD I, 2, 77). Eskil may at this time have been given an important impulse in instituting reforms and new orders, but it should be noted that the immediate result of Theodewin's influence seems to have been a Premonstratensian foundation in Denmark, as pointed out in a forthcoming book by Tore Nyberg of Odense University. For the development of the relationship between the papacy and the Scandinavian church, see Tore Nyberg's *Skt. Peters efterfølgere i brydningstider. Omkring pavedømmets historie. Rom og Nordeuropa 750–1200* (Odense University Studies in History and Social Sciences 58: 1979).

36. *The Ecclesiastical History of Orderic Vitalis*, edited and translated by Marjorie Chibnall (Oxford Medieval Texts, 1973), Vol. IV, Books 7 and 8. For an analysis of Orderic as an historian in the context of his time, see Antonia Gransden, *Historical Writing in England* c. 550–c. 1307 (London, 1974), pp. 151–65.

37. Orderic, Bk. VIII, 26, pp. 310–311: *In saltibus et campestribus passim construuntur cenobia, novisque ritibus variisque scematibus trabeata, peragrant orbem cucullatorum examina.* I am using Chibnall's excellent translation.

38. Orderic, Bk. VIII, 26, pp. 312–13: *Voluntaria paupertas mundi contemptus ut opinor in plerisque fervet ac vera religio sed plures eis hipocritae seductoriique sumulatores permiscentur ut lolium tritico.*

39. Orderic, pp. 314–315

40. Orderic, pp. 318–21. The answers placed in the mouths of the loyalists at Molesme tell us a great deal about monastic attitudes towards peasants. They are looked upon as a lazy lot who have to be kept under control. Moreover their work is 'servile and unbecoming'. Orderic's revelation of his social prejudice is invaluable for any understanding of class attitudes in medieval society.

41. Orderic, pp. 322–23.

42. Orderic, p. 324: *Iam fere xxxvii anni sunt ex quo Robertus abbas ut dictum est Cistercium incoluit, et in tantillo tempore tanta virorum illuc copia confluxit, ut inde lxv abbatiae consurgerent, quae omnes cum abbatibus suis Cisterciensi archimandritae subiacent.*

43. Orderic, 324–27: . . . *multisque bonis in mundo ut lucernae lucentes in caliginoso loco renitent. Omni tempore silentio student, fucatis vestibus non utuntur. Manibus propriis laborant, victumque sibi et vestitum vendicant. Omnibus diebus preter dominicum ab idibus Septembris usque ad Pascha ieiunant. Aditus suos satis obserant, et secreta sua summopere celant. Nullum alterius ecclesiae monachum in suis penetralibus admittunt, nec in oratorium ad missam vel alia servitia secum ingredi permittunt . . .*
. . . *In desertis atque silvestribus locis monasteria proprio labore condiderunt, et sacra illis nomina sollerti provisione imposuerunt, ut est Domus Dei, Claravallis, Bonus Mons et Elemosina, et alia plura huiusmodi, quibus auditores solo nominis nectare invitantur festinanter experiri, quanta sit ibi beatitude, quae tam speciali denotetur vocabulo.*

44. As in H. N. Garner, *Atlas over danske klostre* (Cpn., 1968), p. 75.

45. Niels Skyum-Nielsen, (note 2), p. 120.

46. *Esrom Klosters Brevbog* (*Cod. Esrom.*), ed. O. Nielsen (Cpn., 1880–81; photographic reprint, 1973), pp. 135–6. Also DD I, 2, 107. See also Arne Odd Johnsen, *Om Pave Eugenius IIIs vernebrev for Munkeliv kloster af 7 januar 1146* (Avhandlinger utgift av Det Norske Videnskaps-Akademi i Oslo, II. Hist. Filos. klass. Ny Serie. No. 7: Oslo, 1965). Johnsen points out (p. 43) that the clause *'salva sedis apostolica auctoritate et dyocesani episcopo canonica et reverencia'*

indicates Munkeliv is a Benedictine house subject to episcopal jurisdiction, a so-called non-exempt abbey.

47. KLNMA II, 577–78.

48. For Geoffrey's letter, DD I, 2, 114. For Eskil's privilege, DD I, 2, 126. See the statement in Erik Arup, (note 2 above), p. 225: 'Home from his visit to Clairvaux, Eskil brought the colony of French Cistercian monks, with which he in the midst of Northern Zealand's trackless forest regions founded an abbey in Esrum'.

49. Niels Skyum-Nielsen, 'Das dänische Erzbistum vor 1250', *Acta Visbyensia* III (1969), pp. 131 f.

50. AD, p. 79. The words (*in Warnhem*) are not included in the Hamburg manuscript, our main source for the original Ryd Annals but are in the Codex Arnamagn. 107, written by the Danish Reformation Dominican, Peder Olsen, who had a lost manuscript of the Ryd Annals. See Ellen Jørgensen's introduction in AD, p. 15.

51. *Necrologium Lundense*, ed. Lauritz Weibull (Monumenta Scaniae historica: Lund, 1923), p. 66. For Svend Grathe's charter confirming the possessions of Esrum given the monks by Eskil, see DD I, 2, 107.

52. See the table and explanation in R. W. Southern, (note 1), p. 254.

53. DD I, 2, 114, p. 206: *Siquidem Bernardus amicus vester dormit; sed non totus dormit; vigilat vigilat cor illius.*

54. *Ibid.*, p. 208: *ut prolixitatem si sibi displicuerit mihi dignanter indulgeant; cui multa sug-gerebat affectus.* The *ut . . . indulgeat* clause is a typical epistolary cliché, but the emphasis on the writer's feelings is unusual. Thus a Cistercian writer transforms an old theme by new emotional content.

55. PL 185, col. 335: *Confessus est etiam nobis de pane quem retulit quod nunc usque, cum jam tertius annus transierit, illaesum eum beati viri fides et benedictio custodivit.*

56. PL 185: 1087. Griesser, p. 213. SM II, 435.

57. PL 185: 335: *Nam de expensis dicere non est magnum, quamvis eundem audierimus pro-testantem, quod expenderit in itinere ipso argenti marchas amplius quam sexcentas.*

58. *Cod. Esrom.*, nr. 80, p. 86: DD I, 2, 126. See the commentary in the *Diplomatiarum* by Niels Skyum-Nielsen: 'Archbishop Eskil's privilege for Esrum abbey stands as a monument over his work for monasticism in Denmark. The emphasis is placed on his own activity and on his own and Count Niels's donations'.

59. PL 185: 335: *Ubi quantum fleverit, qualem sese non modo erga eum, que tam unice suspi-ciebat, sed etiam erga minimos quoslibet fratrum exhibuerit, non est facile dictu.*

60. SM II, 186–89, cap. xxxi: 'De moribus domni Suenonis episcopi'.

61. PL 185: 335: . . . *miraculum dignum memoria nuper factum in coenobio quod, ut supra meminimus, in terra sua ipse fundavit.*

62. Weibull, (note 11), p. 279.

63. PL 185: 335. This is probably Niels, who appears in a charter in the Esrum Book, 8 August 1158 (DD I, 2, 127), in which Eskil says Niels gave his property to the abbey and thereafter be-came a monk.

64. PL 185: 336: *Quod ut factum est, Germanica lingua per os ejus coepit horrendis vocibus nequam spiritus exclamare, 'Tollite, tollite, amovete Bernardum'. Et dicebat, 'Heu, quam ponderosus factus es, Bernarde! quam gravis, quam intolerabilis factus es mihi!'*

65. SRD IV, 534. The list was drawn up at Sorø just before the Reformation and has a great number of mistakes in it. See the criticism of it in DD I, 5, 51. We can at least assume that Sorø had a tradition according to which the first abbots were foreigners. Also the mention of two English and one German abbot there in the twelfth century corresponds to the Øm Abbey Chronicle's mention of foreign abbots, SM II, 192-3. Also the EM mentions German and English monks (note 24).

66. Robert witnessed Eskil's privilege for Esrum dated to 1158 (DD I, 2, 126) and signed the foundation charter for Tvis, 24 March 1163 (DD I, 2, 152).

67. See my 'Property and Politics at Esrum Abbey', *Mediaeval Scandanavia* 6 (1973), p. 146, n. 99.

68. Ortved, (note 27), p. 57.

69. Hal Koch, *Danmarks Kirke i den begyndende Højmiddelalder* (Cpn., 1972), pp. 98-102. Also Jørgen Quistgaard Hansen, 'Regnum et Sacerdotium: Forholdet mellem stat og kirke i Danmark 1157-70', *Middelalderstudier tilegnede Aksel E. Christensen* (Cpn., 1966), 57-76, esp. 62-3. The relationship between Eskil and King Valdemar may have been more complicated than Hal Koch imagined. In a forthcoming article in *Historisk Tidsskrift*, 'Kansleren Radulfs to bispevielser. En undersøgelse af Saxos skildring af ærkebispe— og pavestriden 1159-1162', Michael Gelting shows that King Valdemar in the years after 1160 sought to limit Eskil's secular power in his archbishopric.

70. DD I, 2, 126: ... *ac ne Cisterciensis ordinis fratres nobis deessent. ad beatissimum Clarevallensis cenobii patrem dominum Bernardum quamvis multo labore sumptu pervenimus. de cuius filiis semen unde seges postera fidelium animarum pululare [posset] nobiscum in terram nostram adduximus.*
Notice how the sentence ends with three words emphasizing Eskil's own contribution: *nobiscum, nostram, adduximus.*

71. *Cod. Esrom.*, p. 135, nr. 117. DD I, 2, 107, dated between 1151-57.

72. The images of the early charters for Esrum are sometimes close to those of the early charters or writings from other Cistercian houses and especially to the images used in the *Exordium Parvum*. It is possible that Eskil and the Cistercians consciously tried to imitate the international style in describing the roles of new Danish abbeys. This borrowing indicates that Danish charters do more than just imitate foreign models. Compare Eskil's 1158 confirmation with the *Exordium Parvum*. Both mention the monks as poor of Christ, but for completely different purposes: Eskil in order to explain his gifts; the Cistercian writer to explain the monks' role apart from the world.

Ex. Parvum (note 3), p. 77	*Eskil to Esrum* DD I, 2, 126
Ecce hujus saeculi divitiis spretis coeperunt novi milites Christi cum paupere Christo pauperes, inter se tractare	*Quem locum idcirco necessitati pauperum Christi destinavimus. pro eo quod multis habundet utilitatibus ....*

73. DD I, 2, 126: *Postea vero processu temporis numero fidelium ibidem crescente. animadvertentes pauca pluribus non posse sufficere. ne ipsorum necessitati quicquam deesset ....*
74. SM II, 176, ch. 20: *Quidam autem de colonis possessiones suas libenter vendebant; alii vero, qui ditiores erant, valde difficiles efficiebantur.*

75. Canivez 1182, nr. 9. As Southern points out (n. 1, p. 260), 'there is considerable obscurity

in the wording of the prohibition, and this obscurity grows deeper when the rule is amplified in 1188'.

I am gratified to find that R. A. Donkin considers the Cistercians in England also to have frequently settled in already inhabited areas where a peasant population had to be bought out or convinced to leave by other methods: *The Cistercians: Studies in the Geography of medieval England and Wales* (London, 1978).

76. See the imposing description of the boundaries for Dargun abbey's lands given by Bishop Berno of Schwerin in his foundation charter of 30 November 1173: *Meck. Ur.* I, 106, nr. 111.

77. See my Esrum article (note 67), pp. 133-4.

78. *Cod. Esrom.*, p. 55, nr. 39—DD I, 3, 77

79. The image is taken from John 4, 36, but fits in perfectly with the agricultural terminology: *Ut simul gaudeant et qui seminat et qui de seminatis metunt.*

80. DD I, 2, 120.

81. SM II, 140. See Quistgaard Hansen, (note 69), pp. 57-8.

82. SM II, 161.

83. DD I, 2, 120: ... *praesente venerabilis archiepiscopo, apostolicae sedis legato Eschillo atque id ipsum confirmante.*

84. According to Gertz in SM II, 137. The monastic writer says that after the reestablishment of the abandoned Varnhem, the greater part, composing the best of the monks, returned there from Vitskøl. SM II, 141.

85. Ortved, *op. cit.* (note 27). Lauritz Weibull, 'Erik den helige', *Aarbøger for Nordisk Oldkyndighed* (1917), 99-130, dates that *Narratiuncula* from the end of the 1100s or the beginning of the 1200s, assumedly because it would fit in with other contemporary literature about the foundations of Øm, Sorø, etc. He points out (p. 104) that Christina's family bonds to Sigrid indicate that the resistance to the monks was due to resentment against their land holdings and not because of any anti-monastic policy on the part of King Erik. See also Tore Nyberg, 'Eskil av Lund och Erik den helige', *Historia och samhälle. Studier tilägnade Jerker Rosen* (Lund, 1975), 5-21.

86. SM II, 139: ... *abbate Henrico de Swecia descendente et per regnum Danorum transeunte, ut in Selandie civitate Roschildensi synodus magna ageretur, in quo rex Waldemarus et archiepiscopus Eschillus presidebant.*
This phrase contributes to the thesis of early thirteenth century rather than a later dating. The view of the king as equal to the archbishop at a church synod reveals an assumption of church-state harmony and cooperation that belongs to the period of the Valdemars and not to that of the battles between the archbishop of Lund and the king after 1250.

87. Canivez 1134, XII: *Duodecim monachi cum abbate terciodecimo ad coenobia nova transmittantur: nec tamen illuc destinentur donec locus libris, domibus et necessariis aptetur, libris dumtaxat missali, Regula, libro Usuum, psalterio, hymnario, collectaneo, lectionario, antiphonario, graduali, domibusque, oratorio, refectorio, dormitorio, cella hospitum et portarii, necessariis etiam temporalibus: ut et vivere, et regulam ibidem statim valeant observare.*

88. Canivez 1211, n. 41. 1213, nr. 11.

89. DD I, 2, 127 (*Cod. Esrom.*, p. 123, nr. 108): ... *terramque, de qua ante calumniam moverant, pariter michi scotaverunt multis coram astantibus, ut predicte ecclesie iure perpetuo subiaceret.*

90. *Cod. Esrom.*, p. 90, nr. 83. DD I, 2, 184.

91. *Cod. Esrom.*, p. 135, nr. 117. DD I, 2, 107.

92. *Cod. Esrom.*, p. 54, nr. 39. DD I, 3, 77. The charter was issued after 2 November 1178.

93. *Cod. Esrom.*, p. 92, nr. 85; DD I, 2, 128.

94. *Ibid.*: ... *quia in orationibus salus nostra protegitur et regni nostri stabilitas firmatur.*

95. *Cod. Esrom.*, p. 88, nr. 81. DD I, 2, 129. The Sven Grathe model is DD I, 2, 107 (1151-57).

96. *Cod. Esrom.*, p. 96, nr. 90. DD I, 2, 130.

97. *Cod. Esrom.*, p. 94, nr. 87. DD I, 2, 122 (1157-1160). See *Danmarks historie* I (note 2), pp. 276-77, 328-9.

98. DD I, 2, 152 (24 March 1163). See Hal Koch, (note 69), pp. 101-102.

99. Christian Godt, 'Bischof Waldemar von Schleswig und die Cistercienser von Guldholm. Ein Beitrag zur Geschichte Schleswigs im 12. und 13. Jahrhundert', *Zeitschrift der Gesellschaft für Schleswig-Holstein-Lauenburgische Geschichte* (ZGSHLG) 21 (1891), 137-186. Also Hans Olrik, 'Bishop Valdemar og den danske Krone', *Aarbøger for Nordisk Oldkyndighed* (1892), 342-84.

100. Hal Koch, (note 69), p. 526, n. 2. This is a reprint of the article 'De ældste danske Klostres Stilling i Kirke og Samfund indtil 1221', *Historisk Tidsskrift* 10r. bd. III (1936). This note has greatly influenced thinking about the Danish Cistercians and their relations with Eskil. Hal Koch here made the monks into Eskil's men and emphasized too strongly the Cistercian foundations as the result of Eskil's own efforts. But the article is still invaluable as a pioneering study of Danish monasticism.

101. *Cod. Esrom.*, p. 114, nr. 90; DD I, 2, 162.

102. *Ibid.*: *Quid enim vicarius beati Lucii sedi Roskildensis subtrahit, aufert, vel derogat, qui genitricem domini votis supplicibus et munere devoto sincerius colit et amplius honorat?*

103. SRD IV, 470.

104. *Cod. Esrom.*, pp. 94-5, nr. 88-9. DD I, 3, 45-6.

105. Vilh. Lorenzen, *De danske cistercienserklostres Bygningshistorie* (Cpn., 1941), p. 225.

106. Besides Lorenzen, see also Harald Olsson, 'Cistercienserklostret i Herrevad', *Säasä.* Skånsk Samling, del V (1948), pp. 15-27.

107. DD I, 2, 147 (dated 1161-71). For the *Ex. Par.*, (note 3), p. 77.

108. DD I, 2, 143. See Quistgaard Hansen, (note 69). Also Wolfgang Seegrün, *Das Papsttum und Skandinavien* bis zur Vollendung der nordischen Kirchenorganisation (1164) (Quellen und Forschungen zur Geschichte Schleswig-Holsteins 51: Neumünster, 1967), pp. 178-83, 194-99. For the international background, Martin Preiss, *Die politische Tätigkeit und Stellung der Cisterzienser im Schisma von 1159-1177.* (Historische Studien 248: Berlin, 1934).

109. The Colbaz and Ryd Annals give 1162 as the date (AD, p. 43), but the earliest part of the Sorø Donation Book says 1161: SRD IV, 467.

110. As Rozanne Elder kindly pointed out to me in a comment on this passage: these events 'raise the question of just how important to the on-going life of the church papal politics were in the twelfth and thirteenth centuries.'.

111. SM II, 166, cap. VII, significantly entitled, '*Quod domus hec in exordio suo non sit sine fundamento fundata*'.

Non est silendum, quod in primis scripsisse debueramus, qualiter abbas Henricus scipserit domno apostolico super loco, quem sibi Eskillus episcopus offerebat, et quid ei apostolicus rescripserit. Fuerat autem episcopus Eskillus scismate Octoviani maculatus, sicut et quidam alii episcopi et ipse rex, et iccirco abbas distulit inconsulto apostolico locum suscipere de manu eius.

112. SM II, 166. DD I, 2, 157.

113. SM II, 163. DD I, 2, 167.

114. SM II, 164: ... *venerabilem quoque fratrem nostrum Eskillum, Lundensem archiepiscopum, apostolice sedis legatum, virum religiosum atque discretum et, sicut credimus, deo et hominibus valde acceptum, tibi quoque et regno tuo fidelissimum....*

115. Hal Koch, (note 69), p. 103: 'The triumph of the Cistercian party could not have been greater'.

116. SM II, 169. DD I, 2, 176.

117. DD I, 2, 142.

118. DD I, 2, 148: ... *messis enim multa in Dacia iam alba est ad metuendum sed operarii pauci....*

119. SRD IV, 469. Also in DD I, 3, 6, dated to between 1170 and 1186. H. N. Garner, 'Charteuserordenen i Danmark', *Århus Stifts Årbøger* 61 (1968), pp. 54–84. Garner says that according to the archivist of La Grande Chartreuse, Bruno Richer, Eskil apparently in 1156 visited a French Carthusian abbey (p. 61), but no written source is indicated. The same archivist claims that the brothers returning from Asserbo in Northern Zealand brought to France young men who had started their postulancy in Asserbo (p. 62).

120. Louis Bobé, *Danske Slotte og Herregårde* 3, 96–7. DD I, 3, 49.

121. Skyum-Nielsen, (note 6), pp. 10–11.

122. DD I, 3, 163 (dated between 1190–97). The Ribe Bispekrønike, reconstructed by Ellen Jørgensen (KS 6 række, 1 Bind, 1933, p. 28) says that the schismatic bishop-elect Radulf was reconciled with Eskil in 1166 and consecrated bishop after giving property for the foundation of Løgum.

123. Lorenzen, (note 105), p. 106, thinks King Valdemar was involved and may have been the real founder. But I find no evidence for this assertion.

124. DD I, 2, 184.

125. *Saxonis Gesta Danorum*, ed. J. Olrik and H. Ræder (Cpn., 1936), pp. 436–37.

126. For a discussion of the problems in this episode, especially as to the location of the castle mentioned, see Ivan Boserup's and Thomas Riis's articles in *Saxostudier* (Museum Tusculanum, Opuscula graecolatina: (Cpn., 1975), ed. Ivan Boserup, pp. 156–74.

127. Saxo's attitude to the monks will be given more attention at the end of the next chapter.

He says the monks' naïvete was the reason for Valdemar's victory: *Ita religiosissimi spiritus circumventa simplicitas finem proelio fecit.*

128. Weibull, (note 11), pp. 276–79. Repeated in the *Ex. Magnum* (Griesser III, 27, pp. 210–12; also SM II, 430–35) and adapted in the Older Zealand Chronicle, probably written at Sorø at the end of the 1200s, SM II, 48–50.

129. Weibull, (note 11), p. 279: *... noluit esse contentus istorum quinque cenobiorum instauracione/ verum etiam alia multa tam de suo quam de aliorum fidelium dono studuit edificare.*

130. *Ibid.: ... cotidie magis ac magis dilatantur et crescunt.*

131. For an analysis of the *Exordium Magnum*, see my article 'Structure and Consciousness' (note 9). For an attempt to trace the development of Eskil's religious mentality through these sources and his own letters, see my 'Clairvaux og Nordens cisterciensere' (note 5).

132. Weibull, (note 11), pp. 280–81. Griesser p. 212.

133. Weibull, p. 281-2.

134. Weibull, p. 283.

135. *Ibid.: Hec et alia pene universa que supra retulimus ab ipso venerabili et sancto patre audivimus.*

136. Griesser, p. 214. PL 185: 1088.

137. Griesser III, 28, pp. 214-17. SM II, 437-41. PL 185: 1088-90.

138. Griesser, p. 217. SM II, 441-2. PL 185: 1090: *Tales itaque personae tam sublimes honoribus, reverendae dignitatibus, odore virtutum beatissimi patris nostri Bernardi, sacri quoque Cisterciensis ordinis puritate attracti improperium Christi cunctis Aegyptiorum pompis praeferentes maluere sub disciplina ordinis temporaliter potius macerari quam pro impensis sibi favoribus falsis et honoribus aeternaliter cruciari.*

139. Weibull, (note 11), p. 288. PL 185: 450 (ch. 29, 63).

140. Weibull, p. 290.

141. On these changes of mentality and world view, R. W. Southern, *The Making of the Middle Ages*, Chapter V, 'From Epic to Romance', many paperback editions have appeared both in the United States and Great Britain. For Eskil's letter, DD I, 2, 119.

142. See my 'Patrons, privileges, property: Sorø Abbey's first half century', KS, 1974, 5-39, esp. 28-31.

143. SRD IV, 463 ff.

144. SM II, 161: *Nam Johannes nigrorum abbas propria voluntate se cum omni humilitate abbati Henrico tradidit, et de magistro discipulus factus sub regulari disciplina in Vitescola per aliquantum temporis in summa obedientia fuit, semper gemens in contritione lacrimarum, quod in priori ordine inordinate nimis vixerit ....*

145. SRD IV, 467.

146. *Ex. Par.*, (note 3), p. 60: *Nam viri isti apud Molismum positi, saepius inter se Dei gratia aspirati, de transgressione regulae beati Benedicti patris monachorum loquebantur, conquerebantur, contristabantur ....*

For Sorø, SRD IV, 467: ... *et desolatus factus est locus, quoniam dispositione divina locandus erat aliis agricoliis, qui facerent fructum.* SM II, 161: ... *quot fratres in ecclesia de Weng collocarent, que tunc conculcabatur negligentia nigrorum monachorum.*

147. SM II, 169, cap. XII.

148. SM II, 148.

149. SM II, 173-4, ca. XVII.

150. SM II, 175.

151. For whom did the monks write? Since they wrote in Latin, they could only have been intending to be read by clerks and other monks. Most of all they seem to have written for posterity so that their successors would be able to ensure their rights and privileges. Thus the heavy emphasis in the Øm Abbey Chronicle on the inclusion of documents. See especially the Øm preface (SM II, 138), our best statement of intention: *Ad noticiam posterorum transmittere cupientes, quomodo hoc coenobium ... exordium sumpsit ... ut si forte aliquando persona aliqua secularis seu ecclesiastica illud perturbare et possessiones eius diripere temptaverit, cognita veritate fundationis et reverentia fundatorum ab incepto malo opere quiescat.*
Note that the 'reverence of the founders' is ranked equally with the 'truth of the foundation'.

152. SM II, 174.

153. SM II, 175: ... *eo quid rex propter cognationem tenere diligebat mulierem nec volebat eam contristare in vita sua; et iccirco iusticia negligebatur.*

154. SM II, 175: *Unde fratres, sicut semper conquesti sunt et adhuc hodie conqueruntur, nec cessabunt conqueri donec eis iusticia de iniuste sibi ablatis fiat.*
Niels Skyum-Nielsen, in quoting this remark in *Kirkekampen i Danmark* (Cpn., 1971), p. 183, says, 'During the hundred years in which they (the Øm monks) comment on their own and contemporary history, they only emit a few kind words'. This is correct, but it should be added that the author of the early section of the Øm Chronicle had just finished describing how all appeals by the pope to the bishops and king on behalf of the monks had been fruitless: *Scipserat regi et episcopis, et nichil effecerunt.* The Øm monks at the start of the thirteenth century and again in the 1260s were angered that their use of normal legal channels in the church failed to achieve recognition of what they considered to be their rights.

155. SRD IV, 517-18. See Poul Nørlund's mention of this problem in his masterful essay, 'Et Højdepunkt under Valdemarerne', in the collection Johannes Brøndsted and Poul Nørlund, *Seks Tværsnit af Danmarks Historie* (Cpn., 1941: paperback 1966), pp. 89-91.

156. For a delightful popularized account, see Erik Kjærsgaard, *Borgerkrig og Kalmarunion* (Politikens Danmarks Historie 4: Cpn., 1965), pp. 103-109. See also my *Conflict*, (note 6).

157. SM II, 175-76.

158. For Øm's properties before 1180, Poul Rasmussen, *Herreklostrenes jordegods i det 16. århundrede og dets historie.* Den katolske kirkes jordegods i Århus Stift III. Østjydsk hjemstavn (Skanderborg, 1957), pp. 51-53.

159. Johannes Steenstrup, 'Fandtes der i Middelalderen i Danmark eller andre Riger Herreklostre?'; KS 7 Række, 1 Bind (1933), 1-22.

160. The ruins are described in most detail in C. M. Smidt, *Øm Kloster. Cara Insula* (Århus, 1924). Most recent guide is H. N. Garner, *Øm Kloster Museum* (Historisk Samfund for Århus Stift, 1973). I should like to thank H. N. Garner for his help and advice. From 1975-78 extensive

excavations at Øm made under Olaf Olsen, Århus University, revealed much late medieval (post 1450) building in the cloister quadrangle. I shall return to the significance of these excavations in the final chapter. I should like to thank Ole Schiørring, Moesgaard, Århus, for sending me copies of the excavation reports.

161. AD, p. 43.

162. *Die Cistercienser in Dargun von 1172 bis 1300*. Ein Beitrag zur meklenburg-pommerschen Colonisationsgeschichte (Güstrow, 1899). See also Stella Maria Szacherska, 'The political role of the Danish monasteries in Pomerania 1171-1223', *Mediaeval Scandinavia* 10 (1977), 122-155, an abridgement of a 1968 study in Polish. My treatment was written prior to this excellent article, and so I shall only refer to it at points where we differ.

163. Wiese, pp. 6-7.

164. Skyum-Nielsen, (note 2), p. 187. See, however, Szacherska, (note 162), p. 129.

165. Walbert is named in Eskil's foundation privilege for Væ in 1170 (*Scandia* 51, 1951, p. 21), DD I, 3, 13. A papal bull of Celestine III, dated 6 March 1193, was sent to him: *Cod. Esrom.*, p. 13, nr. 5. DD I, 3, 193.

166. *Meck. Ur.* I, nr. 111, p. 106.

167. *Meck. Ur.* I, nr. 114, p. 111, from around 1176. DD I, 3, 59.

168. *Cod. Esrom.* p. 7, nr. 3. DD I, 3, 117.

169. My explanation is based on the assumption that Walbert's first appearance as Esrum abbot has to be dated to 1170 and no later. S. M. Szacherska has a different interpretation of the evidence, (note 162), p. 139, n. 83.

170. *Meck. Ur.* I, nr. 98, p. 94. Berno was himself a Cistercian from Amelungsborn.

171. *Meck. Ur.* I, nr. 111, p. 106. The authenticity of the charters for Dargun by Berno and Kazimir was challenged in 1868 by the editor of the *Pommerschen Urkundenbuch*. But Adolf Kunkel argued convincingly for their validity in his 'Stiftungsbriefe für das meklenburg-pommersche Cistercienserkloster Dargun', *Archiv für Urkundenforschung* III (1911), 23-80, esp. 62-76.

172. *Meck. Ur.* I, nr. 111: ... *dum altare in honore beate et intemerate Dei genitricis semper virginis Marie in prima capellula in Dargon consecraremus, quod et primum consecratum est in tota Circipen, cui et ob hoc iure maior debetur reverentia.*

173. *Meck. Ur.* I, nr. 114, p. 111. Dated 1174, but DD I, 5, 163 gives the date as after 1176.

174. *Ibid.*: ... *dedimus liberam potestatem et perfectam libertatem vocandi ad se et collocandi, ubicunque voluerint in possessione prefate ecclesie de Dargon, Teutonicos, Danos, Sclavos, vel cuiuscunque gentis et cuiuscunque artis homines et ipsas artes exercendi, et parrochias et presbyteros constituendi, necnon et tabernam habendi, sive velint more gentis nostre, sive teutonice et danice.*

175. *Meck. Ur.*, nr. 125, p. 121. Although Kunkel (note 171), pp. 76-7, concluded that this document is a falsification made after 1200, it may be based on a genuine charter destroyed during the abbey's troubles.

176. Wiese, (note 162), pp. 22-4. For the full text of the Annales Colbazienses, see Pertz, *Monumenta Germaniae Historica, Scriptores* XIX, pp. 715-19 (MGH. SS). The full entry for 1188 is: *Conventus qui missus fuit de Esrom in Dargun venit in Hilda* (p. 715).

177. *Meck. Ur.* I, nr. 168, p. 166.

178. Wiese, (note 162), p. 24: 'Die nationale Erbitterung zwang die Dänen zum Verlassen Darguns'.

179. *Meck. Ur.* I, nr. 226, p. 212.

180. For the Cistercian nuns, see Gina Gertrud Smith, 'De danske nonneklostre indtil ca. 1280', KS (1973), pp. 8, 25. Stella Maria Szacherska points out (note 162), p. 151, that one of the main problems which limited Danish growth in the southwest Baltic was 'the lack of available manpower in Denmark'.

181. H. Hoogeweg, *Die Stifter und Klöster der Provinz Pommern* I (Stettin, 1924), pp. 503–4.

182. *Ibid.*, p. 225.

183. *Ibid.*, p. 253, from 1283.

184. *Ibid.*, p. 224.

185. MGH. SS. XIX, p. 715.

186. *Ibid.*, p. 716.

187. Hoogeweg, (note 181), p. 303.

188. Hoogeweg, pp. 230, 235, 244. In about 1186 and 1195 Colbaz sent monks to a daughter abbey at Oliva on the Polish coast. This monastery had probably been founded by 1178 (Hoogeweg, p. 255). Again we hear nothing about Esrum's participation.

189. Even Hoogeweg, who was much more careful than his predecessor Winter, is so caught up by the phenomenon of colonization that he ignored the ways in which the Wendish Cistercian abbeys resembled their southern sisters. Thus he tried to excuse their early acquisition of villages, in opposition to the Cistercian statutes, because of the requirements of colonization (p. 227). But such a practice was equally common in France and in Denmark. It has nothing to do with the special circumstances of the Wendish houses. Thanks to Szacherska's work (note 162), we now have a full evaluation of the monasteries' beginnings that takes into account Danish political policies.

190. Colbaz Annals, MGH. SS., p. 716. Ryd Annals, AD, p. 93. Lorenzen, (note 105), pp. 343–44 for a site description.

191. *Cod. Esrom.*, p. 288, nr. 216. DD I, 3, 55.

192. SM II, 180; DD I, 3, 112. The possessions are described as *'numero multa, sed precio pauca, quia sunt maritima et paganorum incursibus exposita'*. This testament is dated 1183, so even now the coasts were not considered safe. But Sven did give the monks the land and they held onto them, so they apparently had some value.

193. *Cod. Esrom.*, p. 228, nr. 216: *Hanc enim humanitatis graciam priorum temporum adepti fuisse leguntur, qui post brevem regni temporalis amministracionem patrie felicioris principibus meruere perhenniter sociari.*

194. R. W. Southern, *Saint Anselm and his Biographer* (Cambridge 1966). See especially Anselm's letter to Lanzo on the monastic life: F. S. Schmitt, *S. Anselmi Opera Omnia* (Edinburgh, 1946) III, ep. 37.

195. Joel T. Rosenthal, *The Purchase of Paradise. The Social Function of Aristocratic Benevolence 1307-1485* (London, 1972).

196. Niels Skyum-Nielsen, (note 2), p. 109.

197. As in 1211: Canivez 1211, nr. 41.

198. *Cod. Esrom.*, p. 230, nr. 218. DD I, 3. 66. A *herred* is a medieval Danish administrative district roughly like the English county.

199. *Cod. Esrom.*, p. 229, nr. 217. DD I, 3, 103.

200. *Ibid.*: ... *pios et precipue seculi contemptores moliuntur quasi de terra eradicare, famam eorum sinistris oblocucionibus fuscando vel necessarias et iustas possessiunculas iniuste sibi usurpare calumpniando suasque clamando* ....

201. SRD IV, 471: *Unde compassus indigentie dictae domus, specialiter de lignorum inopia, quibus necessario opus habebat pro consummendis aedificiis.*

202. M. Mackeprang in *Danmarks Kirker* (ed. P. Nørlund and V. Hermansen), *Sorø Amt* 1 (1936), p. 18. When completed, Sorø was 67.5 metres long. Other measurements: Århus cathedral, 93m., Roskilde cathedral 84, Chartres 135.

203. SM II, 263–4.

204. SRD IV, 471: ... *litigaverunt habitatores praedictae villae cum fratribus super eisdem terminis silvarum.*

CHAPTER III

1. *Cod. Esrom.*, 54, nr. 39. DD I, 3, 77. Note that Absalon calls Abbot Walbert *amicus noster*, a titulation I do not find in any other of Absalon's letters and which may indicate a personal relationship. The closer we get to Walbert, the more he seems to have been dynamic and decisive in Esrum's early history, perhaps partly because of cooperation with Absalon.

2. S. M. Szacherska, 'The Political role of the Danish monasteries in Pomerania', *Mediaeval Scandinavia* 10 (1977), pp. 134–37, reviews the various trips of Danish Cistercian monks and abbots to the papal court. I have to disagree with her assertion p. 142, n. 99, that Abbot Walbert applied for all four Esrum privileges personally 'which means that he was in Rome in 1178, 1184, 1189, and 1193'. Cistercian privileges could have been obtained by non-cistercian emissaries.

3. M. Tangl, *Die Päpstlichen Kanzlei Ordnungen v. 1200-1500* (Innsbruck, 1894), pp. 229–31.

4. *Ibid.*, p. 230, nr. 12 and 13.

5. SM II, 216: *domus episcopi*. For Løgum, Bishop Omer had a chapel built for himself near the abbey. His successor Bishop Gunner of Ribe was given property by the monks to build a residence for himself at Løgum. SRD VIII, 242 (3 February 1238).

6. DD I, 3, 139. The letter was sent by an abbot W. of Citeaux. There were Abbots William at Citeaux between 1186–89 and 1190–94.

7. *Ibid.*: *Rogantes humiliter et attente, quatinus fratres nostros qui apud vos sunt contra tam evidens mandatum summi pontificis vexari nullatenus permittatis* ...

8. Giles Constable, *Monastic Tithes: From their Origins to the Twelfth Century* (Cambridge Studies in Medieval Life and Thought X, 1964), pp. 270–306, 'The Crisis of Monastic Freedom from Tithes'. Also Louis J. Lekai, *The Cistercians: Ideals and Reality* (Kent State, Ohio: 1977), pp. 65–68.

9. See Hal Koch, 'De ældste danske Klostres Stilling i Kirke og Samfund indtil 1221', HT 10, III (1936), pp. 555–56, reprinted in *Danmarks Kirke i den begyndende Højmiddelalder* (Det Historiske Institut ved Københavns Universitet, 1972).

10. SM II, 184–85. DD I, 2, 173.

11. SM II, 185–86. DD I, 3, 122.

12. P. Jaffé, *Regesta Pontificum Romanorum* II (1888), nr. 15687, 15762, 15764, 15765, 15825, 15959, 15961, 16067, 16215, 16345. This bull, *Quia plerumque veritatis*, was used in the years 1186–88.

13. For Absalon and Sorø, see Poul Nørlund, 'Klostret og dets Gods', *Sorøbogen I* (Cpn., 1923), pp. 69–70. It could be argued that Absalon as a person is not behind these charters issued in his name to monasteries, that they are merely business declarations indicating nothing about his programs or policies. This formalistic approach has relevance for charters issued after 1200, but in Absalon's time, it is hard to imagine documents originating from his circle as nothing more than technical statements. I have been gratified by Aksel E. Christensen's attempt, on the basis of all available sources, whether narrative or documentary, to characterize Absalon's personality: *Danmarks historie I* (Cpn., 1977), 368–69.

14. DD I, 3, 51, p. 74.

15. Nanna Damsholt, 'Abbed Vilhelm af Æbelholts brevsamling', HT 78 (1978), 1–22 (English summary, p. 22).

16. SRD VI, 2–3. DD I, 3(2), p. 429: ... *non doctis sed proficere dictando volentibus haec carmina destinare decrevimus, ut si quid in eis, quod eorum sensum et intellectum exerceat, occurrerit, nobiscum gratiae divinae gratias agant, memorieque commendant.*

17. DD I, 3(2), p. 430: ... *ex eorum nominibus maior auctoritas famuletur.*

18. *The Love of Learning and the Desire for God* (New York, 1961), pp. 181–82. A new edition was published by Fordham University Press in 1974.

19. In Bk. II, ep. 14 (DD I, 3 (2), p. 493), Bishop Absalon of Roskilde supposedly ordered the parishioners of Lyngby and Helsinge to help Æbelholt in transporting stones to the new abbey church. In Bk. II, ep. 13, Bishop Peder of Roskilde (1192–1214) handed over church income from the diocese to Æbelholt (DD I, 3(2), p. 492). In fact Peder gave this income to the church at Roskilde (DD I, 4, 61).

20. In using the letter collection in such a manner, I am taking a step which some Danish historians would not allow. But Nanna Damsholt's work has shown that Abbot William's collection belongs to the European genre of letter writing. If we can use collections containing the letters of men like Peter the Venerable for determining their attitudes to French monasticism, why should it be forbidden to utilize William in looking at Danish monasticism?
I agree with Tore Nyberg's statement in 'Klostren i abbot Wilhelms brev', KS 1971, p. 56, that the letters should not be used as an 'antiquated treasure chest, from which one takes forth some anecdotal piece of information about one monastery or another'. What I seek in the collection is not a string of anecdotes, but a *pattern of statements* revealing the author's attitude towards the Cistercians.

21. Bk. I, ep. 36. SRD VI, 31. DD I 3(2), pp. 482–83.

22. Bk. I, ep. 37. SRD VI, 31–32. DD I, 3(2), pp. 483–84.

23. Bk. I, ep. 38. SRD VI, 32–33. DD I, 3(2), pp. 484–85. The arrangement of these letters indicates that the editor, perhaps William himself, intended to deal with the various ways of ex-

pressing friendship in letters. The first letter (ep. 36) provides a general declaration of affection. The second (37) couples the declaration of love with a desire to lay aside differences. The third (38) expresses love as part of a concrete attempt to right wrongs and clear up accusations. See Nanna Damsholt, (note 15), pp. 14–17, for a more detailed treatment of the letters dealing with friendship.

24. William's style is masterful. He leaves out the abbot of Esrum as an object of personal attack and yet still manages to involve all the monks: *Dicebatur, Pater amande, quod tamen longe sita sanctitatis vestre honore, quod nos more leonum in insidiis, ut religionis vestrae cohaerere volentes a vobis avertere niteremur et cupiditate rerum suarum nostro eos consortio iungeremus.* SRD VI, 32–33. DD I 3(2), p. 485.

25. For more on the problem of recruitment of boys to Cistercian houses, see J. H. Lynch, 'Cistercians and underage novices', *Citeaux: Commentarii Cistercienses* 24 (1973), 283–97.

26. Again William shows an ability to dramatize. He does not just repeat the slander. He makes it into something enormous: *Dicebatur enim nobis, ut vere percepimus, quod in tantam fueramus malitiam devoluti, quod nostrum esset officium vos appellare hominum devoratores.*

27. For more on Æbelholt, see Vilh. Møller-Christensen, *Bogen om Æbelholt Kloster* (Cpn., 1958), esp. pp. 94–96.

28. Bk. II, ep. 27. SRD VI, 46. DD I, 3(2), pp. 511–13. The letter is addressed to Abbot W. of Esrum.

29. *Atlas over danske klostre* (Cpn., 1968), p. 73.

30. SRD VI, 139. DD I, 3, 97. The editors of the *Diplomatarium Danicum* discovered that the documents are William's own draft and not the composition of Abbot Walbert of Esrum. I should especially like to thank Herluf Nielsen, one of the editors of this volume, for making this result and others available to me prior to publication.

31. 'Søborg', *Fra Nationalmuseets Arbejdsmark* (1930), pp. 16–17.

32. Bk. II, ep. 35. SRD VI, 53–54. DD I, 3(2), pp. 526–27.

33. Bk. II, ep. 70. SRD VI, 72. DD I, 3(2), pp. 562–63.

34. A glance at any of the early letters in Anselm's collection (*Anselmi Opera Omnia*, ed. F. S. Schmitt) would make it seem as if he only had spiritual dealings with his correspondents.

35. Bk. II, ep. 72. SRD VI, 73. DD I, 3(2), pp. 563–64.

36. Bk. II, ep. 45. SRD VI, 59. DD I, 3(2), pp. 536–38.

37. Canivez 1205, nr. 10, a perfect example of the male Cistercian fear of contact with women, even eminently royal and respectable ones.

38. The biography of William is printed in *Vitae Sanctorum Danorum*, ed. M. Cl. Gertz (Cpn., 1908), pp. 287–386. William was canonized in 1224. See also Tue Gad, *Legenden i dansk middelalder* (Cpn., 1961), pp. 173–77.

39. See my 'Love, friendship and sex in the eleventh century: The experience of Anselm', *Studia Theologica* 28 (Oslo, 1974), pp. 111–152, for a possible psychological and cultural explanation for Anselm's insistence on the unimportance of frequent contacts among friends.

40. As in a letter to the Slangerup nuns (Bk. I, ep. 28. SRD VI, 26. DD I, 3(2), p. 471): *Sincerus videlicet dilectionis affectus qui inter amicos semel exortus nullo tempore consenescit,*

sed verius cum quid defuerit, mutuis foretur alloquiis et scriptis recentioribus validius incalescit.
Or to the Esrum abbot (Bk. I, ep. 37. SRD VI, 31. DD I, 3(2), p. 483: *Solet enim inter amicos
esse in amore levamen et in dolore remedium, familiare colloquium.* For the problem of sincerity
versus literary convention in such statements, Leclercq, (note 18), pp. 184–85.

41. R. W. Southern, *Medieval Humanism and Other Studies* (Oxford, 1970), 'Peter of Blois:
A Twelfth Century Humanist?', pp. 105–32.

42. Damsholt, (note 15), p. 13.

43. Gina Smith, 'De danske nonneklostre indtil ca. 1250', KS (1973), pp. 1–45. We have no
idea when Slangerup and Roskilde monasteries for women officially were associated with the
Cistercian Order. It is however likely that this link was established by about 1200, at the same
time as women's houses elsewhere finally received official recognition of their cistercian status.

44. DD I, 2, 163.

45. Gina Smith, (note 43), p. 25: 'The White family was not obliged by economic need to put
its women into convents. A combination of religious and sociological relationships probably was
the most important motivation.'

46. The Roskilde monastery of nuns is first mentioned in the privilege of Lucius III to Sorø
from 25 January 1181 (DD I, 3, 100). For the Order's changing attitude towards women, see
Louis Lekai, (note 8), pp. 347–52.

47. Gina Smith, (note 43), p. 7.

48. Book I, ep. 27. SRD VI, 25–27. DD I, 3(2), pp. 469–70.

49. See Tore Nyberg, *Birgittinische Klostergründungen des Mittelalters* (Bibliotheca Historica
Lundensis XV; Leiden, 1965), pp. 18–19.

50. Bk. I, ep. 28. SRD VI, 26. DD I, 3(2), p. 471.

51. Bk. I, ep. 29. SRD VI, 26–27. DD I, 3(2), pp. 472–73.

52. *Ibid.: Quia igitur et vos filiae regis estis et sponsae, sit ab intus gloria vestra, non ab exterioribus rebus.*

53. Bk. I, ep. 26. SRD VI, 23–25. DD I, 3(2), pp. 466–69. Gina Smith, (note 43), pp. 38–39.

54. DD I, 3(2), p. 468: *Non credimus, quot vobis sit necessarium, vestram sanctitatem atque
propositum commonere, nec sit vobis familiare in mensis vestris ebrietatis habere diffugium, licet
consuetudini terrae sit, illud vitium nobis vero sit horrendum . . . .*

55. See note 30. For a full treatment of this dispute and the drafts of charters involved, see my
'Property and Politics at Esrum Abbey', *Mediaeval Scandinavia* 6 (1973), p. 145.

56. SM II, 146–51. Gina Smith, (note 43) says the Ryd Chronicle is incorrect in calling St
Michael's monastery Cluniac and claims that the monks must have been Benedictine (pp. 17–18).
The problem is, as she points out (p. 4) that Cluny frowned on double monasteries, as St
Michael's was.

57. Vilh. Lorenzen, *De danske cistercienserklostres Bygningshistorie* (1941), p. 100. Lorenzen
is negligent in checking written sources, but here he has done a complete piece of work. The Ryd
Chronicle from 1289 says (SM II, 150) that in June the *conventus* came to Guldholm. This agrees
with the Ryd and Colbaz Annals (AD, p. 43). The mistake is the assertion that in the same year
on Ascension Day, Bishop Valdemar consecrated the cemetery and cloister. The date given for
the Ascension is incorrect for 1192 and has to be moved back to 1191.

58. DD I, 3, 216, dated 31 March 1196: ... *commutacionem ordinis nigrorum monachorum ecclesie sancti Michaelis de Sleswyk in ordinem alborum a domino apostolico ob insolencias et enormitates intollerabiles nigrorum ibidem nimis dissolute vite semitas impudenter ambulancium factum approbemus.*

59. Christian Godt, 'Bischof Waldemar von Schleswig und die Cistercienser von Guldholm', ZGSHLG (1891), 138–96. This limited view of the founding of a Danish monastery is partly due to the Slesvig dispute in the nineteenth century and resulting violent nationalistic feeling. Godt's article on Guldholm is an intellectual successor to G. V. Buchwald's article on Øm Abbey. As shown in my book on Øm, Buchwald cannot be trusted: 'Die Gründungsgeschichte von Øm und die Dänischen Cistercienser', ZGSHLG 8 (1878), 1–121.

60. SM II, 150.

61. Hans Olrik, 'Biskop Valdemar og den danske Krone', *Aarbøger for Nordisk Old-kyndighed og Historie* (1892), 342–84, said in response to Godt's article that Bishop Valdemar's preparations for founding Guldholm belonged to the late 1180's or 1190 at the latest, before the dispute between the bishop and the king broke out (p. 363). Olrik's conclusion that political mo-tives did not in any way influence Bishop Valdemar's foundation plans is too categorical, but is a necessary antidote to Godt's purely political interpretation.

62. SM II, 150–151.

63. Bk. II, ep. 11. SRD VI, 35. DD I, 3(2), pp. 489–90. For the question of patronage, see Hal Koch, (note 9), pp. 571–72.

64. Bk. II, ep. 12. SRD VI, 36. DD I, 3(2), pp. 491.

65. Bk. II, ep. 46. SRD VI, 60–61. DD I, 3(2), pp. 538–39. Also ep. 48: DD I, 3(2), pp. 540–41.

66. DD I, 3(2), p. 538: *Nigri consurgunt in griseos, monachi in monachos, fustibus, ut dicitur, et gladiis praeparatis ad bellum, ut iam dies tribulationis imminere credantur.*
The colours given refer to the monks' habits. The Benedictines wore black, while the Cistercians used grey in daily use and white for participation in the office. Thus the contrast is cleverly used by Abbot William to underline the fact implied in the next phrase, *monachi in monachos*: both types are still monks.

67. DD I, 3(2), pp. 540–41.

68. *Ibid.: Ecce ipsi veniunt ad praesentiam vestram tanquam viri, qui fecerint judicium et justitiam iaculis impietati armati, quibus arcem pietatis impugnent, sed non expugnent, quia sapientia semper vincet malitiam.*

69. DD I, 4, 158 (19 August 1209). Bishop Niels of Slesvig exchanged land with the Cistercians in Guldholm so that the bishop got the abbey's goods in return for Ryd as the new location for the monks. The Ryd Annals give 1210 as the date when '*Conventus venit de Aurea Insula in Rus Regium*'. But one of the Danish versions of the Ryd Annals says the monks 'read their first rule' at Ryd on the eve of the Feast of Saint Thomas the Apostle, which would place their arrival at 20 December 1209. Cf. M. Lorenzen, *Gammeldanske Krøniker* (Cpn., 1887–1913), p. 115.

70. C. C. Lorenzen, 'Nogle Bemærkninger om Guldholm Kloster', *Annaler for Nordisk Old-kyndighed og Historie* (1859), pp. 319–26. This little article can be looked upon as a landmark in work on Scandinavian monasteries, for Lorenzen used both written sources for Guldholm and his own personal investigation of the site in order to reach his conclusion.

71. M. Lorenzen, (note 69), pp. 115, 181.

72. Johannes Stüdtje, 'Gedanken über den Wirkungsraum des Ryeklosters', *Jahrbuch des*

Angler Heimatvereins 28 (1964), pp. 90–110, esp. pp. 97–98. See also Hans Joachim Kuhlmann, 'Das Rudekloster und seine Vorgänger St. Michaelis-Schleswig und Guldholm', *Jahrbuch des Angler Heimatvereins* 19 (1955), pp. 81–87.

73. For Sorø, my article in KS 1974, p. 28. For Øm's canals, see H. N. Garner's guide to the abbey, *Øm Kloster Museum* (1973).

74. DD I, 3, 163. Also printed in SRD VIII, 193–94.

75. 1173 is given as the foundation for Løgum in both the Ryd and the Colbaz Annals and has been generally accepted. See, for example, Olga Bartholdy's beautifully written and illustrated *Munkeliv i Løgumkloster* (1973), p. 44. But our earliest (and only local) source for Løgum, Bishop Omer's letter, says that Bishop Radulf made the change of place and of order:

> *Cuius loci et ordinis commutatio et pretaxatarum possessionum prelibata collatio, a prefato episcopo rationabiliter facta et communita, et sanctione apostolica et sui privilegii auctoritate solidissima prefato claustro do Loco Dei fuit in perpetuum confirmata.*

The preceding sentence to the one quoted mentioned the monastery at Seem. Now Omer wrote about an exchange of location as well as of monastic order and mentioned Løgum in the same sentence. Clearly he meant that Radulf had moved the Seem monks to Løgum. In the next sentence he says only that Radulf's successor Stefan approved what had been done: *hoc approbavit factum.* The Latin text is clear. Thus according to Bishop Omer in the 1190s, the move to Løgum was made before the death of Bishop Radulf, which was in 1171.

76. DD I, 3, 163 (pp. 262–63): ... *monachos de Loco Dei cordi nostro conglutinavimus et licet pre angustia facultatum minus, tamen ut eis benefaceremus, operam dedimus, cupientes eorum orationibus a deo recuperare impensam, ut cum forte post villicationem nostra fodere non valeamus et mendicare erubescamus, in eterna tabernacula recipiamur.*

77. *Ibid.: Huius spei gratia religiosos omnes intima cordis devotione veneramur, prelibatos tamen quasi magis domesticos et proprios tot affectu specialius amplectimur.*

78. Note that the Cistercians' right to collect tithes in certain parishes is completely different from their exemption from paying tithes on land they owned. From the very earliest days, bishops like Absalon and Eskil gave Cistercian abbeys the right to collect all or part of the tithes given to certain parish churches (DD I, 2, 147. DAM I, 250). This practice was in conflict with the original Cistercian prohibition but quickly became an important source of income for Cistercian houses in Denmark as well as abroad.

79. AD, p. 93 for 1192 and 1204.

80. DD I, 3, 163, p. 263.

81. *The Cistercians*, (note 8), p. 68. See also Friedrich Pfurtscheller, *Die Priviligierung des Zisterzienserordens im Rahmen des allgemeinen Schutz- und Exemptionsgeschichte* (Berne, 1972).

82. SRD IV, 534 for Sorø.

83. DD I, 4, 48. SRD VIII, 15–16.

84. DD I, 4, 57. SRD VIII, 196.

85. See Niels Skyum-Nielsen's commentary in the *Diplomatarium*. I am indebted to him for his careful analyses of chancellery style and for his datings of documents.

86. DD I, 4, 57, p. 123: ... *ordinem Cisterciensem pre omni religioni qui sub coelo est amandum et honorandum elegisse.*

87. The same attitude is shown in the *Ex. Mag.* from the same period. Both in Denmark and in Germany, Cistercians felt obliged to assert the primacy of their order, a sure sign that its position was being challenged.

88. J. B. Mahn, *L'Ordre Cistercien et Son Gouvernement* (Bibliothèque des Ecoles françaises d' Athenes et de Rome 161: Paris, 1945), pp. 48–49. David Knowles, *The Monastic Order in England 940–1216* (Cambridge, 1966), pp. 348–66.

89. Robert Fossier, 'Les Granges de Clairvaux et la Règle Cistercienne', *Citeaux in de Nederlanden* (Westmalle, 1955), 6, pp. 259–266, a short but very informative article.

90. As Canivez 1182, nr. 9 and 1188, nr. 109. See R. Taylor-Vaisey, 'The First Century of Cistercian Legislation. Some Preliminary Investigation', *Citeaux: Commentarii Cistercienses* 17 (1976), pp. 219–25.

91. SM II, 176–77.

92. SRD IV, 482.

93. DD I, 2, 126. Bo of Tjæreby.

94. James S. Donnelly, *The Decline of the Medieval Cistercian Laybrotherhood* (New York, 1949), pp. 52–62.

95. The suspicion of secular clergy towards monks is reflected in Geoffrey of Monmouth's *History of the Kings of Britain*, where he describes the British king Constans as being unable to cope with the sly Saxon usurper Vortigern: 'It was his own character which made him act in this way, plus the fact that what he had learned in the cloister had nothing to do with how to rule the kingdom.' (Penguin Classics, trans. Lewis Thorpe, 1968, p. 152). The Danish historian Niels Lukman has dealt with Saxo's knowledge of Geoffrey (HT X, 6, 1944, 593–607). Saxo and Geoffrey share the same world view: they are secular clerks seeking a reputation for their literary prowess and admiring military virtues, which they delighted in describing. The antithesis of this ideal is the monk, who fights by praying and has no experience in practical life.

96. Since writing these lines, I have been gratified to discover that Kurt Johannesson in his exciting reevaluation of Saxo (*Saxo Grammaticus: Kompositon och Världsbild i Gesta Danorum*, Stockholm, 1978) also deals with this enigmatic historian's apparent hostility towards Danish monastic activity. Johannesson speaks of a possible 'rivalry at the court of Absalon and King Knud between monks and clerks' and adds '. . . Saxo can have experienced the monastic world as one foreign to him and as an insult to his own intellectual and ecclesiastical ideal' (p. 338).

97. Torben Skov, 'Tvis kloster - en foreløbig orientering om prøvegravningen i 1978', *Holstebro Museum Årsskrift 1978* (Holstebro, 1979). I should like to thank Torben Skov for his kindness in acquainting me with the results of the excavations.

CHAPTER IV

1. DD I, 4, 48. See the commentary. The privilege by Valdemar I (dated to 1202–1204) says clearly that the monks can hold the land freely, also during the period when it is occupied by peasants. The privilege thus hints at a Cistercian intention of consolidating the land into a large holding after the peasants had been removed.

2. Niels Grevsun sold Esrum his properties in Husby and Skærød (1211–14) for twenty marks of gold (DD I, 5, 7). Actually only nine marks were paid to him in horses and money. In 1199 Jens Sunesen, brother of Bishop Peder Sunesen of Roskilde and Archbishop Anders Sunesen of Lund, gave property in Alsted to Sorø in return for 200 marks (SRD IV, 478).

3. DD I, 5, 79 (1216). Pope Innocent III ordered Archbishop Sunesen to see to it that the Ryd monks supported those who cared for their parish churches near Slesvig.

4. SRD IV, 517-18 and 490-91.

5. SM II, 193. Thorkil is characterized as *'in secularibus rebus multum eruditus'*. Significantly he is the first abbot said to have been brought up from youth in the monastery. His predecessor, Niels (1197-99) is criticized for his 'excessive simplicity'.

6. As in Bishop Omer of Børglum's 1219 transfer, with King Valdemar II's approval, of the churches in Nørresundby and Hals to Abbot Brendan of Vitskøl. Omer allowed the Vitskøl monks to install or remove monks or secular priests to care for souls in these parishes without any intervention on his part. (DD I, 5, 157.).

7. Canivez 1258, nr. 52.

8. DD II, 1, 231 (26 July 1257).

9. SRD VIII, 215 (31 March 1246).

10. SM II, 198-201.

11. We lack a full treatment of the development of episcopal power in the Danish church. Troels Dahlerup's *Det danske sysselprovsti i middelalderen* (Cpn., 1961) gives much information. For England, see Kathleen Edwards, *The English Secular Cathedrals in the Middle Ages* (Manchester 1949), especially ch. II, 'The Bishop in his Cathedral Church', pp. 97-135. Obviously the development of canon law (as the publication of *Liber Extra* in 1234) contributed to the crystallization of issues that in an earlier period had not been so clear, such as questions concerning the incorporation of churches under Cistercian abbeys, procurations paid by these houses to bishops, and the obligations of hospitality.

12. We can see a similar development in Norway. See Arne Odd Johnsen, *De norske cistercienserklostre 1146-1264 sett i europeisk sammenheng* (Det Norske Videnskaps Akademi, II. Hist. Filos. Klasse Avhandlinger Ny Serie No. 15: Oslo, 1977), 48-51.

13. DD I, 5, 92: September to December 1216. A medieval copy of the letter can be found in the Bodleian Library, MS Rawlinson c. 533, f. 59r.

14. *Ibid.*: ... *ut videretur non quasi de manibus hominum, sed demonum evasisse.*

15. For an evocation of thirteenth-century Rome, see Robert Brentano's excellent *Rome before Avignon* (London, 1974).

16. DD I, 5, 92: ... *consuluimus si licet esset duri animi vix consilium admittentis ut pro innovandis litteris suis que alios non haberent effectum, ad sedem apostolicam laboraret.*

17. Canivez 1215, nr. 19; 1216, nr. 14. The reason for the Øm abbot's failure to appear may well have been Thorkil's death in 1216.

18. In 1250, nr. 54, the abbots of Varnhem and Ryd were ordered to be punished for non-attendance. In 1251, nr. 65, Tvis was to be disciplined for not coming.

19. Løgum: DD I, 4, 114 (21 January 1206).
Sorø: *Bullarium Danicum* (BD), ed. Alfred Krarup, nr. 11, p. 11 (23 November 1198). Esrum: *Cod. Esrom.*, p. 22, nr. 7. This is only a summary of what must have been a privilege from Innocent III.

20. DD I, 5, 105 (30 January 1217).

21. SM II, 175 = DD I, 5, 110 (31 January 1217).

22. DD I, 5, 101–114, lasting from 25 January to 11 February.

23. For Århus, DD I, 5, 107 (31 January). Same day for Sorø: DD I, 5, 109.

24. Sorø BD 322 (19 February); 324 (29 February); 326 (1 March); 327 (2 March); 328 (5 March); 329 (6 March).
   Esrum: *Cod. Esrom.* 36 (24 and 28 March); 32 (26 March); 27 (30 March).
   Århus: SRD VI, 389.

25. See Friedrich Pfurtscheller, *Die Priviligierung des Zisterzienserordens* (Bern, 1972), esp. pp. 95–129: 'Freiheiten von der Jurisdiktion des Bischofs', as p. 128: 'Innocent III stellt nämlich fest, der Exemte sei *nicht* zum Obedienzeid verplichtet'.

26. BD nr. 214 (22 February 1228).

27. *Cod. Esrom.* 17, nr. 6.

28. *Cod. Esrom.* 35, nr. 23 = DD I, 5, 219 (27 October).

29. DD I, 5, 220 (23 October 1223).

30. Sorø: BD nr. 260, 261, 262, 266.
   Esrum: *Cod. Esrom.* 24, nr. 8 (27 October 1234).
   Løgum: SRD VIII, 190–91 (31 October 1234).

31. See the *Dictionnaire d'Histoire et de Géographie Ecclésiastique* XII, col. 936–37.

32. '*Quia refrigescente caritate*' (23 January 1234), A. Potthast, *Regesta Pontificum Romanorum* I, nr. 9376. Contained in the Sorø Book BD, nr. 246. Other bulls of Gregory guaranteeing Cistercian rights are nr. 8101–8103, 9784, 9788.

33. BD nr. 244 (23 January 1234).

34. In 1233 Esbern Snerling gave Sorø Ørslev and Bringstrup. This transfer looks generous, but the story is more complex. As a grandson of Esbern Snare, he was trying to rectify the long overdue legacy (SRD IV, 481). But on his death his mother Margareta withheld everything from the monks and appealed the matter to Bishop Niels Stigsen of Roskilde. The case was taken to Gregory IX, who in 1237 ordered Archbishop Uffe of Lund to force the execution of the original testament (*Dip. Svecanarum*, Liljegren, nr. 297, p. 289). Such frustrating cases seem typical for Sorø and Esrum in this period. They still acquire land, but only after great effort and expense.

35. J. B. Mahn, *L'Ordre Cistercien et son Gouvernement* (Paris, 1950), 167–68.

36. *Cod. Esrom.* 29, nr. 12 (19 September): excommunications; 26, nr. 9 (22 September): general reconfirmation of Cistercian privileges; 28, nr. 11 (22 Sept.): visitations; 30, nr. 13 (22 Sept.): confirmation of Cistercian immunities; 33, nr. 18 (24 Sept.): examination before ordination.

37. Thus the '*Non absque dolore*' bull issued to Sorø, Esrum, and Løgum in 1234 already had been sent to the German house of Eberbach in 1229 (Potthast, nr. 8354).

38. In the Canivez 1250, nr. 24 text, the Ryd and Varnhem abbots are said to have been obligated to come in that particular year: '... *qui hoc anno debuerunt ad capitulum generale non venerunt.*'

39. Canivez 1217, nr. 38: The abbots of Ås and Hovedø (on Oslo Fjord) were to investigate

the charge that the abbot of Lyse (near Bergen) wrongly appointed an abbot at Tuterø (on Trondheim Fjord). Canivez 1243, nr. 43: The Ås abbot was to bring the decision of the General Chapter to the Esrum and Varnhem abbots regarding the measures they were to take in dealing with a scandal at Hovedø.

40. Canivez 1232, nr. 35; 1233, nr. 53; 1235, nr. 44. All deal with the General Chapter's attempt to get Colbaz and Lukna (in Poland) to help starting a monastery at Paradyz. In 1237, nr. 39, the abbots of Colbaz and Eldena were ordered to inspect the proposed site of another abbey. In 1249, nr. 36, Dargun was ordered to settle a dispute between Klaarkamp in Friesland and Oliva on the Polish coast. In 1259, nr. 56, the incorporation of the abbey at Bukow on the Baltic was handed over to the abbots of Doberan and Neuencamp. It was to be a daughter of Dargun.

41. Canivez 1232, nr. 54.

42. Canivez 1237, nr. 57. The text is representative for the procedure normally to be followed:
Correctio et reformatio abbatiae Colbas de qua clamosa insinuatio venit ad Capitulum generale abbati de Herrisvad committitur qui assumpto secum aliquo abbati ordinis nostri ad locum personaliter accedat et tam in capite quam in membris, quae correctionis digna repererit, corrigat et reformet in plenaria Ordinis potestate.

43. Canivez 1229, nr. 44.

44. Canivez 1241, nr. 72.

45. Canivez 1241, nr. 26.

46. Canivez 1242, nr. 64.

47. Canivez 1241, nr. 49.

48. Canivez 1254, nr. 6.

49. *Ibid.: Cum dominus Cistercii commississet abbati de Sora visitationem filiae suae de Herrivado secundum formam ordinis in plenaria potestate.* Thus the Citeaux abbot had given the Sorø abbot full powers which he himself normally would have exercised on such a visitation. We can see here a tendency that will become more pronounced after 1300. The French Cistercians handed over the administration of their Scandinavian daughter houses to the abbots of Sorø and Esrum.

50. *Ibid.:* The language is very strong, even for the General Chapter:
Unde sit ab ordine constitutum ut si quis abbas alium iniuste deposuerit recipiat talionem, dicti abbates de Sora et de Asylo deponuntur in instanti. Abbas de Esrom hoc eis denuntiet; ista vero sententia, ut a simili praecipitatione in posterum caveatur, in omnibus domibus ordinis habeatur.

51. Canivez 1243, nr. 43. For this revolt and others like it, which were fairly common in the period 1230–1280, see James Donnelly, *The Decline of the Medieval Cistercian Laybrotherhood* (New York, 1949).

52. *The Monastic Order in England*, pp. 654–61, esp. p. 655: 'In the upland abbeys of England, and still more in those of Wales, or the Marches, all recruitment came from the locality, and few of the aspirants were men of any education. In the monastery itself they would receive no intellectual training, and the mental outlook would remain confined.'

53. Canivez 1211, nr. 41. Ås, Nydala and Tvis were charged with the visitation of Lyse in order to find out what wrongs were done by the Fountains visitors, who are said to have acted improperly.

54. Canivez 1213, nr. 11. The abbot of Alvastra was given Lyse as his daughter. In 1214, nr. 24, the Lyse abbot was accused by the General Chapter of refusing to receive the Hovedø abbot as visitor. This indicates that the Alvastra abbot had tried to hand over his duty to a Norwegian abbot and thus caused resentment and resistance at Lyse. For a full review of these events, see Arne Odd Johnsen, *De norske cistercienserklostre*, pp. 37–43.

55. Canivez 1243, nr. 65.

56. Canivez 1250, nr. 50.

57. Canivez 1252, nr. 34.

58. Canivez 1254, nr. 21: ... *quod cum dicta causa iam propter nimiam protractionem factam tediosa, infra sequens Capitulum eamdem causam studeant terminare.* The Esrum-Doberan dispute is an especially valuable illustration of the workings—and effectiveness—of the General Chapter, for we can follow a single dispute through all stages to its final resolution.

59. Canivez 1255, nr. 20.

60. Canivez 1257, nr. 11: *De misericordia concedit Capitulum generale ut monachus ille qui fuit abbas de Esrom et anno praeterito per generale Capitulum depositus extitit, de cetero sit eligibilis dummodo canonicum non obsistat.*

61. Canivez 1258, nr. 52.

62. *Meck. Ur.*, II, 116, nr. 812 = DD II, 1, 260.

63. *Meck. Ur.*, II, 135, nr. 841 = DD II, 1, 266: *Volumus et mandemus quatinus recipientes as abbate et conventu de Dobran xxxᵃ marchas argenti ad pondus Trecense tradatis eisdem omnes litteras instrumenta seu privilegia pertinencia ad abbaciam de Dargun seu ad ius paternitatis quod reclamabatis in eadem....*

64. *Meck. Ur.* II, 135, nr. 841 = DD II, 1, 284.

65. SM II, 230: *Anno domini mcclxiii, in vigilia beati barnabe apostoli, letus et hilacer cessit frater Boecius xvi abbas. In die eiusdem apostoli electus est dominus Thuro, quondam abbas Vite schole, postea Esromensis.*

66. Canivez 1217, nr. 52.

67. Full text in Hans Olrik's article 'Bidrag til Danmarks kirkehistorie hentede fra Clairvaux og Citeaux', KS 4 Række, 3 Bind, pp. 22–23. See also his 'Tilføjelser og Rettelser', pp. 421–25.

68. Olrik pointed out (p. 425) that the same products were still being imported by the citizens of Troyes from Denmark in 1484 and concluded that the Clairvaux monks, regardless of the proviso about private consumption, had actually started a regular trading connection with Denmark in the thirteenth century.

69. Olrik, p. 7.

70. The Ryd Annals (AD, p. 111) merely say that in 1245 'Niels bishop of Roskilde fled from Denmark'. They give the incorrect date of 1248 for his death at Clairvaux (p. 113). The Lund Annals give 1249 but state no reason for his presence there. Likewise the Sorø Annals (1130–1300) give no explanation.

71. See J. B. Mahn, ch. 3, 'L'Activité du Chapitre Général', 197–216 and ch. 5, 'La Querelle de 1263–65 entre l'abbé de Citeaux et les quatres premiers pères'.

72. For this development, see Thomas Riis, *Les Institutions politiques centrales du Danemark* (Odense, 1977), esp. the chapters 'L'exécutif' and 'Le pouvoir judiciare', 283-322.

73. DD I, 4, 55.

74. *Cod. Esrom.* 60, nr. 43.

75. SRD VIII, 15 = DD I, 5, 10.

76. *Diplomatarium Arna-Magnæanum* (DAM), ed. G. Thorkelin (1786), I, 117 (24 June 1234). Poul Nørlund has already pointed out that Sorø had earlier royal privileges, for in an 1197 papal bull copied in Bartholins Collectanea p. 582, the monastery's peasants are said to be free and immune 'from all royal service' (*ab omni regio servicio*).

77. DD I, 2, 107: ... *colonos ipsorum fratrum. de omni quod michi vel meis successoribus debebant absolui servicio.*

78. AD, p. 109: ... *pro iam dicta exsolvit libertate, ita quod non sit eiusdem ducis posteris liberum nec licitum hanc pactionem aliquo tempore infirmare iuxta intestationem privilegii principis memorati.*

79. *Dänische Bibliotec* VI, 156. According to *Jyske Lov* III 9, in which the Cistercians are especially named, the monks could not buy land after the 1215 General Council without having to pay military tax (*ledingsskat*) on it. Vitskøl is thus getting a very important exemption here, something that Esrum seems to lack—and possibly an explanation for the latter's and Sorø's slowdown in new acquisitions after 1215.

80. For the nature of such services (*leding, stud, inne,* etc.), see Poul Johs. Jørgensen, *Dansk Retshistorie* (Cpn., 1947), 407-409.

81. Probably the most complete expression of the early attitude comes in Knud VI's elegant charter to Esrum of 1194 (*Cod. Esrom.*, 59, nr. 42): ... *ne aliquibus premissi religiosi de possessionibus suis molestentur iniuriis, sed emunitatis et pacis securi quiete divinis invigilent servitutibus...*

82. AD, p. 111.

83. *Cod. Esrom.* 61, nr. 44 (28 April 1249).

84. *Cod. Esrom.* 63, nr. 47 (24 July 1249).

85. *Cod. Esrom.* 62, nr. 45 (8 November 1250) = DD II, 1, 14.

86. There is unfortunately no detailed account in English of Danish medieval political history. The best introduction in a non-Scandinavian language is still Lucien Musset, *Les Peuples Scandinaves au Moyen Age* (Paris, 1951).

87. DD II, 1, 12.

88. DD II, 1, 12: *Audivimus querimoniam dilectorum fratrum nostrorum de Viteschola, quod a quibus [dam] exactoribus nostris et multis aliis, frustra impetantur et molestentur super libertatibus sibi a progenitoribus nostris collatis....*

89. DD II, 1, 13. Here Abel actually mentions his brother Erik Plowpenny.

90. SM II, 196-97.

91. SM II, 199.

92. AD, p. 113.

93. As Abel to Æbelholt and to Antvorskov (DD II, 1, 40: 6 June 1251 and DD II, 1, 53: 30 September 1251).

94. DD II, 1, 94 (8 March 1253).

95. Poul Joh. Jørgensen, 276–77, 408.

96. DD II, 1, 78 and 79 (25 September 1252).

97. DD II, 1, 73 (5 August 1252).

98. See Niels Skyum-Nielsen, 'Den danske konges kancelli i 1250'erne', *Festskrift til Astrid Friis* (Cpn., 1963), pp. 225ff. and 'Kanslere og skrivere i Danmark 1250–1282', *Middelalder Studier tilegnede Aksel E. Christensen* (Cpn., 1966), 141–84.

99. *Cod. Esrom.* 227, nr. 214 (25 May 1239).

100. In a privilege by Valdemar II dated to the beginning of his reign (DD I, 4, 59: 1202–1214), Vitskøl had ten holdings. By 1219 the monks had obtained part of Læsø (DD I, 5, 160). In 1252 (DD II, 1, 67), the monks had kept every single one of their old holdings and added at least fifteen new ones. So while Esrum's and Sorø's growth period was prior to 1215, it looks as if Vitskøl's came after.

101. DD I, 5, 81.

102. DD I, 5, 89.

103. DD I, 5, 90.

104. DD I, 5, 157.

105. DD I, 5, 161.

106. Poul Joh. Jørgensen, p. 40.

107. DD II, 2, 232 (29 May 1274) at Lyon.

108. DD I, 5, 197.

109. Gunner's text is 'in partem canonicorum cederent *iure perpetuo possidenda*' while the Vitskøl monks wrote 'canonicorum *usui* cederent'.

110. H. N. Garner, *Atlas over danske klostre,* 92–121. The first indication of the friars' coming is in a bull of Honorius III to Valdemar II asking him to support the Dominicans on their arrival (DD I, 5, 194: 6 May 1221). See also Johs. Lindbæk, *De danske Franciscanerklostre* (Cpn., 1914), 12–17.

111. Here, for lack of Danish sources, I must assume that English and German developments were repeated in Denmark. See David Knowles, *The Religious Orders in England* (Cambridge, 1962), 4–7 and 127–37.

112. One instance of open resistance between an established abbey (Benedictine) in a town and a new Franciscan house can be seen at Næstved. See Lindbæk (my note 110), pp. 33–34, and DD II, 2, 153 (2 June 1270) for an agreement between the two.

113. As in the attempt to start a monastery at Paradyz: Canivez 1232, nr. 35; 1233, nr. 53; 1235, nr. 44.

114. *Westfälisches Urkundebuch* VI, nr. 406, dated 1243-56. The abbot of Loccum informed the council and citizens of Minden that he had given those who were killed on the town's side in a vendetta all masses for the dead offered in the abbey. On his request a larger number of Cistercian abbots gave those killed a share in their houses' spiritual benefits. Among them was Sorø. Many thanks to Niels Skyum-Nielsen for allowing me to see the notes for the *Diplomatarium Danicum* at Det danske Sprogog Litterurselskab, where this entry is included.

115. SM II, 201.

116. *Danmarks Kirker* XXI Tønder Amt (1957), 1052-1954.

117. SRD VIII, 134-35 (23 March 1228); 221 (14 April 1237); 231 (11 September 1238).

118. *Cod. Esrom.*, 116, nr. 100 (17 August 1246): The charter was drawn up 'in the church of the nuns' at Slangerup, one of our few documentary indications of contact between Esrum monks and Slangerup nuns. Those present include master Peder Ranesen, chancellor of King Erik Plowpenny; Master Bo, provost of the church of Roskilde; master Adam, a canon of Roskilde; Tue Bondesen, canon of Copenhagen; Troels, prior, and Jens, subprior, of Æbelholt; master Tode, '*rector scolarium*' in Copenhagen; the priest Asser, procurator of the Slangerup nuns. King Erik, Peder his chancellor, and the Provost Bo of Roskilde affixed their seals. In this assembly of the leading churchmen of Zealand, we can see how the Esrum monks sought and obtained the support of the regional power structure in order to defend their rights and holdings.

119. *Cod. Esrom.* 17, nr. 6.

120. *Cod. Esrom.* 116: ... *ob reverenciam parentum memorum et parentum uxoris mee Malild felicis memorie, qui apud monasterium de Esrom in somno pacis dormiunt et requiescunt.*

121. *Cod. Esrom.* 124, nr. 109.

122. Erik Ulsig, *Danske Adelsgodser i Middelalderen* (Cpn., 1968), 55-58.

123. SRD IV, 535. Although the abbot list is late and defective, the information about the fire may be based on an earlier source.

124. SRD IV, 481-82, 501-502.

125. BD nr. 481 (7 October 1248).

126. J. O. Arhnung, *Roskilde Domkapitels Historie* I (Roskilde, 1937), 61-62.

127. SRD IV, 474.

128. SRD IV, 484; 475 = DD I, 5, 43 (28 March 1214—the issuing of the episcopal charter) and 27 September 1214 (the actual deeding at the high altar in Sorø abbey church).

129. DD II, 1, 231 (26 July 1257).

130. Canivez 1214, nr. 54; repeated 1215, nr. 63.

131. Lekai, p. 386.

132. Canivez 1234, nr. 1; 1235, nr. 2; 1236, nr. 3.

133. SRD IV, 484, 506 = DD II, 1, 142.

134. SRD IV, 481, as dated by Niels Skyum-Nielsen.

135. DD I, 5, 60.

136. DD I, 5, 63.

137. DD I, 5, 65: ... *nos tamen considerata maxima necessitate edificii cathedralis ecclesie que multis retro temporibus usque ad tempora duorum antecessorum nostrorum quasi neglecta fuerat.*

138. Ellen Jørgensen, 'Ribe Bisperkrønike', KS VI, 1 (1933), 23-33.

139. As the description of resistance by the canons to Bishop Elias in the Ribe Bispekrønike (p. 28): *Sed plures tandem eius austeritati contradicebant in tantum quod a regulari tramite deviarent.*

140. Omer (d. 1204) and Oluf (d. 1214) are both said to have been buried at Løgum (Bispekrønike, p. 31). Two other Ribe bishops buried at Løgum are Gunner (d. 1245) and Esger (d. 1273). Gunner is the bishop who helped the Franciscans get started at Ribe, and there is a tradition for his burial in their church (Andreas Nissen, *Danske Bisperækker*: Cpn., 1935, p. 70). But a Løgum inscription with the title *primus fundator* given him in the Necrology together with Bishops Radulf and Stefan indicates he was buried at Løgum (SRD IV, 576, 583). Gunner's support for both Løgum and the Ribe Franciscans points to the possibility in this relatively harmonious time for a diocesan bishop to encourage both traditional and reformed types of monasticism.

141. DD I, 5, 99 = SRD VIII, 215.

142. SRD VIII, 132.

143. *Ibid.:* ... *quod nos fratrum nostrorum de Loco Dei inopiae condolentes....*

144. *Ibid.:* ... *ut ipsi ibidem perpetuum instituant vicarium eidem expensam honestam assignantes, cetera vero ad dictorum fratrum commodum iure perpetuo devolvantur.*

145. When Bishop Jens Krag of Roskilde (DD II, 4, 258: 12 June 1297) gave Sorø the right of patronage to Lynge church in Alsted herred, he reserved the rights maintained by the bishop and the archdeacon of Roskilde cathedral. Arhnung (p. 62) concludes from this and similar provisions in other Roskilde documents that the archdeacon was thereby guaranteed procurations on visiting the church. This exception to the monks' rights does not exist in the Løgum transfer.

146. SRD VIII, 134 (23 March 1228).

147. *Ibid.: Nos igitur, quia omnes religiosos intima cordis devotione in Christo diligimus, prelibator tamen quas magis proprios et dilectos toto affectu specialius amplectimur, omnes has immunitates et collationes, sed et omnes generaliter possessiones quascumque.*

148. Esger however managed to avoid the sentence of excommunication and interdict unleashed by the cardinal legate Guido against many of his fellow bishops in the royal party. See Niels Skyum-Nielsen, *Kirkekampen i Danmark*, 226-28.

149. SM II, 198. Peder Elavsen died in 1246. His successor, Peder Ugotsen, was not elected until 1249 and seems to have begun immediately to harass the monks, also concerning the books (p. 200). As in so much else, the 1240s are a turning point for the Danish Cistercians.

150. SM II, 276.

151. DD II, 1, 57 (dated to some point between 1251 and 1267).

152. SRD VIII, 211 (14 April 1237).

153. *Cod. Esrom.* 124, nr. 109.

154. SRD VIII, 242 (3 February 1238).

155. *Ibid.: ... fundum unum iuxta aquam a Capella domini felicis memoriae, Omeri quondam Ripensis episcopi...*

156. SM II, 216. The passage is meant to show that the monks did not accept that the house belonged to the bishop, but the popular name given to it indicates that the bishop would stay here as a guest of the abbey:
At ille [Bishop Tyge of Århus] *truculentus extendit manum suam ad magnam domum, quae dicitur 'Domus episcopi', dicens: 'Nonne hec est domus nostra?' Et abbas: 'Monachi nostri dicunt eam esse domum suam et non vestram'.*

157. SRD IV, 535: *sacellum episcopi.*

158. SRD VIII, 231 (22 August 1245).

159. SRD VIII, 208, issued at Slesvig: *Nos etiam considerantes, quod nos et nostros sepius contingat gratia hospitalitatis ad idem claustrum divertere et ne propter hoc predicti fratres nimium graventur expensis predictam donationem,* si legitime facta fuerit, *approbamus.*

160. First mentioned in Valdemar II's 1202–14 confirmation of Løgum's holdings: SRD VIII, 196.

161. Bishop Niels of Slesvig had already renewed the privilege sometime between 1209 and 1234 (SRD VIII, 209 = DD I, 4, 171).

162. SRD VIII, 219 = DD II, 1, 56.

163. *Ibid.: ... maxime cum nos et nostros sepius contingat gratia hospitalitatis ad idem claustrum divertere.*

164. Skyum-Nielsen, *Kirkekampen*, p. 185.

165. SRD VIII, 198 = DD II, 1, 196. See the explanatory notes in *Danmarks Riges Breve* for this entry.

166. SRD VIII, 178 = DD II, 1, 224: *... si unquam ad portum nostrum in Obenroe cum navibus suis applicuerint sive ad alios quoscunque portus infra terminos regni nostri.*

167. For the respect Gunner engendered among the other bishops (as seen by Cistercian eyes), see his *Vita*, SM II, 274: *Quandocunque ad aliquod consilium regni dompnus archiepiscopus Uffe et ceteri suffraganei sui episcopi ac ipse convenerunt, ipse in maiori honore aliis, ac si pater esse omnium, ab omnibus habebatur.*

168. DD II, 1, 228 (16 July 1257).

169. Already in a 1250 charter (DD II, 1, 16), Abel admitted that the nuns' labourers had been misused by being made to pay royal exactions from which they legally were exempt.

170. DD II, 1, 229 (16 July 1257).

171. DD II, 1, 230 (20 July 1257).

172. *Ibid.: ... propter quod monasterium ipsum grave detrimentum sepe patitur et sancte contemplationis otium ibidem non modicum perturbatur.*

173. Some examples: SRD VI, 157 (23 October 1248 and 30 May 1249); SRD VI, 158 (11 November 1249).

174. Hoogeweg I, 463-73.

175. *Codex Pomeraniae* I, nr. 400.

176. Canivez 1232, 54; 1273, nr. 31.

CHAPTER V

1. For an account of events at Øm abbey, see my *Conflict and Continuity at Øm Abbey*. I shall not go into detail here but instead will try to look at the Øm disaster in terms of the situation of the Cistercian Order as a whole in Denmark.

2. Lekai, 340-45.

3. SM II, 241 = DD II, 2, 12 (before 21 May 1266).

4. SM II, 261-63.

5. Contained in AD 62-70, 73-125. Some Danish historians refuse to allow the use of the Ryd Annals as an expression of Cistercian perspectives. I disagree: it is inconceivable that an account dealing in such detail with Cistercian events and concentrating on Southern Jutland so clearly should have been composed at any place except the Southern Jutlandic Cistercian house of Ryd. Ellen Jørgensen, one of the leading Danish historians of this century, concluded that the author was a monk at Ryd Abbey who lived in the mid-thirteenth century. This opinion is followed in Herluf Nielsen's article in KLNM XIV 516-18. The Danish versions (and continuations) of the Annals are contained in M. Lorenzen, *Gammeldanske Krøniker* (Cpn., 1887-1913), 61-192.

6. *Danmarks Ældste Annalistik*'s author is extremely cautious about the problem of dating for the Ryd Annals: 'A penetrating investigation of the various Ryd versions' connections with each other and their relationship to other annals, especially after 1261, must be made before it is possible to decide with certainty the date of composition for the Ryd Annals'. (p. 104—my translation).

7. SM II, 146-151.

8. SM II, 147 and 150.

9. AD, ρ 111.

10. AD, 115-16: *Ericus filius eius regnavit, qui multa mala fecit ecclesias spoliando, lesis et iniuriam passis iusticiam nullam faciendo. Monasteria quique, quae patres eius per se et suos edificaverant, per equos et canes miserabiliter attenuavit.* The last charge rings true in the light of Erik's 1282 royal charter (*håndfæstning*) by which he promised monasteries that excessive demands for hospitality would not be made on them (DD II, 3, 45).

11. Niels Skyum-Nielsen, *Kirkekampen*, 147-48.

12. AD, p. 114. For a comparison of all the sources on Kristoffer's death, see Skyum-Nielsen, *Mordet på Kennedy og andre opgaver i historisk kilderkritik* (Cpn., 1973) 243-54.

13. Compare 1241 (AD, 110-111); 1247 (AD, 112-13); 1259 (AD, 114-15).

14. AD, 118-19.

15. SM II, 150: *Sed heu proh dolor! fefellit eum spes eius, et non est datum perficere opus propositum suum tam pium. Nam non longe post captivatus est et de regno expulsus.*

16. SM II, 147: . . . *ut sciant posteri nostri et posteri posterorum nec non et successores eorum.*

17. SM II, 150: *Propterea, Guldholm et filii tui, luge et deplora celerem et nimis immaturum casum patris tui piisimi, quod vivente omnium deliciarum tibi copia affluebat, quo subtracto tu paupercula remanes et inter alias sorores tuas tenuis et despicabilis delitescis.*

18. AD, p. 123: *Iacobus episcopus Sleswicensis privavit monachos Ruris regis decimis et nonnullos eorundem fecit verberari.*

19. DD I, 4, 165 (1209), preserved in a copy of a *vidisse* by Pope Alexander IV from 9 January 1255.

20. Ad, p. 123: *Conventus domus Ruris regis dispersus est.*

21. *Gammeldanske Krøniker*, p. 129: 'Monkene af Rythæ closter skildes af met stoor sorg oc drøwelse'. This is Danish Ryd Annals I, contained in Copenhagen Royal Library MS E don. variorum 3, 8°, from about 1400, in which the narration continues to 1314. See AD, p. 16.

22. AD, p. 125: *Obiit Iacobus tyrannus plus quam episcopus dicendus.*

23. *Gammeldanske Krøniker*, p. 130.

24. Another possibility is that the Danish Ryd Annals (I) were not composed at Ryd at all, but this is doubtful, again in view of the great interest shown here in the history of Ryd Abbey.

25. In 1920 Ellen Jørgensen pointed out that the Ryd Annals (to 1288) 'are actually a royal chronicle from King Dan to Erik Menved' (AD, p. 1). It should be noted, however, that this royal chronicle also reflects *monastic* concepts of royalty and political life.

26. AD, pp. 62 ff.

27. *Vetus Chronica Sialandie*, SM II, 1–72. For dating, p. 7, where the editor Gertz says that the consistent interest for the Cistercians continues down to 1251 and then stops. 'Everything until this year is in my opinion, when one disregards the various additamenta, undoubtedly the work of a single writer, but what is present after 1251 all the way to 1307 could have been added later by one or several annalists just as the various *additamenta*'.

28. SM II, 27–30; 47–52.

29. SM II, 41–47.

30. SM II, 35–37.

31. SM II, 265–78. See my *Conflict and Continuity.*

32. DD II, 3, 70. Also contained in *Pom. UB* II, 407, nr. 1272.

33. Canivez 1273, nr. 31.

34. Canivez 1282, nr. 31: *Super facto de Hylda, patri committitur auctoritate Capituli generalis, ut inquirat diligenter de litteris abbatis Ursicampi ibi raptim* . . . . Ourscamp is a daughter of Clairvaux founded 1129 in the diocese of Noyon in the north of France. See L. H. Cottineau, *Repertoire Topo-Bibliographique des Abbayes et Prieurés* II (Macon, 1937), col. 2160.

35. Canivez 1277, nr. 49 and 82. 1278, nr. 69.

36. Pertz, *Monumenta Germaniae Historica. Scriptores* (MGH SS) XIX, p. 716.

37. *Ibid.*: 1275. *Abbas de Machaplana ordinis Cisterciensis in civitate Tholeto captus, verberatus, cathenatus est a Minoribus fratribus. Quare nobis preceptum est a capitulo generali, ne aliquam familiaritatem habeamus usque ad satisfactionem condignam cum fratribus supradictis.*

38. AD, p. 113.

39. MGH SS XIX, 716: 1273 6. *Idus Marcii audite sunt campane se ipsas pulsantes et in Benedig tempore vespere marchiones terram Stitines et Piricensem graviter spoliaverunt et ecclesiam nostram multum condempnaverunt.* For more on Colbaz during this period, see Hoogeweg I, 233-55.

40. SM II, 196-97.

41. DD II, 4, 156 (24 January 1295).

42. As in the selling of feudal privileges to Eldena on this date: DD II, 4, 155.

43. DD II, 4, 210 (13 April 1296).

44. DD II, 6, 2 (9 February 1306). Two knights sell Bergen's Cistercian house for women property, and Abbot Jakob of Eldena is one of the witnesses.

45. Hoogeweg I, pp. 256-57 (Marienwalde 1294, Himmelstädt 1300). See also the chart, p. xxi: 3 Cistercian abbeys were founded in Pomerania before 1200; 4 between 1231 and 1252, and 5 from 1278 to 1304.

46. See the article of M.-A. Dimier on Doberan, *Dictionnarie d'Histoire et de Géographie Ecclésiastiques* XIV (1960), 532-34: 'Doberan devint comme le rempart de la foi chrétienne de toute la région, en même temps que le premier centre des sciences, des lettres, et des arts' (col. 532).

47. Again the Colbaz Annals, MGH SS, XIX, 716. Also Hoogeweg for Neuencamp (Vol. II, 1925, pp. 121-223) and for Hiddensee (II, 1-70).

48. DD II, 4, 210 = *Pom.* UB III, 270, nr. 1764.

49. DD II, 4, 221.

50. DD II, 4, 252 and 253 (7 and 8 April 1297): . . . *cum illustris princeps Ruyanorum dominus Wizlaus in insula Hyddensee fundari mandasset Cysterciensis ordinis abbaciam et eamdem monasterio Novi campi eiusdem ordinis subiecisset et monasterii eiusdem monachos in possessionem mitti iussisset nos hoc in nostri preiudicium fieri sencientes eo quod predicti insule medïtas et plenum ius atque iudicium ad nos pertineret ipsos monachos super huiusmodi statuimus convenire.*

51. DD II, 5, 25 = *Pom.* UB III, 365, nr. 1886.

52. *Ibid.: Tandem ut verum fateamur nostra propria consciencia nos monente eo facilius cum predictis abbate et fratribus ad concordiam tendebamus/ quo nominimus propter difficultatem. transitus brachii maris quod parochy nostre et ipsi insule interiacet quam maxima et quam plurima animarum pericula evenissee. nam constitit liquido multos parvulos sine gracia baptismatis/ et multos eciam adultos sine sancta communione et extrema unctione et confessione misere decessisse.*

53. For some of the problems created by Cistercian involvement in parish structures, see Lekai, pp. 68-69. Also Hans Erich Feine, *Kirchliche Rechtsgeschichte* I (Weimar, 1954), 361-62, and Troels Dahlerup, *Det danske sysselsprovsti*, 300-319.

54. DD II, 5, 203 (15 May 1302). Also nr. 204 and 208.

55. DD II, 5, 218 and DD II, 6, 23.

56. DD II, 5, 153 (4 June 1301). See Erik Arup *Danmarks Historie* IIA, pp. 219-20.

57. This feeling is reflected in the remark at Øm: . . . *littere nostre in curia Romana acquisite nichil nobis profuerunt* (SM II, 239).

58. SM II, 226 = DD II, 1, 374. These abbots also launched a rather unusual separate appeal to the college of cardinals (DD I, 1, 375 = SM II, 227).

59. See my *Conflict and Continuity*, pp. 78-82 for more background.

60. SM II, 228 = DD II, 1, 376. The names of the abbots are given as A. in Herrisvad, E (Esbern?) in Esrum, Niels in Tvis, Asgot in Vitskøl, M. in Holme, Jakob in Sorø, Jens in Løgum, and Mads in Ryd.

61. SM II, 224 = DD II, 1, 377.

62. Bruno Griesser, 'Unbekannte General Kapitelstatutten', *Cistercienser-Chronik* (dec. 1957), p. 53. I would like to thank Sv. E. Green-Pedersen for this reference.

63. SM II, 225 = DD II, 1, 373 (5-10 May 1263).

64. SM II, 230 = DD II, 1, 399.

65. SM II, 221 = DD II, 1, 379.

66. SM II, 232 = DD II, 1, 417.

67. SM II, 233 = DD II, 1, 425.

68. Niels Skyum-Nielsen, *Kirkekampen*, p. 313, n. 92.

69. DD II, 1, 429.

70. Sm II, 237. The abbot emphasized Margrethe's past generosity towards Clairvaux and begged her to extend the same treatment to Øm and the other daughters of Clairvaux in her own kingdom: *Quapropter regiam vestram magnificentiam imploramus humiliter et attente, quatinus intuitu dei ac vestre reverentia Clarevallis, que semper aput dominationem vestram locum vestri gratia optinuit singularem, dicte abbacie ceteris nostre generationis monasteriis in regno vestro fundatis in suis afflictionibus . . . .*
Margrethe's double standard in favouring Clairvaux but opposing Danish Cistercian abbeys shows how little the structure and wholeness of the Cistercian Order could influence a thirteenth century Danish ruler.

71. SM II, 239 = DD II, 1, 447.

72. DD II, 1, 382.

73. SRD VIII, 239 = DD II, 1, 404.

74. SRD VIII, 131 = DD II, 1, 420.

75. *Cod. Esrom.* 65 nr. 51 = DD II, 1, 466.

76. *Cod. Esrom.* 64 nr. 49 = DD II, 1, 488.

77. DD II, 2, 2. Copies were kept at both Løgum and Esrum and probably at other houses: SRD VIII, 220 and *Cod. Esrom.* 46, nr. 33. See *Kirkekampen*, p. 204.

78. SRD VIII, 200 = DD II, 2, 24.

79. SM II, 265.

80. SM II, 241 = DD II, 2, 21.

81. SM II, 241: ... *timendum profecto exinde nobis erit quod huius exemplo ceteris regni Dacie episcopis modo simili contra ceteras domus nostri ordinis debachandi materia generetur quod utique iam ex quorundam illorum verbis minatoriis nobis innotuit evidenter.*

82. DD II, 2, 39.

83. SRD VIII, 126 = DD II, 2, 26.

84. The one exception to this policy of caution is the willingness of the abbot of Løgum to hide Abbot Ture of Øm at Løgum in 1267 after it was no longer safe for him to be at Øm. Ture also stayed at Ryd and with Jakob Erlandsen at Slesvig during this period (SM II, 256).

85. SM II, 241: *In gaudio exultavimus, sperantes ab eo et per ipsum iusticiam de omnibus in-iuriis ab episcopo sive de aliis nobis illatis acquisituros.* The monks of Øm were being quite naive here, but the following letter from the Danish abbots to Guido shows they felt the same way.

86. SRD VIII, 125 = DD II, 2, 43 (2 November 1266).

87. SM II, 247 = DD II, 2, 46.

88. SM II, 252, = DD II, 2, 47.

89. SM II, 253, 256–61.

90. SM II, 254–55 = DD II, 2, 61. The close of the letter conveys challenge and threat in the most polite language possible:
Dignationem igitur vestram fusis lacrimis imploramus, quatinus amore et honore illius, qui captivitatem nostram sua duxit virtute captivam, dominum episcopum Arusiensem litteris vestris vel nunciis dignemini commonere, ut sepe dictum abbatem et conventum suum desistat pertur-bare. Quod si noluerit, egre non feratis dedignantes, quod non una cum dilecto coabbate nostro et conventu eiusdem causam coram iudice nostro ecclesiastico vel iudicibus ab eo subdelegatis prosequamur, donec super illatis iniuriis aliquod a predicto domino T episcopo iusticie receperimus complementum.

91. SM II, 256–61 = DD II, 2, 74, 81, 82, 85.

92. *Kirkekampen*, 220–222.

93. Peder Olsen, *Collectanea*, AD, pp. 208–209. *Kirkekampen*, p. 227: 'The Cistercians and the Franciscans obeyed the order and closed their churches'.

94. *Cod. Esrom.* 64, nr. 58 = DD II, 2, 100.

95. *Kirkekampen*, p. 258.

96. *Cod. Esrom.*, 66, nr. 52 = DD II, 2, 107; DD II, 2, 110.

97. SRD IV, 516 = DD II, 2, 134.

98. DD II, 2, 216 (before 29 November 1268).

99. Canivez 1268, nr. 37.

100. This is the one instance during this period that the abbey of Ås in Halland was involved in such a common appeal.

101. Sv. E. Green-Pedersen, 'Studier over de danske Cistercienserklostres forhold til ordenens internationale styrelse og til den danske kirke og det danske samfund indtil ca. 1340' (Unpublished thesis at the Institute for History in Copenhagen, 1969), pp. 67–68. Many thanks to Green-Pedersen for allowing me to use this and other aspects of his work.

102. SM II, 258. This was the third summons of Tyge. On the second summons, the abbot of Løgum, Jens, participated. This provides another indication that Løgum alone of the remaining Cistercian houses besides Ryd and Øm played a dangerous game of keeping on good terms with both its local bishop and Jakob Erlandsen.

103. Canivez 1269, nr. 70.

104. DD II, 2, 135 = DD II, 2, 136.

105. SRD VIII, 128 = DD II, 2, 142.

106. SRD VIII, 326 = DD II, 2, 147.

107. DD II, 2, 149.

108. DD II, 2, 154.

109. *Kirkekampen*, pp. 258–59.

110. Canivez 1270, nr. 33.

111. *Cod. Esrom.* 97, nr. 91. The relevance of this exchange to the Øm controversy and the church interdict has not previously been noted. Mills were extremely important to Cistercian abbeys as a source of incomes. See for example Hoogeweg, p. 239.

112. For mills in the context of the economic upswing in twelfth century Europe, see George Duby's excellent *The Early Growth of the European Economy* (London, 1974), pp. 187–88: '... mills remained among the most lucrative sources of seigneurial income'.

113. DD II, 2, 190. Copy in the Løgum Book, SRD VIII, 214.

114. SRD VIII, 237 = DD II, 2, 202.

115. SRD VIII, 126 = DD II, 2, 185, 186.

116. As SRD VIII, 125 = DD II, 2, 43 (2 November 1266). For the Brede controversy in full, Axel Bolvig, 'Stridighederne omkring Brede kirke 1250–1350', *Historisk Tidsskrift* 77 (1977), 85–95.

117. SRD VIII, 117, 121, 122 = DD II, 2, 193, 194, 195.

118. SRD VIII, 237: ... *cum progenitores vestri considerantes devota servitia et voluntarias administrationes, sibi tempore pacis et belli ab eodem monasterio impendi.*

119. SRD VIII, 98 = DD II, 2, 187: a peasant gave the monks property in compensation for a wrong he had done them.

120 *Cod. Esrom.* 88, nr. 53 = DD II, 2, 212.

121. Canivez 1272, nr. 48.

122. Canivez 1277, nr. 61.

123. Canivez 1281, nr. 63.

124. Green-Pedersen (my note 101), p. 85: 'The statutes contain a number of administrative and legislative decisions concerning the Danish Cistercian abbeys. It is most interesting, however, that we know from other sources of a number of matters ... that belonged to the General Chapter's jurisdiction but which are not known from the surviving statutes. The most immediate explanation for this is that these matters were not brought before the General Chapter. The influence of the General Chapter on Danish conditions therefore seems for the most part to have been limited to the matters on which the Danish Cistercians informed it.' (my translation)

125. *Kirkekampen*, pp. 278–79.

126. DD II, 3, 219: ... *literas concordiae inter venerabilem fratrem dominum Petrum Vibergensem episcopum et dictos monachos factae super impetitione iuris sui, quam contra suos monachos habuit.*

127. *Annales Sorani*, AD, p. 124. Ribe Annals, AD, p. 154.

128. Canivez 1291, nr. 8, an unprecedented decision for a Danish house, it mentions Herrisvad's 'intolerable poverty'. The decision points out the duty of abbeys to care for their near neighbours, *'Item cum ad omnes operari bonum, maxime autem ad domesticos teneamus'*.

129. Canivez 1293, nr. 14.

130. Lorenzen, *De danske Cistercienseres Bygningshistorie*, 36–39.

131. Canivez 1291, nr. 14. Another indication of the continuing involvement of Clairvaux visitors with Danish abbeys is the 1288 permission by King Erik Menved and his mother Agnes for the French monks to purchase and export hides and wax duty-free: DD II, 3, 283. The charter mentions frequent visitations by the Clairvaux monks: ... *et maxime ipsorum fratribus. qui gracia visitandi. ab abbate dicti loci* [Clairvaux] *ad filias suas. in regno nostro. vel Swecie constitutas. frequenter transmittuntur.*

132. Canivez 1292, nr. 7.

133. Canivez 1294, nr. 10.

134. Canivez 1293, nr. 31.

135. Canivez 1297, nr. 30.

136. Canivez 1297, nr. 36.

137. Benoit Chauvin, 'Les Décisions des Chapitres Géneraux de l'Ordre Cistercien Concernant l'Abbaye de Balerne aux XIIe et XIIIe Siècles', *Commentarii Cistercienses* (23) 1972, 160–170.

138. Chauvin, *Ibid.*, p. 169: 'Une seule solution s'imposera dés lors pour tenter de redresser, avec quelque succés d'ailleurs, cette situation deplorable: un contract de paréage, association politico-immobilière conclue en 1285 avec un puissant seigneur Jean de Chalon, ouvrant ainsi une nouvelle page de l'histoire de Balerne.'
Note that the Premonstratensian Order in Scandinavia was going through a similar decline in

international contacts. In 1289 it was decided at Prémontré that abbots from the North only had to come to its General Chapter once every four years (DD II, 3, 365). At the very same time as Cistercian visitors to Denmark and Sweden were being resisted, the Premonstratensians were having trouble with collections from Norwegian houses in 1290 (DD II, 3, 420).

139. J. B. Mahn, *L'Ordre Cistercien*, p. 238, sees the outcome of this dispute as leaving the Order's administration intact. But as Lekai points out, the emergence of a body of definitors at the General Chapter as a result of the controversy 'discouraged the attendance of those abbots who had no chance of becoming definitors' (p. 72).

140. Canivez 1291, nr. 8.

141. Canivez 1412, nr. 18; 1419, nr. 27; 1425, nr. 27; 1451, nr. 36. The Danish abbeys were already being taxed in the 1330s and 1340s. See H. Peter King, 'Cistercian Financial Organisation 1335–1342', *Journal of Ecclesiastical History* 24 (1973) 127–43, esp. p. 133.

142. For Margrethe's central role during the minority of Erik Glipping and even after, see Skyum-Nielsen, 'Kanslere og Skrivere i Danmark 1250–82', pp. 169–173.

143. SM II, 208.

144. DD II, 2, 174, 340, 382.

145. Thelma Jexlev, *Fra dansk senmiddelalder* (Odense, 1976), p. 24. Helge Paludan (together with Inge Skovgaard-Petersen and A. E. Christensen), *Danmarks historie* I (Cpn., 1977), 452–53.

146. DD II, 3, 228 = SRD IV, 508.

147. SRD IV, 508: *Senciens autem illic nimiam asperitatem et duriciam a sororibus, reliquit habitum et ordinem et ad seculum est reversa. Inter seculares igitur posita castam duxit vitam . . . .*

148. DD II, 4, 188 and DD II, 4, 204. In 1297 King Erik ordered the peasants and users of the properties of Agnes and Jutta not to pay the income of their holdings to any institution except the Roskilde convent of Saint Agnes. Sorø is clearly implied here (DD II, 4, 269).

149. SRD IV, 508 = DD II, 5, 117.

150. See *Conflict and Continuity*, 95–97.

151. DD II, 2, 121, 122, 123.

152. SRD IV, 505 = DD II, 2, 173. For an analysis of this will, see Tore Nyberg, 'Lists of monasteries in some thirteenth century wills', *Mediaeval Scandinavia* 5 (1972), 60–62.

153. Poul Nørlund, 'Klostret og dets Gods', p. 77. The monk Jonas was according to a now lost gravestone from c. 1300 supposed to have visited Jerusalem twice, Rome thrice, and St James in Spain once.

154. SRD IV, 483, 505 = DD II, 3, 265. The change in conditions could be due to the fact that Juliane had sons who now were grown and would not allow such a generous gift as before.

155. *Cod. Esrom.* 120, nr. 105 = DD II, 2, 229: . . . *claustro Esrom Cisterciensis ordinis Roskildensis diocesis quem locum pre ceteris affectuosius diligo . . . .*

156. As *Cod. Esrom.* 151, nr. 133 = DD II, 2, 387 (1279). For relationships between various branches of the Skjalm family descendants and Jon Lille, see the chart on p. 56 in Erik Ulsig,

Danske Adelsgodser i Middelalder. Full information on Jon Lille's family, pp. 55–61. Also *Cod. Esrom.* 122, nr. 107 = DD II, 3, 151 (1285): Jon Lille deeds Kollerød for the purchase of wax for altar lights and *Cod. Esrom.* 129 nr. 115 = DD II, 4, 27 (1299): another gift from Jon and his wife.

157. *Cod. Esrom.* 118, nr. 102 = DD II, 2, 258.

158. SRD IV, 512 = DD II, 2, 384. See Ulsig's chart and information on the Saltensee of Tystofte line, pp. 66–71. According to Nørlund in 'Klostret og dets Gods', p. 70, this was one of the two branches of the Skjalm family that still benefited Sorø at the end of the thirteenth century. Thus the Saltensees looked to Sorø, while Jon Lille's family tended the interests of Esrum.

159. SRD IV, 510 = DD II, 3, 4. Pittances are extra dishes which supplement the monastic dinner on feast days in honour of patrons. See Lekai, pp. 368–69.

160. *Cod. Esrom.* 172, nr. 159 = DD II, 4, 7. Margrethe asked the archbishop of Lund, the bishop of Roskilde, and Jon Lille to confirm the gift with their seals, another indication of the latter's importance to Esrum. Jon seems to have functioned almost as the abbey's aristocratic guardian until 1306.

161. Nørlund, 'Klostret og dets Gods', pp. 91–92.

162. SRD IV, 522 = DD II, 4, 67.

163. H. N. Garner, *Atlas over danske klostre*, 122–28. I. Lindbæk and G. Stemann, *De danske Helligåndsklostre* (Cpn., 1906).

164. DD II, 10, 116 (1329). For his reconcilliation with the monks in 1334, DD II, 11, 124.

165. As in 1279: SRD VIII, 159 = DD II, 2, 389, when Knud Stubbe deeded money to the friars and land to other Løgum monks, or in 1293, SRD VIII, 233 and SRD VIII, 239 = DD II, 4, 105.

166. DD II, 6, 24.

167. SRD IV, 517–18.

168. SRD IV, 490–91.

169. SRD IV, 503.

170. To the Roskilde convent of St Clare, Peder Saksesen, who had sent his daughters to become nuns there, admitted that he had promised 200 marks money. DD II, 4, 10 (1291).

171. We have a copy of the document containing the 1285 judgment of Bishop Ingvar (DD II, 3, 141), plus the Sorø compiler's version of it (SRD IV, 503).

172. Earlier Roskilde bishops: Peder Jakobsen (1215–25) was the son of Jakob Sunesen and the nephew of Peder Sunesen, bishop of Roskilde from 1191 to 1214. Niels Stigsen (1226–49) was a grandson of Toke Skjalmsen, one of the sons of Skjalm Hvide (according to Andreas Nissen in *Danske Bisperækker*). Jakob Erlandsen (bishop of Roskilde 1249–52) belonged to the powerful Galen family of Skåne (Ulsig, p. 92). Peder Skjalmsen Bang (1254–74) was a brother of the devout Lady Gyde of Broby and thus had a family bond to Sorø (Ulsig, p. 80). Stigot (1277–80) had first been a canon in Århus and then provost in Randers, while Ingvar (1280–89) was a native Roskilde product.

173. DD II, 3, 294.

174. DD II, 3, 298 and 299.

175. SRD IV, 503: *Sed heu! Dictus cocus, videns auxilium suum sibi in morte praedicti domini defecisse, seque perinde non posse in eisdem bonis diu subsistere, transtulit ea in crudelissimum virum dominum Ascerum Jönson militem.* Notice the dramatic quality of the passage. The Donation Book at such points becomes almost a full chronicle of events.

176. SRD IV, 504.

177. SRD IV, 504: *Nec profuit correctionem vel judicium ecclesiae, quia contumax fuit in omnibus et obfirmaverat cor suum duritia nimia, ita quod non erat ultra de ipso spes proficiendi in aliquo.*

178. DD II, 6, 74.

179. Catalogus Illustrium Sorae Sepultorum: SRD IV, 540.

180. Nørlund, 'Klostret ...', 69–72.

181. Canivez 1180, nr. 5. In 1217, nr. 3, lay people were allowed burial in Cistercian cemeteries if their parish priests consented, but apparently the restriction of burial inside churches was still in effect.

182. SRD VIII, 118 = DD II, 2, 268 (29 March 1276). For the Brede controversy in full, Axel Bolvig, 'Stridighederne omkring Brede Kirke 1250–1352', *Historisk Tidsskrift* 77 (1977), 85–95. It was once thought that some of the documents used by Løgum in its defence were falsifications. Erling Ladewig Petersen argued against this view in 'Preaching in Medieval Denmark', *Mediaeval Scandinavia* 3 (1971), 142–71, esp. pp. 170–71.

183. A. Friedberg, *Corpus Iuris Canonici.* Pars Secunda. Collectiones (1881): c. 3 X de Statu monachorum III, 35.

184. DD II, 2, 321 (1278).

185. SRD VIII, 6 = DD II, 2, 398.

186. SRD VIII, 232 = DD II, 3, 74.

187. SRD I, 160 = DD II, 3, 78.

188. SRD VIII, 161 = DD II, 3, 79.

189. For a discussion of growing legalism as a general European cultural phenomenon with application to Denmark, see *Conflict and Continuity*, Ch. VIII, 'The Thirteenth Century Process of Definition'. For the Cistercians and the study of law, Colomban Bock, 'Les cisterciens et l'étude du droit', *Analecta Cisterciensia* 7 (1951), 3–31.

190. SRD VIII, 160 = DD II, 3, 152.

191. DD II, 3, 418 = *Cod. Esrom.* 258, nr. 249 (12 October 1290), where he is called *procurator* or bailiff.

192. SRD VIII, 162 = DD II, 5, 410. SRD VIII, 109 = DD II, 3, 290.

193. SRD I, 293 = DD II, 3, 88 (8 April 1284). In a 1288 charter Duke Valdemar claimed he was the monks' principal defender (SRD VIII, 181 = DD II, 3, 279): *... recognoscentes nos eorundem et unicum defensorem.* Duke Valdemar means this in a legal sense: *... ac etiam aliquem loco nostre substituere cupientes, qui et in singulis placitationibus suis (si opus fuerit) pro ipsis in absentia nostra respondeat.*
Great lords are increasingly defining their duties to Cistercian houses in terms of helping them

to stay out of legal entanglements and thus giving them time to devote to spiritual pursuits, as in a charter of King Erik Menved to Ryd from 1299 (DD II, 5, 1): ... *ut rerum suarum facultates et possessiones tanto securius possideant, quanto in deo et in nobis fiduciam habendo secularium legum causis occupari fugiunt et recusant.* For the first time in decades, a royal arenga brings in a new theme and points to a new social situation in which legalism is a danger to the monks.

194. DD II, 4, 258.

195. DD II, 5, 355 and DD II, 4, 107.

196. *Cod. Esrom.* 99 nr. 92 = DD II, 6, 17.

197. *Cod. Esrom.* 162, nr. 148 = DD II, 5, 119, from 1300.

198. *Cod. Esrom.* 163, nr. 149 = DD II, 5, 158, from 1301. Also 164, nr. 150 = DD II, 5, 287 from 1304, where Atte, priest in Tibirke, expressed his desire to be buried at Esrum.

199. SRD IV, 506 = DD II, 3, 43, from 1282, and SRD IV, 482, 506 = DD II, 3, 93, from 1284: *In istis nichil profuerunt monasterio mediatores sed ipse Petrus rediens ad cor correxit semetipsum et dedit....*

200. A. Schneider, *Die Cistercienserabtei Himmerod im Spätmittelalter* (1954), 89–93. SRD IV, 477 = DD II, 4, 289: *Quibus ita peractis transtulit se ad monasterium gracia permanendi ibique tandem divine ductante spiritu confraternitatem a fratribus devote recipiens.*

201. Esrum: DD II, 5, 119 = *Cod. Esrom.* 162, nr. 148, from 1300. Also at Augustinian Æbelholt, DD II, 5, 118, from 1300.

202. *Cod. Esrom.* 170, nr. 157 = DD II, 5, 40: ... *considerans in rebus hominum nichil firmum, nisi quo saluti anime consulatur.*

203. Nørlund, 'Klostret ...', p. 71.

204. King Erik Menved seems to have become financially dependent on Sorø: DD II, 3, 167 and DD II, 4, 55. Vitskøl's 1289 privilege from King Erik makes no mention of his predecessors' role, a thematic break with past practice that could point to a loss of royal interest: DD II, 3, 347. A significant turningpoint is the first royal burial at Sorø in 1304 of Junker Valdemar, brother of the future king Kristoffer: DD II, 5, 333.

205. SRD IV, 523 = DD II, 4, 284. The new property may have been a location for mooring the abbey's ships.

206. SRD VIII, 240 = DD II, 4, 232 and 233.

207. SRD VIII, 213 = DD II, 4, 339, from 1298: ... *ex quo, ut asserunt, propter confluentiam populi iuxta consuetudinem, immo corruptelam patrie multas molestias, et gravamina incurserant, temporibus retroactis, et similia timent incurrere in futuro....*

208. SRD VIII, 107 = DD II, 5, 10. Another indication that the Herrisvad abbot kept up regular visitations at Løgum is from 1303: SRD VIII, 17 = DD II, 5, 260.

209. DD II, 1, 382.

210. *Cod. Esrom.* 48, nr. 35 = DD II, 6, 8.

211. SRD IV, 482. Nørlund calls these donors 'selvejerbønder' in 'Jorddrotter på Valdemarstiden', *Festskrift for Kristian Erslev* (Cpn., 1926), p. 150.

212. Canivez 1188, nr. 8.

213. C. Weeke, *Lunde Domkapitels Gavebøger* (Cpn., phot. reprint, 1973).

214. *Ibid.*, p. 335: *Et quod nullius nomen scribatur in hoc libro, nisi aliquod beneficium contulit ecclesie, archiepiscopo, vel fratribus hujus ecclesie, canonicis in communi seu capitulo, vel aliquod magnum gesserit memoria dignum, propter quod ipsius memoria in commemoracione fidelium defunctorum sit habenda.*
   For a completely different kind of evidence, see Jacob of Voragine, *Legenda Aurea* ed. Th. Graesse (Osnabrück 1965—phot. reprint of the 1890 edition), p. 221: *Miles quidam dives ac nobilis seculo abrenuntiavit et ordinem Cisterciensium introivit et quia litteras nesciebat, erubescentes monachi tam nobilem personam inter laicos deputari dederunt et magistrum; se forte modicum addiscere posset et sub hac occasione inter monachos permaneret.*
   The implication is that the rich nobleman could not become a monk until he was at least semi-literate. This dilemma must have been faced by many novices from rich families, with the result that some remained *inter laicos*, among the lay brothers.

215. For this problem, see esp. Aksel E. Christensen, *Kongemagt og Aristokrati* (Cpn., 1968), esp. 127–36.

216. Nørlund, 'Jorddrotter på Valdemarstiden', 159–62.

Chapter VI

1. *Cod. Esrom.* 130, nr. 166 = DD II, 6, 91.

2. Erik Ulsig, *Danske Adelsgodser i Middelalderen*, pp. 57–8.

3. Ulsig, pp. 88–89, who in his English summary uses the expression 'chieftain' families to distinguish them from their successors after 1300 (pp. 377–78).

4. DD II, 6, 126 (23 May 1308).

5. Ulsig, 63–64. For Jakob Blåfod, p. 86.

6. Note the details given and the personal element here. Were women donors more careful and precise about what they gave than men?
   Item pro vestibus sororum in communi ibidem. xviii ulnas rubei scarleti/ cistam meam meliorem/ unam sabel. unum mensale novum consutum et lxxx ulnas de gracili tela linea....

7. *Cod. Esrom.* 221, nr. 206 = DD III, 1, 196 (13 September 1341).

8. SM II, 203–206.

9. See f. 28v in the Øm Codex, Copenhagen Royal Library, E. donatione Variorum 134, 4°. There is an excellent photographic reproduction of the entire manuscript in C. A. Christensen, *Corpus Codicum Danicorum Medii Aevi* II (Cpn., 1960).

10. SM II, 203, lines 20–22; p. 203, 16–17; p. 204, 13–14; p. 204, 24–26; p. 205, 1–2.

11. See Gertz's foreword to his edition of the text, SM II, 155–56.

12. See *Conflict and Continuity at Øm Abbey*, Ch. IX, C.

13. AD 128.

14. AD 142-43.

15. AD 24. *Saxostudier*, red. Ivan Boserup (Museum Tusculanum, 1975): Franz Blatt, 'Saxo en repræsentant for det 12. århundredes renæssance', p. 12.

16. AD 142: *Monasterium de Sora fere totaliter incendio periit, sicut invenies in libro Excerpta patrum.*

17. The Øm monks had many such collections, as can be seen in the book list compiled at the Reformation. See *Conflict and Continuity*, ch. XII.

18. SRD IV, 535.

19. AD 142: *Hoc anno fuit magnum bellum in Hispania inter paganos et Christianos, sicut potes invenire in fine libri qui dicitur Herveus.*

20. PL 231: 'Venerabilis Herveus Burgidolensis Monachus'. See Fr. Stegmüller, *Repertorium Biblicum Medii Aevi* III (Madrid, 1951), nr. 3251-3289.

21. AD 142: *Obiit magister Jacobus in decretis, monachus in Sora.*

22. For Brother Jens Jyde of Sorø, who wrote down the medieval laws of Zealand, see Verner Dahlerup, 'Tre litterære munke i Sorø', *Sorø: Kloster, Akademiet, Skolen*, 135-37. Note that Niels Rytze, abbot in 1310, is called *magister* (SRD IV, 495-96). This could indicate legal training, for the Reformation abbot list calls him 'Doctor in Decretals' (SRD IV, 536).

23. AD 142: *Obiit abbas Hemmingus de Sora, consiliarius regis Erici Danorum.* Actually Henning was still alive in 1310 (DD II, 6, 323), an important indication that the Younger Sorø Annals are not completely accurate and that they were composed in the 1340s and not contemporaneously with the events described.

24. DD II, 4, 289 (1298). DD II, 5, 333 (1304). DD II, 6, 185 (1309).

25. AD 143: *Istis diebus et temporibus non erat rex in Dacia, sed regnabant Holsati, in magna malicia multis annis.*

26. AD 143. In 1298 Bishop Jens Krag gave the Sorø monks their first piece of property in Copenhagen that is recorded in the Sorø Donation Book (DD II, 4, 284 = SRD IV, 523).

27. AD 167-188.

28. Erik Arup thought it was written by the knight Bo Falk: *Danmarks Historie* IIA, 106-107.

29. *Yngre Sjællandske Krønike: Baggrund, tilblivelse og værdi* (Odense University Studies in History and Social Sciences 10: Odense, 1973). See also Kai Hørby's review in *Historisk Tidsskrift* 1975, 133-40, where he too rejects the attribution to Sorø.

30. Szomlaiski, p. 17.

31. *Ibid.*, p. 18.

32. *Ibid.*: 'On the basis of the source material preserved for medieval history it is seen that the milieu in Sorø most markedly can be thought to have stimulated the creation of a work like the Younger Zealand Chronicle'. (My translation)

33. Verner Dahlerup (note 22 above), 138-39.

34. Szomlaiski, p. 20 (AD 172).

35. AD 188.

36. Szomlaiski, p. 24.

37. AD 29-31.

38. Tage E. Christiansen in 'Yngre Sjællandske Krønikes Sidste Aar', *Scandia* 40 (1974) 5-33, esp. p. 15, shows that the Chronicle had more than one author. Christiansen thinks the Chronicle was composed 'in an ecclesiastical milieu' (p. 13, n. 44).

39. AD 176.

40. AD 173-74.

41. AD 178: ... *rex Magnum Johannis, canonicum Roschyldensem et Aarhusiensem, ibidem instituere attentabat, quod et fecit, eique in omnibux necessariis suis providebat et diu secum in curia sua honorifice tenuit.*

42. AD 182.

43. Andreas Nissen, *Danske Bisperækker*, 39-40.

44. DD II, 6, 147.

45. DD II, 7, 116. Gudhem Cistercian house for women is located in Väster Götland in central Sweden, not far south of the Cistercian abbey of Varnhem. The nuns' insistence on fishing rights in Viskan may reflect a religious community's need for a ready supply of fish. For Gudhem in general, see Edward Ortved, *Cistercienserordenen og dens Klostre i Norden* II: *Sveriges Klostre*, 363-401 (Cpn., 1933).

46. *Cod. Esrom.* 38, nr. 28 = DD II, 6, 202. The same bull went to the monastery of Saint Stephen in Dijon.

47. SRD VIII, 185 = DD II, 8, 212.

48. SRD VIII, 187 = DD II, 8, 224.

49. DD II, 11, 106 = Sorøbogen, f. 25r.

50. AD 170. For the most recent summary of the archaeology and early history of Knardrup abbey, see Tage E. Christiansen, 'Sognelisterne i Roskildebispens Jordebog', HT 77 (1977) 13-17.

51. DD II, 10, 116.

52. See the explanation in *Danmarks Riges Breve's* translation of this bull: DRB II, 10, 116.

53. DD II, 10, 116: ... *et nonnulli alii laici eiusdem diocesis/ villam Syosum cum iuribus et pertinentiis suis/ et quedam alia bona ipsius monasterii mobilia et immobilia/ in dicta diocesi consistentia/ occuparunt et detinent occupata....*

54. *Ibid.*: ... *ob dispositionem instabilem dicti regni nequeant a dicto regno de dictis occupatoribus habere iusticie complementum.*

55. The Younger Sorø Annals write for 1343 (AD 143): *Hoc anno secundario missus est conventus in Knartorp.*

56. See Ulsig's chart, p. 56. For more on the Skarsholm family, to which Barnum Eriksen belonged, see Ulsig, pp. 83-84.

57. DD II, Lo, 104 (27 February 1329).

58. The traditional and inadequate Danish term is *landsbyvæbner* (for the Latin *armigerus*) and means a man on the lowest rank of nobility who bore arms and owned his own land. The only English equivalent I can find is 'country gentry', which gives an idea of this class's place above the peasantry but below the full nobility. It should be added, however, that Danish historians themselves are not in full agreement about class structure at the end of the Middle Ages, partly because of insufficient source information.

59. DD II, 10, 104: ... *predictam Walburgim restituendam et reintegrandam esse ad possessionem bonorum eorundem plene libere et cum effectu ipsam que ad ea quantum potuit/ restituit et reintegravit.*

60. DD II, 10, 1.

61. DD II, 11, 325: ... *quod horrendum est explicare/ viros ecclesiasticos presbiteros et alios indifferenter/ wulnerare mutilare/ occidere/ capere/ captos detinere/ trucidare et torquere/ eorum privilegia libertates minuere/ auferre/ et quantum in eis est/ in nichilum pro dolor redigere in grave preiudicium ecclesie/ eius ministrorum/ et divinam forensam non formidant.*

62. The best resumé is in Ulsig, ch. III 'Tiden 1241–1340. Overgangen fra selveje til fæste' (The Transition from Landowning Peasantry to Tenantry), 47–54, where other work on the period is discussed.

63. *Cod. Esrom.* 74, nr. 66 = DD III, 1, 302.

64. *Cod. Esrom.* 74, nr. 66: ... *constituimus et ordinamus ipsis fratribus et dominis et eorum familie universe per presentes. tutorem et defensorem virum videlicet nobilem et discretum ... mandates eidem Nicolao firmiter ut dictos dominos et ipsorum familiam ab omnibus eis aliquas iniurias vel molestias inferre volentibus. auctoritate et vice nostra protegat et defendat.* Notice that Esrum monks are called *lords* as well as brothers here, perhaps an indication of a new social attitude towards them.

65. DD III, 1, 369: ... *gravia incommoda nobis et nostro monasterio, pericula et vexationes verisimilter imminebant. precipue si dicta ecclesia ab aliquibus pacis emulis fieret incastellata.*

66. Younger Zealand Chronicle, AD 173, as for 1343: *Sialandia desolatur in pecoribus tam a Danis quam Alemannis, et plures rustici truncantur ab iisdem. Villa Køke comburitur, et plura oppida desolantur.* Sorø had many land holdings just west of Køge.

67. DD III, 3, 124 = Sorøbogen f. 28^v.

68. For incorporation in Denmark, see Troels Dahlerup, *Det danske Sysselsprovsti,* 315–19. For the international development, D. Lindner, *Die Lehre von der Inkorporation in ihrer geschichtlichen Entwicklung* (Münich, 1951).

69. SRD VIII, 133 = DD II, 9, 75: *Reprehensibile iudicari non debeat a quocunque, si propter temporum varietates, statuta variantur humana.*

70. For a summary of the Danish literature on the agricultural crisis of the fourteenth century, Esben Albrectsen, 'Den holstenske adels invandring i Sønderjylland i det 13.–14. århundrede', HT 74 (1974), 81–152, esp. 120–27. Although this article is limited to one part of Denmark, many of its conclusions provide helpful guidelines for this difficult period. Albrectsen uses the studies made by C. A. Christensen on the dramatic fall of land rent in the fourteenth century, its causes and consequences: 'Nedgangen i Landgilden i det 14. Århundrede', HT 10 Række, 1 Bind (1930–31), 446–65; 'Krisen på Slesvig Domkapitels Jordegods 1352–1437', HT 11 Række, VI Bind (1960–62), 161–241; 'Ændringerne i landsbyens økonomiske og sociale struktur i det 14. og

15. århundrede', Ht 12 R., 1 Bind (1964), 257–349. See also E. Ladewig Petersen, 'Jordprisfor-hold i dansk senmiddelalder', *Middelalderstudier Tilegnede Aksel E. Christensen* (Cpn., 1966), 219–244. He is inspired by George Duby's masterful *L'Economie rurale et la vie des campagnes dans l'Occident médiéval* (Paris, 1962). In recent years many new results have come to light from research done in the Nordic *ødegårdsprojekt* (project on abandoned farms). For Denmark, see Svend Gissel, 'Forskningsrapport for Danmark', *Det nordiske Ødegårdsprojekt.* Pub. nr. 1 (Cpn., 1972), 3–71. Also Gissel's article 'Den senmiddelalderlige krise i Norden' in *Kulturblom-string og samfundskrise i 1300-tallet*, ed. Brian McGuire (Middelaldercentralen: Copenhagen, 1979), 183–92.

71. For this development in the order as a whole, see Lekai, 386–87.

72. DD II, 8, 411 (14 May 1322). DD III, 1, 12 (14 February 1340).

73. Sorø: DD II, 7, 99 = Sorøbogen f. 28v (4 October 1313).
Løgum: SRD VIII, 222 = DD II, 10, 51 (1 September 1328).

74. SRD VIII, 124, 126, 129 = DD II, 9, 142 (1 September 1324).

75. DD II, 19, 96.

76. DD II, 7, 294.

77. *Cod. Esrom.* 178, nr. 168 = DD II, 10, 332.

78. *Ibid.:* ... *necnon et omne ius quod nobis racione patronatus in eadem ecclesia competit. et compete potest. in predictum dominum abbatem pro se et suo conventu tenore presencium transferimus/ ordinacionem et provisionem ipsius ecclesie eidem domino abbati quantum ad nos spectat concedentes/ precipue et eisdem domino abbati et suo conventui Esromensi. ex altera parte ius eciam patronatus in eadem.*
The ambiguity of the last line indicates that a problem similar to that debated at Brede had arisen: how to distinguish *ius patronatus* from *ius presentandi*. Normally the first would mean a share in the income of the church but would not necessitate the second, the right to appoint the priest.

79. *Cod. Esrom.* 179, nr. 171 = DD II, 157 (23 March 1332): *Cum instantia cotidiana et sollicitudo ecclesiarum nobis commissarum nos ammoneat ad efficaciter elaborandum/ qualiter deificus cultus/ non imminui sed semper valeat augmentari. quod per viros religiosos sollicicius credentes adimplendum/ ubi eorundem tenuitas poterit aliquatenus relevari.*

80. Tommerup Premonstratensian Abbey received six churches from Archbishop Esger of Lund because of it near total destruction by fire: DD II, 8, 451 and 452 (27 and 28 October 1322). Æbelholt's burden of hospitality was to be relieved by the income from Lille Lyngby church: DD II, 9, 127 (4 July 1324).

81. For Antvorskov: DD II, 6, 250 (9 June 1310).

82. See the early fourteenth century wills in Kr. Erslev, *Testamenter fra Danmarks Middel-alder* nr. 36 (1 June 1338); nr. 43 (28 September 1346); nr. 42 (15 April 1345).

83. DD II, 6, 443.

84. As when Pope Clement allowed the newly-elected archdeacon in Roskilde, who was a doc-tor in canon law and teacher at Paris, to keep the income he had held as a parish priest: DD II, 6, 439 (22 July 1312). See also DD II, 11, 3 (11 January 1333). For the problem of absenteeism caused by the attraction of universities in the fourteenth century see Kathleen Edwards, *The English Secular Cathedrals in the Middle Ages* (Manchester, 1949), especially Appendix I.

85. SRD VIII, 213 = DD II, 8, 134 (3 July 1319).

86. DD II, 8, 410: ... *ad suggestionem et assertionem quarundam clericalium et laicalium personarum dictae nostrae diocesis, saepius et cum instantia postulantibus et supradictis dominis abbate et fratribus constanter et semper negantibus et nullum ius aut iurisdictionem super ipsos nos habere vel unquam obtinuisse dicentibus.*

87. *Ibid.: Nos enim diligenti veritatis inquisitione per capitulum nostrum praehabita supradictam suggestionem seu assertionem non satis probabilem ad tantae rei prosecutionem deprehendimus, sed quasi ab incerto autore primitus emasse unde et minus solidam vel sufficientem iudicavimus.*
The language here is a beautifully balanced combination of scholastic terminology and personal reflection.

88. DD II, 8, 411.

89. DD II, 8, 424: ... *destruximus et perpetuo damnamus omnes literas seu processus pro parte nostra et ecclesiae nostrae contra praedictam ecclesiam Viteschole.*

90. SRD VIII, 213 = DD II, 4, 339.

91. As Tvis: DD II, 6, 131 (25 July 1308). DD II, 7, 333 (1314)—special royal exemption from payment of tolls.

92. Æbelholt: SRD VI, 167 = DD II, 6, 121 (1 May 1308)—privilege for June market covering all tolls.
Roskilde convent of St Agnes: DD II, 6, 152 (27 September 1308).
Næstved Abbey of St Peder: DD II, 6, 168 (1308). Many of these privileges merely renewed charters already given by Erik Menved before 1300.

93. The Younger Zealand Chronicle, AD 168–69, shows other means used, as under 1317: *Rex indixit omnibus clericis et laicis, quod soluerent sibi decimas omnium reddituum suorum et quasdam alias tallias indixit super Hafn, et quod bondones et rustici redimerent sibi decimas ecclesiarum omnium.*

94. A still excellent outline of the outcome of Erik's reign is Kr. Erslev, *Den Senere Middelalder* in *Danmarks Riges Historie* II (no date, but c. 1900), 186–93. Erik Arup in *Danmarks Historie* IIA, 51–60, is a bit too personal and prone to condemn Erik's foreign policy on the basis of the twentieth-century Danish Radical Liberal party's aversion to foreign military involvements.

95. *Cod. Esrom.* 67, nr. 54 = DD II, 5, 113 (3 March 1300): ... *donec cum consiliariis nostris deliberaremur, quid cum ipsis et ceteris claustralibus super huiusmodi libertatibus sit agendum....*

96. *Cod. Esrom.* 69, nr. 57 = DD II, 6, 127 (24 June 1308); 69, nr. 58 = DD II, 6, 129 (29 June 1308); 70, nr. 59 = DD II, 6, 226 (25 March 1310); 70, nr. 60 = DD II, 6, 227—only this last privilege added something apparently new, exemption from payment of tolls.

97. *Cod. Esrom.* 68, nr. 55 = DD II, 5, 148 (2 May 1301).

98. *Cod. Esrom.* 68, nr. 56 = DD II, 6, 54 (2 March 1307).

99. As in 1337, *Cod. Esrom.* 101, nr. 93 = DD II, 12, 34. Another indication of trouble comes in 1362, 104, nr. 95.

100. DD II, 7, 261.

101. DD II, 5, 333.

102. It is interesting that neither Kristoffer nor Valdemar Atterdag wanted to continue the tradition of royal burial at Ringsted. Similarly Valdemar Atterdag's charters mark a departure from thirteenth century formulae in expressing royal devotion to Cistercian monasteries. For Erik Menved it had been important to keep up the traditions that linked him with the early Valdemars. To his successors it seems to have been important to distinguish themselves from Erik Menved.

103. DD II, 8, 189.

104. DD II, 8, 192.

105. DD II, 8, 334. Canivez 1321, nr. 10.

106. DD II, 8, 305.

107. DD III, 1, 6. The original charters from 1320 make no mention of this unpleasant circumstance (DD II, 8, 287, 288). Note that the consent of the Esrum abbot Peder had been sought and given in 1320, an important indication that Esrum still functioned as mother abbey.

108. DD III, 1, 1: ... *mera necessitate conpulsi. non habentes aliam viam nisi quod bona nostra pro summa dicte pecunie/ de necessario alienaremus.*

109. DD II, 10, 21.

110. DD II, 9, 455.

111. DD II, 10, 30.

112. DD II, 9, 470 (1327 for Lund). DD II, 9, 472 (Antvorskov). DD II, 10, 33 for Tommerup in 1328 has the full text, but it is very general.

113. DD III, 1, 57.

114. *Ibid.:* ... *piis locis et ecclesiis per ipsos fundatis, dotatis et locupletatis, in quibus quotidie pro vivis et defunctis gratiarum actiones et propitiationes altissimo pro peccatis et negligentiis offeruntur eorundem per personas, inibi domino famulantes, nolentes in temporalibus sine quibus spiritualia non subsistunt facere decrementa, quinimo de nostris facultatibus, ut beneficiorum per progenitores nostros creatorum participes existamamus, continua facere incrementa.* Compare with Kristoffer I to Vitskøl from after 29 June 1252 (DD II, 1, 67).

115. DD III, 1, 145.

116. *Cod. Esrom.* 74, nr. 66 = DD III, 1, 302.

117. SRD IV 495 and 529 = DD III, 1, 139.

118. DD III, 2, 13.

119. *Danmarks Kirker: Frederiksborg Amt* II (1967), 1042.

120. DD III, 4, 18 (12 March 1353). DD III, 4, 68 = SRD IV, 341.

121. Valdemar's only act of what could express religious devotion to a single church community was extended to Roskilde cathedral, an indication of the growing importance of the church to the Danish monarchy: DD III, 2, 22 (12 February 1344).

122. *Cod. Esrom.* 112 nr. 98 = DD III, 4, 39 (4 July 1353).

123. *Cod. Esrom.* 76, nr. 68 = DD III, 3, 12;77, nr. 70 = DD III, 5, 98; 77, nr. 69 = DD III, 5, 234.

124. *Dipl. Svec.* V 568 nr. 7070 (1 May 1346). *Dipl. Svec.* III 345, nr. 2132.

125. DD II, 8, 3 (18 January 1318). DD III, 2, 127 (4 March 1345). *Dipl. Svec.* V 518, nr. 3911.

126. DD III, 2, 382 (8 September 1347).

127. SRD VIII, 120 = DD II, 9, 139 (22 August 1324).

128. G. Mollat, *The Popes at Avignon* 1305-78 (New York, 1965).

129. SRD VIII, 185 = DD II, 8, 212 (22 April 1320). SRD VIII, 188 = DD II, 8, 157 (22 November 1319)—general declaration of papal protection. SRD VIII, 187 = DD II, 8, 224 (1 July 1320)—monks are given right to inherit.

130. SRD VIII, 187 = DD II, 9, 442.

131. DD II, 11, 106 = Sorøbogen f. 25r.

132. *Cod. Esrom.* 34, nr. 21 = DD II, 6, 201 (2 September 1309); 35, nr. 22 (5 July 1382).

133. As for Sorø in 1329 (DD II, 10, 99), Løgum and Ryd in 1331 (DD II, 10, 336); Ryd again in 1332 (DD II, 10, 377).

134. DD II, 8, 271. For Herrisvad, DD II, 10, 364 (1 May 1332). For Holme helping Odense, DD II, 7, 389 (1316).

135. Canivez 1321, nr. 17.

136. Lekai 97-99.

137. H. Peter King, 'Cistercian Financial Organisation 1335-1392', *Journal of Ecclesiastical History* 24 (1973), 127-43.

138. King, p. 135.

139. King, p. 136.

140. King, p. 138.

141. King, p. 134. I shall consider Arne Odd Johnsen's and Peter King's *Tax Book of the Cistercian Order* (Oslo, 1979) in the next chapter.

142. Canivez 1352, nr. 17. Also Clairvaux apparently came to concentrate on its daughters in terms of finances. There is no direct evidence that Clairvaux maintained direct contact with Danish abbeys, but we do know that it made collections in Sweden, so it is likely it did the same in Denmark: *Dipl. Svec.* V 568, nr. 4070 (1 May 1346). The Abbot Bernard of Clairvaux acknowledges forty gylden which the Alvastra abbot paid through the Varnhem abbot for 1343 and 1344.

143. Canivez 1347, nr. 9.

144. DD III, 2, 374: ... *cum nuper monasterio Hildensi filie nostre dilecte officium visitacionis annue personaliter impenderemus....*

145. Lekai, Ch. VIII 'The End of Prosperity', 91-108, the only general treatment of this period for the Cistercian Order as a whole.

146. DD III, 2, 374: ... *quod nos cum patre venerabili domino Martino abbate/ ac toto conventu ibidem ad hoc specialiter convocato/ ad animum non mirum sollicite revocantes/ discutere cepimus et tractare. quomodo et qualiter ipsum monasterium/ nobile quondam membrum ordinis/ nunc vero ut premittitur/ usurarum voragine ac aliorum gravaminum immensitate/ destructum et quasi desolatum/ ab huiusmodi oneribus per graciam dei aliqualiter posset liberari/* ...

147. *Ibid.: Nos igitur ex tam evidenti informacione certificati/ quod dictorum bonorum alienacio seu commutacio/ ut premittitur fiat/ utile reputamus/ supplicantes vobis ut memorato domino abbati Hildensi et eius conventui in hac parte consencientes/ licenciam eisdem dare dignemini super alienacione seu commutacione bonorum predictorum/ uti expedire videbitur facienda/ ut precio pro eisdem recepto in quantum se extendere poterit ab oneribus et gravaminibus supradictis/ valeant liberari. vel de utilitate ut speratur commutacionis bonorum faciende/ fructum maiorem quam hactenus reportare.*

148. *Cod. Esrom.* 42, nr. 31.

149. An instance of a completely gratuitous bond between a Danish Cistercian abbey and a North German religious community can be seen in a document according to which Abbot Niels of Ryd in 1316 established the brotherhood of Heinrich, provost of the collegiate church in Preetz southeast of Kiel with Ryd Abbey (DD II, 7, 371).

150. DD III, 2, 291 (13 November 1346). Niels Spring, administrator (*previsor*) of the Roskilde Cistercian monastery for nuns (and probably a layman), mortgaged a farm in Svogerslev to a Lund citizen with the permission of the Sorø abbot. See also DD III, 1, 372 (9 October 1343); DD III, 6, 166 (1308).

151. *Cod. Esrom.* 120, nr. 104 = DD III, 3, 587 (14 September 1352).

152. DD III, 3, 307 (about 22 July 1350). In general the Zealand Cistercian houses did not seem to interest themselves in the daughter house of Roskilde in Bergen on Rygen. After 1306 at the latest, Bergen's mother abbey was Eldena (DD II, 2, 74). Also Hoogeweg, *Die Stifter und Klöster der Provinz Pommern* I, 114.

153. DD II, 12, 173.

154. *Cod. Esrom.* 249, nr. 251 = DD II, 12, 110; 260, nr. 252 = DD II, 12, 112. The Hälsingborg citizen obtained *fraternitatem* in exchange. This expression is probably used interchangeably here with *contraternitatem*, which seems to have been quite popular during the period, as at Løgum (SRD VIII, 64 = DD II, 11 114).

155. Instances of Ribe favour to Løgum are many, as in 1308 when the bishop of Ribe arbitrated in a land dispute and decided in the monks' favour (SRD VIII, 150 = DD II, 6, 162.).

156. SRD IV, 499 = DD II, 6, 190.

157. SRD IV, 528–29 and 493 = DD II, 7, 287 (30 June 1315).

158. As at Alsted, where one version in the Sorø Donation Book specifically says that the monks' collection of the annual income was *extra sortem debiti* (SRD IV, 479).

159. DD II, 10, 192 = SRD IV, 479, 490, 520.

160. DD II, 10, 406 = SRD IV, 479, 490, 521.

161. SRD IV, 480, 489, 579 = DD III, 1, 338.

162. SRD IV, 504 = DD II, 8, 193.

332 The Cistercians in Denmark

163. *Cod. Esrom.* 109, nr. 97 = DD III, 1, 64.

164. *Ibid.: ... qui frequentibus meis necessitatibus non semel sed quotiens acciderant tam prompte quam benigniter remedio subvenerant optativo ... pro iam tactis meis perplexitatibus dissolvendis favorabiliter concesserunt.*

165. There are exceptional instances from this period in which a Cistercian abbey gives up land in order to get ready money, as Løgum in 1340 (SRD VIII, 245 = DD II, 1, 73). Also in 1342 it regained a farm it had mortgaged (SRD VIII, 23 = DD III, 1, 231). But later in the decade the monks gained a number of properties and in 1349 themselves loaned money on a mortgage (SRD VIII, 133 = DD III, 3, 129).

166. See Tvis in 1337 (DD II, 12, 68). Payment in three installments at Løgum in 1313 (SRD VIII, 219 = DD II, 7, 91).

167. SRD IV, 515 = DD II, 8, 6.

168. *Cod. Esrom.* 224, nr. 209 = DD II, 10, 237: Brother Knud Jul is named procurator of Sorø in 1310: DD II, 6, 306 = SRD IV, 495–96. He also was one of Sorø's copyists (see Verner Dahlerup, note 22 above, 137–38.

169. Compare DD II, 7, 287 (1315) with its twenty marks of pure silver with the 140 marks given as a bribe to Jens Marsvin in 1310 by Sorø (DD II, 6, 306 = SRD IV, 495–96). In 1312 at Løgum land bought for 25 marks is said to have been worth a fourth of an old mark, indicating a rate of 100 new marks in 1312 as equivalent to one mark before 1300 (SRD VIII, 17 = DD II, 6, 389.

170. As at Løgum in 1320 (SRD VIII, 16 = DD II, 8, 312) and 1343 (SRD VIII, 146 = DD III, 2, 191), or at Esrum in 1339 (*Cod. Esrom.* 156, nr. 142 = DD II, 12, 166). In 1348 when Sorø gained a piece of land, it was specified that the peasant living there was to be allowed to continue chopping wood for his buildings and for his hearth. This is another indication that labour was in short supply and peasants were able to make demands (SRD IV, 523 = DD III, 3, 30).

171. For a similar development in Britain, James S. Donnelly, 'Changes in the Grange Economy of English and Welsh Cistercian Abbeys 1300–1540', *Traditio* 10 (1954), 319–458.

172. *Cod. Esrom.* 152, nr. 135 = DD III, 4, 142 (21 July 1354).

173. SRD VIII, 223 = DD III, 2, 341.

174. Albrectsen, 'Den holstenske adels indvandring', p. 132.

175. SRD VIII, 146 = DD III, 2, 191 and SRD VIII, 145 = DD III, 2, 198.

176. SRD VIII, 155 = DD II, 11, 173.

177. As the substantial gift of Borg near Brede to Løgum by Katherine after the death of her husband, the knight of Henneke Limbæk (SRD VIII, 244 = DD III, 4, 215–22 February 1355).

178. Løgum and Tønder: SRD VIII, 154 = DD II, 7, 11. Ryd and Slesvig: DD II, 8, 364 (1321). Esrum and Søborg: *Cod. Esrom.* 152, nr. 135 = DD III, 4, 42. Esrum and Hälsingborg: *Cod. Esrom.* 259, nr. 251 (1338). Slagelse and Sorø: SRD IV, 498 = DD III, 2, 346 (1347).

179. DD II, 8, 29 (1318). DD II, 10, 20 = SRD VIII, 241 (1328).

180. SRD IV, 497 = DD II, 9, 38 and DD II, 7, 429. The Lord Necrologium mentioned the fact that its canon Trued, who died in 1319, had become a monk at Sorø (Weeke, *Lunde Kapitels Gavebøger*, p. 160.).

181. DD II, 12, 87.

182. DD III, 2, 114.

183. DD III, 3,32 (21 June 1348—Pope Clement VI). DD III, 4, 366 (9 December 1355—Pope Innocent gave him permission to become a Benedictine monk at Odense).

184. DD II, 11, 156 and 157.

Chapter VII

1. SRD VIII, 179 = DD III, 7, 324 (22 October 1265): Duke Henrik of Jutland confirms Løgum's rights. SRD I, 99 (17 October 1376): a property exchange is approved by Niels, Count of Southern Jutland. SRD VIII, 178 (2 March 1383): Adolph Count of Holstein takes Løgum under his protection and confirms its privileges SRD VIII, 84 (15 September 1383): Nicholas his successor does the same.

2. A land dispute is settled with the help of the king and the duke of Southern Jutland: SRD VIII, 164 (1375).

3. Erik Arup, *Danmarks Historie* IIA, 183-84. Esben Albrectsen, 'Den holstenske adels indvandring i Sønderjylland i det 13.-14. århundrede', HT 74 (1974), 108-109.

4. DD III, 6, 120 (31 December 1361).

5. DD III, 6, 118 (31 December 1361) and DD III, 7, 36 (7 March 1364).

6. DD III, 4, 18.

7. DD III, 7, 216 (23 February 1364): Oluf Olufsen Lunge, knight, deeded all his property in Halleby to King Valdemar. DD III, 7, 433 (22 September 1366): Niels Agesen of Karholm, knight, sold all his property on Zealand to Valdemar with the main estate at Annisse. For a similar case at Græsted in 1360: DD III, 5, 496.

8. SRD VI, 172, (1 March 1377).

9. The papal bull of 1377 giving Margrethe and her son Oluf permission to have the bodies of Valdemar and Helvig moved to Sorø is contained in KS 7 Bind (1869-71), 865-66.

10. *Repertorium Diplomaticum Regni Danici Mediævalis (Rep.)* ed. Kristian Erslev II (covering 1351-1400, published 1896-98): *Rep.* 3210. '*Abbas vero de abbatia sua eodem die fratres 3 ferculis bonis ultra refectionem usualem et 1 lagena cervisie almanice reficiat'*. As Ambrosius Schneider points out, pittances in the fourteenth century became even more popular at Cistercian houses like Himmerod than earlier, despite economic decline: *Die Cistercienserabtei Himmerod im Spätmittelalter*, 157-58.

11. Næstved's abbot Troels received sixty marks for a daily mass at the altar of the Holy Cross for Valdemar, *Rep.* 3216. Here we are close to the late medieval practice by which nobles set up chantry chapels to assure masses for their souls. *Rep.* 3186 (29 August 1377): *... et cum reverentia et honore quibus bene decet, cum omnibus sacerdotibus conventus nostri et cum omnibus aliis sacerdotibus secularibus, quod ad hoc possumus obtinere, sollempniter celebrandum.*

12. For the spiritual-emotional side of this relationship, see my article, forthcoming in *Analecta Cisterciensia*, 'The Cistercians and the Transformation of Monastic Friendships'.

13. This is only a possibility. Kristian Erslev pointed out in *Dronning Margrethe og Kalmaru-*

nionens Grundlæggelse (1882), p. 48, that we know extremely little about Margrethe's childhood and upbringing.

14. *Rep.* 3577.

15. *Rep.* 3836.

16. In 1393 she gave Kattrup and Kuserup in Løve herred: SRD IV, 510.

17. KS 7 (1869-71), p. 866: ... *et ob temporis malignitatem in dicta capella cultus divinus minuatur nimis et decrescat, monasterium vero predictum ruinas minetur satis graves....*

18. *Cod. Esrom.* 198, nr. 187.

19. *Danmarks Kirker. Tønder Amt* (Cpn., 1957) 1096-1100. See also Jürgen A. Wissing, *Kloster Lögum* (Apenrade, 1972) 115-18.

20. Ulsig, p. 198, for Margrethe's treatment of the nobility in this matter.

21. Poul Nørlund, 'Klostret og dets gods', *Sorø: Klostret, Skolen, Akademiet gennem Tiderne* (Cpn., 1933) I, p. 75. The last royal person buried at Sorø was Anna, sister of King Kristoffer of Bavaria, in 1446: SRD IV, 542.

22. *Danmarks Kirker* III: *Københavns Amt.* Roskilde Domkirke 2 (1951), pp. 1796-99.

23. Helge Toldberg, *Den danske Rimkrønike* I (Cpn., 1961), 151-52:
   I Roskilde hwiles nw myne been
   som ther staar nw bescrefvet
   Hade jeg haffth nogher huldher wen
   i Sore the hade jeg bleffveth.

24. 'Catalogus Illustrium Soræ Sepultorum', SRD IV, 542: ... *hic primum sepulta, sed posterea per Dominum Petrum Episcopum Roskildensem violenter translata.* See A. Fang, *Roskilde Domkirke gennem 1000 År* (Roskilde, 1960), for a different interpretation of these events.

25. SRD IV, 521-22.

26. A detailed account is given in Johannes Lindbæk, 'Bishop Niels Skave i Roskilde og Sorø Kloster', HT VIII: 1 (1907), 254-283. See also Niels Skyum-Nielsen, 'Ærkekonge og Ærkebiskop', *Scandia* 23 (1955-56), 1-101, esp. 60-61.

27. Alfr. Krarup and Johs. Lindbæk, *Acta Pontificum Danica* IV (1910), nr. 3185 (8 February 1490) and nr. 3187 (4 April 1490).

28. Niels Skyum-Nielsen, 'Ærkekonge og Ærkebiskop', p. 71: 'Truly, 1443 became a year of breakthrough. The decree, which was thought of as a reform, became instead half way a reformation'. (my translation).

29. DD III, 5, 332 (17 June 1360): Esrum's abbot is to install Peder Bodulvsen as chanter in the church of Lund. DD III, 6, 95 (23 October 1361): Ryd's abbot is to install canon Jens Mikkelsen in a new office. DD III, 7, 28 (4 March 1364): Esrum's abbot is to fill a vacancy at Roskilde cathedral. DD III, 7, 38 (7 March 1364): Esrum's and Sorø's abbots plus the Benedictine abbot of All Saints at Lund are to hand over canonries with prebends belonging to them in each of Denmark's cathedrals to persons selected by King Valdemar.

30. DD III, 7 139 (11 August 1364).

31. As help given in the Esrum dispute over Uggeløse: *Cod. Esrom.* 107, nr. 96 = DD III, 5, 362 (19 September 1360).

32. *Rep.* 3418.

33. Bruno Griesser, 'Statuten von Generalkapiteln ausserhalb Citeaux: Wien 1393 und Heilsbronn 1398', *Cistercienser Chronik* 62 (1955), 65-83, esp. 65-66.

34. *Ibid.*, 66-67. See also Edvard Ortved, 'Von Generalkapiteln auf dem Festlande ausserhalb Citeaux während des grossen Schismas', *Cistercienser Chronik* 38 (1926), 279-82.

35. Griesser (1955), 79-83.

36. Griesser, 'Unbekannte Generalkapitelstatuten', *Cistercienser Chronik* 64 (1957), 1-20, 41-60. These are meant as a supplement to the incomplete records in Canivez. The first section, covering 1350-64, gives an impression of disciplinary problems with attendance at the General Chapter (as in 1354, nr. 4, p. 10), refusal by many abbeys and even houses for women to pay their contributions (as in 1361, nr. 5, p. 14) and ravages by war and social unrest making life uncertain (as 1361, nr. 8, p. 16).

37. Edvard Ortved, *Cistercieordenen og dens klostre i Norden* 2: *Sveriges klostre* (Cpn., 1933), p. 19.

38. Arne Odd Johnsen and Peter King, *The Tax Book of the Cistercian Order* (Det Norske Videnskaps Akademi. II Hist. Filos Klasse. Avhandlinger Ny Serie, No. 16. Oslo, 1979). The Danish historian M. Mackeprang published in 1945 the *contributio mediocris* for Danish houses that he had found in Løgum records (*Sønderjydske Årbøger*, p. 85), but he was unable to date this levy correctly.

39. *Ibid.*, p. 31. King concludes that Esrum's assessment 'bore little relation to reality'.

40. *Ibid.*, p. 30. I have averaged out the assessments on p. 78.

41. *Ibid.*, pp. 38, 84.

42. *Ibid.*, p. 34.

43. DD III, 5, 119 (11 May 1358).

44. DD III, 5, 121 (11 May 1358).

45. See note 17 above. Later in the fifteenth century the abbot of Esrum excused his rare visitations at Eldena and Colbaz '... *propter nimiam distantiam ac pericula viarum maxima terraeque marique imminentia raro vel nunquam praedictas filias suas vistare consueverit*'. Canivez 1487, nr. 62.

46. Canivez 1410, nr. 24 and 25. Canivez 1412, nr. 13 and 18. The monasteries were Sorø, Esrum, Ås, Herrisvad, Knardrup, Vitskøl, Varnhem, and Nydala.

47. In the same year (1412, nr. 36), Brother Thurstan of Sorø was allowed to become a monk despite illegitimate birth, perhaps a fringe benefit to make Sorø's troubles more worthwhile.

48. Canivez 1419, nr. 27. Again a consolation was added: Henrik Nigrarus, monk of Esrum, at the abbot's request was dispensed of the disadvantage of illegitimate birth and allowed to hold any office except that of abbot (nr. 33).

49. Canivez 1423, nr. 8; 1425, nr. 27; 1434, nr. 25; 1443, nr. 35.

50. Canivez 1451, nr. 36: ... *multa enormia commiserunt, Ordinem diffamando.*

51. Canivez 1451, nr. 37: ... *abbas de Vitae Schola licet a suo ordine excommunicatus nihilominus celebrat, irregularitatem incurrendo et Ecclesiae claves parvipendendo*....

52. Canivez 1462, nr. 54.

53. Canivez 1472, nr. 44: *multis egregiis laboribus.*

54. Canivez 1473, nr. 51: *gravissimos excessus et enormes abusus.*

55. Canivez 1487, nr. 7.

56. Canivez 1487, nr. 98 and 62: ... *sine tamen preiudicio patris abbatis praedicti quem iure suo propter hoc privare praesens capitulum minime intendit, quotienscumque ipse aut per alium commissarium abbatem huiusmodi visitationis officium voluerit exercere.*

57. DD III, 5, 378 = Sorø Book f. 40r (31 October 1360): ... *in qua nobis ac dictis abbati et conventui precipuum ius competit patronatus.*

58. *Dän Bibl.* VII, 177 (15 November 1371): ... *recognoscimus dilectos dominos hospitalitatis gratia nec alicuius procurationis seu debiti praedicta necessaria nobis ministrasse.* Also 20 November 1361 (date not certain), DD III, 6, 108. The formula is the same.

59. SRD VIII, 199 (14 October 1367), Bishop Mogens. SRD VIII, 198 (18 January 1399), Bishop Eskil.

60. SRD VIII, 239 (17 May 1397).

61. *De ældste danske Archivregistraturer* (ÆA), ed. T.A. Becker, I (Cpn., 1854) and IV (1885). ÆA I, 232.

62. 1377: ÆA I, 234. 1385: ÆA I, 234.

63. SRD IV, 472 = Sorø Book f. 34 (30 September 1375): ... *ecclesiam in Toaker nostre diocesis in qua dictis abbati et conventui precipuum jus competit patronatus, de jure vacantem per liberam resignationem domini Benedicti canoni dudum rectoris ejusdem....*

64. DD III, 6, 343 = SRD IV, 522.

65. *Cod. Esrom.* 180, nr. 179.

66. *Cod. Esrom.* 153, nr. 137 = DD III, 5, 111.

67. *Ibid: Insuper predicti bondones, expressa et viva voce considerantes curialitatem quam sibi dictum monasterium impendisse asserebant.*

68. *Cod. Esrom.* 104, nr. 95 = DD III, 6, 225.

69. Lindbæk (see note 26 above) quotes extensively from a manuscript in the Bartholin collection (D 676) at the Royal Library in Copenhagen in which the course of events is described.

70. Lindbæk, 269–71.

71. Lindbæk, 274.

72. G.W. Woodward, *The Dissolution of the Monasteries* (London, 1969), 3 'The Quality of Religious Life', 30–42.

73. Canivez 1491, nr. 38: *Capitulum generale abbatibus de Sora, de Esrom, et de Herivado, et*

cuilibet eorum, mandat et praecipit, ut modis et mediis possibilibus secundum formam in statutis, privilegiis et diffinitionibus Ordinis contentam et expressam, viriliter et exacte defendant, tueantur, et protegant libertates, immunitates, exemptiones et privilegia, Ordinis nova et vetera, loca et personas Ordinis contra reverendissimum in Christo patrem, dominum episcopum Roskildensem, impetratorem cuiusdam commissionis a Sanctissimo domino nostro papa, sub praetextu falsi, ut videtur, ad visitandum monasteria Ordinis in sua diocesi existentia . . . inhibens districtissime ne eidem episcopo in aliquo contra privilegiorum et statutorum Ordinis praemissorum tenores pareant seu obediant quovismodo. . . .

74. Arup, *Danmarks Historie* IIA, 136–44.

75. DD III, 5, 327 = SRD VIII,153.

76. DD III, 5, 364 = SRD VIII, 156. DD III, 5, 303 = SRD VIII, 91.

77. *Cod. Esrom.* 169, nr. 156.

78. *Cod. Esrom.* 249, nr. 237 and 238 (3 and 22 February 1423): Søborg. 248, nr. 236 (27 July 1429): Roskilde.

79. *Cod. Esrom.* 253, nr. 243 (5 June 1452): Helsingør; 261, nr. 254 (14 October 1451) Hälsingborg.

80. *Cod. Esrom.* 233–39, nr. 221–28.

81. SRD IV, 526.

82. SRD IV, 524–5.

83. SRD IV, 510 and 527–8.

84. Nørlund (note 21 above), 84–5.

85. SRD IV, 523.

86. SRD IV, 523–4.

87. SRD IV, 524: . . . *ut scilicet et ipsi haberentur participes spiritualium bonorum et dictae fraternitatis in Sora in perpetuum.*

88. ÆA I, 225.

89. Ulsig, *Danske Adelsgodser i Middelalderen* VII, 'Sjællands Adel på Dronning Margrethes Tid', 155–197. The Queen bought up two central North Zealand estates, Hørsholm and Annisse, and thus deprived the monks of Esrum of any further share in them.

91. *Cod. Esrom.* 141, nr. 122 (28 June 1485): Berete Bondesdatter, wife of knight Johan Oxe, gave Esrum two farms in return for a daily mass at this altar. She specified which saints or religious events were to be commemorated on each weekday.
Cod. Esrom. 144, nr. 125 (9 October 1487): Niels Brahe's widow Magdalene gave a farm in Skåne in return for a once weekly mass at this altar.
Cod. Esrom. Tillæg 286, nr. 264. Johan Oxe gained an indulgence for all those who visited the altar (4 May 1418). 255, nr. 246 (21 October 1492): Jens Andersen of Helsingør made a gift to the altar.

92. At Næstved there is the same emphasis on masses at particular altars, and in 1388 Peder Finkenow founded the altar of St Olav in order to have a daily mass said: SRD IV, 402.

93. SRD IV, 539–45, 577–87.

94. *Western Society and the Church in the Middle Ages*, 'The Inflationary Spiral, c. 1300-c. 1520', 133–69.

95. SRD IV, 474, 499.

96. Grubbes: see Ulsig, 166–69. For Lunges, Ulsig, 174–78.

97. SRD IV, 476, 485, 486.

98. SRD IV, 476: ... *quod habeat eum fratres in sollempni memoria perpetuo et quod faciant pro eo, sicut pro aliis benefactoribus domus continue faciunt*....

99. SRD IV, 477: *Donationem Folmari atque commutationes Andreae praedictas magna sagacitate optinuit dominus abbas per repromissionem faciendi locationem bonorum ipsis ad vitam tam de collatis aut commutatis, quam de propriis et antiquiis bonis monasterii simul.*

100. *Cod. Esrom.* 104, nr. 95 = DD III, 6, 225.

101. *Rep.* 4072: ... *unde omne jus meum in prefatis bonis in Dominum abbatem et conventum in Sora transfero, tum quod me in sororem spiritualem gratiose collegerunt*.... *Insuper cum me migrare contigerit ex hac luce, omnia utensilia mea dicta bohawae dominis in Sora lego et que post obitum meum in eorum monasterio poterunt inveniri*.... (*bohawae*, in modern Danish *bohave*, refers to all movables).

102. Nørlund (note 21 above), 78–9.

103. *Rep.* 4072.

104. *Rep.* 4213, 4222.

105. DD III, 5, 223–26 = *Cod. Esrom.* 175–177, nr. 164–167.

106. As in 1355: DD III, 4 289 = *Cod. Esrom.* 172, nr. 160.

107. *Cod. Esrom.* 154, nr. 138 (22 July 1415): *Spiritu sancto inspirante considerans novissima mea, nichilque stabile manere sub sole, nisi quod in pias causas et viris religiosis divino servicio mancipatis ad salutem impenditur animarum.*

108. SRD IV, 499, 515.

109. I count thirty-six property transactions in the Sorø Donation Book for the years between 1380 and 1413, many of which appear to have been simple gifts. From 1414 to 1440, only eleven transactions are listed.

110. *Herreklostrenes Jordegods i det 16. århundrede og dets historie*: Den katolske Kirkes Jordegods i Århus Stift III (Cpn., 1957), p. 148.

111. In 1385, Poul Olufsen, a priest in Århus, mortgaged a farm in Firgård, north of Dover (whose church the monks had) and so of great value to the monks: ÆA I, 234. In 1400 the monks got a property in Hårby from a member of the village gentry: ÆA I, 232.

112. Albrectsen (note 3 above), 117–18.

113. Albrectsen, 145–46.

114. SRD VIII, 234: *Quia bellorum importunitate et pravorum insultu terra undique turbatur,*

ne monasterium Loci Dei, quod mei progenitores temporibus retroactis plurimum foverant, ab imminentibus malis ex toto desoletur, ex divini amoris affectu servorum dei in eodem monasterio commorantium assidue peticioni benigniter inclinatus, preconsiderata ipsorum erga me meamque cognationem in quam pluribus charitativis obsequiis benigna voluntate....

115. SRD VIII, 7.

116. For the continuing tradition of Cistercian gain in England from aristocratic families, especially from nobles on their deathbeds, see Joel T. Rosenthal, *The Purchase of Paradise: The Social Function of Aristocratic Benevolence* (London, 1972), esp. pp. 83–84.

117. SRD VIII, 83: *Et insuper indulgeo predictis et fratribus suisque servitoribus et colonis omnem incuriam et offensam, quas mihi vel meis servitoribus intulerant aliquando et promitto, quod ipsis de cetero non imputabitur quovis modo sed ex me et meis fraternam amicitiam et promotionem amodo habeant, ut ipsi pro me iugiter deum intercedant.*

118. SRD VIII, 167. For the earlier dispute, SRD VIII, 164.

119. SRD VIII, 80: *... homo mortalis nihil de mundo auffert preter opera, quibus vel iustificetur vel damnetur.*

120. SRD VIII, 7.

121. *Cod. Esrom.* 197, nr. 186.

122. SRD IV, 499.

123. SRD IV, 360.

124. See the chart of additions in H.J. Helms, *Næstved St. Peders Kloster*, 357–8.

125. Antvorskov's records are so rich for this period that they deserve a study in themselves. See for example ÆA IV, 254 (1393); 142 (1394); 69, 84, 104 (1395); 129 (1396). For 1397, ÆA IV, 94, property mortgage to the abbey; 99, alienates its own property; 139, another mortgage to the abbey; 142, Slagelse citizens sell land to Antvorskov; 174, Antvorskov pays back a large sum on a mortgage; 237, gift of a property in Slagelse by a priest; 229, gains a property in the town of Næstved.

126. ÆA IV, 103. See Ulsig, pp. 173–4.

127. *Rep.* 3002 (1373).

128. *Rep.* 3423 (11 November 1383): Michael, abbot of Sorø, is called by the prioress Margrethe Troelsdatter, 'our superior'. *Rep.* 3836 (21 December 1391): Troels is abbot of Esrum, and the document is sealed in the presence of Queen Margrethe.

129. Nørlund (note 21 above), p. 113.

130. Nørlund, p. 114.

131. Mackeprang, 'Løgumkloster og dets gods', *Sønderjydske Årbøger* 1945, p. 86.

132. KS 7 (1869–71), 865–66.

133. *Danmarks Kirker. Frederiksborg Amt* 2 (1967), 1042.

134. *In 1350 Øm gained six farms (DD III, 3, 370). In 1351 one farm (DD III, 3, 520), and in 1352–60, no farms at all.*

135. The first such is for Benedictine Vor on Mossø near Øm, DD III, 5, 179–81, in 1358.

136. Again the Benedictines are in the lead: Vor, DD III, 5, 270 (1359); Næstved, DD III, 5, 397 (1360).

137. *Cod. Esrom.* 153, nr. 137 = DD III, 5, 111; 152, nr. 136 = DD III, 5, 112.

138. SRD IV, 508 = DD III, 6, 171.

139. DD III, 6, 96 (23 October 1361).

140. *Rep.* 341 (undated but c. 1380).

141. Løgum, SRD VIII, 154 = DD III, 7, 449 (7 November 1366). The lack of records for other mortgagings of Cistercian land may well be due to the monks' tendency only to record property they gained and not to account for what they lost, unless it was an exchange.

142. Løgum: SRD VIII, 83 (25 May 1389). Sorø: SRD IV, 507 (1405), SRD IV, 517 (1417).

143. Lindbæk (note 26 above), p. 264: *Dicti abbas et conventus eosdem incolas... eorumque pueros et proles in dictis suis grangiis seu villis natos et commorantes pro eorum arbitrio vendere et donare consueverunt sepeque vendiderunt et donarunt....*

144. See the helpful article 'Bonde' in KLNMA II, 84–89.

145. See especially the work of C.A. Christensen, Erik Ulsig, and Troels Dahlerup given in the bibliography.

146. *Cod. Esrom.* 264–76, nr. 257. This list has not been treated in detail and deserves further study and analysis beyond my summary here.

147. Poul Rasmussen (note 110 above), p. 63.

148. Canivez 1489, nr. 67: *Quia monasterium de Esrum, ut dolenter accepit praesens Generale Capitulum, in spirituali et temporali regimine plurimum est defectuosum....*

149. The Danish historian Thelma Jexlev of the Royal Archives considers the exactions made on Esrum's peasants to have been demanding. See her *Fra dansk senmiddelalder* (Odense, 1976), p. 44.

150. The list even mentions two abandoned farms in the abbey's home parish of Esbønderup: *Cod. Esrom.* p. 272. Not far away in Græsted parish, a third of the farm is said to 'lie deserted' (*ligger øde*), p. 274.

151. *Landbo* is about the same as the Latin *colonus*, and *gårdsæde* as *inquilinus*. See again the section *Bonde* in KLNMA II, 85.

152. *Cod. Esrom.* 275–76.

153. Olaf Olsen, 'Krønike og udgravning: Øm kloster i historisk og arkæologisk belysning', *Convivium* 1979, 1–22. I should like to thank Professor Olsen, leader of the excavation, and Holger Garner, head of Øm Kloster Museum, for their help in informing me of the results of these excavations.

154. Ole Schiørring, 'Lægbrødrefløjen på Øm kloster', *Løgumkloster Studier* 2 (1979), 1–34. Again I owe thanks to Ole Schiørring for keeping me up to date with his work.

155. Alison Luchs, 'Alive and Well in Florence: Thriving Cistercians in Renaissance Italy', *Citeaux: Commentarii Cistercienses* 30 (1979), 109–24.

156. Nørlund (note 21 above), 114–15.

157. Lindbæk (note 26 above), 282–3.

158. Mackeprang (note 131 above), 20–21. SRD IV, 577.

159. Helge Toldberg, *Den Danske Rimkrønike* I (Cpn., 1961), whose conclusions are based on the work of Johannes Brøndum-Nielsen, *Om Rimkrønikens Sprogform og Tilblivelse* (Cpn., 1930), esp. pp. 81, 96. Brother Niels, mentioned as the author in the Low German edition, is thus considered to have been the final author/editor after a long line of composers.

160. Toldberg I, p. 138. Unfortunately there is no version of the full Rhyme Chronicle in modern Danish. Excerpts are contained in *Danske Middelalderlitteratur* 2 (Institut for Nordisk Filologi, Copenhagen University: 1971), 58–59:

> Ee hvo som så uskellig gør
> at han det hader, som Gud tilhør
> og tager det Gud er givet,
> han må sig vente stort vedermod
> uden han gør derfor skellig bod
> thi lade sig heller blive det
> Da jeg fik Danmarks rige bold
> jeg ingen mand retvished holdt
> Desvær at jeg så turde
> kirken tog jeg sin tiende fra,
> med folk, heste, hunde også
> jeg klostre fattige gjorde
> . . .
> I Finderup blev jeg slagen ihjel
> fordi jeg lev'de foruden skel
> og tog det . . . Gud tilhørte (relative pronoun missing here)

These last lines (In Finderup I was murdered/because I lived outside the law/And took what belonged to God) provide a unique medieval commentary on the otherwise unexplained mystery of the murder of King Erik Glipping in 1286. A talented contemporary Danish writer, Ebbe Kløvedal Reich, apparently without knowing this passage in the Rhyme Chronicle, has written an intriguing historical novel in which he tries to solve the riddle of the king's murder by asserting it to have been the result of an international conspiracy made by the Cistercians, the papacy, and a German crusading order, to subject Denmark to their policies. Abbot Ture of Øm becomes one of the villains of this scenario. The novel is a hardly veiled attempt to provide a medieval instance of what Reich considers to be a constant and growing threat against Danish and Nordic independence. The papacy and the Cistercian Order are for him manifestations of the same autocratic spirit as the capitalist European Common Market is today. Although I find Reich's interpretations of historical events somewhat insensitive to the actual roles of the Cistercians in Danish society, his book does show the continuing fascination such an international monastic order can exercise on a post-Protestant Danish left wing intellectual. (*Festen for Cæcilie*, Gyldendal, 1979). See Kai Hørby, *Status Regni Dacie* (Cpn., 1977) for a more sober review of what can be known about this murder.

161. Toldberg I, 151–52.

162. Toldberg, p. 112.

163. Toldberg, 124–25, 127.

164. Toldberg, 116–17.

165. Verner Dahlerup, 'Tre litterære Munke i Sorø Kloster', *Sorø: Klostret, Skolen, Akademiet gennem Tiderne* I, 141:

Tusind halvfemtesinde type paa det femte Aar
efter at Guds søn fødder vaar
blev jeg til konning i Danmark sæt
med Danes Vilje og god Endrægt
Men siden der efter Aar vel try
blev Cisters Orden stigtet af ny
Da vorde os Gud saa mild og blid,
at vi finge da saa god en Tid,
at bedste Skæppe Mel eller Malt
ej mere end to Penninge galdt.

166. Toldberg I, 141, 149, 152.

167. Canivez 1473, nr. 44 and 45. The decision merits full quotation.

Cum ex studiorum, virorumque litteratorum institutione et conservatione potiores salutis et honoris fructus nasci et prodire videantur, solet Capitulum generale studioso mentis affectu suae considerationis oculos ad talia convertere, quare in diversis terrarum partibus viros doctos, eximios et claros efficere et nutrire cupiens et praesertim in praeclarissimo Daniae regno ac provinciis circumvicinis, praesens Capitulum generale ea qua potest districtione et sub gravissimis poenis mandat et praecipit abbati de Sora, quatinus sive in unum evocando patres eiusdem regni sive alias prout congruentius invenerit, eisdem et eorum cuilibet auctoritate Capituli generalis, in virtute salutaris obedientiae praecipiat et iniungat, quod studium iam dudum per Ordinem declaratum et mandatum reincipientibus ipsum eorum expensis, prout quemlibet concernit, et concernere potest, perficiant, et ad habitandum scolares secundum formam Ordinis ad studendum et proficiendum in moribus et scientiis cum provisionibus necessariis et secundum exigentiam patriae requisitus transmittant et interteneant, nec in dedecus et detrimentum eorundem regni et Ordinis longius tempus et expensas perdent, dicti scholares evagari cogantur aut omnino ignari et indocti ignominiose permaneant.

168. See Lekai, Ch. 7, 'The Challenge of Scholasticism', 77–90.

169. An intriguing and humorous passage included in Peder Olsen's *Collectanea* as part of a dedication of the Rhyme Chronicle to King Christian I jousts with the idea that the brothers should be paid for their chronicle writing, an indication that the Rhyme Chronicle was a work meant as a link with secular society and especially with the monarchy:

Thet er os brødre y Soer pa sagt
at oss shulle rente were til lagt
thet wy shulle chrønicken scriffve
thet er doch ey y sandhet saa
men kunde wy nogen rente faa
wy wille that gerne bedriffve.

Den Danske Rimkrønike II: *Danske Fragmenter* (Cpn., 1938).

170. *Cod. Esrom.* 276, nr. 258 (26 June 1492), a papal bull from September 1487, which was witnessed by the abbot of Æbelholt after the Sorø monk Hans Pedersen asked that it be rendered into Danish *for lefhfolk skild* (for the sake of lay people). The bull was translated into Danish by Master Anders Persen, monk at Esrum, on the request of Abbot Peder of Esrum. *Cod. Esrom.* Tillæg nr. 267, p. 288. (12 January 1494).

171. Verner Dahlerup (note 165 above), p. 145.

172. Kristian Isager, *Skeletfundene ved Øm Kloster* (Cpn., 1936).

173. *Danmarks Kirker. Frederiksborg Amt* 2 (1967), 1052–58.

174. *Danmarks Kirker. Tønder Amt* (Cpn., 1957), 1096–1100.

BIBLIOGRAPHY

A. MANUSCRIPT SOURCES

COPENHAGEN Royal Library (Det kongelige Bibliotek)

MS. Gl. kgl. S. 54, fol.	Løgum Abbey: Peter of Riga's *Aurora*
MS. Gl. kgl. S. 450, fol.	Absalon's Justinus and *Annales Sorani* 1202–1347.
MS. Gl. kgl. S. 2485, 40	Sorø Donation Book
MS. Ny. kgl. S. 13, 8°	Vitskøl's *Compendium theologice veritatis*
MS. Ny. kgl. S. 1173, 4°	Vitskøl Book
MS. Ny. kgl. S.2043, 2°	Edvard Ortved's notes on Danish monastic history
MS. E don. variorum 135, 4°	The Øm Book
MS. E don. variorum 138, 4°	Herrisvad: Biblical commentary
MS. E don. variorum 140, 4°	*Codex Esromensis*

The Arnemagnæanske Institute

MS. AM 29c, fol.	Sorø Book
MS. AM 291, fol.	Sorø Donation Book and Vitskøl narration
MS. AM 455, 12°	Sorø law collection

STOCKHOLM Royal Library

MS. Kung. Bibl. K7	Sixteenth century notations concerning Herrisvad Abbey

B. PRINTED SOURCES (unless otherwise noted, the place of publication is Copenhagen)

Aakjær, Sven. *Kong Valdemars Jordebog* (1945).

Becker, T.A. *De ældste Danske Archivregistraturer* I (1845), IV (1885).

Bruun, Chr. *Broder Russes Historie* 1555 (1868).

Canivez, J.M. *Statuta Capitulorum Generalium Ordinis Cisterciensis*(Bibliothèque de la Revue d'Histoire Ecclésiastique 9–14B: Louvain, 1933–41).

Chibnall, Marjorie. *The Ecclesiastical History of Orderic Vitalis* (Oxford Medieval Texts, 1973: Volume 4, Books 7 and 8).

Christensen, C.A. *Corpus Codicum Danicorum medii aevi* 2 (1960) Includes facsimile of Øm Book.

Christiansen, C.P.O. *Bernard af Clairvaux*. Hans Liv fortalt af Samtidige og et Udvalg af hans Værker og Breve. (Selskabet for Historiske Kildeskrifters Oversættelse, 1926).

Danmarks Riges Breve Det danske Sprog-og Litteraturselskab (1938-).

Dänische Bibliothec oder Sammlung von Alten und Neuen Gelehrten Sachen aus Dännemarch VI (Copenhagen und Leipzig, 1745).

Danske Magazin. 1-6 (1745-52). *Nye Danske Magazin* 1- (1794-).

Dansk Middelalderlitteratur. Institut for nordisk filologi 2 (1971).

Diplomatarium Danicum. Det danske Sprog-og Litteraturselskab (1938-).

Diplomatarium diocesis Lundensis. Lund Ärkestifts Urkundsbog, ed. Lauritz Weibull (Monumenta Scaniae Historica: Lund. III-1900; IV- 1909).

Diplomatarium Suecanum.   I-817-1285 (Stockholm, 1829), ed. J.G. Liljegren
II-1286-1310 (1837)
III-1311-26 (1842-50) ed. Bror Emil Hildebrand

Erslev, Kr. *Repertorium Diplomaticum Regni Danici Mediœvalis.* Danmarks Breve fra Middelalderen, II: 1351-1400. (1896-98).

Testamenter fra Danmarks Middelalder indtil 1450 (1901).

Friedberg, Aemilius. *Corpus Iuris Canonici.* Edition Secunda, Pars 1-2. Leipzig, 1879-81.

Gertz, M.Cl. *Scriptores Minores Historiae Danicae Medii Aevi* I-II; Selskabet for Udgivelse af Kilder til Dansk Historie. 1917-22. Reprinted 1970.

Vitae Sanctorum Danorum; Selskabet for Udgivelse af Kilder til Dansk Historie, 1908-1912.

Greisser, Bruno. 'Statuten von Generalkapiteln ausserhalb Citeaux. Wien 1393 und Heilsbronn 1398', *Cistercienser Chronik* 62 (1955) 65- 83.

'Unbekannte Generalkapitelstatuten', *Cistercienser Chronik* 64 1957) 1-20 and 41-60.

Exordium Magnum Cisterciense sive Narratio de Initio Cisterciensis Ordinis auctore Conrado; Series Scriptorum S. Ordinis Cisterciensis II. Rome, 1961.

Helgesen, Poul. *Skiby Krøniken*, trans. to Danish by A Heise; Selskabet til historiske Kilders Oversættelse. Reprinted 1967 by Rosenkilde and Bagger.

Hasse, P. *Schleswig-Holstein-Lauenburgische Regesten und Urkunden* I -II. Leipzig and Hamburg, 1886-88; Reprinted 1972.

Jaffé, P. *Regesta Pontificum Romanorum* I-II (ad annum 1198). Leipzig, 1885-88.

Janauschek, P. Leopoldus. *Originum Cisterciensium* I. Vienna, 1877.

Jexlev, Thelma. *Lokalarkiver til 1559: Gejstlige Arkiver* I: Ærkestiftet og Roskilde Stift; Vejledende Arkivregistraturer XVII. Rigsarkivet, 1973.

Jørgensen, Ellen. *Annales Danici Medii Aevi*; Selskabet for Udgivelse af Kilder til Dansk Historie. 1920.

Catalogus Codicum Latinorum Medii Aevi Bibliothecae Regiae Hafniensis. 1928.

'Ribe bispekrønike', KS 6R, I (1933) 23-33.

Krarup, Alfred. *Katalog over Universitetsbibliotekets Haandskrifter 1-2.* 1929-35.

Bullarium Danicum. Pavelige Aktstykker vedrørende Danmark. 1198-1316. (1931-32).

Krarup and Johns. Lindbæk. *Acta Pontificum Danica* II. 1907.

Langebæk, Jakob and Suhm, P.F. *Scriptores Rerum Danicarum Medii Aevi* I-IX. 1772-1878.

Lorenzen, M. *Gammeldanske Krøniker*; Samfundet til Udgivelse af Gammel Nordisk Litteratur. 1887-1913.

Meklenburgisches Urkundenbuch. Verein für Mecklenburgische Geschichte und Alterthumskunde I-786-1250 (Schwerin, 1863) II-1251-80 (1864)

Migne, J.P. *Patrologia Latina* 185: The *Vita Prima* of Bernard of Clairvaux.

Moltesen, L. *Bullarium Danicum.* Pavelige Aktstykker vedrørende Danmark. 1316-1536 (1904).

Nielsen, O. *Codex Esromensis.* Esrom Klosters Brevbog; Selskabet for Udgivelse af Kilder til Dansk Historie, 1880-81. Photographic reprint, 1973.

Olrik, Hans. *Danske Helgeners Levned*; Selskabet for historiske Kildeskrifters Oversættelse, 1892-4. Reprinted 1968, Rosenkilde og Bagger).

Otto, Alfred. *Liber daticus Roskildensis.* Roskilde Gavebog og Domkapitlets Anniversarieliste. 1933.

Pertz, G.H. *Monumenta Germaniae historica.* Scriptores rerum Germanicarum XIX, 715-719: *Annales Colbazienses.*

Potthast, A. *Regesta Pontificum Romanorum* I-II. 1874-75.

Powicke, Maurice. *The Life of Ailred of Rievaulx* by Walter Daniel, Edinburgh: Nelson Medieval Texts, 1950.

Prümers, Rodg. and Klempin, Rob. *Pommersches Urkundenbuch.* Stettin, 1868-1907, Volume I reprinted in 1970.

Saxo *Saxonis Gesta Danorum* I: Text ed. J. Olrik et H. Ræder. 1931.
II: Indicem Verborum ed. Franz Blatt. 1957.

Schmitt, F.S. *S. Anselmi Opera Omnia* III, Edinburgh, 1946.

Schneider, Ambrosius. 'Vita B. David Monachi Hemmenrodenses', *Analecta* 11 (1955) 27-48.

Southern, R.W. *The Life of Saint Anselm* by Eadmer. Oxford Medieval Texts, 1972.

Suhm, P.F. *Samlinger til den danske Historie* I-II. 1779-81.
Nye Samlinger til den danske Historie. 1792-95.

Séjalon, Hugo. *Nomasticon Cisterciense.* Solesmes, 1892.

Talbot, C.H. 'The Testament of Gervase of Louth Park', *Analecta* 7 (1951) 32-45.

Thorkelin, G. *Diplomatarium Arna-Magnæanum* I. 1786.

Toldberg, Helge. *Den danske Rimkrønike* I-III. 1958-1961.

Weeke, C. *Libri memoriales capituli Lundensis.* Lunde Domkapitels Gavebøger. 1884-89: reprinted 1973.

Weibull, Lauritz. 'En samtida berättelse om ärkebiskop Eskil av Lund', *Scandia* 9 (1931) 270-90.
Necrologium Lundense. Lunds Domkyras Nekrologium; Monumenta Scaniae historica. Lund, 1923.

C. SECONDARY WORKS (except for periodicals, the place of publication is Copenhagen unless otherwise noted)

Albrectsen, Esben. 'Den holstenske adels indyandring i Sønderjylland i det 13.-14. århundrede', *Historisk Tidsskrift* 74 (1974).

Andersen, Niels Knud. 'Striden mellem Øm kloster og Aarhusbisperne. Et Forsøg paa en ny Forstaaelse', *Dansk Teologisk Tidsskrift* (1939) 129-146.

D'Arbois de Jubainville, M.H. *Etudes sur l'Etat Intérieur des Abbayes Cisterciennes et Principalement de Clairvaux au XIIe et au XIIIe Siècle.* Paris, 1858.

Arhnung, J.O. *Roskilde Domkapitels Historie* I: Tiden indtil 1416. Roskilde, 1937.

Arup, Erik. 'Leding og ledingsskat i det 13. århundrede', *Historisk Tidsskrift* 8 R: V B. (1914-15) 141-237.

    Danmarks Historie I, til 1282 (1925); IIA-B: 1282-1624 (1932) Reprinted 1961.

Asschenfeldt Birkebæk, C. 'Mossø klostrenes omstridte fiskegårde ved Vosgård', *Århus Stifts Årbøger* 56 (1963) 41-58.

Baker L.G.D. 'The Genesis of English Cistercian Chronicles. The Foundation History of Fountains Abbey', *Analecta* 25 (1969) 14-41.

Bartholdy, Olga. *Munkeliv i Løgum Kloster* (Løgumkloster, 1973).

Bloch, Marc. *Feudal Society*, trans. L.A. Manyon 1-2. Chicago, 1965.

Bock, P. Colomban. 'Les Cisterciens et l'Etude du Droit', *Analecta* 7 (1951) 14-20.

Bolvig, Axel. 'Stridighederne omkring Brede kirke 1250-1350', HT 77 (1977) 85-95.

Boserup, Ivan, ed. *Saxostudier*. Saxo-kollokvierne ved Københavns Universitet; Museum Tusculanum, Opuscula Græcolatina 2. 1975.

Bredero, Adriaan. 'Etudes sur la Vita Prima de Saint Bernard', *Analecta* 17 (1961) 1-72, and 18 (1962) 1-59.

    'Saint Bernard and the Historians', *St. Bernard of Clairvaux: Studies Commemorating the Eighth Anniversary of his Canonization*, ed. M. Basil Pennington (Cistercian Studies Series 28: Kalamazoo, Michigan, 1977) 27-62.

Brentano, Robert. *Rome before Avignon*. London, 1974.

Brønsted, Johannes and Nørlund, Poul. *Seks Tværsnit af Danmarks Historie*. 1941. Paperback, 1966.

Brøndum-Nielsen, Johs. *Om Rimkrønikens Sprogform og Tilblivelse*. 1930.

Buchwald, G.V. 'Die Gründungsgeschichte von øm und die dänischen Cistercienser', *Zeitschrift der Gesellschaft für Schleswig-Holstein-Lauenburgische Geschichte* 8 (1878) 1-121.

Canivez, J.M. 'Citeaux (Abbaye)' and 'Citeaux (Ordre)' in *Dictionnaire d'Histoire et de Géographie Ecclésiastique* XIII (Paris, 1953) col. 852 -997.

Chauvin, Benoit. 'Les Décisions des Chapitres Géneraux de l'Ordre Cistercien Concernant l'Abbaye de Balerne au XIIᵉ et XIIIᵉ Siècles', *Citeaux. Commentarii Cistercienses* 23 (1972) 160-170.

Cheney, C.R. *Episcopal Visitation of Monasteries in the Thirteenth Century*. Manchester, 1931.

Christensen, Aksel E. *Kongemagt og Aristokrati*. 1945. Reprinted 1968.

    'Archbishop Asser, the Emperor and the Pope', *Scandinavian Journal of History* I (1976) 25-42.

Christensen, C.A. 'Nedgangen i Landgilden i det 14. Århundrede', HT 10 R., I B (1930-31) 446-65.

    'Krisen på Slesvig Domkapitels Jordegods 1352-1437', HT 11 R, VI B (1960-62) 161-241.

    'Ændringerne i landsbyens økonomiske og sociale struktur i det 14. og 15. århundrede', HT 12 R, I B. (1964) 257-349.

Christensen, Villads. 'Knardrup Klosters Historie', *Fra Frederiksborg Amt* (1914) 72-99.

Christiansen, Tage E. *Danmarks Middelalder*. Nationalmuseets Vejledninger. 1972.

    'Yngre Sjællandske Krønikes Sidste Aar', *Scandia* 40 (1974) 5-33.

Clasen, Martin. 'Reinfeld und seine Äbte', *Schriften des Vereins für Schleswig-Hol-steinische Kirchengeschichte* 2:15–16 (1957–58) 17–84 and 7–96.

Constable, Giles. *Monastic Tithes*. From their Origins to the Twelfth Century; Cambridge Studies in Medieval Life and Thought X, 1964.

Cottineau, H. *Repertoire Top-Bibliographique des Abbayes et Prieurès* I–II. Macon, 1937.

Dahlerup, Troels. *Det danske sysselsprovsti i middelalderen*; Institut for dansk Kirkehistorie. 1968.

Dahlerup, Verner. 'Tre Litterære Munke i Sorø Kloster', *Sorø: Klostret, Skolen, Akademiet gennem Tiderne* I (1923) 132–145.

Damsholt, Nanna. 'Kingship in the Arengas of Danish Royal Diplomas 1140–1223', *Mediaeval Scandinavia* 3 (1970) 66–108.

'Abbed Vilhelm af Æbelholts brevsamling', HT 78 (1978) 1–22.

Danmarks Kirker. Published by Nationalmuseet (1933–), especially: II: Frederiksborg Amt 2 (1967): Esrum klosterkirke, pp. 1041–1062.

V Sorø Amt 1 (1926), pp. 17–108. Sorø klosterkirke.

XXI Tønder Amt (1957–58): Løgum klosterkirke, pp. 1050–1130.

Dansk Biografisk Leksikon, ed. by Poul Engelstoft. Volumes 1–26. 1933–44.

Daugaard, J.B. *Om de Danske Klostre i Middelalderen.* 1830.

Dictionnaire d'Histoire et de Géographie Ecclésiastiques. Paris, 1909–).

Donkin, R.A. 'The Urban Property of the Cistercians in Medieval England', *Analecta* 15 (1959) 104–131.

'The Cistercian Grange in England in the 12th and 13th Centuries with Special Reference to Yorkshire', *Studia Monastica* 6 (Barcelona, 1964) 95–144.

The Cistericans: Studies in the Geography of Medieval England and Wales (London, 1978).

Donnelly, James S. *The Decline of the Medieval Cistercian Laybrotherhood*; Fordham University Studies. History Series III. New York, 1949.

'Changes in the Grange Economy of English and Welsh Cistercian Abbeys 1300–1540', *Traditio* 10 (1954) 319–458.

Duby, Georges. *Rural Economy and Country Life in the Medieval West.* London, 1968.

The Early Growth of the European Economy. Ithaca, New York, 1979.

Edwards, Kathleen. *The English Secular Cathedrals in the Middle Ages.* Manchester, 1949.

Erslev, Kristian. *Dronning Margrethe og Kalmarunionens Grundlæggelse.* 1882, reprinted 1971.

Danmarks Riges Historie II: *Den Senere Middelalder* (no date, but c. 1900).

Historisk Teknik. 1911—reprinted often, most recently 1972.

Fang, A. *Roskilde Domkirke gennem 1000 År.* Roskilde, 1960.

Feine, Hans Erich. *Kirchliche Rechtsgeschichte* I: *Die katholische Kirche.* Weimar, 1954.

Fossier, Robert. 'Les Granges de Clairvaux et la Règle Cistercienne', *Citeaux in de Nederlanden* 6 (Westmalle, 1955) 259–266.

France, C.A.J. 'Lists of Danish Cistercian Abbots', *Analecta* 20 (1964) 185–198.

Gad, Tue. *Legenden i dansk middelalder.* 1961.

Garner, H.N. *Søhøjlandet.* 1965.

Atlas over danske klostre. 1968.

348 The Cistercians in Denmark

'Charteuserordenen i Danmark', *Århus Stifts Årbøger* 61 (1968) 54–84.

Øm Kloster Museum. Vejledning for besøgende. The Abbey of Øm. English Guide; Historisk Samfund for Århus Stift, 1973.

De Venders. Høbjerg, 1972.

Gilson, Etienne. *History of Christian Philosophy in the Middle Ages.* London, 1955.

Gissel, Svend. 'Forskningsrapport for Danmark', *Det nordiske Ødegårdsprojekt* 1 (1972) 3–71.

'Den senmiddelalderlige krise i Norden', *Kulturblomstring og samfundskrise i 1300-tallet,* ed. Brian McGuire (Middelaldercentralen Copenhagen University, 1979) 183–92.

Godt, Christian. 'Bischof Waldemar von Schleswig und die Cistercienser von Guldholm', ZGSHLG (1981) 138–186.

Gransden, Antonia. *Historical Writing in England* c. 550–c. 1307. London, 1974.

Graves, Coburn V. 'The Economic Activities of the Cistercians in Medieval England', *Analecta* 13 (1957) 3–60.

Green-Pedersen, Sv.E. 'Øm klosters grundlæggelse og dets forhold til bisp Sven af Århus', *Århus Stifts Årbøger* 57 (1964) 174–246.

'Studier over de danske cistercienserklostres forhold til ordenens internationale styrelse og til den danske kirke og det danske samfund indtil ca. 1340' (unpublished *speciale* at Det historiske Institut, Copenhagen, 1969).

Hall, Fr. 'Beiträge zur Geschichte der Cistercienser Klöster in Schweden', *Cistercienser Chronik* 15 (1903) 193–95.

Hallinger, P. Kassius. 'Woher kommen die laienbrüder', *Analecta* 12 (1956) 1–104.

Hansen, Jørgen Quistgaard. 'Regnum et Sacerdotium. Forhold et mellem stat og kirke i Danmark 1157-70', *Middelalderstudier Tilegnede Aksel E. Christensen* (1966) 57–76.

Haugsted, Ejler. 'Benediktinernes Kirke i Veng', *Århus stifts Årbøger* 30 (1937) 165–95.

Heffer, M.W. *Die Geschichte des Klosters Lehnin.* Brandenburg, 1851.

Helms, Hans Jørgen. *Næstved St. Peders Kloster* 1-2. Næstved, 1940

Hertzsprung, Ivar. 'De danske Klostres Styrelse og økonomiske Forhold samt Klosterbygningerne i Tiden 1202–1319', HT 7 R, 5 B (1904–1905) 299–364.

Hill, Bennett D. *English Cistercian Monasteries and their Patrons in the Twelfth Century.* Urbana, Illinois, 1968.

'Archbishop Thomas Becket and the Cistercian Order', *Analecta* 27 (1971) 64–80.

Hirsch, Hans. *Die Klosterimmunität seit dem Investiturstreit.* Untersuchungen zur Verfassungsgeschichte des deutschen Reiches und der deutschen Kirche. Weimar, 1913; reprinted 1967.

Hoogeweg, H. *Die Stifter und Klöster der Provinz Pommern* I–II. Stettin, 1924–25.

Huizinga, J. *The Waning of the Middle Ages.* (Harmondsworth; Penguin, 1965.)

Hørby, Kai. *Academia Sorana: Kloster, Akademi, Skole.* 1962.

Status Regni Dacie: Studier i Christofferlinjens ægteskabs- og alliancepolitik 1252–1319. (1977).

Danmarks historie II. Gyldendal, 1980.

Dansk socialhistorie: Middelalderen. 1980.

Danmarks historie II. Gyldendall, 1980.

Dansk Socialhistorie: Middelaldern. 1980.

Jensen, H.N.V. *Angeln* zunächst für die Angler historische beschrieben; Schriften zur schleswigschen Geschichte, II. Flensburg, 1922.

Jexlev, Thelma. *Fra dansk senmiddelalder: Nogle kildestudier*; Odense University Studies in History and Social Sciences, Vol. 29. Odense, 1976.

Johannesson, Kurt. *Saxo Grammaticus: Komposition och Världsbild i Gesta Danorum.* Stockholm, 1978.

Johannesson, Hilding. *Ritus Cisterciensis.* Studier i de svenska Cisterciensklostrens Liturgi; Bibliotheca theologiae practicae 18. Lund, 1964.

Johnsen, Arne Odd. *De norske cistercienserklostre* 1146–1264; Det Norske Videnskaps-Akademi: II. Hist. Filos. Klasse Avhandlinger. Ny Serie, No. 15. Oslo, 1977.

Johnsen, Arne Odd and King, Peter. *The Tax Book of the Cistercian Order*; Det Norske Videnskaps Akademi—II. Hist. Filos. Klasse Avhandlinger. Ny Serie. No. 16. Oslo, 1979.

Jørgensen, A.D. 'Striden mellem Biskop Tyge og Øm Kloster', *Aarbøger for Nordisk Oldkyndighed og Historie* (1879) 111–153.

Jørgensen, Ellen. *Historieforskning og historieskrivning i Danmark indtil år 1800.* Second edition: 1960.

'Djævelen i Vitskøl Kloster', *Danske Studier* (1912) 15–17.

'Studier over danske middelalderlige Bogsamlinger', HT 8R, 4B (1912–13) 1–67.

Jørgensen, Poul Johs. *Dansk Retshistorie.* 1947.

King, Peter. 'The Cathedral Priory of Odense in the Middle Ages', KS 7R, VI (1966) 1–20.

'Cistercian Financial Organisation 1335–92', *Journal of Ecclesiastical History* 24 (1973) 127–43.

Kjerulf, A.C.A. *Esrom Klosters Historie.* 1836.

Kjærsgaard, Erik. *Borgerkrig og Kalmarunion* 1241–1448; Politikens Danmarks Historie 4. Second edition, 1970.

Knowles, David. *The Monastic Order in England* 940–1216. Cambridge, 1940; Rpt. 1966.

The Religious Orders in England I, 1216–1340. Cambridge, 1948; Rpt. 1962).

Koch, Hal. 'De ældste danske Klostres Stilling i Kirke og Samfund indtil 1221', HT 10 R, III B (1936), 511–582.

Reprinted in *Danmarks Kirke i den begyndende Højmiddelalder*; Det historiske Institut ved Københavns Universitet. Historiske Afhandlinger. Bind 8. 1972.

Den Danske Kirkes Historie 1: *Den ældre Middelalder indtil 1241.* 1950.

Kongemagt og Kirke 1060–1241; Politikens Danmarks Historie. Second edition, 1969.

Kornerup, J. 'Minder om Dronning Margrethe Sprænghest i Rostock og Doberan', *Aarbøger for Nordisk Oldkyndighed og Historie* (1877) 55 –66.

'Minder om Cistercienserklostret i Esrom, om dets Stifter og dets Forbindelser med Clairvaux', *Aarbøger for Dordisk Oldkyndighed og Historie* (1879) 1–18, 239® 48.

'Om Esrom Klosters Forbindelse med Venden og de arkitektoniske Spor deraf', *Aarbøger for Nordisk Oldkyndighed og Historie* (1881) 1–37.

Krarup, Jens Kr.   *Løgumkloster før og nu.* Løgumkloster, 1974.

Krenig, Ernst G.   'Mittelalterliche Frauenklöster nach den Konstitutionen von Citeaux', *Analecta* 10 (1954) 1–105.

Kristensen, Anne K.G.   *Danmarks ældste Annalistik*: Studier over lundensisk annalskrivning i 12. og 13. århundrede; Skrifter udgivet af Det historiske Institut ved Københavns Universitet. Bind III. 1969.

Kuhlmann, Hans Joachim.   'Das Rudekloster und seine Vorgänger St. Michaelis Schleswig und Guldholm', *Jahrbuch des Angler Heimatvereins* 19 (1955) 81–87.

Kunkel, Adolf.   'Die Stiftungsbriefe für das meklenburg-pommersche Cistercienserkloster Dargun', *Archiv für Urkundenforschung* 3 (Leipzig, 1910) 23–80.

Ladewig Petersen, E.   'Jordprisforhold i dansk senmiddelalder', *Middelalderstudier tilegnede Aksel E. Christensen* (1966) 219–244.

'Preaching in Medieval Denmark', *Mediaeval Scandinavia* 3 (1971) 142–71.

Lange, Christian.   *De Norske Klostres Historie i Middelalderen.* Christiania, 1856.

Leclercq, Jean.   *The Love of Learning and the Desire for God.* New York: Fordham University Press, 1974.

'Comment vivaient les frères convers?', *Analecta* 21 (1965) 239–258.

Lekai, L.J.   *The White Monks.* Okauchee, Wisconsin, 1953.

Translated and revised: *Les Moines Blancs* (Paris, 1957). and translated by A. Schneider as *Geschichte und Wirken des weissen Mönche* (Cologne, 1958).

The Cistercians: Ideals and Reality (Kent, Ohio: Kent State University Press, 1977).

Lind, J.   'Klosterhaven i Øm', *Århus Stifts Årbøger* 24 (1931) 130–42.

Lindbæk, Johannes.   *De danske Franciskanerklostre.* 1914.

Lindbæk, Johannes.   *De danske Helligaandsklostre.* 1906.

and G. Stemann.   'Biskop Niels Skave og Sorø Kloster', HT 8R, IB (1907) 254–283.

Lindner, D.   *Die Lehre von der Inkorporation in ihrer geschichtlichen Entwicklung.* Munich, 1951.

Lorenzen, C.C.   'Nogle Bemærkninger om Guldholm Kloster', *Annaler for Nordisk Oldkyndighed og Historie* (1859) 319–26.

Lorenzen, Wilhelm.   *De danske Cistercienserklostres Bygningshistorie* (1941) (Volume XI of *De danske Klostres Bygningshistorie*, 1912–1941).

Luchs, Alison.   'Alive and Well in Florence: Thriving Cistercians in Renaissance Italy', *Citeaux: Commentarii Cistercienses* 30 (1979) 109–24.

Lynch, J.H.   'Cistercians and underage novices', *Citeaux: Commentarii Cistercienses* 24 (1973) 283–97.

Løffler, J.B.   *Ruinerne af Vitskøl Klosterkirke.* 1900.

Mackeprang, M.   'Løgum Kloster og dets Gods', *Søndorjydske Årbøger* (1945) 20–127.

Mahn, Jean-Berthold.   *L'Ordre Cistercien et Son Gouvernement des Origines au Milieu du XIIIe Siècle* (1098-1265; Bibliothèque des Ecoles Françaises d'Athènes et de Rome, 161. Paris, 1945.

Manitius, Max.   *Geschichte der Lateinischen Literatur des Mittelalter* II; Handbuch der Altertumswissenschaft, Neunter Band, Zweite Abteilung, 2 Teil. Munich, 1923.

Manteufel, Tadeusz. 'La Mission Balte de l'Ordre de Citeaux', in *La Pologne au* Xe *Congrès International des Sciences Historiques a Rome*. Warsaw, 1955.

McGuire, Brian Patrick. 'Property and Politics at Esrom Abbey: 1151-1251', *Mediaeval Scandinavia* 6 (1973) 122-150.

——— 'Love, friendship, and sex in the eleventh century: The experience of Anselm', *Studia Theologica* 28 (Oslo, 1974) 111-152.

——— 'Patrons, privileges, property: Sorø Abbey's first half century', KS (1974) 5-39.

——— *Conflict and Continuity at Øm Abbey*. A Cistercian Experience in Medieval Denmark; Museum Tusculanum. Opuscula Græcolatina: 1976.

——— 'Clairvaux og Nordens cisterciensere i 1100-tallet', *Løgumkloster Studier* 1 (1978) 11-29.

——— 'Written Sources and Cistercian Inspiration in Caesarius of Heisterbach', *Analecta* 35 (1979) 227-82.

——— 'Structure and Consciousness in the *Exordium Magnum Cisterciense*: The Clairvaux Cistercians after Bernard', *Cahiers de l'Institut du Moyen-Age Grec et Latin* 30 (1979) 33-90.

——— 'Friends and Tales in the Cloister: Oral Sources in Caesarius of Heisterbach's *Dialogus Miraculorum*', *Analecta* 36 (1980) 167-247.

——— 'The Cistercians and the Transformation of Monastic Friendships', *Analecta* 37 (1981).

Meer, Frédéric van der. *Atlas de l'Ordre Cistercien*. Paris-Brussels, 1965.

Mollat, G. *The Popes at Avignon* 1305-1378. New York: Harper, 1965.

Morris, Colin. *The Discovery of the Individual* 1050-1200. New York: Harper, 1973.

Musset, Lucien. *Les Peuples Scandinaves au Moyen-Age*. Paris, 1951.

Møller-Christensen, Vilh. *Bogen om Æbelholt Kloster*. 1958.

Neergaard, Carl. 'Bidrag til Danmarks Klosterhistorie', KS IV, 1 (1889-91) 56-90.

Nielsen, Holger Garner. 'Om tamt og vildt ved Øm', *Århus Stifts Årbøger* 55 (1962) 24-34.

——— 'Øm Kloster. Cara Insula gennem fire århundreder', *Århus Stifts Årbøger* 62 (1969).

Nissen, Andreas. *Danske Bisperækker*. 1935.

Norvin, William. 'Abbed Wilhelms Breve, Samlingens almindelige karakter', *Scandia* 6 (1933) 153-172.

Nyberg, Tore. *Birgittinische Klostergründungen des Mittelalters*; Bibliotheca Historica Lundensis xv. Leiden, 1965.

——— 'Klostren i abbot Wilhelms brev', KS (1971) 44-57.

——— 'Lists of monasteries in some thirteenth century wills. Monastic history and historical method: a contribution', *Mediaeval Scandinavia* 5 (1972) 49-74.

——— Eskil av Lund och Erik den helige', *Historia och samhälle. Studier tilägnade Jerken Rosen* (Lund, 1975) 5-21.

——— *Skt. Peters efterfølgere i brydningstider*. Omkring pavedømmets historie. Rom og Nordeuropa 750-1200; Odense Univ. Studies in History and Social Sciences, Vol. 58. 1979.

Nørlund, Poul. 'Klostret og dets Gods', *Sorø: Klostret, Skolen, Akademiet gennem Tiderne* I (1933) 53–131.
'Jorddrotter på Valdemarstiden', *Festskrift til Kristian Erslev* (1926) 141–170.
'De ældste vidnesbyrd om skyldtaxationen', HT 9R: VIB (1928– 29) 54–95.
Nørlund, Poul and Johannes Brøndsted. *Seks Tværsnit af Danmarks Historie* (1941; paperback 1966).
Olrik, Hans. 'Biskop Valdemar og den danske Krone', *Aarbøger for Nordisk Oldkyndighed og Historie* (1892) 342–284.
Konge og Præstestand i den danske Middelalder 1–2 (1892-95).
'Bidrag til Danmarks Kirkehistorie hentede fra Clairvaux og Citeaux', KS 4R, III (1893-95) 1–25, 421–5.
Viborgbispen Gunners Levned (Selskabet til historiske Kilders Oversættelse, 1892; reprinted Århus 1969).
Absalon 1–2 (1908–1909).
Abbed Vilhelm af Æbelholt. Nordsjællands Helgen. 1912.
Olrik, Jørgen. *Øm Klosters Krønike*; Historisk Samfund for Århus Amt. 1924; reprinted 1954).
Olsen, Olaf. 'Krønike og udgravning: Øm kloster i historisk og arkæologisk belysning', *Convivium* (1979) 1–22.
Olsen, Thomas Hatt. *Dacia og Rhodos*. 1962.
Olsson, Harald. 'Cistercienserklostret i Herrevad', *Säasä. Skånsk Samling* Del V (1947) 15–27.
Ortved, Edward. *Cistercieordenen og dens Klostre i Norden*
    I: *Cistercieordenen Overhovedet* (1927)
    II: *Sveriges Klostre* (1933).
'Von Generalkapiteln auf dem Festlande ausserhalb Citeaux während des grossen Schismas', *Cistercienser-Chronik* 38 (1926) 279–282.
Pedersen, P. Storgaard. 'Tvis Kloster', *Hårdsyssels Årbog* 9 (1915) 1–48.
Petersen, K.N. Henry. 'Øm Klosters Feide med Bispen af Aarhus i midten af det 13. Århundrede', *Historisk Archiv* I (1870).
Pfurtscheller, Friedrich. *Die Priviligierung des Zisterzienserordens im Rahmen des allgemeinen Schutz- und Exemptionsgeschichte*. Bern, 1972.
Preiss, Martin. *Die politische Tätigkeit und Stellung der Cisterzienser im Schisma von 1159-1177*; Historische Studien, 248. Berlin, 1934.
Rashdall, Hastings. *The Universities of Europe in the Middle Ages* 1895. Revised edition by F.M. Powicke and E.B. Emden: Oxford, 1936.
Rasmussen, Poul. *Den Katolske Kirkes Jordegods i Århus Stift*; Herreklostrenes jordegods i det 16. århundrede og dets historie. Østjydsk Njemstavn: Skanderborg, 1957.
Reich, Ebbe Kløvedal. *Festen for Cæcilie: Den hemmelige beretning om et kongemord*. 1979.
Riis, Thomas. *Les Institutions politiques centrales du Danemark* 1100– 1332; Odense University Studies in History and Social Sciences, Vol. 46. Odense, 1977.
Riising, Anne. *Danmarks Middelalderlige Prædiken*. 1969.
Rosenthal, Joel T. *The Purchase of Paradise*. Gift Giving and the Aristocracy 1307-1485; Studies in Social History. London, 1972.

Rørdam, H.F. 'Om de danske Klostre i Middelalderen', KS VI (1867–68) 460–76.
Kjøbenhavns Universitets Historie I. 1868–9.
'Efterretninger om de to sidste abbeder i Øm Kloster', KS 3R, III B
(1881–82) 94–111.

Schalling, Erik. 'Kanonisk eller nationell rätt. Ett bidrag til diskussionen om
1200-tallets danska immunitetsstrider', *Kyrkohistorisk Årsskrift* 1937 (38)
Uppsala) 103–34.

Schneider, Ambrosius. *Die Cistercienserabtei Himmerod im Spätmittelalter*;
Quellen und Abhandlungen zur Mittelreinischen Kirchengeschichte Band 1.
Speyer am Rhein, 1954.

Schneider, Ambrosius [et alii]. *Die Cistercienser. Geschichte. Geist. Kunst.* Cologne, 1974.

Schiørring, Ole. 'Lægbrødrefløjen på Øm kloster', *Løgumkloster Studier* 2
(1979) 1–34.

Skov, Torben. 'Tvis kloster-en foreløbig orientering om prøveudgravningen i
1978', *Holstebro Museum Årsskrift* 1978 (Holstebro, 1979).

Skovgaard-Petersen, Inge, Christensen, Aksel E., and Helge Paludan. *Danmarks
historie* I (tiden indtil 1340 (1977).

Skyum-Nielsen, Niels. 'De ældste privilegier for klosteret i Væ. Et nyfund.' *Scan-
dia* 21 (1951–52) 1–27.
'Ærkekonge og Ærkebiskop. Nye træk i dansk Kirkehistorie', *Scandia* 23
(1955–57) 1–101.,
Kirkekampen i Danmark, 1241–1290. Jakob Erlandsen, samtid og efter-
tid. 1963; reprinted 1971.
'Kanslere og skrivere i Danmark 1250–82', *Middelalder Studier tilegnede
Aksel E. Christensen* (1966) 141–184.
'Das dänische Erzbistum vor 1250', *Acta Visbyensia* III (1969) 113–138.
Kvinde og Slave; Danmarks historie uden retouche 3. 1971.
Mordet på Kennedy og andre opgaver i historisk kildekritik. 1973.

Smidt, C.M. *Øm Kloster. Cara Insula.* 1924; third edition: Århus, 1962.
'Søborg', *Fra Nationalmuseets Arbejdsmark* (1930) 5–18.
Cistercienser-kirken i Løgum. 1931.
Vitskøl Kloster; Nationalmuseets blå bøger. 1938.
'Tikøb Kirke og Esrum Kloster', *Aarbøger for Nordisk Oldkyndighed*
(1938) 21–47.
'Nordsjællands Middelalderborge og største Kloster', *Frederiksborg
Amts Årbog* (1939) 53–103.

Smith, Gina Gertrud. 'De danske nonneklostre indtil ca. 1250', KS (1973) 1–45.

Southern, R.W. *Saint Anselm and his Biographer.* Cambridge, 1966.
Western Society and the Church in the Middle Ages; The Pelican History
of the Church, 2. Harmondsworth, 1970.
Medieval Humanism and Other Studies. Oxford, 1970.

Steenstrup, Johannes. 'Fandtes der i Middelalderen i Danmark eller andre Riger
Herreklostre?'', KS 7R, I B (1933) 1–22.

Sterum, Niels. 'Ikke på klippe, ikke på sand, men på tørv', *Antikvariske Studier*
1977 197–202.

Stüdtje, R. Johannes. 'Gedanken über den Wirkungsraum des Rydklosters',
Jahrbuch des Angler Heimatvereins 28 (1964) 90–110.

Szacherska, Stella Maria. *Opactwo Oliwskie a próba ekspansji duńskiej w Prusach*, Kwar talnik Historyczny. R. LXXIV. Warsaw, 1967.
Rola klasztorów duńskich w ekspansji Danii na Pomorzu Zachodnim u schyłku XII wieka. Wroclaw-Warsawa-Krakòw, 1968.
'The political role of the Danish monasteries in Pomerania 1171-1223', *Mediaeval Scandinavia* 10 (Odense, 1977) 122-55.

Szomlaiski, Leif. *Yngre Sjællandske Krønike*: Baggrund, tilblivelse, og værdi; Odense University Studies in History and Social Sciences, 10. 1973.

Tangl, Michael. *Die päpstlichen Kanzlei Ordnungen von 1200-1500*. Innsbruck, 1894.

Taylor-Vaisey, R. 'The First Century of Cistercian Legislation. Some Preliminary Investigation', *Citeaux: Commentarii Cistercienses* 17 (1976) 203-25.

Thiele, Augustinus. *Echternach und Himmerod*. Beispiele benediktinischer und zisterziensischer Wirtschaftsführung im 12. und 13. Jahrhundert; Forschungen zur Sozial- und Wirtschaftsgeschichte, 7. Stuttgart, 1964.

Tierney, Brian. *The Crisis of Church and State,* 1050-1300 (Englewood Cliffs, New Jersey: Prentice Hall, 1964).

Ulsig, Erik. *Danske Adelsgodser i Middelalderen*; Skrifter udgivet af Det historiske Institut ved Københavns Universitet II. 1968.

Undset, Sigrid. *Kirken, Klosteret, og Pilgrimsfærden*. Tre Essays fra Norsk Middelalder. 1965.

Urban, William. *The Baltic Crusade*. DeKalb, Illinois, 1975.

Van Damme, Jean Baptiste Bouton, and Jean de la Croix. *Les Plus Anciens Textes de Citeaux*; *Citeaux: Commentarii Cistercienses, Studia et Documenta,* II. Achel, 1974.

Wallin, Curt. 'Ärkebiskop Eskil som klosterstiftare', *Scandia* 27 (1961) 217-34.

Weibull, Lauritz. 'Erik den helige', *Aarbøger für or Nordisk Oldkyndighed* (1917) 99-130.

Wiese, Albert. *Die Cistercienser in Dargun von 1172 bis 1300*. Ein Beitrag zur meklenburg-pommerschen Colonisationsgeschichte. Güstrow, 1888.

Wilkes, Carl. *Die Zistercienserabtei Himmerode im 12. und 13. Jahrhundert*; Beiträge zur Geschichte des alten Mönchtums und des Benediktinerordens, 12. Münster im Westfalen, 1924.

Winter, Franz. *Die Cistercienser des nordöstlichen Deutschlands* 1-3. Gotha, 1868-71.

Wissing, Jürgen A. *Das Kloster Løgum im Rückblick*. Erinnerungen, Betrachtungen, und Vermutungen; Heimatkundlichen Arbeitsgemeinschaft für Nordschleswig. Heft 26. Apenrade, 1972.

Woodward, G.W.O. *The Dissolution of the Monasteries*. London, 1966.

Zakar, P. 'Die Anfänge des Zistercienserordens. Kurze Bemerkungen zu den Studien der letzten zehn Jahre', *Analecta* 20 (1964) 103-38.

Esrum. South wing of the household quadrangle of the cloister as seen from the north; fifteenth century, much altered and all that remains above ground of the original abbey complex. (*Photo—the author*)

Esrum. South wing. The legendary 'cellar of Brother Rus' is on the left. (*The author*)

Esrum. South meadow, between the cloister and the lake, still rich grazing land today. (*The author*)

Esrum. Sode meadow, near the site of Sode Mill, to the north of the abbey, and an important addition to Es-rum's possessions during the Øm controversy in the 1260s. (*The author*)

Abelholt. An Augustinian community founded by Saint William at the end of the twelfth century and a neighbor of Esrum. (*The author*)

Skamstrup. The village, together with surrounding lands and other villages, was part of Archbishop Absalon's testamentary gift to Sorø Abbey in 1199. The area is about 30 km to the north of Sorø. (*Photo—Benny Kofoed, Holbaek*)

Rolling grazing and forest lands north of Sorø. Again part of Absalon's testamentary gift to the abbey. (*Kofoed, Holbaek*)

Sorø. The romanesque church in red brick, probably completed soon after 1200 (except for the roof over the nave, originally of wood but covered by stone vaulting after a fire in 1247). Notice the simplicity of design and ornamentation, a sign of faithfulness to cistercian building ideals. (*Kofoed, Holbæk*)

Sorø. The nave as seen from the transept looking north. The frieze of shields from the end of the thirteenth century commemorates the abbey's benefactors. The baroque pulpit is from 1650.

Sorø. West facade of the church (the door is from 1870–71, part of the church's modern restoration which began in 1867). (*Kofoed, Holbaek*)

Sorø. The grave monument of King Kristoffer II (d.1332) and his queen, Eufemia. The figures are each about 2 metres in length. Between them is a c. 75 cm. figure of one of their daughters. Under this sad king, Denmark was leased away to German moneymen. Sorø's Cistercians kept a promise to fetch his body and give it a fitting burial in their church. (*Kofoed, Holbaek*)

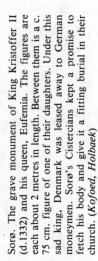

Sorø. Gravestone of Archbishop Absalon (d. 1201), now situated behind the high altar. Abbot Henrik Tornekrans removed the original wooden memorial and replaced it with this imposing Renaissance monument in 1536, the year the Reformation was decreed in Denmark by the monarchy.

Sorø. Tombstone of Abbot Henrik Tornekrans (d. 1538), the last Catholic abbot of Sorø, in the same style as Absalon's tomb. *(Kofoed, Holbaek)*

Sorø. Detail of a medieval abbot's tombstone (notice his staff on the upper left). *(Kofoed, Holbaek)*

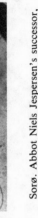

Sorø. Abbot Niels Jespersen's successor, Oluf Lauridsen (d. 1566) is shown on a neighbouring tombstone without the staff.(*Kofoed, Holbaek*)

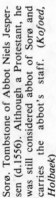

Sorø. Tombstone of Abbot Niels Jespersen (d.1556). Although a Protestant, he was still considered abbot of Sorø and carries the abbot's staff. (*Kofoed, Holbaek*)

Sorø. Early fifteenth century chalk mural of the crucifixion with Mary on the left and the Apostle John to the right, on the west side of the same pillar where a cistercian monk is to be found (cover). (*Kofoed, Holbaek*)

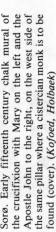

Sorø. The southern transept of the church with romanesque night stairs from a door to what once was the monks' dormitory. Sorø's indebtedness to the Fontenay model for cistercian churches is clear here. Above, the frieze of shields from the end of the thirteenth century. (*Kofoed, Holbaek*)

Pedersborg church a few kilometres north of Sorø. In the twelfth century there was a fortress here, whose owner caused great trouble for the monks. Later a church was built, and in the turbulent fourteenth century, the monks got permission from the bishop of Roskilde to tear down the fortress, afraid that it would again be used to attack them. (Kofoed, Holbæk)

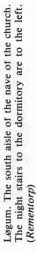

Løgum. The south aisle of the nave of the church. The night stairs to the dormitory are to the left. (*Rementorp*)

Løgum. The restored chapter house, unique in Scandinavia. (*Photo by Bjarne Rementorp*)

Løgum. The east end of the church, with transepts and the east wing of the cloister visible. (*Rementorp*)

A fourteenth-century reliquary chest from Løgum Abbey church. (*Rementorp*)

Løgum Abbey church. Detail of the north door. (*Rementorp*)

Detail of the reliquary chest, showing St Bernard and St Ambrose. (*Rementorp*)

Løgum. The restored east wing of the cloister. (*Rementorp*)

Løgum. Detail of an upper window in the abbey church. (*Rementorp*)

Løgum. The abbey church seen from the north-west. (*Rementorp*)

Løgum. The south-west end of the nave, showing the elegant, recessed high gothic lancets in the west wall. (*Remen-torp*)

Løgum. The marshy land to the southwest of the abbey which provided drainage and pasturage for the monks. (*Rementorp*)

Løgum. The altar, c. 1325, painted in bright red and gold-silver. In the centre is Christ, the Judge of the world. On either side are twelve scenes from the life of the Virgin. (*Nationalmuseet, Copenhagen*)

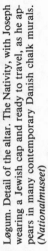

Løgum. Detail of the altar. The Nativity, with Joseph wearing a Jewish cap and ready to travel, as he appears in many contemporary Danish chalk murals. (*Nationalmuseet*)

Løgum. Detail of the altar. The Visitation.

Veng church, a twelfth-century church showing English influence. Originally the home of a benedictine abbey, Veng for a few years housed the Cistercians who founded Øm, a few miles away. (*Rementorp*)

Danish university students, under the direction of archaeologist Niels Sterum, measure the layers of turf in an area a few hundred yards west of Løgum Abbey. The material was used to fortify the embankments of the stream which flowed past the abbey. (*Rementorp*)

Vitskøl. Ruins of the east end of the abbey church with its ambulatory from about 1200. Like Sorø and Esrum, Vitskøl followed the Fontenay model with a rectangular choir and a rounded east end which permitted a number of side altars in niches along the ambulatory. (*Nationalmuseet*)

Myrendalkloster, on Bornholm, 1980. A monastery of Cistercians in modern Denmark.

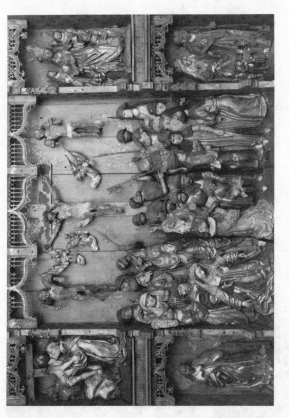

Esrum. Centrepiece of the high altar reredos from 1496, now in the National Museum. The two pairs of moveable wings and predella have disappeared. Above left, the vision of St Bernard. Above right, St Ursula and some of her 11,000 virgins. Below left, Juliana, who whipped the devil with a chain which she has here lost. Below right, Felicitas and another roman woman. At her feet are her seven sons, all martyred in her presence. The altar piece measures 209 x 265 cm. (*Nationalmuseet*)

Esrum. Detail from the altarpiece with the figure of Abbot Peder Andersen transformed, about 1650, into a Protestant clergyman in typical collar. In 1559, the altarpiece was given to St Olaf church in Elsinore, and in 1664, moved again to Holme-Olstrup parish church. (*Nationalmuseet*)

Esrum. Detail of the altarpiece. Bernard of Clairvaux with Christ, a favourite depiction of the saint deriving from a story in the *Exordium magnum* (II, 7) of Conrad of Eberbach. In the background a church and cemetary probably represent Clairvaux, Esrum's motherhouse, to which the pioneer monks hoped to return to die. This scene is a unique representation of cistercian spirituality in Denmark at the end of the Middle Ages. (*Nationalmuseet*)

Øm. Looking from the south end of the east wing of the cloister toward the site of the church, approximately where the figure is standing. (*Rementorp*)

Øm. The site of the library in the east wing of the cloister. Looking towards the cloister yard. The tall structure in the middle marks the site of the well. (*Rementorp*)

Øm. Site of excavations in the summer of 1978 carried out by the Institut for middelalder-arkaeologi at Århus University. The excavated area corresponds to the south wing of the clois-ter, where stone buildings were constructed, apparently for the first time, during the fifteenth century. (*Rementorp*)

Øm. Part of the cellar of the cloister's south wing. (*Rementorp*)

Øm. South wing. Notice the sandy soil and high water level. (*Rementorp*)

Øm. Excavations during the summer of 1975, showing the southwest corner of the abbey garth. (*Moesgård, Århus*)

Holger Garner, of the Øm Museum, tells Danish university students about the charitable and social works undertaken by the cistercian abbeys in the Middle Ages. October 1978. (*Rementorp*)

Øm. Excavations at their completion in late summer, 1978. The outline of the entire cloister is clear, with the 1978 diggings in the west wing prominent. The ruins of the church, out of the picture, are at the upper right hand corner. *(Moesgard, Århus)*

Øm. Graves below the eastern cloister, excavated in 1975. (*Moesgård, Århus*)

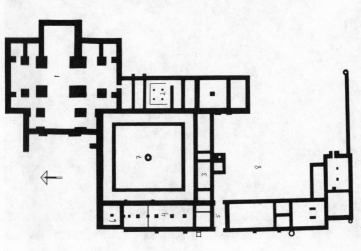

Plan of the Øm Abbey, as known after the excavations of 1975–1978. 1. The abbey church, consecrated in 1257. It was originally intended to extend the church to the west. 2. The east wing, also from 1257. To the north is the sacristy, then the library and the chapter house, which was vaulted. Next to it were the stairs leading to the dormitory. 3. The south wing, built in the fifteenth century, probably from thirteenth-century plans. 4. The west wing, built about 1500. In the cellar were storerooms; they could be entered by the door (5). 6. An earlier part of the west wing. It was once thought to have housed a tower, but recent excavations have not confirmed this theory. 7. The monks' garth with a well and a cloister walk dating from the fifteenth century. Before this time the cloister would have been open. 8. The outer garth, having buildings on the west and south for various activities of the abbey. (From Olaf Olsen, 'Krønike og udgravning', *Convivium* [Copenhagen, 1979] 2–22.)

Øm. An aerial view, 1978. Notice that the west end of the church stops a good distance away from the west end of the cloister. (*Moesgard, Århus*)

INDEX

The alphabetization follows the Danish alphabet, so that the letters *æ, ø,* and *å* are placed after *z*.

12 c. = Twelfth century. 13 c. = Thirteenth century, etc.

For more information as to dates of abbots, bishops or kings, see the respective tables.

For place names and geographical information about them, see J.P. Trap, *Danmark*, Volumes 1-15 (Copenhagen, 1953-72).

abbot, authority of, over peasant labourers, 202

Abel (13 c. duke of Southern Jutland, king of Denmark), 6, 7, 127-8, 160; and Løgum 163, 175; exemptions to Cistercians to show authority, 128; relations with Øm, 128-9

Abraham (12 c. cellarer, Alvastra), 43

Absalon (12 c. bishop of Roskilde, archbishop of Lund), 34, 59, 135, 181; and Cistercian nuns, 98-9, 143; and Carthusians, 67; and Esrum, 56, 60, 84-5, 90; and Guldholm, 103; and Saxo, 110-111; and Sorø, 86-7; and William of Æbelholt, 97; death and burial at Sorø, 92; and tithes, 91; involvement of, with Cistercians, 62- 3, 91-2, 108-9, 110

Absalon Andersen (13 c. descendant of the Skjalm family), 163

Adam of Bremen (11 c. German historian), 17, 34

Agnes, daughter of Erik Plowpenny, 167

Agnes, daughter of King Birger of Sweden, 207

agriculture and images in Cistercian documents, 54; in late Middle Ages, 250-51

Akershus 224

Albert Knoppert (16 c. notary), 27

Alexander III (pope 1159-81), 64-5, 69; and payment of tithes, 91; and parish churches, 175

Alexander IV (pope 1254-61), 136, 143, 158

Alexander the Great 252

Alslev 243, 245

Alsted 170, 182, 213-4, 233

altars 239. (*See also* individual abbeys)

Alvastra 40, 59; foundation of, 41, 43; and General Chapter, 229

Amelungxborn 230

Anacletus (antipope 1130-38), 6

Anders (14 c. abbot, Herrisvad), 212

Anders of Falster (15 c. priest), 245

Anders Erlandsen (13 c. property owner, Rygen), 153

Anders Jakobsen (14 c. landowner), 240

Anders Pedersen Vædder (13 c. landowner), 170

Anders Sunesen (12-13 c. royal chancellor, archbishop of Lund), 6, 34, 86-7, 93, 97, 117, 137, 181

Anders Troelsen (15 c. landowner) 245

Andersen, Hans Christian (19 c. Danish writer), 10

Andreas (13 c. abbot of Greifswald) 143

Andrew (14 c. monk of Esrum), 210

Annales Sorani 1130-1300 (Older Sorø Annals), 17-18

Annales Sorani 1202-1347 (Younger Sorø Annals), 18

Anselm, Saint 11 c., and letter-writing, 84, 97

Antvorskov 169, 246; called hospital, 185; growth of, 248

Api (12 c. peasant near Øm), 110

architecture, Cistercian influence on, 96, 258

arengas 86; of charters and monarchy,
60-1, 84, 127-8, 129; and monastic
intentions, 62; and 14 c. changes
aristocracy 221-2, 239-45. (*See also*
magnates, gentry, families)
Aristotle 252
Arkona 84
armigeri 187, 216. (*See also* gentry)
Arnamagnæan Institute, Copenhagen
University, 19, 25
Arnfast (13 c. abbot, Ryd), 7, 148
Arras, bishop of, 96
Asser (12 c. archbishop of Lund), 5
Asser (14 c. priest of Helsinge), 242
Asser Jensen (13 c. knight), 173-4
Asser Olavsen (15 c. parish priest), 242
Asser Rig (12 c. member of Skjalms), 74
Asserbo 55-6, 67, 90, 252, 258
Augustinians 5, 96; at Æbelholt 96, 98
Aumône, L' 49
Aveholm 56
Avignon 193, 208; appeals to, 194,
196, 218, 228, 231; and great schism
228-9

bakery at Sorø, 134
Ballum 137
Balerne 166
ballads, Danish, 9; Baltic, 37, 41, 80,
82-3, 84, 151, 206, 258
banks, Cistercian monasteries as, 214,
249
Bannebjerg 242
Bari, church of Saint Nicholas at, 169
Barnum Eriksen (14 c. landowner),
194, 241, 246
Bartholomaeus Jensen (14 c.
Franciscan), 218
Basilius (12 c. Carthusian prior), 67
beer 223-4
Benedict, Saint 32, 46, 61
Benedictines, in Denmark 5; and view
of Cistercians, 47-9, 109; and nuns,
247; at Odense, 5, 67, 218; at St
Rêmi, Rheims, 66-7; at Slesvig, 75,
101-2; at Sorø, 74-5, 174; at Kalvø,
75; Cistercian myth of their decline,
74; mistaken house at Esrum, 50

benefactors. *See* donors
benefices 200, 248-9
benefits, spiritual, 239-40, 244; and
parish priests, 242
Bennekin Albrectsen (15 c. monk,
Sorø), 237
Bent Bille (14 c. landowner), 241
Bent Byg (14 c. landowner), 246
Bergen (Norway) 3, 21
Bergen (Rygen) 3, 82, 153
Bernard of Clairvaux (Saint, 12 c.), 6,
22, 41, 95, 108, 150; and simplicity,
64; and style of writing, 105; and
style of life, 218; friendship with
Eskil, 38, 50, 73; Esrum miracles
of, 53; in Esrum altar, 255; the
miraculous in, 54; last days, 51; role
in Scandinavian foundations, 42-44;
Vita Prima of, 18, 21, 31, 51, 71
Berno (12 c. bishop of Schwerin), 80
Bible at Logum 31; biblical metaphors,
55, 99; harvest image, 67; biblical
language in charters, 105-6
biography, of Bishop Gunner 16-17, 35
Birger (14 c. Swedish king), 193
bishops, and Cistercians, in general,
90, 101, 105-7, 109, 145; twelfth-
century cooperation, 91; new
concerns in 13 c., 114, 144; Danish
bishops and Clairvaux, 125;
relations with Cistercians 125-57,
136-42; and stays at Cistercian
houses, 140; and Øm controversy,
158; and harmony with Cistercians
in late 13 c., 179-80; in late Middle
Ages, 198-208, 233-6; problems
with, in 15 c., 226-7
Bjergby 186
Black Death 221, 248
Blekinge 2, 5
Blistrup 178, 179
Bo (13 c. abbot, Øm), 157
Bo Bred (13 c. knight), 173
Bodilsen family (12 c.), 5, 45
Bogislav, prince of Pomerania (12 c.),
82
Bonde (13 c. bishop of Slesvig), 160

Boniface IX (pope 1389–1404), 228–9
Bonmont 49
booths (market), 80–1, 212
Bornholm, modern Cistercians on, 258–9
borrowing, by Cistercians, 211
Boserup 170
Bosjö 247
Bourg-Dieu 188
Brahetrolleborg. *See* Holme
Brede 159, 175–6, 199, 208–9, 243, 245
brewery, at Sorø, 135
Brienne (12 c. abbot, Øm), 65–6; and foundation of Øm, 76, 79
Bringstrup 135, 178
Britain 239
Broby 24–5, 171, 240
Buchwald, G. von, (19 c. German historian), 11
Buckow 231
Burgundy 43, 255; duke of, 97
burial, at Cistercian abbeys, 134, 144; at Løgum, for bishops of Ribe, 138; at Sorø, for Skjalm family, 174–5, and for Kristoffer, 204. *See also* individual abbeys
Buris Henriksen (12 c. Danish aristocrat), 20, 61, 62
businessmen, monks as, 219
Bylderup 141
Byrum 131
Børglum 5, 131; Norbertine house at, 115; bishop of, 130, 191

Cammin. *See* Kamien
canals, at Øm, 79; at Sorø, 103
Canivez, J.M. (20 c. Cistercian historian), 22
Canute (Knud den Store) (Scandinavian-English king, 11 c.), 4
Carthusians, in Denmark, 66–7, 90, 258; and Eskil, 68, 73
cathedrals, building of, at Århus, 137
cattle 58; on Læssø, 132
Cecilie (13 c. benefactress of Esrum), 169
Cecilie (13 c. benefactress of Esrum, sister of Jon Lille), 170

Cecilie (14 c. benefactress of Esrum, daughter of Jon Lille), 183–6
Cecilie, Lady (13 c. benefactress of Sorø), 170
Celestine III (pope 1191–8), 102
cellarer, office of, 215
Champagne 43
chapel, for bishop at Sorø, 134–5, 140; for Valdemar IV, 223; chantries, in Britain, 239; Hiddensee, for lay people, 155
chapters, cathedral, 38, 114; at Viborg, 130–32; growth of, in 13 c., 133, 137–8; at Ribe, 138–9; at Roskilde, 173; 14 c. trends affecting, 200
chapters, monastic in 14 c., 211
charters, language of, 45
Chorin 152
Christensen, Aksel E. (20 c. Danish historian), 4, 12; and Asser, archbishop of Lund, 5
Christian III (Danish king, 1534–59), 8
Christiansen, Tage E. (contemporary Danish historian), 12, 226
Christina (Swedish queen, 12 c.), 58
Chotimar (12 c. founder of Dargun), 80
Christianity, arrival in Denmark, 4; and Absalon, 92; and Eskil, 54, 72–3; and the Cistercians, 43, 109, 257; comparison between Denmark and Wendland, 81; link with the south, 5; spread in the countryside, 37–8
churches, building of, in Denmark, 5, 38; at Løgum, 138; at Sorø, 86, 135; at Tvis, 111; at Æbelholt, 95; at Øm, 134; at Århus, 137
churches, ownership of, 108; at Vitskøl, 165
churches, parish, and Brede controversy, 175–6; and Cistercian acquisition of, 133, 136; and Cistercian involvement in, 154–5, 177, 198; and Esrum, 199–200; and Sorø, 197, 233–4; and Vitskøl, 199; and Øm controversy, 157–8, 198; and testamentary gifts to, 184–5

Circipanien 79, 80–1
Cismar 194
CISTERCIANS (IN DENMARK)
and Absalon, 62–3, 90–2, 110; and
foundations, 2–3, 37–41, 37–41; and
Eskil, 64–74; and Benedictines,
101–2; and spread of Order in 1160s,
64; and recycling of resources, 36;
and General Chapter, 120–26,
209–11, 228–33; and language of
charters, 54–55; and purpose in
society, 42–44; and royal power,
59–62, 107, 126–32, 222–8; and
Saxo, 110–11; and town properties,
237–9; and violence, 192–8
—as exponents of reform, 74–5; as
complainers, 77–8; as lenders,
213–15; as seen through papal
chancellery, 119–20
—change of their status in society,
113–5, 133, 144, 179–82; chronicle
writing by, 21; cooperation with
other interests in church, 118; crisis
in 1260s, 146–7, 156–66; continuity
of structures, 212; crisis in
agriculture of, in 14 c., 248–51
—dependence on bishops, 136–42,
198–203
—end of expansion for, 121, 133,
142–44, 151–2, 155; end of family
generosity towards, 135–6, 181–2,
186; European contacts of, 94
—fate after Reformation, 8; female
donors to, 168–9; friars and
Cistercians, 133
—gentry's dealings with, 239–43;
—historians' view of, 9;
—idealism of, 108, 174–5; isolation of,
182
—lay brotherhood in, 180–82;
—parish churches for, 198–202;
political support for, 6, 109;
political methods of, 76; problems
of travel for, 117; privileges and
tithes for, 90–91
—recruitment rivalry in, 94–5;
relationship to other orders, 246–7;

renewal in 15 c., 251–5; response of,
to lay world, in 15 c., 256–7
—schism and Cistercians, 228–9; social
flexibility of, 215–19; sources for,
15–20, 156, 218–9; late medieval
sources for, 23–7; post-reformation
sources for, 27–30, 115; intellectual
sources for, 30–35; status alteration
in 15 c., 227; early success and
security of, 109–110, 235
—water's importance for, 103–4
CISTERCIANS (IN GENERAL)
—belief in their mission, 74–5
—communication, 70–71; chronicle
writing, 21
—decline of idealism, 108; decline of
central position in church, 114
—financial system, 210; foundations in
12 c., 40, 75
—intellectual activities, 35; international
links, 59
—Orderic Vitalis's view of, 47–9
—parish functions, 154–5
—results of quarrels of 1260s, 166
Rhineland, 41
—shift to East, 114–5; strength of
administration in 13 c., 136; sources
for, change in type, 219
—technical knowledge, 96; tithes, 91;
the *Exordium Parvum*, 56
Citeaux 11, 30, 39–40, 94, 96, 122–3,
141, 163, 210, 212, 221, 228; abbot
of, 91, 97; filiations of, 3, 38;
Orderic Vitalis on, 48; sources for,
21–2
Clairvaux 11, 30, 49, 58, 67, 96, 141,
188, 212, 221; and abbot of, 97, 125;
and burial at, 125, 137, 150; and
filiation of, 2, 39–41; and forms of
piety, 57; and Eskil, 50, 52, 54, 66,
72–3, 108, 253; and General Chapter,
121–2, 124–5, 231–2; and view of
Denmark, 63; and visitations in
Scandinavia, 125, 165; and Øm
controversy, 157; as home for
Scandinavian Cistercians, 44; dispute
with Citeaux, 152; in Esrum altar,
255; sources from, 21–2

Clare, Saint, convent of, at Roskilde, 185
Clement V (pope 1305–14), 193
Clement VI (pope 1342–52), 208
Colbaz (Kolbacz) 19, 31, 184, 196, 212; and foundation of, 82–3, 104; and General Chapter, 121, 152; and localism, 152–3; and papacy, 230–31; and relations with Esrum, 133, 151–3, 233; and the Colbaz Annals, 19–20, 38, 50, 67, 79, 81–2, 152–3
College of St Bernard, Paris 25
colonization 109
confidence, of Cistercians 75, 114
confraternity 178–9, 234, 237–8, 242
Conrad of Eberbach 22, 41–2, 69
Conrad (13 c. abbot of Doberan), 124
Conrad (12 c. bishop of Stettin), 83
Constance, Council of 228
contributions 210, 228–33, 247
convents, female (for Cistercian monasteries for women. See under Roskilde, Slangerup, Bergen), 167–8, 203
Copenhagen 1, 3, 8, 19, 128, 134, 252; and fire of 1728, 17, 34; and church of Our Lady, 184, 186; and Esrum properties in, 26, 237; and Sorø, 180; and University, 27
courtliness 235
crisis, agricultural 216; of 14 c., 202, 248–51; at Eldena, 211
crucifixion 255–6
cupiditas as theme in letters, 99

Dahlerup, Troels (contemporary Danish historian), 12
Dahlerup, Verner (20 c. Danish historian), 34
dairy production 142
Dalby 5
Daler 138, 176
Damsholt, Nanna (contemporary Danish historian), 98
Danes, as settlers, 81; as warriors, 52
Danish, use of 222; in charters, 254–5; in Rhyme Chronicle, 253–4

Dargun 23, 83, 84, 212; and foundation, 79–80; and move to Eldena, 81–2, 103–4; and General Chapter, 114, 121, 123–4, 133, 151, 202; and quarrel with Eldena, 123; and taxation of North, 229
Daugaard, J.B. (19 c. Danish clergyman and historian), 11
DENMARK and coming of Cistercians, 37, 104–5; and coming of Christianity, 2–4; and emergence as political power, 6–7; and geography, 1–2; modern conception of, 1; population, 2; advance along the Baltic, 80, 83; European contacts via Cistercians, 94, 125; end of age of expansion, 133; late 13 c. Baltic decline, 155; nobility of, in 13 c., 181; 14 c. crisis in, 192, 194, 196–7, 202; links with southern Europe, 5; Reformation in, 8; German political influence in, 222; trade with France, 125; role played by Cistercians in, 108–110, 232–3, 258–9; sources for, Cistercian role in, 47, 76; and William of Æbelholt, 97–8
devil 54; at Esrum Abbey, 9, 53; and Eskil of Børglum, 116; in Eskil of Lund's storytelling, 69–70
dictamen 93
Dijon 228
Diplomatarium Danicum 29, 93
discipline, problem of, at Løgum, 107; and Sorø, 167–8
Djursland 16, 84, 238
Doberan 23, 80, 82, 114; and foundations in 13 c., 153–4; and General Chapter, 123–4, 152, 231; and involvement with Erik Menved, 155
Dominic 18
Dominicans 114, 196; and arrival in Denmark, 133; and testaments, 168–9, 179, 184; and Reformation in Denmark, 27; at Roskilde, 167–8
donations-gæsteri 142
donors, and Cistercians 169, 242; and

end of great legacies, 178; and
continuing Cistercian attraction on,
183, 234–5; and social background
of, 181–2; and new interests of,
217–18, 239–40
Dover 189, 214
drainage 103
Draved Forest 176
drinking, at Slangerup 100
Dyreborg 245
Døjringe 178, 213

Ebbe (13 c. bishop of Århus), 130, 137
Ebbe Skjalmsen (12 c. member of
Skjalms), 74
Ebbe Sunesen (12 c. benefactor), 134
education, at Sorø, 254, 257
Eldena 84, 212; and foundation, 81–2,
103–4; and General Chapter, 121,
211–12; and 13 c. growth, 143–4;
and quarrel with Dargun, 123; and
independence from Esrum, 153; and
links with Esrum, 151–2, 157
Elder Zealand Chronicle (also called
Older Zealand Chronicle), 18, 30,
150–51, 189–91, 252, 254
Eleven Thousand Virgins, altar of,
239, 255
Elias (12 c. bishop, Ribe), 69–70
Emborg 8
England 21, 105, 111
Erik Abelsen (13 c. duke of Southern
Jutland), support for Øm, 160
Erik Barnumsen (14 c. landowner), 241
Erik V Glipping (Danish king, 13 c.),
7, 9, 142, 175; and Øm controversy,
160, 163, 170; as protector of Øm,
161; as seen in Ryd Annals, 148;
death of, 79, 185, 192, 193; in
Rhyme Chronicle, 252–3
Erik Lam (12 c. Danish king), 50
Erik VI Menved (14 c. Danish king),
7, 34, 155, 185, 188; and failure of
schemes, 192; and foundation of
Opager, 195; and privileges to
monastic houses, 203–4, 206;
borrows from Sorø, 214

Erik IV Plowpenny (13 c. Danish
king), 7, 33, 129, 148; inheritance
of, 167; and royal privileges, 128
Erik VII of Pomerania (15 c. Danish
king), 1412–39, 226
Erik (13 c. Swedish king), 193
Erik, Count (12 c. relative of King
Valdemar I), 76
Erik, duke of Halland (14 c.), 194
Erik, duke of Jutland (14 c.), 199
Erik, Junker (13 c. member of Swedish
royal family), 163
Erik, Junker (13 c. Danish aristocrat),
163
Erik (13 c. royal chaplain), 163
Esbern (13 c. abbot of Esrum), 157,
162
Esbern (15 c. abbot, Knardrup), 245
Esbern Hammer (13 c. benefactor of
Sorø), 179–80
Esbern Karlsen (13 c. landowner), 170
Esbern Nielsen (12 c. benefactor of
Sorø), 126
Esbern Snare (12 c. member of Skjalm
family), 78, 114, 135
Esbern Snerling (13 c. benefactor of
Sorø), 137
Esbønderup 170, 199, 242, 251
Esger (13 c. bishop of Ribe), 139,
141–2; and Løgum, 158, 176
Esger (15 c. bishop of Ribe), 245
Eskil (12 c. archbishop of Lund), 6,
21, 22, 23, 31, 38, 89, 181; and
ability to publicize himself, 52–4; and
Carthusians, 66–7; and charter for
Næstved Benedictines, 45–6; and
activities in early 1140s, 46; and
interest in Cistercians, 47, 49, 73,
108; and foundation of Esrum,
49–51; and defence of Esrum lands,
55–6, 59–60; and foundation of
Vitskøl, 57–9; and foundation of
Løgum, 105, 138; and role in
monastic foundations, 39–40, 62–4;
and vision in childhood of Mary, 68;
and vision of dead brother, 70–71;
and Premonstratensians, 67; and

uncles' stories, 72; as seen in Øm
Abbey Chronicle, 64–5; as seen by
Clairvaux monks, 69–70; at
Clairvaux, 66–7, 72, 125
Eskil (12 c. uncle of archbishop Eskil),
72
Eskil (13 c. bishop of Slesvig), 141–2
Eskil (13 c. canon of Børglum), 115–7
ESRUM 6, 23, 24, 29, 31, 45, 79, 143;
background for: location, 2, 84;
remnants of buildings, 8; sources for,
15; Esrum Book (Codex
Esromensis), 26, 59, 77, 178, 193,
212, 242, 249–51; Vatican
manuscript, 33; lost Esrum materials,
33; excavations at, 11; Brother Rus
at, 9
—12 c. at: and Absalon, 62–3, 89, 92;
and building of church, 111, 258;
and Abbot William of Æbelholt,
93–7; and Eskil, 54–5, 59–60; and
foundation, 49–51, 104, 253; and
foundation of Vitskøl, 58–9; and
foundation of Sorø, 64, 76; miracle
at, 53; and foundation of Dargun,
80; and end of Baltic expansion,
82–3; and Halland properties, 85, 87;
and Guldholm, 103; and fire at, 106;
and increase in lands, 56, 64, 84, 90;
and investment in crusades, 113;
Saxo's description of its monks, 68,
110; papal contacts, 90; relative
importance of, 96
—13 c. at: and General Chapter,
120–25, 144, 166; and confraternity,
179; and contacts with Eastern Baltic
abbeys, 151–2; and cooperation with
Herrisvad, 123; and papacy, 117–9,
134; and parish priests, 178–9, 216;
and property disputes, 134; and royal
relationship, 126–8, 162–4; and Øm
controversy, 156–8; and property
donors, 134, 182; and female donors,
169–71, 183–4; and paternity of
Dargun, 123–4, 133
—late medieval period at: and bishops,
235; and burial at, 183, 186, 207,
247; and collections of contributions
from, 229–33; and altars, 222, 223,
239, 255–7; contacts with Eastern
Baltic abbeys, 211, 233; and gentry,
216, 239, 241–2; and General
Chapter, 210–11, 228–33; and royal
relationship, 203–4, 206, 207, 223–5,
245, 252; and papal contacts, 209,
228; and relative importance, 231,
247; and properties of, 250–51; and
peasants, 182, 258; and mortgages,
214–5; and procurations from, 228;
and visitation, 245; and towns,
237–52; and Odense, 235; and parish
churches, 199–200, 242; and late
14 c. crisis, 247–8
Esrum Lake 90, 134, 162
Estonia 6
Eucharist 69
Evesham 5
'Excerpts of the Fathers' 188
excommunication, threat of, 120;
outmoded, 208
exemption: Cistercian, from episcopal
jurisdiction, 90, 106, 118, 140, 198,
237; from tithes, 91; from tolls,
125; from exactions on labourers,
127–9, 158, 160–61; compromised
by ownership of parish churches,
137
Exordium Magnum Cisterciense 18,
21, 22, 39, 41; and Eskil, 51, 69–71;
and spread of Cistercians, 42, 150
Exordium Parvum 56, 64, 76, 108
expenses, legal, 241

Falster 2, 5
families, and bonds continued after
death, 169; and changing patterns
of generosity in, 135–6, 184–5,
239–45; and changing practice of
sending sons to Cistercians, 182;
and Knardrup dispute, 194–5
Faurås herred 85
fear, of early Cistercians in going
North, 42–3; of violence and its
threat, 192–8

Felicitas, Saint 255
Ferrand (14 c. lawyer, Avignon), 196
feudal structures, and Danish
monarchy, 155; and Danish
nobility, 181; on Rygen, 153
filiation, question of. *See* **paternity**
finances, of Cistercian Order in 14 c.
210-11; of Cistercians in Denmark,
214-5
fines, judicial 129; and Esrum's right
to collect, 164
fires, at Colbaz, 129, 152; at Esrum,
106, 129; at Herrisvad, 105, 182; at
Løgum, 105; at Oliva, 153; at Sorø,
134-5, 140, 152, 188; at Vitskøl,
165, 182
fishing, at Sorø, 173; and Ås-Gudhem,
193; in Halland, 85; in Southern
Jutland, 140; near Esrum, 251
Flensborg (Flensburg) 3, 8, 237
Flensborg Fjord 20, 38
Florentius (12 c. canon of Lund),
59-60
Folmer (12 c. abbot, Esrum), 50
Folmer Jakobsen (14 c. benefactor of
Sorø), 240
forest, in Halland, 86; near Løgum,
176; of Sorø, 197-8; on Læsø,
131-2
Fountains Abbey 21, 59; and visitation
of Norwegian houses, 123
France 11, 51, 64, 67, 98, 111, 138,
258; and royal dynasty 7; and trade
with Denmark, 125
Franche-Comté 166
Francis of Assisi 18
Franciscans 114; and arrival in
Denmark, 133; and convent at
Roskilde, 168, 185; and Cistercians,
152, 218; and idealism, 108; and
Reformation in Denmark, 27; and
testaments, 169, 179, 184
fraternity. *See* **confraternity**
Frederick (12 c. abbot of Esrum), 64
Frederick I (German king and Roman
Emperor, 1152-90), 6, 64
Frederick II (German king and Roman
Emperor), 1215-50, 119

Frederickssund 204
friars 108, 114; arrival in Denmark;
and Cistercians, 152, 218; fate in
Reformation, 8, 258; and testaments,
171, 184, 185; spiritual role, 139
friendship, in charters, 138, 244; in
letters of Saint Anselm, 98; in
letters of William of Æbelholt, 93,
98, 99
Friesland 165, 209
Fyn (Fünen) 2, 3, 5, 38, 57, 67, 76,
117, 235
Fåborg 67

Gallen 155
Gammel Torv 237
Garner, H.N. (contemporary Danish
monastic historian), 96
Gdansk 152
General Chapter 17, 69, 118, 163; and
burials, 174; and Baltic abbeys, 152;
and attendance, 117, 120, 209-10;
and collection of news, 94; and
contributions to, 229-33; and
continuing importance of, 211-12,
231-3; and Danish Cistercians from
1215-57, 120-26; and Danish
controversies of 1260s, 156, 161-2;
and education, 254, 257; and
financial functions, 210; and meat,
205; and Eldena, 143-4; and dispute
over filiation of Dargun, 123-4; and
parish churches, 136-7; and purchase
of land, 56; and Queen Ingeborg, 97;
and *procurator,* 99; and reforms,
108; and visitation of Norwegian
abbeys, 123; and weaknesses after
1260s, 146-7; during great schism,
228-9; impotence of, for Denmark,
163-66, 186, 236; forbids new
foundations, 40, 51; records of, 22;
travel to, from Scandinavia, 44, 90
General Chapter, Praemonstratensian,
116
generosity, changing royal patterns of,
130; end of spontaneous type, 135;
in late medieval period, 239; of
bishop of Ribe to Løgum, 138-39

Gentofte 62
gentry, rural, 195, 196, 216, 239, 242-3. *See also armigeri*
Geoffrey of Auxerre (secretary to Saint Bernard), 21, 35, 44, 69; and conversation with Eskil, 51-52; and letter to Eskil, 52; and miracle at Esrum, 53
Gerard (12 c. monk of Clairvaux and abbot of Alvastra), 41, 43-4, 53, 58
Gerhard (14 c. count of Rendsborg), 205-6
German-Danish controversies, over monasticism, 11
German historians on Baltic expansion, 83, 109
German monks in Denmark 53
Germany, and church rivalry with Denmark, 47; and Cistercian foundations, 41; and Eastern expansion, 114; and settlers, 81; and political influence in 14 c. Denmark, 222; Federal Republic of, 5, 19, 38; Democratic Republic of, 5
Gertrud (14 c. claimant against Knardrup), 195
Gertrud Jonsdatter (Cistercian nun at Roskilde), 185
Gertrude (14 c. benefactress of Sorø), 241
Gervais (13 c. abbot of Prémontré), 115-6
Ginnegård 106
Glücksborg Castle 103
Glumsten 85-6
grain 251
grange farming 90, 103, 108, 239; at Esrum, 180-81; at Sorø, 136; decline of, 146, 215-6
Gregorian reforms 37; in Denmark, 5
Gregory IX (pope 1227-41), bulls to Danish Cistercian houses, 118-9, 137, 163
Gregory X (pope 1271-76), 163
Gregory of Crescenti (13 c. cardinal legate), 158
Gregory of Tours (6 c. historian), 33

Greifswald 143, 157, 254
Grenå 238
Grib Forest 9
Grinderslev 130
Gro (13 c. monastic benefactress), 168
growth, end of, in 13 c., 144; renewal of, in 15 c., 251-2
Grubbe family 240, 246
Grundtvig, N.F.S. (19 c. Danish clergyman and author), 9-10
Græsted 179
guardian, Franciscan, 201; of parish church, 248; over Cistercian houses, 197
Gudenå 109
Gudhem 193
guest houses, at Sorø, 135
Guido (13 c. cardinal legate), 146, 158-9, 162-3
Guldholm 61, 104. (*See also* Ryd); foundation myth, 75, 149; foundation narrative, 20, 71, 101; William of Æbelholt at, 100-103
Gunderslevholm 246
Gunner (13 c. bishop of Ribe), 139, 140
Gunner (abbot of Øm in 13 c., bishop of Viborg), 16, 162, 218; biography of, 30, 71, 151; mediator in Læsø dispute, 131-2; maintains good relations, 143; and Vitskøl, 139
Gyde (13 c. benefactress of Sorø), 170-92
Gærup 245
gårdsæder 251

Haakon (14 c. Norwegian king), 192, 209
Hälsingborg 204, 212
Halland 2, 5, 84-7, 90, 109, 126, 207, 224, 234
Hamburg-Bremen, archbishopric of, 5, 40
Hamund Hamundsen (14 c. landowner), 214
Hans Laxman (15 c. archbishop of Lund), 227
Hartvig Krummedige (14 c. knight), 235, 241

Havelse 216
Havreholm 90
heaven 107; aristocratic view of, 84; through monks' prayers, 106
Hedeby 4
Heiligenkreuz 188
Heilsbronn 228-9
Heinrich (14 c. abbot of Stolpe), 211
Heinrich (14 c. abbot of Neuencamp), 211
Helena (15 c. aristocrat), 242
Helge (12 c. subprior), Esrum, 96
Helsinge 242
Helsingør (Elsinore) 237
Helvig (14 c. Danish queen), 207, 224, 225
Henneke Olufsen (14 c. landowner), 224
Henning (14 c. abbot of Sorø), 188
Henning (13 c. monk of Sorø), 173
Henning Nielsen Limbæk (14 c. landowner), 243
Henrik (14 c. bishop of Roskilde), 233, 235
Henrik (12 c. abbot of Varnhem, then Vitskøl), 44, 58-9, 64-5; and foundation of Øm, 76; and visits to Clairvaux, 72
Henrik (14 c. abbot of Sorø), 197
Henrik (15 c. abbot of Vitskøl), 32
Henrik Gertsen (14 c. bishop of Roskilde), 191
Henrik Isulvsen (14 c. landowner), 216
Henrik Kristiernsen Tornekrans (late 15 c. abbot at Vitskøl, then of Esrum and of Sorø), 26-7, 252
Henrik Rantzow (14 c. landowner), 244
Henze Krabbe (14 c. Esrum monk), 183
Herbert of Clairvaux, and Eskil, 68, 70; and Liber Miraculorum, 22, 39-40, 45
herbology 190
Herman (12 c. bishop of Slesvig), 60
Herman (13 c. abbot of Colbaz), 151
Herman (14 c. abbot of Esrum), 231
heroes 219

Hervé (Hervaeus), 188
HERRISVAD 3, 6, 8, 79, 105; and foundation, 38-40, 46, 104, 253; and building of church, 63-4, 75; and excavations, 12; and cooperation with Esrum, 123, 212; and controversy at Øm, 156; and daughters of, 76, 160-61, 182; and fire, 165, 182; and gloss on Matthew, 33; and localism, 247; and Transitus super Genesim, 32-3; and General Chapter, 120-23, 165-6, 210, 229; as landlocked a location, 84
herrekloster 79
Hertzsprung, Ivar (early 20 c. Danish archaeologist), 11-12
Hiddensee, and foundation, 153; and pastoral functions, 154-5; and property dispute, 153-5
Hildegard of Bingen (12 c. German mystic and author), 53
Hildesheim 47, 68, 73, 230
Hillerød 56
Hillerødsholm 216
Himmelstädt 152
Himmerod 178
historiography, Danish tradition of, concerning Cistercians 11-12;
— concerning Eskil, 39; concerning papal schism of 1160s, 65-6; on Williams of Æbelholt's letters, 93
— German tradition of, concerning Cistercian expansion, 41
— Medieval Cistercian tradition of, 150-51, 187-8, 190; and Rhyme Chronicle, 252-4
history, Cistercian attitude towards, 203
Holbæk 238
HOLME 3, 38, 76; foundation of, 67, 104; building of abbey complex, 251; and General Chapter, 117, 121, 210, 229; and Øm controversy, 156-7, 161; remnants of, 9
Holstebro 3, 61
Holstein 222, 232, 243-4
Holy Spirit, hospitals of, 171, 184, 185, 217-8

Honorius III (pope, 1216–27), and bulls to Danish Cistercians, 117
Hoogeweg, H. (20 c. German historian), 83
Hornbæk 251
Horsens 3
hospitality (See also procurations), 141–2, 200, 233–4, 255; exemption from, 207; unjust demands of 163, 206
hovedlod, halv 129
Hovedø (Hovedøya) 224; revolt at, 122–3; wealth of, 229
Huizinga, Johan 255
Hulerød 162
Hvide family 6
Højer 244
Hørsholm 134, 185, 197, 258
Hågen (14 c. priest), 216
Hågendrup 234
Hårslev 45

idealism 108–9
Illerup 214
immorality, accusations of, 236
immunities, Cistercian, from bishop and chapter, 119, 139, 227; Cistercian, from royal services, 126
indemnity clause 214
inflation 215; age of, 240, 244
Ingeborg (Danish wife of King Philip Augustus), 93, 97
Ingeborg (13 c. benefactress of Sorø), 135
Ingeborg (14 c. borrower from Sorø), 213–4
Ingeborg (duchess of Halland in 14 c.), 199
Ingefred (widow involved with Hiddensee), 153–4
Ingefred (14 c. borrower from Esrum), 214
Ingemann, B.S. (Danish 19 c. historical novelist), 190
Ingerd Pedersdatter (14 c. benefactress of Esrum), 186
Ingvar (13 c. bishop of Roskilde), 173, 179

Ingvar Hjort (14 c. knight), 172, 174; resistance to Knardrup, 194–5
inheritances, by individual monks, 194, 208–9
Innocent II (pope 1130–43), 6
Innocent III (pope 1198–1216), 116, 117; and Viborg-Vitskøl dispute, 130
incorporation, of parish churches, 136; at Løgum, 138
insecurity, Cistercian feeling of, 75; of life in 14 c., 195
interdict, and Danish Cistercians, 160, 162, 212; as outmoded, 208
interest, payment of, 211
internationalism, difficulty of maintaining, 116–7, 139; impotence of, 166–7, 211; relative abandonment of, 146, 156–66, 222, 258; continuing role of, 212–13, 229–33
iron, extraction of, 85–87
isolation, of individual abbeys, 230–31, 245–8
Itzardus (16 c. papal legate), 26
Ivan (12 c. abbot of Dargun), 81

Jakob (13 c. bishop of Slesvig), 149
Jakob (14 c. abbot at Esrum), 211
Jakob (15 c. abbot at Sorø), 25
Jakob (14 c. legal master at Sorø), 188
Jakob (Count of Halland, late 13 c. exiled Danish magnate), 192
Jakob Blåfod (late 13 c. landowner), 185
Jakob Erlandsen (archbishop of Lund in 13 c.), 125, 142; quarrel with king 146, 159, 179; and Cistercians, 156, 163; and bishop of Viborg, 165; death, 148
Jakob Falster (14 c. canon at Roskilde), 235
Jakob Havre (13 c. landowner), 170
Jakob Herbjørnsen (13 c. landowner), 179
Jakob Jensen (14 c. landowner), 216
Jakob Karlsen (14 c. landowner), 216

Jakob Knudsen (15 c. provost of Roskilde), 234
Jakob Lunge (14 c. landowner), 240
Jakob Nielsen (15 c. landowner), 245
Jakob Poulsen (14 c. bishop of Roskilde), 190
Jakob Roost (14 c. knight), 217
Jarimar (12 c. prince of Rygen), 81, 82
Jellinge family 4
Jens (13 c. bishop of Roskilde), 153
Jens (13 c. bishop of Børglum), 162
Jens (14 c. bishop of Ribe), 198-9
Jens (14 c. bishop of Slesvig), 228
Jens (12 c. subprior at Esrum), 96
Jens (14 c. canon of Århus), 242
Jens (13 c. provost of Viborg), 131
Jens (13 c. provost on Falster), 163
Jens Brostrup (15 c. archbishop of Lund), 25
Jens Dros (13 c. archbishop of Lund), 165, 173, 176
Jens Falk (15 c. aristocrat), 225
Jens Hvid (14 c. abbot of Esrum), 183
Jens Jakobsen (14 c. benefactor of Esrum), 215, 216, 242
Jens Jyde (13 c. monk of Sorø), 34
Jens Kok (13 c. troublemaker for Sorø), 173
Jens Krag (13 c. bishop of Roskilde), 177; burial at Sorø, 189
Jens Nielsen Hviding (14 c. landowner), 213-4
Jens Pedersen (14 c. landowner), 216
Jens Rude (13 c. canon of Roskilde), 173
Jens Urne (13 c. disputant with Løgum), 176-8
Jerusalem 33, 109
Jews 48
Johan (14 c. abbot of Buckow), 231
Johan Oxe (15 c. landowner), 252
Johannes (12 c. dean of Lund chapter), 59-60
Johannes Limbæk (14 c. landowner), 243
Johannites, at Antvorskov, 169; in Norway, 209

John XXII (pope 1316-34), 193-4, 195, 208-9
John (13 c. abbot of Clairvaux), 124
John (early 14 c. abbot of Dargun), 154
Johnsen, Arne Odd (contemporary Norwegian monastic historian), 229
Jon Iversen (13 c. magnate), 177
Jon Jonsen Lille (13 c. benefactor), 134, 169-70, 182, 195, 204; daughter of, 183; testament, 178
judge-delegates 102-3, 209, 235
Judgment Day 62
Juliane, Saint, 255
Juliane, benefactress of Sorø, 170
Juliane, Lady, benefactress of Sorø, 169
jurisdiction, of monastery over labourers, 201-2, 206
Justin Manuscript (Sorø), 187-8
Jutland (Jylland), 1, 2, 3, 5, 38, 54, 57, 61, 109, 111, 115, 142, 157, 204
Jutlandic Law (Jyske Lov), 132
Jutta (13 c. daughter of Erik Plowpenny), 167
Jørgensen, A.D. (19 c. Danish archaeologist), 11
Jørgensen, Ellen (20 c. Danish archivist and historian), 18, 90; and Esrum manuscript, 33

Kalundborg 135, 223
Kalvø 65, 66; Benedictine house, 75; Cistercian monastery, 78, 104
Kamien (Cammin) 231; bishop of, 82
Katherine (13 c. benefactress of Sorø), 173-4
Kazimir I (12 c. duke of Pomerania), 80-81
Keld (13 c. landowner), 140
Keynes, John Maynard 241
Kindertofte 173
king. See monarchy
King, Peter (contemporary British historian), 210, 229-30
Kjerulf, A.C.A. (19 c. Danish monastic historian), 11

KNARDRUP 3, 155, 172, 228, 241; and
foundation problems, 194, 198, 227
knights 181, 187, 195-6, 216, 217, 235,
239, 241
Knowles, David (20 c. monastic
historian), 123
Knud (Saint, Danish king and martyr,
11 c.), 5; Saint Knud's Abbey,
Odense, 67. See also Odense
Knud (illegitimate son of Valdemar
II), 194
Knud Jul (Sorø monk, 14 c.), 34
Knud Lavard (duke and martyr, 12 c.,
father of Valdemar I), 6, 61
Knud Porse (14 c. claimant against
Knardrup), 194
Knud Rød (13 c. landowner), 170
Knud Valdemarsen (also called
Knud VI), (Danish king 1182-1202),
6, 77, 99, 102, 127, 128
Koch, Hal (20 c. Danish church
historian), 12, 13
Kolbacz. See Colbaz
Kollerød 169
Konrad of Bokelem (15 c. Esrum
monk), 228
Kornerup, J. (19 c. Danish
archaeologist), 11
Kristensen, Ann K.G. (contemporary
Danish historian), 19, 147
Kristian (14 c. bishop of Ribe), 200
Kristine (Cistercian nun at Roskilde,
13 c.), 171
Kristine (widow in 14 c.), 214
Kristine (Lady , 14 c. landowner),
185-6
Kristine Jonsdatter (14 c. Cistercian
nun at Roskilde), 185
Kristoffer I (Danish king in 13 c.), 7,
127, 148; privileges to Vitskøl, to
Esrum and Løgum, 130, 142; death
of, 189
Kristoffer II (14 c. Danish king), 7;
burial at Sorø, 190, 223, 225, 227;
foundation of Knardrup, 194;
privileges to Cistercians, 204-7; and
Rhyme Chronicle, 253

Kristoffer III (of Bavaria), (15 c.
Danish king), 227
Krummedige family 235
Krøjerup 173
Kærstrup 235
Kumled 243
Køge 238

labourers. See peasants
landboer 251
landgilde. See rent
landlocked, early Cistercian houses, 84
landowners. (See also magnates), and
Cistercians, 109, 114, 186-7
Langebek, Jacob (18 c. Danish
historian), 24
Langesø 101, 103
Lateran Council, Fourth, 113, 115-6,
127
latinization, of place names, 104
Laurentius, Saint, 46
law, canon, 235; increasing role of, in
13 c. life, 177; in 14 c. life, 209
lay-brothers 251; and importance of,
103, 110; decline of, 146, 155, 158,
165, 180-82, 186-7, 215; at Løgum,
31; at Sorø, 85, 110; in founding
Vitskøl, 58; social background of,
181
learning, at Sorø, 254
Leclercq, Jean (contemporary monastic
historian), 35, 93
leding 127
legal collections 34
legal language 126, 199
legal status, of monks, 197, 235
legalism, increase of, 177, 180
legate, papal, 158-9
legitimacy, of monarchy through
sainthood, 61
Lekai, Louis (contemporary
Cistercian historian), 106, 136
lending, by Cistercian abbeys, 213-4
leper houses 171, 184-5
letter collections 92-3, 97
Liber Miraculorum. See Herbert of
Clairvaux

liberties, of Danish Cistercians, 127-8
Lille Værløse 134, 162
Limbæk family 243, 245
Limfjorden 2, 58, 85, 204
Lindholm 214
litigation, over Halland properties,
85-7
liturgical necessities, for Cistercian
foundation, 58
localism, role of, 134, 139, 187, 212,
246-8; at Sorø, 174-5
Lolland 1, 2, 5, 195
Longinus, legendary Roman soldier, 31
Lorenzen, Vilhelm (20 c. Danish
archaeologist), 12
love, and Saint Anselm, 98; in letters,
97
loyalty, of women, to Cistercians, 171
Lübeck 159, 194
Lucius (Saint, patron of Roskilde
cathedral), 62-3
Ludrö 41
Lund 5, 19, 50, 54, 247; archbishop
of, 25, 40, 46, 49, 89, 141, 146, 148,
194, 234; archbishopric of, 22;
Book of the Dead, 50; Donation
Book, 181; testaments of canons,
217
Lunge family, 15 c., 24, 240
Luther, Martin 9
Lutheranism 257
Lydersholm Mark 140
Lyng 197
Lyse 21; possible absence of lay-
brothers, 58; problems with lineage
of, 59
Læsø 131-2, 205
Løgum 3, 8, 15, 38, 40; and Absalon,
92; and Aurora of Peter of Riga, 31;
and bishops, 90, 140-2, 145, 202,
212, 234, 235; and burial, 243, 244;
and building projects, 251; court held
at, 217; and Brede controversy, 158,
163, 175-6, 208; and Franciscans,
218; and fishing/milling, 141-2; and
gentry, 216-7, 243-5; and General
Chapter, 164-5, 210; and growth,
142-3, 214, 217, 242-5; and

Herrisvad, 182; and papal legates,
158; and papal relations, 117, 119,
193; and parish churches, 198-9; and
peasant settlements, 113; and
procurations, 200; and property
disputes, 176-7, 182; and royal
relationship, 107, 126, 130, 142, 222;
and town properties, 180, 237; and
women, 172;
— foundation of, 67, 76, 104-7;
disputes of 1260s, 156-7, 159;
mortgages, 249; parish priests, 216;
isolation of, 212, 247; Løgum Book,
216; Necrology, 27; in Ribe Bishops
Chronicle, 138-9; tithes and
exemptions for, 106-107

madban 107
Magdeburg 159
Maglesø 173
magnates 142, 201; and attitudes
towards Cistercians, 78, 109, 110,
114, 144, 181-2, 184-7, 217, 221;
and attack on Colbaz, 152; and
Cistercian attention to, 175, 178-9;
and borrowing from monks in 14 c.,
214-5; troubles with, 176-7; and
violence, 192-3; and protection
against, 163; on crusade, 113;
Swedish, and Ås, 208
Magnus (murderer of Duke Knud
Lavard), 61
Magnus Pedersen (15 c. town dweller),
238
Magnus Smek (14 c. Swedish king),
207-8
Maison-Dieu 49
Malmø 8, 238
Margaret, Saint, and altar of at Sorø,
171
Margrethe (12 c. Danish saint), 98, 143
Margrethe I (14 c. Danish ruler), 7,
247; baptism of, 191; and relations
with Cistercians, 222-28, 230,
242-3; and Sorø, 225-7, 247, 252;
and Esrum, 245; and Rhyme
Chronicle, 252-3
Margrethe (12 c. relative of King
Valdemar I), 76-7

Margrethe (13 c. benefactress of Esrum), 170
Margrethe (14 c. Franciscan nun at Roskilde), 185
Margrethe Simbiria (13 c. Danish queen, also called 'Sprænghest'), 7, 148, 170; and Øm controversy, 156-7, 166-7; her devotion to Cistercian Order, 167
Marienhafen 142
Marienthal 230
markets 206
Martin (14 c. abbot of Eldena), 211
Martin (12 c. master of mint), 81
Martin of Tours (4 c. saint), 18
Mary, Saint, 46, 62-3; and Eskil, 68, 73; and Esrum altar of, 255; and church of, at Væ, 67; and church of, at Roskilde, 99; and role in Cistercian Order, 61, 225, and 12 c. literature, 73; and Øm, 110
Mary Magdalene, altar of, 217
masses, in late medieval wills, 217-8, 223, 225, 239-40, 244
meadows, on Læsø, 131-2
meat 204
Mecklenburg 79, 114, 133
medicine 34-5, 190
Merløse 174
Michael, Saint, Benedictine house of, at Slesvig, 101
Michael (14 c. priest), 199
Michael (14 c. priest), 216
Michael (14 c. procurator, Esrum), 215
Michael Skåning (15 c. abbot of Sorø), 234
mills 103; at Esrum, 162; at Sorø, 135, 178; owned by Løgum, 140
miracles 43, 51, 53; at Sorø, 135
missionaries, Cistercians as, 42-3; in Scandinavia, 4, 41
Mogens (13 c. abbot of Esrum), 151
Mogens (13 c. archdeacon of Århus), 175-6
Molesme 48
monarchy, Danish, and the Cistercians, 41, 110; ambiguous royal attitude to monks, 76-7; and involvement in Esrum, 84-5; and literary expression of relationship with monks, 61, 107; and use of Cistercians to assert authority, 128, 144; and relations with Cistercians 1215-57: 126-32, 142-3, 156, 159-60; and Vitskøl's special position for, 130; and Øm controversy, 156, 159-62; insists monks take sides, 145-6; rapprochement with Cistercians, 163-4; as seen in Ryd sources, 149-50; its embarrassment over Roskilde convent scandal, 167; its relations with monks in late Middle Ages, 203-8, 222-8; in Rhyme Chronicle, 252-4
monarchy, Swedish, and Danish Cistercians, 207-8
monasteries, Cistercians for men in Denmark, 2-3; Cistercians for women in Denmark, 3, 98-100; reasons for foundations in the North, 41
monasticism, and attitude towards learning, 35; and dependence on monarchy, 227-8; and French monastic culture in the North, 97; and literary expressions, 46; and myth of late medieval decline, 251-2; as seen by Hans Christian Andersen, 10; hostility towards, in Denmark, 9-11; limitations for, in late medieval period, 196, 219, 227; parish incomes, 199-200
money, in 14 c., 210
Morimund 126, 212; and General Chapter, 123-4, 152; offspring through Doberan, 153-4
Morten Due (14 c. knight), 195
mortgages 179, 237, 242, 244, 246; as monastic policy, 213-4, 238, 249
Morup 86, 90
Mulstrup 197
murder, at Ås, 193
myths, historical. (See also foundation myths, under individual abbeys),

73-4; of Gunner of Viborg, 151; of
Saxo at Sorø, 190
Mødrup 214
Møllediget 103

National Museum, Copenhagen 96, 226
native abbots, in Denmark 106-7
necrologies 240
Neuencamp 211; and Hiddensee, 154
New Doberan 152
Nicholas, Saint, altar of, at Sorø, 171
Nicolaus (14 c. abbot of Colbaz),
230-1
Niels (13 c. royal chancellor and
bishop of Viborg), 139; and Vitskøl,
158
Niels (13 c. bishop of Børglum), 177
Niels (14 c. bishop of Odense), 235
Niels (13 c. abbot of Søro), 173
Niels (early 14 c. abbot of Ryd), 172
Niels (14 c. abbot of Øm), 201
Niels (14 c. abbot of Tvis), 201
Niels (late 12 c. canon at Æbelholt),
99
Niels (12 c. Danish king), 41
Niels, Count (kinsman of Eskil in
12 c.), 56, 59
Niels (15 c. bailiff), 245
Niels Attesen (13 c. priest and donor
to Esrum), 178-9
Niels Clementsen (15 c. Sorø abbot),
25, 240-1, 245
Niels Eriksen (14 c. landowner), 197
Niels Jakobsen (14 c. bailiff), 192-3,
215
Niels Jensen Grubbe (15 c. aristocrat),
242
Niels Jespersen (16 c. abbot at Sorø),
27
Niels Rane (13 c. landowner), 185
Niels Sivardsen (15 c. aristocrat), 225
Niels Skave (15 c. bishop of Roskilde),
25, 227, 236, 249
Niels Stigsen (13 c. bishop of Roskilde),
125, 137
Niels Torstensen (14 c. citizen of
Roskilde), 213

Niels Vind (14 c. landowner), 244
Nielsen, O. (19 c. Danish philologist),
26
nobility, concept of, 181; in Southern
Jutland, 216; and monarchy, 225
Norbertines 115. See also
Premonstratensians
Norway 3, 21, 84, 231; Norwegian
Cistercians and Eskil, 69; and
Hovedø, 122-3
nostalgia, in 13 c. monastic narratives,
149-50, 179
novices, at Clairvaux going to North,
53
nuns, at Bosjö, 247; at Roskilde, 160,
171, 185, 236, 247; at Rygen, 82,
153; at Stettin, 151; at Veng, 76
Nyberg, Tore, (contemporary Swedish-
Danish historian), 12
Nydala 40
Næstved 5; and Sorø, 237-8; 246; and
Valdemar IV, 207, 223; Benedictine
monastery at, 45-6, 184, 203, 215;
growth of, 248
Nødebo 134
Nørlund, Poul (20 c. Danish historian),
12; and Sorø, 24, 238, 241
Nørre Løgum 106-7; 114, 126, 138
Nørre Tranders 202
Nørresundby 177

Octavian. See Victor IV
Odense 37, 194; Benedictine house of
St Knud at, 5, 67, 218; and its
prior, 208, 235; and fire, 129; and
Black Death, 248
Ods herred 245, 250
Östergötland 40
Olav (13 c. bishop of Roskilde), 174
Olav Bjørnsen (14 c. royal official), 223
Oliva 152; fire and attacks on, 153
Older Sorø Annals 187; provenance
of, 189
Older Zealand Chronicle. See Elder
Zealand Chronicle
Olrik, Hans (19 c. Danish historian),
11, 80, 125

Oluf (14 c. bishop of Århus), 234
Oluf Haraldsen, descendant of Skjalm
family, 163
Oluf Tagesen (13 c. landowner), 170
Omer (late 12 c. bishop of Odense),
102; late 12 c. bishop of Ribe, 105,
107, 140
Opager 195-6
Orderic Vitalis (12 c. Anglo-Norman
historian), 47-9
Ordrup 62
Orvieto 163
Oslo fjord 122, 224
Otimar. See Chotimar
Otto, Count of Ravensberg, 13 c., 163
Our Lady. See Mary, Saint
Our Lady, Cistercian female monastery
of, at Roskilde, 98, 143, 160, 171,
185, 224, 228
Our Lady, Cistercian female monastery
of, at Slangerup, 3, 98-9, 186, 224,
228
Ourscamp 152

pagans 84
Palestine 33
papacy, and Cistercian exemptions,
106, 180; and Cistercian visits and
representatives at papal court, 65, 79,
90, 118, 120; and its declining
importance for monks in late Middle
Ages, 186; and Knardrup dispute,
194-5; and late medieval limitations
for Cistercians, 227-8; and Opager
foundation, 195-6; and reservation
of elections, 230-1, 236; and
privileges and bulls for Cistercians,
77, 90, 95, 116, 117-20, 158, 193-4,
247; and Viborg-Vitskøl dispute, 131;
and use of Cistercians, 66; at
Avignon, and Danish Cistercians,
208-9
Paris 254
parishioners 248
patronage, over parish churches, 163,
199, 200, 233, 234-5; for Brede
church, 163-4, 175-6; for

Nørresundby church, 177; by
founders of monasteries, at
Guldholm, 102; at Esrum and Sorø,
137; by Eskil, 253
Pater Noster, church in Jerusalem, 72
paternity (or filiation), question of, at
Dargun, 123-4
payment, for privileges, 127
peasants 38, 257-8; and cultivation of
Cistercian lands, 146, 215, 249-51;
at Esrum, 55, 162, 180-2, 235,
250-1; and Knardrup dispute, 194;
and Løgum, 164, 216, 217; and
Vitskøl, 129, 201; and violence, 236;
and Sorø, 182, 205; importance of,
in 14 c., 186-7; lack of, in Esrum
altar, 256; murder of, 192-3; in
14 c. crisis, 197, 216, 248-9; their
view of monks, 109-10
Peder (early 13 c. bishop of Roskilde),
93
Peder (mid 13 c. bishop of Roskilde),
136
Peder (15 c. bishop of Roskilde), 245
Peder (13 c. bishop of Odense), 161
Peder (13 c. bishop of Viborg), 165
Peder (14 c. bishop of Viborg),
200-203
Peder (13 c. abbot of Ryd), 127
Peder (14 c. abbot of Esrum), 209
Peder (14 c. abbot of Knardrup), 212
Peder (14 c. abbot of Vitskøl), 32
Peder (13 c. prior of Vitskøl), 131
Peder (14 c. canon of Roskilde), 234
Peder Andersen (15 c. abbot of Esrum),
26, 249, 250, 252, 256, 297
Peder Ebbesen (13 c. landowner), 169
Peder Elavsen (13 c. bishop of Århus),
139, 157
Peder Grubbe 241
Peder Jensen Lodehat (15 c. bishop of
Roskilde), 226
Peder Jonsen (14 c. knight), 214
Peder Olsen (16 c. Danish Franciscan
historian), 160
Peder Olufsen (13 c. claimant against
Sorø), 178
Peder Pedersen (14 c. benefactor of
Esrum), 212

Peder Scalle (12 c. claimant against Esrum), 63
Peder Strangesen (13 c. claimant against Sorø), 135
Peder Sunesen (13 c. bishop of Roskilde), 36
Peder Troelsen (14 c. benefactor of Sorø), 240
Peder Tygesen (13 c. landowner), 195
Peder Vagnsen (13 c. landowner), 168
Peder Vognsen (13 c. bishop of Århus), 117
Peder Vendelbo (14 c. knight), 195-6
Pedersborg 161, 174, 197
Peene River 80
pensioners, at Cistercian houses, 241; at Antvorskov, 246
personality, of William of Æbelholt in letters, 95; lack of, in 14 c. sources, 218-9
Peter of Blois 98
Peter of La Celle (12 c. abbot), 66
Peter the Chanter (12 c. Paris theologian), 97
Peter of Riga (12 c. biblical commentator), 31, 33, 34
Peter of Saint Rémi (12 c. Benedictine abbot), 66-7
Philip (12 c. canon of Æbelholt), 94
Philip Augustus (king of France 1180-1223), 93, 95
piety, lay 239-40; 243-5
pigs 85
pilgrimage, request for, 169, 170; and King Valdemar IV, 223
pirates, Wendish 84
pittances 170, 183, 223-4, 225
plague 218, 237
Poland 19, 38, 44, 121
Pomerania 79, 80, 81, 84, 133, 143, 152
Poor Clares, at Roskilde, 185-6
Poppo (10 c. missionary priest), 4
Poul Hvid (13 c. royal bailiff), 163
poverty, as charter theme, 55, 199-200, 215; claim of, in 14 c., 218; of parish churches, 198-9

prayer 219, 222; and money, 205; and prosperity of kingdom, 129
prebends 200
Premonstratensians 227; and Eskil of Lund, 68, 73; and Eskil of Børglum, 115-7; and womens' houses; in Skåne, 46
priests, secular (or parish), 224; and cooperation with monks, 216, 238; and generosity to Cistercians, 178-9, 242-3
procurations. (See also hospitality), at Øm, 156-7; at Løgum, 200-201; at Vitskøl, 200-202; on Zealand, 228
procurator, office of 215
propaganda, in gift to Sorø, 204; in monastic accounts, 151, 193; in property disputes, 168; in royal charters, 128-9; in Rhyme Chronicle, 253
property, purchase of, 55, 64, 108, 214. See under individual abbeys; in towns, 237-8; in countryside, filling out gaps, 239
Property Book. See under Esrum, Sorø, Løgum, etc.
Protestant, abbots at Sorø, 27-8; theology at Øm, 29
Protestantism 244
Pughus 218
Purup 161
Pårup 242

queens, and Cistercians, 225

Ralph (12 c. monk of Herrisvad and bishop of Ribe), 47, 105, 138
Rane (12 c. claimant of Esrum land), 59
Rane, Master (13 c. canon of Roskilde), 173
Rane Jonsen (13 c. political figure), 185
Rantzows 244
rape 236
Rasmussen, Poul (contemporary Danish historian), 243

recruitment, competition between Æbelholt and Esrum, 94–5, 99; crisis of, for lay brothers, 180–82; difficult of, in 14 c., 218

Recuperus (14 c. Avignon lawyer), 196

Reerslev 248

reform movement 108, 115, 200

Reformation 19, 30; and accusations against monks, 236; and Esrum altar, 256–7; in Denmark, 4, 8, 27, 215, 222

Reich, Ebbe Kløvedal (contemporary Danish historical novelist), 9

Reinfeld 232

Reinhold (12 c. abbot of Colbaz), 83

rent system 215–6, 240, 248; at Esrum, 249–51

Resen, P.J. (Danish geographer), 20

resistance, male, to female giftgiving, 168, 170, 172; to new foundations, 194, 196; monastic, to royal decrees, 225. (See also under Øm)

Reval 138

revolt, at Tvis, 161

Rheims, church of St. Denis, 31; Benedictine house of St Rémi, 67

Rhyme Chronicle (Rimkrønike), 34, 189, 222, 226, 252–4, 257

Ribe 37, 47, 119, 131, 176, 196; and Løgum, 217, 234, 237; bishop of, 90, 105, 157, 200; Bishops' Chronicle, 137–9; cathedral chapter, 27, 137–9; schools at, 218

Riddagshausen 230

Ringsted 5; and burial, 204, 223; church meeting in 1170, 6, 104; gifts to, 171, 184; shrine of Knud Lavard, 61

Robert (abbot of Herrisvad in 12 c.), 53, 64, 76

Robert (12 c. Benedictine abbot of Sorø), 74

Robert of Molesme (11 c. founder of Citeaux), 48

Roger (12 c. Carthusian), 66

romanesque style, at Herrisvad, 64

Rome 33, 90, 116, 169

Roskilde 3, 37, 184, 186, 217, 252; and its bishop, 25, 119, 189, 191, 227, 248; and bishopric, 45, 62–3, 155; and canons, 206, 215, 235; and Cistercian monastery for women, 98, 143, 160, 171, 185, 224; and Dominican convent, 167, 185, 228; and Franciscan convent, 185, 186, 228; and Hiddensee, 154–5; and Holy Spirit hospital, 185; and lepers' house, 185; and provenance of Younger Zealand Chronicle, 190–91; and Sorø, 136–7, 171, 173–4, 182, 197–8, 225–8, 236; and Esrum, 228, 234–5, 237; banquet at, in 1157, 57; synod at, in 1158, 58

Royal Library, Copenhagen (Det kongelige bibliotek) 33

Rudolph (13 c. abbot of Colbaz), 83

ruins, of Danish Cistercian houses, 8

Rule of Saint Benedict 32, 46; and hospitality, 141; and Orderic Vitalis, 48

Rus, Brother (folktale), 9, 11

Russia 228

RYD. (See also Guldholm), 3, 7, 19–20; and foundation myth, 75, 149; and bishops, 145; and decline, 182; and Esrum, 193; and Franciscans, 218; and General Chapter, 121, 164, 210, 229; and move from Guldholm, 103–4; and quarrels of 1260s, 146, 148, 156–7, 161, 163; and Ryd Annals, 19–20, 38, 50, 103, 127, 129, 147–51, 173; Ryd Chronicle, 101, 147–51, 152, 219, 252; wealth, 247

Rygen (Rügen), 5, 80–81, 104, 143, 153–5

salt, supply, 80; in Halland, 85

Saltrup 242, 251

salvation, of kings by monks' help, 60–61, 84

Salve Regina 225

Saxo (12 c. Danish historian), 23, 30, 34, 81, 187; and Absalon, 92; and Cistercians, 110–11; and Eskil, 68;

and Sorø, 190; Compendium of, 252
Saxo Torbernsen (13 c. claimant to Esrum lands), 134
Saxolfstorp 90
Scandinavia 3, 4, 21, 58, 84, 96; and church, 47; and church freedom from Germany, 5; and Cistercian foundations, 41; and role of General Chapter, 166, 229-32; and political union, 7
Schaprode 154-5
scholasticism 133
schools, at cathedrals, 218
Scriptores Rerum Danicarum 24
Secundum Registrum 229-30
Seem 5, 104, 244
Sens 65, 66; archbishop of, 97
service, military, and Cistercian tenants, 160
ships 142
shipwreck, as literary theme, 61; right of salvage, 130
Sigrid, foundress of Varnhem, 58
Simon (12 c. bishop of Odense), 67
sindicus 177
sister, spiritual 241
Skanderborg 8
Skanderborg Lake 66, 78
Skanderborg Register 29
skeletons, at Øm and Æbelholt, 34
Skippinge 241
Skjalm family (also called Whites), 17, 75, 92, 99, 114, 117-8, 135, 155, 173; burial at Sorø, 134; continuing generosity via female members, 169; disappearance of, 182
Skjalm Bang (13 c. landowner), 170
Skjalm Hvide, semi-mythical founder of Skjalms, 74
Skjalm Vognsen (13 c. bishop of Århus), 117
Skyum-Nielsen, Niels (contemporary Danish historian), 12, 80, 160
Skærbæk 216
Skåne 2, 5, 19, 38, 46, 54, 57, 67, 76, 184, 207, 247

Slagelse 217, 238
Slangerup 3, 216; Cistercian house for women, 98-9, 224, 228; and Esrum, 256; and king Valdemar IV, 207
Slavonia 228
Slavs 81
Slesvig 4, 5, 20, 103, 113, 159, 161, 184, 217; Benedictines in, 75, 101-2; bishop of, 140-41, 150, 159, 176, 228-9; provost of, 163, 175; dean of, 193
Slesvig-Holsten 3
Smidt, C.M. (20 c. Danish archaeologist), 12, 96
Sminge 65, 104
Smørum 183
Småland 40
Snertinge 126
society, and the Cistercians, 109-10, 257-8; and Cistercians in 14 c., 215-9, 221, 224; and Cistercian status, 235-6; and 14 c. crisis, 248-9; and violence, 192-3; Cistercian attitudes towards, 147, 253-5; Cistercian adjustment to changes in, 183, 186-7; Cistercian influence on, 179
Sode 162, 170
Sorø 13, 15, 23, 24, 29, 79, 143
—background for: location 2, 84; Sorø Donation Book (Sorø Gavebog) 17, 19, 24-5, 67, 75, 86, 114, 136, 167, 170, 173, 178, 181, 219, 240; The Sorø Book 25, 26, 63, 119, 206, 257; Annals and Chronicles, 17-18, 20, 34, 148, 187-91; Necrology, 27, 226; Abbot List, 28, 53; intellectual sources for, 33-4
—12 c. at: and Absalon, 89; and foundation, 64, 65, 104, 253; and foundation myth, 74-5; and foundation of Ås, 85; and Halland properties, 86-7, 234; and other properties, 90; and recruitment, 95; and nuns, 98-9; and wealth, 55; as Benedictine house, 5, 17, 74, 101
—13 c. at: and crusades, 113; and

burials, 134, 169, 171, 174; and buildings, 135, 142; benefactors, 117–8, 134–6, 181–2; and female benefactors, 168–72; and confraternity, 179; and disputes of 1260s, 148, 156; and Erik Plowpenny's daughters, 167–8; and bishops, 136–7, 145; and General Chapter, 121, 123, 166; and lay brothers, 181–2; and international links, 133; and royal privileges and gifts, 126–7, 161, 179; and town properties, 171, 180; and papal privileges, 117–9; and tithes, 114; and nuns, 153; and pilgrimages, 169; and parish churches, 137; and property disputes, 145, 172–4, 178
— late Middle Ages at: and bishops, 197–8, 202, 233–6; and buildings, 258; and burials, 189–90, 213, 223, 225, 245; benefactors, 246–7; female benefactors, 241–2; and contributions, 229; and General Chapter, 210, 230–33; and gentry, 239–41; and last days as Cistercian house, 8, 19, 27–8; and education, 31; and localism, 246–7; and leading position of, after 1414, 227, 232–3, 247–8; and loans on land, 213–4; and nuns, 224, 247; and papal privileges, 194; and peasants, 249; and parish churches, 197, 234; and properties, 214, 226; and town properties, 234–5, 237–8; and Rhyme Chronicle, 252–4; and royal gifts and privileges, 204–5, 225; and self-defense, 197–8; and wealth, 230, 242–3, 247–8; and procuration, 228; as an intellectual centre, 188, 190, 252–4
sources. (See also under individual abbeys), absence of, concerning Læsø, 132; and social change in 14 c., 219; disposal of, by Esrum, 124; by Vitskøl, 202–3; Cistercians seen as aggressive in, 131; nostalgia in, 149; problems in, 187–91, 221, 244

Southern, R.W. (contemporary English historian), 240
Southern Jutland (Sønderjylland) 6, 7, 19, 38, 67, 172, 216; duke of, 102, 127, 163, 177, 208, 222; Løgum as burial church for, 244–5; market towns of, 237; social composition of, 243, 247
Spain 188
Spandet 198–9
spirituality, and Cistercians, 219; and lay aristocracy, 243–5; reflected in Esrum altar, 256–7
stability, of kingdom and monks' prayers, 60–61; and Valdemar IV, 223; in 14 c. papal bull, 194–5
stability, of monks, 107, 228
Stenholt 61, 90
Stenmagle 114, 135, 172
Stettin (Szczecin), 82–3
Stephen (12 c. monk of Herrisvad, archbishop of Uppsala), 47, 105
Stephen (12 c. lay-brother at Esrum), 96
Stephen Harding (11 c. abbot of Citeaux), 108
Stevns 185, 242
Stig (13 c. bishop of Roskilde), 170
Stockholm, Royal Library 40
Stolpe 211
Store Jyndevad 134
Storeå 3
Strippau 211
subsidium. See taxation
Sulpicius Severus (4 c. hagiographer), 18
Sulsted 244
Sune Ebbesen (12 c. member of Skjalm family), 60
survival 257
Suserup 137
Suså 169, 240
Sven (12 c. bishop of Viborg), 72
Sven (12 c. bishop of Århus), 52, 66, 75, 218
Sven (12 c. claimant against Esrum land), 59

Sven Estridsen (11 c. Danish king, 1047-74), 4, 5, 253
Sven Grathe (12 c. Danish king), 57, 59, 61, 127
Sven Simonsen, Danish Cistercian copyist, 32
Svend Lille (14 c. benefactor), 237
Svendborg 129, 148
Sverker (12 c. king of Sweden), 41
Svinninge 241
Sweden 38, 53, 74, 85, 229, 231; and attendance at General Chapter, 117; Cistercian foundations in, 40; insolence toward visitors, 165; king of, 249
Swederus (14 c. abbot of Esrum), 223
Szomlaiski, Leif (contemporary Danish historian), 189-91
Søborg 68, 162, 164, 216, 217, 237
Sønderborg 184
Søsum 194
Søtorp 172-4
Såne 56, 63, 90

tales, in Cistercian life, 70, 158; told by Eskil, 67-72
Tanga 56
taxation 210; of Cistercians by General Chapter, 228-33. (See also contributions); of peasant tenants, 250-51
tenants 155, 215, 239; at Vitskøl, 158; importance of, 202, 216; in Esrum Property Book, 250-51
Tersløse 174
theology, study of, at Vitskøl, 32
Thomas (12 c. abbot of Holme), 67
Thomas Becket 18
Thorkil (13 c. abbot at Øm), 114
Tibirke 178
Tikøb 237
tithes, and their collection, 103, 106, 109, 114, 176; and the episcopal portion, at Sorø, 64; at Colbaz, 83; and exemption from, at Vitskøl, 158; at Esrum, 180; and Fourth Lateran council, 113; as income for

monks, 138; problems with, at end of 12 c. and early 13 c., 91, 107
Tjæreby 45, 55-6, 96
Toelt 90
Toke Skjalmsen 74
Tollerup 234
tolls, exemption from, 206
Torben (12 c. prior of Esrum), 96
Torben Pedersen (14 c. landowner), 235
towns 144; and monarchy, 223; dealings with Cistercians, 217; growth of, and Cistercians, 180, 237-9, 242
Toynbee, Arnold (20 c. English historian), 257
trade, between Denmark and France via Cistercians, 125; for Løgum, 142; in towns, 237-8
travel, monastic, 115-7; difficulty of, in 14 c., 209, 211
Troels (14 c. abbot of Esrum), 224
Troels (14 c. abbot of Næstved), 224
Trund (Trugot) family, 12 c., 53-4
truth, manipulation of, 147
Trøjborg 243, 245
Tue (13 c. bishop of Ribe, and Løgum), 137-9, 140
Tule Boesen (13 c. Skjalm descendant), 169
Tule Ebbesen (14 c. royal official), 192
Ture (13 c. abbot of Vitskøl, Esrum, then Øm), 124-5, 157
Tvis 3, 12, 38; abbots of, 201; and its buildings, 111, 258; and foundation, 61, 64, 104; and General Chapter, 117, 121, 210, 229; and motives of founders, 75-6; and conspiracy of 1260s, 146, 160-61; and Øm controversy, 156-7
Tvååker 86, 234
Tyge (13 c. bishop of Århus), 25, 78, 198, 218; and cardinal legate Guido, 159; and Cistercian cooperation against him, 146; and bitterness in Øm, 150; and legal actions against him, 160-61, 164; stops Cistercian parish functions, 157

Tyge (13 c. bishop of Ribe), 175–6
Tyge Bjørundsen (13 c. provost of Roskilde), 137
Tyge Esbernsen (14 c. landowner), 217
Tyvelse 240
Tølløse 170
Tønder 134, 137, 138, 140–41, 217, 237

Ubbe Tordsen (13 c. claimant against Løgum), 141
Udesundby 186, 207
Uggeløse 204, 207, 214, 235, 241
Ulvilde Håkonsdatter (12 c. Swedish queen), 41–2
universities, in 13 c., 133; in late Middle Ages, 31
Uppsala 47
Urban III (pope 1185–7), and payment of tithes, 91
Urban IV (pope 1261–4), 156–7
Urban V (pope 1362–70), 228
Urban VI (pope 1378–89), 228
Ursula, Saint 255
usury, and mortgages, 213
Utrecht 53

Vagn (12 c. abbot of Løgum), 106
Vagn Nielsen (14 c. judge), 217
Valborg (14 c. benefactress of Cistercians), 195–6
Valdemar (12 c. bishop of Slesvig), 61–2, 101, 141, 149
Valdemar I (The Great), (12 c. Danish king), 6, 33, 59, 63, 64, 65, 75, 107; and Baltic conquests, 79–80, 83–4; and Esrum, 56, 60–1, 68, 84–5, 99; and exemption for Cistercians from services, 127; and Halland, 85; and relations with Eskil, 54, 73; and Ringsted Benedictines, 61; and Vitskøl, 57, 128; and use of Cistercians for spiritual authority, 62; and Øm, 76–7
Valdemar II (The Victorious), (13 c. Danish king), 6, 128; and limited generosity, 130–31; and privileges for Clairvaux, 125–6; and privileges

for Danish Cistercians, 127–8; and Viborg-Vitskøl dispute, 131–2; and Property Book, 34; his death, 119, 141, 148; historical novels on, 190
Valdemar III (14 c. Danish king), 205–6
Valdemar IV Atterdag (14 c. Danish king), 7, 190, 191, 195, 197, 235, 249; and meagre privileges to monks, 206–7, 222–4, 227
Valdemar II (14 c. duke of Jutland), 154
Valdemar III (14 c. duke of Jutland), 217
Valdemar, Duke (brother of King Kristoffer II), 204
Valerius Maximus (Roman moralist), 34
Varberg 85
Varde 216
Varnhem 20, 41, 58, 77, 114; and General Chapter, 122–3
Vatican Library 33
Vejby 216, 235, 242
Veksebo 59
Veng 65, 66, 76, 101, 104, 117
Vestergade 237
Vestervig 130
Viborg 5, 16, 57–8, 128; bishop of, 157, 200–201, 206, 233–4; cathedral chapter, 27; dispute with Vitskøl, 130–32
Victor IV (Octavian), (antipope, 1159–64), 54, 64–5, 69
Vienna 228–9
Viking Age 1, 4, 5
villeins 251
Villingehoved 60
Villingerød 56, 59–60, 61, 90
violence, and Lund, 248–9; in relations between monks and society, 192–8; in fifteenth century, 236
Visby 245
visions, of Eskil, 68–71
visitation 245–6; and Herrisvad, 247; of Danish abbeys by Clairvaux, 125, 175; of Baltic abbeys by Esrum,

151-2, 157, 211, 233; of Denmark, Sweden and Friesland in 1290s, 165-6; of Norwegian abbeys, 123; overdone by abbot of Sorø, 210-11
Visitation, Feast of, 229
Viskan 193
Viterbo 116
VITSKØL 2, 13, 15, 22, 23, 24, 64; abbot of, 124; and foundation, 58, 77, 104, 128; building of church, 111; of abbey complex, 251; dispersion of abbey, 164-5, 182; fire at, 165, 182; dispute with Viborg cathedral, 130-32; and General Chapter, 121, 164, 230, 232; and lineage, 59; and procurations, 200-202, 233-4; problem of its meagre records, 216; and relations with bishops, 139, 145, 201, 235; and relations with kings, 128-30, 205-6; and towns, 239; and wealth, 55, 134; and ruins, 8-9; and Øm, 156-8; Compendium of Theology, 32; Vitskøl Narrative (Narratiuncula), 19-20, 41
Væ 67

Walbert (12 c. abbot of Esrum), 80, 83, 93-4, 96, 100
water level, at Esrum, 162
water supply, at Æbelholt, 96
wealth, comparative, of Danish Cistercians, 229-30, 247-8, 258
Wendland 79-81, 85, 104
Wends 1, 79, 84
widows 147
Widukind (8 c. German historian), 4
Wiese, Albert (19 c. German historian), 79, 82
William, Saint (12 c. abbot of Æbelholt), 17, 74; his central importance, 89; his collection of letters, 92-3; his cult, 143; in Slesvig-Ryd dispute, 101-3; letters to abbots of Esrum, 93-8; letters to Cistercian nuns, 98-100; letters as expression of his personality, 100, 103

William (12 c. abbot of Esrum), 50, 56
Wissing, Jürgen (contemporary German monastic historian), 40
Wizlaus II (13 c. prince of Rygen), 153
women, Cistercian antagonism towards, 76-7; and devotion towards Cistercians, 78, 147, 167, 169, 185; their generosity, 184, 241; in Cistercian iconography, 255-6; and late medieval charges against Cistercians, 236; monastic houses for, in Denmark, 37, 98-100, 143, 195, 227
Wulfard (13 c. priest on Hiddensee), 154-5
Younger Sorø Annals 187-8; political stand of, 189
Younger Zealand Chronicle 189-91, 194
Zarrentin 153
Zealand 1, 2, 38, 49, 57, 76, 84, 85-6, 87, 109, 136, 155, 184, 191, 239

Ølrik Skaft (14 c. landowner), 186
ØM 2, 8, 12, 15, 117, 235; abbot of, 130-31, 201; location of, 2, 84; library at, 35; Skanderborg Register, 216-7; Øm Book (Øm Abbey Chronicle), 16-17, 20, 21, 30, 32, 33, 39, 52, 71, 77, 114, 128, 147, 151, 187, 192, 219; Øm Inventory of 1554, 29, 30
— in twelfth century: foundation of, 65, 76-9, 101, 104; foundation myth, 57, 75, 114; dispute with Margrethe, 76-8; and Eskil, 64; and King Valdemar I, 76-7; and property boundaries, 86; and peasant's dream, 55, 110; and myth of Benedictine decline, 74; and Absalon, 92; canals at, 103
— in thirteenth century: and controversy of 1260s, 30, 78, 115, 120, 125, 146-8, 156-62, 175, 192, 227, 234, 236, 252, 257; and building of church, 134, 145; and General Chapter, 117, 121; and

hospitality, 141; and relations with
Abel, 128-9; and relations with
bishops, 90, 139-41, 145; and
relations with popes, 90, 117-8; and
wills, 168
—in late Middle Ages: and building of
abbey complex, 251; and increase in
property, 214, 242-3, 247-8; and
General Chapter, 230, 232; and lower
nobility, 216-7; and relations with
bishops, 198, 234-5; and the sick,
255; and towns, 238-9
Øresund 64, 98
Ørslev Østre 135
Ørved 67
Østersyssel 234

Æbelholt 34, 89, 92, 94, 96, 99, 143,
186, 202; and parish churches, 200;
and Valdemar IV, 223

Åbenrå 142, 237
Ålborg 177
Århus 3, 5, 16, 17, 25, 194; archdeacon
of, 175-6; bishop of, 90, 117, 146,
234; cathedral of, 157; cathedral
chapter of, 27, 118, 137; provost
and chanter of, 208
Ås, foundation, 85, 104; and fishing,
193; and Danish monarchy, 224;
and Swedish monarchy, 207-8; and
General Chapter, 121-3, 165, 210,
230, 232; and violence, 192-3

CISTERCIAN PUBLICATIONS INC.

TITLES LISTING

THE CISTERCIAN FATHERS SERIES

THE WORKS OF
BERNARD OF CLAIRVAUX

Treatises I: Apologia to Abbot William,
On Precept and Dispensation . . . . CF 1

On the Song of Songs I–IV . . CF 4,7,31,40

The Life and Death of Saint Malachy
the Irishman . . . . CF 10

Treatises II: The Steps of Humility,
On Loving God . . . . CF 13

Magnificat: Homilies in Praise of the
Blessed Virgin Mary [with Amadeus
of Lausanne] . . . . CF 18

Treatises III: On Grace and Free Choice,
In Praise of the New Knighthood CF 19

Sermons on Conversion: A Sermon to
Clerics, Lenten Sermons on
Psalm 91 . . . . CF 25

Five Books on Consideration:
Advice to A Pope . . . . CF 37

THE WORKS OF WILLIAM OF
SAINT THIERRY

On Contemplating God, Prayer,
and Meditations . . . . CF 3

Exposition on the Song of Songs . . . CF 6

The Enigma of Faith . . . . CF 9

The Golden Epistle . . . . CF 12

The Mirror of Faith . . . . CF 15

Exposition on the Epistle to the
Romans . . . . CF 27

The Nature and Dignity of Love . . CF 30

THE WORKS OF AELRED OF RIEVAULX

Treatises I: On Jesus at the Age of
Twelve, Rule for a Recluse,
The Pastoral Prayer . . . . CF 2*

Spiritual Friendship . . . . CF 5

The Mirror of Charity . . . . CF 17†

Dialogue on the Soul . . . . CF 22

THE WORKS OF GILBERT OF
HOYLAND

Sermons on the Song of Songs
I–III . . . . CF 14,20,26

Treatises, Sermons, and Epistles . . CF 34

OTHER EARLY CISTERCIAN WRITERS

The Letters of Adam of Perseigne, I . CF 21

Alan of Lille: The Art of Preaching . CF 23

John of Ford. Sermons on the Final
Verses of the Song of Songs,
I–IV . . . . CF 29,39,43,44

Idung of Prüfening. Cistercians and
Cluniacs: The Case for Cîteaux . . CF 33

The Way of Love . . . . CF 16

Guerric of Igny. Liturgical Sermons
I–II . . . . CF 8,32

Three Treatises on Man: A Cistercian
Anthropology . . . . CF 24

Isaac of Stella. Sermons on the
Christian Year, I . . . . CF 11

Stephen of Lexington. Letters from
Ireland . . . . CF 28

THE CISTERCIAN STUDIES SERIES

MONASTIC TEXTS

Evagrius Ponticus. Praktikos and
Chapters on Prayer . . . . CS 4

The Rule of the Master . . . . CS 6

The Lives of the Desert Fathers . . . CS 34

Dorotheos of Gaza. Discourses and
Sayings . . . . CS 33

Pachomian Koinonia I–III:
The Lives . . . . CS 45
The Chronicles and Rules . . . . . CS 46
The Instructions, Letters and Other
Writings of St Pachomius and
His Disciples . . . . CS 47

*Temporarily out of print   †Forthcoming

Symeon the New Theologian. Theological and Practical Treatises and Three Theological Discourses... CS 41

Guigo II the Carthusian. The Ladder of Monks and Twelve Meditations. CS48

The Monastic Rule of Iosif Volotsky .... CS 36

CHRISTIAN SPIRITUALITY

The Spirituality of Western Christendom .... CS 30

Russian Mystics (Sergius Bolshakoff) CS 26

In Quest of the Absolute: The Life and Works of Jules Monchanin (J. G. Weber) .... CS 51

The Name of Jesus (Irenée Hausherr) .... CS 44

Entirely for God: A Life of Cyprian Tansi (Elizabeth Isichei)....... CS 43

Abba: Guides to Wholeness and Holiness East and West .... CS 38

MONASTIC STUDIES

The Abbot in Monastic Tradition (Pierre Salmon) .... CS 14

Why Monks? (François Vandenbroucke) .... CS 17

Silence in the Rule of St Benedict (Ambrose Wathen)........... CS 22

One Yet Two: Monastic Tradition East and West .... CS 29

Community and Abbot in the Rule of St Benedict I (Adalbert de Vogüé). CS 5/1

Consider Your Call: A Theology of the Monastic Life (Daniel Rees et al). CS 20

Households of God (David Parry).. CS 39

CISTERCIAN STUDIES

The Cistercian Spirit (M. Basil Pennington, ed.) ...... CS 3

The Eleventh-Century Background of Cîteaux (Bede K. Lackner) ...... CS 8

Contemplative Community .... CS 21

Cistercian Sign Language (Robert Barakat) .... CS 11

The Cistercians in Denmark (Brian P. McGuire) .... CS 35

Saint Bernard of Clairvaux: Essays Commemorating the Eighth Centenary of His Canonization.. CS 28

Bernard of Clairvaux: Studies Presented to Dom Jean Leclercq .... CS 23

Bernard of Clairvaux and the Cistercian Spirit (Jean Leclercq) .... CS 16

William of St Thierry: The Man and His Work (J. M. Déchanet) .... CS 10

Aelred of Rievaulx: A Study (Aelred Squire) .... CS 50

Christ the Way: The Christology of Guerric of Igny (John Morson).. CS 25

The Golden Chain: The Theological Anthropology of Isaac of Stella (Bernard McGinn) .... CS 15

Studies in Cistercian Art and Architecture, I (Meredith Lillich, ed).. CS 66

Studies in Medieval Cistercian History sub-series

Studies I .... CS 13

Studies II .... CS 24

Cistercian Ideals and Reality (Studies III) .... CS 60

Simplicity and Ordinariness (Studies IV) .... CS 61

The Chimera of His Age: Studies on St Bernard (Studies V) .... CS 63

Cistercians in the Late Middle Ages (Studies VI) .... CS 64

Noble Piety and Reformed Monasticism (Studies VII) .... CS 65

Benedictus: Studies in Honor of St Benedict of Nursia (Studies VIII). CS 67

Heaven on Earth (Studies IX) .... CS 68†

THOMAS MERTON

The Climate of Monastic Prayer .... CS 1

Thomas Merton on St Bernard ..... CS 9

Thomas Merton's Shared Contemplation: A Protestant Perspective (Daniel J. Adams) .... CS 62

Solitude in the Writings of Thomas Merton (Richard Anthony Cashen)..... CS 40

The Message of Thomas Merton (Brother Patrick Hart, ed.) ..... CS 42

FAIRACRES PRESS, OXFORD

The Wisdom of the Desert Fathers

The Letters of St Antony the Great

The Letters of Ammonas, Successor of St Antony

A Study of Wisdom. Three Tracts by the author of *The Cloud of Unknowing*

The Power of the Name. The Jesus Prayer in Orthodox Spirituality (Kallistos Ware)

Solitude and Communion

Contemporary Monasticism

A Pilgrim's Book of Prayers (Gilbert Shaw)

Theology and Spirituality (Andrew Louth)

* *Temporarily out of print*   † *Forthcoming*